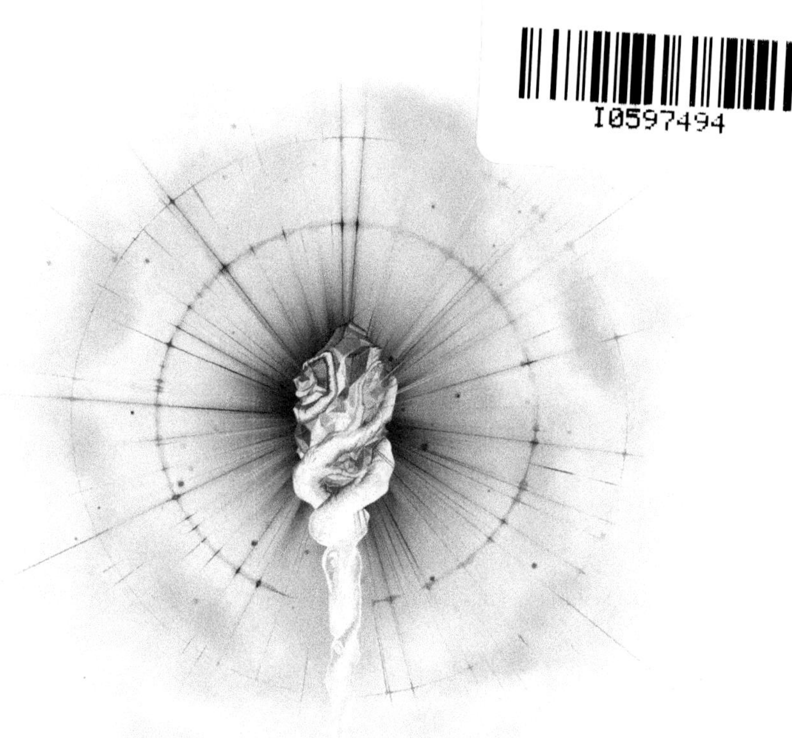

RETURN
OF THE
KEEPERS

KAILEY HOLBROOK

Return of the Keepers – by Kailey Holbrook

Copyright © 2024 by Kailey Holbrook. All rights reserved.

Published by:

Aviva Publishing Lake Placid, NY
(518) 523-1320 www.AvivaPubs.com

ISBN: 978-1-63618-349-7
Library of Congress Control Number: 2024914827

Editor: Ellie Schulz
Cover Design: Helena Winchester
Interior Design: Gorham Printing

Printed in the United States of America

＊　＊　＊

For the dreamers who looked up at the stars

and made constellations of their own

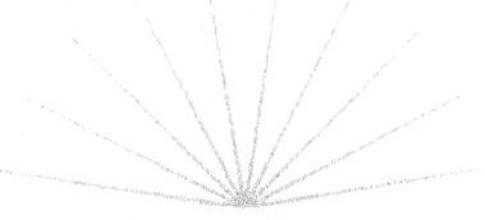

PART 1

Permidia

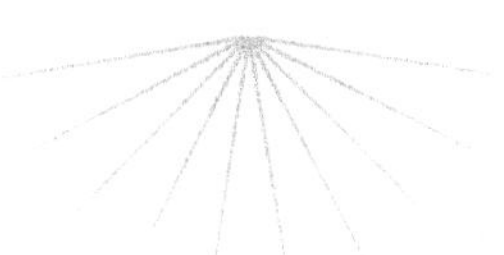

Chapter 1

* * *

Malaya

MALAYA DIED THE day gunshots rang instead of wedding bells, and through the screams and splattered blood against cream-colored clothes, all she could think of were her vows.

She was going to tell James about her life. She would share facts he already knew from her stories, only this time she would piece them together in a way to express how perfect the two of them were together. Malaya was going to explain how dark her life was and how bright people made it. Her family was lost to survival, but having each other made it so much more bearable. It never feels like life or death when the people you love are always living, always coming home with a beating heart or giddy smile. Malaya was going to tell James that though she adored her family, they could never shine brightly as he could.

When her father came home from work with a bruise on his cheek and a blood stain running down his shirt he would use humor to hide Malaya from the truth. He would brush off the wounds and joke that it didn't hurt, that he was a machine, unbreakable. When her mother would return home with only five Corts and a basket of unsold, rotting fruits, she would smile. She would not explain what happened and simply give Malaya pity for what she had to see on her mother's face. But when James came to her with wounds and no Corts, he would look at her and tell her what happened. He would not speak out of anger, or grief, he would just say what happened and leave her with her thoughts. He would tell her that he wanted to make the world a better place so that one day no one would have to work as hard as they did for so little. His light did not come as forced joy or pity, it came as the truth. Malaya would have told him about how bright he was, and how dark her life was without him.

She knew what James was going to tell her. He was not a man of creative liberties, but when he found clever words he used them as often as possible. He called Malaya his little bird after one horrible day in the fields. He told her that a group of little yellow birds suddenly shot up from within the field as if violently disturbed. James knew something was wrong, and though the workers around him told him to stay before someone noticed he was gone, he took the warning and left. The next day he found out that a group of Wardens, the soldiers and protectors of their people, drunk and armed, shot twenty workers in the fields. Malaya was his little bird because she gave him words of warning. James worked off of intellect, Malaya lived off of feeling, and sometimes she could see things he could not. Soldiers are only as good as their ability to hide their ego, and she could tell very quickly when someone was feeling strong enough to get away with murder.

Malaya honestly believed James had no idea what she was going to say, and as he dropped to the ground of the altar, his forehead caved in by a bullet, she realized he would. He would never get to live the life they had been talking about for all those years. He would never know how perfect he was, how perfect they were for each other, and perfect their life could have been.

Malaya knew perfection is a lie, like the idea that true happiness could ever be achieved, but she still wanted that lie. She learned at a young age that comfort was a luxury, and joy was nothing but a small laugh stifled by screams. But James made her believe that perfection existed, that joy and love was not some fantasy. Their life always deserved to be a balance of good and evil, but now it never would.

Malaya didn't know how she ended up on the ground, James's head on her lap and his blood seeping onto her white dress from the back of his head. She didn't know how she could stare at his face for so long and not look away. There was chaos around her and all she could see were his eyes. James had blue eyes, the kind that pierce you when you first see them but become a soft glow the longer you stare. Malaya didn't have anywhere else to look. His face was soaked in blood, half caved in, nothing moving.

The Wardens had killed him. They had found him, and without a word of mercy, shot him point blank in front of his bride. The Enemy. The liars. The torturers. The killers. The *monsters*. Malaya knew most of the people she loved would die at their hands, and part of her knew that this was how James would die, she just hadn't realized it would happen so soon. She felt guilty, suddenly, and it was at that moment that tears started steaming down her face and she cried over the corpse of her husband to be: they never had a chance to say *I do*.

There was one part of James she couldn't warn or protect. There was one place she could not be his little bird: the rebellion. James hated the Wardens, everyone did, but he was one the few who took to action instead of prayers. He had worked to ambush and stop them. He gave donations to as many groups as he could and targeted Warden cargo ships so they would crash right out of the sky. He worked so hard, with so much love for his people, and Malaya could not stop him. She let him risk everything because part of her wanted to believe his work could do something. That one day they could all be free. That one day her father could work without being beaten or her mother could earn enough money to feed her children. That one day Malaya could have a wedding without gunshots or a dead groom on her lap.

James was dead because of what she let him do.

Malaya did not know how she was supposed to react. She thought about trying to shake James, that maybe he was just pretending to be dead, that maybe she was dreaming or he was playing a trick on her. She wanted his eyes to move, to lock with hers, to blink. At the sounds of screams finally reaching her, Malaya forced herself to look away. The Wardens were there, chasing down wedding guests and placing thick metallic cuffs on their wrists or beating them until their bodies could be dragged. Malaya saw her mother being smacked and her father putting up a fight against a Warden. She watched the soldiers shoot her older brother three times in the chest.

Her family had put the wedding together and built it from nothing but scraps. Her mother and brother made the dress, sewing day and night with little pieces of cream cloth they had stolen from the clay walls of the city. They drew designs and dyed the edges to give volume to Malaya's figure. Her father had found the perfect spot out of reach of the Wardens, a little clearing on the river's edge. Malaya could see the city from where she stood beside James, lights and ships moving in and out above miles of farms and factories. Her father had been so proud of the space he found that he vowed to return with Malaya's mother to do their own ceremony since they never had one.

Someone grabbed Malaya from behind and it was at that moment that she realized there was something she could do. She wasn't stuck with James or the bodies of her family, she needed to run and save the people who were left. But the hand on her shoulder pulled her back the moment she tried to get up and run into the fight.

At first, they only held onto her arm, and for a moment she thought it was an aunt or friend, but as they pulled the back of her dress she realized they were not keeping her out of the fight out of love. The Warden tugged her back and dragged her away from James, who, already being on her lap, slid with her for a few feet. She tried to reach out and grab him but missed.

"No!" She screamed and tried to get out of their grasp, but the more she struggled the more hands grabbed her.

She could see the altar, standing as her father had placed it, a small piece of wood carved and placed between her and James. Her brother had made it for the wedding. It was carved to feature a long wind of roots that moved up to a crystal. It was not identical to the pictures Malaya had seen growing up, but she liked how it was almost like her and James's relic.

The Keeper's staff, a piece of the gods to watch over them especially.

Malaya didn't know what to pray for, now that there were so many bodies and so much blood. If the gods had not saved her people for so many centuries of overrule, why would they bring her family back to life now? She wanted to scream for them, to beg for mercy and punish them for their ignorance.

The Wardens threw her to the ground and placed a gun to her head. All she could think was that she was about to die the same way James did.

Malaya heard their voice, robotic and void of emotion due to a filter in their helmets, "Do we need her alive?"

There were still screams in the distance. Malaya recognized her mother among them.

"No. Kill her."

The barrel was pressed harder against her head, and she knew there was nothing she could say to stop them. The only reason they would want her alive was to question her, but that was a fate far worse than death. Malaya realized that dying the way she was about to would be merciful. She didn't want to die, but if she had to this would be the best outcome. James didn't get to hear her vows, but he didn't get to die in pain. Malaya looked up at the sky and, in the final moments she had, she prayed.

Her mother had taught her to speak to the gods respectfully, and quietly. Malaya gave up hiding what she was doing and simply spoke aloud. "*Please.*" She needed the Keepers, she needed their gods, not for herself, not even for her family, who were all going to die, now or in the next hour, she needed them for her people. The Keepers had been gone for so long that some thought that they were just myths, Malaya knew better than that. She knew they were still there, somewhere, waiting or trapped, and they would return. Just not for her.

Malaya had a feeling, and dying alone she had no reason for the gods to even be real. But James was gone, and all she had left was hope.

She died hoping for something that would come much too late to save her.

* ✳ *

Chapter 2

KIRANA

KIRANA SAT ON a bench not too far from a bustling crowd of people. She watched them, picking people out of the crowd to observe. They were all different, after all, in their unique ways. She watched a woman dressed with dark black curls and a ruffled skirt walk in little steps. She was practically skipping. A man passed her by with a thick sandwich. He gorged himself on the contents. Kirana only got a glance but it looked like it was made solely from meats and sauces. A boy walked by, hands to his side and a grin across his face. A girl swayed by with a pink balloon in hand.

The circular platform must have had a hundred people on it, moving around and walking to their own destinations. Kirana always wondered how so many people could have their own lives, walk to their own place, and sleep with their own thoughts. It was almost magical the way people spent their lives. The platform itself was one of a dozen or so, held up by magnets that spun softly. Kirana enjoyed the view almost as much as watching the people around her. She could see so much of her world from the highest platform. Off in the distance, there were lakes and rivers, forests and snow-covered mountains, meadows and prairies. Off not too far from the platforms themselves was her favorite spot; a field with golden blades of grass. During this time in the evening, the sun was setting gently against the field, filling her world with a yellow glow. Kirana spent most of her evenings down in the grassy field, waiting for the quick display of natural beauty.

Her world was called Permidia. The perfect world filled with perfect people.

Kirana loved her life. She loved it with all her heart and soul. She loved the smell of the air, the taste of her food, the sights, and the feelings around her. She loved all of it. Her life was perfect, and there was no doubt of that. There was nothing she could do to make it better.

Kirana put her legs up on the bench and held them close. A woman walked by with a drink in hand, it was steaming softly, and she took a sip. A man moved past her with a screen in hand. Kirana leaned forward and tried to see what he was watching, but, distracted by the new person, she didn't see someone else walk over to her. A boy, eight maybe nine, sat down on the bench next to her. He looked straight ahead as if he too was watching the crowd. There was a pastry in his hand, a soft flaky treat with powdered sugar atop its surface. Kirana found herself leaning away from him, and she should have kept well away but... with a glance around she couldn't see any Nanos. They were normally everywhere, small little androids that floated with lively movements. They flew here to there to make sure everything was perfect.

Kirana glanced down at the boy, and after looking around quickly she put her legs down and leaned over to him. "Hey." He looked over at her numbly. She pointed down to the pastry in his hand, "That looks delicious." He just stared at her. Kirana laughed nervously, "You know it's actually really cool how they make those things. There's this whole process with butter and–"

With a sharp whistle, a Nano suddenly swung by Kirana's head and floated in front of her. They let out a laugh and said her name with violent excitement, "Kirana!" Nanos were adorable little things. They were about the size of her hand; a small ball resting on spinning fans. Their faces were projected in pixels on the ball itself, each expressing a joyful smile.

The Nano flew in front of her as the boy got up and started to walk away. Kirana instinctively reached out to hold him back but forced herself to pull her hand away.

The little android titled its body in the air to mimic someone tilting their head, "Kirana?"

Kirana swallowed and laughed, "What was I doing?" The Nano looked down at her and blinked. There was no point in lying, "I was just going to say hello." She raised her hands in defense, "I didn't–"

"You can't keep doing this. You know the rules–"

"I know. I know."

The Nano's smile fell slightly, "We understand you weren't trying to hurt him, but we're just here to make sure everyone has a perfect day–"

"Again. I was just saying hello. I commented on his pastry." She gestured to where the boy had been sitting, "He was happy to see me."

"Was he?"

No, he wasn't, but Kirana tried to picture him with a wide-eyed grin, a happy look to her happy conversation. She leaned back on the bench, "No."

The Nano sighed, "Kirana, you have to remember you're different."

Those were the words. The two little words. You're different. Different. That word stuck with her every step and every breath, thumping like a heartbeat.

Different.

Different.

Different.

"I know."

No one else wanted to start a conversation with her. No one wanted to stop to talk to her about art. No one wanted to sit and drink warm tea with her. No one wanted to go out and have a picnic. No one wanted a connection. Only solitude.

But her life was perfect.

Kirana knew what it was like to live hundreds of years ago. She had gone through dozens of books about the history of Permidia. All that violence and pain. Those wars caused so much death and suffering. Her world worked to stop that, and they were successful. One of the main reasons for that was that there was no connection between people. If no one spoke to one another no one would start a war or create a conflict. They just… didn't connect. Kirana did, but why she wanted a connection was a question no one bothered to answer for her. But she knew it didn't matter what the science was behind her existence. She could live a perfect life in her unique way.

The Nano let out a soft *bing* and its face lit up for a moment. It let out a chuckle, "Oh goody, it seems Tia is ready to see you."

Kirana shot up from the bench, "She is? Where is she?"

"You asked her if you could go to the field for a picnic last week. She'll meet you there."

Tia was Kirana's sister. Though she didn't want a connection she wanted to help Kirana. She came once a week to sit with her sister and talk. Her conversations meant everything to Kirana, and she rationed herself off of them for the days she spent alone. Tia was incredible; a gorgeous woman and an even better baker. They would be together, eat, and talk. It was the best, most perfect part of Kirana's life.

She jumped up and moved away from the bench, "Tell her I'm on my way!"

"Will do!" The Nano called back, zipping past as Kirana ran through the crowd.

When she got to the edge of the platform she wasted no time in running to her bike and jumping on. Her bike could take her further out into the world if she so desired. Not on the ground, but in the air. Within minutes or even seconds, she could be in the city or somewhere far beyond. Right now, she just needed it to take her down to the fields. Within seconds she popped on her goggles and started the machine. It roared to life and lifted off the ground. She pushed the handles forward and off she went, leaving the platforms and the people behind her. Her bike flew through the air smoothly, obeying her every movement. She kept it moving towards the field of golden grass as she looked back towards the platforms. Kirana wondered what would have happened if the Nano hadn't arrived. She would have gotten to speak to another person, maybe even hear what he had to say, but the look he gave her was enough to leave her without regret. He had not wanted to talk to her, and she knew that as well as he did but... she only wanted to hope, maybe dream a little, about some new person she could meet and learn about.

The platforms behind her each harbored hundreds of people, but they were simply rings around a tall, black tower. It was like the trunk of a tree, letting a world branch out from its center. It was the root of the world's perfection. *The Magistrater's Tower.* Home to their ruler, their savior. The Magistrater created Permidia for everyone out of the goodness of her own heart. She gave everyone their perfect life away from danger or despair, and Kirana gave a small breath of gratitude as she turned towards the grass and headed down to find Tia.

The great field of golden grass was tall and thick, a wonder of nature's beauty left untouched, but within it were small patches of low-cut grass. Kirana had found many across the entire field like the one she had taken Tia to once before. Nothing big, not compared with the size of the area around them, just enough room for a picnic blanket and two sisters. Kirana had come to these small patches hundreds of times and found the largest one to park her bike on the edge of. She jumped off and rolled down onto the grass with a giddy smile.

Kirana lay there for a few minutes until heard a small rustle back the way she had come. She pushed her head back until she could see behind her. The world was upside down but she could see a woman walking towards her. Tia was wearing a pink flowered dress and a wide-brimmed hat with a red tulip tied along it with a bow. Her white gloves and thick stockings gathered blades of grass as she walked uncomfortably through the field. She held her hat from the breeze, unbalanced by the weight of the basket on her arm. "Did we have to go so far?"

Kirana spun around and lay down on her stomach, putting her hands under her chin. "You got grass on your stockings." She said mockingly with a smile.

Tia looked down quickly and wiped her legs, "This was not what I signed up for."

"You signed up for a picnic, and that's exactly what we are doing." Kirana stood up and took the basket out of her sister's hands. She opened the woven lid and pulled out the blanket as Tia laid out the food. Her sister always had an eye for orderly things. She could take ten different types of flowers and create the perfect bouquet. Everything she did turned out perfect. She was a cook who never burned a single meal. She walked with grace and spoke without a stutter. She held herself up with poise and class. Her sister liked to look good; long black hair perfectly braided to the side, her golden brown skin smooth and clean, lips popped with a light pink gloss.

Tia sat down on the blanket, brushing the last bits of grass off her stockings, "You humor me Kirana."

"I do?" She sat down next to her.

"I can't understand why you like this place so much." Tia looked up to the sun, pulling her hat further over her face, "I much prefer the indoors."

"Of course you do." Kirana threw a bit of grass at her dress.

Tia gasped and flicked it off, before laughing and enjoying the tease.

Kirana liked being outside. She liked being in the breeze and being surrounded by nature. The wind, the water, the plants around her. At night, it was the perfect moment for a fire. The only time she spent inside was when she slept, and that was only because the bed was so comfortable. She dressed much differently than Tia. Baggy pants, plain T-shirt, long dark blue jacket and flexible boots. She kept her blond hair short and though most of her attire was for nothing more than the ability to run, jump, and bike, she did enjoy looking nice. She spent time brushing her hair and making sure she remained clean. Kirana figured it was a habit Tia had influenced because, just like her sister, she wanted to look good.

Tia pulled off a small cloth to reveal a plate of pastries. They were warm, still steaming. Kirana's jaw dropped, "When did you make these?"

She shrugged, "I had a few minutes to spare."

Kirana grabbed one and stuffed it into her mouth. A burst of sugar and bread competed for her attention with the inner custard winning as soon as it hit her lips. "Tia, this is amazing!"

"I'm glad you like them." She folded the cloth, "I packed some away for you to take home. But I think you shouldn't have it for dinner."

"Of course, I'm going to have it for dinner, Tia. You can't stop me." She stuffed the rest in her mouth tauntingly, "What do you have planned for today?"

Tia gestured for Kirana to wipe her mouth, "Well, actually, I have to leave earlier today." Kirana stared at her. The disbelief in her eyes poisoned Tia's look of serenity. Her sister let out a laugh, "Do you expect me to stay with you forever?"

"No, of course not." Kirana waved her thoughts away, "I'm just getting greedy with you."

Tia took out a cup from the basket and a large teapot held closed with a wax wrapping, "Let's just enjoy the time we have." She poured herself a cup of steaming red tea, "I want to hear about everything you have done this past week."

Kirana thought for a moment, "Well I found this new spot, deep in one of the old pine forests."

"That sounds exciting. What did you find?"

"A lake! It was gorgeous. The whole forest was dark except this one part. It kind of felt like this place." She gestured to the field, "Sort of magical in its own way."

Tia gave her a warm smile and looked back toward the way she had come. Kirana could tell she wanted to leave and be off on her own. It was selfish to keep Tia away from her perfect life but... Kirana just wanted her to stay.

"There was this old tree in the forest." She crawled around her sister so she was directly in front of her, "It had fallen and you could see the rings in its trunk. There were 147 rings."

Tia rolled her eyes jokingly and took a sip of her tea, "You counted them?"

"I wanted to know how old it was. 147 years old. I was thinking about how many people they must have seen in their years. People who just saw them and now I got to see it too in its final moments. I even saw some people there walking around it."

Tia looked up at her, tea inches from her mouth she set it down in her hand. She tried to hide her worry by acting calm. It didn't work. "Did you… speak to anyone?"

Kirana twisted her jaw to the side, "No." She grabbed another pastry and stuffed it into her mouth, "It's not like anyone tried to talk to me anyway. No one even looked at me."

"That is because no one wants to talk to you." Tia looked up and gave a soft chuckle at her wording, "Not that you are unpleasant of course. You are just… well–"

"Different." Kirana nodded quickly, "I know. I'm different."

Tia put down her tea and grabbed her sister's hand, "That's why I'm here."

Then why was she leaving?

Tia leaned forward and held the side of Kirana's face, "You are perfect. Our life is perfect. You do not need anything else. Do you?"

Kirana shook her head quickly, "I just need you."

"I'm always here for you."

No, she wasn't. "Why don't we go out to see the tree?" Tia took a solemn breath to speak but Kirana wasn't ready to hear her disagreement so quickly and spoke over her, "Just for a few minutes. We can go right now. I'll take you there on my bike. We just look around."

"Kirana–"

"You rode my bike when I first got it. You loved it, I saw the look on your face. Or I can go home with you." Kirana picked up a pastry, "You can show me how to bake these. You know I'm a fast learner, maybe even next time I can make–"

Tia put a hand on her sister's and squeezed gently, "Kirana." She didn't say anything else and instead resorted to looking Kirana in her eyes. Tia wasn't like the boy from before, there was life in her gaze, a connection.

Kirana always wanted her to stay. Her life was perfect. The world around her, Permidia, was perfect. The world had been crafted to make everyone's life perfect. No one suffered. There were no wars. There were no diseases or plagues. People lived in the most beautiful houses in the perfect places. In a cabin along a forest.

In the city hearing the noise of music and life. On a boat resting on the waterside. Perfect in every way. Kirana needed to remember her life was perfect. There was nothing she could do to make it better. She was different but she had Tia to help make up for what she could not have. Her sister was everything she needed, and even if she only came for a little while it was worth it.

"You should go." Kirana put on a quick smile, "I'm just getting excited. I'm good now that you came to see me."

"You are so thoughtful, Kirana." She put her tea down and got up off the blanket, "I'll send someone to clean this up." She wiped her dress, "I will try and stop by for dinner. I can make you that honey garlic chicken you always like." She grabbed her empty basket and left without another word.

Kirana listened to her leave through the grass. The blades shaped around with her movements and finally settled with just the wind creaking them together. Kirana flopped down on the ground and grunted. She pressed her hands into her eyes. Kirana stood up and walked away from the picnic, picking up a small box Tia had left behind for her. She shook it gently and could tell it was pastries. A gift for her absence. It was funny, Kirana could taste Tia more than she could hear her voice or see her face. She hated how much it hurt to miss her sister, how empty it felt to be left time and time again. No one understood what it was like. Even though her life was perfect she kept finding faults and cracks in places they shouldn't have been. Was she at fault? Was her difference a stain on her world? A stain on Tia's life?

Kirana was not perfect, neither was her life.

"*Kirana.*"

It was a whisper.

She looked back the way Tia had gone, "Yes?" She looked around for her sister, but she wasn't there. It took Kirana a few moments to realize how strange Tia's voice was, and even longer to realize it might have not been Tia at all.

Kirana walked forward, "Tia!" As she stepped out into the field the breeze shifted. It changed directions. Kirana felt it flow around her, lift her arms, and rush through her coat. The grass around her bent in all directions, flowing violently in ways it should have been able to. As if it was alive. It grew stronger and stronger.

"*Kirana.*"

It was not Tia's voice. It was someone else. The voice was powerful, but husked, pulling her forward with the breeze. No one had ever spoken to her. No one was like her. No one spoke. And yet, there was someone else. This whisper was carried by the breeze. It was calling for her.

Without wasting another moment she dropped the box of pastries and ran into the field. She sprinted, pushing past cluster after clustering of sharp blades of grass.

She called after it, "I'm here!"

The grass cut her as she pushed herself to move further within. The wind suddenly swept forward, pushing down to form a path before her. It became easier to move through the field, but that was when Kirana heard a sharp zipping sound. She glanced up to see small dots moving from the platforms towards the field. The Nanos. A large group of them were heading right for her, flying forward to overtake her.

They were trying to stop her.

Kirana kept running, trying to find the source of the voice before it was too late. "Wait!" She called out to the person, "Please!"

The Nanos were coming faster, but as she picked up speed the wind started to fade, and the terrain became harder to climb through. As she sprinted forward she suddenly tripped and flew down to the floor. She looked up through the blades of grass as the wind died down and the field returned to its peace.

A final soft breeze flew around her neck, "*Come.*"

She heard a Nano above her and rolled onto her back to look up at them. "Are you alright, Kirana?"

She let out a grunt as she stood up and faced the android. There were more behind the one speaking to her, "What do you want?"

"You were running too fast. We suggest you go slower when you are running through the field."

"I got excited." She glanced at where the wind had been trying to lead her. She couldn't see anything through the grass. "I wanted to see how fast I could run through the field."

The android's expression did not change, "I am here to make sure you are happy and safe. And though you were happy, you were not safe." Kirana stood up straighter and put her cut arms behind her. The Nano suddenly looked surprised, and let out a robotic laugh, "I almost forgot to mention, Tia says she will be over for dinner tonight to make up for leaving so soon."

The timing… It couldn't be a coincidence. Kirana wanted—no, needed—to find out who was calling her. They wanted her to come to them, but what just happened? They were whispering, not yelling from a location. It was as if it came from her mind. Was she just imagining it, so desperate to speak to someone she made up an imaginary person? It was just so real. And the wind, it had never behaved that way before. It felt like the breeze came alive. Kirana thought about running past the Nanos. She could find who was talking if she just moved fast enough, but right now she wasn't even sure they were a real person.

Kirana looked up at the Nano, "I will just go home then."

She walked back the way she had come, moving slowly through the grass to show the androids she was being safe. By the time she made it back to her bike in the small grass clearing half of the Nanos were heading back to the platforms on the Magistrater's tower, and the other half were carefully taking the picnic supplies Tia had left behind in their small robotic arms. Kirana watched them fly together and leave her be. All that was left was her bike and the box of pastries she had thrown down. Half of the cream-filled treats were already spread across the grass.

Kirana looked around the field for a final sign, or the reveal of a person with lively eyes like Tia's. But nothing came for her. The only thing she could hear was the soft dull breeze and a small buzz of a Nano's fans. They didn't all leave, some stayed back to watch her.

Kirana looked out to the field one last time, before returning to her bike.

She decided to leave the pastries behind.

Chapter 3

* * *

GWEN

GWEN PLACED DOWN more items on the table. She laid them out neatly and did her best to make it look like the table was full. There was hardly anything to sell, and hardly any way to make it look like there was. She moved them close to her so she would be able to grab them before anyone could snatch a handful and run off without paying. They were items that took her a long time to make, and she couldn't have them going to waste.

Gwen moved the small post of the stall back so the roof wouldn't fall over. It was heavy but she managed it fine, dragging it along the table. The whole place shook, but that was expected for how cheap it was. The stall was made off of anything she could find, and she kept it all in a small dirty alley down the corner. No one seemed to notice, and everyone figured it was just some extra garbage. A few days ago, however, she noticed a piece of cloth missing. It was supposed to go over the table and now all she had was the rotten wood to place down the handmade items. Gwen didn't mind, she figured if someone was that desperate for a dirty old blanket they needed it more than she did. She knew her display looked cheap without the cloth, but she liked the idea that it was keeping someone warm through the night.

"Daydreaming?"

She looked up. It was Mari. The girl, or rather, woman was leaning on her stall, propping her hip against the side and pouting her lips.

Gwen laughed at herself, "Lost in thought."

"Of course." Mari picked up a bracelet and tried it on. "Who even buys this?"

Gwen shrugged, moving a few items closer to her, "People who like jewelry."

Mari was not a sentimental person. She lived in another house beside Gwen's and as kids they would often play together. When they turned seven, they even worked out in the fields on the same shifts. Mari put her hand out to see how the bracelet looked on her wrist. It looked nice, even on her pale skin. Gwen had hoped it looked nice on everyone, and at first, she had feared that it would only look nice against her own deep brown color since she had been the one to design it. But as more began to sell she realized she was just overthinking.

"How much?"

Gwen hadn't expected her to want to buy anything and quickly spat out a number.

"5 Corts."

"Never mind."

She took off the bracelet and put it back. Gwen was just happy she put it in the right spot. It took her a while to set up everything.

"What are you doing down here?" Gwen asked.

"Shopping, finding food, getting free stuff where I can." She pointed to the ring on her index finger and let out a laugh, "He didn't even notice when I grabbed it off his stall. Too busy looking at all of this."

She gestured to her body as if she was putting it on display. Gwen sighed and shook her head.

Mari whined, "I won't tell these things if you keep making that face."

Gwen was disappointed in her friend. Mari had this enjoyment of getting free things. She stole a lot of items off the stalls and even from larger shops. The problem was that she had never gotten caught, and never had to face any sort of danger. It made her selfish or, even worse, cocky.

"You should give it back."

The thief examined the ring on her hand, "Why?"

"Because it takes a while to make those. He just lost 40 Corts because of you. Do you know how much 40 Corts can get you?"

"Of course I do," Mari glared at her, "But no one was buying his rings. You know old Miller, he never sells anything. So I just… took it off his hands."

Gwen wasn't going to change her friend's mind, and truthfully she was right.

Miller never sold anything. His dusty rings just sat on display while he grew older and older. Gwen put her lips together and kept quiet. Mari took off the ring and slipped it into her pocket. With a small wave, she walked away, "Find me when you're done."

Gwen gave a small smile, but when Mari looked away she looked back down at her handmade items, counting each of them. Friends were valuable to have but hard to keep up with.

Mari had brought with her a wave of bad luck. No one came to Gwen's stall; no one even glanced over. She had some Corts from the day before, but she would need more for the rest of the week. People liked her items, but they would all choose groceries and necessities over a pretty little bracelet any day.

"Gwen!"

She had been slouching in the corner, but at the sound of the voice she stiffened and moved forward. It was Danny. The young boy was running, crashing into the crowd and stumbling blindly towards her. He looked scared, more than that, horrified.

Gwen ran around her stall over to him and he jumped onto her, clinging onto whatever he could hold. Gwen held him tightly, black curls in her hand as he put his face on her shoulder.

"What's wrong?"

Danny spun behind her, holding onto her back. Gwen looked in front of her to see who he was hiding from. When she saw them her heart raced with fear.

The Wardens.

She stood up quickly and kept Danny behind her. The Wardens marched up, guns resting at the ready in their hands. Everyone around them quickly did their best to move away without being noticed. People trapped in their stalls looked down at the floor, not brave enough to make eye contact.

The Wardens, the protectors of the people, but the title had died out long ago. The only protection they did was for themselves.

And their leader.

Their uniforms matched anything around them. Camouflaged with tan and brown colors, their jumpsuits had a scattered pattern of the same blotchy color palette. On top of that rested black and gray armor. Gloves, kneecaps, and a vest. They were not willing to show any skin so, of course, they wore helmets. The whole helmet was black, including the front glass, which was reflective, so when they came up to Gwen all she saw was her pitiful figure, weakened by youth and inexperience. She tilted her head down submissively.

"Hand over the kid." A robotic male voice snapped.

Danny held onto her tighter, and she backed into her stall, "No please, I'm sure there was a misunderstanding. I am his friend. We live in the same household. My father helps his family. I am practically his sister."

"Hand over the kid." He repeated.

"Please," she begged, "Whatever he did I can help fix it."

"He stole an item off of a stall." One of the Wardens was holding a small fruit. Rotten, barely edible. Gwen looked down at Danny. Why did he do it? She figured one of his friends must have dared him to take a toy or some food off a stall, but none of them saw the Wardens on patrol. The Warden who stood before her, the leader of the group, reached out to grab Danny. He screamed and Gwen put up her hands.

"No, please! I can pay them back. I can pay them more than what they would have gotten by selling it." She desperately wanted to see the leader's face, to look into his eyes and try to find some morsel of mercy. She desperately needed to know that the man before her understood that Danny was just a kid. There was a moment of silence between them. The entire street had gone quiet too, but this moment held tension only between her and the Warden. He glanced over to the other soldiers and back down the long street of stalls.

He nodded softly, "20 Corts."

Gwen nodded and slowly moved further into her stall. Danny refused to let go of her and stumbled around him and bent down to her small container under the table. She opened it so only she could see inside and counted the paper bills. She had 30 Corts. She had enough to pay them, but to lose 20 Corts in one day was too much. She didn't dare glance back but she knew they couldn't see into her container. Gwen grabbed 10 Corts and closed the lid.

"I'm sorry I only have 10. It was slow business last week and I only just started–"

They lunged at her and grabbed Danny's arm. The boy screamed and desperately held onto Gwen. The boy's grip slipped and she cried out, "Wait!", diving back down to the tin and pulling out all the money. "I have some extra, it was... I just..." Her heart was racing as she held out the Corts.

The Warden stopped dragging Dany away, holding his arm so high she was afraid they would rip it off. She could hear him sigh from behind his helmet, and after a few horrible moments, they dropped the boy. Danny screamed again and ran back behind Gwen. The Warden stepped right up to Gwen and snatched the Corts out of her hand. She waited as they counted each paper. She stayed exactly where she was, barely able to breathe. He eventually looked up at her, glancing at her empty container, and turning away. The other Wardens walked around the stall back the way they came. Frozen in place with Danny clinging to her side, Gwen watched the Wardens give the money to a stall down the street. But she could tell, even from far away, that they only gave half of what she gave them. Maybe less. They would keep the rest for themselves.

She grabbed Danny by his collar and forced him to look at her, "Why did you steal?" She was yelling at him, but the poor child was too scared to take on any more fear. He ignored her anger and hugged her, sobbing violently. She didn't want to hug him back, gods, she was furious. He could have been taken. She could have lost him, but… that wasn't just his fault. No, she had tried to trick the monsters holding him. She could have lost him and it would be her fault. She dropped down and hugged him back.

He mumbled words with his face dug into her shoulder, "I'm sorry."

She closed her eyes and held him closer.

She wished she could give him a better life.

Chapter 4

KIRANA

KIRANA PARKED HER bike outside and took off her goggles. She sighed, closing her eyes and wiping her face. She needed to just focus on the fact Tia was there for dinner. The voice could have just been her imagination. That was possible, right? Just her imagination. The Nanos were watching out for her safety, and that was it. She just got a little lonely, but no longer.

She could hear something sizzling, some sort of meat being cooked. There was probably sauce too, Tia always added some crazy sauce to all her meals. Kirana realized now how hungry she was, and practically burst through the door at the promise of a heaping plate.

When she walked in the house a wave of heat hit her face. The house was warm and comfortably cozy. She decided to leave her troubles outside the door.

"Well hello." Tia greeted her from the kitchen.

Kirana quickly took off her coat and hung it by the door. As she turned the corner to the kitchen she saw Tia standing over a stove, mixing a bowl vigorously. She had put on the red apron she kept at Kirana's house. She had cooked many meals for the two of them over the years, yet the apron remained spotless. Kirana let out a happy sigh, "I'm so glad you're here."

Tia looked over at her. She was wearing a lively smile as she spun around and grabbed a large spoon. Dipping it into the sauce quickly she glided over and held it up to Kirana. "Try this." She didn't have a choice. Tia stuck the spoon in her mouth and pulled it away quickly. It was worth it. The sauce was delicious.

"So good!" Kirana told her, wiping her mouth. Her gaze found its way to the window. The golden grass just outside. She took a second to watch it, eyes darting around looking for patterns in the wind. She pulled her gaze away and looked back to her sister. But it was too late, Tia had seen her tension.

"What is wrong?"

Kirana shook her head playfully, walking into the kitchen, "Nothing." She grabbed a spoon and scraped the edges of the pot, "How are you?" She was a terrible liar.

"*Kirana.*" Her sister said, stretching out the name in a strange tone.

She glanced out the window, "I just..." She locked eyes with Tia, who waited patiently for an answer. Kirana thought about what she should even say. Should she mention the voice? No, she would just sound crazy, and for now, she just wanted to keep what had or had not happened to herself.

Instead, she decided to say, "Why am I different?"

Tia looked surprised, and then she laughed, turning to the stove.

"You just are, silly." She turned off the heat and moved the large pot away from them. Tia moved over to the vegetables, chopping at them quickly. "Do you have any new drawings?"

"Tia." Her sister heard her tone and looked over. "Why?"

She shrugged, "It's just the way life works."

"What do you mean?"

Tia got out a pan and put it on the already hot stove. She drizzled some green liquid into it and went back to cutting the vegetables. "Sometimes you just are born with unique traits." Kirana laughed at her words and her sister shot her a look, "Stop that now. You are perfect. Different has never meant bad."

"No, it just means I see things no one else sees."

Tia stopped cutting for a moment, before continuing abruptly. She moved to a large handful of green herbs, chopping them up too. "What can you see?"

"People." She felt like the only person who knew there were people around her. Everyone kept their heads up or down while she looked forward.

"What made you think about this today?"

Kirana glanced back to the window, "I think about it all the time. I just– I wanted to get a proper answer."

"Dinner will be ready in a few minutes," Tia told her, wiping her hands on her apron. Still, no spots. "Might as well get cleaned up while I finish."

Kirana didn't want to stop their conversation, especially when she felt like it was going somewhere. So she didn't leave. She just stood there, one hand on the countertop, eyes locked on her sister. Tia kept silent for a moment, before coming over and holding her hands on her own. Kirana felt how warm they were from cooking.

Tia looked her right in the eyes, "I don't have an answer. I wish I did. But this isn't a curse, it's not some bad luck, it's just a trait." Tia moved a piece of her hair behind her ear. "You're perfect."

She looked down at Kirana's hands and let out a gasp at the sight of the cuts from the grass, "Oh my goodness what happened to you." She let go of her and ran back into the kitchen, "Here." She grabbed a small glass bottle and put it in Kirana's hand, "Wash your hands with soap and rinse with this. How did you do this?"

"Some grass cut me." She shook her head, "But I'm fine, Tia." She loved how much her sister cared for her.

Tia was right. They were sisters, and in the end, they had each other. Kirana loved her life, she always would. No imaginary voice could change that.

Kirana moved out of the kitchen and went to the bathroom. She turned on the tap and washed her hands with the sweet-smelling soap. She glanced up and saw her reflection in the mirror. Nothing had changed since that morning, it's not like her hair had grown or her clothes had magically turned yellow. She looked the same... except for the look she gave herself. When she saw her eyes something felt different. Not in a sense that her eyes were no longer a deep blue, but in her gaze. It was as if something deep inside her was sending a message.

Don't give up.

She was telling herself to find the answer because there has to be one out there. But which question did she want answered?

Who was the person calling her or who was she?

Kirana looked away and shut off the tap. Swinging open the door she decided to just enjoy the night with her sister for now. Questions didn't expire, and she only hoped the same applied to answers.

Tia had finished remarkably fast, and Kirana sat down to eat the amazing meal before her. Together the two sisters talked all night, but not about the field, or the questions, but about random small things. Tia never stayed so long and Kirana soaked up every moment she could with her sister. It was truly the perfect night.

After Tia left, Kirana lay in bed staring at the roof of her room. She wished her mind could stop working but it kept playing the voice. She reminded herself of the perfect night in her perfect world with her perfect sister. She forced her eyes shut and told herself that finding the answer to the question would not help her. So with that final thought, she eventually did get to sleep. It was nice when her mind stopped working and peace took over, even if she did dream of the golden field and that strange voice.

She woke up to the smell of breakfast and, through the door, she could hear the faintest hum of a song. Tia? Kirana jumped out of bed and ran to the door and, sure enough, her sister was standing in her kitchen.

Tia flipped a pancake over "Good morning sleepyhead."

"What are you doing here?" Tia had never visited her in the morning. They had lived together before, yes, but since the day she left they had only had dinners and quick afternoons together. What made this day different?

"I have some great news." Tia told her as she placed a warm pancake on a plate. She put it in front of Kirana on a countertop and smiled, "Guess who gets to meet the Magistrater?" She let out a squeal from joy, "You!"

"What?" Kirana felt her stomach curl. Excitement or worry, she couldn't tell the difference, "You're kidding."

"I am not." Tia told her, just as excited. "I was thinking about your questions last night and I had a few favors and I pulled them in to get you a meeting with the Magistrater."

Kirana was ready to celebrate with her sister, ready to jump up and dance around the room, but her words sunk in, and settled, "What do you mean favors?"

Tia went back over her pancakes, keeping her happy smile wrapped around her face. "The Magistrater asked me to meet with her a while back about you, actually. I asked a Nano to contact her for me and ask if you could meet her personally." Kirana didn't respond and she looked over, "You think I would hide another person like you?"

Meeting the Magistrater was an honor too great to put into words. It would be the greatest moment in Kirana's life. The Magistrater was responsible for everything around them. The perfect world was made by her. Millions of people live their best lives because of her. Kirana had never seen the ruler in person, in fact, she never thought she would. The Magistrater was a god compared to her citizens. Kirana learned about her in books and from Tia's stories. Her sister always had a legend to share about the great ruler who could control life itself. The Magistrater was born in the old times; the horrible age of war and suffering. She created a system to help her people each live their perfect lives. Tia once told Kirana she got her power from the joy and content of her people, their lives allowing her to stay powerful and maintain order. The stories said Permidia worked in a cycle, perfect in every way, all because of their ruler.

It's not every day you get to speak to the Magistrater, and it's not every day she wants to speak to you. Face to face.

"Why didn't you tell me you met her?"

Tia blinked softly, "Well maybe we can compare visits once you come back. She's meeting you in an hour."

Kirana waited for the joke to make sense or to see her sister start laughing. She did not. "An hour?"

She winked, "Better eat quickly and go get changed."

Kirana practically dove to the plate of food, eating as quickly as she could and bringing the plate into her room to get changed. She started mentally listing out questions and comments as she dressed. While she brushed her hair she found the perfect greeting, respectful but also relaxed. As she pulled on her shoes she practiced the perfect tone of laughter, soft but perfectly joyful. She slipped on her coat and found the right smile in the mirror, bright but not too hyper.

On the way out and gave Tia a long hug.

"I can't thank you enough."

"You don't have to." Her sister looked her over and squinted at her face, "Kirana. You have crumbs on your face."

Tia grabbed a cloth and tried to wipe them off for her, but with a laugh, Kirana leaned back and took it, "Okay. Okay, thank you." She brushed her mouth quickly and threw the cloth down as soon as she was ready. She turned her head from side to side to show it off to Tia. "How do I look?"

"Perfect, you're perfect."

Kirana took a breath and walked out of the house.

It didn't take her long to get to the center tower. Especially when she was speeding to it on her bike. The Magistrater's Tower was the central point of the city, but for its vastness, it only had one entrance. A grand one with high black doors. Two Nanos were always in front of them, smiling down at the people around. Kirana had visited the doors before, just to get a look. Nothing more than curiosity, until now. Kirana felt like she was in the center of the universe when she walked up to the doors. They were a different shade of the gray exterior of the tower, a sort of lighter tint that reflected off of the sun. Patterns built off of one another until they reached the very top of the towering double doors. In the crack between them glowed a soft golden light. The Nanos floated over to her, and as they did the doors started to move forward. It was a powerful sight to watch them open before her.

"Good morning Kirana." The Nanos bounced excitedly before turning and flowing slowly through the doors. "Just follow us."

Kirana walked behind them, walking to their speed into the room. She looked everywhere she could. The room was a hallway, but, large though it was, it was empty. And dark, as if the entire space was just one large shadow. It was at that moment Kirana realized that this moment, this meeting was not just an honor but also a formal introduction to the ruler that brought the entire world to peace. As they made their way further inside the doors started to close. The shadows became darker, and with a soft thud, she was locked inside. Excitement had become worry, and now it was fear.

The Nanos took her to the end of the hallway where a door stood against a bare wall. It was white with gold-lined edges, something made to look and feel grand. Against the shadows, it simply felt ominous.

"Are you ready?" The Nano asked as if this moment was something to enjoy.

She had no choice but to say, "Yes."

The Nanos moved out of the way of the door as it started to open. Light poured into the dark hallway and spread across Kirana. The room before her was filled with a warm glow, but surely not from the sun. They were far inside the building, certainly not at any wall. And yet, this artificial glow tricked her with the room's warmth. The design was made with lush cream colors, specks of gold patterns, and pops of rose. Not the color, but the actual flower. Pink roses filled every space they could, some hanging from the roof and others spread across pots and vines along walls and floors. The room was high enough to fit a chandelier, and wide enough to have two levels within itself. The first level featured a long wooden table decorated with pink roses, gorgeous decorations, and stacks on stacks of books. A carpet draped the floor in comfort and moved up to the second level; with a throne, and a window. The throne was light brown, a color that demonstrated a well-used gold. The elegant window behind it shaped the light within the room. The warmth, and a shadow. A figure stood beside the throne, her long shadow moving towards Kirana.

"Welcome."

It was her.

The Magistrater.

She was tall, so tall that it looked unnatural. It could have been. She was practically gliding across the room, feet hidden by a long cream robe. The ruler's hands were covered by black gloves. That same dark material covered her neck and head. She had no hair, none that Kirana could see behind the cloth, nor a true face for she wore a mask. Made of metal both silver and gold, and patterned with elegant features, half her face was completely covered. From the top of her head down to her nose was a tangle of metallic artistry. Was she blind?

Something was wrong with her, that was for certain. Edging out of the mask were pieces of her face, black and purple. Like a burn. Like acid.

The Magistrater's red lips curled up into a smile, "I have been waiting a long time to meet you." Without eyes, it was impossible to tell if this was sincere.

She slowly stepped forward into the room. "You have?" The door behind Kirana shut and she flinched at the sound. Everything she had practiced or thought of before entering the room was gone. She couldn't remember anything. Why was she even there?

"I understand you have questions. Your sister has been telling me of your curiosities for quite a while now." Tia had been talking to her? "Ask me anything you would like, I am here to be your answer."

Kirana pulled herself together, straightening her back, "Why am I different?"

The Magistrater smiled. A smirk with more joy than should have been there for such a question. "I love that question." She glided her way over to the table, "For your entire life we have known you were unique. We gave you the perfect life, same as the others, and yet you still longed for connection." She reached out to one of the largest roses on the table, cupping it in her hand gently, "It's admirable, and as you can see I too feel the same remarks to others."

Kirana hadn't even noticed until now, but it felt so important. It was just her and Tia... and the Magistrater. "I'm like you?"

The ruler turned her face back to her, "In some ways, yes. In others, no." She let go of the rose, "I have lived many lives, seen many people come through Permidia and find their happiness. That is my life, a purpose of giving perfection. I will not bind you to such fate, for you deserve the perfect life just like anyone else."

"No." Kirana tried to catch the word before the ruler could hear it. Too late. "Sorry, no I mean..." She searched for the words, "If I am different for a purpose, I want to fulfill that."

The Magister's mood had shifted, and her smile faded down, "I have not answered your question. Why you are different, that is. The answer is... you were a mistake."

Kirana went cold. She couldn't respond, how could she? That was not the word she had expected. It was too... painful.

The ruler tilted her head and pieces of her mask rotated with her movement, "I do not mean to upset you, my dear. But it is the truth. We did not intend for you to be... this."

This mistake.

Kirana shook her head, "I don't understand."

"You don't have to." The Magistrater turned back to the rose and snapped its stem. Pulling it from the rest she walked to Kirana, towering over her. "Your life has just begun. You can still have your perfect life, I promise you that." She pushed the rose towards her and let her take it gently. "And maybe one day we can meet again and use your unique trait for the good of our world."

"What about Tia?" Kirana sounded angry, she hadn't meant to, it was just... it was too much. "Why is she different?"

"She is a wonderful sister, but her connection is limited. She is not like you. No one truly is."

"Except for you?"

The Magistrater shook her head gently, "No one."

The doors behind her opened and she saw the two Nanos outside waiting to escort her out. Kirana looked back up to the ruler and took a step back. She waited for her to say something, anything. But the woman didn't move, she didn't say a word.

Kirana looked from the door to the ruler, "We're done then?"

"Thank you my darling. It's been an honor to meet you."

That was it. That was her answer. *You were a mistake.* It was horrible. She felt worthless, no, useless. Was she a burden on her world? No, the Magistrater had told her she might have a purpose... was that a lie? Did she just have a strange feature no one needed? And what about Tia? Even her sister wasn't like her, not really. Kirana had known that, of course, she had seen it in her perfection. Those clean aprons and perfect words. Kirana was messy and hyper; she had no place in her sister's perfect life.

It was just... Kirana. Alone.

The Nanos guided her back out into the dark hallway and moved her beyond the doors back into the streets of the city. The androids went back to their post as the doors shut. Kirana looked down and realized she was still holding onto the rose. It had been larger than the others, and she wondered if the Magistrater intended that to be some sort of metaphor. Kirana was the only thing not perfect in their world, the same as the rose, and in the end... it was plucked from the rest. Was that a threat? Maybe she was reading it wrong, but her situation felt dangerous. She felt like she knew everything and yet... nothing.

If the world was so perfect... then why was there a miscalculation?

That didn't make sense. There was nothing wrong with Permidia. Nothing off. Nothing damaged. Nothing broken.

Except for her... and the voice.

Was that a mistake too?

No.

That voice was someone like her, maybe, or at least someone who did not belong in perfection. Kirana knew that there was someone out there, someone calling for her.

She looked down at the rose and let it fall to the floor.

She was not different. She was not unique. She would find the voice.

Tonight, in the field.

Chapter 5

✳

GWEN

GWEN HELD DANNY'S hand as joined the crowd in a long, muddy walk home. It had poured earlier that day, and though the fields of crops around them thrived in the water, the people around Gwen did not. She hated the rain. It made her life more difficult because now she would have to go home and clean her boots and pants on top of everything else. Danny's too, and whoever else walked the same path.

She could see their house in the distance. It took a few minutes to get there, but Danny and Gwen didn't say a word to each other or anyone around them, though the others chatted amongst themselves. Gwen had kept Danny by her side the whole time she was selling her homemade craft. He wouldn't let her go, clinging to her as if she would ever let him go. She knew he needed her, and if she had the choice she would have brought him home right after the Wardens left. But there wasn't even a transport to take them back home. The Worker Ship came in the morning and the evening. As soon as someone got to their job they were, quite literally, stuck there for the rest of the day. Besides, Gwen wanted to try and make up the money she lost. She didn't.

As they finally got closer to the neighborhood, many of the people around them started to go into one of the five houses lined up in a stubby U shape. They weren't that nice, nothing stunning to look at or live in. They were long tan huts, with the shorter side facing the main center area. Gwen and Danny's family lived in the center house, and she didn't waste any time getting there. Other places like her own small neighborhood were everywhere, lined up by the fields and small rivers.

When they got close to the door Danny finally let go of her hand and ran for the house. He slammed into the door and threw it open.

"Mom!" He screamed her name.

Gwen took her time to go inside, knowing that Gaia and the others could handle Danny from there. She was honestly scared to go inside. She didn't want to face her family with what had happened, mostly because she felt guilty for all of it. But in the end, she couldn't hide from her family, and it was more selfish to stand outside than face the questions.

Gwen came inside and looked over to the kitchen. Gaia sat in the center of the room, holding onto Danny for dear life. The other people in the room all came around as Danny sobbed, words bubbling with spit and tears.

Gaia looked over to Gwen, who stayed out of the kitchen. "What happened?" She asked in her panic.

"Danny had a close call with a few Wardens."

Gaia held him closer. She was on the floor with him, surrounding him with a warm hug and whispers. The kitchen smelt like some sort of soup, warmth feeding off the stove. The room was small but was big enough to fit George and Mailey, who seemed to be helping with dinner.

The two siblings were Gaia's, and her other son Harold was probably in the kids' bedroom down the hall. Gwen's house had two families, Gaia's and her own. Gaia had four kids of her own, but over the years she had taken in five children off the streets. Gwen had no siblings, it was just her and her father, fragments of what once was. A house of three became two, empty and silent, and her father took in Gaia and her entire family: Her husband Theo, Harold, George, Mailey, Danny, and all the sad little children they kept fed. Gaia's family, Gwen's father, and herself. A big family, a small house.

It was suffocating.

"What happened?"

Gwen turned to face the hallway and saw her father. Gideon stood a bit farther away from her, having come out of the adults' bedroom down the hallway. He always stood up tall, even though he would still be tall if he slouched. He had a muscular build from years of hard labor and wore his usual outfit of browns and grays. The bottom of his pants was lined with mud, and Gwen figured it was from working in the fields that day. She grabbed the tin from her bag and walked over as the people in the kitchen tried to calm down the hysterical Danny.

"He stole something." Gwen told her father quietly, "I don't know why, and I don't want to make a big deal out of it because he knows now never to do it again."

Her father looked down at the tin and she could see the realization coming to him quickly. He closed his eyes, pushing down irritation. "How much?"

"30," Gwen said honestly, "But..." She didn't finish her sentence, wondering if she should even mention it.

"Yes?" Her father asked, seeing there was more to her story.

Gwen fidgeted with the tin, "I lied to them. I said that I only had 10 Corts."

"Gwen–"

"Yes I know. And they almost took Danny. I just... I am tired of them taking everything from us."

Her father put his hand on her shoulder, squeezing it tightly. He glanced behind her, and she realized his touch was more of a warning to keep her voice down than a gesture of sympathy. He leaned forward, "I understand what you wanted to do. What you wanted to prove, but the Wardens... They are superior to us. Did you hear what happened to Malaya and James?"

Gwen shook her head. He looked somber as he spoke, "James got a list of the Warden's schedules after stealing one of their helmets. He took it to Lorenzo and the Wardens found James during his wedding with Malaya. They're saying all the guests were killed or questioned." Gwen knew Malaya well. They used to work together in a milling factory a few years ago and stayed in touch selling craft together now and then. Malaya wasn't necessarily a good friend, but there was still something painful about having looked someone in the eyes and never being able to again.

Her father looked her right in her eyes, not letting her think too long about the death, "We don't make the rules Gwen, we don't rule over our own lives." He came closer and whispered beside her ear, "Yet."

He moved gracefully past her towards the kitchen. His actions were never hard or heavy. He was carried by the wind and walked on the air. It made him seem gentle and had kept him out of trouble all these years. Gwen didn't know how he was able to do such a thing in such harsh situations. She could hear him trying to help everyone pull something together for dinner, explaining that they needed to ration some out for tomorrow as well. Guilt kept hitting her like a punch to the stomach. She knew she would be needed soon, but before anyone called her over she walked over to the bathroom and closed the door.

Gwen sat down on the floor, placing the tin next to her as she moved over to the small vent in the corner of the room. She lifted it off the floor and pulled out the black cloth to reveal a hole. Gwen placed the cloth on the vent lid and put her feet into the hole. She felt around for the first step and then the next one further down. Slowly she climbed down the ladder. When she felt the ground under her boot she moved her hand over to the right where she felt for the light switch. When she found the string she pulled it down and a yellow light filled the room.

It had taken her father a long time to dig it all out, but he had help and a good cause. If the Wardens knew they had built such a place under their house they would be arrested, or worse, but her father had taken that risk with great pride. They had brought down a few makeshift things, broken tables, and a few wooden planks for items, but that wasn't what the room was for.

It was for the books.

Piles and piles of books wrapped around the walls of the short dirt room. All of them were half destroyed, burnt, or ripped entirely, but valuable nonetheless.

Gwen walked over to the small wooden desk in the center of the room and sat down on the bucket under it. She pulled over a large book on a stack of papers and stones. She placed it in front of her and dragged her finger over the indented patterns of the cover. She opened it and started to flip through the pages.

They were all faded, and most had words missing or pictures gone from years of no upkeep. She could read some of the pages, but others were in languages she had never seen or heard before. Gwen had come down to her father's hiding place to read these books. She liked reading about past lives, for that was what every single book was about; history. But she knew it was more than that. Gwen read them because the books were also a crime, and her father had smuggled them into their secret hiding spot. She was breaking the law by dragging her finger along the pages, taking in all the words, and seeing the forbidden languages. It gave Gwen hope. Hope that there was a way to break free from the Magestrater's rule. Every book echoed a single word not written once on the pages.

Freedom.

Her father searched for books about one group of people. Secretly sharing stories about them and worshiping their existence.

They were called the Keepers.

The god-like humans ruled over Hiraeth and other worlds. The only reason people knew about them was because of old stories and her father's books. Gwen remembered her mother telling her about how they ruled over different worlds, keeping the peace.

"Where are they now?" Gwen had asked her. Her mother had been sitting beside her, both of them snuggled up on a dusty mattress Gwen still slept on to this day.

"I don't know." She had told the young Gwen, looking up outside the window of their broken house, "But I like to think they are still out there. Ready to protect us."

"When are they coming back?" Her mother had looked back at her, sharing her perfect smile. "One day."

"But we need them now!" Gwen had yelled at her. Even then the young girl knew the dangers of her own home.

Her mother had bent down and whispered with her happy grin, "You are too much like your father, Gwenith." She tucked the old blanket around her, "But maybe we don't need the gods anymore, maybe we need people like you." She had held Gwen's face in both hands, rubbing her hands over her cheeks.

Even now, Gwen still could feel her mother's hand on the side of her face. Warm, soft, motherly. A loving touch. Gwen flipped another page and saw the picture she could stare at for hours. It was almost destroyed, but she could just make out the outline of an army, or at least it looked like a crowd of people, some carrying weapons, and others too faded to tell. Half of the page was almost completely gone, but Gwen could make out one person.

She knew it was a Keeper. They looked important, a staff held above their head. Glowing bright and emanating power, they led the army behind them.

Maybe we need people like you.

Her mother's words were pure, but she was wrong. Gwen could never be so powerful, not like the Keepers, not like the god her people needed to save them. Fictional or not, they were the only ones who could save her people. She leaned her head against the table, looking at the book from the side. She missed her mother so much. Even the mere presence of her, the energy she brought into a room. She filled it with light, with love.

She *had* filled it. Now Gwen's rooms felt empty. Her life. Her heart.

Chapter 6

KIRANA

KIRANA LAID DOWN on her bed quietly waiting for the sun to set. If she went out during the night the Nanos wouldn't be able to see her, at least, she hoped. Even if it was just a quick look around then so be it. If she found a person, great, and if it was nothing she would return home and live her perfect life. The problem was last time the Nanos came to her quickly, and even though she had not tried to go past them she knew they could stop her. They could not know she was coming, if they did she would be caught. Kirana heard how she sounded, making plans that went against what the Magistrater had told her, after all, the ruler never did anything wrong to anyone. The life she was offering her was pure and considerate.

But Kirana just couldn't let go of a feeling that something was wrong.

She waited a moment, before slowly standing up. She was still wearing her clothes, and with ease, she quickly slipped on her boots, grabbed her coat, and opened the front door. No one was in the house with her, other than a few helper androids, but she wanted to be cautious. She wanted to do this alone. No one else needed to be involved. Especially Nanos. She closed the door carefully and looked out towards the field of golden grass. It was going to be a long walk. The bike was too loud and it would alert someone that she was there within seconds. Walking would be a bit more subtle, but it would take a good portion of the night to get within the field.

She moved away from her front door and started to walk on the pavement. From there she stepped onto the green grass and followed it down to a steep hill. Kirana walked down it carefully but ended up sliding on her boots halfway down. She controlled it and managed only a small stumble at the bottom. She looked around for Nanos or anyone else around. Her biggest worry was that the city before her was still quite awake. The platforms were still rotating, the lights were still burning, and the night birds were out living their perfect life. People out during the night meant that Nanos never went off duty. They went on different shifts but were always around.

Kirana looked back towards the grass and pushed away the first handful of the blades. She stepped in and started pushing her way through. It was hard to get very far because of how thick it was. She knew more clearings would be up ahead, but it would take her a while to get there. She looked around for a change in the breeze or shuffling within the grass, but as she kept going forward all she heard was the small noise the blades made bumping into each other.

"Finally," Kirana said to herself when she finally made it to a clearing.

She took a break and looked around. It wasn't as far in as she had been before and hoped she wouldn't have to venture further to find the person. She stood in the clearing for a moment, looking around. Kirana thought about calling out for the person but figured that would bring attention to her. She waited in the clearing for a long time, but nothing happened. What had she done last time? Something that would make the voice call to her. She was just sitting there on the bench thinking about Tia and her life. Kirana sighed and sat down on the grass. After a moment she lay down and stared up at the sky. She waited a few seconds, listening for things around her, but the longer she stayed down on the grass the more stupid she felt.

"This is pathetic." She muttered under her breath. Maybe she had just imagined someone calling her name. And the breeze must have just been a change in the wind, or maybe part of her little hallucination. Kirana figured she could just go home and continue her perfect life. As she stood up she looked back over the grass, seeing the stars above it.

In one last attempt, she called out, "Hello!" Her voice carried far in the silence, "I came! I'm here!"

She glanced over to the city, but she didn't see anyone coming her way. She waited. She listened. Nothing happened. Maybe it was just her imagination. Kirana turned to leave. That's when she felt the wind on her face. It had picked up. It moved around her, in almost every direction. She looked around and felt it move through her coat and up to her hair. Then it went ahead, parting the grass and creating a path for her.

"*Kirana.*" The voice called.

She hadn't imagined it.

Someone was calling her.

Kirana looked back up to the city, and surely enough she saw the Nanos were no longer staying away. Three of them were coming down to her. But this time she wouldn't let them stop her.

Kirana started to run; she ran through the grass, letting it hit her face as she pushed through the golden blades. The wind kept going behind her as if pushing her forward. She went straight ahead, hearing the Nanos move closer and closer. When Kirana heard one land she dove to her right, diving onto her stomach and hiding in the grass. She heard Nanos look around for her.

"Kirana?" The Nano called sweetly, but she didn't answer.

Kirana realized there was no way they couldn't see her. They were technological masterpieces, and she guessed they knew exactly where she was. Kirana didn't have much time. She looked around for the source. It was somewhere near.

"*Come.*"

It was the voice, only now it wasn't in her head. It was in the field. It was calling her from up ahead.

Kirana got up and ran. The Nanos saw her and flew after her. She kept going. She kept running. She stumbled past thick batches of grass. She pushed her way through until she made it to a clearing, the largest one she had ever seen. Only this one wasn't cut or naturally short. It was made by pushing down fresh blades of grass. The wind seemed to move all around it, centering around something that made Kirana stop running. A stone, one that looked ancient and hand-carved with words around the edges. It was sticking out of the ground; words and patterns along its ragged edges glowed white, before changing to yellow, blue, red, and green. It moved through all the colors, but Kirana barely noticed. She was looking at what was above it.

Floating up off the stone was a mighty staff surrounded by glowing particles of light. It was long, a brown wood swirled from the bottom to the top where the final edges curved around a crystal. The large crystal was unlike anything she had seen before. It changed colors too, but she could tell its main color was white. The crystal bore particles of each color, sweeping through the air and circling the staff.

Kirana was frozen, staring at it for too long. When she heard the Nanos coming closer behind her she managed to move forward just in time before they were able to reach her. She could feel their metal hand barely miss her arm. Kirana moved forward to the staff. It was the source. She just needed to take it and run. She would show it to someone. The Magistrater, Tia, anyone. It was something big, something important, and she needed to know what it was. And if she could get away with it maybe it could lead her to the person calling her name. This staff was for her. It was her guide.

Kirana reached out and grabbed the staff, ready to run with it past the stone. But something happened. It felt like a surge of energy went right through her. Like a rush of energy, yet she couldn't move. Kirana felt herself lift up and saw white particles move around her. She let out a scream as something within her burned and an explosion burst from the crystal. The Nanos were swept away, creating a trail of grass with them. She then felt what she could only explain as a great mass of power moved through her. There was a much larger blast and suddenly Kirana couldn't move. Her body locked in place, stuck and rising into the air with the staff.

Then she felt something hit her, like a kick, like something was pushing her back. Yet pulling her too. In every direction moving her back. She folded in and felt her body push through a force. Wind, thick as water. She pushed through and watched the world around her morph and fold in. She felt her body shift into something new. Somewhere new.

She opened her eyes as the breath from her lungs left suddenly. Her whole body felt compact and trapped in a small space. She couldn't move, she couldn't breathe, she could just look around her. She was floating in an eternity of space. A galaxy of light colors and white streaks. Stars blended into lines and rushed around her, reflected by a cut between this strange world, like a body of water below her. She tried to move, tried to find some way out of this, some way back to Permidia. She pulled her body and strained her limbs, but she was helpless to the trap. She was running out of air, her lungs thumping for volume.

As she felt herself pump her chest for long overdue air the sight before her changed. The world before her grew darker, before suddenly a light shot out before her eyes. Before her, shaped by the world of distant lights, were people.

Figures. Four of them. They unveiled themselves one at a time before they all came together in a single line facing her. They each stood with their own glory, holding weapons and featuring different traits, from the shape of their hair to the color of the lights that moved around them. Though the breath within Kirana's lungs was fleeting, the figures brought a new sense of life to her struggle. These people before her were the reason she was there. They called for her. They needed her. She needed them.

But she was suffocating. She was running out of time. She started panicking, trying hard to breathe as she felt herself become dizzy and delusional. Kirana tried to move, but couldn't. It was as if someone was drowning her in sand, pressure building all around her. She forced her eyes to the side and saw the staff. The thing that had brought her here. It was out of her hand, an inch away. She reached for it, trying as hard as she could to get it back. She stretched out her arm, flexing her hand until her finger brushed the wood. Then she grabbed it. The world around her expanded into a bright, blinding yellow, before settling into a deep gold. Like a sunset. Kirana felt herself being pulled forward before falling suddenly to the ground. She took in a gasp of air, but her head spun around and her whole body flooded her with pain.

Before she knew it she was lying on a wet muddy floor.

Passed out.

Chapter 7

* * *

GWEN

GWEN WENT OUTSIDE with a bucket, carrying it by her side as she got to a line of people in the center of the small cluster of houses. There, they had a water pipe. There was only one for everyone to use, which meant about 50 people shared the same water. Gwen didn't mind the wait all that much, over the years it was more of a routine than a chore. There were many things she had to get done in the day that felt long and sometimes even painful, but for a few minutes, she got to just stand there in the line and be still. The breeze was strong that night, flowing through her hair and contrasting her silence with a soft whistle. It was comforting, above anything else. With Danny being cared for in the house and her family safe, she was able to breathe.

But in her stillness were people who desired noise rather than peace. It was always the aunties who liked to go out and gossip with each other while they waited in line. Winny and Margee were the worst of them, and tonight, they were directly in front of Gwen.

Margee started their nightly conversation, "Johna was all up in arms about the cut pay and Gabriel threatened to give her to the Wardens if she didn't stop, and I quote, *starting rebellions.*"

"Gabriel has been quite strong-minded lately. Is he single?"

"Winny! You are married."

"I was trying to set him up with someone else, I am very much happy with Ricky."

"No, you're not."

"No, but he brings a lot in a certain department–"

"Shut your mouth. There are children around."

"Fine, but have you heard the rumors?"

"No. What rumors?"

"I heard that Gaia and Gideon are having an affair."

Gwen looked up quickly as her stomach turned. She felt her mouth move, trying to form words, but she just couldn't say anything.

"Really? I thought that's been happening for a while now."

"No, I think it's still going on. I just wonder who started the whole thing."

"Gideon. He's the one who–"

Finally, Winny glanced back around them, and saw Gwen. They knew who she was, they knew her family too. The aunty shut her mouth and looked ahead. Margee glanced back as well and immediately looked forward. They didn't say anything after that.

Gwen hated it when people spread rumors like that. Especially when they were about her father. Just because he helped Gaia support her family doesn't mean they were sleeping together. She suddenly hated herself for taking an interest in the gossip. If it was about anyone else she would have been intrigued. Entertained.

Time seemed to pass slowly after that, in the silence of the night. Light conversations buzzed but she didn't let any of them settle in her mind. She kept her head down, and when it was her turn, placed the bucket down on the ground below the tap. She started pumping the water, pulling the lever back and forth until it came pouring out. Gwen watched until it was filled enough for her to be able to carry it back. Then, she picked it up with both hands and started back to the house, letting the man behind her fill his containers.

Gwen looked ahead at the house, letting out a sigh as she adjusted her grip on the bucket, but before she was even able to get halfway to the door something caught her eye. From so far away it looked like some sort of shape in the mud between two houses. At first glance, it looked as if someone had just kicked up some mud, so Gwen kept going and pushed the door open.

Harold took the bucket from her. "Thanks." He said, moving it to the kitchen. He then gave it to Gaia, who dumped half of the water into a small container on the floor and started using it to wash the dishes and plates.

"Give the kids some water before bed." She told him.

Harold nodded and carried it off to the bedroom. Gwen watched him, still standing in the doorway. A breeze filled her hair in a swift gesture and flooded back out of the house lightly. Such a gentle push, yet it was enough to make her glance back at the lump of mud. She was worried it was a person face down and slowly dying. The thing was, people like that had usually been beaten by the Wardens, which meant they were trouble. Helping a criminal meant she was one as well. But there were also the drunks from the city. It was a far walk, but if you had enough of that vile liquor you could do anything. But maybe it was someone from her neighborhood. Someone who tripped over a rock and hit their head. Gwen decided she could at least check it out, and if the person tried to attack her she could always just run back to the house or call for help.

"I'll be right back." She told Gaia, not waiting for a reply as she left the house again.

Going around the side she walked through the mud, lifting her boots higher as she walked. As she got closer she saw the shape of a person and slowed her pace. She squinted in the dark, finding certain colors. Black pants, black boots, dark coat, blond hair, pale skin. She moved closer. As she moved closer and closer she eventually saw blood along the girl's face dripping from their nose and mouth. Her head was planted down on the ground with half her face along the mud. The girl's eyes suddenly drifted open slightly, her eyelid trembling. Her head lifted slightly but then fell back down to the mud. A breeze suddenly moved past them both, pushing the girl's mud-filled hair over her face.

She was hurt.

"Dad!" Gwen called out behind her. "Gaia!"

She bent down to her level, letting mud get on her knees as she lifted the girl up as best she could. She wiped mud off her face and away from her eyes. It was odd. She wasn't bruised or bleeding from a wound. But rather, she just had blood coming out from her nose, mouth, and ears. It was pouring out slowly, more so from her nose than anything else. It was as if something inside her was gashing and flooding out.

Gwen heard someone coming and saw her father and Gaia running over.

"What happened?" Gaia asked, alarmed as she knelt beside Gwen.

"I don't know," The young girl responded quickly, "I just found her like this."

Theo stepped around the group and looked forward past the trees. The other neighborhoods were only a speck in their vision, lights dimmed by the orchards and farms that separated them.

"We shouldn't take her inside." He told them.

"Why?" Gaia said, already lifting the girl away from Gwen.

Theo rushed back over, "She was probably drunk, or running from Wardens."

"She is too young to be drunk, Theo. And Wardens aren't on nightly patrol yet." Gaia started to lift the girl, "Gwen help me get her inside."

She did, grabbing the girl's legs and helping lift her. The blond girl's head rolled to the side, eyes closed fully, and mouth hanging loose.

"You just going to let them do this, Gideon?" Theo asked him. Gwen didn't hear an answer, and as she started walking backward towards the house she peeked over Gaia's shoulder to see her father bending over something. He lifted it up and from where Gwen was it just looked like some sort of stick or branch. It was very straight and unnatural, and for some reason it caused her father to become speechless.

"Harold!" Gaia called, "Open the door!"

Gwen heard the quick footsteps and the back door opened. She carefully walked through the doorway, glancing back behind her as moved inside to the larger bedroom. She saw the kids around her getting up to look at what they were doing, and she was happy to see that they knew to stay away.

"Get her in the kitchen." Gaia told her, not paying any attention to the children. Gwen listened and moved across the maze of matrices and blankets. When they made it to the kitchen Gaia and her placed the girl on the floor.

Harold came into the room behind them, studying the girl, "Who is she?" He sounded disgusted.

"She's hurt, go get the last bit of water. We need to clean her up."

"Why? What if she is wanted by the Wardens?"

"She's not."

He glanced back towards his father, "What if she's drunk? You don't know what she did to deserve this."

Gaia shot him a look, "Go get the water and help us clean her up."

Harold left the room without another word, letting his face do the complaining. Gaia shook her head as she grabbed a cloth from behind her. "I swear that boy is growing up to be just like his father."

Gwen laughed at the joke, before realizing it might not have been. When Harold got them the water they started cleaning the mystery girl. Gwen saw now that the girl couldn't have been older than herself. Eighteen or nineteen, something like that. Her face kept twitching and wincing, but after a few minutes, she settled into something more peaceful. The blood finally stopped spilling out of her nose.

Gaia picked up one of her hands and looked at them closely, dragging her fingers over her palm. "Feel." She told Gwen, sticking out the girl's hand towards her.

"What?" She laughed at the offer, before realizing Gaia was serious. Gwen rubbed her hand and found it was smooth. Completely smooth.

"She hasn't worked a day in her life." Gaia dropped her hand down, hard. She stood up as Theo walked into the room, Gideon behind him.

"What's wrong?" Her husband asked, glancing down at the girl.

"She hasn't done a day's worth of hard labor. Her hands are smoother than Danny's."

Theo looked down at the girl and then back up at his wife, "You don't think–"

"She's a Warden." Gaia finished his sentence, "She has to be."

"Then she needs to put her where we found her." Theo moved past Gaia, ready to pick the girl up.

"No." Gideon told him, grabbing his shoulder to pull him back.

"Gideon–"

"Just give her the night, if she is a Warden they might pay us for taking care of her."

"No." Theo shrugged off his hand, "It's not worth the risk."

Gideon looked at Gwen for some help. It was in his eyes that she found a message, or rather, a warning. He needed her to say something. To do something to let her stay. But why?

It didn't matter.

She turned to Theo, "She saw me. She opened her eyes. She knows what I look like. She saw this house."

Gaia put a hand over her eyes. She was scared, and now her husband was too. The house was filled with terrified people, all of them, except for her father.

"We could put her in the room below the house," Gideon suggested, giving Gwen a small nod of thanks.

Gaia shook her head quickly, "We can't keep her with the books."

"Would you rather keep her with the kids?" He waited for an answer she could not possibly give him, and in the silence, he bent down and lifted the girl. Gwen moved to help him and followed him as he carried her to the bathroom. She pulled out the vent and cloth and looked to her father for what to do next.

"Hold her here for a minute." He put the girl on the ground, "If you lower her down I will catch her." He kicked the door shut and started down the hole.

"Why–"

He put his index finger to his lips, before climbing down and disappearing into the basement. Gwen went over and grabbed the girl's head, pulling her up on her lap so she would be more comfortable. The stranger didn't look like any Warden she had seen before. On rare occasions, she had spotted Wardens without their helmets, but they looked nothing like the peacefully sleeping girl before her. No, the stranger looked gentle. The blood that had been across her face added some strange sense of danger, but with it all wiped away she was nothing but a pretty woman with soft features.

Gwen peeked down the hole and waited until she saw the yellow light. When it flashed and turned on she heard her father call from below. "Lower her down."

The daughter moved the girl back, before pushing her forward, feet first into the hole. She held onto her shoulders until she saw her father had grabbed her entirely. Gwen then climbed in herself. Her father pulled the girl over the dirt ground to some blankets they kept in the cold room. Gwen laid them out and he put her on them.

"Stay here." He told Gwen, going back to the ladder. When he came back in she saw he was holding something. It was the stick she had seen before, covered completely in mud she could make out no details.

"Clear the table." She did. Moving the books away from the center table over to the piles along the walls. He placed the strange stick on the table and grabbed a cloth from the corner of the room.

"Don't touch it." He told her, "If this is what I think it is I shouldn't be either."

Gwen watched as he wiped away part of the mud from the widest point right at the top. The room had a bright yellow glow to it already, but as soon as the mud was cleaned away the room grew brighter. From beneath the mud was a golden glowing crystal. Gideon worked quickly to wipe away more of the mud, and when he was done he threw the cloth aside and stepped away.

"Do you recognize it?" He gestured to it.

Gwen leaned forward to look at it closer. She felt her own eyes widen and her jaw started to drop as the realization came to her.

"It's the staff."

Her father nodded.

It was the Keeper's staff. The staff of the gods. The symbol of hope, peace, and protection. The ancient relic. The staff that was in every book in their room. The item that laid the foundation for entire religions.

Gwen looked over at the girl, "She's a Keeper?" Gideon didn't answer, his eyes were locked on the crystal. Eventually, he took in her words and stepped away from the table to the girl. He bent down to her level, examining her as he had done with the staff.

Gwen stood above him, trying to study the girl as he did, "She doesn't look like a Keeper."

"What does a Keeper look like?"

Gwen shrugged softly, "I don't know, like a god, or a warrior, or a divine power. She looks... She looks human. She was bleeding."

"Who said Keepers can't bleed?" Gideon stood up and moved over to the stack of books, searching through them until he found the one Gwen had been looking at that same day. He put it down on the table and picked up the staff carefully, placing it against the wall. He gestured to the book, "We need to look for anything on the staff, and anything on Keepers who wield it."

Gwen glanced down at the girl. When she looked back at her father he was already vigorously flipping through the fragile pages. "We've already read the books."

He pulled a new book closer to him, eyes wide against the page, "Well now we can read them with new eyes. There might be something we missed."

"And then?"

He looked away to think, and when he found an idea he turned back to the book, "We can bring her to someone. Trent, maybe, or Lorenzo. She can't stay here, not just because of the Wardens but because she is far more precious than you could possibly imagine."

"You really think she is a Keeper?"

Her father looked up at her, and in his eyes, she saw a focus she had not seen in a long time. A sort of intensity that was clouded not by fear or anger, but simply by determination.

"Whether she is or not, she has the staff, and that can only mean one thing. The Keepers have returned."

Chapter 8

✶ ✻ ✶

KIRANA

KIRANA STARTED TO wake up, and suddenly everything hurt. Her head felt like it had hit a wall on all sides. Her body ached from injuries she couldn't identify and shere exhausted. She was laying on something hard and moved her hand around to feel some sort of itchy blanket. She slowly started to open her eyes. Everything blurred as her eyes stung and burned. She took deep breaths and blinked until she started to see clearly. She was in some sort of room, the walls made from dirt and clay with no windows. The room was filthy, and filled with damaged books and broken items. As she looked around she spotted two very important things. The first was a ladder mere paces away. She had a way out. The second was a person sleeping on the table. His hands were on a book, but his face was planted down in front of it.

Did he bring her here?

Wait, did that mean... he was like her?

He didn't look like any person she had seen before. Dirty and dressed in a brown vest, brown shirt, brown pants, and brown shoes, he didn't look like any person she had seen before.

Kirana tried to sit up. She managed to get up a few inches, holding herself up by the side of her arm. She felt something on her face and wiped her nose. When she looked down at her hand she saw blood. She tried to remember anything, but the last thing she could recall was that strange suffocating world and the figures. Then she fell somewhere. The voice she heard sounded like a man's, so perhaps

54

it was the person sleeping at the table.

There was a creak of metal against metal, and a new source of light came through the room from the top of the ladder as someone started coming inside. Kirana rolled herself around with a grunt, trying her best to at least sit up. She felt weak, a feeling she was unfamiliar with. It wasn't about pain, but rather exhaustion. Whatever had happened to her drained almost entirely. By the time she had rolled over onto her stomach, the person was at the bottom of the ladder, watching her.

It was a girl, or rather, a woman. She had deep brown skin and curly black hair that fell to her shoulders. She looked about Kirana's age, 18 years old, maybe older. She had her hands out as if to calm Kirana down.

"Don't worry," The woman told her, "We aren't going to hurt you."

The man at the table woke up suddenly and shot to his feet. He didn't even look over at the new woman in the room and instead locked eyes with Kirana. She had never seen such life within a gaze. He was almost speaking to her through his stare, something she had only caught between glances from Tia. The people before Kirana were like her, they sought connection, even through a single gaze.

The woman put her hand to her chest, "My name is Gwen." She pointed to the other man, "This is my father; we found you outside in the rain."

Father? Kirana knew what that was. Though she had never had any parents growing up she was well educated on what life was before the Magistrater. Tia was very fond of knowledge, and she pushed Kirana to know about their history. Together they read books about what life was like, living out wars and countless horrific events. People lived in groups, and more often in families. Maybe having a father was part of this girl's perfect life, like Tia was to Kirana.

Gwen. That was the girl's name. Kirana looked from her to her father, "You want to talk to me?"

Gwen glanced over at her father, "Yes. We are farm hands, I sell a few items down at the market but mostly–"

"You talk– You talk to people and you want to?" She gave out a small laugh as she tried to get up again. The rush of adrenaline got her to her feet, but with a stumble, her legs gave out and she onto a hard dirt floor. The two strangers rushed over to her and started to pull her up.

"Take it easy." The father told her, "You were out the whole night."

They held her up as she continued to look from person to person. She couldn't help a giddy smile from filling her face. The two of them walked her over to the table and put her down on a chair. Well, a bucket, a broken metal one at that. Kirana held herself up on the table with one arm. "I have so many questions." She laughed once again.

Gwen clenched her jaw, "We do as well. But I think we should get the most important one out of the way." She glanced at her father and took a breath, "Are you a Keeper?" Worry stretched across her face.

"A what?" Kirana wiped under her nose again. She saw now how much dried blood was on her face. She must have looked psychotic, and couldn't help but laugh at the thought, "Do you guys have a cloth or something–"

"A Keeper." Her father repeated, "You have the staff. It was glowing around you, and it still is." He gestured to it in the corner of the room. Kirana looked back over to it and saw he was right, it was glowing. A bright and strong yellow, or gold. That was new.

"That thing is dangerous." She pulled her sleeve up and wiped her face, "I found it near the city. It took me... I guess here." She looked around before focusing back on the girl and her father, "But it led me to you two. Are there others? Also, where are we exactly? I don't want to be rude, this is very exciting, but I'm a bit concerned about how I arrived here."

"You aren't a Keeper?" The father's voice had dropped into some sort of sadness Kirana couldn't quite identify. Like a sort of grief, or perhaps it was just fear. Whatever a Keeper was, it sounded important.

Gwen gestured towards the ladder, "You are just on the outskirts of the city. By the orchards. We work in the farms down the road. There will be a lift soon, it's already morning."

"What orchards?" Kirana gave a small laugh and smiled, "Look, I haven't met anyone like you two and I want to keep talking, but right now I need to go find the Nanos or the Magistrater or... someone." She pointed to the staff, "That should not be in our hands."

"Magistrater..." Gwen repeated. Her tone had changed, and it was only then that Kirana felt the true energy of the room. The people before her were not happy to see her, they were angry. The woman straightened her back, "Are you a Warden?"

Kirana gave another laugh. "A what?" Why were they throwing around strange words? Surely they too were excited to see her, or maybe this was normal to them.

Maybe there were more people like them. She glanced up at the ladder, and the urge to climb it and look around for more people filled her with hope.

Gwen glared at her, "Don't play dumb, are you–"

The father stepped closer to her, putting his hand up to stop his daughter from speaking, "You are in Hiraeth. Do you know what that is?"

Kirana shook her head, "You're saying a lot of strange words I don't know. Can we go–"

"I think you traveled much farther than you anticipated." He pointed down to the table and turned a book around to face her. Kirana leaned forward to look at it fully. It was a picture in some old broken book. The picture was incredibly faded, but she could still make out a person, a figure holding the staff.

Her staff.

"What is this?"

"It's a book about the Keepers. The gods who protected the worlds."

Kirana flipped through other pages, looking for something else. Anything else. But some pages were unreadable, others ripped and faded completely. The father moved around the table to face her. He grabbed the staff and put it on the table. "Do you remember what happened? How did you find this?"

Kirana reached out her hand and touched it lightly, pulling her hand back quickly to see what would happen. Nothing. She went to pick it up, seeing how it wasn't taking her anywhere or releasing the strange blast of energy.

"I just found it. It was floating, so I grabbed it."

"Then you arrived here?"

Kirana nodded.

The father pulled the book away from her and flipped through the pages. He went to the beginning and held it up to show her a picture.

"These are the Keepers."

Kirana looked at the picture, leaning forward to see it fully. There were four warriors and a staff behind them. The people looked like the ones she saw in the strange, suffocating world. Four people. They had weapons, almost like the ones in the picture. Only… different. Like the picture in the broken book, her memory of the figures was faded.

The father pointed at the staff. "Our ancestors used to write down stories about how a group of gods kept the peace between dimensions."

"Dimensions?" She repeated with a laugh.

"Different worlds." He tapped on the page, "These stories tell us of the different dimensions separated by vast planes of existence. It is as if our world is duplicated into four, separated by barriers of time and space." Was that what that strange world was: a barrier? "Every time a Keeper died or the entire group faded away, another would replace it. For each person, there is one dimension, and assuming you came from another world yours would be–"

"Permidia." She looked back to the ladder, "What are you saying?"

He pulled the book away from her to face her properly, "I have been keeping these books because I have held hope that the Keepers will return. We haven't seen them for so long. Most people consider them legends, mythical gods, or just fictional stories. But you're proof that they are real. You're the first one, the leader, the one to wield the staff. Whatever you are, you're important."

Kirana suddenly laughed, it wasn't on purpose, and she quickly tried to collect herself. "I'm so sorry. This is all… so much." She stood up, feeling her old self coming back already. She figured she was strong enough to climb up the ladder. "I will just go find a Nano and talk to the Magistrater–"

"No!" The father shut the book, "That villain can't know about the Keepers."

"Villain?" She stepped away from him, "How could you say that?"

He shook his head quickly, "She's a tyrant. She'll kill us all if you go to her."

"She is our *savior*, she makes every life perfect. Just because you are like me doesn't mean you get to talk about her that way."

"Savior?" Gwen repeated as if lost in translation.

Kirana shook her head and looked from person to person, "I'm still really excited to meet people like you… but if this is important then this needs to go to the right person. If that's you guys then great. Keep it. I am going to step outside." The father came after her, but it was clear he didn't have a proper plan to stop her. She stood there and watched as he questioned grabbing her or shoving her back to the table. But in the end, he stepped back and let her leave.

Kirana just needed to get back to Tia and find the Magistrater. Even if she was on the other side of Permidia there would still be Nanos around she could talk to. She left the staff down in the small dirty room and climbed up into the room above. She was willing to leave it there and never see it again. All it had done for her so far was give her a nasty nosebleed and pounding headache. As

Kirana peeked her head through the hole she saw it was a bathroom. A really filthy one. This was someone's idea of a perfect life? She pulled herself up, still unbalanced but managing her strength. As she walked out opening the door she looked around the hallway she was in. Kids ran past her suddenly, and she heard a rustle of noise coming from the other small rooms. One kid stopped and stared at her. His eyes got wide, studying her and inching away. He was like her. Kirana smiled at the kid but he just ran down the hall to a woman already staring back at her.

"You stay back now." The woman put herself in front of the kid as if to protect him.

"Hi." Kirana waved and brushed her hands on her pants, "It's so nice to meet you. I'm–"

"Gaia, it's fine!" Gwen had come through the bathroom and squeezed past the Permidian.

"Is she a Warden?"

"She's not." The answer didn't seem to make Gaia more comfortable. She took the kid away to another room, safe from whatever harm she thought Kirana would bring. Gwen turned to her, "Let me show you something." And walked to the front door.

Kirana followed her, looking around at the strange house she was in. Everything was so minimal. Dust and dirt lined every surface. Broken items were scattered around without a place to go. Gwen opened the door for Kirana and let her step outside first. It wasn't until that moment that Kirana felt truly, and uncontrollably, afraid. Her heart was racing, her breath heavy, her eyes widened as she looked around her. At the world. In a *new* world.

She stood on a hill that seemed to be slightly elevated from the view before her, and so she felt as if could see the entire world. The nearest sight were trees, forests lined too symmetrically to be natural. Then there were houses clumped together in strange rows between long stretches of farms. Every building was lined up symmetrically, leading up to a city, but not anything like the Permidian city Kirana knew. No, the buildings looked as if they had been built on top of each other creating a rising slope of clay and dirt. Nothing looked planned, simply built with the hope of staying upright. It resembled an ant hill, only with elements of metal holding up entire sections of the city and lining streets and platforms. Ships circled the buildings and moved to and from the farms and far beyond.

All of the structures before her, from the trees and farms to the great city, were leading up to the grand and menacing sight before her: the Magistrater's Tower, dark and towering over all before Kirana. The city she had known all her life was gone, replaced by dirt and shadows. Her world, her city, was filled with light. All the lights were gone. She stood in the choke-hold of a shadow.

This couldn't be. It was impossible. The sight before her was almost a strange and altered copy of Permidia. A word kept ringing through her head and thumping with her fast heartbeat.

Dimensions.

Kirana turned to Gwen, who had remained beside her in silence.

"*Hiraeth...*" Kirana started to say, suddenly giving in to the idea that what the two strangers were saying was very important and concerned Kirana and the strange staff.

"Dimensions are supposed to be partly identical in some way." Gwen told her, "Do you see anything that looks familiar?"

Kirana nodded, looking back to the city, "The Magistrater's Tower, it's different but I would know it anywhere. But It's... It's so... menacing."

She saw Gwen look up at it from the corner of her eye, taking a moment to see fully. "The Magistrater is horrible to us." She told Kirana, "I don't know what she makes you believe back in your world, but here, she works us to death. Producing crops and materials that are sent off gods know where. All she gives us are the scraps."

Kirana shook her head, closing her eyes. It couldn't be true. The Magistrater wasn't a villain. She gave everyone a perfect life. But yet, there was a question the Permidian never bothered asking.

At what cost?

"Shit." Gwen muttered under her breath. Kirana looked back up and saw a ship in the distance. They were different from Permidian ships, wide, bulky, with rust and stains along metal walls. There was no elegance to them, no clean cut or white color, there weren't even windows, just bars spaced out along the walls. Their gray color matched the still-dark morning sky. Their bright headlights made them look controlling and, in a way, Kirana could not understand, superior. Looking back she realized how dark Gwen's neighborhood was with only a few dim lights within the houses. There was an imbalance here, some strange new hierarchy that made Kirana very afraid.

"Inside." Gwen told her. She grabbed her arm and pulled her back to the door. Kirana didn't have a choice but to go with her. For someone Kirana's age, the girl was much stronger than her. Gwen pulled her back inside and shut the door. There were more people in the front room. Gaia had a crowd of children around her, two of which looked barely younger than Kirana herself. Everyone looked over at the Permidian with the same intensity, even the children seemed to know how to match the fear.

"The Wardens are here." Gwen told them as she rushed inside.

Gideon pushed past the group and grabbed Kirana by her coat, "Get downstairs and don't make a sound."

"No!" Gaia moved past the kids and blocked their path to the bathroom, "We are not keeping her here."

Gideon tried to push past her before a new man, much larger than he was, moved beside the woman, "If they find her they will kill you, Gideon."

"She's not a Warden—"

Gaia shook her head violently, "Does she have her worker's ID? Paperwork? Gideon if they find her here without anything they kill you and leave all of us—" Gwen moved beside Gaia and tried to speak, but the woman interrupted with fierce anger. "It doesn't matter! The Wardens are never out this early."

"Who are you?" The new man asked Kirana firmly.

The room went silent. Kirana locked eyes with the woman and tried to think of a good answer. "I'm Kirana." She didn't know what else to say.

"She's on the run." Gideon continued for her, "From her family, not the Wardens. We will take her into the city and get her somewhere safe."

Kirana looked up to Gwen's father. He was lying, but why? Did he not trust the people around him? Did he not trust Kirana?

"Gideon—" Gaia started, but he let go of Kirana and rushed past her back to the bathroom without another word.

Gwen followed quickly, and soon everyone was moving. Kirana didn't know what they were preparing for, but everyone started moving things around, grabbing items, and throwing them in small bags. She moved aside as Gaia gestured for the kids to follow her further into the house. As she moved them all away, a young boy about 13 or 14 years old grabbed his boots and put them on quickly. Before going to the front door he ran up to Kirana, "Get out of here." Before she could respond he grabbed a small bag and ran out of the house.

The new man from before came up to Kirana immediately after, bending down to her level to whisper through the chaos, "If you get us caught, I will kill you." She backed up to the wall but said nothing. There was so much anger in his eyes that she fully believed he had the power to hurt her. After one long look at her, he swung open the door and left the house. Gaia returned and, without another glance at Kirana, followed the man.

This was not right. This was not how any of this was supposed to be. Kirana had been searching for people like her for her entire life, only they were not like her at all. Kirana felt as if she dug up a great crate of treasure without realizing it rested in quicksand. She was sinking, and soon she would be drowning.

Gideon rushed back out of the bathroom carrying her staff. It was wrapped up in cloth thick enough to hide the glow. He glanced around to an older girl in the back of the house with the kids, "Don't tell them anything. She was never here." With that, he grabbed Kirana's arm and pulled her outside of the house. She tried to resist, but like Gwen, he was strong. Strong enough to hold her up even if she refused to walk. She was grateful that he let her go a few steps out of the house. The ship was nearing them now, ready to land. Gwen stood beside them and her father walked swiftly with her, expecting Kirana to follow as he let her go. She did, and without hesitation.

But why? What reason did she have to join them? Or rather, what choice did she have? Where else would she go? To the Wardens? To the Magistrater? The ruler was her savior, she must have had her reasons for this place. Yet, those reasons were costing Gwen and Gideon's family their perfect life. There was something very dark about the world around her, not only through the Wardens but also the people. They had so much connection but also much fear and anger. Kirana needed answers and the people around her were willing to help her learn. Stuck in the dark they were guiding her, and, for the first time in her life, there was danger to being alone.

And so, she followed, and she would not leave without knowing what was going on, and how she connected to all of it.

As soon as she stepped beside Gwen, the girl glanced over, focused but calmer now that they were on a path away from danger. "I'm sorry, this is all happening so fast. We're going somewhere safe. We can talk there. My name is Gwen. I am a Hiraethan."

How Kirana had longed for someone to say that to her in Permidia. To speak to her like that. This was what she had wanted, in a way. They had called her a Keeper from those books not just because she had the same staff, but because she had found her way to them. So, with a glance back to the ship landing in the area of dusty clay houses, she took a breath and smiled.

"I'm Kirana. A Permidian."

Chapter 9

* * *

Gwen

GWEN HELD HER bag close to her. She was good with chaos and good with finding a sense of control within it. She had found a way to prepare like this was just any other day of work. She packed her bracelets and handmade goods in her bag, hiding the tin of Corts beneath it. She tied her boots on and tapped them as she always did on the wall outside her house. She lied to herself and said she was leaving her house with a dear friend and her dearest father. They were going to work with a long stick wrapped in cloth. It wasn't abnormal to bring a tool to work, though most of the time the Wardens kept them at check-in for fear of people using them for tasks outside of their jobs, some required the workers to take and bring back tools. The staff did not resemble a tool, but in a crowd, she prayed no one would pay too much attention.

"The Wardens don't usually go inside the houses." Gwen told Kirana as she adjusted her bag, "They might just knock on the door and ask if everyone has their Worker's ID. A random check, nothing more."

The girl beside her leaned closer, whispering as if telling a secret, "What are Wardens?"

Gwen had never heard that sentence before, and it sounded childish. Even Danny had never asked such a question, he just knew. Everyone knew, except her. Gwen's father answered quickly, "Wardens. The enemy. The traitors. They go around hurting people. They work for the Magistrater under the idea they are here to create order and productivity."

"They tried to take one of the kids yesterday," Gwen added, thinking of how scared Danny must still be. She longed to give him a better sense of stability, but with the staff in their possession she feared they were far from safe, "You don't… have anything like that?"

"Not really, no. We have kids though, a few of them. I saw one yesterday."

Kirana was strange to Gwen. Her answers to their questions seemed obvious, and yet to her were necessary to say. The differences of their worlds were clear, and Gwen hoped once they were safe she could learn about what life truly was like for the people in Permidia.

Gideon took a strip of cloth out of his bag. The staff was glowing brighter through the fabric, so he tried to bundle it tighter. Gwen found herself staring at it regularly, glancing over now and then just to watch it glow. She had been staring at it for years in her father's books, and seeing it in real life was unfathomable. She selfishly wanted to use it herself, just hold it and see how her ancestors would have used it. But that wasn't her priority, and at that moment it was just a walking target.

"Can you turn it off?" She asked Kirana, gesturing to the staff.

Kirana scrunched up her eyebrows, "Off? Like not glowing? I don't even know what *it* is."

Gwen shook her head quickly, "I'm just asking. It's drawing a lot of attention."

Her father finished hiding the glow and ignored their conversation, "You said the Magistrater gives everyone a perfect life, right?" Kirana nodded. "So you were never attacked or threatened."

"Never," Kirana responded as if they were weightless words.

Gideon glanced around as they walked along the path. So far, no one was close enough to hear them, "Tell us about your life. What do you do in your days?"

"I ride my bike. I hang out with my sister, Tia. I watch people…" Both Gwen and Gideon looked over to Kirana when she stopped speaking, and the girl quickly tried to think of something else to say, "I… My sister makes us food. I read a lot about our history. I talk to our Nanos."

"You don't work?" Gideon asked, and when she shook her head, he looked over to Gwen longingly. Gwen couldn't imagine a life like that. It sounded like a fairytale, but if the gods were real, maybe that dream world could be too. Kirana must have lived like a Queen. Her every need was attended to, her every want answered. It made Gwen hate the happy girl beside her, though she tried not to show it. It was a life she wanted her people to live. Danny would get to play all day, have a full belly, and a real bed. Gaia would have real food to cook with, sharing meals with everyone around her without running out of ingredients. Theo wouldn't have to work so hard. Harold wouldn't stress about managing their Corts. Her father could have a library of books that he could spend days reading. And Gwen, well, she would just be happy to watch them all smile.

Kirana shrugged and shook her head, "It's the perfect life."

"What did you mean when you said *people like us?*"

She gestured to him, "People who want to talk. To connect. Permidian doesn't do that."

"What do you mean?" Gideon asked.

"I'm the only one who wants other people. It's the perfect life. You don't have to worry about other people. It's just you, no real feelings, just contentment."

Gwen looked up at her father expecting to see the same shocked expression on his face, instead, he looked forward and stopped speaking. Gideon was known for being unreadable, but as his daughter, she knew certain features of his expressions. He was thinking—plotting—but he was also afraid. She saw it by him merely turning his head towards her. He wanted to glance at her, to see her, but he chose against it. He didn't know what to do, not yet, and he was afraid of what his lack of understanding would do to his daughter.

The path they took was connected to another neighborhood, which was connected to another, and another, all forming a long road heading towards the city. The path started to get crowded as they moved further down. The sun was blazing, yet the ground remained soggy and damp. The weather was still settling from the recent storm.

As they moved into the next neighborhood they saw a new Warden ship land in the center of the neighborhood's small quartyard. The Wardens were everywhere, marching out of the ship to each house.

"That's them," Gideon told Kirana as he moved to the other side of the Permidian. He and Gwen were shielding her from the Wardens. "Don't say a word, just keep your head down." She did so, and Gwen could see a stretch of fear line her expression. Kirana didn't seem to know how to wear worry, or how to hide it.

The Wardens were going door to door, all of them repeating the same line, "Stand aside. We will be doing an involuntary search."

"Does this happen every day?" Kirana whispered. Gideon gestured for her to be quiet, not bothering to answer the question. The Wardens had done this before, sure, but not like this. Not at this scale.

Something caught Gwen's ear. "Have you seen this girl?"

She glanced over and saw they were holding up a screen. She was too far away to see the person in the picture, but she had a pretty good idea as to who it was. Gideon reacted by speeding up. Hopefully, they would just look like they were just late to work. Gwen felt a knot in her stomach grow the further they walked. Wardens had seamlessly doubled, watching everyone with a newfound care for their monstrous work.

Gideon took off his jacket and put it into Kirana's arms, "Put it on."

She did so, fumbling but quickly taking off her long coat and slipping on his jacket. She flipped up a hood that barely hid her face and kept her coat close to her chest, holding it as Danny would a stuffed toy. A childish comfort. The Wardens watched them pass, but with such a large crowd of workers, it would be hard to spot them. Gwen tried to hold her breath steady but she could barely find the air to do so. She felt off balance, heart pounding and head spinning with fear. She tried to kick some dirt on Kirana's polished boots and clean pants.

"Is everyone's life like this?" The girl whispered to Gwen as they walked onto a larger path. It was more crowded, but they were still in the Wardens' view.

"Like what?" Gwen asked, glancing around quickly.

"Terrible, dirty, constantly in danger?"

Gwen looked over at her, seeing if she was really serious. It seemed she was. "Some lives are worse. We have it good. Some people don't even have a job, or a house."

"The Keepers, they helped people, right?"

Gwen nodded, "They united every world, protecting the people and spreading their wealth. Everyone wants the gods to return and save them. Not that you're the person to do so." She found distaste in her words and tried to swallow it down.

"If it's the Magistrater's fault why has no one taken her down?"

"It's not that easy, she has an army. They are at our house right now."

Gideon made a sharp noise to shut them up. Both of them listened as they approached their destination. Gwen went down that same path every day. She went to the same place in the same routine. Every day she got herself ready and walked to the Worker ship. The ships were made to bring stacks of people from job to job across Hiraeth. The passenger ship was nothing impressive. Wide and rusted from years of use, it was fitted with five levels, each with a short roof and dozens of clumped chairs. A large ramp opened at the back, revealing each level and the stairs on both sides.

Once they made it to the ramp of the ship Kirana seemed to be more curious, peeking up from under her hood to look around. Gwen didn't know why she was so intrigued by the ship; she assumed Permidia had vehicles too. Gideon guided them over to the stairs on the side. It would be more cramped at the top, so no one would notice them as much. He walked in first, leading the way. Gwen held up the back, keeping Kirana in sight. When they made it to the highest level, they stayed in the line kept by the crowd. The roof was low, so low that she had to bend her head slightly to not hit the rusted metal plates that hid the ship's inner workings. Chairs were lined up in rows, back to back until they got to the wall. The line walked along the allies made between the chairs.

Gideon went to a corner seat. With his back to the wall, he tucked the staff behind his chair out of view. Kirana sat next to him, but as Gwen moved to sit in the next seat someone grabbed her and pulled her down towards them. She pulled away quickly, knocking into someone in the line. Frantic and ready to run, it took her a moment to see who it was.

Mari.

"Did you see all the Wardens around?" She asked, pulling Gwen down again so they could be next to each other. The Hiraethan looked up at her father, but he didn't exchange any glances. He looked calm, as if his daughter had just gone to sit with a friend during the morning ride to work. She didn't share his mastery in wearing a mask and was grateful that Mari was oblivious to her fear.

"It's weird." Was all she managed to say, before pulling out of her grip and sitting next to Kirana. Though Mari followed her and sat on Gwen's other side, she remained silent. That was good. Gwen kept her eyes down to the ground, trying not to spark any conversations.

There was a sharp noise from her father, and she glanced up at him. He tapped his chin and lifted his head, an indication for her to do the same. She clenched her jaw and pulled her shoulders back. Mari didn't talk to her, yet. Perhaps she would be content in analyzing Gwen's face for secrets. She followed her father's instructions and made sure she wouldn't find any.

The ship suddenly rattled and started to take off. They all felt it rise and Kirana clung to the seat. "This feels a bit dangerous."

Gwen didn't bother to respond. It was a stupid thing to comment on.

Mari leaned over and looked at Kirana, "Who's she?"

Gwen went cold but Gideon spoke up quickly, "Her name's Yara. Gaia took her in a few nights ago. Mother died up in the city and she had nowhere to go."

"Poor thing." Mari whispered, "She looks sick." Gwen looked over at the Keeper to find she was, in fact, very pale. The perception of sickness was better than fear, and so she decided to not edge on any other opinions and settled Mari with a quick nod.

The ship moved forward, pushing everyone to the side. Gwen knew many of the people around her, and if this had been a normal morning she might have even spoken to them. Though the ship was not a place of much joy, it was a rare moment that they were there together. Gwen recalled a time when Jerold's son Ben first started working alongside him. Jerold made such a big deal about the trip that his happy energy spread through the ship. They made it a lot of fun for the kid, so much so that everyone else had a good time as well. People started cheering and laughing. That was until the Wardens came up to check on them, and then the young Ben found out the truth about traveling on the ship. You were stuck with the enemy, with nowhere to go, and nowhere to hide. His father came out of the ship with a black eye and broken nose. Ben came out with a bruised cheek and broken heart.

Even now, Wardens were starting to come up and check on everyone. Kirana spotted them and ducked her head. These soldiers were on edge, but not committed enough to find the Keeper. The staff was well hidden, as was the god. For now, they were safe. Things went on as normal. The ship continued to land and take off again and again to different farms and facilities. When it got to Gwen's normal stop, Mari waited for her to stand.

"I'm going to sell more craft." She told her quickly. "Just cover for me."

"Cover for you?" Mari was loud. Too loud.

"Please, Mari." Gideon said from the corner, locking eyes with the girl, "We need this."

Hearing the intensity in his words, she found her sensibility, shut up, and walked away.

They were on the final stretch of the trip to the city. There were still many workers, but no longer a full crowd to hide the three of them. When the ship landed, everyone stood up at once. Her father did his best to hide the staff as he lifted it and placed it beside him.

When they got down the stairs Gideon took them away quickly. The ship landed on a platform off the city balanced on thick pillars of wood and metal. The city wasn't crowded with as many Wardens as Gwen had expected. They must have known Kirana would be in the neighborhoods, but how?

It was safer now, especially as they started to exit the platform and move into the sloped streets of the city. Gwen moved beside her father, "Where are we going?"

"We just needed to get away. We still do." He looked back towards Kirana, who lingered at the back, eyes darting across the city. She looked so obviously new to the world.

"Are we going to Lorenzo?"

Gideon pushed both her and Kirana forward so that they would follow the natural flow of the crowd, "I have a friend who can keep her for the time being. I'll contact Lorenzo and make a plan."

Kirana and Gwen followed Gideon as they moved off the platform into the true Hiraeth streets. Gwen's stall wasn't too far from where they were now, and she hoped no one she regularly saw would find her walking to some new place. The city was, as always, loud and crowded. It was a place for quick work, rather than daily jobs in the fields or factories. People came to sell their goods like Gwen or became one of the many beggars who would eventually find themselves in the Warden prisons. Gwen had no idea who her father's friend was, or why he would choose the stranger over larger public figures like Lorenzo, but she trusted in his plan.

As they moved through the city streets Kirana kept bumping into Gwen, trying her best to stay close. She was still pale, but her fear was being swayed by curiosity. Gwen tried to understand what she was going through. After spending her entire life alone with no one talking to her, Kirana was suddenly thrust into a new and very dangerous world with people she had been looking for her entire life.

Kirana looked up at Gwen, "What are they doing?" She pointed to a man behind a stall yelling out for people to buy his rugs.

"They're selling rugs." She answered honestly, "Everyone is trying to survive. Make a living–"

There was a scream as Gideon grabbed Gwen and Kirana and moved them all towards the stalls. A woman was thrown into the crowd, crashing into a group of people and rolling down the steep street. She got on her knees and put her hands above her hand, pressing her fingers together with her head bowed. "Please!"

Walking down the street to get her was a group of Wardens. The leader moved to her and grabbed her by her face, his other hand holding his gun to the sky. Gwen hadn't anticipated hearing a gunshot, so when one shot she and everyone around her ducked down at the violent sound. Kirana put her hands to her ears and let out a scream. The Warden threw down the woman as another stepped forward holding out a single apple and showing off to the crowd.

"These are stolen goods! Thieves are as good as those who buy from them!" He threw the apple down at the woman, hitting her ribs, "You will acknowledge the rules we command or we will tear the stolen goods from your *stomachs*!" He went back to kick her stomach, sending her to the ground.

Gwen went cold as Kirana yelled out, "Stop!" Before putting her hands over her mouth.

Gideon grabbed her and pulled her behind him as the Warden looked over through the crowd. The people parted, trying not to get in the way of the monster's wrath. With Kirana hidden, Gwen stayed where she was, and got on her knees.

"Forgive me." She begged.

The Warden marched towards her and as she looked up he smacked the back of his hand across her face. Gwen slammed to the ground and stayed there, face turned to the thief. The woman was watching Gwen with such worry, and after a moment she smiled a small, hopeful smile. She was grateful for the act of rebellion. The second Warden pulled out a small dagger from his belt, grabbed the woman's hand, and cut off her finger. She didn't even scream, she just stared at her gushing hand as they started to drag her down the street.

The Warden before Gwen gave her one last look before following the others. Gideon rushed to Gwen's side and pulled her up to her feet, forcing her to walk. Kirana followed behind them as they moved back into the crowd. They didn't say a word, they just kept walking, and walking, through each street, and past each stall, until finally Gideon stopped in front of a building, swung open the emerald green door, and pulled her and Kirana inside.

Gwen had never been to the shops before, and it felt like a place she should have gone to long ago. It had tan walls hidden by colorful fabrics and rugs. Wooden furniture held dozens of home goods. Pots, pans, plates, glass panels for windows, utensils but no knives, and a great many rows of fabrics covering the walls. Shy her father had taken them to this one specifically was beyond her.

Gideon grabbed Gwen and held her as soon as the door was closed. He grabbed her face and looked at her, checking how much the Warden had hurt her. "Are you okay?"

"I'm fine."

He kissed her forehead before grabbing Kirana and pulling her further inside.

"I'm so sorry." Kirana turned from him to Gwen but neither of them responded. "Why did they do that? They just–" She stopped speaking and put a hand over her mouth.

Gideon pulled her to the counter where a man was waiting. He was a plump fellow with white skin and saggy cheeks. He was not as colorful as the room around him but his attire would have stood out in the average Hiraethan crowd. He wore a dark lavender shirt with a loose, thin coat wrapped around his waist and trailing down to his shins. It was decorated with spots of flowers around the edges, ones that matched his spectacles, which had long metal vines along the sides. But to Gwen's disappointment, his clothes were dim, well worn and spotted from the years. She wished she could have seen him decades before wearing the bright colors.

"Gideon." He said loudly, before putting his voice into a whisper and looking from Kirana to Gwen, "You brought friends?"

"My daughter." He gestured to Gwen and grabbed Kirana, "And someone I think you might want to meet."

He handed the man the staff and went around the countertop. Kirana looked over at Gwen, perhaps searching for the reason they were there. She simply shrugged in response to prove that she too knew nothing. As her father ducked down out of sight, the man started to unwrap the staff. Seeing its brightness, he snapped at Gwen, "Shut the window." A small window was carved into the wall by the door. She drew the thin curtain across it, glancing outside as she did. A patrol of Wardens were coming. A small group, normal. Nothing to fear. The ones from before would be long gone by now, off sending the fingerless woman to prison. Gwen thought back to her and Danny's encounter the day before and how close both of them were to receiving similar punishments. She wouldn't consider it mercy, it simply luck.

There was a click and a creak as Gwen turned around. Her father was pushing the back wall, and as he did it turned. It was a door.

"Gideon." The staff was in full view, and the man seemed completely struck by its glow. He looked straight at Kirana, "Who are you?"

Kirana looked over to Gwen before answering, "I'm Kirana." Gideon grabbed her arm and pushed her into the next room. Confused but not knowing what else to do, she went in and looked around.

The man rushed up to Gwen's father and let out a laugh, "You found the staff?" He kept his voice so quiet Gwen had to move closer to hear what they were saying.

"She did." He pointed to Kirana, "She arrived here from somewhere else."

"With the staff?" He gave a small bounce as he got excited.

"With the staff." Gideon looked over to Gwen as if he had forgotten she was there. After a moment to think he moved to her, "We need to know everything we can from her. Whether she is a Keeper or not, something has returned."

She looked back at the new man as he moved to the window and peeked outside, closing it sharply as soon as he got a good glance. "Why did we come here?" She asked her father.

"This is Trent, he's a friend of mine. We'll talk in there." Gideon put a hand on her shoulder, "I'm sorry this is all happening so fast, but if this girl really is the Keeper then we need to know everything we can."

She nodded quickly, "I understand, Dad."

He looked at her as if this was their last moment. Gwen knew then that though they had found a space to hide, they were far from safe. Gideon turned and walked into the backroom.

She followed without hesitation.

Chapter 10

✴ ✴ ✴

KIRANA

KIRANA PEEKED INTO a box on the wooden table in the center of the room. The new space was small. It matched the room she woke up in back at Gwen and Gideon's house with similar clay and dirt walls, only it was better kept and well decorated. There was a gorgeous red rug under a redwood table lined with boxes of various ancient-looking items. Along the walls stood shelves of other boxes filled with stones, books, and relics all organized either by category or color. The fabrics Trent had at the front of his store matched the ones spread across the walls and strung from shelf to shelf. Kirana was used to designs being symmetrical, or at the very least well organized, but the room looked as if it had been built over time, added to without any clear plan. But there was beauty to the informality of the space around her. Kirana was still recovering from seeing the woman's finger get sliced off, but at least now she was somewhere safe.

The box she looked into was filled with jewelry. Rings, necklaces, broken chains, and discarded jewels rested in small subsections. She noticed very quickly that they all matched each other in some way. Most of them were yellow or gold, and the ones that weren't seemed to all have the same symbol marked on the center: the staff.

Both Gwen and Gideon paced the room moving from shelf to shelf and looking in every box. They spoke to each other in sharp whispers Kirana couldn't catch, and received the intensity of their words through their short glances. When Gwen came by her, Kirana eyed the spot the Warden had hit her and whispered, "Are you okay? I'm so sorry. I didn't mean for that to happen. I just—"

"I'm fine." Gwen gave a small smile as she spoke, and Kirana sensed, by how well she was able to brush off the violent incident, that it had happened to her before. The whole situation didn't feel real yet. It felt like she was dreaming, and at any moment she would wake up in her bed, wrapped up in Permidian silks and sheets. Kirana moved out of Gwen's way and back to the table where she was eventually offered a chair by the new man.

Trent pulled a seat beside her on the table and smiled, "How are you feeling?"

"Scared." She answered honestly, smiling back out of gratitude for his kindness, "And a very confused."

"Well, you should be safe now." He took off his spectacles and put them on the table with a breath, "You're Kirana." She nodded, "My name is Trent." He gestured around the hidden room they had entered, "Welcome to my little rebellion."

Gideon moved beside him, "He's a historian. He's studied the Keeper for decades, same as I have."

Trent nodded, "I collect relics and artifacts about the Keepers. He reads and keeps the books, I examine the books and keep the items."

"What items?" Gwen asked abruptly from the other side of the table. She turned to her father, "You found relics?" It was clear she knew very little about the *little rebellion.*

Gideon grabbed the box Kirana had been looking in, "People keep things in their family." He put down one of the necklaces. It was tarnished and very old, made entirely from a thick sheet of silver that was molded to look like the staff. "Most of them are family heirlooms. Religious keep-sakes Trent collects and studies. He knows more about the Keepers than I do. A brilliant mind and good friend."

Gwen looked over to Trent, observing him, "Why haven't I heard of you?"

"I'm not a part of Lorenzo's rebellion." He stood up and moved past Gideon, "Lorenzo doesn't care for the Keepers as much as your father or I do. He wants to fight back but we know the only way we can truly win is with the Keepers." Trent, as gently as he could, took the staff from the other side of the room and placed it on the table, "I must let myself have a bit of excitement over this. I have spent my whole life wishing to find this. Never knew I would—" He laughed again, not hiding it this time, "And an even better find, is the Keeper!"

Kirana let out a laugh but said nothing. She didn't know what she could say. *Yes? Thank you?*

Trent leaned forward on the table, his eyes darting across her, "It is so incredible to meet you. It's an honor." He put out his hands and Kirana gave him her hand. He held her the way Tia always had, and Kirana felt both a sudden longing to find her sister and the realization she was no longer the only one who could care for Kirana. Trent stared at her as he spoke, "Where are you from, Kirana? Not here?"

"No, I don't think so. I'm from Permidia."

Trent thought for a moment, "Never heard of it."

Gideon placed a new box on the table and moved around to Trent, "I haven't either." He glanced at Kirana and looked back, "But her world is supposedly perfect. The Magistrater is their savior and the Keepers don't exist."

Trent blinked and let go of Kirana's hand to lean back and think. He eventually nodded, "Alright, so things have changed." He looked back to Kirana, "Can you tell us about your world? It'll help us."

"Help you do what?"

Trent gestured around him, "Learn. About you, about the worlds, about the Keepers." He moved around the table quickly and took his seat again with giddy excitement over Kirana's question. Gideon and Gwen listened in on the conversation, but Trent made sure Kirana felt as if it was just them speaking. He smiled at her, "You are the first person to travel across worlds in centuries. We know almost nothing about the other worlds, so our excitement is in the knowledge you possess, and what you can connect us with by traveling."

"I'm sorry, but I am so confused." She masked her panic by smiling back at him, "I don't know anything about the Keepers, or why your people keep getting hurt."

"You don't know anything about the Keepers?"

She shook her head quickly, "I know nothing."

Gideon moved around the table and knelt in front of Kirana beside Trent, "We need to know the information you have. We can explain everything later but we're short on time. Do your people worship the Magistrater? Is she your god?"

"Worship?"

"The Keepers are our gods, who do your people pray to?"

"My people just live their lives." Trent looked up at her and waited for more. Kirana looked around the room and took a breath, "I don't know what is going on. I don't know why you are asking me these things and I have questions too."

"We need you to answer ours, Kirana. This is life or death for us." She realized Gideon had a notebook and pencil in hand. They wanted her every word written down to be kept like the artifacts in the room.

It was too much, "I think this is life or death for me too then and... how I am supposed to answer your questions without knowing what you are asking me? I don't even know where I am or what you are calling me or what *thing* is." She pointed down the staff.

Gwen shook her head quickly, "Don't call it a *thing*."

"Then tell me what to call it!"

Gideon put his finger to his lips and pointed to the door they had come through, "Your life may have been perfect, Kirana, but ours is not. You need to trust us and do as we say. You may be confused but we are desperate. The information you give us could change the tides of our very century."

"Dad." Gwen intervened, "If she doesn't know what is going on then she can't answer our questions."

Trent nodded, "She has a point, Gideon." He gestured to a chair at the wall.

Gideon took a breath but did not move to the chair, "Trent, the Wardens are everywhere. We shouldn't stay here for too long. We'll take her to Lorenzo when we're done and find somewhere to hide her."

Kirana put her hands up, "Who is Lorenzo?"

"One of the greatest leaders in Hiraeth." Trent answered, "He leads a much larger rebellion." He gestured around the small room with a laugh before turning back to Gideon, "We're safe here. I will go out if a Warden arrives and deal with their questions. If worse comes to worse you know how to get out of here. And Gwen is right, if Kirana understands then we can get more information from her. Where are the Wardens looking for her?"

"The neighborhoods."

Trent nodded quickly, "Then we're fine. We're safe here and if they arrive I will go talk to them. We have time."

Kirana felt the energy in the room shift with that final thought of safety. Trent leaned towards Kirana. She found both Gwen and Gideon leaning in with him to listen as well, and suddenly it no longer felt like she was being questioned, but simply being let into a conversation. It was nice to be around so many people like her. Without the danger, she was able to take in the wonder of the world she had entered.

"The Keepers were gods that ruled over every world." Trent gestured with his hands on the table, miming out different places, "Four worlds that make up a team of four Keepers."

"What do you mean by *worlds?*"

"Back hundreds of years ago there was some sort of event. We don't know what it was exactly but we know it had to do with that very crystal." Trent gestured to the staff, "It was powerful enough to split one world into four different dimensions. At first, they matched each other but as time went on they changed. Each world had different people, different cultures, and different languages. They were separated and could only be brought together by the Keepers. The ones who could travel between."

Gideon swung one of the books around and put it out on the center of the table. It had a picture like the one he had shown Kirana before. The four figures and the staff between them, "Each world has one Keeper to rule over them. Together, the Keepers united the worlds and kept the peace between them. They say the most recent ones were even able to create a gate. People could pass freely between each dimension."

Kirana squinted at him, "The most recent ones?"

"When one Keeper dies another takes their place. A never-ending cycle of gods."

"Gods?" Kirana couldn't help but laugh. When no one else seemed to find the humor of his words she stopped quickly, "They're gods?"

Gwen nodded, "They're very powerful. There are records of them possessing gifts. They have a connection to their people and to the world they come from and that gives them abilities beyond any others. There are stories about them having powers that save their entire world from enemies and starvation and… everything."

Kirana looked down at the book, "So someone died and now I'm here?"

Trent shook his head, "We haven't seen any sign of the Keepers in centuries."

"Why?"

Gideon shut his eyes, "The Magistrater destroyed them. Killed them and kept them dead. The staff disappeared the moment she came to power."

Kirana felt everything start to hit her, "Why now? Why me?"

"For whatever reason you were able to find the staff, and now the cycle has begun again." Gideon told her firmly, "Only the staff knows the answer to why you were chosen."

"It's a piece of wood." She gestured to the staff.

"It's also this." Trent tapped the glowing crystal with his pen. "It's called *Rhodonite*, a crystal fit for a god. It's an energy source."

"Like a battery?"

Trent waved away her words, "Batteries store energy. The crystals are the energy. The weapons the Keepers used were powered by these crystals. One small piece of this could power this entire city. There is an old myth that said the source of the Rhodonite fell from a collapsed star, and that it is, in fact, a star itself." He shrugged, "Not sure if it's true but it makes a good story."

"So how much Rhodonite is there?"

Gwen put a hand to her heart, "There are pieces of it everywhere. Within us and the worlds around us. The Keepers can connect to it more than anyone else. That's how they're chosen. The worlds choose the Keepers through the staff."

Kirana remembered the figures from before. They each had a weapon in their hands. "Where are the other weapons? Other Keeper weapons?"

"No idea."

"But when the staff disappeared did the other weapons go with it?" She looked at everyone and leaned back, "You don't know that much, do you?"

Trent started to put up a fight, but Gideon spoke first, "That's why you need to tell us more about your world. Your people, the Magistrater, the staff. This is the first contact we have had between worlds in centuries."

She nodded quickly, "Permidia is run by the Magistrater. She gives everyone their perfect life. There are cities, towns, lakes, rivers, towns, apartments. People can live in the center of a busy city or live in a quiet cabin. But they are all alone."

"*Alone.*" Gideon grabbed his notebook from before. He started writing her words down, "Keep going."

"No one wants human interaction. No one wants connection. They all live their perfect lives alone. So, is it normal to feel connection here?" Everyone nodded. "Well, I don't have that trait. I wanted human connection. I had my sister, Tia. She liked to speak with me, but she would only visit once a week."

Trent squinted at her, "But surely you would lack social skills. Doesn't all of this shock you?"

"I studied it."

He squinted at her, "You studied us?"

"I studied the history of my world. Or I thought it was history because honestly, it looked a lot like this world. Everything was destroyed, lots of corruption. I understand some of the things around me. I know how a shop works, I know about money but... It just feels like I jumped back in time before the Magistrater saved us."

"You were studying our present lives, Kirana, not our history." Gideon wrote vigorously, "Does Tia work with the Magistrater?"

Kirana let out a laugh, "What? No. Of course, she doesn't. But she should be safe."

"She had no connection to the Magistrater?" Gwen asked, forcing her to think harder.

Kirana shook her head firmly, "She never... well. She got me..." She shook her head again, "She's not working with her."

Gideon looked up, "She got you what?"

"To speak with her."

"Who?"

"The Magistrater."

Everyone stared at her with widened eyes. There was a heavy silence in the room, and from what Kirana could tell no one was even breathing. Trent let out a gasp of air, "You spoke with her?"

Gideon pushed the notebook aside, "What did she say?"

"I don't know." Kirana tried to remember the conversation, but she was distracted by the alarm on everyone's faces, "She just told me I was different. She told me I was a miscalculation."

"A miscalculation?" Gideon stared at her, "A miscalculation of what?"

"The perfect world. I am Permidia's fault. A mistake. My perfect life has to do with connecting with other people. I wasn't allowed to be with anyone but my sister but–"

"How is that perfect?" Gwen interrupted.

"Love is not worth the pain." Kirana nodded to her own words, "Without connection, there are no wars, no fights, no pain."

"No love?" Gwen said it like it was some horrible concept.

Kirana shook her head quickly, "But it works. It's perfect."

"But if you were a miscalculation it isn't perfect." Gideon stared at her, "Who made the miscalculation? The Magistrater?" She nodded, "Does that make us musculations too?"

"I... No, Permidia is perfect. It just is. This is somewhere else." Kirana didn't want to start any conflicts with the people she was with, but they were wrong, they had to be, "Maybe she's just working on it. Maybe there is a reason for all of this."

"A reason?" Gwen let out a sharp laugh, "Love is not worth the *pain*? You don't know what *pain* is. How can you, of all people, judge the value of love?"

"I want love. I want connection, but it doesn't work. Permidia is perfect–"

Gideon gestured to her, "Where do you think your clothes come from? Who makes them? You look well-fed, where does your food come from? Your water? Your technology? Your entertainment?"

"It's not like I could question the perfect ruler who created everyone's perfect lives! I thought she was a hero!"

Trent brought his finger to his lips, "Be quiet."

Kirana stood up and pushed the chair away, "Why would she be hurting you all? She's powerful. As powerful as the Keepers you're all praising."

"You never thought to question the price of perfection?" Gwen clenched her jaw, "She's hurting our world. People are dying, or living life waiting to die. They are being hurt. They are being taken from their families. You wanted connection, we want it too. We just want to love, but she has created an imbalance. There is too much pain in our world. And now you're here to save it."

"I'm–" Gideon moved towards and put his finger to his lips and she backed away from him. Lowering her voice she forced herself to calm down, "I'm not a god. I don't understand any of this. I don't know how you expect me to save an entire world. Alone."

"You're not alone." Trent gestured to his books, "You have a team waiting for you. You just need to find them. As the leader, the first Keeper, the first chosen by the staff, it is your job to find them."

"I don't want this."

"Well, you have it." Gideon snapped back, "And you're the only one who can do something. You can do anything with that staff. Inspire, protect, command, rule, *attack*. We need you."

"I saw the Keepers." She pointed to the staff, "Before I came to... to this place I was somewhere else. It was like I was in space or something. This light galaxy... and there were figures."

"How many?"

"Four people."

"You are here for a reason. You're a god. Your vision showed you who you need to find, what you were destined to create."

The Magistrater had spoken to her about fate. She said something about the purpose of giving perfection. Was this perfection? No, the ruler was hurting their people, for what? One world to live above the others?

Kirana shook her head quickly, "I was just following a voice. I just found the staff. I took it to give to the Magistrater. Are you sure that..."

He stared at her, "What?"

"Are you sure she's evil? I mean... maybe this is all a system. Maybe she has a plan–"

Gwen looked at her as if she had said something impossible, "How can you say that?"

"You get to love!" She gestured to all of them, "That is the greatest gift I can think of. She could have separated you all but she kept you together. That's mercy–"

Gideon flinched at her words, "Watching everyone we love die is not a gift. My brother, Tristen, was deaf and was shot for not listening to a drunk Warden's orders. I had a friend named Cassidy who was strangled for the fun of it. My father died out in the fields, my mother died trying to get his body so we could give him a funeral. The Magistrater sends us working day and night until our hands bleed." He gestured to Trent, "His wife was killed the day after their wedding. His sister can't work because she fell off of a city platform and no one came to help heal her broken spine." He pointed at Gwen, "I have had to raise my daughter alone because her mother was beaten to *death*–" His voice broke with the final word and he had to stop for the sake of remaining calm. Kirana knew there were so many more stories he could have told if he had the strength to remember them all.

He stepped forward and Kirana walked back into the shelves behind her.

Books tumbled off and she hurried to pick them up and place them back. "I'm sorry."

"You can fix this. Don't you get it?" He gestured to her, breathing out as if already disappointed in their proclaimed god, "You are the first Keeper, the leader, Kirana. We have been waiting for you for centuries. You have the potential to change *everything*. No one can save us but you."

"What am I supposed to do? *Kill* the Magistrater?"

"Unite the worlds. Protect our people."

When he stopped talking no one else spoke up. Gwen and Trent watched Kirana with the same patience as if it was the Permidian who would decide their fate.

In all of Kirana's years alone, a room had never felt so quiet.

But suddenly, there was a loud knock from the other room.

Everyone's head shot to the door before they remained completely still. After a moment, Gideon glanced up at Gwen. Behind his determination, Kirana saw his fear. Trent sucked in a fleeting breath and rushed back to the door. Without a word, he went through and closed it quickly behind him. It was only then that Gideon took a step away from Kirana and walked to his daughter. They exchanged whispers as noise came from the other room. Kirana moved to the door carefully and put an ear to the wood.

The front door unlocked and opened. Then there was a voice.

"Stand aside. We will be doing an involuntary search."

Footsteps echoed, but it was hard to tell how many Wardens were there.

"Of course," Trent said as they walked around the room. It sounded like they were tearing the place apart, working quickly and with little care for the shop. "May I ask–"

"Who works here?"

"I do. Alone. I haven't had many customers today."

Kirana flinched as she heard a knock on the wall. A hand scraped the surface before suddenly stopping. "Is this your only room?"

Gideon came over to Kirana and put a hand on her shoulders, pulling her away from the door to the other side of the room. He had the staff wrapped up in the cloth already and swung it onto his back with a new strap attached. He pointed up to a small tinted window on the ceiling as Gwen pushed her chair underneath it. Kirana heard more knocks on the wall behind her as Gwen got up on the chair and pushed open the window.

"What is this?" A Warden asked firmly as the noises suddenly stopped.

"This is my only room. The wall is thin."

Gwen jumped off the chair and pulled herself through the window.

The wall suddenly shook with a violent crash as a Warden yelled, "Open the door!"

Gideon pushed Kirana up on the chair as Gwen reached down to give her hand. The Hiraethans worked together to throw Kirana up and onto the roof.

Just as she landed beside Gwen, there was a loud, thundering *bang*. Kirana flung her hands to her ears, as the box next to Gideon broke with an invisible impact. It was the same noise as before, the one that came from whatever the Warden had been holding before. She realized very quickly that it was a weapon and a powerful one at that.

Gideon, no longer staying quiet, jumped up off the chair and pulled himself up onto the roof beside his daughter. He pulled Kirana up and the three of them started running.

The buildings were all of different heights, different sizes, and sometimes even different shapes. But they were all small, so the changes happened quickly. As soon as the group had sprinted far enough they had to leap onto a new building. One, two, three, buildings they jumped, sometimes small leaps, other times it took everything Kirana had to make it to the other side. As they kept running a new set of buildings came before them, taller ones. They were heading down the city slope toward the miles of farmland, but there were clusters of high buildings around them still.

Gideon pushed them both to a wall and looked over the side to see if they were being followed. Kirana and Gwen looked with him. No one was there. Somehow, the idea of not knowing where the Wardens had gone terrified Kirana more than seeing them.

"What happened to Trent?" She asked Gideon, but he didn't even look at her, and with a push he kept them running forward.

As they sprinted ahead they were forced to jump across a huge gap between two buildings. Both Gwen and Gideon landed on the other side but Kirana went chest first into the edge, starting to slip. The two Hiraethans ran back and pulled her up as something metal hit the side of the roof. A hook, piercing clay. A rope tied to it. Kirana looked down to see a group of Wardens climbing after them, a hand reaching up to grab her leg. With a scream, Gideon pulled her back up onto the roof and forced them to run faster.

But suddenly the Wardens were everywhere, appearing behind walls and chasing them with the weapons held high. Kirana heard more of the *bangs* as pieces of clay beside Gwen and Gideon broke. At one point, out of view from the Wardens at least, Gideon stopped them and grabbed his daughter.

"What do we do?" Gwen asked, her voice pitched from fear.

He held her shoulder and walked her back towards a gap between two buildings, "Get to Lorenzo." Then he pushed her. Hard. So hard that she had no time to react to what he was doing, falling backward into the alley. Kirana tried to reach out to grab her but he was faster. Gideon held onto his jacket still around her shoulders and locked eyes with her, "Do what you were chosen to do. Protect."

Kirana was then pushed back, only her scream was louder. She fell back with the push and hit the wall of the building, before going down onto the hard floor. She winced in pain, as Gideon leaped over the gap. Disappearing.

Kirana felt the sting of bruises forming around her sides, her arms, her legs, and her head. But there was no time. Gwen, hurt just the same, went right beside her and pulled her back up. They both heard something move in the street beside them and put their backs on the wall. A group of Wardens came rushing past them in the direction Gideon was going. Gwen's father was leading the enemies away so his daughter and the girl he believed was god could get away.

"What do we do?" Kirana asked Gwen. There was another *bang*, then another, and another. Each time Kirana flinched and winced from the noise, "Who is Lorenzo?"

"A rebellion leader." Gwen looked back around the alley; there were boxes and crates stacked at the end.

"We need to find him. That's what Gideon said. Where is he?"

Gwen didn't answer, her eyes were locked on the boxes. She suddenly sprinted towards them and started climbing up towards the roof.

"Gwen!" Kirana ran after her and attempted to scale the crates just as she did, only to find herself much slower. When she reached the rooftops Gwen already leaped to another roof in pursuit of her father. Kirana had no idea what she was doing or what was truly going on, but she knew running back into danger was only going to get them hurt. And yet, what else could she do but follow her? The two of them ran after Gideon, following the groups of Wardens who had not looked back just yet.

Gwen stopped at the edge of a rooftop, staring at a gap too large to jump across. When Kirana reached her she stopped to catch her breath and looked ahead to see the Wardens scattered and running with their weapons raised. She could see how hard Gideon was working to stay out of sight. This was his home, he knew how to hide within it, but how long could instinct last against the power the Wardens held? They were trying to kill him, not capture or question, kill. The danger had hit her long before, but in that moment Kirana realized Gwen was about to lose her father, and then they would hunt too. This was what Gideon was talking about; Hiraethan fear for those they love, always in danger.

"Stop!" Gwen yelled as loud as she could, waving her hands up to get Warden's attention. A few of them glanced over. She was distracting them, leading them away from her father.

Kirana, out of breath and panicking, gesturing back the way they had come, "We can't–"

Gwen put out her hand, "Give me the staff."

"What?"

"Give me the staff!"

Kirana didn't move. She knew there was no way for both the two of them and Gideon to get away. But the rage and determination in Gwen's eyes would not be put out by Kirana's fears. It was fueled by love. She needed to save her father, no matter the cost.

Gideon's words came to mind: *Do what you were chosen to do. Protect.*

"Please." Gwen begged her, "Help me, Kirana."

Kirana looked towards the Wardens, choosing not to find time to hesitate as she ripped the cloth from the staff's crystal, "Wardens!" She screamed at them and held up the glowing staff sky. The Wardens stopped and stared, almost all of them no longer in pursuit of Gideon.

Gwen ran to Kirana and put out a hand to take the staff. Kirana let her, knowing she would do a better job at showing it off. But as soon as the Hiraethan touched the wood, something changed. At first, it was a feeling, a source of energy Kirana could sense in the air. The city noise went quiet. There was a force of energy. It was powerful. It felt strong enough to push Kirana off the roof entirely, yet it did nothing to her but move her hair back and strain her eyes. A burst of golden light expelled out around Kirana as she backed away slowly.

Gwen was floating in a nexus of golden light. Sparks and particles moved all around them across the rooftops. It took Kirana a moment to realize it wasn't coming from just the staff, but also from Gwen herself. Then, only moments later, she fell to the ground and the staff rolled out of her grasp. Gwen looked more terrified than Kirana had ever seen, her whole body shaking as she looked from the staff to the Wardens.

Kirana wanted to know what just happened. It felt so important but there was simply no time. The Wardens were coming for them, finished with their useless chase with Gwen's father.

Protect.

Kirana dropped down to the staff. It was no longer glowing and taken on a lightless white color, that of normal crystal. Kirana grabbed Gwen and tried to pull her up. Gwen looked locked in fear, eyes darting from the Wardens to the staff. As Kirana forced her to run, she became focused again, taking the lead as soon as she was done with fear. Gwen grabbed Kirana and forced them both to jump down the nearest gap. Kirana forced herself not to scream and hit hard clay and dirt with a tumble. This time, she wasted no time in indulging herself with pain. She shot up and ran with Gwen as the two of them darted into the streets. They were on a new platform, wrapped around a series of buildings and doors that smelt like wood and glue.

Gwen moved them along this lumber district, sliding past workers moving polished furniture and large logs from building to building. She took Kirana far up the street until it ended and slipped them both down a thin set of stairs. They ended up in a more crowded space, a landing platform much like the one Kirana had just been in. Everyone there looked on edge, all of them having heard the same violent noise from the Warden's weapons. It was a marketplace with stalls all around them. Gwen walked through the crowd as fast as she could with her hand still wrapped around Kirana's wrist. Further into the crowd, Gwen let go of her so they could walk like the people around them. Kirana hadn't wanted her to let go. She wanted to be guided, or maybe just to be held. She looked at each person around her and expected to see a Warden with their weapon raised for her head.

Kirana followed Gwen and eventually was led to a stall. In the midst of her panic she only caught the end of Gwen's conversation with the woman selling fruits.

"And *you'll* get the Corts for me?"

"Just give them my message. Lorenzo will pay you."

The woman on the other end of the stall looked aged. White hair and a wrinkled face, but she had strong eyes and a look of determination that flavored her old age. As she walked out of the stall, Gwen took her place and gestured for Kirana to duck down below the table. With a cloth dangling over the side she was able to hide there, for now. Gwen grabbed a piece of string on the table and did her best to tie up part of her hair. She looked like she was going to cry, but did her best to bite back tears.

Kirana clung onto the staff until her knuckles turned white. She was so terrified, but finally, she allowed herself to take in what just happened. She understood the most terrifying aspects of her situation: Gideon was gone, Trent was gone, the Wardens were trying to kill them for the staff or for Kirana, maybe both. What took her longer to understand was the more magical elements of what had occurred. The staff had been glowing that yellow light all day, all night, from the moment she landed in Hiraeth. Suddenly, that energy went into Gwen. No, it came from Gwen. Like it had for Kirana.

Four dimensions, four Keepers. That included Hiraeth.

That included Gwen.

Chapter 11

* ✳ *

GWEN

GWEN REMEMBERED THE day she first saw a corpse. She had been playing outside early in the morning before her parents went to work. She remembered holding her doll's hand and bouncing her along the ground, before suddenly running into something. Someone. Their neighbor, David, lay with his face planted in the mud and his leg twisted to the side. She screamed and ran home to find her mother, crying and guiding her to David. She remembered the panic in her mother's eyes, not just because he was dead, but because her daughter had been the one to find him.

That night, she sat beside Gwen in bed and held her close, "I'm sorry you had to see that Gwyneth. David was a good man."

Gwen started crying again, "Why did he die?"

"We think the Wardens found him in the orchards and shot his leg." She winced, "Do you know why I am telling you this?" Gwen shook her head, "Because danger is all around us, and that is the reality of our life. You need to know that, sweetheart."

"What if they take *you*?"

Her mother's face dropped as she clenched her jaw, "Sometimes I wonder if they'll hurt you too." She held Gwen tighter, "I feel helpless. The Wardens are villains, and your father and I are trying to fight back. Our people are hurting, and I want to believe we can make a difference but... people keep dying, no matter what we do. We can't win just yet. That's why we pray to the Keepers, my darling.

89

When I'm scared and feeling helpless, I send out a prayer to our god hoping they can protect you and your father. I pray that they'll stop a Warden or guide a bullet away from our family. I pray that they'll return and free us from the Magistrater."

Gwen's mother was a strong believer in the mythology of the Keepers, praying as much as she could for the wellbeing of her family. Gwen simply couldn't believe that she—a Hiraethan girl, her daughter—was the Keeper she had been praying for all those years.

When she held the staff she felt herself lift and glow, experiencing feelings of power and strength unlike anything she had ever known. It terrified her. Gwen understood the Wardens and the threat they posed, but she didn't understand the staff, and somehow that was much more frightening.

"Are you okay?" Kirana asked after a few minutes in silence. She was still tucked under the stall and clinging to the staff.

Gwen shook her head after seeing no one close enough to hear them. She spoke in a whisper, "What just happened?" Kirana didn't respond and Gwen resisted the urge to look down at her. She had to look like any other vendor. "My whole family is at risk now and I can't–" She clenched her jaw and took a deep breath, tears forming again, "I need to find my father."

"Gwen." She looked down at Kirana. She was crying. Clutching the staff with reddened eyes, "Is it even possible for us to go find him *now*? After..."

Gwen shook her head again, it was all she could say to their horrible situation. "What happened?" Her voice cracked, and still, Kirana didn't answer.

Someone nearby looked over the food displayed as a group of Wardens came rushing by. They looked around the crowd, not in the stalls, but that would not last for long. When the soldiers were out of view Gwen took a breath and spoke her mind, "I'm not a Keeper. I'm not a protector. That was an illusion." She shook her head, "I don't know how I can reach my father. I need..." She laughed at her thought, which only made her want to cry more, "I need a god."

Kirana looked away, holding the staff closer to herself, "I'm so sorry Gwen."

"We're not gods. We can't be." She thought of her mother praying for divine safety. "The gods are supposed to be powerful rulers."

Kirana put the staff on the ground, "How can I fix this?"

"Fix what?"

"This world?" Gwen looked at her. The tears were gone. Kirana was shaken, but the tears were dry now. She looked determined, "This isn't fair. None of this is fair. On you or your people."

Gwen looked around before crouching in front of Kirana, "We can't just save them all."

"The Keepers mean something, don't they? They're gods?"

"Yes."

"If I was brought here to be a Keeper then maybe I just need to be one." She shook her head, "I don't know what to do. I don't have some godly powers but I can't walk away from this. I think I just got a second chance to fix this world." She laughed as tears filled her eyes, "I lived my whole life reaping your labor, and I never even questioned it. I came here looking for people like me and... I found you." She took a breath, "I want to help you and your people so that maybe one day we can all love each other without being stopped by the *Magistrater.*" Kirana spoke with the same tone of disgust Gwen had heard from every Hiraethan who had said the ruler's name. Kirana finally understood.

Gwen put a hand to her heart, holding her family there with it, "I wish there was a god to come down and save us, but you're not going to do it. You're up against an army of Wardens and we don't even have a weapon."

"I have to try." Kirana took a breath and wiped her tears before they could fall, "I will fight, I will lead, I will give hope, but I *will* do something." She straightened her back, "I am going to find the other Keepers."

"How?"

Kirana shook her head and looked away, "I don't know, but this is wrong and if I am the only person who can fix it I owe it to everyone to try. I'll travel and I'll find the other Keepers and I'll fight and I'll protect and I'll do whatever I can to stop the Magistrater." Kirana locked eyes with Gwen, "I don't know what I am going to do, exactly, or how I am going to find the Keepers, but you are one of them, Gwen."

Gwen looked down at the staff.

But maybe we don't need the gods anymore, maybe we need people like you.

Her mother's own words suddenly became ironic, and now Gwen wished more than anything she could look up and respond with such simple words.

Maybe we need both.

Gideon and her mother had been the perfect balance between action and prayer. They did as much as they could without being targeted by the Wardens and left the rest of their work as prayers to the Keepers. Gwen wondered if she could complete their work, and finally help her people as the god they needed her to be. The god her mother prayed for.

Gwen looked up at Kirana, "I want to save my people."

Kirana locked eyes with her, staring deeply as if checking that the Hiraethan was telling the truth. "Are you sure?" She asked, a warmth in her words but fear in her eyes.

Gwen nodded again, "I can't live another day, watching my family, my friends, and my people die in the streets. All because of one dictator who wants power. And… I haven't done anything to stop her or the Wardens. I didn't know how. I was just a powerless citizen. I still am but now I have the potential to be something more but…" She clenched her jaw, "But I am blind."

"Then let's find a way to see through the darkness. Because that's all it is, the dark. We aren't blind Gwen, we just haven't found the light."

"The light…" Gwen looked down at the staff, "There's an old story called the Keeper's Compass. It tells us how they found each other, following the light of the Rhodonite."

"So the plan would be to go to the other dimensions and locate the Keepers with the glowing light. Two more dimensions, two more Keepers. We learn how to be gods along the way. Then we start building rebellions and find more in other worlds."

"Unless there are no Wardens there. We don't know what these places could be."

"But we do know a god is waiting for us there." Gwen found hope in Kirana's eyes, maybe even a sense of excitement.

"You should be scared, Kirana."

"I am." She said as a grin grew across her face, "But it's so…" She searched for the right thought, and settled on a word that looked sweet against her lips, "Exciting."

She was naive if anything else, and yet, her joy was something refreshing. For all the grief in Gwen's life, she found Kirana's joyful determination to be true. Her intentions were made by her heart, not some saddened mind. But she was inexperienced with pain, she had no idea the cost of fighting back, even with the title of a god.

Kirana leaned forward, "The problem is I have no idea how to travel through dimensions. Let alone if I can bring you."

"How did you get here?"

Gwen was ready for a thoughtful answer. She was disappointed to see Kirana shrug and smile. "It was an accident. I just grabbed and suddenly I was lifted into the air like you were. Then I was somewhere else."

"Hiraeth?"

Kirana looked ready to say yes but stopped herself. A second later she shook her head, "Somewhere completely different. But it wasn't another dimension, it was just…" She tried to find the right words, "Between, it was just *in-between*. I was just floating in this new world, and there were people there."

"Are you sure this isn't another world you jumped through?"

"No. I could feel it was like a crack or… or a gap of some kind. There was no ground either. Just a void. And there were four people. Figures. They looked like the people from the book, only they were silhouettes, and then I was dragged here."

"Can you–" Gwen heard the sound of metal crashing together in the distance. She shot up and looked around. There were no Wardens around her, a concept that scared her greatly. They were normally everywhere, patrolling or standing by, but now they were gone. Gwen stayed up at the stall a few moments longer and looked for signs of the soldiers. She caught two women moving quickly up the street while glancing back the way they had come. She heard a quiet murmur as those around her noticed the absence of danger. Gwen looked down the way the two women were glancing back and heard what sounded like two metal pieces being bashed together. It wasn't a machine, the material was too thin, it sounded like pots. A Hiraethan was banging metal together, and though it was far away, by the abrupt stop Gwen recognized it was a warning. Those types of signals normally happened in the fields to alert others to a patrol or ship coming to watch them work. The fact that someone was warning the entire street meant something big was coming.

Gwen ducked back down to Kirana, "We need to go. Now."

"Go where?"

"Can you travel, right now, get us away before they can find us?" She pushed the staff to Kirana's chest, "We're being cornered."

"What about your father?"

Gwen felt Kirana's words stop her for a moment. She didn't know what to do, but with how close the Wardens were she wondered if there was even a way to stay in Hiraeth, let alone find her father. If he was smart he would have stayed hidden or journeyed to find his daughter with the Keeper. That fact that he wasn't there right now showed her that there was no way she could ever make it to him. Her family would run, they would make it to Lorenzo, and they would be safe. Gwen knew the importance of the staff and its Keeper, and she knew the best way to protect them both was to run.

She ignored Kirana's question and held onto the staff, "You're right, we have the potential to be gods. I can't let my people down." She made sure that sentence settled with Kirana, though she knew it would never live up to Gwen's Hiraethan understanding. All those nights her mother spent praying to the gods for their return, all those secret worshipers begging to be saved, and suddenly it was becoming true.

Kirana was the hope they had kindled for centuries.

Gwen could hear people moving faster down the street and shook the staff, "Go."

"You saw what happened the first time I traveled." Bloody nose, unconscious, knocked out all day, and weak even when she finally gained consciousness. "Don't let me die." Kirana gave a nervous laugh and Gwen recognised her fear masked in humor. With a breath, Kirana pulled herself together and closed her eyes to focus. She watched as the staff glowed ever so slightly under the stall table, a soft white glow that moved with Kirana's breaths.

This was the moment Gwen would leave Hiraeth. Leave her home. Not just the city or her neighborhood, but the world itself. She would be alone with a stranger following her destiny as a proclaimed god. It seemed idiotic, but it also felt right. As if there was someone there with her telling her to do it. A hand on her shoulder, a kind word in her mind. A light breeze filled her hair and she smelt the air around her, somehow already homesick for something she had never experienced leaving. She was determined to return to her world in victory. Her people had kept her safe for her entire life, whether it be her father or her mother, or Gaia or Theo, or the old man who snuck her five Corts for dinner, or the woman who gave Gwen her old shoes, it was finally Gwen's turn to save them.

The feeling Gwen had when she first touched the staff returned. She felt connected to it once again and as she watched the Rhodonite glow white the stalls and marketplace started to flatten and morph before her. The view before her dissolved into a bright light that forced her eyes closed. Gwen took in a breath of air she had never tasted before, cold and unwelcome in her warm Hiraethan lungs. Then suddenly the ground beneath her disappeared. At first, Gwen thought it was just a sick feeling in her stomach, like falling in a dream, but as she collapsed to a hard floor the pain reminded her she was far from asleep. Her legs hit the ground and she fell onto her side, rolling onto her back.

There was light all around her, but it didn't feel like it was coming from the sun. No, Gwen had felt the warm rays on her skin her whole life. This new light was not anything natural. As her senses returned she watched the light before her eyes altered. A shadow fell over her, and it took her a few moments more to realize that it came from a large ship. It was larger than her own house, at least five times the size. The underside featured metal lumps and an array of wires, with the two engines spewing out heat and faded smoke at the back of the ship. Gwen knew the Warden ships well, and it was not one of theirs. When the ship passed, she saw there were more above it. Dozens if not hundreds of ships flying past each other at ridiculous speeds. They were flying high above the tops of large buildings. Her eyes followed the rooftops, each structure a different height. Different in every way. Though they were all made with modest gray concrete or lined with metal and plastic, they featured loud elements to draw her eyes across each building. Bright words lit up with eye-burning colors. Music blasted out of doors and holes within the very walls of the buildings.

As Gwen turned her head, following the buildings down to their lowest level, she was forced to go onto her side and held herself up as she saw what was directly around her. She was next to an overbearing structure, a building that could have been as tall as the Magistrater's tower itself. The entrance had a large open door with a neon sign in bright blue reading, *Dingers*. The entire wall and door frame were made from colorful pieces of plastic and large dazzling feathers. The window looking into the first floor showed a bar. Hiraeth had them too, but not like this. Someone inside was chugging something green and bubbly. The way the bearded man poured it down his throat it might as well have been thinner than water. When he finished the whole place exploded with a collective cheer, the music inside went up and lights flashed in celebration. Gwen flinched away and forced herself to her feet.

This world was nothing like Hiraeth.

Nothing.

Her world was infected by the disease that was the Wardens, but at its heart, it was a place of grace and beauty. It had mountains and fields of grass and flowers, it had rivers and lakes and oceans, and it had plants of all types grounded in crimson dirt and clay. But the world she found herself in was not infected, it was just... dead. There were no plants, or mountains, or flowers, or anything real of any kind. There was just metal and plastic and horrible lights that burned her eyes. As Gwen looked around, she saw the people of this world, and she could see even from a glance that they were just as fake as the rest of their city.

They all seemed to walk alone, each of them contrasting the other with extreme accessories, colors, or fabrics, all of which featured a signature mask. One woman wore a dress shaped like a tube accessorized by an oval-shaped mask. A man passed by with a suit on that seemed to change colors with every step he took. Gwen could hear music coming from his mask. Someone in a large orange coat with a black mask shaped to look like a human face walked right up to Gwen, and she was forced to step aside before they could walk right through her. Suddenly it seemed like everyone was walking right into her, and Gwen dogged person after person as she tried to grapple with where she was.

It was true chaos, and she knew then and there had it was because there were no Wardens. For now, that would be a good thing for the Keepers.

Gwen went cold. "Kirana!" She looked around for her, but there were too many people, and no one seemed to even notice Gwen as she frantically moved through the crowd while attempting to not get lost herself. In her frantic pursuit, she ran into someone on the ground.

"Sorry." She muttered, trying to move away. But something caught her eye. Gwen looked back down to an old man holding Kirana. She locked eyes with him, his own looking frantic and psychotic. He had sores surrounding his mouth and creeping up from under his orange beard. She realized then how young he might have been, and simply looked aged from whatever he had done to himself.

He stared at her as if waiting for Gwen to do something. "Let go of her!" She yelled at him, giving him the signal he needed. As soon as she opened her mouth he dropped Kirana and ran away, back arched and shoulders hunched. He looked like an animal scurrying away from a predator and hid in a dark alley just a few feet away. It was where he was taking Kirana.

Gwen dropped down to Kirana as people started to walk right over her. The

Keepers needed to get out of the crowd, and not knowing where else to go, Gwen moved into that same alley and watched the man run further back away from them. She couldn't see anyone else with him and prayed his fear would last. When she had Kirana by the wall she knelt over her. She looked alive, but her nose was gushing out blood.

There was a noise behind Gwen, and she turned her head. Her eyes darted around the dark alley until they landed on something just at the end. It looked like some sort of machine or a robot. It was small, very small. Two tracks moved back and forth as it went over a piece of metal. It was blocky, with a small square head, and a slightly larger square body. Lights, wires, and panels of metal all around it. It moved over the piece of metal and looked over to the Keepers. Gwen saw now it had a screen for a face, its expression shown in pixels. Its eyes lifted suddenly as if the robot was surprised. Gwen realized why.

It was holding the staff.

All of a sudden its tracks spun and it shot forward with its human-like voice crying out in a panic. Its head moved back with the amount of speed it carried. The staff moved with it into the alley.

The Keepers were being robbed.

"Stop!" She cried after it. Without thinking Gwen turned herself around and started running after the robot. And yet, she couldn't. She turned back to look at Kirana. There was no way Gwen could just leave her, but she couldn't just let the robot get away with the staff. Lose the Keeper or lose the staff.

"Shit!" Gwen ran back and knelt by the unconscious girl, shaking her violently. "Kirana!" She needed her to wake up, "Kirana! We need to go! Wake up!"

She looked back down the alley. The thief was getting away.

"Damn it! I'm sorry for this." She slapped Kirana across her face. She winced and opened her eyes, finally awake. Gwen started pulling her up, grunting as Kirana refused to give her any help. She let Kirana lean against her as they stumbled forward into a run.

"Wait–" Kirana told her, trying to resist and pull away from her.

"They took the staff!" Gwen yelled at her. She was starting to panic.

"Who–" The Keeper tried to ask as Gwen made her run faster.

"I don't know, but we need to find them."

PART 2

Telematic

Chapter 12

✳

KIRANA

KIRANA FELT SICK and tired, and she knew it wasn't because she had traveled dimensions. This time it felt easier, like she had already paved the way through the strange in-between world. She was hurting and exhausted because she had to drag Gwen with her.

By focusing on the staff she was able to *feel* the in-between world. It was a sensation her first trip had given her, and one that felt so familiar to her already. The world morphed around her as she focused on going back into the void, and as she pulled herself forward, hands gripping the staff and dragging Gwen with her, the air left her lips and she was frozen in the in-between. As soon as she opened her eyes, she saw Gwen before her, only she was not awake. Her eyes were shut, her mouth open and her head hanging low. Her body seemed to be able to move in the world as her body drifted up and down, unlike Kirana who was stuck in the position she arrived in. Getting them both there was easy, but deciding where to go next felt nearly impossible. Last time someone or something had pushed her into the new world, and this time she had to do it herself. Kirana could feel the different places around her, and the more she looked around the more she could spot them. Hiraeth was behind her, and from what she could tell it gave off a yellow glow. There were two places in front of Kirana, each with their own color and space. The worlds were almost calling to her, each with their own voice and soft touch.

That was, however, before she remembered she couldn't breathe. Her lungs stung, and her head spun with fear. She pushed them towards the first world that called for her, one that felt like a sting of mint pinching her skin, alive in flavor. She pulled Gwen with her, feeling the fabric of the world break and bend to her will.

After that, Kirana couldn't recall anything until she was slapped across her face. She was able to walk as she tried to shake herself awake. Someone was helping her along: Gwen. Kirana put her hand to her pounding head and tried to get her senses to cooperate. She could hear Gwen talking to her but could not process what she was saying. Touch came to her first and she put a hand to the bottom of her nose and wiped away blood. Kirana tried to focus on where they were. Trash and dirt lined concrete and metal walls, and it took her a second to realize people were there too, many bodies with their backs to the walls and thin blankets around them. Though it was hard to take in what she was looking at, Kirana noticed how thin they were, and how many were extending their bone thin hands out to her.

"Kirana." Gwen's voice finally reached her, "Did you hear me? Someone took the staff."

"What–"

Kirana slammed against something in front of her. She grabbed onto it as her upper body almost fell past it. A metal railing. Below her were concrete levels with a large hole in the center she nearly fell into. It was almost impossible to see the bottom, which seemed to be the only place without the bright neon glow of blinding signs.

Grunting and seeing Gwen looking around quickly, Kirana finally got a chance to see where they were. The city in Permidia was organized, clean, and fresh. This city was chaotic, a mess of a hundred things all around them. Even the people on the street next to them seemed a mix of a hundred things. Different colors, layers of clothes, masks, and hats. No one matched one another, no one even looked at each other, and though it was very different from Permidia, Kirana recognized the lack of connection. But she knew that it wasn't the same as her world. The people were creative simply in their fashion choices, and she was startled to realize the people of this new world might have chosen to be alone willingly. It was an idea Kirna couldn't fathom nor had the time to.

The area she and Gwen had entered seemed less chaotic than the city street they had come to. Very few signs lined the walls and the few groups of people kept to themselves a few levels down. The walls were bare with a dull gray color, wires, and a few blacked-out, boarded, or broken windows featured almost randomly on each wall. Down about 5 levels Kirana saw something zoom away into a lower alley.

Gwen pointed down, "That's it!"

It looked like an android, something only slightly larger than the Nanos back in Permidia, but Kirana didn't see the staff on him. Gwen sprinted after it, running to a staircase wrapped in a chain fence. Kirana took a deep breath and tried to keep up. She nearly tripped down every step as they went down faster and faster. When Gwen got to the bottom she no longer waited for Kirana and sprinted down the alley. Traveling through the dimensions had left Kirana exhausted, but even at full strength she knew Gwen would be faster than her. She was a Permidian who only had to run if she wanted to get somewhere a little faster, Gwen was a Hiraethan who had to run for her life. Kirana stopped at the bottom of the staircase and took a moment to catch her breath before hurrying after Gwen.

Gwen had her target set and there was nothing that could stop her. While Kirana slowed and looked around at the sights, Gwen never slipped for a moment. The Keepers ran through a busy plaza filled to the brim with people and shops, they sprinted across empty bridges, they climbed up and down stairs and through it all Gwen never lost sight of the little android for a moment. That was until Kirana ran through the crowd to find her standing still and looking all around her.

"I lost it." She put a hand to her head, breathing hard, "It was so easy to see I don't–"

Kirana put her hands on her knees and tried to get enough air to speak. Eight flights, she counted four flights, that was 128 steps. She tripped down 37 of them. "We– We should... You... You should..." Kirana leaned against the railing beside them and put a hand to a stitch. There was a hole beside them, a long gap between the two sides of the streets. Kirana looked down to see other platforms lined up and leading down to complete darkness. She looked back up to Gwen, "What direction did it go?"

Gwen pulled herself up onto the railing to look around, "It was going in all directions, I just..." She jumped down, "Wait here. Don't talk to anyone."

Kirana didn't argue. She leaned against the railing and watched Gwen slip back into the crowd. The Keepers had found themselves in what resembled a neighborhood, that was if a neighborhood was also the busiest city street lined with small shops and an array of colorful characters. Each building matched each other down the long road; two stories tall, a pale blue color, a green door, and black windows. It looked like no one was inside any of the houses, and as Kirana studied the corners she saw what looked like black cloth wrapped around the class. It was strange to think that such extravagant people would bother to hide away from attention. Kirana looked around at the crowd and found herself excited by the idea of a whole new culture she could experience. She could talk to anyone around her and they would talk back.

Kirana glanced around for Gwen and, ignoring her original instructions, stepped away from the railing and into the crowd. She wanted to get to a higher level so she could search for the android as well, but as she made her way to a box tall enough for her to climb, Kirana heard something in the nearest alley. It sounded like wheels spinning out on the concrete. It reminded her of one of the androids used in Permidia further away from the city. If there was water on the pavement they would skid and slide. This noise matched that. Kirana, still digging her hand into her stitch, walked into the dark alley. A small android rolled back and forth before zooming forward, only to go nowhere. A small metal wire was wrapped around its wheel, keeping it there as it extended its little arms toward the other end of the alley. As Kirana walked closer it heard her and tried to scurry away.

"Danger!" It yelled out, its voice boyish and face framed by a pixelated screen.

Kirana walked right up to it and knelt out of reach, "You stole our staff."

"Liar!" It pointed a metal hand at her.

"Where is it?"

Its face flashed white for a moment and he stopped moving, "No."

"No?" Kirana glanced back hoping she could spot Gwen. When the android tried to dash forward again she put out a hand, "I can help you, but only if you tell me where you put our staff."

Again, his face went white, "I can not. You are not authorized."

Kirana nodded, she understood from experience that questioning androids was a useless task. She lost count of how many times she had cornered a Nano and begged for answers. But if she was not authorized, then someone else was. "I can still help you, then maybe you can show me who you belong to?"

The android's body leaned away from her, "Why?"

"Because you need help. Here." She reached out and grabbed his head, lifting him up before his wheel could spin again.

"No!"

"Stop spinning." She tried to stop his wheel from moving but it was no use, "I am trying to help you."

A voice said from behind her, "I can help."

Kirana shot up and, still holding onto the android, looked over to someone behind her. Though the man stood away from the nearest light, she could see he was dressed in a striped formal suit. He swung a red bag around loosely and Kirana heard glass tipping onto one another inside as he moved so he was in the center of the alley.

"That's kind of you to offer but I'm okay, thank you." She pulled at the wire again.

"How about some Korts."

Korts sounded like something a Hiraethan had said before at the stall. Finally, a similarity to Hiraeth, but one she could explore later. "I don't need any right now."

"Oh come on, it's easy money. I'll give you 60 Korts for just taking off your coat."

"Really?" Kirana considered it, "Why?"

He stepped closer to her, and as soon as he moved into the light Kirana noticed how grimy he was, not just from the stained suit but also his bright yellow teeth curled into a smile. "I'm always looking for beautiful specimens like yourself."

Kirana realized very quickly that the man before her was someone she needed to run away from, but by how he was positioned she would not be able to get past without being grabbed. Besides, she was holding onto the android, and she was worried the wire was attached to something that would keep them tied to the alley. But before she could do or say anything, she saw someone else walk into the alley: Gwen.

The man looked back and, almost as soon as he saw her, hunched his shoulders and turned around. Gwen watched him and stood out of his reach as he slipped back into the crowd.

Kirana shivered and let out a laugh, "That was creepy."

She winced and walked closer, "There is another one like him further down the street."

"Why are you upset?"

"I'll explain later." Gwen looked down at Kirana's hands and saw the android, "You found it!"

"Him." The android corrected.

Kirana realized he was no longer trying to escape and picked at the wire around his wheel, "Poor thing was stuck." She yanked and the wire flew off. "How does that feel?"

The android's head turned all the way around so he could face her, "Unexpected."

"Can you show us who you belong to?"

His head turned to the side and his pixelated eyes blinked before he looked back and nodded, "I like you!"

Kirana smiled, "Well that's nice."

She tried to set him down but Gwen ran over and grabbed her arm, "What are you doing."

"He's going to show us who he belongs to."

"He's going to run away." Gwen waited for her to do something, and with no response, she looked down at the android, "Where is the staff?"

"Gwen, his programming stops from telling us."

"But it doesn't stop him from showing us where his master lives?"

The android shook his head quickly, "Unauthorized word."

"Kirana." Gwen took a breath and gestured to the street, "We know nothing about this world but I can tell you right now how fake these people are. They are wearing literal masks. We can't trust them. This isn't Permidia."

Kirana stepped back, and bit down her anger, "I know that. I know this isn't some perfect world but we can't... What else are we supposed to do? Do you know how to hack an android?" The android let out a gasp and Kirana patted his head, still focused on Gwen, "Let's just try. If I am wrong then... we'll chase him again."

Gwen looked down at the android and studied him for a moment, before looking down the alley and stepping back, "Fine."

Kirana set the android down and he rolled slowly past Gwen towards the street. His wheel didn't seem to be damaged, so by how slowly he was moving Kirana figured he was showing them the way. She gave Gwen a playful nudge, "See."

"Luck, Kirana. We have luck. For now."

She shrugged as the two of them walked out of the alley and followed the android, "You call it luck, I call it faith. As a god, I expect a little more faith from you too."

It turned out that the person the android belonged to did not live far from the alleyway. In fact, they were in the same neighborhood the Keepers found themselves in. Kirana liked watching the city without having to run around so quickly, and though the walk didn't show them some new extravagant piece of the world, it was nice to experience it as any other person would.

The android stopped in front of the stairs of a house. It looked like any other building on the long street with its green door and blue-tinted walls. Kirana found no defining features to it, which would make finding it again a difficult task.

Gwen picked up the android and gestured to the door, "How should we do this?"

"Well we saved their friend, maybe they'll just… give it back?"

"No. They'll want something in return." She looked down to the android, "What's your name?"

"Ben E."

"We'll offer them Ben E, and if they don't give us the staff we throw him over the railing."

Kirana let out a sharp laugh, "Gwen, I don't think that's smart–"

"I don't want to, but we have to do whatever it takes to get the staff back." She gestured to the door again, "If you knock I'll stay down here. If they chase me, hide."

Kirana looked from Gwen to the new frightened android, before giving in and walking up to the door. She didn't want to threaten the owner, and maybe it was a bit foolish to believe they would like the Keepers for saving their friend, but she wanted to have hope in the people of the new world. It was only yesterday that she was longing to find the source of that voice. Even in such dangerous times, she was still the Permidian who wanted a friend. Kirana knocked on the door and stepped back.

A voice called from inside, "I'm busy!"

"Hello!" She called, glancing back at Gwen, "We need to talk!"

The voice didn't speak for a moment, and when it did she could hear the person right behind the door, "What do you want?"

"We have Ben E. We–"

The door opened just a crack and a light brown eye darted over Kirana.

"Where is it?" Gwen asked, stepping forward.

The person spotted Ben E and opened the door, "Stay back." He pulled something out of his pocket, a tool-like object similar to what the Wardens were holding when they chased Kirana in Hiraeth.

At the sight of it, Gwen put up her free hand to the side of her head, "There is no need for that."

"Put him down." He glanced over at Kirana as she looked behind him to see inside his house. The whole place was a mess. Loose objects were everywhere, metal parts and trash seemed to be placed anywhere it could fit beside plates of old food and empty bottles. Kirana could see above was the second story with a steep staircase by the doorway leading up to another small room. This was his house.

When the man turned the object, or rather, the weapon's round barrel to her she looked up at his face. This was the first face she had seen from the new world. His mask on the metal table in the house, he stared at them with nothing to hide behind. His skin was a golden brown, dirty and spotted with ash. He looked as messy as the room behind him, a stubby black beard wrapped carelessly around his face and his hair tied back into a bun, greasy and tangled. At first glance, she figured he was as messy as both his attire and house, but looking at his face she saw something beyond that. He looked intensely focused, his body still and expression sharp, but his eyes moved slowly. Kirana got the impression he was worried about his android, but not driven to do something reckless. He was precise, studying the two Keepers. When Kirana had studied Permidians they were always easy to read, as if there was only one side of themselves to truly show off. The man before her was far more complicated than anyone she had met before, maybe even more complicated than Gwen.

Kirana glanced back at the Hiraethan who stared back with an intense worry. Kirana realized how much weight the weapon in the man's hand held, and she remembered exactly what those Warden weapons had done in Hiraeth. She stepped away from the stranger, "Your android stole something from us. We need it back."

"What did he steal?" He asked, confused.

"Our staff." Kirana realized how absurd such a statement sounded, but found no other definitions or descriptions to help them.

The man looked from Keeper to Keeper before looking over to his right. He let out a laugh and, as if in disbelief, shook his head. He put the weapon in a small holster on his leg and walked past Kirana. Gwen stepped away from the door and he walked right past her, pointing to his android, "Just hold him for a minute." He walked up to his neighbor's house and knocked on the door. "Stinger!" When no one answered he kept knocking and refused to stop.

The door swung open and a woman barged out, forcing the man to step back, "What? What do you want Tech?" Her voice had a smooth melody to it, each word strung with a defying intention. She did not look like a polished woman, but someone attempting to be neat. Her white hair was pulled over her head in a single wave with loose stands ruining the idea of fluency. Her clothes came together in rings. Clips, bracelets, shoulder straps. Rings wrapped down her chest, her stomach, and her pants. There were piercings along her eyebrows, nose, and ears. But rather than looking like she had a theme to her attire, she simply looked messy.

Tech gestured to Ben E, "Did you reprogram my android?"

"You never–"

"He's not a thief, he's my helper."

"I can take the code off, I just sent him out for today." She leaned against the door frame, the rings of her shirt bending as she looked from Kirana to Gwen, "Who are they?"

Tech laughed and gestured to them both, "These are the people you stole from. The people who came to *me* and not you. Because you use *my* android."

Stinger let out a laugh and patted him on the shoulder, "Well isn't that fun." She stepped out of the doorway and walked to the Keepers. As Gwen stepped back Kirana swallowed and stepped in front of her. The woman stopped mere inches from her, "You look clean." Her breath smelled like garlic, "What did he take?"

"Our staff." Kirana felt herself leaning back and forced her body to remain still. She wanted to be strong in such a situation and found it hard to hide her fear. What helped her was remembering Gideon's stoic stature, and how he had asked her to do one thing: protect.

Stinger leaned over and smiled at Ben E, "Good job." She gestured to the android for Tech to see, "I told you he could be useful."

"He is useful." Tech walked over so he could stand beside her, and though he leaned over her and dominated some aspect of power from his height, he kept a smile fixed on his face, "Now take off the coding."

"I will, I will." She waved her hand in his face before turning back to Kirana,

"So what do you want?"

"We want our staff back."

"100 Korts."

Gwen said from behind, "We are not paying you–"

"120 Korts."

Kirana did not know the true value of the numbers, but she knew they would only increase so long as they fought against Stinger, "No, 100 Korts is fine."

"We don't have 100 Korts," Gwen told the woman from behind.

"Not my problem."

"Except it *is* your problem." Kirana didn't know if intimidation would be the best way forward, but it was worth a shot. Stinger held all the power, and to win Kirana would have to take some back, "That staff is worth more than you could imagine." Stinger looked amused at the thought. Kirana nodded with a smile, "But not to anyone but us and the *Wardens*. They'll kill you if they find it here. That is your problem. Better give it to us than risk your life for something no one else wants."

Stinger thought for a moment, "*The staff.* That's a pretty dull name. Got another?"

"We *will* get the Wardens." Gwen said, but the woman ignored her too and turned back towards her house.

"Stinger." Tech said as he walked beside her, "We talked about this. Ben E is not yours, he is mine. You can't use him like that."

"You're such a baby, Tech." She groaned, "I just made 100 Korts off a business deal you were too afraid to take."

She grabbed the doorknob and tried to close the door, but she was stopped when Tech grabbed the frame, "He's not–"

She glared at him, and suddenly both of their smiles were gone. This was no longer a joking matter, and Tech seemed to understand that another word would mean danger, so he let go and, without another word, Stinger slammed the door shut. Even with the weapon on him, she was more powerful. That meant that the Keepers were up against someone even such an object couldn't defeat so easily.

Kirana let out a breath, and it was only then that she realized exactly what had happened. They lost the Keeper's staff. They lost their way back to Hiraeth. They lost their way to find the next Keeper. They lost *everything*. She turned back to Gwen and took Ben E from her hands. Kirana ran back to Tech and pushed the android forward so the man could take him, "He knows where it is. Can you ask him?"

Tech took back Ben E and held him up, "Where did you hide their staff?"

The android's face flashed white, "Unauthorized personal."

Tech shut his eyes and took in a deep breath, "I swear to the gods, she believes can do whatever she wants with no consequences."

"Then you can help us get it back, to get back at her." She pointed down at Ben E frantically, "Just hack him or something. Steal what she stole from us."

He shook his head and set his android on the ground, "I'm sorry, but there is nothing I can do. The best thing you can do now is get 100 Korts and pay her before another buyer shows up."

Ben E rolled around the ground and stopped in front of Kirana, he looked back at Tech and pointed up at her, "But I like her."

Tech squinted down at his android before looking up at Kirana, "Why?"

"She saved me."

The intensity in the man's look dropped. His eyes went still and he studied Kirana once more, "You saved him?"

"He got stuck on some wire." She gestured down to the android, "We were following him because he stole our staff and found him in an alley."

"So why did you save him?"

"I... I don't know." She answered honestly, shrugging and stepping back towards Gwen, "He just needed help." Kirana expected Tech to walk away. She thought that she and Gwen could have a conversation and regroup once they had found some sort of advantage in their horrible situation. She expected to be treated as she had been by the crowd around her: ignored and shunned.

But Tech didn't leave, he followed her, Ben E on his heels, "Wait." She looked back and he looked from her to Gwen, "Who are you?"

Gwen put her hands in her pockets and shook her head, "We are just two people who really need that staff back. Are you sure you can't help us?"

Still, Tech did not leave. He stood there for a moment to think, "Stinger won't budge, and you two don't look like the most credible people either." He gestured under his nose and then pointed to Kirana. She had almost forgotten about her nosebleed and now, putting a hand to her face, felt how far the stream of blood had carried. "I can't help you get the staff back but you can take some medical supplies." He pointed to his house, "I have bandages and some drinks."

"You're helping us?" Gwen asked, bewildered.

Tech shrugged and gestured to his android with a smile, "You saved my friend, I owe you." Ben E looked at Kirana and tilted his head with a smile.

Kirana looked over to Gwen and, as expected, she didn't seem to like the idea. It was justified to believe the man before them could harm them, and honestly, as soon as he would shut the door they would be locked in his house without any advantages in a fight. But Kirana felt like the man was different, like he wanted to help them, like he was telling the truth. She didn't know if Gwen could see what she saw, but with a shrug and nod towards his house, she tried to show her that he might not be as bad as she thought. If no world can be entirely good, then no world can be entirely bad. If Permidia is a lie, then so is the dark, fake world around them. Gwen glanced back towards the alley and then to the crowd around them. Kirana got the impression her decision was being made based on other immediate dangers, the least of which was the man before them. She nodded once and refused to meet eyes with Kirana, perhaps hating the idea but having no other option to present.

Kirana nodded with her and turned to Tech, "We'd like that. Thank you."

Tech started to walk to his house before turning back and looking at Kirana, "But seriously, who are you."

Kirana took a breath, "I'm Kirana. This is Gwen."

Chapter 13

GWEN

GWEN DIDN'T TRUST Tech. What kind of name was that? *Tech*. It wasn't even a real name. He was strong enough to run and climb quickly through the city, but there were aspects to him that seemed more dangerous than his physical abilities. He was charismatic, in a way that made lies easy to miss. He was smart, and she suspected he could perceive them incredibly well, which meant lying wasn't a great option anymore. Gwen had no problem with filtering through or telling lies, but she was worried about Kirana. The Permidian was new to everything around them. It had only been a few hours since she woke up, and felt like only now, with both of them exhausted from running and hiding, that they could finally stop for a moment. The new world wasn't safe, but that moment, sitting outside Tech's house against a bar wall, was the safest Gwen had felt all day.

She took a moment to look outside the nearest window. It seemed from outside that they had been blocked, only now, from inside, she could see down the entire street, and no matter where her gaze fell there was something to watch. Shops, people, signs, stalls, ships, each of them their own unique piece of the city. People stood silent in groups, yelled at each other, passed bags around, and passed bottles from mouth to mouth. Signs changed so quickly Gwen could barely read them. Some spoke about a new bar with the world's best drinks, and others showed pictures of people, either dressed in fine attire and placed on the sign around art or left in an unflattering frame with a price above their head. But though the world around Gwen was enough to keep her attention, the ships drew her in more so than anything else. They were almost as unique as the people around them. They soared across the sky blasting their music and blinding viewers with lights. The music was different from Hiraethan music. It was robotic, and though very few songs had lyrics the ones that did spoke too quickly for her to understand. The music she knew was softer. The voices were calmer, singing tones and not just saying words quickly. They used string instruments and soft drums. Gods, she wished she could find something familiar in the strange world. A piece of home would do her good.

Tech was seated across the room at a metal table pressed against the wall. On it was an array of tools and gears that pushed away to fit Ben E. Tech seemed to be checking him for something, perhaps whatever Stinger had placed within his programming. Gwen didn't bother to watch what he was doing simply because she had very little knowledge about technology. The Wardens only gave basic information to workers, which was most often how to turn on and shut off a tool. Gwen had seen androids before, but all of them had been made by the Wardens. Ben E didn't look Warden-crafted. The metal was darker, shinner, and placed unevenly across his bumpy surface. No, she suspected Tech or some other person in the new world had made him themselves.

Kirana nudged her softy, pulling her out of her thoughts, "You okay?"

Gwen nodded, "It's been quite a few hours."

"That it has." She put the back of her head on the wall. "Can I ask you something?" Gwen nodded. "What is that thing in his holster? The weapon."

"A gun." When Kirana said nothing in response Gwen felt herself go cold, "Kirana, it's a gun. Do you know what that is?"

"It's familiar." She tilted her head side to side, "I skimmed the Permidian history book talking about weapons. I learned about swords and cannons but I stopped when the names got so complicated." Kirana thought for a moment, then nodded once she had a realization, "I think Tia talked to me about them. They're dangerous."

"Kirana, they'll kill you in one shot. A bullet could fire from across the street and it will still kill you. If someone points a gun at you, don't fight them. Submit."

Kirana squinted at her, confused by what Gwen was saying. She laughed, perhaps figuring Gwen was being over dramatic, "Give up?"

Tech had given Kirana a wet cloth to wipe away the blood, so now she looked almost as good as new. In fact, she looked the same way as she had when Gwen and Gaia had cleaned her yesterday, and somehow it still shocked Gwen to see how Kirana looked so clean, so fresh. She was beautiful, there was no doubting that, and she wore her looks well. Her energy practically lit up her expressions, whether it was a grim emotion or a happy release, she remained pretty. Gwen found it refreshing to see someone so happy, to see their eyes open so wide, but it scared her. Kirana didn't understand how bad the world could be, she didn't even understand what the man in the striped suit wanted. Gwen didn't know if she could take care of them both, she didn't even believe she could take care of herself.

Gwen sighed and decided now was as best a time as any to start teaching Kirana how the worlds worked. "My dad has this one story he would always tell me. It's called, *The Keeper's Short Becoming*. It was what he feared would happen if the Keepers returned in a dangerous setting, with the Wardens and constant fear." She pointed to Kirana, "Once all the Keepers die, the staff chooses the next leader. They wield the staff and become the first Keeper, destined to find the others and begin a new era of the gods."

"What does this have to do with guns?"

"There was one Keeper, the first Keeper, named Zhao. The staff chose Zhao in a time of war, and when he should have waited and prepared with his people, he jumped from dimension to dimension trying to find his team. In the end, the opposition killed him before he could even find one of the Keepers, and the staff remained dark for five years. He left the worlds in a war with no gods to bring peace." She locked eyes with Kirana, "You are the new leader, Kirana. I am the second Keeper. We both owe too much to these worlds to not fulfill our destinies because we are reckless or greedy."

"Greedy?" Kirana squinted and laughed.

"My point is, we have to be careful everything we do has consequences." She pointed subtly to Tech, "He could have killed you."

The idea of such danger affected Kirana. She clenched her jaw and glanced over to the man, "Do we need a gun?"

Gwen surprised herself by realizing she never intended to get ahold of a gun. Certainly not to fight a Warden, that was suicide, but now the situation had changed. Not only was she a god supposed to fight evil, but she was also in a world that required more protection. "It would be smart. But I don't want to just ask for one." She nodded to Tech, who, at that moment, stood up.

He walked near them towards a cupboard and pulled out two bottles, both white in color with a matching orange pattern at the bottom. He handed them to the Keepers, "It's Flix, I don't have anything else. Unless you want Belic."

Gwen didn't recognize the words he was saying, and simply shook her head, "Flix is fine."

He knelt down in front of them, "Do you have 100 Korts?"

"No." Kirana said, laughing at the idea.

"Where do you work?"

It was hard to lie in a place you didn't understand. Lies are based on reality, but what if you didn't understand reality? "We're between jobs right now." Gwen kept her face still, eyes locked on Tech hoping he would believe her based on how confidently she spoke.

"That's not Flix." He pointed to the bottle in her hand, and when neither of the Keepers responded, he sat down on the ground, "Flix isn't a real drink. Why are you lying?"

"Why are you testing us?"

"Where are you from?" He asked, looking from Keeper to Keeper.

"It doesn't matter." Gwen opened the bottle and the drink inside let out a sharp noise. She looked inside and saw what looked like clear water with bubbles. "What is this?"

"Sparkling water."

Kirana drank hers and whispered, "We have this in Permidia."

Gwen set her drink on the ground beside her, "We don't have a job, we don't have Korts. I am very grateful for you giving us shelter, but it seems you want to know something about us, and we need to know something about how to make Korts."

"You want to trade?" He asked, and she got the sense he was willing to listen by how intrigued he was. It seemed, there was something he wanted. Gwen had been right, he did want something from them.

"What do you want?"

"Answers." He shrugged off the comment, "You're different, I want to know why."

"And you'll tell us how to make Korts?" Kirana moved her legs so she sat crisscrossed on the floor, "Can you show us?"

"Show you?"

He laughed but Kirana leaned forward, "What else do you want?"

"Korts."

"We can do that."

From the metal table, Ben E shook suddenly and came to life, "Sir!" Tech jumped up and moved back to the table. The android looked up at him, "No resident virus."

"Check again." Tech told him, eyes locked on his android.

As he gave more instructions Gwen whispered to Kirana, "What are you asking for?"

"A tour guide." She smiled at the idea, "He has a gun, he knows the world, he knows how we can make Korts and, I'm sorry, what information could we possibly give him?" She waited for Gwen to give her an answer, and when she didn't Kirana continued, "I would much rather pay him money than our secrets. I mean, are they secrets?"

Gwen shrugged, "I don't know."

Kirana pointed at her reaction, "Exactly, we don't know. We do know that Korts is valuable, so let's not share anything, do the work under his guide, pay Stinger back, and get our staff."

Gwen let out a laugh, she couldn't help it, "Kirana, that's a good plan."

"You look surprised."

"I am." She answered honestly.

Before Kirana could argue Tech kneeled in front of them again, "You can pay me?"

"How much do you want?"

He thought, and Gwen felt herself lift at the idea he might just agree to their deal, "I have a job to do today, and they'll pay you 75 Korts each for it. That's enough to pay me and Stinger."

"What's the job?" Gwen asked before Kirana could agree.

"Selling." He said, smiling down at her, "Can you be charismatic?"

"I can sell things." Gwen thought back to her stall in Hiraeth, "It just depends on what we're selling."

He shrugged and stood up, "Depends on the day." He pulled down his sleeve and looked at something on his wrist. It looked like a thick bracelet with a screen on top. Gwen glanced at Kirana to see if she knew what it was, but as always, Kirana just seemed curious, so it was hard to tell. Tech gestured to the door, "We'd have to leave in five minutes. It's in a place called the Stonewall Nook down in the Lockwood district."

"Is that real?" Gwen asked.

He laughed and wagged his finger at her, "This time, it is."

Kirana stood up as well, "So you'll help us?"

"I'm not about to turn down 50 Korts." He laughed at the thought and walked further into the room.

Kirana glanced over to Gwen with a smirk. The Keepers had a plan, they had a way to get the staff back, find the next Keeper, and even return to Hiraeth. Gwen let out a small prayer, asking for some piece of power that could help them on their journey. It may have been ironic to pray to a god she now had the title of, but she hoped that the old Keepers could see them, that they were watching with more divine power than she or Kirana had. They needed a miracle, one they could not give to themselves.

Tech took the full five minutes to get ready, and in that time Gwen let herself rest. She figured it would be a while until they got the opportunity to be both still and safe. She also forced herself to down the horrid bubbly water, and though Kirana seemed to like it, Gwen found its burning sensation to be anything but refreshing. But still, it tasted like water, and right now that was exactly what she needed. Tech filled a brown bag with bottles, gears, tools, and objects Gwen couldn't quite identify. When he was ready, he slipped his mask over his face and let it hang around his neck. The mask was made from metal with two dark eyes and tubes around where his mouth would be.

He gestured to the door, "You ready?"

"I think so." Kirana said, patting her pockets as if she had anything to bring with her. Gwen put her own hands in her jacket and felt the pocket knife. It felt reassuring to have such protection, even if it was useless against a gun, it was still something.

Tech put on the mask, "We'll take a ship to get there, just follow me." His voice came out robotic and Gwen stepped back when she realized how similar he sounded to a Warden. When he moved by she looked over to Kirana hoping the Permidian was able to connect him to danger only to see her looking curiously at the mask.

The walk through the city was not pleasant. Hiraeth's city was crowded, but it was also calm. People moved together, all flowing with the commonality of knowing who held the danger. In the new world, all strangers were dangerous, and if Tech had so easily pulled out a gun on someone knocking on his door, then anyone could. Gwen kept her hands in her pockets and walked beside Kirana, allowing Tech to lead them forward. He was their shield, a barrier from the strange people of his world.

The ship Tech had been referring to looked like the equivalent of Hiraeth's worker ships, only much smaller and more colorful. It was parked on the edge of one of the long drops, packed with people and filled with blue and purple smoke. There were no seats inside, only rubber ropes that hung from the ceiling. When Gwen found her place in the crowd and grabbed on the ship shot forward, wind rushing in from the open door. Gwen watched as the street went out of view as the ship climbed higher and higher out of the platforms and reached the height of the buildings around her.

She stepped back and bumped into a person behind her. A man with a collar that reached the bottom of his eyes glanced down at her, before looking back to a screen in his hands. There was some sort of game on it, his fingers jumping around and a small character following his movements.

"It's called Climbly." Tech said from her side, his mask back around his neck, "You've never seen it before? The game's pretty popular down at Buck's Place." When Gwen did not answer he lowered his head and asked, "Do you know what Buck's Place is?"

Gwen straightened her back, "You ask a lot of questions."

"You don't give a lot of answers." He glanced down at Ben E as the ship turned. The android was sitting between his feet so he wouldn't roll away. "When we get to the market I'll show you around and get you started on whatever we've been hired to sell. If you do a good job you can get another job there later on."

The ship started to go down and Gwen hung onto her rope, "A market?"

"It's small but the people there pay well, a bit close to the Warden's facility but they won't be too close. Is that alright?" He looked down and Gwen saw him waiting for her to react. Kirana had already told him the staff was only worth something to her and the Wardens, and now it seemed he was testing Gwen to see if this was true. Maybe the information he wanted was about their connection to the Wardens.

She nodded, "We'll be fine."

Kirana pushed past the crowd to stand next to Gwen, "I have a question."

Tech raised an eyebrow, "Okay."

"What other jobs are out here? I overheard those two talking about being bodyguards." She gestured back and Gwen saw two people dressed in large black coats at the back of the ship, smoke pouring out of their mouths and noses.

"Some people need bodyguards, delivering services are dangerous but are in high demand. Most want people to just go kill someone bothering them, which is pretty easy because both of them are drunk. We're going down to Monix, it's more of a working district but the easiest way to get Korts would be to just work in the bars or clubs, they are always looking for people with fresh, *dazzling* faces." He sang out the word and looked back at the two of them. Gwen turned her head away. She didn't like how much people fantasized about looks in the new world.

Kirana moved against the wall so she stood beside Tech, "So you sell things, that's your job?"

Tech gestured to himself, "I can do a lot. I'm a thief, a beggar, a good drinker, a good shot, and a pretty decent cook."

Kirana leaned forward to look at him, "You cook?"

"I do." He tapped his head, "I've got the best recipes. You could give me pretty much anything and I'll be able to make something with it."

Kirana let out an amused gasp, "Like what?" Gwen shot her a look, but the Keeper just turned her attention back to Tech, "I've seen a lot of meat around, do you guys have pastries?"

"Not a lot." He shook his head, "If you get extra Korts after all of this you should go to Chop's shop in Ginish. He makes the best meats in the entire city."

"*Chop's shop.*" Kirana repeated, "Where else should we go?"

Tech took a moment to think, and through his thoughts he glanced back down to Gwen and shook his head, "Learn how things work before you run to indulge yourself in anything."

Learn. He knew they didn't know a lot about the world, could that be why he was helping them, to know who they were and where they came from?

The ship shook as it landed next to a new platform and the crowd all started to leave. Unlike the Hiraethan worker ship, the transport seemed to only have one stop. When Gwen walked out with the crowd she was shocked to find the only space to walk was a thin platform that led into a literal hole in the wall. As she stepped out she realized how high the ship had truly taken them, and how needed rails were as the people around her pushed their way forward. She moved beside the ship and held onto the door as the crowd rushed past her.

Gwen forced herself to breathe. The situation felt too dangerous, too risky. She was a Keeper now, a god, and she couldn't help but think what good would this do for her world? The best case scenario would leave Kirana and Gwen back where they started, maybe with more information, or maybe with scars.

Gwen put a hand to her chest and stayed there until her heart slowed to a calm beat.

A breeze filled her hair and she looked out at the city around her, at the long drop before her. Yes, this place was dangerous, but in some strange way, it was also beautiful. Her world would always be the true sense of beauty for her, but she could not ignore the feeling the city before her carried. She would survive this, she had to. They would get the staff and find the next Keeper. They would make the team of gods and begin the journey to free their people from the Wardens and almighty Magistrater.

Kirana walked out with Tech and moved over to Gwen. At the sight of her, breathing and holding onto the door for dear life, Kirana put out her hand. "You okay?" Gwen took her hand and they stood at the center of the platform, "We're okay, this is a great situation."

Gwen looked up at Tech who had walked ahead, "It's still dangerous." As Kirana followed her gaze she preempted her argument and cut her off, "He isn't helping us because he is kind. He wants to know something about us. Something worth spending this much time in our company. He's dangerous, not kind. I need you to trust in my experience."

Kirana scoffed, "He's not a Warden."

"There are still dangerous people besides Wardens, even in Hiraeth. Here, everyone seems so much colder, and alone, and that can only grow into hatred and selfishness. He's selfish, not kind."

Tech looked back and gestured for them both to follow. Gwen gave Kirana a look before moving forward, and in response, the Keeper whispered, "He's still different, I can feel it." Before Gwen could argue, Kirana looked forward and walked with her into the hole, eyes wide, "This place is amazing."

Gwen looked ahead expecting to see a room much like the streets they had just come from, only to find space before her like nothing she had seen before. In Hiraeth, places often stayed the same when in the same vicinity. The style was governed by what the Wardens let them keep. One of the most exotic places she had been to was Trent's shop, but even that had the same Hiraeth look as everything else. The further Gwen went from the Magistrater's tower the more differences she noticed, but they were always small. Towns by lakes and bodies of water always had a little color to their designs. The brown clay wall became a red clay wall to the west. Those in the mountains and working in mines had stone roofs and very little wood used. But this new world had no consistent features. The three of them had been walking aside metal, concrete, and dirt, and suddenly they were in a brightly lit room lined with stone walls. Wooden stalls lined the long hallway evenly with the same simple design to each of them. Light came from small bubble-like balls resting against the stalls. They were lined together, strung like vines.

Tech was waiting for them, leaning against a wall with his mask hung around his neck, "Welcome to the Stonewood Nook."

The place was crowded, and they clustered together closer at a wall as a large group went back towards the ladder.

"This is where we can make Corts?" Kirana seemed hopeful.

Gwen was not, "What exactly do you want us to do here?"

"Ruby and Card Face run a small business dealing goods." He gestured around the Nook, "This is a new territory they hope to begin sales at. The two of you will get the supplies and return when you've got the Korts."

"The two of us?" Gwen glanced back at the ship, which still had not taken off, "Where are you going?"

"I'll get you guys set up, then I have to leave for a bit." Gwen must have looked disappointed, because he pointed at her reaction and shook his head, "I'm giving you a lot for 50 Korts. Since you two don't seem to understand how things work around here, the very least you can do is be grateful that I am helping."

"We are grateful." Kirana reassured him as she gestured down the Stonewall Nook, "Whatever it takes, we'll do it."

Gwen winced at her words and Tech watched her reaction. Without a comment, he moved forward and pushed Kirana inside, "Then let's get to work."

Chapter 14

*   *   *

KIRANA

KIRANA DIDN'T TRUST Tech. Not completely at least. He confused her, but if they weren't in such a dangerous situation she might have enjoyed his company. She had never experienced a complex person before. Gwen was amazing to speak with, but this new man had so much to hide. He was different from those around him but seemed to so naturally fit in with the crowds. He smiled when needed, his expressions used as a tool. He loved his android and cared for him enough to help his saviors. He wanted to know who Kirana and Gwen were for some reason beyond the features he had shown the Keepers. Kirana wondered what he would turn out to be.

The market before the Keepers was unique for its calm environment. Compared with other streets and shops they had passed through it did feel less chaotic, but to her Permidian standards, it was still a mess, and still loud. There were so many more conversations going on between people inside and outside the stalls. The place echoed soft noises into a collective murmur.

The people in the Stonewall Nook were less extravagant than those the Keepers had passed before. They still had flare, but they seemed less flashy. Their colors were toned down, their accessories had little to nothing jaw-dropping, and no one dressed out of the aesthetic of the Nook. Was it planned? The stall owners and the stall themselves were the most in theme with only small pieces of unique displays. They fitted their shops with small pops of colors, most of them being green, but kept the classy and less chaotic feel of the entire room. As Tech led them further inside Kirana caught glimpses of everything around her. If there was also a theme for the products being sold, she couldn't find it. She saw cooked meats, raw meats, mechanical tools, metal gears, wires, androids, watches, and something called *adult toys* that didn't look like any toys Kirana had seen before.

Tech took a turn when they reached a section of the Nook without any stalls. A variety of people sat at each of the six round tables, but Tech moved directly to one on the left. Three people stood around two people dressed out of the theme of the Nook. Ruby and Card Face.

Kirana assumed Ruby was the one dressed entirely in red. Her stiff outfit was fitted with layers of red gemstones that matched her makeup and eye color. Card Face must have been the other figure seated in front of her fixed with a stern expression and hidden by large sunglasses. A large fur coat hid most of his outfit, the edges of which were patterned with the four card symbols.

At the sight of Tech, Ruby laughed and swung her legs onto the table, "I heard you were working again, you dumb bastard."

Tech extended his arms out, laughing with her, "You know me, Ruby."

She leaned over the table and looked down at Ben E, who, in response to seeing her, spun around. She laughed and kicked her feet up, "Ben E!"

Card Face lifted his chin towards Gwen, and as soon as he spoke Kirana felt the section of the nook go quiet, "Who are they?"

Tech gestured to Kirana and Gwen, "Workers. They're here to help me."

"When I told you about this job, did I tell you to bring in more of your savior projects?"

Kirana exchanged a look with Gwen.

"They're hard-working." Metis put a hand on Kirana's shoulder and pointed at her face, "Look at her, who wouldn't buy something from this dazzling face?" He laughed at his words, and when Kirana looked up she saw how hard he was trying to keep on a smile. The situation felt too tense to be completely safe, and Kirana glanced back at Gwen, not wanting to give into the idea that the entirety of the new world was dangerous but allowing her the courtesy of this moment.

Card Face rolled his tongue under his silver teeth, "75 Korts."

"That works for them."

"But not you?" Ruby asked, slamming her feet on the ground and letting out a squealed gasp, "Are you leaving again?"

"Where are you going?" Card Face asked, and once again, the Nook went still.

"I have some errands to run." He let go of Kirana, "But I'm leaving you with two very–"

"You did this back in my bar, Tech. You may have paid your debt, but I haven't forgotten." Tech looked as if he was trying to find the right words, and when he couldn't think of what to say he simply gave up and looked to the side. Card Face leaned back in his chair, "If these two fail to be as excellent as you, I might just require your service again. Is that a deal you are willing to make?"

"Yes, I am."

Kirana looked over to Gwen once again, but was cut off by Ruby, "You!" The woman pointed at Kirana, "Who are you?"

Tech gestured to her, "This is... Summer."

Card Face smiled softly, "She reminds me of you." He placed a finger under Ruby's chin, who laughed at his touch. "Do you want work, Summer?"

"No, thank you." Kirana put her hands in front of her, "This job is all we need."

"She sounds so cute." Ruby said, before looking over at Gwen and frowning, "You look angry. Are you angry?"

Gwen forced a smile, "I'm just focused."

"Let me guess, you're more of a grounded woman." Card Face said, clasping his hand, "Summer's cute but you're gorgeous. Some people like to be intimidated. I don't get a lot of workers like you."

Tech moved forward and clapped his hands together, "What are we selling?"

"Fairies." Ruby gestured to one of the three people around her, "Only this time when you smoke them you don't get those purple-stained teeth." She licked her lips as a man placed a black crate on the table.

Tech took it and moved back the way they had come, "Thank you my darlings!"

Ruby laughed but Card Face remained stoic. Gwen rushed by, pulling Kirana with her. When they were out of view Gwen let out a shudder but said nothing. It was then that Kirana realized how similar Card Face was to the man in the striped suit, and it was then that she realized exactly what the two of them wanted.

Tech walked back to the platform and knelt to open the crate. He took a moment and let out a breath, shaking his hands softly.

Gwen stood beside him, "What was that?"

"I didn't think they would be here." Tech wiped down his face, "They're never here."

"They wanted us to work for them, Tech. As what? Slaves?"

He opened the crate and pulled out two thick bracelets like the one on his wrist, "Put these on."

"No." Gwen said, throwing her hands up.

"Gwen." He said, eyes locked on her, "They won't hurt you."

"They just–"

"If you do anything wrong it will be my fault." He pushed the other watch on Kirana's hands, "They were joking. They do that to everyone."

Gwen wrapped her arms around herself, "Will they take us?"

Tech took this question very seriously. He shut the crate and stood up, "No. I promise." He stared at Gwen and clenched his jaw, "Can I ask you a question?"

"Sure."

"Did some lock you away, and only now you escaped?"

Kirana realized how obvious such a story would seem. The Keepers knew nothing about the world around them, so clearly they must have been kept from seeing everything. Locked away.

"You don't have to tell me." Tech swallowed, "I know it's hard. I mean I don't know but…" He sighed, "I knew someone who had a similar situation. He acted a lot like you two: very confused." He put a hand to his heart, "I promise they won't hurt you. I'll make sure." He extended the bracelet out once again and, this time, Gwen took it. He nodded and put on a small smile, "I'm sorry, for everything that has happened to you, but there is something I need to ask."

"Alright." Gwen said.

"Did the Wardens take you when you were children?"

The question gave way to so much information, so when Gwen looked over Kirana nodded. They knew about the Wardens, they could lie about what happened. Kirana was, technically, kept locked away her whole life by the Magistrater. In a way, so was Gwen. Together they could make such a lie work.

"Yes." Gwen answered, keeping her eyes on the ground.

Tech let out a breath, "Then I really need to talk to you when I get back." He looked over to the ship as it started to shift and stir, "Get your Korts, and stay out of trouble. I'll be back in two hours."

Neither of the Keepers complained. Tech looked at each of them before slipping on his mask and walking into the ship with Ben E. Within seconds, the ship detached from the platform and flew off.

Kirana looked over to Gwen with a laugh, "What was that?"

"He was kind." She let out a laugh, "You were right."

"Everything is working out." Kirana smiled and watched the ship fly away, "Maybe this was all meant to be."

Gwen tapped on the watch Tech had left them, "What is this?"

"I have no idea." Kirana looked down at her own and tapped on it, and the screen glowed. It asked two questions, one on each side of it. *Activity* or *Korts*. She pressed Korts, and the band around her arm glowed, fading in and out as the screen gave two choices again. *Give* or *Take*. Give Corts or take Corts. At the top of the screen, she saw a number next to a letter. Ko. As in, there was no money on the watch?

"The Corts is stored here." Kirana pointed to the watch.

"It's in there?" Gwen shook her head, "How would it fit money? That thing is tiny."

"Digital Corts." Kirana laughed and showed her the screen, "They spell Corts differently here. It's with a K."

Gwen rolled her eyes, playfully this time, "That's not important."

"No, but it sure is interesting. We should collect fun facts about each world, something fun to tell the next Keeper." Gwen gave a small laugh and Kirana felt so privileged to have made her happy. The situation was not peaceful, it was danger-ous, but now that they had found kindness and hope there was room for enjoy-ment. Kirana smiled at her, "We'll be okay."

"I think so."

Kirana bent down to the crate and pulled out one of two small crates filled with long pipes, "Let's get started."

Selling Fairies was easier than Kirana had anticipated. All it took for people to pay was for the screens of their watches to be pressed together, so interactions could happen quickly. It seemed people knew what it was well before she named it, and the more she said it allowed the more people came over. It became more of a game when people stopped buying it quickly, and suddenly it was her turn to make them like it. She would stop those who did know what Fairies were and have them describe it to her.

"It's a rainbow of fire."

"It's shit, but the shit's good."

"You light the tip on fire and suck it."

It was so incredible to see people talk with their own personalities and beliefs. Some of the people seemed to really like Kirana, and not only was that a great way to make Korts, but it was also a great opportunity to make friends. She had never felt so fulfilled by the company. They were more dangerous and reckless than the Hiraethans but there was a beauty in their madness. Gwen was still worried, and in her worry, she sold fewer Fairies.

"They like a show." Kirana said, pushing her hair back dramatically, "Entertainment."

Gwen tried to copy Kirana, smiling and talking, and in the end, the two of them sold nearly all of their Fairies.

That was when Ruby appeared. Kirana turned around after making three more sales to nearly crash right into the red woman. "Ruby."

"Hello, Summer." Ruby had been seated when they last spoke, and now Kirana realized just how tall she was, her shoes extending her height by a few inches. She chewed on a red candy in her mouth, "Is Tech back yet?"

"Not yet." Kirana placed the box to her side, "Why?"

"We have a job for him." She pointed down the Nook, "It's further down in Lockwood. He said he would have a full shift so we planned for him to just do it. When will he be back?"

Kirana glanced behind her to see Card Face standing at the round table, eyes locked on where the ship should have been. She realized very quickly that Tech was in trouble, both for leaving and for leaving Kirana and Gwen in his place. He had helped the Keepers so much already, so what else could Kirana do but return the favor? "Why don't we take the shift?"

"You two?" Ruby asked, amused by the idea.

Gwen came over and stood beside Kirana, "What's going on."

"You two are going further down the Nook into the Lockwood district to sell more Fairies, shouldn't take more than an hour. Card Face wants to knock out two territories in one day." She stuck out her tongue and gagged, "It's kind of stupid but I'm not about to say no."

"It's for Tech." Kirana told Gwen, "We'll be back in time to meet him here."

Gwen looked from Ruby to Kirana and nodded softly, "Alright. Do we get paid more?"

Ruby laughed, "You're so serious. What's your name?"

She glanced at the stone walls, "Stoner."

"I like you." Ruby glanced back to Card Face, "I'll see what I can do. But you better leave now. We have a crew waiting down there who wanted this delivered in this shift, *exactly*. Very particular people." She pointed down the Nook, "This place goes on for a while but eventually you'll back it back to the alleys. Take a left and a right and just go down that alley for a few minutes. You'll see people everywhere." With that, she walked away.

Gwen turned to Kirana, "So now we're leaving?"

"We're expanding our services." She stood up straight, "Business is fun."

"And we'll be back in time?"

"Yes, we will."

Gwen twisted her jaw to the side and nodded, "Okay. Let's go."

Kirana smiled and the two of them walked past Ruby and Card Face further into the Stonewall Nook. Ruby had been right, the Nook went on for quite a few more minutes, and when the two of them finally did react at the end they watched it morph into a concrete alley with very few lights or people. They took a left, then a right, then continued straight, occasionally going up or down a staircase.

"I like you like this." Kirana said, nudging Gwen lightly, "You're not worried."

"Kirana, I am so very worried, but something about Tech helping back there felt so reassuring." She sighed and winced, "I might have misjudged this place."

"I think you did."

"When we arrived it was all so terrible. Then the staff was gone, you were bleeding, we had just escaped the Wardens, my father..." She stopped talking and looked to the side.

Kirana adored Gideon. He was truly the first person she met beside Gwen and, even in the short time they had together, she knew he was special. The people of the new world intrigued her, but she knew he held more value than all of them. He was powerful and he was smart, smart enough to escape the Wardens and survive.

Kirana remembered what he had told her, his final words to the Keeper: *Do what you were chosen to do. Protect.*

That was her purpose, but in all honesty, she had no idea whether he was referring to Kirana protecting the worlds or his daughter. She decided his words would mean both, and took Gwen's hand, "We'll go back to Hiraeth, I promise."

"This world may be safer for the time being." Kirana laughed at her words and Gwen shrugged while still smiling, "I know, I know. I want to go home, but I need to be a Keeper. This is important. We finish this job, we go back to Stinger, we get our staff, and we find the next Keeper. Then we can–"

Kirana spotted something up ahead and cut Gwen off in her excitement, "Gwen!" She looked over at Gwen and shook her head, "Sorry. I'm sorry that's important but... look!" Before the two Keepers sat a cream-colored bike with no wheels.

Gwen looked at Kirana, "It's a bike–"

"It's my bike!" She ran over to the bike, brushing her hand over the surface, "Gwen this is mine! This is from Permidia."

"Are you sure?"

Kirana nodded quickly, "I mean, I don't think this specific one is mine but it's the same model." She looked back up to Gwen, her mind working fast, "Gwen, Hiraeth works in agriculture, right? Farms, cattle, factories."

"Mines, fisheries." Gwen continued.

"Yes!" Kirana yelled, jumping up in her excitement, "This place is a technological city! They produce technology!" She snapped her fingers, "And entertainment! Permidians live in solitude, they take in entertainment, maybe it comes from here! Comfort and entertainment from here."

Gwen laughed as Kirana jumped around her, "Kirana, calm down."

She took Gwen and spun her around, "Gwen we're Keepers! We are learning about the worlds! This is–"

A scream burst through the alley.

A blood-wrenching, child's scream.

Gwen grabbed Kirana's arm and looked around the empty alley, "Ruby said people would be here."

Kirana put down the crate of Fairies and started to walk slowly down the alley.

"Kirana." Gwen whispered, following behind.

The two of them moved up a staircase to reveal another empty alley before them. The scream had been so loud that it felt impossible to locate. But they had to, they couldn't just leave a child. Right?

Gwen pulled Kirana back, "We don't have a weapon."

"You have a knife."

"I have a very *small* knife, Kirana."

She walked up the next set of stairs, "We can't just leave a child here."

"We can't fight someone. If they have a gun they'll shoot us too."

"But we're–"

Kirana stopped at the top of the stairs, and when Gwen saw it too she put a hand to her mouth and let out a horrified gasp.

Hanging from the roof, a stuffed toy tied to their hand, was a little boy. He was strung up by his neck, eyes wide open.

Gwen looked away but Kirana looked beyond him. There was a large room just behind the hanging corpse, and within it was something all too familiar.

Pink roses.

The Magistrater's Roses.

Chapter 15

* * *

GWEN

GWEN THOUGHT OF Danny. She thought of Danny, hanging from the ceiling. She thought of Gaia finding him. She thought of the little stuffed toy Gaia had made for him, tied to his little hand.

Kirana, who was still looking forward, put a hand on Gwen's shoulder, "There's something up ahead."

"We need to go back." Gwen had her hands around her eyes. It was so quiet, and in the silence she felt the absence of the murderer around them. The monster that killed the child could be there, waiting.

"I've seen those roses before." Kirana said as she let go of Gwen's shoulder, "Wait here."

Gwen turned around and grabbed her arm, "Don't." She kept her eyes on the ground in hope that she wouldn't have to look at the child, only to see a pool of his blood stained against the concrete floor. How long had he been there? Why had no one helped him? She let her eyes wander and saw the roses. They were sitting in large baskets, most of them a light pink color. Kirana pointed at the flowers and Gwen spotted a white piece of paper tucked between the petals.

Without another word, Kirana took Gwen's hand and they started to walk further inside. The two of them inched past the body of the child and pool of blood until they were in the next room. Gwen was listening for movement, for the sound of someone running, for the sound of someone breathing, but all she heard were the sounds of the Keeper's footsteps and a soft dripping. She looked to her left and let out a soft scream at the sight of more bodies. More children. They were hanging, all of them.

Kirana ran forward and grabbed the note off the roses. It was a letter with a bright red seal pressed on wax. Kirana tore it open and started to read, her voice shaking, "I heard your heart outweighs your reason. One of the children is alive, do you save them, or run? My soldiers are nearby, they'll know when you arrive. I am curious to see which way you struggle." She showed Gwen the page, "This isn't for us."

At the top of the page, it read: *For our dearest Telematic Hero.*

"Kirana we need to go." She shoved the letter back into the flowers, "If she finds us here–"

"One of them is alive." Kirana looked from corpse to corpse before her breathing went heavy and she pressed her trembling hands into her eyes, "This is the Magistrater."

"What?"

"When I met with her she had roses everywhere. I don't..." Kirana shook her head, "We have to save the kid."

Gwen didn't want to argue against protecting a child, but what could they possibly do? And gods, they still had to get the staff. If the Wardens found them it would all be over. Gwen was trying to think for the future, but at the thought of Danny, she realized that they couldn't just leave, no matter the consequences. They were the Keepers, this was what they were chosen to do, even at such a small scale, a life was a life.

Gwen ran to the right side of the room, "Check for a pulse." She was shaking her head as she spoke.

The bodies had been hung low to the ground, perhaps to help the Telematic Hero find the survivor. As Gwen pressed her fingers into the wrists of dead children she looked around for cameras. The room was a large alley, and like the allies from before, it was filthy. She couldn't tell junk from cameras even when moving up close to the walls.

Gwen counted the bodies: 20. There were 20 children and only one with a soft heartbeat. They were all strung up by their necks, how could the Keepers possibly heal them? What if there wasn't a survivor at all?

Kirana continued to run around frantically, pressing her hand to each chest in hopes of feeling a heartbeat. Gwen stepped back and forced herself to look at the bodies. The children looked vastly different from each other either by age, skin color, or clothing. Most of their eyes were open, and Gwen realized they had not been strung up at all, but had died by being hung where they were now. She looked for the children with their eyes closed, someone the Magistrater would have left. Ten of the children's eyes were closed. She looked at their clothes, she listened for a breath, she watched their fingers hoping to see a twitch or a flicker of life. Nothing. No one moved. It was all silent. Gwen was ready to say that it was a worthless search, that the Magistrater was trying to trick them, but then she remembered it had not always been so quiet.

Someone had screamed, someone was alive, but there was no way they could have yelled out while being hung. Gwen looked around the sides of the room for a hiding place, somewhere the Wardens could have tucked a child out of view. There was junk, but only metal scraps. Gwen looked back to the center of the room, to the roses. She ran to it and ripped the flowers away, digging her way to the ground. As she tore away the stems and petals, she saw a layer of metal.

Kirana came running over, "The child?" She ripped away the last few roses to reveal a box, or rather, a coffin.

It was then that Gwen heard something behind them, and for a moment it was just footsteps until a gunshot rang through the alley. The Keepers took cover behind the metal box and looked over the roses to see light coming from down the alley. The Wardens were here, and yet, they weren't shooting at the Keepers.

"Who–" Kirana started to say, but Gwen cut her off by trying to open the box. She pulled violently at the edge but it wouldn't budge. She pulled out her pocket knife and slammed it into the crack. She lifted the blade up but it was no use, the box was sealed. The gunshots continued to fire from the alley as the Keepers did everything they could to open the box, and when the room suddenly went silent, they were forced to stop and wait.

Gwen was ready to see the Wardens appear over the stairs, she was ready to see the barrel of a gun and then a bullet shooting for her head. She was trembling. She kept her knife, now bent and useless, held up in defiance. But a Warden did not appear in the alley. It was a man.

It was Tech.

He came running up the stairs and stopped when he saw the body of the child.

He ripped off his mask and put a hand over his mouth.

Kirana jumped up and over the box, "One of them is alive!" She pointed to the metal box, "We can't get it open."

Without looking at Kirana Tech ran to the box and slid down to its side, "Ben E!" The little android rolled so quickly that he cracked into the metal. His little hands pressed together and a blue knife appeared. He pressed it into the metal, slowly melting the rim with his hot blade.

Tech jumped over and slid into place beside Gwen, "What are you doing here?" He sounded angry as if she had done something wrong by trying to save a child.

"Why are you here?" She asked, and it was only after said it that she realized how important of a question it was. Why was Tech there? How had he found them? She looked back the way he had come, back towards the sound of a gunfight.

He didn't respond to her question, he looked over at her, blinked once, and pulled his bag over onto his lap. From it, he pulled out a small gun. "Shoot the Wardens. As soon as the kid is free we're running. Follow my lead and never stop running."

"You're him." Kirana said, her eyes wide, "You're the Telematic Hero."

He looked ahead and used both guns to shoot someone in the alley.

It was the Wardens.

But not the Wardens Gwen knew. They were dressed in a black uniform, not brown. A jumpsuit with armor plates. Not a single piece of their skin was showing. Gloves, boots, a vest, a helmet with a glass front. They were the same, except for the complete black color. In such a colorful world, they stood out as something incredibly menacing.

Tech pushed the gun into Gwen's hands, reached into his bag, and pulled out what looked like a grenade. He pulled out the round wire on top and threw it into the alley. A huge puff of blue smoke filled the alley, reaching the Keepers in a blue fog. Tech jumped over the box and tried to rip it over with Ben E's help. The metal was moving now, peeling open ever so slowly. Gwen and Kirana reached over and pulled it back, fingers digging into the hot metal. Ben E's knife did enough work that, within a few seconds, the metal lid flew onto its hinges. The child inside let out a gasp for air. She couldn't have been more than 4 years old.

"You're okay." He told her, slipping on his mask and grabbing her. She clung onto him for dear life. "Ben E!" The android's knife retracted back into its hand

and it sped back into the alley. Tech looked back to Gwen and put out his hand, "Hold on and don't let go."

Kirana was right, Tech was the Telematic Hero. Gwen took his hand, Kirana grabbed her wrist, and the three of them started running. The blue smoke blinded Gwen, stinging her eyes and causing her to nearly trip down the entire flight of stairs. Tech didn't slow down, he guided them forward but never stopped. As they moved out of the smoke Ben E came speeding by and rolled ahead of them. That was when Gwen saw them, the Wardens, an entire group of them. Ben E was the first to arrive, and when he was at their feet his head suddenly spun. Perhaps fearing the android was a bomb, the Wardens pointed their guns at him and shot. Only nothing happened. Their guns, all of them, stopped working. Gwen saw sparks coming off Ben E's head and realized he was distorting the guns in some way she did not understand.

Tech let go of her and started to shoot the Wardens, and that was when Gwen realized she had to do the same. She had to shoot the Wardens, fight them, all of them. A Hiraethan girl with the opportunity to kill the Wardens just as they had killed her people. It was terrifying, and for some reason, horrific. She had always seen the Wardens as monsters, but now, with the gun in her hand she saw them as people. Gwen hated it, she hated how much mercy she had and in that moment she decided to get rid of it all. They were the enemy, and she could not hesitate to kill them, after all, they never did. She shot the gun, pulling the trigger as she had seen the Wardens do. Her bullets flew wildly and the gun pushed her back every time she shot, but she didn't stop. The Wardens were attempting to run forward, to get to the Keepers before they could be shot. Their armor was stopping some of the bullets, at least enough to keep moving forward. Tech placed his bullets in their necks, wrists, shoulders, and finally, on one of the last Wardens, Gwen shot one herself. Their head flung back and their body was hurled to the floor. She killed them.

Kirana rushed to one of the bodies and grabbed one of their guns. Then they were running again, and Gwen's first kill was left as another step in their journey.

Tech moved them around the allies until they were finally back onto the city streets. The crowd brought a sense of protection, but they were far from safe. The Wardens were following them, either from the allies or by waiting on the streets. As a patrol came from across the street Tech shot at them and suddenly, for the first time, the people reacted. They ran, took cover, and hid from the fight. Tech took them down street after street, down and up stairs, until finally, there were no gunshots. They each started to slow. Tech led them to a fairly empty street, a few people lining the walls and staying clear of others. They all seemed sick, drunk, or high, and none of them were good people to bring a child to. The concrete roof was low and doors lined every wall without windows. When they finally stopped it was in one of the smaller streets in front of a metal door tucked into the wall.

Kirana, panting and gasping for air, bent over at the wall and threw up. Gwen put a hand on her back and looked over to Tech as he flipped over a panel on the door and pressed a button inside. Gwen moved closer so she could hear what he was saying.

He took off his mask, "It's Tech. I've got one." He flipped down the panel and mouthed the word *one*, before wiping down his face with his spare hand. The little girl was still clinging to him, her face on his shoulder.

The light remained red for a moment, before flashing green. The doors did their best to creak open as Tech pushed them the rest of the way. He knelt down and slowly got the girl to stand on her own feet. He held her shoulders, and though he did not smile, his expression remained soft, "How old are you?"

She didn't answer.

"You're very strong." He told her, "And now you're safe. I promise. Have you heard of Martha?"

She shook her head softly.

Tech glanced up at Gwen. It was clear he didn't like that they were there, hearing all of this. "She'll take care of you. Just go down this lift and you'll be safe. Follow the red wire." Tech spun his bag around and pulled out a small tube. He shook it around and cracked it in the middle. A green light started to glow through it, and he handed it to the girl. "I'll come to see you soon, okay? You're safe now."

He pushed the girl into the small room, and though she continued to look terrified, she did not resist. Gwen didn't understand what was going on. Was the room a hiding place? Tech shut the doors and the panel flashed red again, before dark. The sound of creaking metal came from inside the room, but no screams. The girl did not make a noise. From what she could tell by the fading noise, the room was moving, it was taking the girl away. Tech saved her.

Tech turned around and slid down the metal doors onto the floor. Ben E rolled around him and sat against his leg, looking from him to the Keepers. Tech looked up at Gwen and, though his anger had worn off with the run, he wasn't exactly thrilled to see them still around. "What were you doing there?"

"What just happened?" Kirana asked, wiping her mouth.

Tech looked forward in a sudden realization and winced, "Oh gods." He put his hand over his eyes, "You didn't give Card Face his Korts."

"We– We didn't really have time." Kirana put her hands on her hips, still catching her breath.

Gwen glanced at the metal doors, "You save children?"

"The Wardens take them, they take little kids from the lowest parts of the city. They find the orphans or lonely wanders and drag them away. No one ever sees them again." He gestured to Gwen and Kirana, showing that they would have been the first survivors.

"But you stop them." Kirana knelt beside Tech, "You're the Telematic Hero."

He shook his head, "I don't know why they call me that."

"Because you save *children*." Gwen gestured to the door, and when Tech didn't respond she looked back the way they had come, "Where do the Wardens take them?"

He laughed, "You know, I wish I knew, but I can't just let them take a group of kids just to see where they go. I can't do that to them." He put a hand on Ben E, "They must have known I would be down there, that has never happened before. The Wardens don't just waste kids like that."

Kirana pulled the letter out of her pocket and handed it to him. Without a word Tech read it over, his eyes wide. Kirana leaned forward, "Those roses were from the Magistrater." He looked over, just as shocked as Gwen had been. Kirana nodded, "We took the shift that you were supposed to take."

Tech nodded and tucked the letter in his pocket, "Either Card Face set me up or let some information slip, either way it's not good."

"Tech." Gwen said, and when he looked at her she felt guilty for trying to change the conversation, but she had to, "I'm grateful for what you just did to save that poor girl, but we need our staff back, or we need 100 Korts."

Tech didn't respond at first, he took a moment to close his eyes. He looked shaken, and rightfully so after the escape they just pulled. He sighed, "You weren't taken by the Wardens, were you?"

"What makes you say that?"

"You don't care."

He gestured to Gwen and she waved her hands as if she could push away such an idea, "Of course I care, Tech. They're children."

"But they're not you. So you lied to me." Tech took a breath, "You would have changed everything." He laughed at the idea, before his expression grew somber and he looked ahead.

Gwen thought about telling the truth. She could have told him that she and Kirana just came from a different part of town, that their past was hard to talk about but had nothing to do with the Wardens. But the way Tech talked about the kids, the fact that he had a title for his heroic actions, and the way had managed to grab the almighty Magistrater's attention made Gwen want to use his sympathy for their benefit. Kirana looked ready to confess their truth, but Gwen didn't let her. She spoke first, arms folded over her body, "They did."

Kirana looked over, and though the Keeper seemed to always have different opinions on a situation, this one seemed to affect Kirana the most. She looked disappointed at what Gwen was doing, and yet, she said nothing.

Tech locked eyes with Gwen, "I need you to tell me everything you remember."

"Then I need you to help us get the staff. After that, we can tell you everything we know." That was the truth, Gwen and Kirana had so many secrets to share that one wouldn't hurt the world's hero.

Telematic's hero, that was the world's name. *Telematic.*

Tech let out a breath and stood up, "Let's walk."

"Just no more running." Kirana laughed, but she was honestly pleading. As Tech moved forward, Ben E rolling beside him, Kirana stood beside Gwen and whispered, "We can't lie to him."

"You think I like this?" She asked, and there was more anger behind her words than she intended. Gwen didn't want her to think she was cruel. She liked Tech as much as Kirana did, but she had to think beyond the world they were in. Kirana's people were safe, Gwen's were not. "A little lie, that's it. We need him on our side."

"He'll help us even if we tell him the truth, Gwen." Kirana said, her eyes soft, as if to convince Gwen that a loving act was all they needed.

"I want to believe that. You were right, there is good in this world, but we can't take chances. Not with something this important."

"I trust you." Kirana walked forward after Tech, "If we need to lie then we'll lie. I just don't want to ruin what we might have found here."

Gwen nodded but said nothing. Kirana was right, Gwen's lie could ruin their trust, but for now, that was worth the risk.

The three of them walked back through the streets. Tech took them down an alleyway and up a new ladder. This would be the highest level Gwen had gone to considering how tall the ladder was. When they reached the top she was met by a view of the city. The building they were on was raised higher than she had expected and gave way to a downward view of the city. Gwen walked to the edge of the building and looked at it all.

It was then she spotted something the world had been missing: The Magistrater's Tower. It towered over everything else, and yet it didn't dominate the space. It was the center of the city, with roads, and streets, with traffic flowing in circles across symmetrical lines. This was not the chaotic city she had first entered. There was order to it, organization behind it all. There was noise, yes, but now it flowed into a melody. A hum only the city knew, harmonizing with every part of the world. Every place was unique, but from up high it was all just the same city of lights, a balance between the setting sun and rising star-filled sky.

Kirana came beside her, wind sweeping her hair back evenly, "All I have known my whole life was the embodiment of a perfect world. The perfect cities, the perfect mood, the perfect lights. But this..." She shook her head, "I never knew there was so much beauty in balanced things." She looked at Gwen with a sense of serenity. The Hiraethan had almost forgotten how new she was to the world. This was not her first city, but it was her first experience with a piece of chaos. For all of its violence and destruction, it was still a home. Hiraeth was the same. Filled with despair and pain, but alive. Her people valued good moments because they knew the worst ones. The only reason the city before them looked so beautiful was because they had seen the darker sides of it.

Tech moved beside her at the edge and pointed next to the Magistrater's Tower, "King King can get you Korts. He owns half the districts out there, one of the richest people in the city. He gives out loans to people who need them, and in return, you do some jobs for him."

Gwen didn't like the idea of being in debt to anyone, especially in the city they were stuck in, "We don't want to do any jobs."

"That's fine, there are ways to deceive him, especially if you're willing to leave this part of the city and go away." Gwen looked over to Kirana. They could leave the entire world as soon as they had the staff. "You need to be smart. He needs to know you aren't some druggy who will up and run. He'll ask you to do a job, it doesn't matter what job, you just say yes."

Kirana looked up at him, "What would we be agreeing to?"

"Best case scenario: a few days working in the bar or polishing his guns. Worst case scenario: he asks you to kill someone." He glanced at Gwen, expecting her disapproval. She bit down her thoughts and let him continue, "That is something he will expect to be done. If it's not he will know. The thing about acting smart is that he expects better things from you."

"You've done this before then?" Kirana asked, crossing her arms the same way Gwen was.

Tech nodded, "I've worked with him three times. The first time I just needed some extra Korts. I got 300 and he gave me a job down at the bar. I did it, I paid off my debt and left. The second time I got stupid, I thought I could outsmart him. I was going to get the Korts and run for it. But he knew well before I entered the room. I got jumped and was stuck in his factory for three weeks. Then he let me go. On the third try, I knew better than to cross him. I came in looking for a new loan, something bigger. It had been a few years since I had last been there and he could see something had changed in me. So he gave me a bigger job. He wanted me to kill a small gang for him."

Kirana squinted up at him, "You didn't do it?"

"He said they were stealing his products. It was bad for business and he was right to want to get rid of their production, but they were just kids selling it for extra Korts. A group of them trying to get food. They were living well. I knew they would stop as soon as I gave them a hard talk. I got them out of town and told King King I took them out." He sighed, "The next day I went to see King King and he locked me up in a backroom and forced me to work for a month. He always knows."

Gwen shook her head, "Then why are you offering this as an option for us?"

"You two have nothing here. You came from somewhere far away, a place you don't want to tell me. That's fine. Go back there. Get your staff, get a ship, and fly away."

Kirana nodded quickly, "As soon as we get the staff we're gone."

"So you ask for the Korts, act smart, get a flexible job, *agree* to it." He glared at Gwen, "Then give me the Korts and I will get it to Stinger. You will have your staff by the time you leave his bar."

Kirana squinted at him, "You're leaving us there?"

"I go inside and I am dead." He tapped the mask around his neck, "I come with you and I'll be wearing this, and at some point, you give me the Korts and I'll sort out Stinger. Ben E will stay with you in case something goes wrong and I'll be waiting outside with the staff."

"How many Korts should we get?"

Tech shook his head and put a hand on his chest, "100 Korts for Stinger, I don't need my share anymore. Just get your staff and tell me everything you know, then you're free."

Gwen found herself trusting Tech now that she knew he was the Telematic Hero, but part of her still wondered if all of this was a setup. He saved a child, yes, one child. She wanted to believe that he wasn't lying, but if he was the consequences would be deadly.

She looked over to Kirana, hoping to catch her before she could say yes too quickly, only to find her already looking over. Kirana glanced at the city and took a breath, before looking back and mouthing the word: *faith*. Was it foolish to trust someone so easily? Gwen looked out at the city, at the beauty around her, and thought about Hiraeth. She thought about the Wardens, the long work hours, and the horrific conditions some of her people lived in. She thought about her mother, her father, Gaia, Theo, Lorenzo, the rebellion, Hiraethan music, and Hiraethan food. Her world was a balance of good and bad, and though she did not trust Kirana to always see the bad, she did trust her to see the good. Kirana saw the good in Tech, she saw a person she had been searching for in Permidia. Gwen did have faith, she had faith in Kirana.

She took a breath, the wind flying through her hair, "Let's do it."

Chapter 16

KIRANA

KIRANA KNEW SHE could talk her way into getting a loan from King King. It would be the same as speaking with Card Face, and if he was more charismatic, he would be like Ruby. Kirana could feel her experience grow, and as it did, she connected each person to what she had always believed to be true from watching Permidians: every person was a unique formula made up of memories, trauma, and the people around them, and within their complexity were weak points. King King was not just a businessman, he had a life, maybe even a spouse or a child. He might have loved poetry or had a sweet tooth. There was always something about a person that made them unique, and so now it was her job to see who King King was and use what she was learning to trick him into believing a false image of herself. Tia used to tell Kirana the one thing she should never do is lie, because that was immoral, especially between sisters. Kirana lied often by saying she was fine with Tia leaving so soon or commenting on how perfect her lonely life was, but now she would have the opportunity to lie completely. It felt good to be so far from her Permidian morals. Being a god demanded new skills.

Kirana was back to her normal self. Stronger and healed from the journey. She was prepared to fight or run again, though she would prefer an easy journey from then on. Once Kirana and Gwen got the staff back all they needed to do was find the Keeper and move on to the next dimension. It would be dangerous, and yet again everything they had done so far seemed to be reckless, this new plan was no different. Danger was involved in any path they chose.

Tech led them down the streets once again, slipping on his mask he moved through the crowds of people with ease. Kirana was getting tired of being around so much noise. She could already hear the ringing in her ears and felt nauseous from how much music and talking was around them. Constantly. It never stopped. Even as the sun set below the high city buildings the people and busy nature didn't change. It was as if no one had a perception of time. Night or day, it didn't matter.

Kirana hoped the next dimension would be quiet. She wanted people around, just without the need for useless background noises.

Tech suddenly took off his mask, slipping it into his bag behind his back. Kirana looked around for the reason and realized it just in time.

A group of Wardens.

She put on her hood and gave Gwen a nudge. Gwen's jacket didn't have a hood, and so to avoid the Wardens she was forced to look in the other direction just as they passed. There were ten of them in two rows of five, marching to a rhythm that didn't match any music around them.

Kirana glanced back to see if they were gone before moving over beside Tech, "We didn't see Wardens up here before, is that normal?"

"They're usually in smaller groups." He looked down the street and saw Kirana with her hood still up. His eyes went soft, "Are you okay?"

Tia had taught Kirana about trauma not in one of their lessons but in their day-to-day life. It was when Kirana was about ten back when her sister lived with her. They used to talk and play all the time. Tia seemed so much more alive back then, though Kirana suspected it was just her exaggerated image of a detached sister. One day, Tia had eaten one of her meals so quickly that she started to choke. After that, Kirana used to watch her eat and make sure she had small bites and chewed fully. The idea that her sister could choke haunted her. It was silly, and looking back Kirana felt embarrassed to know how low her pain tolerance was in the perfect world, but Tia had used the situation to teach her a lesson.

"You have trauma, Kirana." She had told her, sitting at the end of her bed, "Trauma is a bad memory that enhances your fear. You might be afraid of bugs, but you're traumatized after one of them stings you. You remember what it felt like to feel so much pain, and it hurts to have any situation remind you of that."

Kirana remembered that now, the lesson Tia had given her, and thought about the trauma she would have if she had been kidnapped. Tech was assuming the mere sight of a Warden would make her afraid, so she gave in to that idea and looked afraid. She clung to her hood and swallowed, "I'm fine." She tried to make her voice crack so it would sound like she was lying.

Tech nodded once and looked ahead.

The lessons Kirana had learned in Permidia seemed so useless at the time, but now she started to think back to her history lessons and small conversations with Tia. But Kirana knew the most important thing she could do was learn from experience. For now, she would practice what she believed was the foundation for every challenge that would come before them: lying.

"We stole the staff from the Wardens." Kirana pulled off her hood as Tech glanced back, "When we escaped we grabbed it and ran and then lost it to Ben E." She looked down at the android who, after hearing his name, looked up expectantly, like a pet expecting a treat. She pointed back at Gwen, "We were sheltered and kept locked away for most of our lives." She tried to spread pity through her words, "The city is new to us, I want to explain everything the Wardens did but for now…"

Tech nodded, "They kept you away from everything, you don't have to explain."

Kirana smiled at him, happy with his reaction and he pointed at her face, "You take life with such joy. It's nice to see." He laughed and looked down at Ben E, "Maybe you should run off and steal staffs more often."

The android shook his head quickly, "No thank you. It was a rather draining experience."

Tech patted Kirana on her shoulder, "I'm sorry you've been through so much before this." He walked forward, gesturing to them to follow as he put on his mask, "Come on. We're almost there."

Kirana moved over to Gwen and walked beside her, "Lying is kind of fun. I think this is turning out great."

"Last time you said that we walked into the corpse of a hanging child—"

She waved at her words, "We're okay now. We have a plan."

"I'm not jinxing it this time." Gwen put up her hands, a smile on her face.

Kirana smiled back and said nothing in hopes that she wouldn't ruin the mood. It was so nice to see Gwen happy. She hoped her smile would stay a little longer.

As the three of them walked further down the street Kirana suddenly realized how close they were to their destination. Plastered on a large building was a huge sign that read, *King King*. It had a crown on its first King. It wasn't very original, but it seemed to draw a crowd. Almost everyone they were walking with was headed for the same place. People in all shapes and styles stood outside the building, enjoying muffled music from each floor. As they got closer she saw some of them had settled outside entirely, drinks in hands and conversations flowing. Some people danced to whatever beat they could find through the walls. Most of them, however, were standing outside the grand entrance. Two large silver doors lined with a neon red rim.

Tech stopped them far from the building. He gathered them at the railing beside a rusty metal stall. The man inside turned, expecting customers and finding their pit stop an annoyance. Tech waved him off before gesturing to King King's building, "When you're ready go up to the guards and tell them you're looking for a loan."

Kirana gave a nervous laugh, "I thought you were coming in?"

"I will, but once I have the Korts I have to bring it to Stinger first."

Gwen shook her head, "We need more details. What will happen when they give us the Korts?"

"Just go ask for King King once you're inside. If you get a loan you will be set up accordingly." He tapped his head, "Act smart. I suggest you negotiate. He's going to give you a bad deal, you can model it to what you want. If you want him to spell it out for you, act cute. If you want him to treat you with respect, act like you own the building... in the most respectful way you can."

Gwen looked down the street, "You'll be here?"

"I'll be a good distance away, but I'll be watching." He pointed down at Ben E, "You can take him with you, and if anything goes wrong he should be able to help. He's also linked to my datawatch so he'll keep me updated on what is going on." Tech leaned forward, "I'll go in with you with my mask on. Ask for the Korts upfront, give it to me, and I'll run off to get the staff while you do the talking. Easy as that."

"I feel like we're going in blind." Gwen said in all honesty.

Tech pointed to himself, "I'm right here, this isn't an issue. Just relax. You're a fighter, Gwen. Negotiate for what you want." He gestured to the entrance, "You ready?"

Gwen looked over to Kirana and they exchanged a glance before both nodding. The three of them walked away from the stall and up to the entrance of the large, bright building. The doorway was embedded within the wall and framed by a golden arch. The line to get in was filled with large groups of thematically dressed people. Within a minute, the three of them were standing in front of the doors before two large guards. Almost every part of them was big; their hands, heads, stomachs, arms, legs, and feet all oversized.

With Tech staying behind, Kirana took the lead and stepped forward. The guards quite literally looked right down at her. Kirana felt like they could flick her away.

"Business?" His voice was so deep his words vibrated in his throat.

Kirana put her hands on her hips. She couldn't decide whether to smile or look stern. Her face flickered until she settled on a glare, "We want to see King King... to get a loan."

One of the men put up his datawatch. He flicked it up and Kirana was excited to see a hologram appear in the form of a screen. She had seen holograms in Permidia. Screens were more common but some shows needed to be watched from all angles. Kirana especially liked dancers. They would hop around her room in their little hologram and she would try and copy their movements. Sometimes Tia joined her, and the two of them would joke around with the little hologram. It was a nice reminder of home, at least the good part of it. They pressed a few buttons and after a look at numbers and charts, it disappeared. Gwen seemed much more shocked by it, and Kirana remembered how little technology was in Hiraeth. It might have been her first time seeing such a thing.

"Under or over 1000 Korts?"

"Under." Kirana glanced at Gwen, unsure of her answer.

"First time?"

"Yep. But we are very excited to meet—"

They covered the hologram with their hand after a blue light flashed across the screen and nodded to the other guard.

Within a second the large doors before them slide away from each other to reveal the room before them. The music and lights matched the other parties Kirana had seen before, loud and messy, but this one had a sense of elegance no other place had achieved. Glass seemed to be the main theme as everything was made from it. Either reflective or just transparent, it made the lights reflect off of every surface. People danced, drank at the bars, talked, smoked, and went crazy in the center of the room. At each of the corners in the room were round tables with a shelf of bottles on the walls and stools in front. The room itself was long, stretching far and creating enough space for people to move around and be comfortable in. But there weren't only customers in the glass room, there were also incredibly tall people holding trays. From what Kirana could tell they were wearing stilts to extend their legs. They wore the same outfit, a suit covered in shards of glass. Every part of them was reflective, and as they moved around the light jumped from one person to the next. They passed out drinks and took empty glasses back to the bars.

The sight of this extraordinary room caught both of the Keepers frozen at the entrance. Tech must have noticed their shock because he pushed Kirana and Gwen forward and walked them inside. Once in the room fully the doors slid shut. Kirana looked behind and saw it was a mirror too, so when it closed the whole room came together.

The music pumped through their bodies and the very walls shook. Kirana looked down at Ben E to find his little arms waving at his side, his head bouncing on his body. The music was so loud it was pulling him apart.

Gwen put her hands over her ears and looked at Tech, "What do we do?"

Kirana could barely make out her words, "I don't know!" She looked back around the room and took a second to look at her reflection in the mirror. She still had blood across her face and took a moment to try to scrape it off.

The music died down as the beat suddenly changed. As if on cue with the music, a voice called from above her, "You are here for a loan?"

She turned around to see one of the taller people. It was a man dressed up with a tray in one hand and a white cloth in the other. He was smiling down at them, a sight Kirana didn't feel comfortable with.

Gwen nodded quickly, "Yes, we need to speak with King King."

"How many Korts?"

"1– 200 Korts." Gwen said, and Kirana nodded softly to confirm her raising the amount needed. A little Korts wouldn't hurt anyone. Besides, they could always give it to Tech for all his help. It was what he had asked for in the first place.

The man had been leaning down to speak with them, but now put his hand to his ear and stood up straight. He seemed to be listening to something, or someone. When he leaned back down he handed Kirana a glass filled with a yellow liquid. "King King will speak with her." He pointed at Gwen.

Kirana went cold, "No, we will speak with him together."

He shook his head and lifted his eyebrows up and down, "King King won't like to hear that." His smile didn't flicker or flinch.

"Kirana." Gwen shook her head, "We can't get on his bad side."

Kirana looked to Tech for support, only to find him at the bar in the corner of the room. He was keeping a low profile, and though that should have been a warning for Kirana to obey King King's authority she continued to argue, "We're a team. I should be going in with you."

"What if they don't give us the loan?"

"Then we make up a new plan!"

Gwen shook her head firmly, "Kirana I don't want to go alone but if I have to I will. We'll be free after this. Just trust me."

If there was one thing Kirana could not deny, it was her trust in Gwen, and though she wanted to fight for them to stay together, she gave in and nodded.

The tall man smiled, "A Suit will bring out your due amount shortly. Your friend shall be back when King King has finished with her. You may stay here and enjoy the Belic.

What was Belic?

Then he gestured towards the only thing in the room that wasn't reflective or made of glass. A door on the right wall of the room. Metal with no windows, and it was tall enough for the man to fit through. Gwen bent down and picked up Ben E as the man guided her to the door. Kirana watched as he saw the android but did not comment on him. That was good, for now everything was still going to plan, only without Kirana there to help. Her stomach twisted as she watched Gwen walk through the door, the tall man following behind her. The door closing was a dangerous last chance for her to stop Gwen from going alone, but she didn't take it.

Kirana fiddled with what was in her hand. The glass of yellow liquid was thick and barely filled the glass. She knew it was alcohol, and hoped she didn't have to drink it. She knew what it was because of her studies, and pushed down her curiosity for what she knew was a terrible drink. Belic. Was that what it was called? She sniffed the liquid and realized it was the strong smell she had been breathing in all day. That and whatever else was in the streets.

As the tall man had said, one of the other tall workers came over with a metal box in hand. They opened it for Kirana and revealed a gold and silver datawatch inside. She took it carefully and yelled over the music, "Thank you." She ran over to Tech and sat beside him, "We've got it."

He took the watch from her and inspected it.

Kirana glanced back at the metal door, "She's okay, right?"

"She'll be fine. They're just talking about the job they'll give her in return for the Korts." He tapped it, "Looks like everything is here."

Kirana smiled and nodded, "I knew everything would be fine. I knew we could trust you and I knew this plan would work."

"Because you're naive." He put the datawatch on his wrist above his own.

Kirana stared up at him, "Well no… I'm just positive. Gwen always sees the worst in people."

"I know you'll share your story later but can I ask you one thing?" She nodded. "You were clearly given a very comfortable life before you escaped. So do you miss the life you left behind?"

Kirana thought about Permidia. She thought about Tia and her silk sheets. She thought about warm breakfasts and fresh air. She shrugged and decided to answer honestly, "I think so. I lived a good life."

"Because someone lied to you." Tech looked at the bartender on the other side of the bar. She wore the uniform like the others but didn't seem to have any extensions to make her taller. She was washing a cup and had their back turned to the two of them. With a glance back Tech took off his mask so he could lock eyes with Kirana, "I think it's time you rethink the life you lived because I guarantee you everything you thought was good was cruel. You think you're positive when you're just ignorant. Gwen doesn't see the bad, she sees the truth."

Kirana was offended by what he was telling her, and yet she had nothing to argue with. He was wrong, Permidia wasn't a lie, it was perfect. Kirana lived the perfect life and looked at life from a positive view. And yet, he had a point. All those memories of Tia were exaggerated. Kirana knew Tia would never dance around a hologram with her or give her lessons out of the goodness of her heart. Tech was right, Kirana's life was a lie, and yet somehow that was so hard to fully understand.

All of Kirana's life had been about perfection, and now she could barely find the good within it.

Her silk sheets were probably made by a Hiraethan, maybe even by Gwen. Her food had been grown through blood sweat and tears, all to be made by an emotionless sister Kirana had convinced herself was the greatest person alive.

Tech stood up, "I'll be back in 10 minutes. If Gwen's back before I get here, wait outside."

Kirana was still lost in what he had told her and waited too long to respond. He slipped through the crowd and walked back out the doors.

The bartender finished polishing a glass and grabbed a large bottle of the same yellow liquid Kirana had in her cup. She put it above Kirana's glass, only to see that she hadn't drunk it yet. The bartender was surprised and looked over at her, as if to study her. She walked away cautiously. Kirana figured she would have to drink the liquid if she wanted to blend in.

She lifted the glass to her lips and took a small sip. It wasn't small enough. The taste was overwhelming. Bitter, and hot. She stuck out her tongue and her gasps of disgust were thankfully hidden by the music. It was horrible, truly disgusting. She didn't understand why people would want to drink so much of it but she did understand their need to puke it all over the streets.

The woman came back again with the bottle and held it over the glass again. Kirana waved her away, "I'm taking it slow." She swallowed down the taste.

"You want something else?"

"Do you have water?"

The woman just stared at her, and after a moment pulled her gaze away and looked at the people dancing. Kirana moved side to side to try and get her attention, but it seemed she was being ignored.

For the next few minutes, Kirana just sat there, waiting for Tech or Gwen to return. She felt truly alone in the chaotic room, overwhelmed by music and the horrible drink. Kirana couldn't shake what Tech told her, and as she looked around she saw beyond her need for a connection. The people in the room were dangerous. They were drunk, high, or crazy enough to dance their way through the night. It was funny, the longer she waited for Gwen and Tech the more she wanted it to just be the three of them again. It seemed that connection worked best in small, but valuable quantities.

It was hard to keep track of time, but after five different songs Kirana figured it had been well over ten minutes, and that was when she started to worry. Gwen was still up there with King King and Tech was nowhere to be found. What if King King was hurting Gwen? What if he had stolen her? What if Tech ran into the Wardens? What if the staff was gone?

Her heart raced as panic took over. She nearly screamed at the sound of something being slammed beside her. She looked down to see a screen on the table. Tech, standing right above her, pushed it in front of her, "Who are you?"

Kirana's face was on the screen. It read:

Lost Warden, return for a reward of 5,000 Korts. Alive, unharmed, to the Magistrater's Tower.

Tech swiped it out of her hands, "You're a Warden?"

She wished she could see his eyes, "No. We're not–"

"Wardens are everywhere. Large groups, big guns. I just saw them come down with people in handcuffs. Dozens of them."

She shook her head, "I'm not a Warden!"

"You lied to me!" The bartender came over with a glass of Belic and tried to hand it to him. He took it and slammed it in front of Kirana. "Is this what you wanted? Me to give you the best situation–"

Kirana stood up and stepped away from him, "Tech, we're not Wardens. They're just calling us that."

"Then who are you?"

"I'm a Keeper!" She yelled it out too loudly and put her hands over her mouth as she looked around for who might have heard her, "Tech, please. We have information we can give you–"

"So were you taken by the Wardens or not?"

He was looking for a real answer this time. A full explanation. But Kirana didn't answer. How could she? He would know if she lied. Lying felt wrong, it felt too personal, so she gave up and told the truth, "We lied to you, Tech. I'm sorry, we needed the staff. But we have information. We can still help–"

He glanced behind Kirana as the front doors opened again. The guards looked inside and he quickly sat at the table, "I will give you the stupid glowing staff back if you just leave me alone."

Kirana nodded frantically and sat beside him, "It's a deal."

The bartender came back and put a drink in front of Tech. He held it in front of him, spinning his finger around the rim of the glass. He couldn't remove his mask, but something told Kirana he desperately wanted to drink it. She took a moment to breathe, adjusting her shirt and jacket before turning the chair back around and picking up her glass. Before the bartender came around she spilled her drink onto the floor and looked innocently for a refill. The bartender came back around and filled it up, this time without any suspicion.

Kirana let herself take a breath, they were almost in the clear. Tech would give them staff in return for them to leave and never return. Then the real search could begin, and they would find the next Keeper. She let herself laugh at the way he referred to the staff. *Stupid glowing staff.* She lifted the glass to her lips but stopped suddenly.

Stupid glowing staff.

Glowing staff.

Glowing.

The Keeper was nearby.

She put the glass down, "It was glowing?" He didn't answer. "When did it glow?"

"Stinger said it was dim before."

"Before what?"

"Before I arrived."

Kirana leaned closer and waited for him to turn to her. When he did, she asked the question, "Did you ever touch the staff?"

"No, apparently Stinger hid it in my apartment after you said the Wardens were after it. I checked it out and it's still there, glowing like a beacon for everyone to see."

Tech never touched the staff. It glowed around him. Tech wasn't some setback, he wasn't some obstacle, he wasn't some random person who had been kind enough to help them.

No. He was a Keeper.

Chapter 17

* * *

GWEN

GWEN WISHED KIRANA had come with her. She wasn't comfortable exploring the new world on her own, but she knew arguing against King King would mean losing the Korts, maybe worse. She had a feeling that if they did as they were told and acted the right way, nothing would happen. Gwen wanted Kirana, but she didn't need her there. The Keeper offered her comfort but not physical support, and yet still without her, Gwen felt exposed. She was on her own. Truly, on her own. No family. No friend. No Hiraethan with her. No stranger she learned to trust. Ben E sat in her arms but he was just another android, a little friend who she would have to look after if something went wrong. No, Gwen was completely alone.

Behind the metal doors was a long hallway that seemed bare and matched the alleyways they had been in under the city. She was surprised to find how ominous the hallway felt when compared to allies. The music was strangely muffled from the mirror room, sending vibrations across the walls and floors. It was like a murmur of voices she could not reach. The people who could help her were completely out of reach, no matter how loudly she could scream. There were doors along the walls like the one she had just walked through. She couldn't hear anything inside and stepped a few paces away as she passed them. The hallway was a dead end, but the tall man guided them to a left turn halfway through. From what she could tell they had traveled the length of the room. Gwen looked down each path and realized there were two rooms carved out with the hallways.

He stopped at a chain door against the wall and opened it up. She stayed back and glanced inside. It wasn't a room. It was a hole. A dark hole.

Was he going to throw her down it?

The man glanced over to her as she got ready to run, but he just laughed at her, "It's a lift."

She didn't know what that meant. There was a sound coming from the hole, and suddenly something came down from the top of the doorway down into the hole. It was a room, a small room. It came to a complete stop once the two floors met each other. The tall man then opened the door and walked inside, waiting for her.

"That's quite a reaction. Have you ever seen a lift before?"

She remembered the little room Tech had sent the girl into, and though she did not understand what was before her, she had no choice but to step inside with the man. The man shut the door and pressed one of 5 buttons on the side next to the doorway. Then the room shook and Gwen put her hand on the wall to stabilize herself. She felt the whole place move and realized what this was for. It lifted them. Was King King too sophisticated for stairs?

The Hiraethan could see through the doorway and watched as the hallway disappeared. They moved up and for a while, all she could see was a concrete block moving past them. When she saw a crack as a new doorway appeared, she stretched up to see what was on the next floor. This one had loud music like the one she had been in, only this one seemed more chaotic. Someone from inside actually howled and another person poured their drink on them. Gwen continued to watch until another concrete block came back into view.

She glanced up at the tall man, who looked down at her, not saying a word. The Hiraethan then looked away, deciding not to ask what they were doing. Silence felt powerful in such a noisy world, and as a Hiraethan, she knew how to keep quiet. All of her people had learned to be silent, whether to hide from the Wardens or just stay out of the way. They had learned that noise was the first thing the Wardens noticed in a situation, and with the Hiraethan's flowing movements they continued to not threaten the soldiers. So she used her Hiraethan strength and kept herself still and silent. In response, the man glanced down at her now and again, and she was proud to see him so uncomfortable.

The next few rooms were blocked off by pieces of cloth or planks of wood. Then after that, the doorways were lined with beads she couldn't see through, but as they passed a strange pink light came into the lift as they passed by. And the smell. It smelt like flowers. Which was strange considering she had not seen any such plant in the large city. The next room was blocked off very well with a solid black cloth. She could hear a few noises inside, most sounded like breathing, as if someone was wearing something filtering their voice. But it was still very quiet, and the only light she got to see through a small crack in the doorway was a heavy blue light.

As they passed room after room, she tried to sneak a peek inside. When they got to a certain level the button the Tall man had pressed flickered off and the lift stopped. Unlike the door they had entered to get inside the lift, this door was clean and almost professional, with a gold frame with no holes or windows. It opened on its own, revealing the room before them.

The lift seemed to be in the center of the room. One surrounded by windows and carpeted floors. Pillows and blankets were everywhere, and the only real part of the room was another blocked-off space before them. Gwen stepped out of the lift and looked around. There were many people along each large pillow. They held burning sticks and smoke filled the air as soft music played from a woman on a large stringed instrument. There was a variation of thematically dressed people as there had been everywhere else in the strange city. Those fully dressed lay down in the comfort of the room. They seemed relaxed, or rather, high. The other people in the room were busy but hid it well. They walked in tight clothes, showing off limbs and sections of themselves. They walked as if all eyes were on them and sure enough, those lying down watched. The people around her seemed like a mix of men, women, and those she could not identify, pairing up with the opposite or same gender. No one seemed aggressively sexual, they just seemed amused with each other, staring with drooping eyes and hanging mouths.

Gwen coughed as the wave of smoke hit the back of her throat.

She didn't understand how King King's business worked. Did the people even pay Corts to come here?

The Tall man walked out with her and gestured to a door directly across the room from the lift, "I'll make sure King King is ready for you. You may wait here until I bring you in." He pointed to a set of red chairs beside the door.

Without another word Gwen walked over and sat down, watching as the man opened the door, ducked his head, and walked inside. For a while, Gwen sat there and watched the people around her. She did her best to not breathe in the smoke too deeply and fiddled with Ben E anxiously.

The android let out a shudder, "Please stop." He pushed her finger away.

"Do you know anything about him?" She whispered, trying to prepare for such an important meeting.

"He's six foot three. He uses his right leg more than his left. There is a dent on his right palm. He is very powerful."

"How powerful?"

Ben E's pixelated face went into a frown and he shook his head, "Dangerous."

Gwen took a breath and coughed. She missed Hiraeth so much. She missed breathing in clean air. Gods, it had been so long since she had felt the breeze and not some drifting smoke from ships or smokers. "If anything goes wrong, please contact Tech."

"I will!" Ben E said happily. His joy reminded Gwen of Kirana, and she found herself missing her company. For all of Kirana's inexperience, she was fun to be around. Hiraethans were quiet and tamed, the people of the new world were loud and mysterious, but Kirana was happy and bright. It was so nice to be around, even when her joy meant she was naive and far too trusting.

The Tall man reappeared a few minutes later and held the door open. Two men walked out wearing tight dresses and lengthy heels. They were smoking a long golden stick, red smoke pouring over their ruby lips. One of them glanced at Gwen and mouthed the words, *good luck.*

Gwen let out a breath, stood up, and stepped inside.

As soon as the Tall man shut the door Gwen felt the music and murmur suddenly go silent. The room was sealed from the chaos of the world and the other room. It was clean and crisp. It still had the technology and metal as everything did, but this time it wasn't so crazy and bright. There was no music, just the muffled beats of distant parties. Gwen looked around to see four men in the room like the ones in front of the entrance, only these people were slightly smaller and easier to fit in the room.

Bodyguards.

They stood at all the four corners of the rooms. They stared at a certain spot on the wall, not bothering to even glance over at her. Behind a clean and well-organized desk sat the final person in the room. King King had chocolate black skin, a smooth bald head, and well-styled with make-up around his eyes. Behind his reflective lenses was a golden eyeliner that traveled up around his eyes and moved to the back of his head. One hand rested against the desk, fiddling with a bronze knife. He was strong, both by his general muscular figure and the way he held himself. Even sitting down, his presence loomed large in the room.

"Sit." He gestured to a chair in front of the desk.

Gwen hesitated, not wanting to move away from the door, "I would rather stand."

He didn't seem annoyed by her comment, but there wasn't any sign of a smile on his face. Gwen wondered if his mouth could even move up, it looked like someone had glued it down from years of glares. He wanted her to stay in the room, to be at his level. To help show she wasn't about to run away she put Ben E on the ground next to her. The android looked up at King King and nodded to Gwen with a frown as if to remind her of how powerful he was.

"You want a loan?"

"Yes."

"How much?"

"200 Corts." She kept her head held high. Extra cash wouldn't hurt them, and Kirana didn't seem to argue when she told the Tall man downstairs.

King King put his elbows on the table and leaned closer towards Gwen. "That's rather low. You sure you don't want more?"

Gwen thought about it, but eventually shook her head, "200 Corts is all I need."

"Very responsible." It sounded almost genuine, like he was giving her advice. That made her relax ever so slightly. King King stood up from his chair, "Your friends have the Korts, so let's talk about payment."

Gwen nodded, "Maybe I can pay you later. When I get the Corts back. No work necessary."

He shook his head, "That never works, no one ever pays me back."

"Then what do you want?" Gwen tried not to show her fear, keeping her gaze forward she didn't dare look at the guards around her.

King King grabbed a bottle from somewhere under his desk. He got two cups from the same place and put them on the table. They were small, which made her realize how strong his drink was. She hoped the second glass wasn't for her.

"For one month you work for me, then you are not only free but on my good side."

"What work?"

"This is always in demand." He gestured out of the door to the backroom, "You can start tonight if you want. Even now if you're so daring."

Gwen didn't look back, "I know what women do when they work for you–"

He gave a smileless laugh, "Women? What makes you think I want women? Gender's dead, darling. But those *people* are nothing to spit at. They do fine work in making my customers happy. You don't even have to have sex with anyone, just get them high and watch them believe you did unspeakable things." Gwen leaned back and kept her mouth shut. King King shrugged, "If you have some other skill, by all means, choose another job."

He was a horrible man, acting like what he did was pure and helpful. Sure, the people behind her were probably making a good amount of Corts, but they shouldn't have to do such things just to get some low-cut wages. Gwen knew of a few women like that in Hiraeth. They were rare, and almost always desperate. It was a quick way out of discomfort, and she wished they didn't have to sell themselves like that. Her father had always told her there were other ways to survive, and perhaps he was the reason this hate was so embedded within her. This was the first time Gwen had seen it exploited in such a way, and she hated King King for it.

"What other jobs do you have?"

King King poured the liquid into both cups, filling them up to the rim, "How do you feel about blood?" She didn't answer, and he continued without a response, "I have a few people on my tail. You could go kill them for me. Then you're free."

Gwen didn't say a word. She was shocked about what he was asking her to do, and she missed her opportunity to say yes and run for it.

He went on, "Or you could go work getting me some more business. Five loan customers and 25 drinkers." He picked up the glass of alcohol and looked her up and down, "But it's a pity you won't wear our uniform. I can tell you would draw the finest customers."

Though she couldn't see his eyes, she could feel his gaze across her body. She nodded quickly, "It's a deal. Yes."

He didn't speak for a moment, he just watched her. "That was quick."

Shit. "You found my skill. I'm a good salesman. That's my skill."

"How convenient." He nodded softly, "It's a deal as soon as you tell me what you need the Kort for. Company policy."

Could she tell the truth? She could, she had no allegiance to Stinger, besides, if King King went after her it would be well deserved, "I woman named Stinger stole from me and my friend. We need to pay her back."

King King rolled the glass on the table, watching her, "You and that girl?" He had seen her, how? Gwen glanced at a screen on the desk, and when King King caught her gaze he flipped it over, "I see everything. So tell me, who was the other man?"

Gwen remembered Tech's stories and clenched her jaw. King King waited, and when he found himself in her silence he sighed, "What are they called?"

Gwen didn't know what to say. She realized then she might not have to say anything at all. They had the Korts. One quick turn around and she could try to escape. But they would risk everything. Gwen would risk her life. Was Tech worth that much? Yes, he was. He was the Telematic Hero, he saved the children of his world. He was nearby too, King King would catch him or wait for her to give him up. No, she was a Keeper, she had to start acting like one.

"His name is... Tallon. He came for a quick drink."

King King didn't say a word, he waited a moment, before looking up at one of his bodyguards. Then back to her, "I am starting to not like you, and people I don't like never end up living well here. Lies look terrible coming out your mouth."

Gwen nearly took a step back to the door and caught herself with a sway, "What their name is doesn't matter... I will come back to work for you. Tomorrow–"

"Lies again dear?" He stood up and with a quick lift, downed the first glass. He slammed it down and grabbed the second glass. With a slow tilt, he let the alcohol spill across the desk.

The glass was meant for her, it was the formal agreement to seal the deal.

She started to step back towards the door, "I am not lying. Please."

"Why are you protecting him? Do I know him?"

"I will come back tomorrow–"

"I despise lies. The deal–" He stopped speaking and looked behind Gwen. Everyone turned to see Ben E balancing on a small table by the door. His little hands were stuck in the keyhole, and as he turned from Gwen to King King, he pushed his hands inside and the door unlocked. It had been locked. They had locked her inside.

Before King King could say a word or the bodyguards could react, Gwen lunged to the door, grabbed Ben E, and ran. The Tall man was at the lift, and at the sight of her running he spread out his hands. He looked eager to grab her, moving into a stance that could support her weight.

There had to be another way out.

She sprinted past the tall man to the other side of the long room, looking for something, anything. The people around her smoked their drugs and watched curiously as she turned around looking for a place to escape. There had to be stairs or a ladder or a window or… gods, anything would do.

"I need a door!" She yelled to the people around her and then to Ben E. The android responded by pointing at the wall.

She saw it. A door, neatly hidden against the wall. She would have missed it entirely.

Gwen ran to the door and peeled it open, crushing her fingertips into the edges of the wall. When the door was open she pushed a man and his pillows out of her way. As she went through she tried to slam it shut, but someone's large hand blocked it. Stronger than she was, the bodyguard opened the door and Gwen ducked as they tried to grab her. She turned and saw a staircase. She leaped to it and ran as fast as she could. The Hiraethan needed that knife, she needed something. A weapon of any kind. Just something she could use to defend herself. But there was no time. The guards were right behind her. They were fast too. She continued to turn down the concrete stairs. Her hand on the rail she pulled herself to the next flight as fast as she could. The music was starting to return, but so were the loud crashing footsteps above and behind her. She could see them passing by as she turned.

Suddenly the lights went out. In the darkness, Gwen lost track of the steps and slipped. Falling down a flight of stairs she rolled and landed on her face. She got back up, cheek thumbing with pain and arm twisted she lunged forward again. The lights were flickering on and off, and she realized it might be some sort of silent alarm. That, or they were trying to slow her down. It was working.

When she got to the bottom of the stairs she jumped down the steps right into the door. She twisted the door knob and ran. She was in the hallway from before, the one between the rooms. She knew where to go.

Gwen ran as fast as she could down the hall, pumping her arms and holding onto Ben E for dear life. She could see the door at the end of the hallway, but the bodyguards were right behind her. She pushed herself forward as fast as her body would let her go. She felt tears form in her eyes as she prayed to the gods to let her run faster. The door was just up ahead. She could hear the Guards behind her. If she couldn't get the door open they would catch her. If she didn't open the door fast enough she would be trapped.

"Kirana!" She screamed down the hall towards the door.

She threw herself at the door and twisted the door knob. But it wouldn't twist. The door was locked. She pulled it back and forth, shaking the frame before pounding on the door.

"Help!"

Someone grabbed her hair and threw her to the ground. She hit the concrete head-first. Pain filled her skull as they grabbed her ankle. Ben E rolled out of her hands and hit the wall. A guard appeared in front of her and kicked the android across the hallway. Gwen watched as his gears spilled across the floor as he lay motionless.

"Ben E!"

They pulled her away from the door.

"Someone help me!"

They dragged her along the floor down the hallway.

"Kirana!"

She screamed as hard as she could. Scraping her hands on the floor in a last attempt to get away. Gwen kicked and screamed, but she was trapped. They were going to take her back. King King would keep her in his whore house. His little speech about the good work his people were doing was a lie. Was that her fate? Working to pay off an unpayable debt? Working for others' pleasure? For King King's pleasure...

"Help me!" She cried one last time as they turned into the next hallway.

They were going to the lift.

She tried to grab onto the corner. Her fingers scraped the sides of the wall and she managed to grab onto the edge. But a spare bodyguard came over and kicked her fingers against the wall. She screamed and let go as a guard grabbed the back of her hair. He pulled her up and wrapped his hand around her throat.

"Hey!" Gwen knew that voice. "Put her down!"

It was Kirana, Tech right behind her with his gun drawn.

Ben E had called them.

The man holding Gwen twisted her around with him so he could see Kirana. She was standing at the end of the hallway, a metal pole in hand. She was ready to fight them, even without a gun.

The guards charged for them.

Gwen counted how many guards there were. Five including the one holding her. The four remaining split up into pairs to run at Tech and Kirana. Tech took the first one out quickly and ran forward through the hall. The other guard had a gun, but Tech was faster. He shot them down as Kirana faced her own problems. She managed to swing at the guard to get him to go back, but with a second attempt to hit him, he caught the pole and sent a fist to her head. She flew to the wall and coated the concrete in blood.

But that was all Gwen got to see because the man holding her suddenly started to walk her into the lift.

She kicked and tried to pull away, "Kirana!" She screamed.

The bodyguard got her inside and shut the door. He grasped Gwen's neck and pinned her against the wall with a single hand. Suddenly she couldn't breathe. Again she tried to hit or kick him, but nothing was working. Even when he took his time to hold the door shut she couldn't do anything to get him off her. Kirana came to the door and tried to pull it open.

"Let her go!" The guard pressed the buttons by the door and the top one lit up. Kirana desperately tried to pull the door open, but the lift was going up. "Gwen!" Eventually, the man let go of the door and pointed a gun at Kirana. Without any other option, she dove away a series of bullets that kept both her and Tech out of view. When the guard stopped shooting the lift had moved up too far up for Kirana or Tech to fit through.

"S... St..." Gwen tried to tell her about the stairs, trying to find a way to say it without using air. "Stair... air..." She couldn't.

She wasted her breath. Her lungs became flat. Uselessly flapping up and down. Her heartbeat rose and all instincts told her to breathe, to fight, to survive. She wiggled around, finding a few pockets of air and staying conscious as the lift stopped at the next door. Gwen needed a way to slow them down. She reached out her leg and kicked the panel with the buttons. She kicked and kicked until each one lit up.

The bodyguard grabbed her leg and threw her across the room to the other wall. Gwen fell to the ground and gulped in the glorious filthy air. Tears fell down her face in hot streaks as she sobbed thankful cries of life. She looked up at the man. He didn't grab her again. He just stared. It was all he needed to do to keep her from running.

When they got to the next floor the lift stopped thanks to Gwen pressing the buttons. But nothing happened. Gwen looked around for Kirana, for Tech. But no one came. Then they moved further up. And on the next floor, the same thing happened again. The bodyguard was annoyed now. He glared down at Gwen and pressed the top button again and again in hopes of speeding up the journey. No one came to the lift, and it moved up.

When the elevator stopped the third time the bodyguard took a deep breath through his nostrils to calm himself down. Gwen knew one more stop and he might just kill her.

She needed Kirana to be at the next level. She prayed to the god who had found her. She prayed for the Keeper to be at the next level. But no matter how hard she hoped, there was only so much luck the world could offer her. When the lift stopped again no god was waiting for her, it was just the sheet separating them from a noisy music-filled room.

Gwen looked up at the man in the hope of finding some sense of mercy, but he didn't even look at her. She didn't know whether to beg or stay silent and, in the end, she was too afraid to do anything but stay still and breathe. She was preparing herself for the worst, and the worst came. The man grabbed Gwen by her jacket and pushed her against the wall. She knocked her head against the metal and suddenly her vision spun. She realized how many hits she was taking to her head. Too many.

But her pain was met with the grace of the gods. Her prayers were answered. With a sharp slide of metal, the cloth peeled to the side and Tech appeared before the guard, gun raised. A shot ran through the lift and both she and the guard fell to the ground. The room shook with their fall as Kirana came rushing into the room.

She dropped to Gwen's side, "Gwen!" Kirana tried to find a place to hold her. Gwen offered her hand and she took it, pulling her up. When they got out, Gwen expected them to make a run for it, but instead, Kirana hugged her. "I'm so sorry."

Kirana held her so tightly Gwen couldn't slip away. Nor did she want to. The hug felt so loving, so… familiar. The feel of Kirana's jacket, the mere smell of it, was Hiraethan. It was Gideon's jacket. Through the chaos, Gwen hadn't seen that Kirana was still wearing her father's jacket. She held the god tighter and tried to pretend it was him, that he had protected her once again. That was a nice thought, and however much she was grateful for Kirana, she wished more than anything that he was the one holding her.

Kirana pulled away and guided her through the room, "Tech has the staff. We need to run."

"I messed up–"

Tech pushed Gwen further into the room, not caring about her injuries, "We need to *run.*" She looked down and saw Ben E in his arms.

"He saved my life"

He shook his head and continued down the steps, "It doesn't matter." That was when Gwen realized something had changed. He was angry, not at King King or the guards, but at the Keepers. Gwen looked over to Kirana, who in response let out a breath and decided against explaining.

The three of them moved towards the stairs, Kirana supporting Gwen as she tried to get herself back together. They hurried down the steps as the lights continued to flash. For now, there was no one to stop them as they made their escape. Perhaps King King underestimated Gwen's ability to take down four guards. Rightfully so, but he forgot to take in mind she had backup. When they made it to the bottom level Kirana let go of Gwen and the three of them sprinted for the door.

When they got to it Kirana twisted the handle. It was still locked.

Tech pushed her away and turned his bag to face him, grabbing something from inside. It looked like some sort of complicated tool, one with a technological element Gwen had never seen before. A trigger rested against the tube and on Tech's finger, and when he pressed down fire shot out of it. He started burning the side doorknob. Gwen and Kirana covered their eyes as the metal melted against the heat until finally he jumped up and kicked the door open. Just then, Gwen saw the bodyguards coming for them, running down the hallway at top speed.

King King had caught on.

The three of them ran into the large glass room. A few people looked over, but no one paid enough attention. Other than for the workers. They spotted them and started moving towards them.

"Move!" Tech said, glancing back.

The entrance was opening for a new set of guests, thank the gods, and the three of them sprinted past both the new people and the guards outside. Tech now led them away, holding his android for dear life. Kirana tried to help Gwen the best she could, but it was up to herself to stay upright and keep moving. Even as she felt faint or completely dizzy, she kept herself running. She was getting better, or at least she would once they stopped running. Kirana glanced back to see who was following them, but Gwen didn't let herself for fear of tripping or falling behind.

The group dodged people in the crowd and kept running. Faster and faster. Tech led them down multiple corners until they were back on a recognizable street. Gwen could see Tech's place up ahead and they all ran faster towards it. When they reached his door he swung it open and held it for the Keepers. When they all got inside he slammed the door shut and ran over to his window. He ducked down and looked around the street.

"Gwen–" Kirana was trying to whisper something, but was too out of breath. She held a stitch on her side, "Tech... Tech... He–" She swallowed hard.

Gwen put her hand on her shoulder, "Breathe."

Kirana did, and there was a moment when they all took a second to calm down. When the second was over, Kirana grabbed Gwen's shoulders and forced them to meet eye to eye.

"Tech... is... the Keeper."

Gwen looked over quickly, "What? How do you–"

"He knew... He said it... glowing."

The staff was glowing?

That was impossible. There was no way the man they had been following around all day could be the same man they were looking for. And yet, he was the only person willing to help them. He was the Telematic Hero, the savior of his world and little children. If Tech was the Keeper it would be a very ideal situation for the Keepers. Everyone was together and ready to move on.

But there was one problem.

Tech turned to them and held the gun up to Kirana's head, "Get out."

He didn't want them there.

Chapter 18

* * *

KIRANA

KIRANA KNEW IT would be easy to get Tech to touch the staff. Forceful or not. All she needed to do was throw it at him, or make him pick it up. Something small and effortless. But once she did that, the problem would be getting him to sit down and talk.

Tech moved his gun from Gwen to Kirana before grunting and putting it away. He swung his bag to face him and put the damaged Ben E inside. He pointed to the other side of the room, "Your staff is under the floor panel. Get it and get out."

Kirana looked over at Gwen and ran past Tech to where he had pointed. She clawed at the floor panels until one of them came loose. Around her, Tech walked from place to place grabbing items and boxes and pushing them into his bag. Kirana pulled out panel after panel until a bright blue light was revealed. Her staff was tucked with the cracks of the floors, but it was such a glorious sight to see it again. She pulled it out and looked at Tech as he moved to his desk by Gwen.

Gwen glanced at her, wondering what she was planning, but Kirana couldn't communicate her ideas through a look, so she turned back to Tech.

"Now go!" He yelled at them, again glancing outside through the window. "King King will be after me again, and this time he won't stop. Then I guess the Wardens will be here too considering you're one of them."

"Tech–"

"Leave!"

Kirana stepped forward, "Why don't we–"

"Get out or–"

Kirana threw the staff at him. It wasn't a hard throw. It was light enough for him to catch. But instead, Tech ducked and the staff crashed behind him.

"Get out!"

Gwen pointed at the window, "They're here!"

Tech ran over and looked out the window. Kirana could see the guards running beside other people. They were all rushing down from the other platform across the large gap, just starting to walk on the bridge over. Tech grabbed his bag and pushed everything he could inside, slowly moving towards the door.

Kirana ran past Tech to grab the staff, but when she turned around he was at the door.

"Don't follow me!" He slammed the door behind him.

Gwen gestured to him, "What happened?"

"He thinks we're Wardens." Kirana swung the door open, "We can't let him get away."

The two of them sprinted out the door and leaped down the stairs. Quickly realizing Kirana still had the metal pole, she put the weapon in Gwen's hand. She spun the staff in her hand and the two of them ran after Tech. The group of King King's guards and other killers were right on their heels, and as Kirana looked back she saw them notice the three of them running and started to charge. Tech turned up ahead down a new street, but when Gwen and Kirana arrived at the corner they realized it was not a street at all. It was a crack between two houses barely a foot wide. Beyond it, the back alleyways.

Gwen didn't hesitate for a second; turning to her side she moved through at top speed. Kirana was next, holding the staff in her left hand so it was facing the enemy. She squeezed in and tried not to panic about how narrow the gap was. She turned her head so she could see the street they had come from. Just as her entire body was inside the crack she heard a loud noise. A bang, and something whizzing through the air. Suddenly she saw a long blue streak of light hit just beside her head at a strange angle. A long spike bullet stuck out from the wall.

Kirana quickly moved through faster. They were aiming from the other side of the large drop, but it would be a clear shot if they got to her fast enough. She couldn't see Gwen up ahead and there wasn't enough room to turn her head. Kirana was a barrier for her, even if that strange spike hit her the enemy couldn't reach Gwen.

"Tech! Stop!" Gwen yelled ahead.

Kirana could hear her footsteps quicken, and it was clear she had made it through to the other side. Which meant Kirana was almost through as well. As she slid against the wall with her hand stretched out she finally found the edge. She pulled herself through just as she saw the enemy arrive. A few raised their weapons and she dove out of the narrow space to the right. The blue line the spike made traveled past her head and onto the wall of the alleyway.

The space they were in was larger than the ones before, and this time there was barely any trash left on the side. She never thought she would long for garbage to return, but they needed cover. King King was right behind them with his fast weapons, and they would be out in the open, a clear target.

Kirana ran after the others down the larger alley. Without the Kirana, Gwen seemed to move faster. Faster than Tech. Her steps were so well used she might as well have been running on air. She ran right next to him. She talked to him, saying something Kirana couldn't hear, especially over what was happening behind her.

There was a loud explosion, and when Kirana looked behind her all she could see was smoke. There were screams in the distance, and more explosions suddenly went off in a rhythm.

King King *really* wanted them dead. But why? All they did was steal a few Korts. He had been more tactical when he forced Tech to return and pay his debt.

There was a turn up ahead, one that would give them all cover. But they were all still far from it. Tech and Gwen continued to talk, and he eventually turned and pushed her to the wall. With a stumble and eventually a fall, Tech was able to slow her down and move ahead. Kirana sprinted as hard as she could and managed to catch up to her.

"He won't listen!" Gwen rubbed her shoulder and pushed Kirana forward so they wouldn't stop running.

"Just–"

There was one last explosion and Kirana and Gwen looked back. Smoke was everywhere as debris and dust filled the air. Kirana saw figures, ones heading straight for them. Kirana looked forward again. Tech turned the corner. They were getting closer. The enemy wouldn't be able to see them within a few seconds, and that might have been all they needed to get to cover.

"Kirana!" Gwen's voice scratched Kirana's very soul. She had to slow down to look, but when she did she almost stopped running entirely.

It wasn't King King's men.

No.

It was the Wardens.

More than ten of them, and their weapons were raised.

"Go! Go!" Kirana screamed. Gwen ran ahead and turned quickly as Kirana slipped and stumbled until she managed to sprint to cover. Just then Kirana heard the sound of gunfire. As she sprinted forward the spikes landed on the wall, sticking into the concrete.

The Hiraethan gave out a panicked gasp as they continued to run.

"What are those things?" Kirana sucked in breaths, trying anything to get rid of the stitch in her side. It was not the time to be a bad runner.

"They're Spikers." Gwen yelled back, "Wardens use them to slow down the people they want to catch."

"Those are different from the ones in Hiraeth. They have spikes–"

"Different guns for different ways to hurt someone!"

Kirana shook her head quickly, "Hurt? They want us alive!" Was that better or worse than being hunted and killed?

She looked ahead to where Tech was. He was ready to turn again, but this time he had stopped. Kirana and Gwen were able to catch up and stopped next to him by the wall.

"Tech, we need you to listen to us–"

She followed his gaze to the next turn. The corner was blocked. A chain fencing with warning signs signed by the Wardens. It was locked with a heavy chain. The lock was on the other side of the gate.

There was no way out.

"We'll fight them off." Kirana spun the staff around in hand, "Just get that open and run."

Tech looked at her, still panicked but now surprised.

Gwen ran up to him and put out her hand, "Give me your gun."

He pulled it behind him, "No–"

"Tech!" She kept her hand out, "None of us want to die here. We lied to you because of how important the staff is. It was wrong. You're a good man and we shouldn't have used you like that, but we need to survive this. And so do you."

Tech looked from the fence to Gwen, and slammed the gun into her hand.

Gwen gestured to the fence violently, "Hurry!"

He knelt down and took out a tool from his bag, frantic but finding the strength to stay focused. Kirana and Gwen moved back down to the corner. They just needed to surprise the Wardens and get the guns out of their hands. Anything to buy Tech some time.

"Remember." Kirana told Gwen, "They want to slow us down, not kill us."

Gwen had the gun up and ready to fight as they stayed close to the wall, hearing the Wardens get closer. "I never said the spikes couldn't kill you. It is just normally used to slow someone down before they kill you."

Kirana took a stuttered breath, "Then stand back. Shoot from a distance."

Gwen moved back away from her and Kirana got ready to take the first hit. She held the staff up and got ready to drop it down and shatter a Warden helmet.

The footsteps got louder, until the first Warden showed himself. He was rounding the corner and with one hard swing Kirana pushed the staff's crystal to his helmet. With a crack it bounced off the screen and sent Kirana back down the alley. The Warden fell as the others came. That was when Gwen came into the fight. She had stepped away from the wall to get a clear shot, but she was messy. The bullets flew in all directions rapidly, none of them finding a body.

A Warden charged at Kirana with his gun. The back of his gun. She tried swinging her staff at them but he dogged her unbalanced attack and pushed the gun to the side of her face. Her head flew back and she retreated. But the Warden kept on her. He hit her side, a blow that made her crumble onto the wall. When he lunged at her she pushed off the wall and changed her grip on the staff. She forced the end of the staff into the Warden, piercing him between his plates of armor. As he fell she ripped the staff out of his stomach, but one kill took too long. Someone grabbed her from behind by her hair and threw her to the ground. There was a gunshot above her and she was able to stumble back to her feet as a body dropped in front of her. Grabbing the staff, Kirana ran for Gwen. But the Wardens outnumbered them. Kirana had miscounted, there were more than ten Wardens, there were fifteen, maybe more.

Gwen was their threat with the gun, so she was their target. As she shot at each soldier one Warden managed to slip behind her. Kirana tried to scream out for Gwen to run, but her voice came too late. She watched as he hit his gun to the back of Gwen's head. She was already too injured by King King. She gave in and crumbled to the floor.

Kirana tried to run to her, but she couldn't get there. Something hit her. Not a bullet, too light. Something smaller. Lighter. It stuck to her. Before she could reach for the item it released an explosion of energy. It felt like fire spreading across her body that shook her very bones. She let out a scream and collapsed to the floor, trembling until the fire stopped.

Kirana's body trembled as she tried to force herself to crawl. Two Wardens grabbed her and pulled her up. One hit her in the face and swung their boot into her stomach. They let her go and she fell back to the wall. She couldn't hold herself. She fell back to the floor on all fours.

She spat out blood and tried to breathe.

The staff.

She had dropped the staff.

The Warden had it. She could see them standing with it, just looking at it. She caressed the wood with a gloved hand.

Gwen was awake. Kirana could see her eyes. She was helpless. The Warden closest to Kirana knelt in front of her. She didn't touch Kirana, just tilted her head to study her face. Was she admiring the blood she had splattered across the Keeper's face? Kirana was a blank canvas from their artwork.

She put her hand to the side of her helmet. "We've captured the Keepers." Another Warden came over and suddenly kicked her side, jabbing their foot between her ribs. She fell back to the ground with a painful gasp. She couldn't fight them, no one could escape. The Wardens started to relax and move around as two of them held a gun to Kirana's head. One of them was holding onto the staff. She needed it. She needed a gun. She needed a miracle.

Tech.

She needed a god.

There was suddenly a parade of noises. Gunfire shot through the air and hit the Wardens before her. Their bodies fell. So did their guns. So did the staff.

Kirana forced her body to her knees and smiled at Tech, their teammate, their savior, but as he ran towards her his gun was not pointed at the Wardens. No, he was aiming for Kirana. Tech ran to her and put his gun to her head. He didn't even look at her, he just held the gun to her skull and stared at the remaining Wardens.

There were only ten left. They all stood in the same manner. Frozen in shock. Kirana assumed they planned for everything, but how could they have prepared themselves for this? Another person was ready to kill their gods.

"Bring her to me." He had his mask on, his voice robotic once again.

The Wardens had their guns to his head. No one shot.

One of them stepped forward, "Walk away."

"I can't do that."

The Warden lowered his weapon. No other soldiers followed his lead, they stayed where they were, like statues, or silent bombs. "These people are none of your concern. You are the one we see in the pipes, are you not? The hero who saves children? These are no children. You have no place here. Put down your gun and you can walk away."

Kirana looked up to Tech to beg him to help them, to stay. If he dropped his weapon, the Wardens would take her and Gwen to the Magistrater and gods know where else. He had no way of knowing the dangers ahead of them, and he had no reason to save them. But the Wardens were right about one thing, he was a hero. If only he knew how much he was destined to change, how powerful he could become. A symbol and a true Telematic hero not just for children but for his entire world.

Maybe he did know, deep down, the fate the two Keepers sealed for him.

He shook his head, "I can't do that."

Tech stepped forward with them. Gun still on Kirana, he reached down for the staff. As he gripped the wood Kirana could see him try to bring it up slowly. But he couldn't.

There was an explosion of light as a gust of energy swept through the air. Kirana watched as the Wardens before her were flung back to the wall. They hit the concrete with enough force to keep them motionless on the ground. Gwen lifted her head and watched with the Kirana as Tech's body was lifted. He floated above the world around him, surrounded by blue light and particles. It was gorgeous, as if the seas and the sky had come alive as one. When the light faded he dropped back down to the ground. He landed on his feet but stumbled back and fell to his knees. The staff rolled away from him, no longer glowing its bright blue.

Would he trust the Keepers now?

Kirana forced herself up, pushing past every aching part of her body she stumbled forward into a run and got to Gwen's side. The Wardens were getting up. She grabbed Gwen's gun and searched for a way to use it. A trigger, there was a trigger. A way to shoot it. A Warden moved up, gun raised. Kirana put her finger on a small lever and pulled it. A bullet shot out and her body shook by the force of it. She widened her stance and pulled the trigger until she finally succeeded and the Warden stayed down. She shot frantically at all of the soldiers before grabbing Gwen by the arm and forcing her to stand. Gwen obeyed and, like Kirana, made herself ignore pain altogether. Without any help from the Keepers, Tech stood up and ran for the fence. He ran faster than the both of them and Kirana prayed he wouldn't leave them like that. She grabbed the staff off the ground and pushed her body further. The Wardens were alive, she was not a good shot, but now they were injured. As the three of them ran she heard the ring of gunshots. Pops of concrete flew around her as the bleeding soldiers tried to aim with pain. They couldn't. They didn't have the time. Kirana rounded the corner and kept going. They all did. All three of them ran out of the alley.

Sprinting together as the Keepers.

Chapter 19

GWEN

GWEN NEEDED A break from all the running. From all the fighting. She was tired of being out of breath and bruised. She was fed up with all the knocks to her head. But they were still running. If they stopped running they would be killed. Gwen would choose pain over death any day. With blood along her face and her hand wrapped around her side, she ran forward until they made it back out onto the street.

Gwen could see King King's men running around like lost puppies. The Wardens must have scared them away. When Tech saw them he ran in the other direction. The Keepers followed him without a second thought. This next street was not as busy, and there was no gap in the center of the walkway. The buildings, smaller than she had seen before, were all shops. Horrible smells carried from the doors, poisoning her panting breaths. People with blankets over their heads watched them closely, their eyes unblinking and pupils narrow.

Tech started up a line of stairs along the building and they followed. Up and up they went until Tech started to slow into a jog, then a walk. Gwen was grateful, she needed to catch her breath. Tech kept them walking up the stairs before turn-ing onto a new level. The platform was in between the edge of a round building making a small O shape. The only way to get there was up or down the one set of stairs. The building looked abandoned. The windows were smashed and the place seemed soundless. For the first time, they had arrived in a quiet spot in the city, ominous, but quiet. Up ahead there was a small break between the building creating an alley. There was a wall at the back, making it more of a cave than a room. Large metal boxes gave way to horrible smells, and Gwen realized that in the new world, peaceful places were just abandoned dumps.

Tech was the first one to go into the little cave. He walked to the back of the room and looked around each box. As he did, Kirana went past him to the back wall and slid down to the ground. Gwen stayed standing at the entrance. Gods, she wanted to sleep. To close her eyes and let her injured body rest. It would be somewhat safe to do it now. But first, there was one last problem to deal with.

Tech.

He noticed her lingering at the front, and even as he searched the room twice over he said nothing. When his search was complete he slumped down on the side wall, taking off his bag and settling. Gwen gave in and walked to the opposite side. When she dropped to the ground her body shifted into a slush, and she felt herself through both suffering and satisfaction. But if she was alive, she would be alright. Her main injury was a knock to her head. She would need medical help, or at least a day to rest. She wondered if they would be lucky enough to have either. Other than her head she was simply weak. A few bruises here and there but nothing serious. A Warden had kicked her in her stomach, and she now felt the pain they left with her. Gods, it was horrible. It was like they were having fun. She didn't doubt that idea. Her father used to call them satists, as most Hiraethans did.

Gwen looked up at Tech and saw he wasn't resting at all. He was staring at the staff. He was probably thinking through what just happened. Gwen couldn't tell what he was going to do, and the idea that his emotions would lead him to do something crazy scared her. He wasn't injured in any way. Maybe a bit out of breath, but he was fine. They had taken the beating for him, and perhaps that was the only reason he was still there.

Tech looked over at Kirana, "Who are you?"

Kirana looked horrible. Blood along her face, forehead sweating against her flush complecture, and yet she still looked up at him, and spoke with as much power as she could master, "Do you know who the Keepers are?"

He took a second to think, eyes moving to the side as if he was searching through old memories. It was a good sign, it meant that he was ready to listen and give thought to what they wanted to tell him.

"The gods?"

Gwen stood up straight to try and make herself seem more godly herself, "You would have heard legends, or people to worship. Stories like the Keeper's staff." She waited for his reaction, and though he took time to think he eventually just shook his head. "Or the Keeper's Chambers?"

Tech nodded, "I know that one. The library." He took a second to think, and when he was done his mood shifted. He glared at Kirana, "What is going on?"

"They're like warriors. People who protected everyone. Like a ruler."

"Like the Magistrater?" There was disgust in his voice.

Gwen cut in, "No. Not a dictator. They were protectors of the people. They were rulers of... of different dimensions."

Tech didn't say a word. He looked from person to person, before sliding his bag in front of him and taking out gears, tools, and the little Ben E. Tech shook his head, "I'm so stupid."

"You're not–"

"I've heard of you guys. Cultists who try to recruit people by getting them high and sending them on some spiritual journey."

"We're telling the truth, Tech." Kirana glanced at Gwen, trying to figure out what to do or say. "I know we lied before and I am so sorry, but we really needed the staff so we could find the next Keeper. Which happened to be you." She gave out a laugh that turned into a cough.

Tech started to open Ben E's panels and pull out wires, reworking and fixing what the guards had done to him. Tech wasn't interested in anything the Keepers were telling him. Gwen suspected any history lesson would just be seen as obsessive cultish behavior. How could they convince him that he was a god? How could they convince anyone? It was such a strange story, with dimensions and a magical staff, but why did Gwen believe it so easily?

She knew that answer.

Gwen pushed off the wall and walked over to Tech, she sat down in front of him but he didn't look up. "I am from a world called Hiraeth. It's different from this one. For a start, there is only one city. And the rest of the world is just towns, farms, and grassy hills. Kirana is from a world completely different from both of ours. Permidia. Where no matter who you are, you live the perfect life."

He waved in her face, "I'm not listening to you." He grabbed a small tool and used it to scrape away a piece of small metal within Ben E's gears.

"I felt it too."

He stayed still for a moment, before looking up.

Gwen mimed the staff in her hand, "It felt like… a light was set off inside me. A glow. The staff was a switch and I was the bulb. It activated something within me. Something that was always there. Always waiting."

Tech clenched his jaw, "What drugs did you give me?"

She locked eyes with him, "You know that wasn't drugs."

"Gods aren't real." He let out a laugh and grabbed a small wire beside him, "And if they were I'm not one of them. And neither are you two. I mean, shit, you're just two people who can barely shoot a gun" He glared up at her, "And you're liars"

Gwen nodded, "I shouldn't have lied. I thought it would be for the best. We just really needed the staff back." When Tech didn't acknowledge any of her words, Gwen stood up and walked to her side of the wall.

Kirana spoke again, "In Permidia no one wants to connect. And you'd be surprised how little conflict there is because of that, but there is also no love." She took a deep breath, swallowing again. It looked like she was in pain.

"But you do?"

All Kirana did was nod, and Gwen decided to continue for her, "She was the only one who wanted human connection. She's like us. And when she found the staff, it took her to Hiraeth, where she found me. I am a Keeper, she is as well. Growing up I learned all about the legends and the history of my world so I know a lot about them. Kirana is our leader, the owner of the Keeper's staff, and we are part of her team."

Tech shook his head, "Please stop talking to me. I just need to fix my android."

"Please Tech, we wouldn't–" She was going to say; we would lie to you. But that was too soon.

Tech shook his head, perhaps knowing what she would have said, "And all for what? So you could recruit me into your cult?"

"Not a cult." Gwen pointed at the staff, "We can show you. Tomorrow. We can take you to another dimension."

He put down his tool and placed his hands on his knees, "Take me there right now."

Gwen looked over at the very injured Kirana, "It takes a lot of effort to travel–"

"Do it. Right now, or I leave."

Gwen shook her head and tried to sound less cultish, "There are four dimensions, we can take you to any of them tomorrow."

"Telematic is just one of–"

"Telematic?" Kirana leaned forward, "Is that the world's name?"

Metis grabbed his bag and Ben E, and walked out of the alley.

Gwen stood up with a grunt, "What about the Wardens?" He stopped walking. She walked closer, "Why would they come after us if we were nothing? Why would they not kill us? Because they need us alive! Those... those *monsters* want us! They have every power in every world, but they want us. They *need* us."

He glared back, "Then why are you doing this?"

"What?"

"If you're the gods, then why are you going through all this trouble? What do you want from me?"

She knew what he was asking, "I am tired of not being able to do anything to help my people. They die just as much as yours. Maybe even more. Wardens kill everyone, capture everyone, and hurt *everyone*. If there is some hope that I can be some great savior, then I'll take it, because no one else can help them but the Keepers. I followed Kirana to Telematic. To you." She looked him dead in the eyes, "Tell me you don't think that the kids you saved need warriors to protect them. To help them live their best life. Off the streets."

This hit him, more than anything they had said. If she had proven their value with the Wardens then now she had just proven their cause.

He squinted down at her, "You want to help your people?"

"That's all I have ever wanted." She gestured back to Kirana, "We don't have a lot of proof right now, I understand that. But clearly drugs can't make you float just by touching wood and clearly we are different. Kirana was sheltered her whole, perfect life. Disconnected. I was kept at gunpoint, scared for my family and my people. You can see that, I know you can. We can take you to another world. Tomorrow."

Tech had something to say, she could tell. But something was stopping him. He winced but eventually made himself speak to her, "I am not a god. Okay. I am not some... dimensional protector."

She sighed. Her breath was mixed with both relief and disappointment. He seemed to believe them, but not himself. She understood that. "What about the power you felt? The staff chose you. And... well from what I have seen I think it's right. I saw what you did for that kid. I know for some reason, you don't want to be the hero. But maybe, just maybe you are. Maybe you're the only hero who can save your world."

Tech ignored her words, "If I join your little cult, what happens next?"

"You come with us to the next dimension. There we find the last Keeper. Then after that, we make a plan to overthrow the Magistrater."

"What!" He laughed, his voice echoing. He put a hand over his mouth and bit down his voice, "She can't be overthrown. She has an army."

"Then we'll just have to make one ourselves." He rolled his eyes, but she wasn't joking, "I'm serious. Our efforts could ripple across all worlds. Hiraeth is already building an army. Rebellions are everywhere. We just need to unite all the dimensions. Your world, my world, and the one we will go to next."

"So what is the plan?"

She sighed, "We talk, I tell you and Kirana everything I know about the Keepers, then we make a real plan, a very specific plan, and we unite the team of gods, then we unite our worlds."

He stared at her for a moment, and in that moment she could see him rethink a thousand things. To help him she shook her head quickly and said, "You don't have to choose to stay with us. Even if you believe us this is still your choice. But for now, at least let us show you the possibilities."

Still, Tech did not respond. He stood there, one hand on his hip and the other around Ben E, thinking. Gwen decided to leave him there and not pressure him with information or more begging. Gwen walked back to the wall and settled near one of the metal boxes. She nuzzled by its side and rested her head away from the aching spots she would deal with tomorrow. If Tech didn't join them then so be it, there was nothing else she could do or say that would sway him. Right now she just wanted sleep and the time to heal.

For a few minutes, she stared at where Tech had been and waited for a sign of him returning there. Whether he had left entirely or was standing at the entrance was beyond her, and she was too tired to take the time to watch him. More time went by and soon she gave up waiting for him. She just slept. Surprisingly, she did, in fact, sleep.

When she woke up it was hard to tell how long she had been out for, and when she looked up she saw nothing but concrete above her. There was no way to tell where the sun was. She looked over to Kirana and saw the Keeper slumped down on the ground, cheek to the floor, and hand wrapped around her stomach. Gwen felt herself go cold at the sight of her father's jacket. It looked dirty, with blood against its side. She wanted to take it back, to keep it safe, to have it close. But the Keeper needed it. Gwen tried to pretend it was her father watching over Kirana, not because he was dead, but because he was present with her. He was holding Kirana together, keeping her safe. Gwen couldn't deny her jealousy. She wanted him with her.

Gwen looked to where Tech had been and there, sitting and staring at her, was Tech. He came back for them. Did that mean he trusted them? Maybe. Gwen glanced back at Kirana and decided the Keeper would need her sleep. She pushed herself up and walked over to Tech, slumped down next to him.

He seemed surprised by this but said nothing.

Gwen gave him a small nudge to his side, "What's your name?"

He raised an eyebrow, "You know my name."

"Tech's a nickname."

"We don't use names here. Just nicknames. You get named by your friends." He pointed to her face, "But that's not the case where you two come from, is it? *Gwen.* Is that a… Herathan name?"

"Hiraethan." Gwen corrected, "So you don't have a name?"

He looked away, before glancing over to Kirana. Then to the staff. He turned back to Gwen and lowered his voice, "Are we really going to do anything for our people? I mean, you can't even shoot a gun."

"We are the only people who can go from world to world. Unless each dimension works together how could we defeat the Magistrater?"

"But it seems impossible." He shook his head, thinking to himself more than speaking aloud, "I don't want to give my loyalty if you're not going to do anything with it."

"We will. We need you." She looked down at the gun in his hand and gestured to it, "I've never used a gun before. I mean, I've seen them being used, but I never actually held one. I know nothing about fighting and war, but I know that we have to do… something."

"Starting with gathering the team."

She nodded and locked eyes with him, "You can trust us."

"I have known you for less than a day."

"How about this." Gwen stood up straight, "If we're right, if we're really the Keepers, then think of what you can do for those kids." He looked away and she sighed, "We targeted your weakness, Tech. But I was thinking about my people. They mean everything to me, but I want those kids to be safe. The Magistrater takes and takes. She steals your technology and sends it to Permidia." Gwen pointed at Kirana, "She sends food from Hiraeth. She sends those kids to work somewhere, for her system."

"Why?"

"I don't know." Gwen answered, honestly, "But we're the only people who can figure this all out, and who can change it."

Tech looked over to her, his eyes soft, "Okay." He crossed his arms and leaned further back on the wall. "Metis."

She squinted at him, and laughed, "That's your name?" He glared at her and she swallowed a second laugh, "I'm sorry. I'm sorry it's a nice name."

"Humor doesn't suit you." He shrugged, "No one else knows that name."

"Well, your parents must know, right? I figure your friends give you nicknames and your family gives you–" He looked over at her, not saying a word. She looked away, "Thank you, Metis. I promise we won't take your loyalty for granted."

He sighed and slid down onto his side, "We'll see. Tomorrow."

Gwen stood up without another word and went back to her little corner. She glanced over a Kirana at the wall. Something about her sleeping felt familiar, and she realized about that time last night she had just found the Keeper. Gwen didn't understand how it could feel so long ago.

She couldn't help but miss her home. Being surrounded by people. Helping the kids and Gaia and in return being cared for by her father. Her life wasn't necessarily bad. She still got to laugh at home and smile with her family. With her friends. With her fellow workers and those she loved. Of course, there were the Wardens, the dictatorship, the long hours of work, and the Corts they never got. Her life was hard and painful, even with the love. She remembered how terrified Danny was when the Wardens grabbed him. That's why Gwen left. For him. For all the kids in that small house. For all the children across her world. For the parents who couldn't afford shoes or proper dinners. For the people who resorted to terrible things to make enough Crt to buy food. She did it for her people.

And it is painful now, maybe even more than before, but Gwen knew her pain would be rewarded with their happiness. And for that, she had to try.

Metis understood that. He saved his people and did more than she ever did before finding Kirana. He was already a hero for his people. Gwen wanted to be just that. A hero for her people. He was a better fighter. He knew his world well. He was older than she was, but surely not by that much. His beard made him look older, but his voice and energy were young and immature. He had seen many things in his years and it made him strong. She felt so young, so weak. If he had done so much, why couldn't she have? Lorenzo was there, waiting for her. His doors were open to people who wanted a change but she never took it. Was it because of her family? Surely it was. She couldn't just leave them. But… maybe it was also because of fear. Even now, she had kept Kirana from exploring the world for fear of finding danger, it was the reason she had lied to Tech in the first place. All because of fear.

She rested her head on the metal box nearest her and tried to sleep again. She didn't need to think of the past, she had too much ahead of her to wonder what might have been.

She just needed to sleep.

Chapter 20

METIS

METIS WASN'T A stranger to sleeping on the streets. He had done it before, but he found himself missing his bed this time. It was a nice one too. Soft and comfortable. He had saved a lot of Korts to get it, and now some King King member was claiming it as their own. Truthfully, Metis had no idea what would happen to his place, but he knew he wouldn't be the one living in it. He couldn't count the number of homes he had gone through in his lifetime. Too many.

When he woke up he felt his upper lip move up as he smelt the air he had been breathing all night. He must have just been able to ignore it, but now it hit him. Metis sat up and looked at the two women in the alleyway. Neither of them were up yet. Gwen lay opposite to him against a metal crate and Kirana on the floor at the back wall. Without waking them Metis got up and put on his bag, which he had made sure was packed before going to sleep. He didn't trust the sneaky druggies in the area they were in, especially with Ben E tucked inside.

Metis sat down near the stairs and pulled his android out again. He wanted to make sure Ben E was ready for whatever was about to happen next, whether it meant running from King King or traveling *dimensions.*

Metis didn't believe Gwen and Kirana, not entirely, at least. Their story was crazy, and he had every right to believe they were just as insane, but he couldn't deny what he felt when he held the staff. Gwen was right, it felt like a light bulb had been turned on. He was in the air, floating not because of the staff but because of himself. Metis didn't know what he believed, but Kirana and Gwen were unlike anyone he had met before. He had thought they were cruel to lie to him, but it turned out they were just protecting their people. It was a loving act, something Metis hadn't seen a lot of from his own people. If they were telling him the truth, that he was a god and they had the potential to take down the Magistrater, he would listen.

As Metis closed Ben E's panel the android shook to life. His face flicked to life and let out a robot scream. Metis put a hand over his speaker, "Be quiet."

Ben E looked around, "Did I die?"

"For a few hours."

Ben E was Metis's closest companion. He had one of the best-programmed personalities Metis had ever seen, let alone helped create. "Happy Sleep?" His voice had a sort of tang to it, like a mechanical accent that might have just been rust in his circuits.

"Yep." Metis looked down the stairs to try and see if the sun was up yet. They were high up so there should have been at least some source of daytime. From what he could tell it was dark, but brightening. Morning... ish. "Come on." He told Ben E as he packed up his tools and headed back to the others. His android quickly followed him, making a loud clicking sound as he passed over the concrete walkway.

Gwen was awake when he arrived, her arms crossed and head against the wall. She looked over at him, "You're still here."

He shrugged, "Looks like it."

Kirana started to wake up at the sound of their voices. Slowly she pushed herself up onto the wall, "Good morning." She said with a husky voice.

Gwen stood up and walked over to her, "You feeling better?"

Kirana nodded, picking up the staff from the ground. "Just a bit bruised." She lifted her shirt and showed where someone had kicked her. She looked down and was a bit shocked when she saw a huge purple spot against her rib cage. "Oh. That's worse than I thought."

Metis looked up to Gwen to see her reaction. Though she seemed worried about Kirana, she showed no signs of disgust. It was clear she had seen her share of injuries before.

Metis took a breath, "Okay. So let's go."

"Go where?" Gwen asked, and in response he squinted at her and laughed. His reaction helped her remember. She put a hand to her head, "Right, to another dimension. Kirana?"

Kirana stretched her arms, "Hiraeth or the next one?"

"Can you even travel?" Gwen asked.

"I'll just be knocked out for a bit. We're just proving who we are, nothing big. We'll pop in and out." Kirana looked over at Metis, "I'll go unconscious for a bit, but if we're in a safe place I can just take a few minutes to recover and we'll return here to talk." She put out the staff and Gwen grabbed it. Kirana looked up at Metis, "Just hold on."

He glanced behind them, "We're doing this now?"

"You wanted to do it last night." Gwen gestured to the staff, "We'll do what it takes to prove ourselves to you."

Metis had to admit, he was becoming worried with how honest the women seemed to be. He grabbed Ben E and put a hand on the staff. The wood was warmer than he expected, as if it didn't apply to the cooler temperature around them. Kirana closed her eyes and for a moment Metis felt nothing, until something clicked. He felt a familiar pull and suddenly the world was morphing before his eyes. Metis was leaving Telematic, he was leaving his world. This was really happening; he had been chosen by the staff as the next god. Fearing what was about to happen, he let go of the staff, "Wait." He shook his hand out as his vision returned to normal.

Kirana dropped to her knees and wiped blood from her nose, she groaned, "Please don't do that again."

Metis shook his head and glanced back down the alley. When he looked at Gwen she was already staring at him, "Do you believe us now?"

"Maybe." He shook his hand out again, "But I can't just leave."

"We aren't going to." Gwen said calmly, "Last time we left Hiraeth to escape the Wardens. This time we can go slow, talk, prepare, and plan."

Kirana wiped her nose and smeared the blood on her pants, "A plan would be nice." She gestured to Gwen, "She knows a lot about the Keepers. She can tell us everything we need to know."

"But what happens next?" Metis asked.

"We go to the final world and get the final Keeper." Gwen crossed her arms, "Then I suggest we go to Hiraeth to one of the more fortified rebellions and start spreading the word. Start building... something." When Kirana and Metis waited for more she glared at both of them, "This isn't the plan, I'm not just making up a plan. It's a suggestion."

"It's a good suggestion." Kirana reassured her. She looked up at Metis, "So we'll talk."

Metis looked back down the alleyway, "Do you mind if I leave, just for an hour or two."

"We can take you to the next world, Metis." Gwen said, gesturing to the staff, "We can prove–"

"I believe you." He put up a hand, "But I can't just leave. I need to make sure everything is alright here." Leaving Telematic meant not saving any more kids for a little while, which also meant not seeing Martha or helping her with payments. He needed to make sure now was a good time to leave his entire world behind.

Kirana sighed, "I mean if you have to. How far is it?"

"Is what?"

"Wherever we're going."

Metis laughed at her determination to stay as a group, "I'll be faster on my own. Just stay here and rest." In all honesty, the two of them looked like they needed another day's worth of sleep. They both had blood on their faces and clothes, bruises deep in their skin, and a look of exhaustion that was enhanced by a rough sleep.

Gwen looked him up and down, "You're going to see the kid?"

He was shocked she had guessed his intentions so quickly, "I was. I need to make sure the kids are alright."

"There are more?" Gwen asked, shocked.

"Martha looks after them." Metis hesitated to tell them more before but now decided to share the information, "She takes in lost kids and gives them food, a bed, clothes. I bring in the kids and give her Korts so she can sustain herself."

Kirana put a hand on her heart, "That's amazing."

"Do you mind if we come?" Gwen asked, "I'd actually like to see what she does. Besides, we should stick together."

Metis sighed. He had wanted to talk to Martha alone, but bringing the Keepers wasn't the worst idea. It wasn't dangerous by any means, safer even, so he wouldn't lose them in the city or get them killed by leaving them unarmed and injured. He nodded, "Okay then. Let's go."

Metis decided to lead the Keepers through the busy streets and not the more isolated alleyways. He knew it was dangerous, but it was the fastest way to get to Martha. Kirana instinctively put on her hood and Gwen just kept her head down, adjusting her hair to hide parts of her face. It took them only a few turns and three flights of stairs to get to the right street. They saw one Warden patrol but navigated around them with ease. Glancing around at the people who passed by, he walked back to the metal doors and knelt beside them.

Kirana stood beside him, "Did Martha take care of you?" She said it like it was some secret, even if she didn't bother to lower her voice.

He thought about lying but decided against it for fear of Martha saying something to them. "Yes." He pressed the red button and waited a moment before saying, "It's Tech, I need to talk to you."

Gwen stood beside Kirana, "Do all the kids come back to help her?"

He closed the panel, "No. They get selfish."

"But you're not." Kirana smiled at him, a giddy grin across her face.

"No I am." He laughed, "Trust me, when I want something, I go and get it. I just happen to have some moral values."

The lift came within moments and he pulled the doors open for the Keepers. Gwen took her time to get inside, feeling the floor and putting both hands on the walls for support. He guessed she had some trauma from her incident with King King. He pulled the doors shut but said nothing about it to her. She needed to deal with it alone. She didn't need some stranger she barely knew to tell her how to feel better.

When they reached the bottom he pulled open the doors and stepped out first. He landed in a puddle of water and quickly brought out his bag, reaching inside he searched for his flashlight.

Kirana and Gwen moved around him, looking down the dark room before them.

"We should find a light." Kirana told them. Metis brought out his flashlight and turned it on, shining it in her eyes. She put up a hand, "Yeah, like that." He put the flashlight up and looked around the room.

Pillars were scattered across the room, all of them a part of a detailed system to hold up the city above them. His world was messy and unorganized for almost everything, except for the city's structure. The Wardens built it decades ago, if not centuries, creating a system that could pump or pull water through the city. Water was one of the most dangerous threats in Telematic, for the city was built on top of a vast sea. The walls of the room the Keepers stood in were lined with entrances to pipes. They were made to drain out or pull in water from one side of the city to the other. They didn't work well, in fact, sometimes they just made things worse, but so far they had never pulled too much water through these pipes, making it an empty space for people to travel through or live in. Metis shined his flashlight to the ground so the Keepers could see the largest pipe in the area, a giant hole in the center of the large space around them. The hole was a long drop down into the true waters of Telematic.

Metis walked across the wet open space to the hole and glanced down, seeing the waves pass by and hit the concrete below. Ben E knew to stay away from the edge and rolled through the puddles to the other side of the room.

Gwen inched to the edge of the hole, "Water?"

"The ocean, actually." He said, stepping back and walking away.

"The city is built on top of the ocean?" She seemed surprised, and Metis had to remind himself she was from another world.

Metis shined the light on the tunnels. He wanted to make sure they were going down the right one because some of them led to dangerous areas he never wanted to visit again. Martha's tunnel had a small symbol carved above and below the entrance. "It's where we get our water. We filter it and bring it right up to our homes."

"Where is the surface?" Kirana asked.

Metis glanced back to find her looking down the hole, leaning over it. "I would step back if I were you. No one will be able to save you if you fall in."

Gwen stepped away from it, "Has anyone before?"

Metis could name hundreds of times someone did. The easy ones to forget were the drunks and the stoned morons who wandered down without a light. The ones that stuck with Metis were the kids who fell in. Normally they were heading over to Martha and just didn't have a light on them. A while back, he had been taking a few there, when a kid tripped over the edge and fell down into the water. Metis would dive down to the edge to try and find them, but by the time he got there the only thing he could see was the splash. The current was so strong it would take them immediately, and the kid would be pulled around before either hitting a pillar hard and dying or running out of air.

The worst ones, the ones that left him waking up in a sweat in the middle of the night, were the ones who were able to grab onto the edge. They fell near the wall, and could just grab onto the corner. They would pull their head up and cry out as the current started to push them to their death.

They would scream a hopeless word, "Help!"

One time, and it only happened once, Metis got to see the look on a little boy's face as waves crashed around him, and he screamed, "Please! I don–" *I don't want to die.* Metis heard it over and over again. He could still hear the wave coming and the pound against him, pulling his little body down under the city where no one would ever find him.

Metis hated the water, he hated how many children he had seen go down into those waters. Not just in that room but everywhere. It was like the world knew he was the one trying to save the kids. As if the water was trying to remind him of old times. How much guilt could he possibly take?

"Has anyone before?" Gwen asked again.

"A few times." He answered honestly, "Mostly drunk idiots or stoners who come down here without a light." Metis looked back to make sure Kirana was away from the edge as well. She stepped back and walked towards him, listening to his words and staying clear of the death trap. Metis stepped up into the third tunnel against the wall and walked ahead.

He kept the flashlight up and around the tunnel. When they got to a turn he quickly moved through it and saw light further down. He walked towards the small door made of scrap pieces of metal and plastic and pulled it open slowly, peeking inside.

Martha had found this abandoned place a few decades ago, long before Metis was even born. She suspected it used to be used as a space for the Wardens who managed the pipes and water currents, but based on the water damage and reminisce from stolen electronics, she had suspected it was a failed workspace. The room was shaped like a square, a wide and tall space fitted with a long row of pillars on either side of the room. On the left were the beds and cradles. On the right were long tables fitted with plates and forks ready for the next meal. At the end of the room sat two separate rooms, one on the right and the other on the left. Martha suspected they were offices for the high-ranking Wardens, and used one for the bathroom and one for her own personal room. The space was cold and dull, the concrete gray and soggy, but Martha had tried to lighten up the place through the years. She decorated the space with bright orange lights, most of which were strung together along the wall. She decorated the room with red carpets that had turned a light brown through the years. But best of all, she gave the children colored chalk and let them fill the room. The floors were lined with stick figures, animals, and flowers, but the back wall was their main canvas.

Most of the kids were from the pipes and had either lost their parents, had run away, or never had parents to begin with. They came from all sides of horrible situations, some even from gangs and cults. Martha was a saint, but she didn't get the credit she deserved for all the children she raised. Most of the kids went right back to the situation they came from, and almost all of them never came back to see Martha or help her with the next generation. Metis was one of the few who stayed with Martha and did his part, away from his situation.

Metis walked inside and saw the many children scattered mostly around their beds. At the sight of him, they all froze, wondering what sort of person was coming into their home. They had been warned about the drunks, druggies, and those desperate enough to find them, but at the sight of Tech, their faces expanded into a wide grin.

The first child who had seen him laughed and jumped up off the floor, "Tech!"

The other kids now saw him too, getting up and going over just as fast. The kids ran around him, excited as ever. They jumped around him and started talking over each other, spitting out sentences with the same constant jumping.

"Where is Ben E!"

"I lost a tooth!"

"Dolly pulled my hair!"

"Sticky and Bucky got into a fight!"

Metis put his hands up and laughed, "Okay! Okay! I want to hear *everything*, but I need to speak to Martha first. Alright?"

"She's cooking!" A little boy with two front teeth missing yelled as if they were miles away.

"Good. I need to talk to her." He looked across the room and saw Martha at the kitchen, her back facing him. She only looked over when she heard new footsteps, and Metis looked over as well to see the Keepers step inside.

Gwen took her time going through, making sure she did not present herself as a threat to the children. Kirana was not as graceful and walked quickly over to

Metis and the children, the staff at her side.

The children all behaved differently when meeting strangers. Those who had been raised in the safety of Martha's gaze looked excited. Yes, they knew the dangers of new people, but they had hope for the love the strangers could give them. Those who had seen the true horrors of life stood away, looking around for a path to escape. There were only a few kids here who had seen enough cruelty to stand tall and glare at each Keeper. If Kirana or Gwen dared to move towards them the kids would attack. They knew how to defend themselves, and would most likely be the ones who never came back to help Martha with other kids. Not because they were selfish, but because they had no love to give.

"Hello." Kirana gave a small wave before looking at Metis and pointing towards Martha, "Is that her?"

Metis looked over to Martha at the countertop to find her staring right back at him. She stood over by a makeshift counter made from rusty metal and melted plastic. She looked upset, very upset. Her gray hair and slight wrinkles made it worse for some reason. As if age enhanced a stern look, or maybe it was just the knife in her hand. Her large dress and apron matched each other, and he couldn't believe she still found a way to look elegant when they were living off dirt and charity.

One of the kids let out a happy gasp as Ben E rolled into the room, "Ben E!"

Metis gestured to their bedroom, "Why don't you guys play with Ben E for a bit while I talk to Martha."

Ben E was a common attraction among the children. Through the years Metis had found many of the children liked to bond with the android more than him or any other person. Ben E wasn't a threat, he was just a friend. The android sped past the kids towards their beds and with a laugh the kids scattered after him.

Metis walked over to Martha who, seeing Kirana and Gwen were with him, had returned to her chopping. It looked like cooked meat on the countertop, all ready to be served on a large platter. At the table sat three kids: Fisher, Mercy, and the girl he had saved with the Keepers. He walked to Martha first, leaning against the countertop and smiling, "Is she alright."

"Who are they?" Martha nodded back to Gwen and Kirana who had stayed back by the table.

"They helped save her." He looked back at the girl. She was staring at the table, her hands placed in front of her and fingers twitching now and again. Her blond hair was cut short around her ears, blackened at the ends perhaps by dirt or oil. Metis took a breath and turned back to Martha, "She looks shaken."

"She hasn't spoken once. When she eats I'll check if she still has her tongue." Metis winced and Martha stopped cutting the meat. She wiped her hands on her apron and turned to him, "You need to talk?"

"In private."

She raised an eyebrow and looked over to the Keepers, "Which one of you is pregnant?"

Gwen gave Metis a hard look, wide eyes telling him to explain. He laughed at her comment and waved his hands, "They are not pregnant–"

"Then why are they here?"

Metis gestured to her room, "Please, let's talk."

Martha nodded and threw the rest of the meat on the platter, "Help me get the kids dinner, we'll talk while they eat." Metis nodded and took the platter off the table. He set it down in the center and started to dish up the meat onto 23 plates. Martha came over with a larger pot and started spooning rice onto the meat as the children rushed over. Martha handed Gwen a small plate, "Share." She gestured to Kirana and pulled Metis to her door.

The room itself was completely modest. She had a gray bed, a dresser, and a chair in the corner beside a box of fabrics and needles. That was it, that was all she afforded herself to have.

Martha sat down in her chair, "So why are they here?"

"They helped save the girl." He leaned back on her dresser, "I need to ask you something." She nodded. "Do you know who the Keepers are?"

Martha looked shocked by his question and pointed to the door, "The staff? You think they're the Keepers?" She laughed, "You can't be serious."

"I think they are, Martha."

"Do you have proof?"

Metis thought for a moment. He knew describing how it felt to use the staff would only make Martha believe he was high at the time, but he had to try and explain, "They think I am one of them." That sounded stupid and childish, he took a deep breath, "The proof was when I magically floated into the air and a burst of light flew out of me."

Martha leaned forward to look in his eyes, "So they are drug dealers."

"I wasn't high. I wouldn't be telling you this if I wasn't certain that they were telling the truth."

"Do you trust them?"

"For the most part. But the Wardens are after them. They're everywhere. And the two of them know nothing about the city." He took a breath and leaned back, "I know this sounds stupid, and for all I know they could be lying, but if they're not... Martha, I could find out where the Wardens are taking those kids." He pointed back to the door, "They could change everything."

"Tech." She waited a moment so they would lock eyes, "Why are you here?"

"I need to know if you'll be alright without me."

Martha's face dropped, and Metis suspected his words proved he was completely serious about the Keepers. "What are you talking about?"

"If they are telling the truth, if the staff is real, if the *gods* are real, then they'll take me to another dimension." He winced at his words, "I just need to be sure–"

"Tech." She stood up and walked over to him, "You're going to leave?"

"Do you think–"

"You should." He hadn't expected her to agree so quickly, and so forcefully. She took his hand and held it in her own, "I think you should go far away from here."

"You believe me?"

Martha glanced at the door, "My aunt used to tell me about the Keepers. I never believed her, but when life got hard I did what she told me to do and prayed. I asked the gods to help me and my children. If you think you found them, or even just the staff then I trust you to learn the truth and be careful."

"You want me to leave?"

She dropped his hand and gave him a light smack on his shoulder, "Of course, I don't want you to leave, Tech. But this is a good time."

He shook his head, "With more Wardens more kids–"

"I think you need to go, Tech." She took a breath, "If not with these people then alone. You need to go away for a little while."

Metis leaned back, "What happened."

"Stick didn't talk to you?" He shook his head. "He was down in the Firelane district and he saw an old beggar." Martha twisted her jaw, "He was missing his left eye."

Metis's eyes went wide. His heart raced. He felt his stomach crawl under his cold skin. *The Master.* That name. It felt like it was opening old wounds on its own. *The Master. The Master.* His name echoed in his mind, and all Metis wanted to do was let the world hide him away from that name. "What else?"

"Stick said he looked exactly how you described him. White beard and all. He stopped Stick and…" She took a breath, "Asked if he wanted to upgrade." Metis went cold. The kids made a loud cheering noise and Martha clicked her tongue, "Take your time." She patted his shoulder softly and it took everything he had not to flinch. "Stick can help out more and I have some Korts saved up I can use. For once in your life, Tech, allow yourself to not stay in this situation. Do what you need to in order to save those kids, and stay away from the Master." When she shut the door Metis put a hand over his chest and tried to breathe.

Stick was always sharing something to create chaos. Maybe he was just drunk or high, or maybe he was just bored. Sure, his friend knew what the Master's return would mean to Metis, but maybe he just forgot. It could just be some old man who matched his description. After all, Stick had never met the Master. It could just be a close call. That's it. A close call.

This sounded like a warning.

That was impossible.

The Master was gone. He had been gone for 11 years.

11 years, and 3 months. Metis had only recently stopped counting the days.

Metis knew it was unlikely. He knew the chances of Stick finding him were low. He knew that if the Master was alive he could not hurt Metis. He was old, he was dying, or dead.

But if it was true, and the Master had truly returned, then perhaps it was a good thing he was leaving the world.

With Martha's blessing, he could go with the Keepers and escape for a little while. If Kirana and Gwen were telling the truth then he would be able to truly help the kids.

All while staying away from the Master.

Chapter 21

GWEN

GWEN WATCHED AS Metis spoke to the kids and said his goodbyes. From what she could tell, Martha was his mother figure, and though she had many other children to worry about she still had time to care for Metis. Martha was what Gaia was to Gwen.

Kirana was crouched down on the floor looking at one of the youngest kids. Barely a one-year-old. She rattled a toy in their face, trying to make them laugh. The baby was on the verge of tears.

Gwen moved over to Kirana and took the rattle from her hand with a laugh, "What are you doing?"

"Playing? I've never seen a baby before." She wagged her finger in their face.

Gwen laughed, "Seriously? What, does paradise mean no diaper changes?"

"I guess." The baby let out a cry and she shot back, "It's so loud."

"*He* is so loud. Not it. *He.*" Gwen handed the baby its rattle and let it throw it around, "Danny was this old when Gaia moved in with my family." She looked back to Martha, "I miss them all so much."

Kirana grabbed her hand and held it, "We'll go back to Hiraeth as soon as this is all over. One more Keeper and you'll see your family again, I promise." She looked down at the baby, "That bike I saw, right before everything happened. We should ask Metis more questions about the technology here.." She gestured around them, "The Magistrater doesn't seem to announce the purpose of her system, but from what I can tell she is using the worlds to make Permidia perfect. Hiraeth gives Permidians food and Telematic gives Permidia technological advancements to stay comfortable and entertained."

Gwen nodded, "She's created a system only Permidia profits off of."

"But why?" Kirana asked and Gwen simply shrugged. She had no idea what the Magistrater wanted to do with the world, but so far all it had done was hurt Hiraeth and Telematic. Kirana sighed, "We need to stop her." She grabbed the baby's hand and shook it gently, "People shouldn't have to live like this when others live so beautifully, all because of one person."

Gwen found herself so grateful to hear Kirana say that. She smiled at her and nodded, lost for any other words. At the sight of Metis jogging over to them the Keepers stood up.

He clapped his hands together, "Okay, I'm ready to go."

"Good, because Gwen and I came up with a plan." Kirana smiled and placed the staff to her side, her other hand on her hip, "We don't know what the next world will be, and when I travel I sort of just arrive in certain spots."

"You can't control our location?" He seemed surprised.

Kirana laughed, "I am learning. It's pretty difficult, and in the end, it's sort of to do with feeling. I can feel the world and its people when I enter it. Soon I hope I can just picture a spot and we'll end up right there, but since we don't know what we're jumping into, we'll pop in, look around, and then come back here to get the supplies we need. Water, forests, desserts, another busy city, lots of dangerous people." She counted out the possibilities and laughed, "But for now I think the best thing we can have is a gun."

Metis tapped on his bag, "I've still got mine. I'll ask Martha for another."

"When we get the final Keeper we'll go straight to Hiraeth and go to Lorenzo's rebellion. Gwen says he'll take us in and help us get settled."

"And after that?"

Gwen shrugged, "We made a better plan."

Metis nodded and stepped back towards the kitchen, "Okay, let me ask for a gun." He pointed to a group of kids, "Get Ben E."

Kirana nudged Gwen, "*Now* things are working out–"

"Do not finish that sentence." Gwen laughed and stepped towards the kids, "I swear to the gods, Kirana, if you jinx us one more time–"

"Okay, okay." Kirana put her hands in the air and looked towards the android, "Ben E!"

His head peeked out from within the crowd and he rolled over to Kirana quickly. She bent down and picked him up, "You ready to explore a new world?"

His head shot back and his pixelated expression changed to a smile, "Sure!"

The gun Metis got from Martha looked the same as the one they had used before, only this time it was slightly larger. He handed the gun to Gwen and she held it by the barrel, not wanting to appear as if she would use it any time soon. She hoped she wouldn't have to use it all, that maybe this next world would be, at the very least, somewhere quiet.

The three of them walked through the dark streets again, trying to find their way back to the main levels. Gwen looked around at the trash and junk against the walls. It still felt dangerous, even with no one around them. She hoped the next dimension would be less chaotic. Something green would be nice. A single tree or a patch of grass would help. And no noise. Just the wind in her ears. "There are no alleyways in my world. And I mean *none*. Every single space is used in the city."

Metis looked over at her, he seemed thoughtful, "That sounds weird."

"Well, it is a different world."

"Same planet though? Right? You're not just hopping universes or something."

"Different dimensions"

"How do we know that for sure?"

Kirana grinned, eager to answer the question, "The worlds are built the same way. Everything pours out of one spot. The Magistrater's Tower." She spun her hands around and wiggled her fingers, "The tower's the same in every single world. Location, color, shape. Always the same."

Metis stopped walking as they made their next turn. The new alleyway looked cleaner, but the horrible smells remained. Gwen put a hand to her nose and regretted breathing in the air around her. "Did something die?"

"Two cats and an old man." Metis gestured around the small alley, "No one will come down here."

Kirana nodded, bouncing around and stretching her back, "Okay. When we're ready I'll take us to the next world. And whatever happens, just make sure you protect the staff..." She took a second to look at Gwen. Gwen twisted her jaw to the side but said nothing. Losing the staff wasn't something Kirana would forget anytime soon. "And please don't let me die." Kirana laughed nervously, as if her survival was a joke.

Metis took a deep breath, "Alright. Let's go travel dimensions."

"And you're alright to leave?" Gwen asked.

He nodded quickly, "This is the best time to leave. And I am ready to see if you two are actually telling the truth."

"You know we are." Kirana placed the staff in front of them, "Just hold on and don't let go, alright?" Gwen and Metis nodded and she closed her eyes. For a moment nothing happened, and Gwen watched as Kirana's face twitched and pulled. Then suddenly, she felt herself being pulled forward as the world around her melted and morphed. The view shifted as she felt her body lift. As light flashed before her eyes the ground beneath her feet suddenly disappeared and, still holding onto the staff, she fell to the ground. Letting out a scream she twisted and landed on her back. Grunting in pain she took deep breaths until her body settled on the new surface. She forced her eyes open and felt her pupils shrink as the bright sky shined down on her.

Gwen put her hand up to block the sun and looked at the sky. If anything, it looked empty. Not a single cloud, and yet the normally sky blue color was dull and brownish as if there was something above her filtering the color. She squinted and saw the color moving and shifting, like dust in the wind.

She turned her head over to see what was around her.

Nothing.

There was nothing around them.

The ground was dust, white dust that moved as she breathed out. A small breeze moved an entire space of dust away from her, up into the air she breathed.

It was just… nothing.

She pulled herself up and looked in every direction. Endless miles of dust and flat surfaces extended around her. It was quiet, deathly quiet. After all the noise her ears now rang in the silence, and she could only imagine what Metis was going through.

She looked over at him and Kirana. Metis was looking around quickly, just as shocked as she was, if not more. Kirana was lying on her back, eyes closed with blood running down her face from her nose.

"Where… Where are we?" Metis spun around in a panic. He put his hands to his ears and took deep breaths.

"Where is everyone?" Gwen asked, knowing he wouldn't have the answer. She realized how her voice sounded without any echo, without having to yell over music, conversations, or the basic noise the city made. Silence had never felt so powerful, so overwhelming.

"It's so quiet." Metis's tone had become softer, poisoned by a great discomfort. He breathed faster, trying to take in the noiseless environment. Gwen hadn't expected him to react this much, but compared with the constant noise in Telematic it made sense. Not only that, but they had now officially proven to him that they were the Keepers.

"Are you alright?"

"You're gods." He looked at her as if seeing her for the first time.

She nodded, "So are you."

He didn't respond, and instead looked around the strange new world with his hands over his ears. The two of them sat in silence and took in the great nothing around them. The world felt dangerous. The dust seemed to move around and up into the air with the smallest breeze. The white dust was everywhere. Blocking the sun, filling the horizon. Gwen tasted it on her lips. She felt it enter her lungs. She could breathe fine, but it felt suffocating.

Gwen looked back at Metis but said nothing. They both spent a long time just looking at the view, waiting for something to happen.

But there was nothing.

Gwen looked back down at Kirana, who stirred and started to move around. She was shocked to see her eyes open.

"Kirana?" Gwen moved beside her, kneeling.

"Where..." That was all Kirana could say. She was exhausted from the trip, but she looked better than normal. There was less blood, and her consciousness was returning faster. Gwen hoped the more they traveled the better she would get.

Gwen looked over to Metis, "We need to see if there is anything out there. Like a forest or a town."

He gestured to the vast nothingness before them, "So what, we split up and just start walking?"

She shrugged, "Got a better idea?"

He clenched his jaw and looked around. He didn't. So he pointed forward and nodded, "This way has some really good energy, it feels promising."

He was being sarcastic. It seemed his panic was gone, and now he was just annoyed. Gwen figured he was expecting somewhere more exciting, but she was just happy to be away from Wardens. Gwen looked down the opposite direction to Metis and decided that would be the best way to go. Metis dropped his bag down by Kirana and took out Ben E. The android came to life and looked around.

"Wow!" Its voice was still amplified. Gwen hid a laugh as it tilted its head and wiggled its wheels at the sight of the dust. It was so human.

"See all the dust?" Metis gestured around the empty space, "Go find something other than dust."

Ben E looked around and then picked a direction. "Roger!" He said, moving away from them. Gwen could see the dust sticking to his tracks. She looked at her clothes and saw she too was covered in the white powder.

When she looked up Metis was already walking away, "Don't go too far from Kirana."

He turned around to face her and, while walking backward, gestured around him with a smile, "Not sure where else I could possibly go."

Gwen rolled her eyes, "Just don't get lost."

He nodded dramatically and turned his back to her.

Metis was a fun companion to have on their team. He was humorous, yes, but also kind and well skilled. There were aspects to him she still didn't understand, but for the time being she decided to do what Kirana would do and take a chance to make a friend, to find the fun in getting to know someone new. Gwen turned her back to him and Kirana and started walking.

And so she walked.

And then she kept walking

She walked, and walked, and walked, and walked on and on.

Until she turned back and saw Kirana was just a small dot behind her, fuzzy with the particles and heat. With no clouds, it felt like one of those deserts she had read about in her father's books. Perhaps the world was a desert, but it didn't look like the pictures. There weren't dunes or deep mounds of sand. The ground was solid with a coating of powder on top. She bent down at one point to look closer, and brushing the dust away she saw a level of hard dirt-like material. She was able to take out a chunk and found it most similar to some sort of metal or concrete. White, like the dust. And the ground was flat, as if someone had smoothed the land down. One thing was for certain, the world around them was no nature feat.

Gwen took off her jacket and put it above her head to create some sort of shade. When she almost lost track of Kirana she turned back without any new sight to be found. When she returned she wiped sweat from her brow and sat down next to Kirana who had managed to wake up on her own. She had streaks of blood under her nose and a tired look in her eyes, but she was awake.

"Any luck?" Kirana probably guessed what they were doing. Gwen shook her head, adjusting her jacket over her head. Kirana squinted up to the sun and took off her own jacket to do the same. No, not her jacket, Gideon's. There was more blood on it now, and already Gwen could tell the heat was bending the very material it was made out of. It was burning away her father from its fabric.

"Kirana–"

"Oh!" Kirana looked over quickly, "Did you see it?"

"See what?"

"The in-between." She looked hopeful, "I never asked if you could before, I wanted to see if you could see the figures like I did."

Gwen had not thought about the in-between until now. She shook her head, "I didn't see anything. I just arrived here."

Kirana squinted at her, "You just..." She glanced at the staff, "I guess it's because I take you through the world. You're just a passenger."

Gwen nodded, hanging her head and trying to rest in the heat. "I guess so."

Metis came back a few minutes later, wiping dust and sweat off himself. "Anything?"

"Not a thing." He slumped down beside them.

Kirana sighed, "We should keep looking, or go back to another world and get something to block the sun with."

"Or maybe we should just go back and never return." Metis suggested, "This is a wasteland, no one could survive in this." He hated where they were, and Gwen couldn't disagree. It would be nice to return somewhere with clouds. She thought about suggesting Hiraeth and Lorenzo's rebellion. She could check on her family and introduce Kirana and Metis to the rebellion. But when she looked down at the staff she saw the crystal had the slightest glow. A pinkish color, perhaps a light red.

There were people... but where?

Metis pressed his datawatch and moved it up to his mouth, "Ben E, we need you to come back now." He put it down and thought for a moment, "He might overheat soon. I should have thought about that before I sent him out."

Kirana tapped Gwen's leg, "Guys–"

"Can't you just–"

"Guys!" Kirana used the staff to pull herself up.

Gwen and Metis turned to see what she was looking at. There, hazed by the dust, was a ship. It was hard to make out entirely, but it was flying close to the ground, gray and clearly metal. It made a line of dust as it traveled at top speed through the wasteland.

Something in the nothingness.

Metis ran back to his bag and grabbed some sort of long glasses. He dove down to them and gestured for Gwen to do the same. He was getting her to hide. She didn't understand the point, there was nothing they could do to hide themselves in such a place.

He held up the glasses for Gwen to see, "Binoculars. You know what these are?"

"No."

"I do." Kirana answered, reaching out for him to give them to her. He didn't right away, instead, he moved the small dial on the top and looked through them with complete concentration.

"It's too dusty, I can't see it clearly." He whispered as he moved his head with the ship. He handed them to Kirana, who used them the same way. When she was done she gave it to Gwen who mimicked what they did. When she looked through them she saw everything in the distance much closer. More visible. It was incredible. The ship looked large, something for cargo or passengers. It didn't look like anything made to fight, not like the Warden's.

She pulled the glasses down, "Can it see us?"

Kirana took the glasses out of her hands and looked through them again, "I mean we were looking for them, they aren't looking for us. So I want to say no–"

"Sir!"

They all let out a scream and turned around. Until they saw it was Ben E. The android stood innocently behind them.

"Ben E, don't do that!" Metis told him, looking back at the ship before moving over to his android. Gwen and Kirana followed and saw there was something in his hands. A piece of metal.

Metis took it and held it up, "It must be from the ships."

"Who could live here?" Gwen gestured back to the land around them.

"If we follow them we will find out." Kirana told them both, "It has to be going somewhere, maybe to a town?"

Gwen nodded, trying to keep an eye on the ship. "If the staff gets brighter we will know where to find the Keeper."

The group gathered their things quickly. Metis pulled out a knife and ripped off part of his sleeve. He got Ben E to raise his arms and hold onto the cloth as shade. Metis used the rest of his coat and put it over his head as Gwen and Kirana did the same. Gwen felt sorry for him when she saw he was wearing a long-sleeved shirt, and hoped he would roll up his sleeves to cool down.

The three of them started walking down the wasteland.

Walking on and on. Right where the ship had been.

Walking and walking. In the blazing heat.

On and on. For 30 minutes.

On and on and on and on. For 40 minutes.

On and on and on…

"You okay Ben E?" Metis asked, panting hard.

The android laughed and yelled, "Not really!"

"I think I messed up with his volume when I fixed him." Metis laughed before wincing, "How far is this thing?" He wiped the sweat off his face.

"Just keep moving." Kirana tried to sound inspiring, but her words came out in a slur of exhaustion.

"You're not the one who is carrying the bag." He laughed at her before wincing.

Kirana gestured to the staff, "You're not the one who just traveled through dimensions."

"We all did." He looked over at her, "Why do you get so hurt?"

Gwen took a deep breath, wishing the heat away, "Kirana travels through another dimension first. We call it the *in-between*."

He seemed interested now, "What do you mean?"

"Every time I travel I go somewhere else." Kirana explained, "We call it the in-between because it's almost like a… well it's an in-between. I go there through the staff and find each world we need to go to."

Metis put out his free hand, "Can I see the staff?"

Kirana didn't hesitate to hand the staff to him.

He studied it, feeling the texture and weight of it. He held it up to his eyes and looked through the crystal. "What is the crystal?"

"Rhodonite." Gwen explained, "One of the most powerful materials in the world. The staff is one of the only sources of it as far as we know."

"How much do you two know about the Keepers?"

"Not a lot." Kirana laughed, "It's not like there was a guidebook on how to be a god." She nodded to Gwen, "She knows a lot though. Her father used to keep books about the Keepers, he was a historian."

Gwen looked over and felt her heart sink at Kirana's words: *used to, was.* She stayed silent and repeated the words in the present tense. Her father *is* a historian, he *keeps* books. That hadn't changed.

Gwen waved her hand in front of her own eyes as a gust of wind moved the fog around them for a moment. It was then that something came into view. They all stopped walking, squinting through the dust. Before them was something bigger than anything she had seen before. So tall that even from such a distance she had to lift her head up to see it all together.

A giant gray cube, as wide as a city and as tall as the Magistrater's building itself, revealed itself to the Keepers through the haze.

Each Keeper took a step back in fear.

Metis gave a staggered breath, "What is that?"

Kirana took the staff from Metis and held it in front of them, "A sign of life." The crystal was glowing brighter, now clearly a deep red color.

"Is..." Gwen glanced back up to the building, "Is red a bad sign?"

"Red's a nice color." Kirana thought for a moment, "It's just also the color of blood so... maybe."

It took them several minutes to get closer to the giant cube, and the closer they got the better they could see it. The walls were effortlessly smooth with sharp corners and a slightly reflective metal surface. There were lines where the metal plates ended and began, but they were just as neat as the rest of it. Gwen could see in the distance another ship approaching. It entered through what she could only see as a small hole. It was a city, an entire world in one controlled space. The more they walked towards the cube the bigger it seemed to get. Until finally they were standing right before it. The entire structure stretched for miles, and any chance of seeing the top was long gone.

Gwen reached out and touched the warm surface, "Metal."

She knocked on it. No echo. It wasn't hollow. These walls were thick. Impenetrable.

Metis dragged his hand down the wall, "How did they get the material?" Neither Gwen nor Kirana responded. They had no answer. "Where do you get this much metal from in a wasteland?" He turned back around and looked across the flat, dusty world.

Kirana shrugged, "There might be a mine or something inside, or somewhere else in the world." She looked down at Ben E, "I mean, where do you get your metal?"

"What do you mean?"

"Telematic is built on water, how do your mines work?"

Gwen could tell she was looking for a genuine answer. But Metis had none. "I never thought about it. I just… buy metal, or go find scraps on the streets." She could tell the idea of not knowing scared him.

Gwen looked down the long wall of metal. There was a noise as if something was coming towards them. She looked to their left and saw part of the wall moving back into itself, before moving to the side as a ginormous door opened in its place. Then there was a noise behind them. Gwen looked back to see a ship approaching.

"Guys… Guys!"

There was nothing else they could do to hide. The ship was coming towards them, aiming for the door. They just stood there and watched, praying that the people wouldn't be looking out for strange visitors. The ship started towards the hole, slowing down as it aimed itself.

"Come on!" Kirana told them, starting to run over to the open gate.

"Kirana!" Gwen tried to call her back, but Kirana was trying to take the opening gate as their only opportunity to get inside. Gwen sprinted after her, pumping her arms back and forward, she felt off balance because of the jacket she was holding and slipped it back on as she ran. The ship entered the gate and with a sharp slide of metal, it started to close. Gwen and Kirana crouched down and threw themselves through just in time. Metis came a few seconds later and was forced to roll under the door. Ben E, the slowest of the three, sped inside with a robotic yell as it came crashing down.

Metis stood up and Gwen turned around to see where they were. They were in

the open, in clear view to anyone who might so much as glance back. She needed
to move but... she couldn't. She was stuck looking at where they were.

It was perfect.

Every inch of the place seemed symmetrical and lined up straight. The only
colors were defining whites with a few grays and blacks. The ships were dark gray.
The walls, floor, and roof were all white with light gray lines as if for professional
decoration. Kirana had brought them into a huge hangar filled with vehicles. The
room had to be more than four stories tall and was made in a way to store ships.
One ship was hung from the roof, then another below it, and another one at the
bottom. There were three levels, each floor made from a strong weaved wire she
had seen in fences. Gwen could see right through them and quickly noticed how
their shape was an outline for the ships to fit into. With a short platform on either
side of the vehicle for people to enter and exit through.

As the ship that just came in lowered down to the ground under two other
ships the doors opened. Five people came out the door.

Five people.

Five Wardens.

"Gwen," Kirana whispered harshly, grabbing her arm and pulling her away.

Kirana pulled her over to a large cluster of boxes. All of them were made of
plastic and felt as stationary as everything else in the room. Gwen had only been
looking at the first half of the room, and now saw the other half was filled with
large crates. The Keepers were hidden by stacked, small plastic boxes, but behind
them were metal crates placed on top of each other.

A storage depot.

They moved through the rows of smaller boxes until there was a break in the
line. There they were able to stick their heads up and look around. Wardens were
everywhere. More so than Gwen had first realized. They were coming out of the
ships, walking along the platforms, coming in and out of doors at the walls. But
they were different. Again, their uniform had changed. Those who came out of the
ship were dressed in their signature jumpsuits. Gloves, helmets, and the works.
Only it was a light gray, with their armor plates and vest a clean white. Those who
were walking around the ship had different uniforms. Some wore jackets of whites
and grays in some sort of formal appearance, others had on dark gray jumpsuits
with no armor, and some even wore t-shirts with their jackets tied around their

hips or completely out of view. Gwen knew Wardens well, they were always strict and uptight, ready to kill and punish. But now they felt relaxed, to the point in which everyone's helmets were off. Gwen had never seen one without their helmet on. It felt unnatural. Monsters weren't supposed to wear the face of humans.

"Guys," Kirana whispered, lifting the staff for them to see. It was glowing red, brighter than ever before.

"General Allen." The voice was coming from above them in some robotic tone. The words rang through the entire hangar with a loud echo. "General Allen report for briefing in A-1-25."

"There are only Wardens." Gwen said, stating the obvious and only truly understanding what such a statement meant after she spoke. The realization hit her and she looked over to see Kirana wearing her same worry.

"This is the Warden's world."

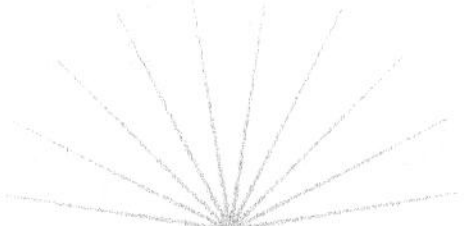

PART 3

The Ward

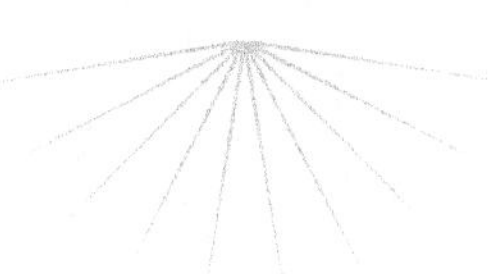

Chapter 22

KIRANA

KIRANA COULDN'T BELIEVE how much the Warden's headquarters looked like Permidia. It wasn't just the organization, or how clean it was, or even how symmetrical every object was to one another. It was the feeling, the energy. Kirana felt a great tension that should have been eased by the perfection around her. Everything was perfect, but she felt misplaced within. Different once again, just like she had been in Permidia.

"They have their own world?" Gwen whispered, voice quiet but still panicked. She watched the Wardens leave their ship and greet other soldiers. It was weird to see them without a helmet, and even weirder to see them talk and laugh. They seemed so human, so normal. There was a certain style everyone seemed to follow. Their uniforms all had the same formal fashion, crisp and clean. Their hair was either short and gelled back, or long and tied back with more gel. No inbetween. There was a right and a wrong way. A straight line. Human, perhaps, with the culture of a machine.

"This makes sense." Metis turned to Gwen, "Did you honestly think the Wardens just lived in the Magistrater's Tower? If they cover two dimensions, *at minimum*, they would need an entire population. Like this." Gwen was still watching the Wardens, and with a gentle nudge he got her to look away. He leaned in, "The Keeper is here. They're a Warden."

She flinched at his words, "We don't know that." Gwen had grown up watching the Wardens keep her world in a chokehold. Kirana had spent one day under their rule, and by the time she left the Wardens were enemies in her eyes. She could only imagine how Gwen felt about this whole situation. It was just a few days ago that the Wardens had separated her from her father, and then her family. Kirana didn't know how they would recruit a Warden to their cause, but she knew it would be a more difficult task to convince Gwen that the team needed a Warden as a Keeper. Their world was, after all, a stark reminder of Permidia, which meant there were cracks in their perfection, and perhaps situations in which the Wardens became the victims to the Magistrater's rule. Kirana knew they were the enemy but suspected there was more to their story than she had seen from Hiraeth and Telematic. If the staff chose someone, it was for a reason.

"We should look around." Kirana lowered the staff down to the ground, keeping it hidden behind the crates. The red glow would attract attention, especially around people who knew to look out for the staff, "We need to see what this world has to offer."

She heard footsteps from the other sides of the crate. The Keepers dropped down and did their best to crawl along the crates. The more they walked along the rows, the more cramped the area became. Stacks on stacks of small crates became rows upon rows of large metal containers nearly double Kirana's height. The Keepers snuck away from the Warden's view, peeking around the corner of the crate they took cover behind.

From what Kirana could tell, no one was working around them. She turned back to Metis and Gwen, "We should go inside. Have a look around."

"We can't just go inside." Gwen's words were fueled by anger. She held herself with her arms folded over her chest. "Kirana, they know what you look like, they might already know what Metis and I look like too."

Metis tugged on his shirt's collar, "And we can't go in looking like a Telematic and a Hiraethan."

"Then we'll make a plan."

Gwen clenched her jaw and peeked around the corner. Kirana suspected Gwen was mad at her for even suggesting going near the Wardens. But Kirana could tell there was more fear clouding her thoughts than a need for revenge. She wasn't comfortable in the world, and Kirana wished she could help by taking them back to Hiraeth, but she couldn't. Not yet. They were the Keepers, they had to complete the team and learn about the worlds. That included the Wardens.

They all looked back around the crate with Gwen. The Wardens were distracted. They were either speaking to one another or doing their tasks. Kirana saw they were unloading the ship that had come in. Wardens pushed small crates like the ones the Keepers had hidden behind out of a cargo hold. They hovered above the surface as the Wardens pushed them onto small gray lines on the floor. Kirana had thought they were decorations until the crates shook themselves onto the line and were shot forward toward the other stacks.

"Magnets." Metis whispered to the both of them, "I've never seen technology be used like this."

"Like what?" Kirana whispered.

"Productively." He looked at Kirana, directing his next words to her alone, "It's kind of exciting."

Kirana nodded because, honestly, she agreed. For all of Gwen's troubles, learning about the Wardens was needed. They weren't the true enemy. The Keepers were trying to get rid of the Magistrater and her reign, not her soldiers. What were the Wardens after all? Did they support her completely? Were the citizens of this world turned evil by some manipulation? From what Kirana could see so far, they were just people under her same rule as Hiraeth and Telematic. The world belonged to them, and though they benefited from the labor of those they oppressed, perhaps there were problems they faced as well.

Kirana held up the staff for her team to see, the crystal shining against the crate, "The Keeper is here. Warden or not, we have to find them."

Gwen shook her head, "If they are a Warden then we need to leave. Now."

Metis stepped away from the crate and looked down the alleyway they were in, "I saw a door at the back wall, we can slip inside through there."

"It's not worth it." Gwen looked to Kirana for support, "They'll kill us."

"The Wardens–"

"No. If the Keeper is a Warden they will try to kill us, Kirana."

"What if they can help us?" Metis stepped closer to her, "You told me the staff chose me. Right? It chooses people. So it chose a Warden here. There is a reason for that, right? Someone was born to be a god."

Kirana nodded, "It's our job to find them. Right? Gwen of all people I expect you to understand–"

"Yes." She answered fiercely, "There is a story about Paloma's Keepers, about how they tracked down every Keeper from world to world, holding out the staff and letting hundreds of their people hold it. Not just because they wanted to find the Keeper, but because it was the one chance that others had to hold such a powerful relic. That's what the gods are, symbols. The Wardens don't deserve their own Keeper. They don't deserve a *god*." Gwen looked at Kirana and waited for her to understand. Kirana found herself shaking her head softly, already disagreeing with such a harsh intent. The Wardens were people, human beings, and it was at that moment that she realized Gwen might have believed they were less than Hiraethans. Gwen clenched her jaw and looked away, outvoted.

Kirana gestured down the column of crates, "We have some options here. We can go in now, sneaking in or disguising ourselves, or we can go back to Telematic or Hiraeth and come back later."

Metis shook his head, "I don't think we should come back later." Gwen laughed and he simply shrugged, "We got lucky when the ship came in. We're inside, that might not happen so easily twice."

"Kirana can bring us back here. To this spot." Gwen told him.

Kirana shook her head, "But someone could be working here. I can't just bring us to this exact spot. What if someone put a crate here and we end up stuck in it? I can barely navigate the in-between, I don't know the rules of dimension travel yet."

"We can't just sneak in."

Metis looked back over at Gwen with a new look on his face. Not one of unease or worry, one of thought. He had an idea. Kirana didn't know if she should have been excited or terrified. The man was, after all, from Telematic. A world of chaos and reckless actions.

In the end, she was right to be worried.

Metis pulled his bag around and took out a long wire, "I can kill three Wardens, then take their uniforms."

Gwen quickly tried to speak, mouthing the start of words until finally finding the right thing to say, "No. Metis, no."

"We're here." He gestured around them, "Gwen, this is a good opportunity."

"This is happening too fast. Kirana?"

Kirana shook her head, "I'm sorry, he's right. No one's seen us, the Wardens think we're in Telematic, most of the soldiers here don't know what we look like–"

"You're assuming that." Gwen pointed at her face, "They've seen you. They have photos of you everywhere."

"Gwen." Metis said, holding the wire with one end in each of his hands, "We'll be careful."

She threw her hands up and stepped away, "Fine."

Metis and Kirana exchanged a look before he looked at Ben E and pointed towards another path created by the crates, "I need you to look around, stay out of sight, and be silent. We need to find a way inside without too many people seeing us."

Ben E gave a quick nod before quietly rolling beside the crates. Metis turned and went another way, leaving the two Keepers alone. Kirana stood beside Gwen and smiled at her, "Everything will–"

She put up a hand, "You don't know that. You and Metis don't know the Wardens, I don't even know that well."

"He fights them all the time."

"I've seen them do horrible things." She winced, "I can't just put on their uniform and be one of them so that maybe we can find a monster to add to our team. I'm not bringing one of them to Lorenzo, Kirana. Not to my family."

Kirana knew there was nothing she could say that would persuade Gwen to see the Wardens as anything but monsters. But if there was one thing she was certain of, it was that Gwen was wrong. Kirana saw herself as an unbiased party in the mix of so much separation between the worlds. The Wardens were as new to her as the Hiraethans and Telematics, and for the time being, she would treat them as she had all the others: with an open mind. So for Gwen, all she could say was, "I'm sorry."

Metis appeared a minute later, dragging a Warden body with him, a woman with dark black hair and a hooked nose, "They're sitting ducks." He said it as if it was a fact, and not a mocking comment. Kirana got the sense that he too would remain unbiased for the time being. He gestured to the nearest crate, "Get it open."

Kirana walked over and, as quietly as she could, unlocked the metal door and pushed it open. Inside were boxes on boxes of items, much like the ones from before. Metis pulled the Warden inside and looked from Gwen to Kirana, "I think she'll fit either of you." He dropped her and ran back outside. Gwen came around and looked at the Warden. She seemed speechless, unable to decide between anger and gratitude.

Kirana set the staff on the ground and started to take off her coat, "We get in and get out."

"They'll know. We'll be too suspicious."

"Do you want–" Gwen shook her head and Kirana started to take off the Warden's armor. Kirana smiled at her, "We stay together and look around. If we can find the Keeper then we grab them and run. We can explain everything to them later."

Gwen said nothing. Her anger faded, and she lowered her head. Kirana wanted to comfort her, but for the time being, they needed to focus.

Metis came back through the door with another Warden, a man with tan skin and brown hair. Then finally with a female Warden who he dropped beside the others. He shook out his hands, "I feel awful. This isn't exactly a great way to start a mission."

"You kill Wardens all the time." Kirana took off the woman's boots, "How is this different?"

"They didn't do anything to deserve to die." He shook his head, "But we need this." Metis started to strip down the Warden and Kirana was quick to do the same. She left the other woman for Gwen, who eventually rejoined the two of them. The woman Kirana had looked like any other person she had met. When resting, or rather, lying dead on the floor, she seemed completely normal. If someone had asked Kirana where the woman was from, she would not be able to say. She could be a Hiraethan, a Telematic, or even a Permidia, and Kirana would not be able to tell the difference. She pulled off the jacket, her boots, and the pants, and took off her clothes once she was ready.

Putting on the Warden's clothes was rather easy. For how complex the armor looked on the soldiers it was still practical. The jumpsuit was entirely gray and black. A belt wrapped around her waist with holsters and items of all kinds. Kirana searched them quickly and found a small screen and an empty gun holster. Along the jumpsuit were pieces of well-crafted armor plates. They felt different than she had imagined. They felt soft, and though they pressed firmly against her body they weren't uncomfortable or restricting. The armor plates were stark white and had pristine quality to them, to the point in which they were nearly reflective. A large piece on her chest, another on her shoulders. They carried down her arms then to her thighs and stopped where her boots began. She was ready to walk out with her hair down when she saw the woman had her hair in a bun, a rubber band holding everything in place. Kirana took it out and let the woman's greased hair fall flat on her face. Kirana pulled her own hair into a short ponytail and folded down any lumps she could. She put a hand to her face and felt dried blood and dirt across her skin. She used her old shirt, which now had turned from white to a dirty cream, and wiped her face down until she felt at least partially clean. Kirana could only do so much without a mirror, but it was better than nothing.

Metis's Warden armor looked different from Kirana's. His uniform had smaller armor pieces, and on his chest was a strange symbol. She looked down at her symbol and compared the two. Her chestplate featured two lines and a star in between them, but his contained four lines on each side of the star.

He noticed the differences as well, "It's fine." He shrugged it off, "If I'm superior to you two that might come in handy later."

Kirana looked over to Gwen. She looked the same as the Keeper, better, even. Her uniform looked more fitted to her figure than Kirana's, and with Martha's gun in her holster, she looked supplied and ready to do Warden work. Her arms were pulled away from her body, her shoulders slumped. Her eyes were on the ground. She was so repelled by the armor she wasn't willing to feel it on her skin. Kirana tried to walk towards her, to help in whatever way she could, but when Gwen looked up and saw her, her face dropped. She looked shocked, maybe terrified, by what she saw. Metis confirmed Kirana's fear by shaking his head and saying, "You look just like a Warden. That's good."

Gwen blinked and looked away.

Before Kirana could say anything to her, Gwen walked beside Kirana to her pile of clothes and took out Kirana's jacket, holding it before her. She didn't do anything with it, she just stared at it. In Kirana's confusion, she remembered suddenly that the jacket was not hers to begin with; it was Gideon's. It was the last remembrance that Gwen had of him. Of Hiraeth. Gwen put the jacket to her face and held it there.

Metis looked over at Kirana for an explanation. She shrugged softly and decided against debriefing him on Gwen's history. It wasn't fair for the explanation to come from someone who only saw a small part of it. After a few seconds, Metis reached into the crate and pulled out a knife. He held it out to Gwen as she looked up, "Take a piece, keep it somewhere close." He understood exactly what she needed. Gwen took it and cut out a piece of the front. Within a minute, the jacket was returned to its hiding place, and the piece was stuffed under her shirt, resting gently against her heart.

Metis bent down and grabbed the body she had undressed, "Kirana." He nodded to the Kirana's Warden and she followed his lead by dragging them further into the crate.

It was so strange to see dead bodies. Metis had used his wire to strangle them to death, keeping them quiet and forcing them to die slowly. Kirana found death a lot easier to handle than she had first expected. She realized this wasn't the first Warden she had killed at all. No, she had killed Wardens when they chased her and Gwen. She had stabbed one through the stomach with her staff. Kirana was a murderer, and she was fine with that. If Telematic had taught her one thing, it was that not all people were worth her love and time. The Wardens tried to hurt Gwen and Metis, and Kirana realized, looking down at the dead Wardens, that these weren't the last people who would die in the name of love and connection. She had to accept that now before things got worse.

"*Death.*"

Kirana looked over at Metis, "What was that?"

He was standing on the other side of the crate, watching as Ben E climbed up using his little arm. "I found a door." He said proudly.

Metis pointed down at his android, "I'm assuming I can't take him."

Kirana laughed, "What did you mean, *death?*"

"I didn't say anything." He picked up his android, "So we just leave our stuff here and come back for it later?"

"I guess." Kirana looked down at the bodies. It sounded like a man's voice, deep and soothing. She put a hand to the Warden's neck and tried to feel for a pulse.

"I'm fine to leave my bag, it's just tools and gears." He thought for a moment, before pointing to his datawatch tucked under his Warden sleeve, "I can have Ben E navigate the hallways to get back to us, but that feels a bit risky."

"*Control.*"

Kirana knew that voice. It wasn't coming from the corpses or Metis, it wasn't coming from anyone at all.

It was the voice that had called her to the staff.

She had never considered who was calling her name that night, lost in meeting

Gwen and learning all of the Magistrater's secrets. There was someone out there, speaking to her and trying to tell her to *control.*

"Kirana?"

Kirana stood up and grabbed the staff. She took it back to the bodies, away from the other two. She was a god, this was her power. Dimensional travel. She was the only one who could reach the in-between, so there had to be something there that she could control. It was worth a shot. Kirana put the staff out in front of her and took a deep breath. She searched through the air, through the space they were in. She felt the urge to travel but did not pull herself through. Instead, she pushed the staff to the in-between, and let go. With a burst of white light, it disappeared in her hand.

Gwen and Metis rushed to her side.

"What– What did you do?"

Kirana put her hand out and tried to reach for the staff. She found it more difficult to take the staff out of the in-between than put it in, but she could feel it. She could sense its location before and around her. She reached out and grabbed the hilt, pulling it back through and showing off the staff to her Keepers.

She smiled, "Well that helps."

"A lot, actually." Metis laughed, "You really are a god, Kirana."

Kirana had spent a grand total of one and a half days as a Keeper, and though she had so quickly gotten used to being part of the ancient team and wielding the staff, she considered herself to be a god. This power that she had, to travel through dimensions, was the reason they were all standing in the Warden's world. It would be the reason for their success. The Voice was helping her, guiding her along a god's journey. She smiled to herself and decided, just for the time being, that she wasn't going to share the voice with the team. Kirana had a feeling that if they knew that her power was coming from an external source, they wouldn't respect her as much as a god. She wasn't lying by any means, simply withholding how she *learned* to do such an act.

Kirana bit down a wider grin and gestured to the staff, "So we'll just bring it out now and then and check how bright it is. We should still wrap it up, just in case we need to bring it out around other Wardens."

Metis and Kirana searched the crates until they found one filled with long pieces of fabric. The material matched that of the uniform, thick and dense, they were able to hide the glow. If they squinted they could just barely see it, just enough to track down the final Keeper. When it was ready, Kirana pushed it back into the in-between and shook out her empty hands.

Kirana looked at Gwen, and at the sight of more worry she moved over to her, "If anything goes wrong, we'll run. Okay? I'll grab the two of you and we'll leave. Just like that." She snapped her fingers.

Gwen smiled back, "I trust you, Kirana."

Her words touched Kirana more than she expected. So far their journey had been filled with fights, chases, and running, so for Gwen to put her trust in Kirana meant she was giving her very life. Kirana glanced back towards the bodies, to where she had heard the voice, and allowed herself a bit of pride as a new god. She was getting powerful, slowly gaining experience from their journey.

Kirana smiled back at Gwen and took a breath, "I think we're ready to go."

Chapter 23

Metis

METIS DID NOT hate the Wardens. He knew they were the ones taking the children, and he understood their purpose was to hurt his world, but he knew where their orders came from, and it was far beyond the loyal soldiers. The Magistrater was the cruel one, barking down orders for her own devious rewards.

The Master was like that, sitting atop his throne and giving orders. The Master was as close to a father as Metis ever had. Back in Telematic, finding a real family was a gift, and to Tech, he had the best one. He didn't know who his biological parents were or if the Master was in fact his father, but it didn't matter. The Master was everything to him, and Metis loved to listen to him, to do as he asked. Being the Master's little soldier gave him purpose, it gave him love. Metis would have done *anything* for the Master's love. He would have burned the world to the ground if it meant that the Master would smile at him, tell Metis sweet-sounding words, pat him on the shoulder. Metis did unspeakable things and returned home for that little piece of love. He broke families, killed, hunted, and kidnapped. But the love he received was no excuse. Metis knew the destruction he was causing; he just didn't care.

Even now, one of the main reasons Metis had wanted to leave Telematic so quickly was because he feared seeing the Master. What if he offered his love once again to Metis? What if Metis gave in, addicted to his false care?

Metis wondered if the Wardens were stuck in that same loop, trying to get a piece of love or some other reward in return for their cruelty.

Gwen saw them as monsters, Metis saw them as victims to an oppressor, no different than what he once was.

Getting out of the ship depo was easier than he had expected. With their faces out but turned away he expected to draw some suspicion, but no. From what he could tell, no one cared to watch them. He received glances, but most of them simply looked him up and down and then went on with their business. Metis didn't look like a Warden. They were all carefully groomed with their hair tied tightly back and no beards in sight. For the time being, Metis just looked like a messy version of them, and not a threat. That was good.

Metis took the lead, Kirana right behind him and Gwen huddled in the shelter of their shadows. Kirana didn't look worried or even slightly out of place, if anything, she looked at home. Her head was held high as she smiled at other Wardens. She was a good observer, and quick to understand body language. She watched the other soldiers and copied them. Metis tried to copy her in return, leaving Gwen the outcast behind them, too scared to give in to the enemy's nature.

They were moving through the hallways of the building swiftly, but without a destination in mind, they were quickly lost in the maze. The hallways were identical to one another, featuring the same large white walls with light gray floors and practical decorations of gray and black patterns on the edges. Doors were everywhere, some small and others large, but from what Metis could tell they matched each other and featured no number or sign to show what was on the other side. So the Keeper just kept walking forward. Eventually, Metis moved to one of the doors in a rather empty hallway and turned the doorknob. It shook but did not twist. He looked to the side and saw a panel with no buttons. Just a lump in the wall. Did they need a key? Did they *have* a key? He searched through the pockets of his uniform, opening each holster on his belt. Nothing.

He nodded to the door, "Do you have anything?"

Gwen shook her head but Kirana held up her screen, "Maybe it's this?" She walked over and pressed it to the lump. Nothing seemed to change, and sure enough, the door wouldn't open.

Metis tried to find something on him that could work as a key and noticed something along his arms. The small armor plate along his forearm had strange electrical patterns on the sides. The key might be more practical than he thought. He pressed his arm to the lump and sure enough, it glowed a bright green. Metis smiled to himself, realizing the Keepers might just have access to all Warden rooms. That would come in handy later on. He twisted the doorknob and opened the door. Inside he found a small meeting room. Dark, with few lights on the walls. Empty. The Keepers went inside and he shut the door.

Kirana put her hands out and closed her eyes, reaching forward as a white light grew around her fingers. Within a few seconds, the staff appeared. Kirana wiped her nose and looked down at her hand, "I still bleed." She held out the staff and squinted, "Do you think it got brighter?"

Metis shook his head, not bothering to look at the still faint glow, "So the crystal glows when we're near the Keeper, right?" Gwen nodded. "Okay, so it's a compass. We can't check it too often so why don't we section off parts of the city."

Gwen pointed at the door, "I say we go up and further back. If it's brighter there than we know it's not on this side of the cube."

Metis smiled at her, "Looks who's gotten into some team spirit."

She didn't smile back, "Well I was thinking… what if they aren't a real Warden."

"What do you mean?"

Gwen hesitated, but spoke her mind, "It's more likely that the next Keeper is, at the very least, somewhat connected to our cause."

"Which is?"

"To take down the Magistrater. To protect our people." She gestured to Metis, "I mean, that's exactly how we found you. You were born to protect your people. Maybe there is someone like you here."

Metis clenched his jaw and resisted the urge to shake his head. He wasn't a protector of his people, no matter the name they had given him. *Telematic Hero.* Metis wasn't born to protect his people, he was just a man trying to fix his mistakes. For now, Gwen and Kirana didn't need to know that. What they did hope was that the staff chose him because of what he had become, not what he once was: a monster.

Kirana tucked the staff in, trying to hide the glow as much as she could behind the fabric, "You have a point. But we can't just eliminate every other Warden because they—"

"I understand that." Gwen gave a nervous laugh, "But come on, it's not a Warden. They're the enemy."

Metis looked over at Kirana, who quickly glanced around the room, ignoring Gwen's denial, "Let's go across the cube first. Then we can move up and go from there." With a single nod from each of them, she pushed the staff forward back into the in-between and moved back to the door, "We'll bring the staff back out when we get to the other side. I think we have time to look around too so–"

She opened the door and stepped out. In front of her, Metis saw someone passing by. Yes, they had passed other Wardens before, but this person was different. It wasn't that he looked or dressed strange, but that he glanced over at them with sharp eyes and slowed down to a stop.

"What are you doing in there?" He walked towards Kirana.

The Keeper laughed, "We're... Well—"

The Warden looked past her and locked eyes with Metis. A frown carried across his entire face, "Why are you escorting the Second Lieutenants?"

Second... what?

The Warden sighed, pinching the bridge of his nose. He looked tired, like he had encountered this sort of situation before. "Get out."

Kirana obeyed, so what else were Metis and Gwen supposed to do but follow? They all stepped out into the hallway, Gwen lingering behind them. This was her worst nightmare, and he stepped in front of her hoping to, at least somewhat, shield her from the encounter.

The Warden faced Metis, ignoring Kirana entirely, "Have you just finished your last mission?"

"Yes."

"Then you can report to the guard mission, as a short punishment." He took something out of his pockets. It was so close to his gun that Metis got ready to grab his own. He was grateful to see the Warden bring up his screen instead. The man walked right up to Metis and grabbed his arm. He resisted the urge to pull away and let the Warden tap his screen against his right arm. With a green flash, he felt a short vibration go up his arm.

The man looked at the screen, "Willis Haroldson." He looked up to Metis, and back down to the screen, "You forgot to shave?"

Metis touched his beard and laughed, "Just came back from Telematic. Got lost, didn't have any... tools."

The Warden put his screen away, "You will report this incident to your superior commanding officer. Go to C-25-60 for your mission briefing. I will be sure you make it there." He turned to Gwen and Kirana, "Both of you will report to training immediately."

Kirana looked at Metis, but he had no way of communicating a plan. If they were to separate he would have no way of reaching them. If they could speak he could give them a time or a place to meet back up, assuming this new Warden was following him. But this interaction had caused too much suspicion. If he so much as found a photo of the real Willis Haroldson or investigated them, he would find three different people wearing the wrong uniforms, holding the Keeper's staff.

"Did you hear me!" He pointed down the hallway to the left turn, "Training room. Now!"

"Yes... Sir." Kirana grabbed Gwen's arm and pulled her down the hallway. She looked back and opened her mouth to say something, or maybe just mime her intentions, but the Warden was watching her, and she was forced to disappear behind the wall with no plan.

Metis looked back to the Warden. "C-25-60." Not knowing what else to do, he gave a small bow before walking past him in the direction Gwen and Kirana had gone down. If he could catch up with them then they could run.

"Haroldson!" Metis froze. Had he done something wrong? He forced the fear out of his expression and looked back. The Warden pointed down the opposite direction Gwen and Kirana had gone, down the other hallway. "You must have been gone a long time."

"It's been quite a day." Metis laughed and walked into the other hallway. When the Warden was out of his view he looked down the other hallway. Kirana and Gwen had walked into a more crowded space. Clumps of Wardens came in and out of doors. It took him a while to search through the crowd, and by the time he spotted someone who might have been Gwen, he heard footsteps.

The Warden was following him.

Metis cursed under his breath and kept walking down the hallway. What could he do now? Willis Haroldson was dead, tucked in a crate far from him. If they looked hard enough they could follow the Keeper's tracks right back to the bodies. This had never happened to Metis before. Yes, he had killed before, but he never had to hide the bodies. If he did, he would just tuck them in an alleyway. No one would bother retracing his steps or finding the person. But this was different. Metis was in danger, and right now the only thing he could do to avoid suspicion was to follow the orders he was given.

C-25-60.

That sounded like some code. Metis had heard it before, at least, something of the same nature. A-1-25. Someone had called a General to a location. It might just be a room number. A strange one at that. The Warden had told Metis to go down the specific hallway, which meant somewhere in this direction he would be able to find the location. But Metis didn't have a map on him. Did he? He slowed down, glancing behind him as he took out the screen from his holster. He pressed on it and it activated without any passcode. In the top left corner, it read *Haroldson*, and the rest of the screen was a series of symbols and data marks.

Metis pressed the one that looked like some sort of map. But nothing showed up on the screen. It was just a transparent view of what was before him. He held up the screen as he walked through the hallway. Maybe it was some sort of virtual system. Metis held it up to a door. There, the screen changed. It read, *F-1-80*.

It was the room number. Metis looked left and right. Same for each door. *F-1-81. F-1-82.*

C-25-60.

That sounded far away.

Metis looked around before a group of Wardens passed by from behind him. They spoke with one another, glancing at him but not looking long enough to see how lost he was. Glancing back down the hallway, Metis decided to follow these people. They might show him a better way of getting around; after all, the cube was the size of a city. There had to be some form of transportation.

He followed the group down a series of hallways. To his surprise, they didn't seem to mind him tagging along. He received a few glances but nothing more. Metis realized something, looking at the Wardens so unguarded and relaxed: they were safe. This world had no criminals to take down. No Hiraethans could take their revenge. No Telematics could wander in with a gun. They were locked in a metal cube with only their people in their own dimension far from everything they controlled. Even the Keepers, who they were looking for, were not a threat. Gwen and Kirana were young after all, neither of them good fighters or powerful gods. And the Wardens thought they were in Telematic. So why would they suspect Metis?

When the group stopped at a door he moved around them, getting away from their intended destination. He would have walked away entirely if it wasn't for the doors opening sideways. He looked back and saw a small room with walls made of glass.

It was a lift.

Metis got what he could only describe as a terrible idea, but he had to act quickly and he had no other ideas. Metis went in with the group and stood right in front of the doors. They were close to him, and though he would be the first to leave, all eyes were on him.

Metis glanced over to the panel at the side of the doors. Buttons from A to H, then buttons from 0 to 9. Someone reached past him to the panel and pressed down on D, 3, then 0. C-25-60. C could be the section of the building, a cube divided into eight parts. 25 might have been the level, and 60 would be the room number. He leaned over and pressed C, then pressed 25.

The other Wardens didn't seem to mind him, but he didn't dare look over to double-check. He got ready for the lift to move up, as all Telematic lifts did. Up or down. That's how they moved.

But he was wrong.

Up wasn't the direction they went. The so-called lift wasn't that at all. It shot sideways, moving faster than he could have imagined. It threw Metis off guard and he stumbled with the lift. He crashed into another Warden, a blond woman who tried to quickly move out of his way. He stumbled away with a small sorry, giving a smile and trying to act normal. He could put on an act, and he could play it well, just not in a world he knew nothing about. These were the first Warden faces he had seen, and most of the time, he worked so quickly to get the children free that he barely got a chance to hear their voices. For how many times he had fought the people around him, he knew nothing about them.

The lift, if he could still call it that, moved up and Metis managed to stay steady. From what he could tell, the room moved in all directions. But still, he couldn't stay still. The lift suddenly moved back, and again he stumbled, barely catching himself. None of the other Wardens flinched. They stood like statues, swaying now and then but never truly moving. Metis desperately tried to copy them. To stand still. He put his hands to his side, brushing the holster of his gun. Just in case.

He heard a noise behind him. A sharp squeal. Metis thought it was an alarm and put a hand on his gun, but when took in the noise fully he realized it was coming from someone behind him. A Warden. They were... laughing. Someone's hand was suddenly on his shoulder. Metis writhed at the touch but didn't let himself move out of it.

"Looks like someone got some Quorts from Hiraeth." His voice was husked, well used. Metis glanced back to see a nearly bald man standing uncomfortably close to him. He was smiling, "Let me guess, you spent it on some Telematic Sunshine?" He gave a wink and playfully shoved him forward.

Sunshine was a drug. They thought he was on edge because he was high or had drugs on him. That was good, Metis knew how to play a druggy. He laughed, "Well what else could I possibly buy down there? That place is a shit town."

The Warden laughed and Metis felt like he was drowning. The air was thick with tension, like smoke, but only he could see it. For now.

The man leaned against the glass wall, still smiling, "You got any on you?"

The blond woman gave a breath of annoyance, "Don't give him anything." She glanced at Metis, "He won't pay you back. And one more mess up and his Sergeant's going to kill him."

Sergeant? Metis just nodded.

The Warden waved his large hand to shoo her away, "She's being uptight. But seriously." He locked eyes with the Telematic man, "You got any?"

No? Yes? What could he do? Could he get anything out of this conversation other than a lack of suspicion? Friends? Allies? Maybe some information? The Keepers were in the Warden's world to find the final Keeper, but also to learn about the dimension. So Metis decided he would play out the situation and learn more about the soldiers.

He glanced over at the woman and bit down a fake smirk, "How much will you give me for it?"

The woman shot him a look, "Don't. I am serious." She looked him up and down, "Whoever are you?"

"I got moved." He winked, "And who said bad behavior doesn't get you places?"

She rolled her eyes and seemed to bite back a comment. The other Wardens in the lift were all intrigued by the conversation but stayed out of the way. Metis moved beside the bald Warden in the lift, leaning against the glass wall with him.

"I've gotten into so much trouble lately." He gave a tired laugh, "Gods, I hate going to the Sergeant."

"You've got that right. I hate those cells."

Cells, as in, a prison for Wardens. A place for the outcasts. Metis nodded softly, "That place sucks. Every time I hear that room number I want to shoot myself."

He pounded his fingers between his eyes and mouthed the sound of a gunshot.

The man laughed at him, a chuckle that vibrated the very room, "One day, buddy." He wiped the sweat from under his nose, "But seriously, can I get some of the sunshine? I'll pay you back."

"He won't!"

The man waved the woman away again, "I will. Okay. I can pay you right now."

Metis lifted his hands, showing they were empty, "I don't have it on me. You think I'm that stupid? I've got…" The light in the lift changed. "Some…" The view outside the glass shifted.

What was once rows on rows of concrete now extended into a new room. A new space. A new *world.* The place before him was large enough to fit an entire city within it. As they rose with the lift, higher and higher, the view only grew. The view was lit with beams of sun rays that fell through the glass roof. The light changed colors with stained glass panels along the edges, marking the walls with beams of reds, yellows, and oranges. The light reached down to the surface, to the plants. Greenery was everywhere, trees and vines swallowed every part of the ground, climbing up the wall and around a center building. Within this space were walkways and small scattered buildings, and the rest were plants. All of it leading up to one structure. One giant black tower as tall as the cube itself.

The Magistrater's Tower.

Metis was star-struck. The tower was there, it was truly right before him, the same as it was back in Telematic. It was surrounded by plants. Real plants. He had only seen them out of pictures and stories. The closest he had ever gotten to one was when he found a small sprout in a pile of trash. He was seven at the time, maybe younger. He didn't know how it got there, but by the gods he wanted it to stay. After showing it to the Master they spoke about trees and bees and things Metis couldn't even fathom. But that sprout died, smashed against a fist.

The Master didn't like to learn about plants, he was more fascinated by people, living organisms. Metis would beg for books about plants and pictures to stick to his walls, but the Master would get him diagrams and explain how the brain connected the nerves and how bruises healed. The Master loved people, maybe not their souls, but their bodies. He wanted to understand how they worked, and then, how to improve their features. Metis adored the Master, his father, his teacher, but plants were his own little joy. It was strange to think he had been so quick to run away from the Magistrater's roses when had freed the little girl with Kirana and Gwen's help. He had been so close to the plants and he had pushed through. Now, Metis allowed himself a moment to look at what he had always dreamed of. He wanted to go to those plants, he wanted to walk on grass, he wanted sunlight on his face, he wanted water on leaves, and a breeze to fill his dirty lungs.

He didn't want blood, he wanted a flower. He wanted a rose.

The man snapped in front of his face, "You good?"

"Yeah." Metis was not alright.

The lift suddenly stopped. He caught himself against the glass and as the doors opened. He looked back to see a hallway identical to the one before. The glass panel above the series of buttons read, *C-25*.

Metis smiled at the Warden, stepping back out of the lift, "I'll get it to you later."

The Warden tried to argue but he turned away and walked down the hall. He glanced back to check if they were following him and made sure the doors closed before moving on. Looking around, the hallways were empty. The Warden following him wasn't there yet, so could Metis run for it? He needed to find Kirana and Gwen or find more information. The one thing he wouldn't be able to find was the Keeper, not without the staff. He wondered if the Keepers would go on without him, or follow *him* instead. They knew the room number after all. The Warden had said it in front of them. At this point, it seemed almost necessary to go to that spot. If Kirana and Gwen were smart they could find him there, and if not... Well at least the Warden following him would see Metis was a loyal Warden.

Using the screen he did his best to follow each room number. It took him several minutes to find room 60, which had been quite a walk away. At the sight of the right door, he put his screen away and prepared himself for whatever was inside. He tapped his gun to make sure it was still ready to be used and tried to fix his hair up, flattening lumps at the top and pulling the rest of it back as far as it would go. With a final brush of his beard, he turned the doorknob and slowly opened the door.

The room was much different than how he had imagined it. Crisp and clean like all others were. Only this one had levels to it. More than 20 people were walking around or sitting on blocky white chairs lined up in rows. The seats were placed on a long staircase that rounded and faced a single platform at the bottom.

There were screens on the three walls and a round table in the center. Metis stood at the highest point, meaning the person on the platform could see him. This Warden wore a completely white uniform. Not a jumpsuit, but rather something more formal. A jacket, gray in some places, with symbols along his chest. He peered up at Metis, before moving to the back of the room, somehow signaling everyone around him to start to sit down. Metis moved with them, finding a seat at the back so no one could see him well. The seats were nearly all full, meaning he had two Wardens next to him, and many more in front. There was a beady-eyed man next to him, glasses resting on his nose. His skin was a golden brown, and his hair matched Metis's, only put together. On his other side was a person with curled orange locks. For how messy they should have been, they were able to tame them into looking formal.

Metis felt completely out of place.

"Good evening." The Warden from the platform walked to the center table and pressed a button. Within a moment the lights dimmed and a screen came up from the table. It lit up and gave the illusion of something 3D. Metis was blown away by it. Stunned so much that he almost forgot where he was. It was so crisp, so clean. It wasn't just blue, but other colors as well. It didn't glitch nor had anything wrong with it at all. It was far beyond his datawatch or anything he had seen in Telematic. He wondered what inventors they had in the building. He hoped he could bump into them, at least to sneak in a small conversation.

"Over the next 3 weeks, you all will be assigned to task 106. Guarding the Magistrater's Vault." Metis watched the screen, it looked like a door in a long hallway. It moved around, flipping the 3D scale.

"Now let's all go through the mission tasks." The hologram stayed where it was, and now the man before the Wardens started talking.

And he kept talking.

Going on and on.

On and on.

On and on.

"Then you will report to room E-50-97. You will move there from 12 hundred hours to 1215 hundred hours. Then you will have from 1215 hundred hours to 1220 hundred hours to attend to any conflicts before reporting to room C-25-90."

Metis couldn't pay attention. He expected something important, like a briefing about a new mission on Telematic. Maybe even something about the kids they were taking. Anything. He looked over at the door, wondering if he could slip out or even make a run for it. He had been there long enough. Kirana and Gwen should have arrived by now.

But he couldn't slip away.

Standing at the door was the Warden from before. The suspicious Warden. He was already looking at Metis, and when they locked eyes Metis turned back to the platform. The man was watching him. Carefully. Surely a high-level Warden had better things to do. Metis's heart started to race. He sat up straight, putting his hands on his lap and copying anyone around him.

This Warden didn't just suspect him, he might have even understood who he was. If this was a high-level Warden then maybe he had been tasked to watch out for the Keepers. Anyone out of the ordinary.

Metis was trapped.

✳ ✳ ✳

Chapter 24

GWEN

GWEN DIDN'T WANT to play the part of a Warden. She didn't want to walk in their shoes, she didn't want to wear their armor and act the way they did. She wanted to shoot them dead. She wanted their armor to be scattered with their blood, not filled with her own body. She hated the way the material felt on her. She hated the holsters and the armor plates. Gwen looked down at her hands, at the gloves that had grasped Hiraethan throats and Danny's little arm. The only thing she liked was the gun strapped to her side. She tapped it and found the hilt. She needed to be ready to grab it. Just in case.

Kirana glanced around and stopped when she saw no one was around. Listening carefully, she took the silence as a sign they were truly alone. "We need to find an elevator."

"A lift?" Gwen looked down the hallway, "I don't know if we have any other choice at this point."

The plan was to find Metis first. If the two of them found the new Keeper, they would likely need to grab him or her and run, leaving Metis behind. So, instead of searching for the new Keeper, they were following the hallways and looking for the room number.

It was funny, the Wardens were idiots. They thought they were so untouchable that the idea that the gods had returned didn't make them fear an infiltration. No, the Keepers could get by, Gwen was learning that quickly. She liked the superiority she felt over the monsters; for once in her life, she was manipulating them. Still, there was danger, and this time, it seemed Kirana understood that. As they passed groups of Wardens Kirana took the lead and walked just like the other soldiers, protecting her team.

Gwen gave small prayers as they walked to ask for the next Keeper to not be a Warden. Maybe the next Keeper was a prisoner. Maybe they secretly started a rebellion against their people. Gwen didn't want to think of the enemy as people, because they weren't, but if there was one soldier who saw the damage they were doing... maybe the staff could see that too. They needed a hero, not a heartless kill-er. Gwen wasn't going to let the enemy into the team, let alone back to her world.

Kirana took out her screen, "We need directions." She started pressing but-tons on it. Gwen didn't take out her own for fear of doing something wrong with it. She had no experience with technology, and if a Warden saw that they might notice more faults she was showing. Her fears were spread across her face, her worry was brighter than the staff.

She hated this damn Warden World.

As the two of them walked down new hallways hoping to run into a lift, Gwen heard the sound of voices coming from a large open door in the middle of the hallway. As the two of them walked by, Gwen turned her head away, not risking a glance inside. As she continued forward Kirana stayed back just on the edge of the doorway, her eyes narrowed as she peeked around the corner to look back inside.

"Kirana?"

She looked up, "It's a party." She laughed and walked back over to Gwen, "They're celebrating."

"Why are you happy?" Gwen pictured them celebrating the murder of one of her own people. When she locked eyes with Kirana, Gwen realized why she was so excited, "You want to go inside?"

"I think we should."

Gwen stepped back, "No." She whispered, "We need to find Metis."

"We have time." Kirana gestured to the door, "They were drinking, Gwen. Their guard is down. We need to learn more about the Wardens and right now we have the chance to be one of them and get valuable information."

"Not like this. Not now. Please, Kirana–"

"We won't get another opportunity like this." She walked to the door and smiled, "We'll leave in a few minutes. Trust me. We're safe."

Gwen had no other choice but to follow her. She wasn't about to walk the Warden hallways alone, searching for Metis or the next Keeper without the staff. Kirana was playing a game with their situation, trying to build knowledge for a Keeper they could never accept. To keep calm, Gwen told herself that she was learning more about the enemy, finding their weakness by acting like one of them. She ignored Kirana's naive plans, straightened her back, and walked into the monster's lair.

Gwen was expecting to walk into a conference room or a dull communal space. Instead, she was met with what looked like a Warden party. There had to be at least twenty Wardens inside, all standing around a large centerpiece in the middle of the room; a hologram featuring a spinning map of light brown buildings and scattered red dots. Gwen recognized it was Hiraeth, but she had no idea where it was in her world. The area was too small to be the city but far too large to be a neighborhood. It must have been somewhere far out beyond the mountains, perhaps a mining village. On the other side of the room was a large window that overlooked a much larger room that appeared empty. Gwen watched the window a moment longer and saw a small box rush by along the wall, then another. It looked the same size as the lift back in Telematic and figured it was some strange Warden transportation system. Fast and violent like their people.

None of the Wardens had their helmets on, in fact, Gwen couldn't see them anywhere. As the Keepers had walked down the hallways she had spotted a few wearing their helmets, but they were always marching in a small group, training, perhaps. Others had their helmets to their side or completely out of view. These Wardens were celebrating a victory, safe in their little lair.

Kirana nudged Gwen and pointed subtly to a group of Wardens in the corner of the room.

A Warden with deep black skin and a wide frame stood in front of a group of people in the same uniform as the Keepers. He spoke to the people before him, gesturing with a glass of bubbling white liquid.

Kirana leaned over to Gwen and whispered, "He must be the leader. Look how they're listening to him."

Gwen studied the Wardens around him. They were all wide-eyed, nodding as he spoke. The longer she watched them, the more she realized how none of them blinked. She also noticed a very common detail about the Wardens' faces:

they were smug. Even when listening to someone above them, they remained superior in their own minds. They believed they were better than those around them by listening to him speak, by taking in his words. Gwen caught one of them glancing over at another, watching to see what everyone else was doing. While watching this Warden, Gwen got caught in their look and the two of them locked eyes. Gwen looked away quickly and saw a tray of glasses filled with a white liquid inside, bubbling softly.

"What do you want to do here?" She asked Kirana, still upset that they were stuck with so many Wardens.

"I'm going to talk–"

A voice called from behind Gwen, "Are you Giriman?"

She turned around to see the Warden she had locked eyes with standing right behind her. The Warden had bright orange hair and blotches that were so clustered it was hard to make them out as groups of freckles. Her eyes darted across Gwen's face as she waited for an answer.

In the end, Kirana spoke up first, "I'm Giriman."

The Warden's mouth curled up into the smug expression. She extended her hand and Gwen stepped back so Kirana could shake hands. "Cyra Dowson. How is your arm?"

She looked down at Kirana's arm and the Keeper pulled away quickly, "Better than I thought it would be." She put a hand on her shoulder and stretched her joints, "Hurts though, but I'm always pushing through."

"I never thought you would be blond." Cyra glanced down at Gwen and reached past her to grab a glass off the nearby tray, "They put us in those damn helmets and then force us to come here and celebrate when we have not even seen each other's faces." She held the glass up to her lips before stopping to look at Kirana, "You look gentle. Kind. Not what I would expect from you."

"Looks can be deceiving."

She smiled at Kirana and handed her the glass, leaning forward as she did. She whispered, "Take my kill again and I will strangle you in your sleep." She patted Kirana's back and pointed to a group of Wardens, "They're playing a game, you should join." She scrunched her nose and went back into the room.

Gwen looked at Kirana, "What was that?"

"Apparently they're not above killing each other." Kirana laughed before her expression became something more unsettled, "We'll be careful." She walked toward the group Cyra had pointed to.

"Kir–" Gwen called after her before putting a hand over her mouth. She followed Kirana into the crowd, "*Giriman.*"

Kirana joined the group as they all started laughing, one of the Wardens even having to hang onto another for fear of falling down. He was a tall dark skinned man with a slim figure. For a horrifying moment, he reminded Gwen of her father. Kirana laughed with them and took a sip of her drink, "What are we playing?"

"Who are you?" The tall Warden asked.

Before Kirana could answer the Warden he was leaning on pushed him away, "You're so hostile today." She was Warden with a softer face than those around her, full cheeks and lips.

"I'm Giriman." Kirana answered, and the group gave a collective look of realization.

The softer faced Warden smiled and gestured to herself, "Beckett." She looked Kirana up and down, "We're seeing who got the worst kill. I heard you stole Cyra's victim. I'd love to hear how you did it."

Another Warden laughed at her, "Oh come on, you're just stalling."

"I will be moving to the Justice force soon, you little Army folks can do your little Hiraethan cleanings in one of those muddy fields. I'll be drinking Belic at my desk."

The group laughed and the tall Warden leaned on her once again, "You Justice force troopers think you are so special. Stuck on your asses all day while we do the real work."

"I got my fair share of kills, Clint." Beckett locked eyes with him and suddenly her expression was more aggressive than happy, "I got five of those druggies in one shot. Killed the little one too with my bare hands. I still have bits of his throat in my *gloves.*" She rubbed her hands in his face and as the group laughed Clint threw himself back and walked away. Beckett only laughed harder, "I wish we weren't in Hiraeth. Telematic patrols always get the better kills."

A Warden with her glass already empty shook her head quickly, "Those dumbasses have never caught the Telematic Hero." Kirana and Gwen exchanged a look. "If I was sent into that city I wouldn't just put the kids into the ship, I would set up a trap and lure him out."

Beckett shook her head, "They tried that already. If it worked we would have heard about his capture."

"Well we never heard about the Child Reaper." A Warden said, shrugging, "That serial killer stole hundreds of children and then vanished. They might have gotten him, but we would never know. Higher command just thinks it's a bit above us." He pointed at Beckett, "Not for you, of course, *Justice* Trooper."

The group laughed but Beckett shook her head, "Do you remember what our sergeant used to say?"

Clint peeked back into the group, a full glass in his hand, "What did you shave with, *private*? A bowl of milk and an angry cat?"

The whole group laughed as Beckett raised her glass, "Pride yourself on what you do for your people and do what you do for yourself. That's what I've done. I've set my legacy, and I'll continue to. For my people, and for myself." She lifted the glass, "To our mighty Magistrater. May her divine powers continue to bring us honor."

"Hail be." The Warden repeated as one, even Kirana joining and raising her glass. Gwen didn't care how suspicious she looked, she didn't raise anything. She cursed the Magistrater silently.

The Warden turned to Kirana and gestured, "So Giriman, what was your worst kill?"

Gwen prayed that Kirana would turn around and leave, that she would excuse herself and never speak like one of them. But she didn't, she stepped forward and smiled, "I… stabbed one of them with a rusty metal pole."

"That's nothing." One of the Wardens told her, and to Gwen's horror Kirana just laughed.

"I watched them die. I didn't just kill them, I let them bleed out. Their child was there, watching." She stared at the ground as she spoke, and Gwen stepped forward so she could see Kirana's eyes. "I put a dagger through her throat so they couldn't exchange any words. Her little kid was covered in her blood." Kirana's eyes were cold. "Then I killed them both, and left them in their house for the rest of the family to find." She smiled, "Wasn't even a part of the mission."

Gwen had tried to not think of her mother during her time as a Keeper. She knew the Wardens were terrible people, but thinking further would only make her helpless to their true cruelty. But now, hearing Kirana's words, she saw her mother's face. Beaten in and bleeding, eyes open and still. Their Warden gloves on her beautiful figure, throwing her onto the kitchen floor.

A new Warden smiled and raised his glass, "Now that, that deserves some recognition. You must be proud, that's quite a kill. Cyra has every right to be mad, you'll be recognized for your service with that kind of story."

Gwen felt sick. She turned away to leave and Kirana followed her quickly. As she pushed through the room of monsters Kirana grabbed her arm and stopped her from leaving, "What are–"

"How could you say that?" She put a hand over her mouth, physically sick by what just happened. She swallowed and prayed she would not throw up. She couldn't get the image of her mother's corpse out of her head, "You have no right to say that."

Kirana glanced around and lowered her voice, "Gwen this is good, we're learning about them. This is why we're here."

"How could you say that?" Gwen felt her eyes sting and she hated the idea that she was crying. It felt so pitiful. The Hiraethan god, crying because she couldn't hold herself together long enough to be a good spy. She was failing her people, and Kirana didn't seem to care. She blinked her tears back and pulled out her grasp, moving to the door and walking back into the hallway.

Kirana followed, closing the door behind her, "Stop!" Gwen looked back. "I don't mean those things. Obviously. I am not one of them." She gestured to the door, "Do you understand what we just learned?"

"They're monsters."

"They're people who were raised to be monsters." She walked right up to Gwen, "You can't see it, can you? They pride themselves on death, so what else could they brag about but murder?"

"It's cruel."

"It is!" Kirana sighed, "Gwen, it is. For Hiraethans, for Telematics, *and* for Wardens. They might *all* be soldiers. All of them, raised so they can only be seen when killing. That is cruel."

"You don't understand." Gwen shook her head, "You don't know death, Kirana. You have never lost someone to those... *monsters*. They have a choice."

"Do they?" Kirana asked, but Gwen just shook her head.

"I don't care, Kirana. I don't care how they were raised. They have hurt me and my family too much to ever be redeemed. This is my worst nightmare, and you seem very comfortable in it."

Kirana waved her hands in the air, "I do not like this. But Gwen, I spent my entire life watching Permidians." She lowered her voice and looked around, "I know people. I was obsessed with finding a connection with just one person in my world. I can see what is going on here without Hiraethan or Telematic bias. Tell me right now if I am doing a bad job at being the leader of the Keeper. Because from my view this is what is needed. Who is the real villain, Gwen? The soldiers or the ruler who forces them to kill?"

"She doesn't force them."

"She manipulates them. She lies to them. She puts them in a society that values one thing. It's the same thing she did to me in Permidia. I understand them, Gwen. I hate them for what they did to you and your people, but I am not going to forget who the real enemy is. The staff chose someone here, a Warden." She stepped forward and pressed her hands to her chest, "Tell me right now if, as a Keeper, I am not doing my duty to complete the team of gods. Tell me right now if your books said anything about one world being worse than the others. That unity was not deserved because of who they were forced to be."

Gwen couldn't argue. She just shook her head and eventually gave up on saying anything. She couldn't agree with Kirana, she really couldn't. Gwen hated how helpless she felt, stuck with so much hate after so many years of blood and death. She wanted Kirana to understand, but deep down she knew Kirana was right. It was her duty to the staff to unite the worlds and the team of Keepers. So there was nothing Gwen could say, she was just stuck, standing and shaking her head, eyes to the ground.

"We'll find Metis." Kirana said eventually, "I'm—"

The two of them heard someone coming down the hallway and stopped talking. Kirana gestured forward, ready to walk past the new Warden and continue on their way. But as the strangers rounded the corner, Gwen stopped walking and stared.

The Wardens had different uniforms for each rank, and Gwen had noticed the lower the rank a person was, the more armor they had on them. The high-ranking Wardens wore fashionable materials and had no reason to wear such protection. These strangers, these new Wardens, were dressed unlike any of the soldiers around them. They wore dark orange jumpsuits, a belt, and black shoes. Their uniform wasn't flattering or even Warden-like in any way. Their greasy hair was cut short or left hanging. They didn't look at the Keepers and kept walking forward. There were three of them, two men and a woman. One man held a box of glasses like the ones inside for the celebration, the other man was holding a closed crate, and the woman was carrying white cloths, careful to hold them away from herself. Gwen and Kirana watched as they walked past, footsteps quiet in the empty hallway, and walked into the celebration.

When the door shut behind them, Kirana turned back to Gwen, mouth open in shock. "They're not all soldiers."

"They looked like servants." Gwen laughed, before realizing how she sounded and shaking her head, "Kirana, one of them could be the Keeper. The Keeper is not a Warden."

"We don't know that for sure–"

Another voice spoke from behind them. "Were those the Malfunctions?"

Two Warden walked into the hallway, a woman with black hair and a man with blond curls. The woman had spoken. As she adjusted her gloves she walked towards them, smiling, "They have the good stuff?"

Malfunctions. They weren't Wardens after all.

"Yes." Kirana said with a laugh, "You two are here for the celebration?"

The woman smiled and extended her hand, "We're stopping by. I'm Giriman." Gwen went cold, and for a moment Kirana did not shake her hand. When she did, the woman laughed, "Am I not what you were expecting?"

"Of course you..." She swallowed and tried to let go of her hand, "We should go. Thank you."

Giriman did not let go of Kirana's hand, "Do I know you?"

"Well, we were on the same mission."

"You look young." Giriman looked from Gwen to Kirana, "Who is your com-mander?"

"Why?" Kirana asked, suddenly defensive. She swallowed and quickly corrected herself with a laugh, "I apologize. The two of us were just called in by General Allen. He is asking for our help. We shouldn't leave him waiting too long."

She was referencing the man on the speaker. But he was a General, not a Commander? Could they be the same thing? Gwen was drowning in questions. She couldn't breathe.

Giriman stared down at her, "The General needs you?" She nodded, and the smug expression returned, "Let's call him, I'd love to hear what he needs you for." She let go of Kirana's hand and grabbed the screen from her belt. "The celebration is for your return from Hiraeth on a successful mission, so we would love for you to stay."

"I would gladly call him myself if you would prefer." Kirana had raised her tone, spitting back each word with a sharp wit. "So I can explain that you were the one who made us late. Once that's done you can complain to him about your *little* celebrations."

"*Little–*" The blond man stepped forward, "How dare you–"

"I dare, sir. I dare very deeply. Now if you excuse us, we would not like to be late. I know you may be jealous of our improvement in company, but that is no reason to hate us." Before either of them could respond Kirana grabbed Gwen and pulled her down the hallway, "Give the other our regards!"

Gwen glanced back as they turned the corner to see Giriman watching them both, eyes narrow as if trying to concentrate on their features.

Gwen had an awful feeling that the Warden had seen the Keeper's faces before, or maybe they were just that bad at being spies. But it was clear that Giriman knew something was wrong.

Kirana started walking faster, and when they were in an empty hallway took as many turns as she could to avoid being followed. "We need to hurry." She sounded scared, truly scared, "We just need to find Metis. Then we can get the Keeper and leave."

"We don't need to find the Keeper right now."

Kirana glanced back behind them and again shook her head, "If we come back again they'll be ready for intruders. They know something is wrong, our window is between now and when they realize we're here."

"Kirana–"

"We'll grab the Warden Keeper and run."

Gwen remembered the Malfunctions and shook her head, "Even if they're a Malfunction, Kirana, we can't stay here. They'll lock us away or kill us, and it'll be so easy for them here."

Kirana clenched her jaw, "We get Metis, we get the new Keeper, and then we get out. We just have to move quickly."

Chapter 25

METIS

METIS NEEDED TO leave. It had to have been 30 minutes of him just sitting there. Listening to the man drone on and on about some mission he wouldn't even be going on. Metis wanted to know about the Telematic kids being taken. He wanted to hear a briefing about how and where they would be taken. But the mission was some sort of guarding post, so it was unnecessary to stay. He needed to regroup with Kirana and Gwen, and only then could they look for the Keeper. He leaned over to look at the door again. The Warden was still there. Not only that, but he was listening to every word of the briefing. Did he think it was some sort of grand speech? Gods, the Wardens were true psychopaths.

He turned to the man sitting beside him, "Hey, how long do these usually last?"

The Warden glanced over and then looked back to the platform.

"Do you not know?"

The man didn't answer him.

But someone else did, "The same as always."

Metis looked forward to the woman in front of him. Her head was turned forward. Short black hair straight as could be and lined up neatly around her neck.

He leaned forward, "So is it going to wrap up soon–"

"Be quiet and wait." Her voice was grounded, forged to be sharp and powerful. The Wardens seemed to have a way of being rude to each other and not just the people of the other worlds. Metis knew his own people could be cruel, but there was still some sort of softened pleasant energy around. Through all the crime and deaths, people were trying to live their life and live it well. Everything was usually done to have a good time. People stole to buy drugs to have a fun night out. People killed to get rid of a guy who was stopping them from enjoying their life. People drank to kill the unwanted emotions inside of them to have a fun day. Wardens were completely different. They were rude to each other perhaps based on some competitive system. They were soldiers given orders and praised for their ability to kill. One mission after another. It was boring and cruel, and Metis could barely sit through one mission briefing.

He wondered how many times the woman had been on missions and in briefings. The same procedure every time. Was that her life?

"How–"

"We have done this hundreds of times. Be quiet."

He glanced back at the Warden by the door, "I was just joking. But this guy can really talk."

"So can you." She spat back, head turning slightly. He was getting on her nerves.

"Who here has been stationed in Telematic?" The Warden on the platform asked, managing to grab Metis's attention.

About half of the people raised their hands beside their heads, the woman in front of him being one of them. Metis realized very quickly that most of the people around him could be one of the Wardens who take Telematic children. If he could talk to one of them, maybe integrate, he could get more information. So he too raised his hand.

The woman must have heard him move around because she suddenly glanced back. Metis studied her as she glared up at him. Her brown eyes were narrow, sharp at the edges. They seemed cold and focused. Her white skin was spotless, her lips thin, and her jawline straight as a gunshot. She took in a deep breath as they lowered their hands together.

"What?" He asked.

"Who are you?"

He smirked, "Why, you wanna buy me a drink?"

Her expression changed from a place of hatred to something violent. He leaned away from her, fearing that she would jump up and try to hurt him. She looked ready to.

Suddenly there was a hand on his back. He was pulled back out of his chair and fell onto the floor. He stumbled to his feet and stepped away from the man.

It was the Warden who had been watching him.

"Report to your Commander!" He looked over to the woman, "Both of you."

Metis quickly realized how quiet the room had become, they were all staring at him. If this was happening in Telematic there would be someone cheering for a fight or passing around drinks. Having some fun.

Not here.

It was interesting to see how two cultures valued violence so differently. In Telematic it was profitable, fun, and loud. For Wardens, it was a delicate art that happened quickly and silently. They were soldiers, but they were strategic. Violence was only as good as its outcome. If Metis threw a punch and missed, Telematics would cheer or boo, but Wardens would simply frown upon his failure.

The woman didn't complain, she didn't even look angry, she just stood up and walked to the door. The man didn't even look at her, he was locked on Metis, "Who is your commander?"

"Her's." He gestured to the woman as she walked out the door.

The Warden titled his head, "Lieutenant Colonel Allen?"

Wait... that was the General from before.

"No." Metis straightened his back, "That would be General Allen, and he's no longer commander. And... that's not my commander... sir." He hoped that was true, he hoped more than anything that it was true. The Warden before him tightened his jaw and nodded, allowing Metis to realize that it was.

"I will make sure you arrive at *your* commander, and if you aren't there, you will wish you were born a Malfunction."

Metis leaned away, not understanding the threat but figuring it was something deadly. He walked around him as carefully as he could and headed to the door. He swung it open and walked out of the room, shutting it quietly. He had no idea where to go but knew he had to go somewhere. Either run and find the others or find the Commander. He had two choices.

But as Metis turned to look down the hallway he saw something flying towards him. A fist. It hit his left cheek. He was thrown to the wall and used it to stay standing up. Looking up at the person before him he saw the woman. She shook her hand out. Yeah, he hoped her hand would hurt after that.

"What was that for?"

Metis held the side of his face as the woman walked right up to him. She stopped inches away from him, "Stay out of my way." Menacing as always. Her breath was hot, and strangely had no smell to it. Just plain old air, just as plain as she was.

She swung around him and walked down the hall. She was going to go to the Commander, the Commander he also needed to go to. Of course, Metis could never follow her there. He knew the moment someone connected the dots to his lies they would figure out who he was.

But something was grabbing his attention. Something, or rather, someone. The woman had worked in Telematic. He didn't remember her by any means, but there was a high probability that they had met before. Whether on a patrol or by sending wild bullets after him, they had met each other. She was one of the soldiers who hunted people in pipes and scraped kids off their metal homes as if they were mold. She was one of the people Metis protected the kids from, and normally the right answer would be to kill her or simply run away, but this time he could do more than that.

She knew why the Wardens were down there. She knew the mission, she knew the goal, she knew where they took the kids. And it wasn't just her, because perhaps this commander she was meeting knew more as well. They were superior to her, they might know more secrets than she did.

Gods, they could know everything. Metis could learn... *everything.* He could save the kids. He could stop them at the root of the problem. Metis would be the true Telematic god, finally saving lives. Even if it meant losing Kirana and Gwen for a few more minutes, it would be worth it.

He ran after her.

"What's your name?"

He stepped into pace beside her. Honestly, he had expected her to fight him again, maybe swing another punch. But no, she didn't even flinch. Her expression was so hard to read, it was as if she was a marble statue, stuck with a stone-cold scorn.

She looked up, squinting, "Do we not know each other?"

"I don't think so, no."

"You don't know who I am?" He raised an eyebrow, and she looked back in front of her, "Why do you want to know my name?"

He shrugged, "Just wondering."

"R. O." She stretched out the letters as if she had a disgusting taste on her lips.

"Are those your initials?"

She didn't respond, only glared up at him once before stopping at a new door. Metis realized it was the one from before. The lift. She pressed a button for it to go up.

He put his hands behind his back, "So, are we in trouble?"

"You're the one in trouble. I have done nothing wrong."

The doors to the lift opened. The woman entered first, walking right past him and pressing various buttons very quickly. Metis slipped in and saw she pressed in a code. B-105. That was much higher than where they were now and in an entirely different area. Kirana and Gwen would not be able to find him, but he would just have to risk their separation for a little longer. The lift moved like before, only this time the Telematic man was ready. He grounded himself and only stirred slightly as it moved around. RO, however, didn't even sway, and when he tripped near her with a sudden movement all she did was continue to look forward.

He stood back up straight, "So you've been to Telematic. Where were you last?"

She looked up at him slowly, "Who are you?"

"I'm new. Got transferred for some... behavioral issues." He shrugged it off with a quick laugh.

"I know the Commander well, and he won't like you. So wherever you were *transferred* from, I hope you will enjoy an even worse position. Or at least be grateful I didn't get my hands on you first."

"But you did." He gestured to his face, "I am sorry about getting you in trouble, by the way. You didn't do anything wrong, I did."

"No you're not," She spat back, "Not yet at least." The way she said it made Metis truly fear the woman beside him. He studied her again. She looked strong, with perfect posture and with muscular build. She was small, much shorter than him, but he knew she could probably attack him again if she wanted to. Metis could hold his ground, but something about her presence made him fear her greatly. As if she could truly harm him.

The lift moved up one final time before the doors opened again. RO walked out first, moving along quickly. This hallway seemed more prestigious than the others. Well decorated and comfortable, the style had changed from white, black, and gray, to white, black, and orange. Warm lights hung from the walls with plants featured between each of them in small maroon pots. What were previously doorways were now short hallways leading to large wooden double doors. Metis had to hold himself together and not run up to the plants to feel them, to see what they were like, growing and living in Warden's world. He glanced down at a wide-leafed plant and brushed his hand against it. It felt like plastic, and Metis realized he wouldn't be able to tell if it was real or not.

He took a quiet breath, "So there is no hope for me once you speak with the Commander?"

"None." RO told him factually, turning into one of the shorter hallways. Up ahead he saw the double doors, the Commander surely on the other side. His heart started racing as they neared the doors. Metis had a plan, and by the gods, he hoped it was worth it. He needed it to work.

RO knocked on the first door and stood, ready to open it.

"Come in." A male voice called out.

She pulled the door open and went inside. Metis followed quickly, doing his best to keep up with her. The room inside was smaller than he expected but well-furnished. Chairs, tables, decorations, all of it around a wood desk. Behind it sat a Warden. He looked to be in his late forties. Overweight, but hiding it well with a thick jacket. His dark hair was cut short, trimmed, and gelled. The Commander in all his glory.

RO stepped in front of the desk. She spread her legs shoulder width apart, hands behind her back, "Sir, this man has been completely out of line. We were sent here due to a commotion he made during our latest briefing."

Though the Telematic man was scared, he did not show it. He copied RO and gave the impression of someone calm. Someone calculated. The Warden looked up to him and studied his pose, "Who are you?"

Metis glanced at RO, "May we speak in private, sir?"

"Why?"

"This sort of matter is at a higher classification than RO."

RO stared at him with widened eyes. Was she shocked or simply angry? Did it matter? Some part of her believed him. That was the thing about lies, if you hold them as secrets no one can tell if they are true until you unveil them. And even then, the words have a new value to them. Permidians, Hiraethans, Telematics, and Wardens, in the end, they were all people. And people were curious creatures.

So was the Commander.

He leaned back in his chair, "How high of a classification?"

"Who holds our highest rank, sir?" Metis gave a small gesture to show that whoever this person was had sent him. In a world with no chance of invasions, he might just be able to pull off a nameless mission.

"Chief Haunton?" He turned to RO, shifting his mood, "You can head to the detainment center."

The woman was speechless for a moment, stuck in a formal stance and unable to break out of it. She forced herself to, "But sir—"

"I see that man has a bruise on his face. Did you give it to him?"

RO looked from him to Metis, struggling to answer. She was a proud soldier, she couldn't just lie. She knew that.

The Commander gave a wave of his hand, "Tell them of your actions, I will give them a proper report and you will be out within two days."

RO looked up to Metis. It was a gaze that carried both anger and disappointment. She had never asked for this, and for that he was sorry. But this was more important than her feelings. She collected herself with a breath and turned to the door. Metis watched her leave carefully. He watched the doors slowly close, and when he heard the final click he waited a few moments more. Five seconds, enough for her to leave the hallway.

When the time was right he grabbed his gun and lifted it to the Warden. But when he looked back the Commander was standing. A gun in his hand. In a panic, Metis shot at his shoulder. Two bullets rang through the room as one hit the Warden's lower arm and another hit the wall behind the Metis. The Commander let out a screech of pain and held his arm. Metis jumped over the desk and slammed himself into the Warden, grabbing the gun. He pulled it out of the man's hand and ran back. Holding up both guns the Warden slid down the wall and landed on the floor.

What just happened?

Metis looked at the door. Anyone could have heard the gunshots. What if RO was coming back? What if she was getting more people?

"You should have shaved." The Commander coughed, clutching his arm with a bloody hand, "Or is facial hair something too sentimental for a Telematic to give up so soon?"

He knew.

Metis put one gun in his holster, "You know who I am?"

"Tech, I believe."

That was not his name. He didn't let it affect him, "We need to talk."

"You're reckless, but not stupid." The Commander nodded to the gun, "You've shot at Wardens before, haven't you? That was a good aim, better than most of my people."

"Then you should know to be careful." Metis crouched down, glancing at the door again, "I want information. You give it to me and I'll leave you alive."

"Sympathy for the enemy? A strange taste for the Telematic Hero."

That name… that name did hurt Metis. He showed it on his face and shut his eyes to block out any emotion at all. Too late.

"That is you, isn't it? The do-gooder who saves the children of their world. From the stories I've heard, it's no wonder you were chosen to be a Keeper." Metis tried to speak, but the Commander cut him off, "I know the questions you will ask me. They will be basic questions until you find the heart to say the real reason you are here, and by that time it will be too late for both you and I."

"I have other questions to ask."

He scoffed, "That may be true. After all, you must be curious about the world you are in. You would naturally want to learn about my people, but that is not why you are here. If you were truly here to learn about the Wardens you would be with the other Keepers, or at least trying to find them." They locked eyes, and suddenly it felt as if Metis was weaponless, and the man before him had a gun pressed to the back of his head, "Ask me."

Metis gripped the gun tighter. He was in control, and though his intentions could be seen quickly, they were still his own. The man knew nothing about him, only the basic facts. No one understood exactly why he was doing all of this, no one ever would.

He stared the Commander down, "Where are you taking the Telematic kids?"

Chapter 26

KIRANA

KIRANA KNEW SHE was moving too fast. If any Warden spent too long looking at her they would see her panic. They could reach out and grab her, or pull out their guns and shoot her. It would all be over like that, the Keepers dead and the staff stuck in the in-between. Gwen, now walked beside her, moving just as fast. The crazy lift had taken them to a new level with doors marked with new codes reading, C-25-68 and C-25-66. They followed it together, and by the time they reached the right door, Wardens started pouring out of the room. The Keepers stood to the side, but Kirana made sure they were in view so Metis could find them. As the crowd started to move past them and thin out, no one approached. They waited, looking into the empty room and soon empty hallway.

Gwen pulled Kirana away from the door, "He's not here."

"Where is he then?"

"Do you think..." Gwen did not bother finishing her sentence, and Kirana understood what she was trying to say.

She shook her head quickly, "They would be on high alert, not relaxed like this. Intruders would be a big deal, and they would know he's a Keeper, which would–" A cluster of new Wardens came into view and she shut up quickly. She hadn't expected everything to become complicated.

Gwen gestured down the hallway and they walked away from the new cluster of soldiers, "What do we do now?"

Kirana looked around quickly, trying to find a new plan, a new idea. Anything.

Gwen was terrified of the Wardens and Metis was missing, which made her the leader. But Kirana didn't know what to do. She thought she had a way to get past the Wardens but now it all felt too complex. It was her choice now, danger or danger. One wrong move and someone would end up dead. Or worse. Not knowing what else to do, she pulled Gwen into the empty room, shut the door, and pulled the staff from the in-between. It was still covered in the Warden fabric, and before they had wrapped it enough to hide the glow entirely. Now, the red light was flooding through.

Gwen looked back to the door, "Could The Keeper be here?"

Before Kirana could answer, the light dimmed rapidly.

"What?" Kirana shook the staff, "Stop. Stop!"

Gwen put a hand on her arm, "Don't shake it."

The light only got dimmer, "How—"

Gwen looked up suddenly, "The lift." The Keeper was in a lift as they spoke, going down. "But what about Metis."

"He's not here." Kirana gestured around and forced herself to lower her voice, "Why didn't he just stay here?" She closed her eyes and pinched the bridge of her nose, "I don't know what to do, Gwen. But right now we have two choices: find Metis or find the next Keeper."

She hated Metis for not being there for them. Didn't he know they heard the room number? The Final Keeper was *so close*. That was his fault, not hers. She would never leave him behind but... for now, they would have to prioritize their efforts.

She locked eyes with Gwen, "We find the Final Keeper, we have a way to find them. Metis can either find us or—"

"Or we come back and get him." Gwen said, eyes glossy but expression stern. "He's smart, he'll be okay. We move fast, we get the Keeper, and in the worst-case scenario we leave with them and come back for Metis."

Kirana nodded and looked out the door. As she did, she saw a group of Wardens getting into a new lift, "The lift is back." She ran outside after them.

"Stop!" Gwen called, catching her as they walked into the hallway. The doors to the lift were closing and Kirana was forced to sprint forward to catch them. Gwen grabbed her and nodded to the staff still in her hand. The staff's glow was still dimming. The Keepers had to take the lift if they ever hoped to catch up to the Final Keeper, but they would need to keep it out in order to see how close they were. It would only be for a minute. The staff was still wrapped up in the cloth so they could lie about what it was. The situation would only last for a minute. Kirana glanced back and let Gwen think. After a moment, Gwen looked up, nodded, and the two of them slipped inside.

The Wardens stood at the back, leaving Kirana and Gwen at the front with their backs to them all. Kirana looked to the panel and saw this group was heading to D-10. But where had the Keeper gone? Gwen glanced at her for more instructions, but there was none to give. She leaned over and pressed H-1. The lowest she could go. They could get a better sense along the way.

The elevator moved to the side and slid down. Kirana forced her body to stiffen and stay still. She glanced down at the staff. It was getting brighter the further they went down. Too bright.

"What is that?" A Warden stepped forward, looking at the staff. She didn't look curious, she looked suspicious. Dark brown skin lined with a tight jawline. She looked like Tia, in a way. But different eyes. Heavy eyes. She didn't blink.

"It's evidence." Kirana swallowed a lump in her throat and smirked, "Why do you want to know? Trying to take credit from us for getting it?"

The room went quiet. The woman put her hand out, "Let me see it."

Kirana didn't have a gun. She had the staff. "No. It's not–"

Someone moved behind Gwen. Another Warden had grabbed his gun and pushed it to Gwen's head, thrusting it into her hair, "Drop it."

Gwen had pulled out her gun to protect Kirana. She didn't drop it.

Kirana swung the staff around as fast as she could, hitting the man's face and forcing the gun away from Gwen's head. The bullet landed on the wall with one loud *bang*. The room erupted with movement. The woman next to Kirana lunged forward and pushed her to the door of the elevator. Gwen spun around and shot the man before he could recover from the blow. Kirana pushed the staff between her and the woman, lifting it and clocking her chin. She pushed her head up in one blow and slammed her knee into her stomach. Gwen raised her weapon to shoot another Warden, but she was too slow. They grabbed her arms and slammed her into the wall, pushing her against the cracking glass. The woman before Kirana reached for her weapon as the Keeper spun the staff around and drove the end into her stomach with a scream.

Her triumph ended when a gun slammed into the side of her face, forcing her to let go of the staff. When she tried to recover they came at her again, kicking her to the elevator door. Gwen let out a scream as the Warden twisted her arm. She dropped the gun. Kirana swung a fist for the Warden, who ducked and slammed their shoulder into her back. Kirana fell head-first onto the glass wall. Gwen kicked the Warden's knee, and with a crack and a scream the soldier loosened their grip. Gwen pushed them away and dropped the gun. She lifted it and shot the Warden. Kirana spun around against the wall, only to see the soldier holding a gun to her head. The Keeper froze. She didn't know what to do. She didn't know how to get away. Gwen pushed herself up and shot the Warden first. It was smart, it was calculated, and if Kirana hadn't been leaning against a cracking wall it would have gone perfectly. But when the Warden's head caved in with a bullet, her finger twitched the trigger active. A bullet shot beside Kirana and the glass wall gave out.

The Keeper felt her body fall back. She saw Gwen racing to her but they missed each other by a second. With a scream, Kirana fell out of the elevator entirely. But the gods were on her side. They chose to keep her alive, they chose to give her a token of luck. The fall lasted less than a second before she landed on the ground. It was a hard fall, but it was not deadly. Her body screamed out in pain as glass shattered around her. She took deep breaths, trying to recover but knowing there was no time to. She needed to move.

"Gwen!" She yelled up as she shut her eyes, letting out pain in grunts and short spurts of screams. She forced herself to stand, to walk along glass and blood. The body of the Warden lay near her. Twisted and snapped. The staff stuck out of her and turned to the side. Kirana walked to her. She placed her foot on her body and pulled the wood out of her stomach. Kirana stared at the body before her. That was her doing, she did that. She was met with two feelings. One of fear, and one of pride. Yes, she had taken a life, but she had been able to do it. It felt good. She knew she would be able to do it again. For her, for Gwen, and her Keepers.

The elevator landed in its usual spot and Gwen jumped out, "Kirana!" She stood in front of her, examining her face, her hands, and her body. The Keeper was bleeding, cut, and bruised. Her uniform was stained with blood and covered in glass. Gwen glanced around them, "We need to go." She took the Keeper's hand and placed a Warden's gun in it. Kirana looked behind them. There were people in the garden space where she had landed. They were running towards them.

The window was shrinking.

With a shaking breath, she forced herself to move to the nearest door, and within seconds, she managed to start to jog away. They moved into the hallway and ran for their lives. Turn after turn they eventually forced themselves to walk, to look normal. But that was impossible, they were bleeding, guns drawn and staff half exposed and covered in blood. Kirana pushed the glass off her uniform and tried to cover the staff. The crystal was glowing brighter and brighter. The cloth could not stop it from shining through the hallway. Nothing could.

Kirana didn't know what to do. Metis wasn't with them. They couldn't just leave him, but what about the Warden Keeper?

Gwen looked to Kirana, "Who do we get now?"

"Both."

"Metis or the Keeper. Kirana, we can't do both." Her words were covered in fear. Real fear. This situation was worse than it was in Hiraeth or Telematic. They had no allies and no natural advantages. Time was fleeting, and she was right, they could only make time for one thing.

Kirana put a hand to her chest. Her breaths were flustered. She could barely breathe. "I don't know what to do."

"We should find Metis."

Kirana shook her head, "No."

"Kirana–"

"He wasn't there. We don't have time."

"We can't–"

She glared at Gwen, "You agreed to find the next Keeper."

"That was before we were nearly attacked, Kirana. They know we are here. It's over."

"Warden or not we need to find them. This is our only chance to even get a glance at who they are."

"You–" Gwen clenched her jaw, forcing herself to not cry. Kirana couldn't tell if her tears were out of anger or fear. "I am not choosing him because I hate the Wardens. We can't leave him here. Not now."

"We have a compass for one person. *One.* We don't have time to find him."

Gwen didn't respond. They just kept moving. As they passed Wardens they started getting glances, but as soon as one of the soldiers dared to move their hand with their gun Kirana would turn and shoot them. The staff was getting brighter and brighter. The Keepers moved around the area, following the glow as closely as they could. Eventually, they found where the Warden Keeper was.

In a long hallway sat a single door, darker than others, gray and black standing out amongst gray and black. There were no other doors, there were no other possibilities. There were no other people. The Keeper was behind the door. Kirana walked up to it and put her hand on the metal frame. There was no doorknob.

Gwen nodded to the panel on the wall. It looked like the one Metis had shown them. The one that had unlocked with his arm. Gwen pushed her forearm to the panel. It didn't light up. It didn't flicker. She pressed it again and again. Nothing happened. Kirana tried the same thing. Nothing.

"We need someone else." Gwen looked around the hallways, "Someone superior to us."

Kirana didn't even know what they would look like. How could they find someone like that now? There wasn't even anyone in the hallways... Suddenly, Kirana realized how quiet everything had become. There should have been more people around them. Yes, they had been careful to act normal in the hallways, but surely the Wardens were smart enough to find them. She looked up to the corner of the hallway and saw a camera. In every corner, in every crevice possible, was a small white box with a black dot in the center.

They knew. They were just waiting for something.

Kirana closed her eyes for a moment. Was it her fault? She was trying to lead them through the world and now she was the reason they could be stuck there forever. She needed to get smarter. She needed a plan, a way out of what she had brought them to. If not for her stake then for Gwen's, for Metis. But they were running out of time. Kirana was running out of time.

"*Sacrifice.*"

She looked to Gwen, "What?"

Gwen pushed her arm to the panel, "It's not working."

That voice... That wasn't Gwen.

She looked around the hallway for a source. No one was there. No Warden. It wasn't from a person. It wasn't from anything at all. It felt like... something within her.

It was him. It was the voice that called her name. The voice that led her to the staff.

Gwen stepped away from the door, her breaths were as heavy as her words, "Kirana what do we do?"

"*Sacrifice.*"

The voice was guiding her. He was showing her a way to save her Keepers.

Sacrifice... Kirana knew what to do.

She pounded the staff onto the door, "Hey!"

Gwen tried to pull her away from the door, "Kirana–"

"We need help!" She put a hand on Gwen's shoulder and squeezed until she stopped pulling her away, "They're here!"

For a moment there was nothing. Before a voice called from the other side of the door, "Who is here?"

"The Keepers. They're coming this way. Let us in!"

"Who is your Commander?"

There was a noise down the hallway. It sounded like people. It sounded like people moving towards them.

"Let us in!" Kirana pounded on the door, "They'll be here any minute!"

After a moment, an awful, thoughtful moment, the door opened. A man looked around out from the corner of the door carefully. A mess of orange hair circling his head matched a long brown jumpsuit. This man was not wearing any armor. He was not in a uniform Kirana had seen before. As he saw them his eyes suddenly widened. She lunged for the door and slammed into it as he tried to push it shut. She squeezed her body inside and pushed the door onto the wall, keeping the man behind it. Gwen came rushing inside, holding her gun up and looking around her.

Sacrifice.

Kirana threw the staff into the room. Gwen looked back at her as she gripped the door's side, "Find Metis. Find the Keeper."

Before Gwen could make it to the door the Keeper took her gun and shot at the panel inside the room, before swinging the door shut and aiming another bullet to the second panel. She shot at it five times, just to be sure. Five times for Gwen. When she kicked at the door to make sure it stayed closed. She could hear Gwen trying to open it on the other side.

"Kirana!"

Kirana looked down the hallway where the noise was coming from. She mustered up whatever strength she had left and ran for it. By the gods, she ran. She sprinted down every hallway, she took every turn she could. She moved past every room and pushed off every wall, until she turned a final corner and her path was blocked. A group of Wardens ran towards her, guns raised. She slipped at the sight of them, stumbling back the way she had come. Not towards Gwen, she couldn't take them back to her. She ran down the next hallway and the next, until she managed to find her way into the Warden garden. She ran onto the grass and into the maze of hedges, trees, and flowers.

The Wardens were right behind her, following her and finding ways to cut her off even when in the garden. Kirana kept running, but soon her luck ran out, and something flew past her. Not a bullet. Not a spiker. Two little dots that hit the tree beside her. They weren't fast enough to go through her, so why shoot them?

She tried to go back the way she had come but the Wardens were catching up. There was another *bang* as the circles flew around her. This time, they hit her. They stuck to her armor, and as she tried to claw them off of her they let off a sharp click. A burst of energy filled her body suddenly. Not like the staff, not something good, not something powerful, something deadly. The energy shook her very bones. Her body tensed and with a scream, she dropped to the ground. It didn't stop. Her body shook violently on the ground, and when it finally stopped she couldn't breathe. Her body trembled. She couldn't move, stuck not by force but by trauma. By fear.

To make the whole situation worse, Kirana looked forward to seeing flowers before her. Beautiful, meaningful, roses. The Magistrater's roses. She wanted to scream. A hand grabbed her, then another, and suddenly she was being pulled up. She was useless. She couldn't resist. If her body had been weak before then now it was just broken.

The Wardens pinched her arms back and she forced her head up. A Warden walked towards her. He looked… happy.

He looked proud.

He was young, not just by age but by the inexperience in his eyes. He had this spark that was getting its fill by simply looking at Kirana. "Is this our god? She looks more like a child."

Something pulled her arms behind her back and she found the motivation to lunge forward and try to escape. They would not let her out of their grasp.

The Warden grabbed her face, "She acts like a child too."

He let go of her, and her head threatened to drop down again. She wouldn't give in, "I am not a child. I am a *god*."

"It would seem so." He waved to someone behind him and stepped away from her.

They were going to do something with her. She knew that. She knew they would keep her alive, for now. She knew they would go after the others, whether that was Gwen or Metis. She knew that her plan had gone wrong. She didn't know if it was her fault. She didn't know if she was supposed to choose guilt or revenge. She didn't know how they would escape.

But it didn't matter. Gwen got away. Metis was still safe. They could do this. They could find the Keeper and get away. She wished she could give them an easier trip out of this place, but she couldn't. This was as much as she could do for them.

A Warden came in front of her with a machine she couldn't identify. It looked dangerous, shaped like a human face with wires stretched across the forehead and eyes. Someone grabbed her head from behind and they pushed the machine onto her face. With a small burst of energy, she felt her head fall, and stay down. Her eyes closed, her body went limp, and before she went unconscious she made a silent promise.

She would do anything in her power to get back to her team.

Chapter 27

* ✳ *

METIS

METIS DIDN'T REMEMBER the first time he saw the Master work on a client. If anything, it was simply a normality, and only years later, after Metis had gone to the true city, did he realize that blood and pain were not normal. Only after everything did Metis realize not all children grew up as an extra hand in surgery.

Metis grew up in the Master's shop, down in the lower pipes. It was one of the worst places in the city, just behind the Wasteland: a series of collapsed platforms barely standing, filled with garbage and forgotten bodies. It smelt like rotten meat and piss. Every house was twisted or tilted, half destroyed and barely standing along the fast-moving channel in the middle of the street. A place for the lost and forgotten.

Metis hadn't known anything else. The Master kept him home, kept him safe. The shop was small, half working area, half living place.

The Master saw himself as some sort of miracle to society, so Metis did as well. He worked with prosthetics, trying to get Telematic to *upgrade* and *advance*. He worked on a smaller scale, replacing limbs with simple designs, but to him, that was child's play. In his spare time, he worked on advanced inventions far beyond Metis's comprehension. Day and night, it was all he did. The Master would talk about how brilliant he was and how his intellect was far beyond those around him. Truth be told, he was a genius, and his goals were never too far from reality, but Metis saw him as a god. His father, his master, a divine figure he had the honor to work with.

"You are my apprentice." The Master would tell him with a smile, "You get to help me and our world."

Once Metis was six, he was pronounced old enough to go outside, to scavenge. He used to go into the Wasteland or run down the streets to find wires, metal plates, batteries, and anything that looked shiny and useful. It felt purposeful. One pat on the head and Metis was practically glowing. Even if he had been followed home, scared away with a gun, threatened… it didn't matter. As long as the Master was satisfied, it was justified. Metis put himself and others on the line to get those items to him. At first, he did it for his world and for his father's goals, but over time it grew into an obsession for the Master's praise, for his god to smile down at him. When Metis came home with an abundance of items the Master would talk to him and laugh. When Metis came home with only a handful the room would go still and cold, and suddenly the Master was busy with other more important matters.

Looking at the Commander now, Metis thought about the Master and all he could do to the Warden. That was the thing about old memories: the worst ones always become lessons. Metis knew he was skilled enough to give the Warden upgrades. He looked at his gunshot and traced where the bullet would have gone. Metis could fix him, not just heal, but fix. It was a horrible trait to have.

Metis's gun was still aimed at the Commander, but he no longer had to hold it to his head. The Warden understood the threat.

"You're different than we pictured you, Tech."

Not his name. "How so?"

"We always saw you as something flimsy. Someone reckless for the fun of it." He pulled a hand away from his arm and reached below his desk, "There is a bottle of Belic, mind if I pour us a drink?"

Metis held the gun up again, "I don't plan on getting to know you one-on-one, Commander. Put your hands on the desk and answer the question."

He looked disappointed, but put his hands back on the table, "Fine. You wish to know where the children are taken."

"Yes."

"But you haven't asked *why*."

Metis glanced back at the doors. How much time did he have? The gunshots were loud, anyone could be coming. But if the Commander was truly going to tell him something of interest he needed to listen, to stay longer. Was it a trap?

He might just give in if the right information was shared.

"Fine. Why?"

"Because they are worthless."

Metis stared at the Commander for a moment. He thought about how easy it would be to shoot him there and then, to cave his proud Warden face in with a single bullet. But he couldn't, not yet.

The Commander pointed at him with his good hand, "That look. It's that look that we could never put down on a data file. You see them as so much more. You see them as worth something."

"They're just children."

"Your people are selfish, what makes you different?" The Warden waited for an answer. He locked eyes with Metis and became patient. Metis did not speak, he simply looked away. He wasn't there to be interrogated, he was the one there for information. He had the gun. He had the power.

"Where do you take them?"

"You're a Keeper, are you not?" The Warden shrugged softly, "You should have been able to connect the dots by now."

"What dots?" He glanced back at the door again, "Just answer the question or I'll make sure you're not left with any good arm."

"Did you live in the pipes?"

Metis lifted the gun higher, "Where."

"I will tell you where." The man got softer, "If you tell me who you are first."

"No." He stood up, "Do you not see your situation here? I have the gun. I can kill you in a second–"

"But you won't." The Commander laughed, "Not until I give you every answer you need. Then you'll kill me. At least give me this, Tech."

Not his name. "Fine." He sat back down, "There isn't a kid in Telematic who didn't grow up in the pipes."

"Is your name Tech?"

No. "Yes."

"Why do you save the children?"

"Because they're kids. They're just kids, and you take them away from their families. That is reason enough." That was a lie, but the Commander didn't need to know his every motivation.

Metis grew up watching the kids in the pipes. One step down and the Master and him would be there with them. He didn't like to talk to them when he was younger, but he would watch them play and scavenge. Most of the kids lived on their own, or in their little groups. Sometimes they were even recruited into gangs. Metis had the adults do one of two things with the children: have pity and love, or have greed and anger issues. Metis wasn't saving them from anything, he knew that, but he couldn't just let the Wardens take them somewhere worse. He couldn't just let them die. Not like that.

The Commander watched him carefully, "Do you honestly think we have no mercy?"

"It crossed my mind."

"I have a child." This shocked Metis. He had never pictured a young Warden before, let alone with a family. "Her name is Luna. She just turned eight."

Metis knew what made a good parent. It wasn't in the way an adult supported a child, but in the way they set them up for life. Yes, kind words build golden hearts, but sometimes you need to get hit to learn how to fight. Parents need to be hard, but not strike long-lasting fear. They need to be caring, but not overprotective. He had seen two sides of such a balance with two fathers. On one end, a man who spoke loving words over a beating. On the other end, a man who comforted his child into weakness. Neither father was good, and neither one made good children.

What was the man before him? A Warden, yes. A liar, maybe. But a father always had a love for their child, it just depended on what type of love.

"How is she?"

The Commander hadn't been expecting that question, it caught him off guard, and for a moment he allowed a small sliver of fear to take over his expression. Wardens were good at acting tough and pushing forward. In their culture they were strong or they were weak, and there was no inbetween. Metis wondered if the man had brought up his child to make him feel guilty. It was backfiring now, making the man feel guilty instead. He loved his child. "She's at the top of her classes. A good shot."

"You train kids?"

"We train the next generation."

"Doesn't that scare you?"

The Commander's eyes flickered somewhere for a moment before his face settled back on something smug, "You have a knack for finding emotions. Have you always been able to do that?"

Metis leaned back in his chair, "You don't have to die."

"You have such a sympathy for people. Why?"

He shook his head, "Because no one else does. Not even your people. Do you realize the power you hold? Don't you see the good you could be doing?"

"We are doing good–"

"You're not. In Telematic you're just patrolling the streets for… what? You don't stop murders, you don't stop drugs, you don't stop any basic crime? The only thing I have seen you do is shut down a business. Once. I've seen it once. It was the only good thing you people have ever done." He gestured back to the door, "I am not here for this, alright. I am trying to help my people, I just want to save them. I don't want to leave Luna without a father but what if she was one of those kids? Think about that."

The Commander closed his eyes. Whether it was in pain, annoyance, or fear, Metis could not tell. Nor could he understand who it was for. Himself or Luna? He opened his eyes and stared back at the Telematic man, "We don't kill them. We use them."

Metis leaned forward, "For what?"

"For our projects."

"What kind of projects?"

"The kind you need thousands of workers for."

Metis shook his head firmly, "I need specifics. I need coordinates."

"We don't keep them in Telematic."

His heart started to race, "Where?" This entire time, through everything, Metis had been right in the middle of the fight. Maybe the Keepers were right, he had been chosen for this. His work, his cause, his actions, they were all linked to the Magistrater, to the Wardens. To the Keepers.

He was a god.

This was his purpose.

Swept up in his revelation, he didn't hear the noise behind him. By the time he caught onto a creek of a door, it was too late. He tried to get up from the chair, but as soon as he started to move there was a small *bang,* and he felt something hit his back. He tried to ignore it and turned around to fight. But he couldn't. A stream of violent electricity pumped through his body in a wave of cold fire. He shook under his skin and the gun dropped from his hand onto the floor, then he dropped to the floor. When the electricity finally stopped he tried to get himself to move, to escape. But he couldn't. The Wardens grabbed him, pulling his body around and back up. His legs nearly collapsed under his weight.

There was a gunshot. Metis stayed still. He waited for the pain to hit him, for his blood to start spilling out onto the Wardens' floor. But there was no pain. He looked up to see the Commander drop onto his desk, before sliding off onto the floor.

"No!" Metis tried to get out of their grasp. The Warden who had shot him looked proud. He looked *proud.* "He didn't do anything!"

The Warden was young, maybe even younger than Metis. "All he had to do was sit there and wait." He put his gun away, looking at Metis, "I should thank you, clearly he was not fit to be a Commander."

"He had a daughter, you *monster!*"

He turned to another Warden behind him and laughed, "That electric shot sure did a lot more damage to the other god."

Other god...

"Take him to the detainment facility. We can give him some time to recover before the Magistrater arrives."

The Magistrater was coming. She was coming... to see them. To see him. The Warden didn't need to put a gun in his face to threaten him, he knew his words, he knew his tone. He had manipulated Metis into standing still. Something cold was suddenly pressed against his face, and within seconds a wave of energy flooded through his head. His body gave out, and soon he was unconscious.

For a while he felt nothing, he saw nothing. As time went on he got glimpses of the world around him. His senses activated in flickers, now and then trying to pull him back to consciousness. He could hear voices, and the thump of Warden boots. Then it went back to black. He could feel his feet dragging along the floor. Then black. He could see a hallway, a life, and a floor scattered with broken glass. Black. Then for a while, there was nothing, just a deep sleep he could not pull out of.

When his body finally came back to its senses he forced himself awake, blinking and forcing his eyes open he saw a dark space around him. The rooms had been entirely white, until now. Now, the walls were black and gray. He was lying on his side, head pounding. As he tried to move his body ached. His brain threatened to peel out of his skull. He didn't let it. He tried to bring his hands beside him, only to find them in handcuffs behind him. With a groan he rolled onto his back, pulling his legs up he tried to fit them through his arms. Weak and not that flexible, it took him a while to get his hands in front of him. By then he had gathered enough strength to stand. Slowly he rose off the floor. With a stumble, he nearly fell forward, but something caught him. His arms pulled back around to face the other wall. He looked to find the handcuffs chained to the back wall.

The handcuffs themselves were strong, mechanical, and well-designed. It would take a key or maybe a switch to get them off, nothing he could manage without proper tools and a full hour's work. He looked around the room. It was larger than he had expected. Poles lined one side of the long room, shadowing a dark concrete floor. The other side of the room had layers of beds and a small section cut off for what he expected was a bathroom. This place was intended to hold soldiers, not real prisoners. That made sense. Why would a world prepare for prisoners if everyone was a soldier? This was the best option for Metis's detainment.

It took Metis a while to notice someone sitting on a top bed. They were covered by shadows but looked comfortable in the darkness. "What did you do?" She asked.

It was RO.

He noticed now her hands were free. By the fact she was so curious he assumed she had no idea that the Keepers were around her. Or rather, in front of her. Metis looked back down at his chains and went pale. He was trapped with a skilled killer. The only advantage he had now was that she had no idea who he was. He needed to keep it that way.

"I lied to the Commander." He told her with a shrug, "He got angry and I hit him." Metis didn't like shaming the dead, even if he barely knew them. He forced the image of a grieving child out of his head. It was his fault, but he could deal with guilt later. "I'm sorry I got you sent here." He gestured around with his handcuffs, "It's been a crazy day."

"Who are you?"

This would be the second time she asked him that question. Metis looked up to find her sitting on the bed with her legs on the floor. She had been able to spin around so quietly. There was anger behind her words, he could see it, she wanted the power behind knowing his name.

Her people already knew who he was, or soon she would learn too. "I'm Metis."

She squinted, "A Telematic name?"

"My mother had a sense of humor."

RO jumped off the bed, landing softly and walking over to him. She pulled something from her belt and held it up for him to see. A datawatch. Metis was confused as to why she would have a Telematic device until he looked down at his wrist and realized he was gone. He instinctively walked towards to get it back but was stopped by the chains.

"RO–"

"What is going on outside, *Metis.*" She extended his name and let the final letter last too long for comfort.

"How would I know?" He put out his hands, "Give it back."

"I know someone came in before you."

"Before me?"

"The door opened. I heard a commotion. They have not come inside yet, are they lined up outside?"

Metis took a piece of the truth and laughed, shaking his head quickly, "I was knocked out. I didn't see anything." He put his hands as far out as they would go, "Please give it back."

She twisted her jaw and raised her chin, "Why do you have this?"

"I stole it. It's a trophy from a guy I killed in Telematic. My first."

"You keep this thing as a trophy?" She studied Metis, looking him up and down, "You heard nothing?"

"To be very honest with you, RO, I would tell you everything I knew. But if there was someone out there, I didn't see them."

She rolled the datawatch in her hand for a moment, taking her time to think before suddenly smiling, "You're pathetic." She tossed the datawatch and Metis caught it, stepping back closer to the pole, "You keep that damn thing on your wrist all day?"

Metis looked up at her as she walked back over to the beds, "Did you search me?" He slipped the watch back on, "Stay away from me–"

"Or what, Metis." She climbed up and returned to her original spot, "You'll run after me? You'll chase me down? You'll climb up here and take back your Telematic trophies?" She leaned back into the shadows, not bothering to wait for a response.

Metis glanced down at his datawatch, opening it to check if RO had changed anything on it. He wondered now how the Wardens had missed it when they searched him. It would have been hidden under the cuffs, pushing down onto his wrist. The watch was thin enough so that when the Wardens pushed the handcuffs on the thick metal hid it from view. If they had searched him they would have probably looked for weapons, not watches.

A datawatch was nearly useless away from Telematic. It was a communication tool and a Korts-keeping device. It was other things as well, of course, but nothing as useful. After all, he didn't have any Telematic people to connect with.

Except, Metis did.

He had Ben E.

Doing his best to slip it up his wrist, he started scrolling through the systems. But what about RO? She would easily hear him in the already silent room. He would just have to improvise.

He called Ben E and, placing his hand over the speaker to muffle the noise, yelled to RO, "Hey these handcuffs are tight, do you mind coming here to help loosen them for me?"

The Warden didn't respond, but Ben E did.

"Where, sir?"

He dug his hand into the speaker. Metis A joke. "If you heard something outside the prison, or barricades I guess, do you think they'll come in here?" Metis had glanced down for a moment, and when he looked back up RO was watching him. Her eyes lit up in the shadows. She didn't blink.

Ben E responded again, "Where?"

"Do you mind if you come down here and loosen these cuffs?" His heart was racing, "Just track me down and give me a hand."

Ben E had a tracking system, he had just forgotten. Metis didn't make him for full productivity, he made him to be... someone in his life. Not that he was the one who made him, exactly, he just got to choose the personality. He remembered how the Master had laughed at his request, but still, at the end of the day, after the long hours, he would get right to work on Ben E. Metis had watched him make every part of the android and even got to help along the way. Ben E was a symbol of happy memories, good times, and laughter. Yes, Metis had improved parts of the android so they could fight off Wardens and save the stolen children, but he couldn't just change Ben E's nature.

Metis knew the Master did horrible things. He knew his father hurt people, including Metis. But Ben E represented the love that he had grown up with, no matter how fake it seemed. Now and then, when alone with Ben E, Metis would hear him talk and think he was the Master. They had similar voices, perhaps it was a gift from his father, and still Metis had no idea whether to scream at the sound or laugh at the Master's humor. He chose to be ignorant and selfish, keeping Ben E and not bothering to think of what it truly meant to him or the Master's legacy.

"Oh!" The android gave his robotic laugh, and before he could respond Metis fumbled to shut off the call.

He smiled at RO, "Help a friend out."

"*Friend.*" She sunk back into the shadows and went out of view, "You have no idea who I am. *Metis.*"

Her words were so frightening that he found himself scared to respond. After a moment he decided he might as well, "Who are you, then?"

There was no answer.

Metis took a deep breath and sat down at the pole, giving in. It was then that the silence of the room hit him. He could hear himself breathing, the moving of the chains, but nothing else. RO was soundless in an empty room. He listened to anything beyond the door. It too remained quiet. Perhaps the metal was too thick for noise, but RO had been able to hear things. Surely something would come through. No. If there was no one else beyond those doors then RO was the only one there. She was the only Warden in the prison.

Metis didn't know the situation. He was making assumptions but he didn't have any other choice. The Warden from before had mentioned another god had been captured. It seemed that either Gwen or Kirana had not been careful, they slipped, and one or both of them was locked somewhere else in Warden's city. Metis tried to think of what could have happened to them, and more importantly, why they weren't there in the detainment center. The Keepers were following the staff, something must have gone wrong and they were desperate enough to let themselves be known to the world.

If one of them were still out in the world, alive and hidden, then they would be after the next Keeper, not him. Metis needed Ben E to rescue him so he could try and escape. But honestly, sitting there, chained to the pole and relying on the android, he was losing hope.

The Keepers needed a miracle.

Chapter 28

KIRANA

KIRANA PUT HER head back against the concrete wall. She was sitting on the floor in a long empty cell. It was just wide enough for her to sit and long enough for there to be a large gap between her feet and the door. She was wearing handcuffs, large ones that stopped her from moving her wrist around. The Wardens were taking every precaution to keep her from escaping, but the idea that they thought she was so powerful felt good. It was a lie, and sitting there alone she realized how helpless she truly was. She was meant to be the leader of the gods, yet there she sat, alone and without hope. Metis was gods know where and Gwen was running from the Wardens, and it was all her fault for not protecting them. She was a Permidian in search of connection, but the moment she found them she let them slip away.

Feeling such loss reminded Kirana of the day Tia left her, the beginning of her desire for other people in her life. It was the day after her 12th birthday when she awoke to find the house empty. Her sister lived with her, cooked with her, ate with her, and slept in a room right next to hers. They did everything together like a little team in their perfect lives. That morning Kirana expected to find her in the kitchen or getting dressed, but when she went into Tia's room she found the cupboards empty and the walls bare. Tia was at the front door with a small baby blue suitcase, white gloves, and tidy hair.

Kirana had run up to her, "Where are you going?"

"You look so grown up." She pointed at her figure, "You've become quite a mature young lady, so now it's your turn to get your own house."

Kirana remembered feeling so scared, and she fumbled her words over a fast, fake smile, "With you."

"No no, just you." Tia grabbed the doorknob, "Come along, I've found you a nice place on the edge of the field you like. I think you're going to like it."

"Where will you be?"

She pointed out the door, "In the city."

Kirana quickly tried to shut the door, "No, no it's fine, we're fine here."

"Living your days with me shouldn't be a part of your perfect life–"

"But it is! It is, please Tia. I don't want you to go!"

Tia bent down and held the side of her face, "I'm not going anywhere. Just because we're not in the same house doesn't mean we won't see each other." She beamed with joy, "Think of the fun we will have."

Kirana grabbed her waist and held her, silently vowing to never let go until her sister stayed. She sobbed into Tia's dress, "*Please!*"

"Kirana let go of me."

"You can't–"

Tia had nearly tripped back and, scared of hurting her sister, Kirana let go. Tia bent down and held her shoulders, "Have you ever considered my life?" Kirana remembered how cold that moment felt, how horrified she had been to hear those words. Tia pushed a piece of Kirana's hair behind her ear, "I will visit you, Kirana. But our time living together is over. I need to have my own perfect life, and it is time for you to live just like the rest of our people."

Kirana sobbed, "But I love you!"

"And I can't." She smiled softly and shrugged, "You just never saw it. No one is like you, Kirana. You're different, and I'm not."

Before that moment, the memories Kirana had of her sister were so bright and happy. All she could remember was how loudly Tia could laugh or how much mess they made together in that kitchen. After Tia's goodbye, those memories were ruined by Kirana's fear of having ignored all the signs. She couldn't tell, even now, if Tia had once truly loved her, or if Kirana had been ignorant and oblivious.

Sitting in the cell after losing Gwen, Kirana had never felt more certain that Tia may have never loved her, and those memories were stretches of her hope for a loving sister.

Kirana missed Gwen so much. They had met each other while running and bleeding, but the connection had always been there. Kirana had found love and now she had lost it. It felt the same as losing Tia, the same heartbreak. The only difference was that Kirana felt more powerful. She was imprisoned and helpless, she couldn't deny that, but with the Voice whispering in her ear and the title of a god, Kirana felt as if she had the potential to be powerful. Not yet, not while sitting in the cell at the Warden's rule, but soon. Then no one would be able to take Gwen away from her again, and Kirana would never experience the helpless heartbreak of losing someone she loved again.

Kirana could hear someone coming. Her first thought was Gwen and she got up quietly to check. The metal door had a small window right at eye level, and carefully she looked through it. The two Wardens posted outside her door were stepping forward from their posts to greet someone coming down the dark hallway. Not Gwen. The two Wardens reached over and opened the door. Kirana stepped back.

The high-ranking Warden, nearly armorless with three stars on his chest plate, stood framed by the doorway. He looked old, gray hair cut short around his ears and stern expression lined by wrinkles. The other Wardens, helmets on, walked into her cell. Kirana didn't move until they grabbed her arm and forced her out. They pulled her forward and moved her out of the doorway. There were more Wardens scattered everywhere, all of them watching her with the same look: pride.

The high-ranking Warden walked up to her, "There was an old story our superiors used to tell us as children. They said the Keeper's goldy powers were commanded by both the connection to their worlds and the hate they fostered for their enemies. I'm curious, how mad would you be if we strung up your Telematic friend on display without his head?" Kirana could barely process what he had said, and by the time she had her body start shaking. He smiled, "I've always wanted to see the godly power. The thing you should know about my people, little Keeper, is that we're always looking for more ways to become stronger. You'll be good for us."

"He's not–"

The Warden behind her pulled her away and walked her further down the hallway. Kirana clenched her jaw and did her best to control her breathing. She looked around for something. Anything. She glanced from Warden to Warden, staring at their guns. If she wanted to escape she would need a weapon. And her team. And her staff. And the other Keeper...

The Wardens went up the stairs and pushed her up to follow. She did so, though every step she took made her wonder if she should just bolt there and then. If she even managed to break free of their grip she knew there was no possible way to escape from there. She was walking the halls of some strange, small, and dark hallway which only had one cell and a series of stairs. As they walked up the stairs she looked through the doorways into other levels and saw dozens upon dozens of Wardens watching her. If she ran, they would hurt her and she would hurt their ego. Then they would break her. Up and up they went. Higher and higher. Until they stopped at the top floor.

Kirana suddenly realized she needed to focus on her own safety, rather than the idea of escaping. Kirana needed to survive whatever diabolical room the Wardens had prepared for her. She looked around the new floor, seeing how it only had one of the long hallways. It led to a single gray door. She looked down and saw light peeking out from within the room. Orange light.

As they neared, she felt the two Wardens suddenly let go of her, and she instinctively stopped where they left her. One of the Wardens opened the door and Kirana decided the best thing she could do was stay there. Running would only get her less mercy. The Wardens didn't see her as a threat, and for now, that had kept her from being tied up and dragged. They knew they could catch her, and she did as well, so what else could Kirana do but stand her ground and look through the door?

She expected to see a torture room. Something filled with machinery and blood. She prepared herself to walk in with her head held high against all odds. She got ready to yell at high-ranking Wardens or stay perfectly silent despite their questions. But that was not what she faced before her. The room wasn't dark, nor covered in blood.

It was a dining room.

A nice one at that. The Warden's world had styles with grays, whites, and blacks, patterned with a Warden style and decorated with a few plants here and there. This room felt like the furthest thing from a Warden room. The walls of white and gold looked like the Magistrater's throne room. There was only one piece of furniture, a long wooden table. It was covered in blooming bouquets and a garden-like spread of plants. Roses, tulips, all of them pinks, reds, and golds. Plates and chairs were fitted together to seat more than 20 people. But no one was there. The only person was seated at the end of the table.

A Warden.

Only, they did not look like the Wardens Kirana had seen before. Yes, this person's uniform matched that of their people, but it was different. Black, much like the Telematic uniform, and covered in decorative gray stripes. The Warden wore an array of black armor along their body, each piece well polished. Though there was a plate of food before them, their helmet remained on.

The Warden stood up when they saw the door open, "Kirana."

One of the Wardens pushed Kirana inside and she stumbled through the door. As it closed behind her she felt the handcuffs around her wrists loosen, and suddenly fall. She was free.

The Warden gestured to the seats before them, "I can only imagine how hungry you are."

Kirana looked around the room. The only door was behind her, certainly locked and guarded. This environment was some sort of trick, she wouldn't fall for it. Kirana approached the table slowly. She looked from the food to the Warden, and grabbed the first knife she saw, putting it up to the stranger, "I would rather die than eat with you."

"How dramatic." The Warden sat back down, "And you have no idea who I am. Please put down the knife, that's useless here."

Kirana didn't put it down.

The Warden sighed, "If we wanted you dead we would have killed you back in Hiraeth. The only reason you were able to get so far was because we didn't want to hurt you." They paused, and shook their head, "I guess we did end up hurting you. I apologize for that, my people take violent actions to achieve their goals. It's our fault, really, we train our people to be killers and then expect them to act with mercy at our command."

"Who are you?" Kirana adjusted her grip on the knife. She didn't know what else to do. To simply drop it felt like she was giving in to this trick. She couldn't do that.

"I am Chief Haunton. Right hand to the Magistrater." Kirana's reaction must have been obvious, because the Warden laughed and gestured to her face, "You assumed she works alone? She is powerful Kirana, but even gods need a team."

"Just you?" Kirana glanced around the room, wondering who else could be watching.

"I am what my people call a Specialist. There are a few dozen of us for missions of dire importance based on the Magistrater's orders. But I am *the* Specialist. I am second to the Magistrater and above all Wardens. I am the one who puts her plans into action. I oversee everything. Including you."

Kirana looked around the table. She would need a bigger knife.

Haunton gestured to the seats again, "I simply want to talk. There is much to discuss."

"I have nothing to say to you. You or the Magistrater. Except to call you all villains and evil, cruel people who let entire worlds suffer."

The Warden leaned back in their chair, "We knew you were a Keeper."

Kirana stared at the Chief. She tried to find something to say. Anything. But she couldn't. In her silence she found herself waiting for more.

"The staff doesn't normally do that. It should have accepted you as the first Keeper and dropped you back into your world. Instead, it shot you right to Hiraeth. A mistake on our part."

"Mistake..." She held the knife higher, "The Magistrater said I was a miscalculation."

"The Magistrater lied, she wanted you to search for better answers, and thus, allow the staff to present itself to you. You were not a mistake." She laughed, "You were the calculation of the century."

"How did you know?"

Haunton put their hands together, and for a moment sat in silence, "I can't answer everything you ask. The Magistrater wished to inform you of these things herself, as soon as she gets here."

She was coming...

Kirana slowly walked to Haunton, tucking the knife closer to her body and holding it with both hands, "Tell me how you knew."

"You're not a threat to me, Kirana. I could take you down in seconds, and I'm not even armed. Those Hiraethans gave you the title of a god, but that doesn't mean you are all-powerful. Right now, I am all-powerful. And I am all-knowing. So I suggest you listen to what I have to say because unlike you or any of your teammates, I know about the Keepers. I have studied them for 16 years with resources sent straight from the Magistrater."

Kirana wanted to know what Haunton had to say. She truly did, but part of her recognized that anything the Chief said could be a lie. She looked around the room for a way out, a better weapon, another person, anything. But Kirana was stuck there, not yet being harmed and at the mercy of the Chief. If she fought Haunton she would never learn what they had to say, even if it was lies, it was important to hear. Slowly, Kirana lowered the knife. Pulling up a chair, she sat down, the knife still held to her side.

Haunton tilted their head, "I love how you long for knowledge. Growing up you were quite the explorer." Kirana went cold at the thought: the person before her had watched her her entire life. The Chief leaned forward in their chair, "The Keepers have been here in each world for centuries. Their main goal and purpose is to keep each world connected. They are the unbiased leaders of each dimension, keeping the peace within and between."

"You make them sound like heroes. So why are you against them?"

"I am not. Neither I or the Magistrater have been. The Keepers are the reason for many of the things before us. The technology we have, the weapons, the language we speak. Their crystals power everything. The *Rhodonite.*"

"There are more crystals?"

Haunton shook their head, "The Magistrater will tell you more about Rhodonite."

"What can you tell me then?"

"I can answer your questions about my people, about the world you snuck your way into, and some aspects of the Keepers. For example, the one concept I hope to explain to you is how horrible the Keepers truly were. Their main purpose caused millions to suffer and die. They were tyrants."

Kirana scoffed, "I don't believe that."

"Heroes are mislabeled by their temporary solutions. They thought connecting each world would make each of them equal. They thought they could prosper off of each other's advances. That goal was impossible."

Kirana shook her head, "It's not."

"You have no idea what you are saying. You've been a Keeper for only a few days. You think like the gods before you. But I know the history. Their connection and desire for equality in everything always ended in wars. Even when people lived the best lives, they found problems. Hate is fueled by comfort. The Keepers were useless with their causes. People suffered endlessly until the Magistrater ended their rule."

"You're joking, right?" Kirana let herself laugh at the Warden before her, "People don't suffer now, then? I have seen their worlds. People are dying out there!"

"You don't—"

"I do understand! I know why Permidians are kept away from each other. I understand the Magistrater's cause. But I know that in every world you are hurting people. In Permidia you tamper with people's natural emotions to give them perfection. In Hiraeth you make people work for the Magistrater to have a cause—"

"Wrong." The Chief snapped back. Their tone had changed. "Without the Magistrater the Hiraethans would not be the Hiraethans. They would live in different places across the world. They would hate each other and fight and suffer. The Magistrater is their enemy so they can be a community."

Kirana shook her head, "That's horrible."

"Whatever we do, people suffer. This system we have designed doesn't work perfectly, but that's the point. The perfect society only thrives in Permidia, a place with no human connection. That is the only way to achieve peace. You will see that when the Magistrater arrives." Haunton pulled down part of their sleeve to see their watch. They analyzed something, and looked back to Kirana, "She will be here shortly; it seems there was something she needed to attend to."

"What does the Magistrater get out of all of this?"

"Peace." Haunton extended their arms out, "She will explain the true extent of her system when she arrives. You will understand very soon that she is one of the kindest people to have ever lived. The merciful god."

Kirana went cold, "She's a god?"

"What did you think she was?" Haunton waited for an answer but Kirana had none.

Back in Permidia, Kirana had learned about gods from books about ancient religions and mythologies. The Magistrater was a ruler, not a god. She was powerful, not divine. When Kirana met the Magistrater she had thought of her as a kind and strong leader, the one who could bring and maintain perfection for all not because of some magical abilities but because of her intellect and years of experience. Perhaps this was why the worlds needed the Keepers: no one else could kill a god. Kirana felt herself grow pale as the weight of everything she was supposed to do hit her suddenly.

The Chief sighed, "You know so little about the worlds, Kirana. Within the next hour the Magistrater will be finished explaining everything and you will be on our side."

Kirana shook her head, "Never."

"Did I give you a choice?" Haunton leaned back, hands on the arms of the chair, "Did you know that Wardens grow up learning about the Keepers? Legends, mostly, but just enough to understand the tyrants that the gods always turned out to be. The Magistrater made sure every soldier disliked the Keepers to prepare for the day you arrived. Not enough to kill you, but enough to make sure that if they were the ones to bring you in, they would be rewarded above all others for their contributions to their people. The Magistrater has been preparing for you for centuries, embedding your existence within cultures for generations. The staff took you away from us and ruined our initial plans, but if you believe that will last, then you underestimate how much we want you. You are ours."

Kirana glanced around the table. That's when she saw it. Stuck in a golden brown chicken was a bigger knife. She looked back to the Chief, but her gaze was followed quickly. Haunton sighed and got up. As soon as she did Kirana jumped up from the chair and ran to the knife. She tore it out of the meat and held it up.

The Chief stood away from the table and put out her hand, "If we have to force you into submission we will. I am not afraid to hurt you to make you understand we are not the villains."

"Like you hurt every other world?"

Haunton nodded, "We do what we must."

"Even your people?" Kirana studied the Chief closely, "You suffer too."

"We all suffer, Kirana. We gave you the perfect life; endless food, water, safety, entertainment. The moment we dared to end the excess of *company* you decided your life was not perfect after all. You searched for problems when you had none."

"You're wrong." She shifted her grip on the knife, ready to face the Warden before her, "You manipulated me into thinking my life was perfect and I was the only fault within it. You made me feel worthless, and guilty because I took Tia away from her perfect life."

The Chief's sigh turned into a laugh, "Do you not hear yourself, Kirana? You created problems. This would have never happened if you were like the other Permidians. No conflict–"

"No love."

The Chief lifted their head, "I do hope we can work together soon, after you learn the truth of your ways and realize your mistakes. It may take a few cuts and bruises, but in the end, I believe we will make a good team, for the betterment of the worlds."

Kirana stepped back, adjusting her stance with the knife raised, "Why don't you remove that helmet and face me?"

"I can't do that."

"You're that ugly?"

Haunton twisted their head around and laughed. They tapped below their chin and looked up, "This better?" Their voice had changed. It sounded like a woman. Her words were strung together like honey, stinking together in one smooth medley, a sweet, sticky mess of words. The robot tone stopped Kirana from hearing her fully, but she knew that was all she was going to get.

Kirana leaned back and shrugged, "Still ugly." She shot forward. Kirana ran at the Warden, lifting the knife and thrusting down when she got to her. But Haunton was fast and stepped to the side. As Kirana passed her, she pushed out her leg and kicked the Keeper's side. Kirana tumbled to the ground. She held onto the knife and pushed herself back up, swinging the blade right to left at her. The Chief stepped back. She moved to the side, avoiding every slash. Haunton reached out with Kirana's next swing and grabbed her arm. Within a second she brought her helmet down and slammed it into Kirana's face. She dropped her and Kirana fell to the ground, nose bleeding and head spinning. She crawled back and stood up away from the Warden.

"I won't listen to the Magistrater. You can't make me listen to her." She held her bleeding nose, her forehead bruising.

"We can make you do anything, Kirana." Haunton stepped closer as the Keeper backed away, "And if I can hurt you this much imagine what the Magistrater will do to you."

Kirana hit the wall and held up the knife. The Chief came right up to her and stepped right into the blade. She was inches from being stabbed and she didn't care.

Haunton leaned closer and whispered, "Imagine what she will do to your team."

Chapter 29

✳

G W E N

GWEN WAS TRAPPED in a prison, but she was not a prisoner. Not yet at least. Gwen had to remember that. There was no gun to her head, there were no chains wrapped around her wrists. She was free, even if she was still being hunted.

After pounding on the door, screaming for Kirana to come back, Gwen eventually turned around and faced the room she was in. The door Kirana had pushed her through led to some sort of office-like space with a large metal door at the back wall. A desk sat on the left, rounded and nearly empty except for a large screen placed on the side.

The man who had let them in stood beside the door, eyes wide and watching her. He looked like the Malfunctions from before, dark orange and shaggy hair. The Wardens were all clean and tidy, but the man before her had stains along his clothes, face, and ginger hair. His eyes were a bright green, wide and frantic, his right eye twitching every so often. Gwen stood by the door and waited for him to do something. She expected him to pull out a weapon and she held her own gun ready to be raised. Gwen waited to see what he would do, if he would jump her or yell out for the Wardens either in the hallways or behind the large door behind her.

In the end, he stopped blinking and spoke first, "May I assist you?"

She glanced at the panel Kirana had shot, and looked back to the Warden, wondering if he was just playing games with her. Maybe he was unarmed and was trying to trick Gwen into believing he wasn't a threat. They were not the bloodthirsty monsters she had seen in Hiraeth, but they were still a part of the

Warden's world. She pulled up her gun and stepped away from the door, "Get behind the desk."

The Malfunction didn't even flinch at the sight of the gun. He turned around and walked back to the desk, "Do you need to see the prisoners?"

Gwen walked with him and stood in front of the desk, "Open the door."

"Which one, sir."

Gwen looked back to the door, and in a moment of curiosity, dropped her gun. The man did nothing. He had seen her and Kirana walk through. The staff was lying on the ground. Did he still think they were Wardens? "Who do you think I am?"

He squinted, "I do not know how to answer that question." He blinked and swallowed, "You are a Second Lieutenant. I apologize but I do not know your name."

Gwen glanced over the Malfunction and the desk in front of him. He was unarmed and unaware of who she was, so she decided to take a page out of Kirana's book and learn more about the Warden's world, "What are Malfunctions?"

He looked alarmed by such a question, and yet, he answered, "A Malfunction is a failed Warden. A Warden who did not meet the criteria of a strong soldier. Those left over."

Failed Wardens. The Wardens, the horrible soldiers, hated themselves enough to disregard their own people.

She looked around the room and saw the staff on the ground. Gwen realized quickly that she might have been right to assume the Keeper wasn't a Warden. They could have been a Malfunction. She grabbed the staff and walked around the desk to the man.

"What is your name?"

This shocked him. "Are you feeling quite alright sir?"

"Tell me your name."

"Clay."

Clay. A material, a tool. Not a soldier. Not a person.

Gwen held out the staff towards him, "Hold this."

He reached out and her heart raced with anticipation. When his hand gripped the wood she braced herself for a blast of light. She took a short breath and waited. But when he grabbed the staff the light did not fade. No burst of energy.

No floating body. No Keeper.

Gwen clenched her jaw and took the staff back, "Who else is here?"

"Two Wardens."

"Where?"

He pointed to the large door, "There."

Gwen decided it would be best to keep up her act as a Warden for Clay and said, "I have been sent here to bring them into the fight. Can you unlock the cells?"

"No cells. One of them has been handcuffed. You can use your key to unlock it, sir." He gestured to her forearm.

Gwen stepped away from the desk and up to the large doors, "If someone comes, I need you to bang on the table. Hard."

"Yes sir." He looked forward, staring at the blank wall in front of the desk. Gwen watched Clay and took a moment to wonder what their team could have looked like. She had no idea what Malfunctions were, but she knew they mattered. Clay would have been a god for his people, the oppressed, and fought back to take their world. He deserved to be a Keeper. This prison was for Wardens, but she hoped that maybe, just maybe, she would find someone just like him in the cell.

When she got to the larger doors, a small blue light shone through the crevices. Alarmed, she stepped back, gun ready. Glancing back at Clay she saw he had some sort of control panel in his hands. He didn't care that the gun was off him. Gwen wondered if the promise of death was given daily to the Malfunctions. She needed to learn more about them, but right now her focus had to be on the next Keeper, Warden or Malfunction. The doors started to slide open, and she quickly realized how unprepared she was for any sort of meeting. She pushed her gun back into its holster and stared at the glowing staff in her hand. What could she do with it? She couldn't just leave it behind, could she? No, the last time she left it it was stolen, she couldn't risk that, not in the place she was in. She was forced to hold the staff out in the open.

The room before her looked like a bedroom. Rows on rows of bunk beds lined the walls, with poles on the other side. The first person she saw was a man chained to one of the poles closest to the door. It was Metis. She hadn't expected to see him.

"Metis?"

He looked just as shocked to see her, and as he got ready to say her name or smile, he looked from the brightly glowing staff to one of the beds.

Gwen followed his gaze to the second person inside. A woman dressed simi-larly to Metis. Short black hair and pale white skin. She walked lightly, shoulders pulled back in perfect posture. It was then Gwen realized that the woman before her was, unconditionally, a Warden. The soldier locked eyes with Gwen. That look, that gaze, that cold-hearted stare filled with pride and death. It was what Gwen had always expected to see behind those Warden helmets.

The monster before her was the final Keeper.

The woman's gaze fell to the staff. She looked shocked, but quick to hide it. "What is–"

"The Keepers are here. They're being chased down as we speak. We got their staff." Gwen said, and she decided not to say anything else. For once in her life, Gwen had power over a Warden. With a gun in her holster and the woman believ-ing that she was still being imprisoned, Gwen could do whatever she wanted. So she stood up tall and said nothing else.

The Warden waited, but in their silence eventually spoke up, "What can we do–"

"I'm here for him." She turned to Metis, who had been able to keep his reac-tion to her presence quiet. He looked tired, weak, but alive. He hadn't been beaten nor showed any signs of horrible injuries; he could run, he could hide, he could fight. That was what mattered.

He mouthed the words, *it's her*, and nodded towards the Warden.

Gwen pressed her forearm against various spots on his handcuffs until it sud-denly flashed white, and with a small click, loosened. As if the metal was suddenly burning him, Metis ripped them off and rubbed his wrists and forearms.

The Warden stepped closer to the Keepers, "May I ask–"

"No." Gwen still didn't look at the Warden. She gestured into the other room for Metis to see, "We need to go."

Metis could see her anger. He could see that she was trying to leave the so-called Warden Keeper behind, but she didn't care. She wasn't about to give the Warden the staff, let alone a place beside them on a team of gods. Gwen didn't know how she expected Metis to react, but she hoped he would give in and fol-low her lead.

He did not.

With a turn of his head, Metis looked back to the Warden. He straightened his back and held his chin high, "I am a Keeper."

Gwen felt her breath catch in her throat. She looked back to the Warden and found the woman staring at him, not angry, not hateful, just shocked. After a moment, the Warden's head dropped slowly, her eyes still and glaring. "*Metis.*" Gwen wanted his name out of her mouth. "You're the Telematic." She looked at Gwen, and her gaze shifted.

Metis put up his hands, "RO. We don't want to hurt you. But we need to talk."

RO glanced outside the room, seeing now that it was just the three of them. She looked back at Metis and smiled ever so slightly, "The Keepers." Her eyes went to Gwen, "You think I'm scared of a gun?"

Gwen pulled out her gun and aimed it at the Warden, "You should be."

Metis reached out and tried to push her arm down, "Don't–"

She stepped away from him, "I'm not doing this. We need to go." She glanced back to the open doors. Clay remained at his desk, staring ahead at the blank wall. "Kirana is on the run, they might have even caught her by now."

"Gwen–"

RO spoke with a laugh, "*Gwen?*"

Metis stepped beside Gwen, putting his hand out, "Give me the staff."

"We're not taking her."

"Taking her?" He acted as if the idea was something horrible. He lowered his voice, "We need to talk with her."

"She's a Warden."

"All we can do now is bring her with us."

Gwen gestured into the other room, "We need to find Kirana. We are running out of time."

"Give me the staff."

He tried to reach for it, but she stepped away again, pulling the staff away from him, "I'm not doing this."

"Don't let your ego–"

"My ego?" She gave a laugh, a horrible, joyless laugh, "Do you realize what she has done in the name of the Magistrater?"

"We won't until we ask her." He stepped away from her and walked to RO, "We need to talk."

Gwen called for him, "No!"

He ignored her, walking right up to the monster, "You're a Keeper."

RO was shocked by this, more so than Gwen had expected. This news was alarming to her, at least, for a moment. Soon she was back to her normal expression, only this time with more humor attached to a smirk, "Am I now?" She turned her body to face Metis entirely, "So you've been parading the entire building looking for the one *Warden* Keeper. What was your plan? To grab them and run? To never get caught and walk out of this without injury or punishment?"

"The Magistrater is evil, RO. You're on the wrong side."

She bit down a smile, "Am I?"

Gwen stepped closer, "She's not going to change–"

Too close.

RO lunged forward at the very moment Gwen least expected her to. The soldier was fast. Gwen tried to shoot the gun but she was too slow. RO pushed her arm up to the sky. The bullet went off and landed on the ceiling with a loud *bang*. With one fast swing, her fist collided with Gwen's chin. It knocked her head back as her teeth shattered against each other. Gwen stumbled back and fell to the ground. The gun was ripped out of her hand as she tried to jump back up. RO slammed the back of the gun across her face and Gwen was sent back to the floor. The staff rolled off her hand to the floor as something cold pressed against her head. She didn't dare try to get up again.

"RO..." Gwen could see Metis in front of her. The Warden was behind her holding the gun against the side of her face. Her heart raced as she forced her body to remain still.

"I am not scared of a gun." RO was leaning close to Gwen, her mouth above her ear, "Because *you* are the one holding it."

Gwen could see Metis's reaction; the horrified look on his face. He had his hands lifted, ready to submit to the Warden. "People are suffering, RO. You can see it. Please. I know you can."

"I can see it." There was no emotion to her words, "But it's something I enjoy watching." She pushed the gun hard against Gwen's head and leaned back over her, "Your people especially. I've never actually been to Hiraeth, but I can only imagine the power my people hold in such an order. It's people like your father who break the rules... and then things get messy."

If Gwen had any power or determination left, it died in that moment.

"RO." Metis tried to push the attention back to him, "We only want to help."

She ignored him and spoke into Gwen's ear, "Where is your mother? I couldn't find her in the reports. You live with that other family, yes? But they're not truly yours."

Gwen couldn't respond. She just... she couldn't. She was angry, yes, and that should have been enough to fight back, but she knew there was nothing she could say at that moment to make it better. She would only make it worse by saying names, lies, or cursing the armed Warden.

"Don't do this." Metis pleaded.

The gun was lifted from Gwen's face. She didn't move, not yet. With the softest of footsteps, the Warden walked around Gwen and stepped in front of Metis, "I suggest you rethink your loyalty, Telematic. If you go willingly, my people will not harm you."

He shook his head, "You know that's a lie."

"I admire your need to fight." She bent down, "But your priority is set in the wrong place."

She reached down to something on the ground. It took Gwen a few moments to comprehend what RO was doing. Gwen forced herself out of fear and into thought. She forced her eyes to focus and take in the situation.

RO was picking up the staff.

"*No.*" Gwen muttered softly under her breath. Not her, anyone but her. Not the Warden who prided herself on murder and violence against Gwen's people. Not the monster who cursed her father and went searching for Gwen's weaknesses. "*Please.*" She begged the staff to choose Clay or a Malfunction. Anyone else.

RO laughed, "Maybe one day–"

There was a blast of red light as RO gripped the wooden staff. The light flooded the room with a great force of energy. Metis stepped away from RO as her body was lifted off the ground. The red light covered every inch of the room, feeding into the next. Red particles flew from her body and the staff itself. Gwen lifted her head to see the figure of RO stretched wide in the air. Metis was on the ground, crawling back in complete shock.

The Warden didn't deserve to be granted a godly title. She didn't deserve to be chosen. Gwen cursed the very staff that had brought her to the Warden, to her den of bloodthirsty soldiers. They had put a monster in a team of gods. The blast, the choice, it meant nothing to Gwen. RO may have been chosen, but Gwen would never see her as a god.

When her body fell back to the ground RO stumbled, barely able to stand properly. She dropped the staff, and Metis dove for it. As he did, RO pointed the gun for his head and shot. Gwen let out a scream as the bullet nearly flew past Metis's ear. He pulled the staff up and swung it for RO's head. With a hard swing, he knocked her to the ground. She bounced off the floor once, before her body went limp.

Metis ran over to Gwen and knelt beside her, "Are you okay?" He put out a hand and she took it. When she stood up the pain hit her suddenly. Her vision blurred. She wasn't focused. Her brain throbbed with distractions.

She put a hand to her head and let go of Metis, "What do we do?" She stood over the unconscious Warden, "She can't come with us."

"Gwen–"

"We need Kirana, Metis." She looked back to the doors. Clay wasn't at his desk. "Shit!" She ran to the other room. It was empty, "He's gone!" He must have seen the blast of light and finally realized that Gwen was lying.

Metis ran to RO's side, picking her up and swinging her over his shoulder.

Gwen stood in his path, "We can't just carry her!"

"What choice do we have?"

"We can leave her." She pointed to the ground, "We don't need her."

"We *need* her." He pushed the staff into Gwen's hands, keeping the gun for himself, "The staff chose her for a reason. I don't know why, I don't know… Gwen, I don't know anything. But it's better to take her than leave her behind."

She pointed to the door, "Kirana–"

"Do you want all of this to be for nothing?"

Gwen had no way to argue that point. Metis was right, this would all be for nothing. But maybe it already was. "Fine. We take her."

RO was not a god.

She was a loyal monster.

The door to the room suddenly swung open. Metis reacted quickly, putting up his gun and shooting first. The Warden flew back and Metis dropped RO. He leaped past Gwen to the door and threw himself onto it, slammed it shut. Gwen came beside him, pulling the Warden's body out of the doorway.

"Get the desk!" Meits yelled as he held the door closed.

Gwen ran over to the desk and tried to push it forward. Gods, it was heavy. It screeched across the floor, agonizingly slow. She pushed and pushed and when she finally got to Metis she slipped it awkwardly beside him. He moved with her and they tried to push together. The door opened again but with a determined push, the two of them slammed it shut. Gwen saw something roll under the desk and into the room. It was made completely of metal and rolled fast through the room. It looked like a bomb.

"Metis!" She kicked it to the other side of the room, and it was then she realized what it was exactly. It was an android. It was Ben E. The poor little guy smashed into the wall and fell to the floor.

"Don't kick him!" Metis yelled, before refocusing on the door.

Stepping back the Keepers realized that their only escape was blocked.

Metis ran back into the room, running past RO's body, "Find something."

"Like what?" Gwen tried to follow his frantic movements.

"A way out. Anything!" He turned to his android, "Ben E! Find a way out!"

Running from room to room Gwen searched for a vent or a secret door or… something. She slid her hands across walls, looking up and down each one. Moving into the first room once again she looked up to see a small vent door. It was high up on the wall but it looked large enough for her to fit through.

"I found—"

There was a crash behind her and she looked back to see the metal door bent and breaking. "Metis!"

He came running. She pointed to the vent and he put out his hands, "Get it open."

She stepped on his hands and he gave her an extra push up to the vent. She clawed at the door and ripped it off the wall. She pulled herself up and she looked inside. She expected to see an empty vent, but as she tried to push herself inside, she was met face-to-face with a person. She screamed and dropped down, crawling away from the vent, "Someone's in there!"

There was a hard crash from behind the door and suddenly the desk swung away. Metis ran back to it, pushing the desk and keeping the door closed. A gun was jammed in before Metis could shut it once again, and suddenly bullets spun through the air. Gwen put her hands over her head and tried to duck down. She felt two bullets hit her armor, pushing her to the wall but not passing through her. Metis let out a scream, but before she could look over a piercing pain shot through her leg. She fell to the ground clutching her thigh. She got shot. Not a graze, not a scratch, it had gone through her. That had never happened before, in all her years of seeing bullets, they had always been aimed at someone else. Gods, it was horrible. She looked to Metis in a flash of pain to see him shooting at the hand peeking inside the room. He shot the hand until the palm was caved open, forcing the Warden to retreat. She could see blood staining his armor at his shoulder. His right shoulder. He was forced to use his left hand to shoot.

Gwen looked back up to the vent to see the person leaning out of it, staring from Keeper to Keeper. It was a woman with dark skin and a ruffle of curled locks. She pulled herself forward and dropped down to the ground. Gwen, panicking because of the pain in her leg, swung the staff at the stranger, hitting the side of her face. The woman fell to the ground. She was dressed in the same uniform as Clay. Unarmed. A Malfunction.

"Ask her!" Metis yelled from the desk.

Gwen forced herself to stand and turned the end of the staff to the Malfunction's head, "Where is Kirana?" She screamed at her, "Where is my *Keeper?*"

The woman nodded her head violently, "She has been taken."

Metis pointed his gun at her, "Tell us how to find her!"

The woman pointed to the vent, "I can help you."

"How?"

"You can escape through the vent."

The door nearly swung open again and Metis grunted as he pushed himself against the desk, "Don't listen to her Gwen!"

"Why would I lie!" The Malfunction turned back to Gwen, "Just look!"

Conflicted and out of time, Gwen jumped to the vent. Catching herself on the edge she looked through it. Her eyes went wide, "There's a room in the vent!"

"What?" Metis was nearly shot back with the table. The Wardens were getting inside. He couldn't keep the door closed anymore. "Hurry!"

Gwen dropped down and forced a scream down her throat as she slipped against her injured leg. The Malfunction ran for Metis. He got ready to shoot her before she slammed herself into the table to help him push the door. She was helping them.

"Go!"

"What?"

"Get in the vent!"

She wasn't helping them. She was saving them.

"Get the Warden in the vent and run for it. They'll explain everything there."

"Who–"

"Keeper!" She locked eyes with Metis, "Do us the service of saving our god."

Chapter 30

✳ ✳ ✳

METIS

METIS HAD GOTTEN kidnapped once, back when he was the Master's child. He was trying to collect pieces of metal in an alley when suddenly two men grabbed him from behind and took him away into the pipes. They locked him down in one of the small rooms they had found, similar to the space Martha lived in with the kids. Metis remembered feeling helpless as they forced him into the corner, threw bottles at him, and beat him up. One of the men had even talked about throwing him down into the water. When their little party was done and everyone had drunk enough to sleep the next few days away, the one in charge had looked over at Metis and grabbed him by his shirt. Metis was then hurled at the wall and went unconscious. He never knew what they did to him that night, if they did anything at all. All he remembered was waking up with a thumping headache in his bed. At the bottom of the bed sat the Master, cleaning one of his knives. Metis remembered the smell of blood, the house always smelled that way after his father's appointments with clients.

"You need to be more careful, my boy." The Master had looked over, spots of blood covering his face. He placed the knife next to Metis, "There are dangerous people in our world. May I be honest with you?"

Metis had nodded, staring down at the knife.

"This is a good situation." He smiled softly and pointed to the other room, "Now we have people to work on. We can practice." He took a breath and wiped the blood off his face with his cloth, "Sometimes, when bad things happen, the best thing you can do is keep moving with your progress. Everything is a step towards advancement. You will learn two lessons today, my boy." He grabbed Metis by the bottom of his chin, "First, I will teach you how to drain a corpse of his blood and check his blood type. We'll need that for later. Second," he held Metis's face tighter, "you will understand that one day I will not be able to save you, and it will be your turn to take the step forward. Next time someone takes you, take something back. You are *my boy*, Tech, just do what I would do, and keep moving towards progress."

The Master stored the kidnappers' bodies in the small room down the hallway. He used them as demonstrations for Metis, showing the young boy exactly what he did. Metis had seen corpses before, but he had never been allowed to work on them. With the Master's guidance, he replaced limbs with machinery. He opened a heart and replaced organic tubes with plastic pipes. He cut open a throat and practiced replacing their trachea with a glowing cylinder. He pulled off their hand and reconnected thin wires to nerve ends.

Those days, learning from the Master with the corpses, were some of the best days of Metis's life. As he pried open the dead, his father spoke about everything he could improve in a human body. Metis would sit there and stay silent, listening to the genius before him. The Master would move his hands from one organ to another, holding limbs up for the young boy to see, and then get to work. As the Master practiced and taught his craft he grew cheerful and celebrated with Metis.

"One day I will be a god." He said over a large, hot meal, "This world will see me as what I am. If you work just as hard as you did today and listen to my wisdom, you will help me get there, my boy."

"I'll be like you?"

"You'll be beside me." He put a hand on Metis's head and shook around his hair, "*My boy.*"

The month after that fateful day was the start of the downfall. Metis could not bring himself to hate the Master, not that part of him. Their life had been bloody, but there was love, back then, Metis would always believe that.

So now, bleeding out and fighting for his life, Metis couldn't help but think of his father. What would the Master think of him? In a way, Metis had done what he asked. He had followed RO to the Commander and got information about where the kids were being taken. He had turned a bad situation into something good, and now he had to do it again.

Metis let go of the table. Bewildered and shocked by the heroic actions of the stranger from the vents, he ran to RO's side and grabbed her. As quickly as he could he pushed her up and into the vent. Gwen was already through it, and he prayed she would catch the Warden as he pushed her inside.

"Ben E!"

His android rolled to his feet and Metis grabbed him and threw him inside.

Metis looked back at the woman, but she was too focused to notice him. Her eyes were locked on the door. She looked ready to die. For what?

The Keepers.

He dove into the vent.

As he pushed himself through he could only see metal around him. It was too dark to see anything else, and suddenly his body dropped. He muffled his yell as he fell onto a hard concrete floor. He looked back to the hole as the light changed. Bars matching that of the vent door were put up in their right place. The woman had covered their tracks. He heard running, then a clatter of a crowd. Shadows flew past them as he remained very still. The Wardens ran into the other room. He heard one final gunshot, and then a body drop.

A hand grabbed his shoulder and he looked back expecting to see Gwen. It was not. A skinny man with messy black hair and a uniform like the woman's put a hand to his lips. Metis looked around for Gwen and RO and found them in a different section of the small room. Gwen in the corner of the room with the staff held close, and RO lying on the floor, still unconscious. Light came from poorly hung bulbs in a few corners. Metis could make out figures of other people. They crouched down, their heads already touching the low roof. They were all looking at him, eyes wide.

The man in front of Metis gestured down what looked like a small metal hallway. A vent, only much larger. He got low and moved through it, waiting for the Keepers. Metis looked at Gwen and they exchanged looks of confusion and fear. The new people weren't Wardens, so who were they? It felt like they were in an entirely different world. Nothing around them looked like anything of Warden origin. If anything, it felt like Telematic. But more trusting. The people had soft eyes, tired, but kind. Metis could see it, and by the way the woman had sacrificed herself he figured he owed them all his trust. If it was a trap then they were already too far in it to go back.

Metis had to make the best out of the situation, so no matter where the strangers took him, he would move towards progress.

He took a staggered breath and crawled towards the vent.

For how thin the metal felt against his weight they made little noise. There must have been concrete all around them, supporting their bodies. This place was built for people who walk through, so why not build a hallway? It was poorly done too. It felt like the alleys in his home city. They were built around pre-existing places, molded for extra space. So who were these people?

They kept moving through, sometimes taking strange turns or curving along rounded corners. Metis followed the man in front of him. He glanced back to find Gwen behind him. She was struggling to keep up with her injured leg, but Metis could tell by the angry determination on her face she wasn't looking for any pity. Metis was struggling too, his shoulder continuing to test his ability to not gasp or cry out. It was dark the entire way through, the only light coming from horribly placed bulbs. His eyes got used to the dark but it didn't make it much easier to travel through the tight space. The sight of a light feeding into the hallway gave him hope, and soon the man in front of him was standing up and walking into a new room. Metis wasn't as graceful, his knees cracking and muscles straining from the constant crawling. He went back and helped Gwen up, allowing her to lean on him and the staff. Behind them came two people holding RO. They picked her up and walked her further into the room.

The ceiling was still low, only just high enough for him to stand properly. The room featured rows on rows of brown sheeted beds. The room looked well maintained with minimal supplies. A few make-shift dressers were placed in between furniture, and rooms up ahead gave way to more small hallways.

Metis turned to the man he had followed inside, "Who are you?"

"My name is Zero." He put a hand to his chest. His voice was quiet, as if all he had ever done was whisper, "Do you know what we are?"

A woman came over to them, gesturing to Gwen, "Please, come sit. My name is Flint."

Gwen looked up to Metis, "I met one of them. They're not Wardens." She limped over to Flint and looked up at her, "You're Malfunctions?"

Malfunctions.

Zero nodded, "We are." His body language was jagged. He moved in flashes, sometimes even small twitches. He seemed smart, but his intelligence was hidden by fear. He pointed up, "We're not them."

A Malfunction came out of the hallway, a few feeding out now and then. It seemed there were more of them in the small room than he had seen. One of them carried Ben E and Metis was quick to take him back, cradling the android in his arms.

"Why are you helping us?" Gwen said from the bed, "Clay turned us in."

Zero shook his head, "Clay is loyal to the end. Most are."

"Are you?"

"We are loyal to *our* people. Not them."

Metis looked back towards the hallway, "Who was she?"

"Patch." His eyes glazed over for a moment. He swallowed and looked away, "She believed you could help us."

Flint stepped forward, "But first we need to help you." She pointed to a cluster of Malfunctions at the end of the room. They were waiting by the next hallway, "We can take you to your Keeper."

Metis looked at every person in the room. Each one of them shared the same expressions, the same body language. They were terrified of what they were doing, but they were willing to do it. "What are Malfunctions?"

This was not a conversation they had often. Zero took a moment to find his words, "We are those who could not meet the Warden's standards. Physically, mentally, emotionally. We are analyzed when we are babies and then separated. Wardens do the real work, Malfunctions do the little work."

"Like what?"

"Cleaning, prepping ships, fixing weapons. We unpack shipments. Make meals. We do everything a Warden should not have to do."

"And you live here?" Metis glanced down at the concrete floor. Their living situations were close to what he once had with the Master, living bare-boned against cold concrete floors. Metis rubbed his forearm.

"There isn't a lot we can do." Zero put his arms around himself, "If the Wardens see us, they'll hurt us."

Metis squinted at him, "What do you mean? You're not allowed to be seen?"

"We work when they are not there. And if we work a job where they can see we need to be very *quiet.*" He spoke the final work silently, as if it was a dark secret. He swallowed, "Most of us have been scared into complete submission."

"That's horrible." Gwen spoke from the bed. Metis glanced down at her leg, it looked bad. They needed to get her a medical kit as soon as they could. She leaned forward, "You've been treated as objects your entire life." This was the first sympathy he had seen from her during their time in the Warden's world.

Metis looked at Flint and Zero, "What made you defective?" It sounded horrible to say, and from their reactions it wasn't something people asked them often.

Flint pointed at her leg, "My left leg is longer than my right. I walk with a limp."

"I had a mental defect." Zero tapped his head, "I struggle to read."

Metis squinted at him, "But you were a baby. How can they know that?"

"They have really good tests."

Gwen stood up using her good leg, "You're fighting back now?"

"We have been, in a way. We are trying to make our lives easier but one mistake and... we die. We figured the only way to truly make an impact was to take over the system. Or change it entirely. Even then, the Wardens outnumber us. We are powerless."

Flint moved suddenly in a flow as if settling into something smoother. She gestured with both hands to the staff in Gwen's hands, "But you're here. The Keepers."

"You're here to help us." Zero stepped closer to Metis, reaching out as if he wanted to touch him.

Metis took a step away from them both, glancing down as more Malfunctions came out of the vent. "We need a minute. To discuss... all of this."

Flint went over to Zero and pulled him away, "Hurry. They'll know where you are soon enough."

"What?"

She didn't stop walking away, "We don't have much time. When we get you to the Keeper, jump to another world and run."

It was then that Metis realized the Malfunctions around him were all ready to die, just like Patch. They had sealed their fate long before helping the Keepers. Metis wanted to change their fates. He wanted to be the god they saw him as and save them. But how could he? They were lost in the dark surrounded by soldiers and bullets, and it would be hard enough to save Kirana and Gwen alone.

He could almost hear the Master telling him to use the situation well and get all he could out of it. Even corpses have a purpose, in the end. But if there was one difference between the two of them, it was that the Master saw himself as a godly savior of humanity, willing to risk the world for the sake of his work, and Metis saw himself as a guilty savior of his people, willing to risk himself for the sake of his world. No matter how desperately Metis wanted his father to be a good man, to be the man he thought he was, the man he killed for, the Master was not good for his world, and certainly not good for Metis.

The Malfunctions were right, Kirana was their way out, above all else, he had to keep her safe. Gwen needed to survive for her people, and he owed it to her to protect her from the Wardens. He thought about grabbing someone else, they could take Zero or maybe Flint. But Kirana would have to be willing, and he doubted they would find her in any good condition.

No, it was just the three of them.

Selfishly, he wished for any guilt he would surely be given from this experience to be wiped away from his consciousness. He was done feeling the weight of people's deaths on his shoulders. They were pulling him down, drowning him, and gods, he knew he deserved it. But they didn't.

Metis looked down at Gwen to find the same expression on her face. She sank back down onto the bed and he knelt in front of her.

"How do they know about us?"

"They want to change the system, and so do we. I'm sure they heard stories about us and think we can save their people."

"Where would they hear stories?"

"From books." She put a hand to her heart, "Wardens took every artifact from Hiraeth, who's to say the Malfunctions didn't get a glance? The Keepers are bringers of peace and order. They unite people. Do you realize what hope we bring them?"

He closed his eyes, and wiped his face, "We didn't do this right, Gwen."

She winced softly, trying to hide her regret, "I know." She smiled down at him, her eyes red, "Why didn't you wait for us."

Metis laughed at her, and clenched his jaw, "I was followed, and then I followed someone else. I wanted to learn about the worlds. I'm sorry, Gwen." He looked over at the group of Malfunctions, "So now we fight with them, get Kirana, and run."

"And then make sure the next generation doesn't live like this." She stood up carefully, leaning on the staff, "We just have to make sure of something, Metis."

"What?"

She locked eyes with him, "That we don't undervalue the change we can bring to these worlds. Whether by hope or by war. We mean something." She glanced across the room and looked at RO. The Warden lay on the bed, a few Malfunctions staring at her with a strange numbness. Gwen looked away, "It should've been them. Not her."

"Gwen–"

"You agree?"

He shook his head, "The staff chose RO–"

"Maybe it got it wrong." She moved past him towards the group of people.

Ben E shook to life in Metis's arms. His head twisted up, and he pointed at Gwen, "She kicked me."

Metis smiled down at him, "She got confused. She thought you were a bomb."

The android looked around the room, "They seem nice."

"Get ready to turn off Warden guns."

"Are we saving children?"

Metis took a deep breath, "We're saving our friends. Just stay quiet, turn off the guns, and stay close to me or go straight to Kirana."

"Yes sir!" Ben E smiled up at him.

Metis followed Gwen, and the Malfunctions reacted to their movement. Two of them went back over for RO and picked her up once again. Metis wondered how she would react to being in such a place. Did she hate the Malfunctions? She must have, she was a Warden after all. Soon they would be able to sit down and ask these sorts of questions. Ones where they would learn of her true opinions. His first thought was whether or not they would need to tie her up to have a decent conversation.

Zero gestured down the hallway as the cluster of Malfunctions moved around them. He addressed the Keepers, "We saw them take your Keeper to one of the higher facilities. They had a group of us set everything up for her. A dining room, with enough food and space to feed thirty people."

Metis didn't know what he was expecting to hear, but it was not something as peaceful as a dining room. "What are they doing to her?"

"It's a meeting. We can take you directly inside it, and defend you along the way."

Metis looked around him to find weapons in the Malfunctions' hands. Guns, daggers, spikers. The Malfunctions treated the weapons like something delicate, holding them as if they had no idea how to use them properly. He pointed at the guns, "My android can turn off Warden guns, but that means you can't use them either."

Zero nodded as the Malfunctions around him with guns started walking back into the room, "That's fine, we have other weapons."

"How many of you are there?"

"In total, I have no idea. Millions of Malfunctions, I suspect."

Metis shook his head, "How many of you are fighting back?"

Zero didn't answer. He didn't seem to want to. Flint stepped forward, "They're afraid. Of dying or getting a worse punishment. They're just... robots. Androids with no expression for feelings. It's hard to build a team of defeated people."

Metis counted the people around him. Nine Malfunctions. Nine out of millions. The only ones who weren't broken to the point of complete submission.

Nine Malfunctions and three Keepers, it would have to do, "Show us the way."

The journey to this dining room was a long, uncomfortable trip. They were cramped together in the tight metal and concrete rooms. Adjusting his eyes between each bulb of dim light, Metis could make out paths untaken. The hallways stretched further than the rooms he had been in by what felt like miles. They were not built for productivity, and yet the people living in them could navigate them well. Gwen and Metis were slowing them down, partly because of injuries, and partly because of their basic physical ability. Metis knew how to navigate strange spaces, but even in Telematic, they were usually open. He had to climb, jump, or swim, not crawl.

At the sound of a voice Zero ran ahead quickly. His speed was impressive, and within seconds he was too far away for anyone to see him properly. They had to stop at various turns and climbs for Gwen. She was getting weaker, but by the gods, she was pushing through. He was hurt the same, losing blood at a steady drip.

Zero was the only Malfunction in front of Metis, so when they walked through a small room it was him and Metis who went in first. Zero suddenly stopped when he saw someone inside. A woman with salt and pepper-colored hair walked up to him, "What is going on?"

"They're asking us to stay out of the hallways. They are searching for someone."

"You–"

"Are you arguing against them? Stay away. We have to get to our rooms."

Zero was a strange little man, but a determined one nonetheless. Metis made himself take in what the people must have been thinking at that moment. They were walking to their deaths, sacrificing everything for the Keepers and the future of their people. They must have been terrified, and Metis hated that their last moments would be so violent. They were going to die in a fight or soon after when the Warden would catch them.

The climb up was the hardest part. They travel across ladders on ladders. Poor Gwen, already weakened by blood loss, was forced to push through and use both of her legs. At some point along the way, Metis wondered if the trip should have been done over many days. He had no way of knowing how far they had come and how far they had left to travel.

But suddenly Zero stopped them a turn, twisting around in the cramped area, "We are here."

"We are?"

Zero put a finger to his lips, "We know our way."

There was a small crash of some sort, like glass breaking. Metis tried to identify what could be breaking before he remembered the dining room.

Zero moved around the corner towards the noises. Metis was followed quickly and met him side by side. The two of them peeked up through the vent door, which was on the floor of the wall.

Metis had seen fancy places before. Some stores, mostly ones fitted with bars, were for those who had saved enough Korts to die fat and festive. The rooms were decorated well, with walls of reds, blues, and grays. He had seen some lined with fake gold, some featuring paintings, and a band playing soft melodies. But the room before him was unlike anything he had seen before. The fake gold had become real, paintings were not needed along walls of intricate patterns, and the soft melodies became the thud of glass and objects crashing to the floor. He heard what sounded like a body, and then a gasp of pain. He moved Zero aside to get a better look at the room. Through the metal bars, it was hard to see things clearly, which helped them hide but not scout out the room ahead.

He could make out the table, but it was on its side. Food, glass, plates, silverware, and flowers were scattered across the ground. Kirana was lying on her side, desperately trying to get back up. She was bleeding, bruised, and cut. She had landed in glass and let out gaps of breaths from the shards digging into her gloved palms. Metis went cold at the sight of a Warden rounding the corner. The person was unlike any soldier he had seen before. Dressed in full black armor they might as well have been from Telematic, but no. They were too different. Their uniform was a reflective black color with gray patterns, well-made with more protection. Their helmet had one long glass panel in the front. They looked advanced. They looked skilled.

They looked deadly.

And yet they did not hurt Kirana. They waited for her to get back up. They were not trying to kill her, just to hurt her. He watched them, studying their body language. Maybe it was just his lack of a proper view, but the Warden was not trying to attack the Keeper at all. If anything, they were just standing there. Was Kirana causing the fight?

Zero pushed him back away from the vent so they could talk, "Send your android in first. Once she's unarmed we'll go in and fight her. Two of us will drag the Warden to your friend. Once you're together, leave as fast as you can."

"When *she's* unarmed?"

Zero nodded, "Chief Haunton." He directed the name down the vent. The name became a soft echo of murmurs from the other Malfunctions. Metis tried to watch their reactions, but it was hard to read people already destined to die. They were already afraid, but too determined to gather more worry. Metis was forced to ask, "Who is she?"

"The right hand to the Magistrater."

Metis and Gwen looked at each other, sharing the same worry.

Zero had a thick dagger in his hands, but only now did he hold it ready, "When she's unarmed."

Metis put a hand on Zero's shoulder, "Thank you, Zero." It was the least he could do for a man with minutes left to live. With a final breath, Metis prepared himself for a fight and brought Ben E forward, "Here we go." He crawled towards the vent and pushed the vent open as Kirana got up off the ground and held up her knife. As quietly as Metis could, he pushed the vent door open and leaned it against the wall. He brought Ben E up and placed him on the glass-covered floor. He whispered, "Turn off the guns," and the moment he let go of his android, Ben E sped forward into the room.

At the sight of him, Kirana let out a happy cry, but the Warden was ready. She drew her gun and pointed it at Metis's head. He ducked back as bullets flew into the vent, before suddenly stopping. Ben E had stopped her gun.

"I know this trick." Haunton said, almost sweetly.

Metis took a final breath of courage and dove through the vent. As soon as he was out, the Malfunctions came running out from behind him. Like RO, they were quiet. Soft gestures mixed with careful footsteps as they got their feet and ran for Haunton.

Seeing the Malfunctions, the Chief did not move back. She shot forward towards Kirana, grabbed her by her hair, and slammed her down into the table.

"Kirana!" Metis called out as Kirana's body dropped to the ground. She didn't move. Their only way out was unconscious.

Metis took a panicked breath and ran back to the vent as the Malfunctions ran forward. He pulled Gwen out, the staff in her hand, and helped her run to Kirana's side. Metis watched as Flint came charging at Haunton, two daggers in each hand. She let out a scream, stabbing through the air. The Chief dodged her blow and spun around her. Haunton put her arm around Flint's arms and grabbed the Malfunction's throat. With one horrifying pull, she ripped the woman's throat from her neck. Flint couldn't even scream. She dropped to her knees, clawing at her neck before falling to the ground. Haunton was holding both her trachea and tongue. By the time Gwen and Metis made it to Kirana, Haunton threw Flint's throat to the side and ducked as another Malfunction threw a dagger for her helmet. While low to the ground, she grabbed a broken plate and swung it, like a frisbee, into another Malfunction's head. It hit his mouth, cracking his jaw but not killing him right away. No, it just stopped him from breathing, leaving him to claw at the plate lodged deep in the back of his mouth.

Gwen dropped down and rolled Kirana onto her back. Metis put his ear by her mouth. She was breathing. "Kirana!"

Something flew over the Keepers. A chair. Metis stood up and watched the wood shatter around the Chief. She looked over and Metis ducked down as she threw the broken leg of the chair to the Malfunction behind him. Metis nearly slipped on the glass and ran back to the vent where RO's body lay. He grabbed her by her arms and looked back as Zero tried to jump up and drive his dagger into Haunton's head. But she simply turned, grabbed his arms, and threw him to the ground. Before he could get up, she drove her boot into the back of his head, forcing his face into the ground. Again and again, until he went still.

It took everything Metis could not to scream. He dragged RO to Kirana as Gwen tried to wake her up. He slipped on something wet and fell to the ground. He crawled forward, dragging RO with him to the Keeper's side. Metis looked down at his boot to see Flint's throat squashed under his heel.

Metis remembered how the Master had cut open the kidnapper's throat and labeled every part of it. Metis could recite it by heart: epiglottis, laryngopharynx, vocal cord, larynx, trachea, esophagus. He let out a small scream as he knelt in front of Kirana and tried to open her eyes, "Kirana, wake up! We need you to wake up!"

He looked up and watched the Chief kick at the side of a Malfunction's leg, cracking their bone and sending them to the ground. Another Malfunction came from behind and managed to hit Haunton with his knife. But the blade didn't go through her armor. It scratched the surface. Metis watched as the Malfunction realized it was all over, and looked up at the Chief. She grabbed his neck and whispered something into his ear. The man screamed before she pushed her fingers into his eyes and let him fall to the floor in pain. Metis looked around for the other Malfunctions, but all he could see were bodies. The room was silent except for the final victim's screams. Metis and Gwen watched as the Chief moved over to the table and wiped her gloved hands on the tablecloth.

The Malfunction clawed at his eyes. "Weaver! Weaver!" He screamed.

Hauton used the cloth to wipe the piece of her armor that had been scratched. She looked down at the Keepers, "This was a smart plan. I did not expect you to come up with anything close to this." She put the tablecloth back down and picked up a spoon, "Or maybe it was just luck." She threw the spoon back and it hit the screaming Malfunction between the eyes, sending him to the ground, twitching but silent.

"Ben E!" Metis screamed, unsure of where his android was hiding. He waited a second, just one second, to allow his android to stop jamming the guns, before he raised his own gun and tried to attack the Chief. But by that time, Haunton had raised her own gun and shot for him. Metis felt his hand burn as a bullet shot through his gun and sliced his palm. He dropped his gun and ran to the nearest body, grabbing their knife and standing in front of the Keepers.

"I know you." Haunton approached slowly, "You have quite a few names. I have to admit it was hard to learn exactly who you are."

The Chief looked down at Gwen and Metis did as well. Kirana was waking up, her eyes fluttering open and breaths becoming heavy.

Haunton sighed, "I took too long." She shot forward and Metis got ready to defend the Keepers behind him. Haunton had one hand out ready to grab him and another ready to block the knife. Metis put both his hands up and tried to grab her extended arm. He used the knife to drive it into the hand he had caught, but he hit one of the many armor plates and it didn't pierce through. The Chief threw him to the ground as Gwen appeared at their side. Gwen shot at Haunton, trying to find a way to hurt the beast before them. But as soon as she started firing the gun, the Chief stepped away from Metis and lunged for Gwen. Haunton grabbed the gun from her hand and used it to hit Gwen across her face. She went crashing to the ground and Metis tried to get up and run to her but the Chief was not done with him. She slid to his side and pressed her knee into his throat. She pressed her gun to the side of his head. Metis gasped for air, clawing at her armor.

Haunton's voice was hidden by a robotic mask, "This certainly was not our plan. The Magistrater was hoping to speak with Kirana alone first. Not you. Not yet."

He tried to speak but the only thing that came out was a whistle and spit.

She pushed down against his throat, "You have a tendency to make trouble where you shouldn't. Don't you, Tech."

Not his name.

"Metis."

His Keeper name...

"Reaper."

Not... no. She knew his name.

With a sudden crash, something smashed against the Chief's head. Ceramic fragments hit Metis's face as the gun moved off of his head. Haunton was not hurt, she was not knocked out, but rather, shocked. Her body had shifted, and in that time her boot did as well. Metis pushed himself free of her and rolled along the glass. Kirana stood in front of the Warden, hands bloody and her body shaking. Haunton stood up and turned to face her. Metis watched as something shifted in her. The Warden was wearing a helmet, yes, but that was not new to him. Telematics always wore a mask. He had learned over the years that there isn't much of a difference between those who hide their face and those who share it proudly in a fight. It's the body language that shows the attacker's intentions, and then it is the energy. He could feel it change. The only reason the four of them were alive was because she needed them.

But now it was different.

Now she was ready to kill.

Reaper.

Haunton knew that name. What else did she know about him?

The Malfunctions were dead, all dead. How many more would die because of them as punishment? How many people would die because of the Magistrater?

Because of him.

Reaper.

He was not the Reaper.

He was a Keeper.

He raised his gun to the chief's head and fired. As the bullet expelled from his grasp, he suddenly realized he did not have a gun. Yet, he was holding something. He could feel the trigger around his finger, metal and... wood? A bullet, flying hot and blue, spun through the air to the Chief's head. It hit the side of her helmet. With a sudden crash, he heard the glass shatter. The screen broke and fell to her side onto the floor with a gasp of pain.

Metis looked down at his hand to see a gun wrapped up in his palm. It wasn't anything he had seen before, let alone had been holding moments before. It looked... ancient. Made of metal with a clear Telematic influence, but the hilt was made of wood... real wood.

Kirana ran to him and grabbed his arm, snapping him out of his state. He leaped down to RO and pulled her back to Gwen and Kirana. Every Keeper grabbed onto Kirana for dear life. Metis clutched RO with everything he had left, forcing an injured arm to work in his favor. He watched Gwen pick up Ben E and cling to Kirana. Kirana tried to gather herself and raised the staff.

"Kirana!" Haunton screamed. She was not dead. She looked up at them.

Through the broken portion of the helmet, he could see a streak of blood along the middle of her nose and her dark brown eyes.

Metis could feel the world morph as he shut his eyes. His body twisted through a shift of energy. He felt nothing beneath him for a single moment, and then suddenly it went solid again. He let go of RO and let her drop to the ground. He let out a short scream before his arms gave out and he lay down beside the Keepers.

They were alive.

Metis put his forehead to the ground and counted.

Patch, Zero, Flint, unnamed, unnamed, unnamed, unnamed, unnamed, unnamed.

Dead because of him. He replayed Flint's death over and over again and again. He forced himself to see her suffer. To see her eyes. Green, they were green. Burning him with what should have been a spark of life. They were empty now. As was her throat.

He let out a sob as he remembered what the Master taught him. Part of him believed that he could have saved Flint, whether by protecting her or healing her after. Metis had learned so much from his father, and yet, so many years later, he still let people die.

When Metis was the Master's son, he had been too young to be able to count as high as his death toll. He wanted to remember everyone he had failed over the years, so that maybe one day he could make up for the number, or at least try.

Right now, the only thing holding him together was the fact that he had saved three Keepers. That was good, that was a start. The four of them would save their worlds, that number was everything he had ever wanted.

They had completed the Keepers.

PART 4

Wandering Travelers

Chapter 31

✳ ✳ ✳

GWEN

GWEN WAS EXHAUSTED. Gods, she needed rest but her mind was screaming out dangers. They were in Telematic, and in such a world anything could hurt them. Kill them. What if King King's men were around? What if Card Face found them? What if there was someone worse? The Wardens, were they still around? What if they came upon the gods sleeping in some corner? And RO. They had a monster of their own right next to them.

Gwen forced her eyes open and saw they were in an alley. Kirana was next to her, staff in one hand being held by both her and Metis. The Hiraethan released her grasp from the Keeper's wrist to see a well-formed red handprint along her skin. She slowly got herself up and pulled herself against the wall. Her leg shouted out in pain but she did not let it stop her from moving. The Hiraethan had been hurt badly before, but she had never been shot. Though other people she knew had gotten a warning shot from a Warden, she never had such a problem. The worst she had gotten was a broken leg. She fell out of a tree during a harvest and landed on her right leg. After getting pulled off the field by annoyed Wardens her father found her and brought her back home to Gaia, who, working without a medical kit, pushed the bone back into place and tied it up. For two months, Gwen spent her days with a stick tied to her leg. An injury like that could leave anyone limping for the rest of their life, and Gwen's family was willing to sacrifice Gwen's two month pay for her future health.

That pain might have been worse. She took a few more deep breaths, a hand placed around the wound on her thigh. Metis started to get up, his arms trembling under his weight. He looked around the alley.

"Where are we?" She kept her voice to a whisper.

He didn't seem sure. Holding his bleeding shoulder he stood up and stumbled towards the end of the alleyway. Gwen could see what looked like a dim street. They must have been quite a few levels down because she couldn't see any ships or even the sky. Metis came back quickly after glancing around, "I'll explain where we are later, but we should be away from the Wardens. We're pretty far from the Magistrater's building."

Kirana's head suddenly twisted towards the Metis, "The gun."

"Holy shit." Metis came back and bent down to look at her, "You're awake?"

"The gun." She repeated, doing her best gesturing to what was in his hand. He looked down at it as if forgetting it was there.

"It just appeared. It felt like... like I always had it."

Gwen was not very familiar with guns. She just knew the basic look of them and how to steer clear of those who held them. But she could tell that this certain gun looked strange, in the sense that it did not resemble anything she had seen before. It had an organic look to it. The center handle was made of wood. Just like the staff. There were lines of glowing blue light that led down to the wood and up to the two barrels on top. Like an energy source. No Warden had ever held such a weapon, she knew that much, and considering how much damage it did to Haunton it wasn't something just for show. It was powerful.

"The Keepers..." Kirana's eyes closed again.

Gwen continued for her, "The Keepers each have their own weapons, I guess they just appear for us." She gestured to it weakly, "It's made from the same crystal as the staff. Rhodonite–"

"Oi!"

Metis looked up at the voice as Gwen remained very still. She couldn't run away, couldn't fight. She could barely move.

"This isn't your territory." The voice said, "You want to speak to Tito about this then be my guest but I'm on my night shift. So beat it." Territory? Gwen glanced up to see a woman standing at the end of the alleyway. She looked thin, starved even. Her arms were crossed and one leg was stuck out at a tilt. She was dressed in a feathered skirt and bra under a large coat. Her mask was in one of her hands, though honestly with the amount of makeup on her face, she probably didn't need one at all.

Metis leaned closer to Gwen and Kirana and whispered, "I have a place we can go, it's not too far, but I need to take two trips to get you guys there."

He looked back up to the woman and shot her a look, "Give us a minute!"

"No finishing, get going."

Metis gestured to Gwen for her to grab his arm and she did. He pulled her up and let her lean against him for support, he noticed Ben E still wrapped up in her other arm.

He let out a breath at the sight of him safe and looked up at Gwen, "Thank you."

Ben E pointed at the woman at the end of the alley, "Should I disarm her gun?"

The woman stared at Metis and he waved his hand in front of the android, "He's been on the fritz lately. Saying things he doesn't mean."

"He can disarm my gun?"

Metis walked them towards the woman and laughed, "Of course not. Look at him." He held Ben E up and the android's mouth curled up into a cute little smile, eyes squinting.

Gwen was slow with a limp, and bit down a wince every time she had to use her injured leg. It was as they approached the stranger that she realized what the two Keepers looked like. They were dressed like Wardens and bleeding from all ends. Would the woman run to get the soldiers? No. The woman didn't seem bothered, even by the blood. With a small glance at both of them, she pushed a long, white tube into her mouth and pressed on the side of it. In an instant, a small flame appeared. She sucked the tube, and suddenly the fire went out. A trail of ash followed the embers, and when she pulled it out of her mouth she tapped it and let the ash fall. She let a rush of purple smoke leave her mouth and watched them get to where she was standing.

When Metis saw her smoking he gave a small laugh, "Tito's got you on Fairies again?"

She glared at him, "You working for Card Face or something?"

"Brush, actually." He gestured to Gwen as they started to walk away, "Card Face got his own place to work out of. Brush just gives us some blood and expects us to find some ego heroes to seduce." Gwen looked over at Metis, wondering if he was making up such a harsh situation. When the woman laughed Gwen realized he might have been telling the truth about some other gang leader named Brush. The two of them picked up their pace down the street.

"You alright?" He asked her without a whisper.

She glanced around at the people on the street with them, "Will they turn us in?"

"For the injuries?"

"We look like Wardens."

"Not Telematic Wardens." Gwen recalled the Wardens she had seen before, back in their first standoff. Even with armor on, the Keepers looked nothing like the full black uniform used in Telematic. Metis shook his head, glancing around, "My people wouldn't care if we had the full set of armor on. No one cares."

Gwen would never truly understand the Telematic culture, but she could see it was selfish. People did things for themselves, and then they walked away. They had sex with anyone they wanted, whenever they wanted. They drank themselves dead. They gambled and played. They shot each other for no reason but for fun. All for fun.

When Gwen and Kirana were selling Fairies for Card Face, she had to practically entertain them just to get their attention. She had tried to act like Kirana, a curious new specimen for them to inspect, and it worked. The Telematic people consumed everything they could from their lives. There was no community, there was no love. There was just enjoyment with a lining of dirt, grim, and piss.

She missed Hiraeth. She missed her father, Gaia, Theo, Harold, and the kids. She wanted Lorenzo to protect them, to support them so they could, in return, help him. She missed the breeze and smell of clay. She missed the quiet. She missed her home.

The new street looked different from the places they had been before, and sure enough, it was far from the Magistrater's building. The street they were on didn't have any ships flying close, only the traffic above them heading in different directions. It was quieter, and the lights were no longer shooting out at all angles and blinding her. Gwen could see now that Telematic was busier towards the Magistrater's building. The buildings were taller and more compact. The lights were brighter and changed to the beat of the music she could still hear from such a distance.

Metis took them down a long line of buildings and, even though they were dressed as blood-wrenched and bleeding Wardens, they didn't get a single glance. Metis turned down into an alley, which at the end of it, had a metal door. He went over and pressed on the panel. Almost immediately, the doors opened, and Gwen realized it was a lift.

The two of them got in, and suddenly the room lifted. It felt like the one at King King's building, and Gwen put a hand to her throat in remembrance of that horrible moment. She could still feel the bruise. They would all need some time off. Gods, she needed sleep.

When the doors opened Gwen saw an entirely new street before them. It looked darker, whether by the lack of bright lights or by the shadows of the build-ings around it. Though there were buildings before her, nearly all of them were under four stories. They were in a valley of skyscrapers. A pocket of what Telematic would consider small buildings. People walked by through bars and clubs that matched the dark, grimy mood of the street. Metis walked out of the lift quickly and moved them down the street towards one of the first buildings. Above a single glass door was a sign that said, *Bot's Bar.*

Where was he taking them?

Without any hesitation, Metis moved them to the door and swung it open. As they came inside she realized how quiet the place truly was. A small soundtrack played in the corner of the room on a record player, but it was soft. Hiraethan, even. She glanced around and saw that this place was a bar. A bar, filled with people. This time, they looked. They studied Metis and Gwen.

"Metis." She whispered to him.

He ignored her and turned to the bar. There, behind the countertop was the bartender. He wore a long vest with tight pants and a very baggy collared shirt. All black except for a few blue patterns on the vest. His hair was cut short on both sides with a messy lot of brown and blue hair at the top.

At the sight of Metis, he seemed alarmed, and it took Gwen a few moments to realize that he wore such a shocked expression out of worry.

"What... what did you do?" He waved their hands in the air and walked away, "Forget it. Just get inside." He moved to a back wall and pushed it forward. It wasn't a wall at all, but a door. It matched the one Trent had back in Hiraeth. What did this stranger have to hide?

"Thank you." Metis guided Gwen to the countertop as the bartender lifted the small door and let them past the bar and into the back room. It was a work room, from what she could tell, with a large table in the center and different stations on each side of the room. Racks of metal and wires sat everywhere, and tools lined up in every place they could. It was cramped, a bit messy, but well-kept. Metis helped her to the back wall and she used it to slowly drop down the floor.

He moved back to the door, "I'll be back. Stay here." Then he was gone.

Gwen sat there for a few minutes. In that time she did not let herself rest. She stayed alert, listening to the noises outside. Nothing happened. Nothing changed. Even with the strange reaction from the people in the bar, no one bothered to get up or run away. But why did they look? No Telematic person had looked at them like that before and studied them carefully. She put Ben E down beside her, and though he was active and rolled around the room, he did not bother Gwen. Perhaps he understood that she needed a moment to herself. Gwen still did not understand how androids could be so human-like.

When Metis returned he was carrying the Warden.

"I have no idea how long she's going to be out." He said, setting her down on the center table, "But I hit her pretty hard."

Gwen looked behind him, "Where's Kirana?"

He glanced back and walked back into the bar. When he came back he was dragging Kirana with him. "She's fine." Gwen tried to get up to help but found herself suddenly weak. Her body slipped back to the floor and she begrudgingly let Metis handle her. He placed Kirana, blood dripping down her nose and cuts across her body, next to Gwen. "She walked the whole way here, just passed out at the door." Metis put the staff at her side before going back to the table and finally sitting down himself.

He took a deep breath and shut his eyes. All of a sudden, he was just as tired and injured as Gwen felt. It was as if he had just dropped a mask. He had even fooled her. Gwen took another breath herself. Finally, she felt somewhat safe. Who knew whether Telematic could offer any comfort or familiarity, but after what they went through, anything would. The door opened slowly, and Bot looked inside. He walked over to Gwen with a comforting look and found Metis behind the table. He held out a small gray box, "I think you might need this."

Bot seemed trustworthy, which surprised Gwen since King King and Card

Face were the only other Telematic bar owners she knew. She had expected them all to be businessmen with a knack for using blood, Corts, alcohol and sex for profit. But not Bot. He looked a bit harsh at first with his expression stuck on something stern and judgmental, but he had a gentle manner beneath the surface.

Metis took the box with his eyes still closed and handed it to Gwen. She took it and looked at it fully. As soon as she saw the large red cross on the top she realized it was a medical kit.

She looked up at Bot, "Thank you."

Bot gave her a half-hearted smile and looked down at Metis, "Is anyone looking for you?"

Metis nodded and looked up, "We'll be out of here as soon as we can. I'll tell you everything–"

"Once you're rested." Bot pointed at the medical kit in Gwen's hands, "Do what you need." And with that, he stepped back to the door and shut it quietly.

Gwen didn't open it yet, she held it down beside her. "Thank you, Metis."

He nodded and pointed back at Bot, "He's trustworthy. We should be safe for now. We'll at least have enough time to make a plan and rest."

"I'm also thanking you for everything you've done for us since... well since we met you, really."

He shrugged, "Aren't we a team?"

She shook her head, "I've known you, what? A day? You saved my life. And Kirana's. Thank you."

Metis smiled at her, "Well you did save Ben E. He means a lot to me." He looked around the room, "Where is he?"

The android came rolling out from under a countertop, a small blue tube in his hands, "Scavenging!" He put the tube in Metis's hand proudly.

Metis smiled down at him and patted his head, "Good job. You've done enough for today. Find a corner and shut off for the night." The android rolled away, zooming past the table and placing himself in one of the corners of the room.

Gwen watched as his face flicked off. Her gaze moved back to the table, and she stared up at the unconscious Warden.

Metis noticed her staring, "Are you alright?"

"No." She shook her head, "But I understand what you two are trying to do. I just can't accept a monster as a god." She placed the box down and looked down at her leg. Blood didn't have a real impact on her, and she was thankful for that because an injury like that might have made someone else throw up.

"That's going to need stitches." Metis gestured to her injury, "Did it go through?"

Gwen glanced around her leg. She couldn't see, so she felt around her wound and found the hole. Wincing, she nodded, "Yes."

Metis leaned forward and took the box back. He looked through its contents and pulled out a few items, handing them to her. A bottle, a cloth, a small box. She lifted the bottle, trying to see what the liquid was. It looked clear, like water.

"Oh." He said, before letting out a small laugh. He moved closer to her and took the bottle back from her hand, "This will clean the wound." He grabbed another bottle from the box, "These pills will help stop some of the pain. I assume you don't have this in Hiraeth."

"We don't." She let out a laugh, "Of course we don't. The Magistrater had all this medicine and all she gave us was... nothing."

Metis started to open the bottle, "Nothing? You don't have any kits?"

"Medical kits? Well, we have a few doctors, but they're all Wardens. The Warden doctors are reserved for dying workers and... well, Wardens."

She watched him pour the liquid on the cloth. He held it up, "This might hurt, do you mind?" He gestured to the injury, and she nodded. Carefully, he placed the cloth against the wound. She hadn't expected such pain, and she let out a small scream, clutching around the wound. Metis pulled away the cloth.

"*Might* hurt?" She glared at him.

He grabbed another cloth and started to pour more liquid onto it.

She put a hand over her wound, "That was enough."

He pulled it towards him, "This one's for me." When he put the cloth to his shoulder he didn't look nearly as affected, just a small flinch. He dug through the box again and pulled out more items. "There is some stuff in here to close up the wound, we just don't want it to get infected. You should take a pill now so it can kick in before we do anything else."

Gwen grabbed the pill bottle and took one of the green pills. She held it up, "What do I do with it?"

"You swallow it. Don't chew."

She put it in her mouth and forced it down. It tasted horrible, like rubber. "So you've done this before?"

He nodded dramatically, "I've been shot a lot." He nodded towards the door, "Telematic isn't exactly the safest place."

"Everyone just carries around guns?" It was a genuine question. Even though she had experienced the world herself she still felt like she didn't understand any part of it.

"Pretty much. Though the Wardens like to keep that under control. They don't like anything threatening their protection." He looked up for a moment, thinking about something. He shook his head, "I mean, they take away the best of anything. If it's better than their equipment then Telematics have no right to have it. You can carry around guns, so long as the Wardens can kill you faster." Metis glanced up at RO, "I agree with you, you know."

Gwen looked up, surprised, "You do?"

"She's a threat, I think Kirana recognizes that too. The two of us aren't against you, we're just trying to do our duty as the Keepers. Complete the teams, unite the worlds." She must have looked disappointed because he shook his head at her, "I'm never going to agree with you fully, Gwen. You and I have two different relationships with Wardens."

"They take children, you should hate them more than me."

"True, but I hate the Magistrater more than her pawns. I am also a strong believer in second chances." He pointed at RO, "If she can understand the wrong she has done and change for the better, then I will always accept her as a god. That is one of the most admirable things people can do."

Gwen smiled at his words, "It's funny, I feel like I don't know you that well."

He gestured to their gunshot wounds, "We nearly died together, I think we know each other pretty well."

"History is important to me. I believe that where people come from defines who they are." Metis glanced up but said nothing. She shrugged, "If you're willing, I'd love to hear about your history. You're still pretty mysterious."

Metis pulled out scissors and a strange blue patch from the box, "Alright, you want to share stories?"

"Like what?"

"I don't know, your life's story, your first fight, your first kiss, your first, your last. Throw in some stories about the Keepers too, I want to know more about gods. I'll just tell you my version of whatever you share." He pulled a plastic layer off the blue patch and adjusted his grip on the sticky side of it. He held up the scissors to Gwen and gestured to her leg.

She took them as he moved back to the box, "Hiraeth is very different from Telematic."

"No technology right?"

"None. It's just the ships. Everything is just crops and cattle and some factories. There are a few towns and cities centered around mines or fishing, but that's about it. The Magistrater created large districts and forced my people to work in each given place. If you don't have a job, you can't buy a house. If you're homeless, you'll be taken to prison. If you're a prisoner, you're forced to work a relentless job."

"What do you produce?"

"Nothing is made from metal or plastic. I've never worked in one of the factories before, but from what I've heard it's mostly packaged goods. Hiraeth's produce is almost always about food, and if it's not then it's more to do with construction. Clay, dirt, brick, coal." Gwen cut a small hole around the wound. The Warden clothes were hard to pierce through, but with enough effort and a sharp pair of scissors, she had it open. Metis placed the patch down over the wound. There were tabs on the end closest to him. From what she could see, pulling on them would help shut the wound.

Metis took the scissors from her and got to work on his own shoulder, "So what was your life like before all this happened?"

"Well, I lived with my mother and father in a small house with another family. I started working to make small things we could sell, like bracelets. Then I went to work with my father when I was five. I climbed trees, planted seeds, and picked fruits. I earned some extra money for my family and the other one living with us. We had 12 kids in the house with us–"

"12?" Metis looked shocked, "That's almost as much as Martha has. Your family just took them in? Just like that?"

She nodded, "My home has a lot of love. A world of pain makes healers."

"So a world of comfort makes killers." Metis glanced towards the door, "But it's hard work to be healers, I imagine."

"There were a lot of mouths to feed. I was an only child and my grandparents died before I was born, so we had room to share. We took in the family and all of their kids. Soon everyone was just one family. My father, Gaia, Theo, and their kids."

She watched him pull the small tabs on his shoulder. Slowly but surely, they held the wound shut, "So you have a whole family back in Hiraeth?"

Gwen shook her head, "Whole is the wrong word. It's not whole. Not really. About nine years ago my mother had left the house to work, and I had to stay behind because I had a hurt leg or something like that. There was a knock at the door and I answered it." She paused, looking down at her wound. Why wasn't she afraid of blood?

Metis heard the silence and looked over, "And?"

Gwen nodded her head and wiped down the wound before holding out her hand for a patch. He handed it to her and she continued, "It was the Wardens. I had seen them before, but this was different." She glanced up at Metis, and she could see by his worry that he was connecting the dots. She continued, "They were carrying her. She was dead. Her face was all... beaten up and they held her up like she was something worthless. Like she was *nothing*." That image crept back into her mind, one memory that would never be forgotten. Would never fade with time. Would never go away. They had held her mother on her back, her neck bent and hung so low that it lined up perfectly with the young Gwen's eyeline. Her mother's eyes were open, one bloody and swollen. Blood dripped down her hair and out from her mouth.

"They put her down on the kitchen floor and told me she had disobeyed the rules. That was all they said. Then we had a funeral and I grew up. I went to work. I took care of my family. My father told the Keeper's stories. We kept the books secret. I watched people I knew join rebellions and try to fight back. I watched them die, or suffer, or hide. I worked every day, for my entire life. And then Kirana showed up."

She looked up to see his reaction. He shook his head softly, "I'm sorry, Gwen. No child should have to go through that."

She smiled at him, "Thank you, Metis." This conversation was helping her trust him more. Metis went back to her patch and pulled the taps. It hurt, yes, but not as much as that horrible liquid had. "How many times have you done this?"

He laughed, "I've done this hundreds of times."

"Hundreds?"

He didn't look up at her, and for a moment he stayed silent. She realized quickly that he wasn't exaggerating the number.

When the tabs had all been pulled he went back to the table and leaned against it, "I never met my parents." He put the box on his lap and looked through it, "I kind of just showed up. You know? Martha took me in when I was seven or eight… maybe nine. She raised me until I was 14 years old. Then I started living on my own."

He grabbed a small blue bottle from inside and opened the lid. With a small swig, he downed the entire contents. He blinked it down with a small lick of his lips. Was that… alcohol? In a medical kit? Gwen waited for him to continue talking, but he didn't.

"I'm going to help RO first. How's Kirana?"

"That's it?"

At first, he looked confused, before realizing she was talking about the story, "I'm sorry, I don't really have anything like your story."

She didn't believe that. "Try harder. You can always tell me a story about where you were before Martha."

He took a moment to think, and Gwen was happy to see that it looked like he was really trying. After a moment he shook his head, and straightened his back, "A person's history is not as important to me. I think a person is defined by what they do after a bad situation. You come from a good situation." Gwen laughed and shook his head, "You had an entire family to look after you. You have love and food–"

"And Wardens." Gwen reminded him.

"I'm sorry about your mother, but I am glad you had other people. I'm just saying a lot of people don't have what you have." She stared at him and he sighed, giving in, "I used to live with someone else, before Martha. My… *father*." He said the word in a single breath and clenched his jaw, as if saying the name put a disgusting taste in his mouth. He smiled, "Your father kept books about the Keepers, right?" Gwen nodded. "Mine used to keep… books about people."

"Phycology?"

"Surgery." Metis glanced down at her gunshot wound.

"He was a doctor?"

He shook his head, a plain expression resting on his face, "I have other stories.

More recent ones. I can tell you about the time I got a loan from King King or got high and found myself in the middle of a Warden's headquarters. I could tell you how I met a bartender that I loved dearly who ended up being a cold-blooded killer."

"Did they try to kill you?"

"I think they still are." He gave a playful smirk, "I am sorry, Gwen."

"About what?"

"Your mother shouldn't have died like that. It's not fair, on her or you." He took in a deep breath, "Grief is a spectrum. I think death affects everyone in different ways. I hope, for your sake and ours, that the Wardens who hurt your mother know what they did. To feel the guilt you want them to."

Gwen had never thought about the Warden's guilt. It was an idea that seemed unrealistic. They were murderers. It's what they did. "I don't think they feel guilty. But thank you Metis."

"I hope we don't die." He bought back his humor and gave a small laugh.

She decided to laugh with him, tired of being stuck in danger's choke hold. She just wanted to breathe, to stay still, and maybe, just maybe, smile. "I don't think we will. Not yet at least. We have work to do."

He gestured back to the door, "Want a drink?"

"I need to sleep."

He nodded softly, "Understood." With that, he stood back up with the medical box in hand, "I'll patch RO up, and from what I can tell Kirana just needs some rest. We can all talk tomorrow."

"Metis." She forced him to lock eyes with her before she spoke, "Have you ever faced death?"

He looked numb. No reaction at all. "I told you, Gwen, I'm Telematic. No one here hasn't had their share of death."

"What side were you on?"

He hesitated for a moment, before his smile dropped, "Honestly, Gwen. All of them." He turned away from her. Ending the conversation without answers.

Gwen leaned back against the wall, and she found herself feeling safe. She was exhausted, but she finally did not have to push through the pain. She could sleep, rest, and heal. Ready to close her eyes, Gwen looked up at Metis as he pulled out bandages for RO's head. So far in their journey as Keepers, it was Metis who took care of each of them. He protected, rescued, and now healed them all. He may not have believed history was important to a person, but Gwen did, and now he had made her curious as to what past had molded his kind spirit.

Was he truly kind, or just guilty?

Chapter 32

✳

KIRANA

KIRANA FELT LIKE she was always unconscious. Every time they traveled, after every fight, after meeting Haunton… She was sick of it. For once, she wanted to fight, run, or even hide without having to be dragged around by her team. Kirana knew her purpose as a god was to protect not only the worlds but also her team. The first Keeper. The wielder of the staff. The leader. She had not met the expectations those titles required of her. Kirana thought about the Voice. If he could help her again then maybe she would be strong enough to do what was needed. Kirana felt helpless. She felt weak. She hated it.

The least she could get was a bed. Concrete may have worked for the first few nights, but she was done with it now. She wanted her old bedroom, and she didn't feel guilty for such a thought. Her bed had been perfect. Soft, but firm enough to hold her body in a warm embrace. She needed that more than she ever did during her time in Permidia. Kirana would have also liked a nice hot meal, and her mind went straight to Tia's pancakes. The best part about her food was the presentation. Tia used to melt down thick chocolate and drizzle it over the steaming pancakes. She would place strawberries around the rim and sprinkle powdered sugar any place it could fit.

As Kirana started to wake up, face planted once again on the cold dirty ground, she realized it had been three nights away from Permidia. That short? It felt like years. She knew Tia was working with the Magistrater, or at the very least had lied to her about Permidia for years, but Kirana found herself missing her old home.

Her bed, her food… but that was all she could list. She did not miss her routine, her people, or even Tia. She missed comfort.

As Kirana started to move and get herself up she found herself feeling better than before. Somewhat, healed, perhaps. It was hard to tell. Haunton had not broken any bones; in fact, she had barely touched her at all. Every attack Kirana had made was quickly returned upon herself, rather than the Warden. Bruises and cuts spread across her body. She was still wounded, and in some cases, still bleeding. It wasn't enough to cause severe problems, she wasn't about to pass out again from blood loss, but Kirana hoped there would be time to heal before the next fight began.

Gwen slept beside her, head tilted to the side. Kirana looked down to see a gunshot wound on the leg. She turned away from such a horrible sight. It looked like they had patched it up but… it was so gruesome. She wondered if she could wake Gwen to see if she was alright. Could something like that kill her? From blood loss or… something? She watched Gwen take a breath. She was alive, at the very least, but she needed her rest.

Metis was in the room with them, sitting at a small table by the wall. He seemed energetic for someone who had just infiltrated the Warden's headquarters. Kirana pulled herself up and got herself to stand. It was only then he noticed her.

He glanced over at her, keeping his voice down to not wake up Gwen, "You seem okay."

"Do I?" She looked at herself. Cut and bleeding in several places, still bruised from past fights. "I feel terrible."

"I mean… you don't look that tired." He set down a metal slab on a table and pulled open a drawer to his side. The room was some sort of workshop, one that Metis seemed to understand quite well. She walked over to him to see what he was doing. With different tools and a series of wires and metal pieces laid out, Kirana identified pieces of Ben E scattered around. The android sat in front of Metis, wires connecting the pieces of metal to his inner workings. At the sight of Kirana, he smiled and waved.

"What are you doing?" She asked Metis.

He gestured to Gwen, "She got a good kick at him, I want to make sure he's okay." He thought for a moment, before turning away from his android to whisper to Kirana, "I also want to make sure he isn't bugged–"

Ben E gasped, "I am not bugged!"

Metis waved his hands around the android's face. "Be quiet." He hissed softly, turning back to Kirana, "From what I can tell the Wardens didn't get a chance to put something on him."

"Like what?"

"The Wardens have these small chips that work as communication devices. It's usually for people but I've heard they can sync it to android's memories. I can't find one on him." He started putting the metal pieces back into Ben E and pointed around the room, "This is one of the most peaceful spots in Telematic. Bot owns the place. He's trusted me with this for years."

"A workshop?" Kirana laughed, but he quickly shook his head at her.

"In a world like this, you need a place to escape to. Bot only lets a few people in here, and he protects them with his life. I've seen him shoot a man for coming in here after one of us."

She glanced towards the door, "Does that include Wardens?"

Metis glanced away for a moment, before nodding, "When Wardens intervene, they are brutal. They only come down here for certain jobs, and even then, the only thing you can do to survive is lie and run."

Kirana glanced back as Gwen moved her head from one shoulder to the other, still sleeping, "Let's talk outside. She needs her rest."

Metis put the final piece back into Ben E and closed up his panel. He picked up his android and gestured for Kirana to follow him to the door. As they moved past the center table Kirana realized the Warden Keeper was sleeping on it. She stopped at her side and tried to get a better look at their new Keeper. RO looked angry, as if her dreams were some sort of battle.

Metis tapped Kirana's arm and gestured to the door, "I'll explain outside."

She nodded and the two of them made their way out of the room. The bar on the other side seemed, as Metis put it, peaceful. The only similarity she could see between Bot's Bar and King King's Bar was that they both sold alcohol. That was it. Bot's bar was quieter, and the music was calmer. No one was dancing or walking around on stilts. It was still Telematic, of course. People were dressed in flashy outfits, sitting alone and sipping on brightly colored drinks. The walls were red with faded gold patterns but were covered with posters with objects and people. But in the end, everything was toned down. Kirana did notice, however, that the people inside held a new sort of tension. They looked over as they walked into the room. Some glanced, others stared, but nearly all of them took their turn to watch the newcomers.

A man with a gorgeous blue vest and a tassel of brown hair was behind the bar with them. He went over to them carefully, glancing at Kirana but focusing on Metis, "Got a good night's rest?"

"Night?" Kirana glanced at the glass door. It was impossible to tell the time of day. She felt rested, maybe she had slept the entire night.

Bot glared at her, "Who are these people?"

"Friends."

"What type of friends?" Metis tried to answer but Bot cut him off, "Did you make a team?" Bot must have known he saved kids. Kirana wondered if Metis came into the bar looking hurt often. Clearly not with other people.

"Yes, I did. But we're not staying long."

Kirana squinted up at him, "We're not?"

Metis glared at her and gave her a small push behind him before turning back to Bot, "We just needed a place to crash. We'll be gone as soon as the others wake up."

The bartender sighed, "Tech, if it's the Wardens after you then you need to leave as soon as possible. You know—"

"I know the rules."

Bot nodded and moved past them without another word. He closed the bar's door onto the countertop and moved to the customers.

Metis glanced down at Kirana, "He means well. He just doesn't like people he doesn't know."

"Why?"

"This is Telematic, Kirana. You could easily be a psychopath with a hidden knife. Besides, if the Wardens come here and find the four of us they'll kill Bot and his customers. He's just being careful." Metis glanced around and spotted something on the bar. Going over to it he picked it up and handed it to Kirana. It was a pile of clothes. "We should get changed; I'm pretty sure we can slip away if we look like everyone else here, but not in Warden armor."

Kirana flipped through the clothes in her hands, "When did you get this?"

He gestured to the door, "I snuck out last night and went looking for some equipment. I had to find extra parts for Ben E anyway and I figured if we meet any new Wardens around here we might need to be able to blend in a bit better. Considering…" He hesitated before pointing from his face to her own, "They know our faces now. That's very important."

Kirana nodded, "They've always known my face."

"Well, now I'm pretty sure they have a high-resolution photo of each of us. They might even be studying how we walk, talk, fight. I'm guessing they'll be handing it out for everyone."

That was dangerous. Kirana had been careful to hide her face before but now it was different. The Wardens would be able to track them with the tiniest details. Metis's beard, her blond hair, Gwen's movements. The trail of information they left behind would be a problem, no matter the dimension they decided to stay in.

She glanced towards Bot, "We can't just leave." She gestured towards the back room, "This is a good place to stay."

Metis wiped his face down with his hand, "Yeah, I know. I can talk to Bot but this isn't a hotel. He doesn't just give out rooms. He calls that workshop *the place for hidden artwork*. And we're bleeding all over it."

"*Artwork?*"

"Wardens like to keep track of inventions around the city. That's what they go around looking for, children and technology. Bot gives a few special people a place to do their work without fear of it being taken away." Metis pointed down at Ben E, "I had a group work with me here, it's how he can disable guns."

Kirana leaned back against the wall, "Where else can we go?"

"A few places. I mean I can pay for the motel. Something cheap for a night." He looked down at his datawatch. He had managed to keep track of it through all the chaos. Pressing at the screen his eyes went wide for a moment and he put it away, "But I may be a bit low on Korts at the moment, so maybe not a hotel. I can ask a few friends though, or maybe we just try and get my old place back."

Kirana shook her head, "We need something permanent. A place to stay." There was a noise from the back room. Maybe Gwen was waking up.

"What about Hiraeth?" He crossed his arms and leaned against the bar, "It doesn't have to be here."

She shook her head, "Hiraeth is too dangerous. At least here we don't have to worry about the Wardens that much. When I was there, I couldn't go three steps

without having to dodge a patrol of soldiers. But there is nothing to build here."
She laughed and swung her hand around nervously, "I mean, what are we going to
do? Find weapons? Find people who want to fight? Soldiers? I don't even know–"

Metis put up a hand, "Slow down."

She took a breath, "I don't know what to do. We have everyone and now we
have to do something." She thought back to Gwen and remembered the name,
"Lorenzo." Kirana locked eyes with Metis, "We can go to Hiraeth and meet up
with Lorenzo."

"Who?"

"He's a rebellion leader or something. He has a whole system set up. Gwen
knows him well, her family is staying with him, maybe we can set up a meeting
and get some help."

Metis tilted his head side to side, "I mean, sure, but we aren't exactly ready to
start fighting a war... are we?"

Kirana hadn't thought about that. She shrugged, "I mean... one day I think it
would be good to start fighting. The Keepers are supposed to unite the worlds and
keep the peace, and so far the only way to do that is to take down the Magistrater."

"So a real war?" Metis laughed but his eyes were locked in a worried expression.

"I think we should go see Lorenzo. The rebellion might already be planning
something. If Lorenzo wants to take down the Magistrater he needs every world
to help him. Because in the end we're not just fighting the Wardens, we're fighting a god."

"The Magistrater is a god?" Metis thought for a moment, "We have to defeat
a god?"

Kirana clenched her jaw and nodded, "We will get our power, just like you got
that weapon." She tried to sound powerful, as if she knew everything would be fine.
Kirana thought about the Voice and prayed that he would continue to guide her
as time went on. The Keepers really did need power if this was the start of a war.

"I hope you're right." Metis gestured back to the room, "The Warden's name
is RO."

There was more noise from the back room. Was Gwen moving something?

"*R.O.*" Kirana repeated the letters, soaking in the name before realizing how
strange it was, "Just two letters?"

Something fell from the backroom before the noises settled. What was Gwen doing?

"Would you rather have three?" Metis laughed before settling into a more stern expression, "It's just her name. But we need to watch her, Kirana. She's a loyal soldier. Nearly killed both me and Gwen, and one of us had a weapon. She's skillful–"

Kirana went cold, "Watch her." She glanced back to the door. There were more noises. "Metis!"

He was already running to the door. Too late. The door swung open.

RO came barging through it, one hand wrapped around a gun and her other holding Gwen's head. "Stay back!"

Kirana and Metis froze where they were standing. Gwen tossed and turned but was not able to find a way free. RO pointed the gun to the wall next to Kirana and shot it. She let out a scream and Gwen stopped moving.

RO put the barrel back to Gwen's head, "Where am I?"

No one spoke, not even the customers at the tables. The only true voice was the one singing the joyous song. No one dared to turn off the music.

"Where!"

"Telematic." Metis's voice cracked, and he swallowed quickly to get it right, "You're safe."

"But you're not." RO locked eyes with him, "I have three Keepers, don't make me kill one to prove to the other two to not cross me."

Kirana watched her movements. RO looked unsteady, hurt, though she refused to show it. Her eyes glazed over for several moments, her stance shifted and shook, and her head dropped up and down. The Warden was not going to be standing for very long, yet Gwen could not slip away. Kirana didn't want her to, not yet. The crazy woman had a gun, and she wanted to shoot.

"What do you want?" Metis asked.

"You're going to come with me. I'm going to turn you in."

Back to the Wardens. Back to Haunton...

Kirana caught something moving out of the corner of her eye. She looked over to see Bot slowly moving behind the Warden. In his hands were... handcuffs?

"Listen to me RO." Metis put his hands up, "You're a Keeper–"

"It doesn't matter. I am a Warden, and you are terrorists. You should be grateful you aren't dead already."

Bot moved closer. Kirana tried not to look at him. She tried not to draw attention to him.

Metis put his hands up, forcing her to stay focused on him, "Do you honestly think your people will accept you like this–"

A flicker of hate, and maybe fear, came over her face, "Of course they will."

"I don't believe that."

The bartender opened the handcuffs and pushed it down onto RO's hand still holding the gun. He pulled her body around to face him and pushed the other end onto a bar. RO tried to shoot the gun and Kirana ducked as bullets flew around the room. Metis moved forward and pulled the gun out of her hand. Gwen slipped out of her grasp and ran to Kirana, dropping to the ground and clutching her injured leg. Metis jumped back as RO reached out to grab her weapon. Angrily she pulled at the handcuffs. Again and again, she lunged forward trying to pull her arm free. Again and again, but as her energy wore off she slowly slid down the wall and to the ground, sitting in defeat.

She glared at the three of them, "What do you want from me?"

Chapter 33

GWEN

GWEN MISSED SO much about Hiraeth. She missed the sound of her people's voices and that sweet melody of prideful songs. She missed the gleam of golden light against the mountains and the curves of every building. She missed the breeze in her hair and the warmth of true sun on her face. She missed her family. She wanted to know they were safe. She wanted to know they were alive, at the very least. Maybe, just maybe, they were doing better than she was.

Gwen had been sleeping when someone had grabbed her. At first, she thought it was Kirana, but suddenly the metal barrel of a gun was pressed to her temple and a hand wrapped around her mouth. She tried to fight it or make some sort of noise, but the Warden was strong, and stronger than Gwen even with the injury.

One bullet and it was over. The monster was willing to kill without hesitation. Gwen wished the others could see the Warden was never going to do anything good for them.

"Are you okay?" Kirana whispered to Gwen.

She didn't like that question, it was pointless. She wasn't okay and Kirana knew that, so Gwen didn't bother to answer and pulled her jacket on. The outfits Metis had gotten from before would serve them well. She didn't know how he managed to find their sizes but he had done well to get them the right fittings. Her pants were loose and her top was a bit too tight around her arms, but she could move freely. The loose pants felt better against her wound. He had even managed to get her a Telematic jacket. It felt expensive, but its most important feature was its hood. She would be able to hide her face away when need be. Gwen had tucked the small slip of her father's jacket into her pocket and brushed it gently every time she could.

Kirana looked more Telematic than Gwen did with her outfit having various colors to it. Her plants were a dark purple shade, well fitted. Her shirt, however, was too big. It looked old and well-worn. Kirana showed visible dislike to it as she pulled a coak over her shoulders. It looked like the one she had worn the night they first met. It dropped down to her shins, only instead of being a plain gray color it was fitted with patterns of dark blues and yellows.

Kirana stood up and offered her hand. Gwen took it and leaned against her as they went back into the main room. RO was still handcuffed to the bar. Gwen got a better look at her now; sweat across her brow, body hung in defeat, but eyes sharp and glaring. RO looked hurt, more so than anyone had realized, and that included herself. That was good, the more injured she was the less of a threat she posed. Metis was sitting against the bar, head resting on the wall with his eyes closed. He looked tired. As soon as they came forward he opened his eyes and looked them up and down.

He smirked, "You two look Telematic."

"I'm not loving the look." Kirana gestured to the baggy shirt as she tried to tuck it into her pants.

"I actually like mine." Gwen moved over opposite Metis and slid down the bar, "Thank you for getting these."

Gwen looked up to Metis to find him staring at RO, only with a different look than her own. He seemed sorry for the Warden. He pitied the monster.

Metis turned back in time to catch Gwen's glare and quickly shot her a look, "Don't do that." He whispered.

"Do what." She didn't whisper. She didn't care if the Warden heard her.

He pulled himself up, leaning closer so RO wouldn't hear him, "We just dragged her from everything she knew to a chaotic world with three gods claiming she was one of them, and when she tried to escape we tied her to a pole." He was mad at her reaction, but he had no right to be.

Bot spoke from behind the bar, "Tech I swear to the gods if she is a Warden she needs to leave." Bot had quickly closed the bar after RO's attack. No one got shot, thank the gods, but it seemed the bartender wasn't about to take any more chances. He dropped something onto the countertop: a ring of keys. "I am leaving this mess for you to clean up. You all need to be gone by the time I am back– I'm serious, Tech."

Metis leaned back on the bar, "I understand."

"Good luck." The front door slammed shut.

Metis looked at RO again, and after a moment stood up and walked into the backroom. When he came back he was holding the medical kit. Gwen hoped more than anything that it was not for the Warden, that maybe Metis needed something inside. But no, he knelt in front of RO, just in arm's reach. He had the gun to his side, not on him directly but close enough to keep her from attacking. She glared up at him, jaw hanging low and her breathing deep.

He shook the box, "May I?"

She clenched her jaw, "Fuck. You."

He put the box next to her, "We aren't trying to hurt you." She tried to speak but he kept talking, "That was not our plan. Believe me when I say that everything that just happened was our worst-case scenario. But it got us to you, RO. We had to find you, and we tore through an entire civilization to meet you. Face to face. I only ask that you listen to what we have to say because you are a part of this."

"A part of a terrorist organization?" She gave herself the pleasure of a small smirk, "No. You have me mistaken for a coward."

"You're a Keeper–"

"A fool?" She thought for a moment, before glancing at Kirana and Gwen, "You consider me at their level?"

Gwen glared at her, trying to get RO to lock eyes, but the Warden's gaze simply glazed over the room as if she wasn't there.

Gwen had seen Hiraethans fight back before. It wasn't rare and extremely dangerous. It happened when someone's anger boiled over beyond rage and crossed into a hate worth dying for. The fight was quick. Two, maybe three hits and a bullet would echo through the streets. Then another, and another, and another. Sometimes at the body, other times at the people around the Wardens. Hiraethans were angry by nature, but it was out of determination, a spirit and a fight within their hearts, ready to escape from the world that burned them *every day*. Gwen had seen it. She had watched people she knew, sometimes even friends, break.

The first time was when a man had simply had enough of taking orders and received ten bullet wounds and one firm kick to an already dead body. Gwen learned later that day that he had lost his baby sister two nights before after her arm was caught in one of the factory gears, and the Wardens were ordering him to take her place so production would not slow. The second time was the true breaking, the moment when a mother's child was kicked away by a patrolling troop. They kicked the child into a pile of debris. The kid went headfirst into a pole, which broke through his little skull and came out the other end. With one twitch his body was limp, but his mother was not. Gwen had been so focused on the child that she hadn't even seen the woman grabbing a piece of the debris. The mother jumped onto the back of the Warden and slammed him to the ground. With one hand she pulled off his helmet and with the other, she hit his head again and again with the chunk of concrete. Five shots to her back and the Warden was carried off to a doctor.

Gwen had never seen what those Wardens looked like under the mask, but she knew, gods she just knew, that they looked the same way RO did. Their ego harmed, and willing to kill for the pleasure of seeing someone else's pain.

Kirana got up and moved away from Gwen up to RO. She sympathized with the Warden too…

"My name is Kirana. Do you know who I am?"

"The First Keeper."

"The Permidia Keeper." Kirana said, not exactly correcting her but simply filling in a second title. Gwen was shocked to see RO react to her words. She knew what Permidia was.

Metis leaned forward in his curiosity, "You know Permidia?"

"We all know Permidia. It's a concept."

Kirana gave a small laugh, "Concept?"

"Permidia. Where everyone lives a perfect life. Happy and fat. I had no idea it was a real place." She looked Kirana up and down, "You seem like the type."

"How so?"

RO shifted forward, "Weak, fragile, naive. Your eyes are filled with dreams, not goals. You have no idea what you are doing because you come from the perfect world."

Metis leaned closer, "How many worlds do you know of?"

RO's eyes narrowed and with a glance at the two of them, she leaned back, "If you're interrogating me you better put that gun up. I won't talk until I'm bleeding head to toe."

RO looked over at Gwen. She seemed to think the only person willing to do such an act was Gwen. Gwen was hurt to find herself wanting the Warden to feel such pain. She hated the Wardens, and any type of torment they felt was well deserved, but she wasn't supposed to be the person who would inflict such things. She wasn't a killer, she didn't want blood on her hands, she just wanted to help her people. She wasn't a warrior, she was barely a god. She looked down at the floor. She would not seek out blood, she would not stoop down to a Warden's level just to see them suffer for their actions.

"The Magistrater is giving everyone in Permidia the perfect lives, but to do so she takes from every other dimension. She forces Hiraethans to work and produce, she takes technology from Telematic and leaves the people in chaos." Metis titled his head, "You know Hiraeth?"

"I've heard stories."

"Then you know how hard those people are working, all for some other world to thrive."

Kirana nodded quickly, "She's a perfectionist. She believes that perfection can only be achieved when people are separated and lack connection to one another. Haunton told me it was to avoid conflicts." Gwen, Metis, and RO looked at her with a quick turn of their heads. Kirana backed down, "We need to talk about that later. She told me a lot."

"You spoke to her?" RO seemed shocked.

"She spoke to me, actually." Kirana straightened her back, "She was answering any questions I asked."

Metis threw his hands up, "What did you ask?"

"A lot of things, she answered less than half of them honestly, but I'll explain later." She turned back to RO, "We are here to overthrow the Magistrater and save our worlds from her system."

RO tilted her head to the side, "Do you believe perfection is a lie?"

"What?" RO waited for her answer, and Kirana glanced over at Metis, trying to find the right way to answer, "I…"

"Permidia is the perfect world, so what will you do with it once the Magistrater is gone? Destroy it? How can you destroy a dimension?"

"Perfection is a lie." Kirana said quickly, making up for her hesitation. She gestured to Metis and Gwen, "We're still a bit confused, about everything. I was stuck in Permedia believing the Magistrater was a saint my whole life and Gwen and Metis were trapped under her rule. We're still learning. The Magistrater believes that perfection can be achieved by removing love from people's lives. That is not perfection."

"So you believe perfect can be achieved?"

Once again, Kirana hesitated to respond.

"The Magistrater created her own form of perfection, are you sure it is not the only one that works? Does it work?" RO asked.

Kirana shook her head but didn't answer for a moment. When she did, she sounded uncertain, "Perfection wrong. It's not right for–"

"And yet it works."

There was a pause, a moment in which everyone waited for each to say something more. No one did. Their explanation was over.

Gwen put her head against the wall, "The Warden doesn't care what we have to say."

RO clicked her tongue, "No no, this is all extremely interesting. They've got me on the edge of my seat with their fairy tales."

Kirana gave a nervous laugh, she seemed to take the comment personally, "*Fairy tales?*"

Metis leaned forward, "Why don't you believe us?"

"The system works." She looked at Kirana, "What did Haunton tell you?"

Kirana leaned back, she didn't want to say. Metis stared at her until she started speaking. A trick or not, the other Keepers needed to know. "She said the Magistrater chose to be the villain, that she was the only thing stopping them from fighting each other. A common enemy."

RO gave a small hum, "The Wardens do the same thing. Without us there is chaos."

Gwen gave a sharp, joyless laugh, "That's a lie!"

"The truth hurts, especially–"

"The system gets millions killed! That is not a system, that is not order, that is a monster's control!" Gwen turned away, "It makes sense you don't know that, after all, you're just a mindless pawn in her game."

"Mindless pawn?"

Metis waved his hands in the air, "Stop. That's not the point. We aren't here to fight each other, we're here to unite everyone."

RO glared at him, "Unite everyone?"

"We can create our system. Together." He finally found the right words, "The Magistrater is trying to separate the world to create the perfect society. But there is beauty in messy groups of love and, yes, chaos. We deserve to find our community."

"Only a Telematic would say that."

"Yeah, no shit. Because I live in a world where people can be and do whatever they want and they choose to be selfish and greedy. I hate it. I hate that those who need love and care are sent down into those... those pipes." He was getting angry, and he had to stop talking to re-gather himself, "We need a government, something to bring equality to each world, not just one."

"Equality is a lie–"

Gwen stood up, wincing with her leg but not letting it stop her, "I can't do this." She moved towards the back room. As she got to the door there was a loud knock at the front door, "We're closed!"

"Open up!"

She froze. The voice sounded robotic, filtered from behind a helmet.

It was a Warden.

Metis lunged at RO and forced his hand over her mouth. She managed to yell out half a word before being muffled. With her free hand, she tried to push him away, and he was forced to hold both her head and body to keep her quiet.

Kirana gestured to the back room, acting as if hiding was an option. The Wardens knew someone was inside. Gwen hadn't been thinking, she just... gods, she thought it was Bot or some Telematic knocking at the door. Did they know her voice? If they did, the Keepers were as good as dead. Kirana stood up slowly and gestured to the backroom. She mouthed the word *staff.* They could escape, just like that. It could work.

But Metis wasn't moving with them. He was stuck with RO, his hand around her mouth and her hand stuck to the pole. They couldn't take her, they had to leave her. Gwen tried to gesture him into the backroom so they could make a run for it, but he didn't move.

"RO, please." He whispered to her, "We just want to help our people." He removed his hand slowly, "Don't you want to do the same?"

"My people live their best lives." She whispered, but why? "They support a greater cause and become incredible soldiers."

"Why did you take the staff?" She didn't answer. "You knew how it worked. You knew all you had to do was touch it. Didn't you." RO took a breath and got ready to yell something. He put his hand over her mouth, "You wanted to know if it was true. RO please, we can help you. Gwen is biased but I want to help the Wardens."

She hated how he used her name as if she was a bad example. He didn't understand.

The knock came back, louder this time, "Open. The. Door."

"I spent less than a day as a Warden, and I hated it. Maybe it is a different experience over time or maybe I saw the bad side of things, but it was horrible. I can't imagine living like that for my whole life, I don't think I could do it. To be forced to be a soldier every day for your entire life. To be tested and tormented for weaknesses. I saw the Malfunctions, I saw how they are treated. Even the Wardens are stuck in this horrible cycle of strength and weakness. All the while, the Magistrater uses your people to control entire populations to benefit *one* world. But we aren't forcing you to go against your people. The staff chose you, but your fate is not sealed just yet. You can go back. But we're going to keep fighting. Not just for our people, but yours as well."

The Wardens outside started to move. Everyone listened carefully, before hearing them walk away. They thought Gwen was just a Telematic, they weren't after the Keepers. It was just an inspection and one they didn't have the heart to do fully.

He let go of RO's mouth and pulled her up with him. Grabbing the keys off the counter top he unlocked the handcuffs.

RO didn't run, she just stood there, swaying and breathing hard, still clearly in pain.

Metis turned to face Kirana, "We need to leave."

Gwen watched as RO grabbed a bottle from the bar and tried to stop her, "Metis!"

Metis turned around and swung the bottle across his face before leaping over the bar and throwing the bottle at Gwen. It hit her arm and shattered on the floor. RO faked the pain, she made them all believe she was injured and tired.

RO swung the door open and ran outside.

Metis's cheek was already swelling, but he ignored the pain and jumped over the bar. Kirana was right behind him, and before Gwen could yell for them to stop they were both out the door. She tried to run after them but her leg wouldn't let her do anything more than walk. She leaned against the bar and watched the door close.

Two gods believed in the Warden, one did not. The odds were in RO's favor.

In the empty bar, Gwen found herself helplessly alone.

She wanted to go home. She wanted to find her family. She wanted to rest. She wanted to stop running. She wanted to stop fighting. This Warden, this monster that the others allowed to stay with them was stopping the Keepers. RO could kill them and she would like it. Gwen could picture her, a gun in hand and a smiling grin across her face as she shot the Keepers. Until the Warden was gone Gwen would not feel safe. She would feel stuck at the end of the barrel, waiting.

For her entire life, all she had done was wait. Wait for the Wardens to let her pass. Wait for the Wardens to calm down. Wait until the day is done to breathe. Wait to see if her family had survived the day. Wait for water. Wait for food. Wait for her mother to return home. Wait for her mother's death to be repaid. Wait for her father to save her. Wait for the Keepers to return.

Wait.

Then she was a Keeper, and the waiting was over.

So why, in all the gods' names, was she still waiting?

Gwen wished she had never told Kirana or Metis that they needed all of the Keepers working together, united as one team, because though that was what every book and story had told her, she could not allow herself to believe that Wardens deserved a god. The situation was tearing Gwen between the mythology she had believed her entire life and her Hiraethan hatred for the Wardens. She was still waiting and it made her feel so helpless. Why was she still a Hiraethan girl trapped in a violent world? Gwen was supposed to bring her world back to peace, to unity, yet she had done nothing but wait.

Gwen leaned against the bar and cried. Her eyes had betrayed her by allowing her to look weak. For all her experience with grief and sadness, Gwen had not learned how to stop crying. She waited for herself to stop crying.

A minute went by without any sign of the others returning. She wondered now what to do if they didn't return at all. She would be alone, lost in a world she didn't understand, with a priceless staff only Kirana could wield. When the doors opened Gwen expected to see the Keepers. It was not. It was a Telematic man and an old one at that.

He peeked inside, "Excuse me, are you open?"

"No." Her voice was hoarse.

"My dear, are you alright?" He stepped inside. The man was old, older than she had first thought. A thick white beard and a thick crowd of white locks on his head folded over half of his face. She could see his eye, not two, but one. The other was hidden by a grimy patch stuck in his socket. It looked painful, and suddenly he seemed dangerous. Those who could endure pain had suffered through too much to be safe.

"We're not open."

He put his hands together. Was he acting respectfully? "I was just hoping to visit that young man with you..." He gestured outside, "Your friend. I apologize I don't know what he's called these days. Tech, perhaps? Reaper?"

Metis... "Now is not the time–"

"I don't mind waiting." He went inside and shut the door. With a small smile and a quick bow, he walked over to one of the chairs and sat down. Behind him came another figure, a customer from before. Then another.

"We're not open!"

They all ignored her and took a seat away from the first man.

Telematic continued to surprise Gwen, but now was not the time for strange new figures in her life. They needed to leave, she knew that much. With a quick wipe of her eyes, she limped into the backroom and grabbed the staff. As soon as Kirana and Metis were back they would leave, for good. She didn't care if Hiraeth was crowded with Wardens, it was time to go home. It was time to take the Keepers to Lorenzo. To safety.

Without the Warden.

Chapter 34

METIS

METIS TURNED THE corner with Kirana and saw RO. The five Wardens hadn't noticed her, not yet at least. Metis pulled out his second gun and handed it to Kirana as he took out his new Keeper weapon. The gun was incredible, and honestly, he was excited to use it again. Metis had watched Haunton walk right through his bullets, but the Keeper's gun had been able to pierce her helmet, carving all the way through. Beyond its technological advancement, the gun felt like his own, as if it were an extension of his arm.

Metis couldn't help but wonder what the Master would think of it. His father always dreamed about advancing Telematic and creating an invention to set himself up as a godly inventor. He wanted fame. He wanted the world to know his name, to bow before his genius. The Master was skilled, Metis had to admit that, but he was no god. Young Metis was his first worshiper, but he was also his father's only helper. A young boy with no skills to match his father's.

Metis was seven when he first saw someone die at the hands of the Master. He had seen people die before, corpses and all, but he had never truly seen the Master kill someone. The client was a large man whose arm had suddenly gone limp after he had tried a new drug on the streets. The Master promised him a better arm than the one he was born with and gave the client his latest prototype. The procedure went as it always had: Metis brought the Master tools as he put the man asleep and started tearing away his limb piece by piece. It was normally peaceful, but something went wrong. There was so much blood, to the point in which Metis had no time to clean the floors between new cuts and spills. The Master got frantic, demanding strange tools and yelling orders at Metis, before suddenly stopping. Metis remembered how cold the room felt, and he reached up to feel the man's wrist the way his father had taught him when looking for a pulse. But as soon as he touched the body, the Master had swung the back of his hand across his face, sending him to the blood floor.

"You should have moved faster!" He grabbed Metis by his collar, "You didn't listen to me, boy. You were slow."

"I'm sorry." Metis pleaded, looking up at his father's cold eyes. He truly believed he was responsible for the man's death. That was the first time Metis felt guilt, and it wouldn't be the last.

The Master walked out of the shop to clear his head and came back to hug Metis and apologize. Those soft words when the Master calmed down meant everything to Metis. That was not the last time a client died on the Master's chair, and it was not the last time he gave his son guilt for being too slow or grabbing the wrong tool.

When Metis turned nine, the Master told him that he had outgrown the small-scale operations they were running. So he thought bigger, and expanded.

He got a partner. A man named Mixer.

Mixer was a genius. The Master had found him in a small hide-away spot for inventors in Telematic, much like Bot's Bar, only for chemists. Metis had stayed home, and when his father returned he was wearing a giddy smile, laughing about a man he met who could finally help him advance Telematic. He never told Metis exactly what the two of them wanted to do, nor allowed him to work with them anymore. Mixer also brought with him a team of rough but loyal workers.

Metis hated the new man. His father was no longer concerned about him; in fact, they spent less than an hour together a day. The Master sent Metis out to get scrap metal that was never used. He felt useless, and he wanted to prove himself to his father. He didn't care if some surgeries could lead to him getting hit or yelled at, the ones that went well made the Master smile and praise Metis. That was all he wanted.

Metis rolled his new Keeper's gun in his palm, thinking about the gears and magical elements his father would love to examine. He pictured his father asking him questions about how it felt to wield such a weapon. If there was a bond between the owner and gun, the Master would be more qualified to answer his questions. His father was a dangerous mix between a master in mechanics and organics, and Metis was constantly reminded of him whether he was looking at Ben E or any random person. He saw gears and organs, and then he saw his father.

Metis put his gun up beside him and forced Kirana not to run. He moved her towards the edge of the street. Stalls lined the edges of blank walls, it would have to do as their cover. Together they stood in front of the nearest one, just out of sight with a small crowd. The man behind the stall tried to push chunks of warm uncooked meat into their faces. Metis was forced to hold a slab of bare meat to keep him quiet.

"Troopers!" RO yelled out as she pointed back to Bot's Bar, "The Keepers are here, call it in!" Her yell had turned into screaming. It wasn't out of panic, but anger.

The Wardens turned and spotted her quickly. There was a moment of realization. They must have heard of RO's disappearance. Metis figured the Wardens must have found some footage of their time in the prison or maybe were able to connect enough dots to figure it out on their own. But they knew RO went with the Keepers, they knew she was a god. Something about that seemed... wrong. What would be their reaction to her?

The leader, the one in front with a gun already in his hands, turned his body into a new stance. He spread his feet shoulder-width apart and raised his head high, confronting her. RO had stopped walking, and it was at this moment she sensed a shift. She tried to step forward, but as soon as she did the Warden raised his gun. "Stay where you are!"

Kirana grabbed Metis's arm and pulled him further along the line of stalls and people.

"What are you doing?" RO snapped at them, "You need to call this in! The Keepers–"

The Wardens all raised their guns. The leader stepped forward, "Hands up! I will not ask again."

She didn't. RO started to step away from them, "What did I do?"

"Hands!"

"I'm not one of them! I am Lieutenant RO, I work in the Firelane district. I was posted–" The Warden walked up and pushed the gun to her face. RO might have been faking how extreme her injury was, but another blow to the head still did enough damage to force her to the ground.

Metis turned to Kirana, "Are we saving her?"

She looked nervous, unable to decide on the right answer. She put the gun up beside her, "I mean… what else can we do?"

He agreed. Pointing his gun around the corner he aimed it at the Warden above RO. With an echoing shot, the blue bullet shot through the helmet. It was powerful still, yet he felt no knockback when using it. The weapon was light, easy to swing, and quick to work in his favor. It was his own, and yet, he still thought about the Master while using it. The other Warden looked for the source as he and Kirana attempted to take out the rest. She missed. Metis took out all five, and Kirana did her best not to hit Telematic people crossing by.

When the last body fell, Metis ran out to RO. She scrambled to her feet, dazed and quick to stumble away from them, "Stay away from me!"

"RO–"

She turned and walked away, "Leave me alone!"

Kirana ran after her, "Don't you see? Your own people–"

RO turned to fight the Keeper but Metis stepped between them, "I'm sorry, RO." He put up his hands, "But they betrayed you."

She let out a breath that seemed to shake her. It looked as if she hadn't let herself comprehend the situation until that moment. Her body softened, and she put her arms around her, defeated.

Metis put his gun away and put up his hands, "They just took everything away from you for nothing."

"I am a traitor." She seemed to truly believe that.

"You're a god." Kirana moved beside Metis, "Who do you think sent those soldiers after you? Your people or the Magistrater?" The Warden didn't answer, but she didn't try to walk away either. "She turns you against each other. She forces you to fight, like this." She gestured to the bodies, "Do not see our violence as the work of traitors, see it as our willingness to work for our cause. We are not soldiers, but we are willing to fight for that choice."

RO glanced down at the bodies of the Wardens. Still, she did not walk away.

"Come back with us." Metis tried to sound as genuine as possible, "We can talk and you can question us. If you go back to your people after we talk, fine, great, you chose a valiant cause. A loyal one. But right now you have nowhere else to go."

"Ask us anything." Kirana told her without hesitation, "You can take our answers back to the Magistrater if you want, or you can stay with us and we will figure something out."

Kirana extended her hand, an offer of acceptance. The Warden was not rash; even in her state of confusion and pain she took her time to think about this offer. After a few moments, she glanced down the street. Metis hadn't forgotten she worked in the Firelane District. It was a dangerous place in Telematic, one crowded with some of the smartest and most technologically advanced gangs. The whole district was crowded with enough guns and drugs to help make some new ideas for inventions that gang leaders like King King or Card Face would pay thousands for. RO knew Telematic, she could find her way to her people, but when she turned back to Kirana it was clear that that choice was not something she could just make. She knew there were consequences now. Either choice would leave her on the wrong side, but in the end, she made her decision.

Pushing Kirana's hand away she walked past the two of them back to the bar.

RO would have made it there if it weren't for the shout.

"Help!"

Telematics have a strong tolerance for strange and gory elements. Everyone stood out, unique in their fashionable ways, and sometimes people took it a little too far. Metis had once seen a man walking around in a white shirt splattered with blood. He was trying to draw attention to himself by resembling a killer, and someone not willing to clean up after a gory kill. The crowd around him took notice, but tolerated the gory details of his attire.

But even Telematics had their limits. Metis was working with Ruby at Card Face's nearest bar when suddenly a woman walked inside dressed in an outfit that was bloody and, from what he could tell, resembled human skin. When gore became too violent, they called the Wardens. The Wardens only came if the threat could harm their own people as well, so Telematics only called in the worst of the worst crimes, kills, and exotic inventions.

A man, dressed in dark clothes and bright blue accessories, stood in the center of the street staring down at the bodies of Wardens. With a scream and a cry for help, he started running down the street.

Kirana ran up beside Metis, "Do we need to go?"

He shook his head, "We'll be okay for now, but we should–"

The man started gesturing down the street to someone or something out of view. Within the next second a group of Wardens were walking out into the street.

Metis pushed Kirana into a run, "We need to go. Go!"

RO was already running for the bar as the two other Keepers ran after her. When they made it to the door, RO waited and let Metis enter first. He swung the door open and found Gwen standing mere feet from the entrance with the staff.

"Hiraeth. Now."

Kirana and RO came after and with a hard push, the Warden shut the door behind them. Gwen's reaction was expected: she was angry. But this time she seemed to have more intentions with her hatred of the Warden.

"Let her go."

RO stepped forward, "I'm coming."

"No, you're not." Gwen didn't even let herself contemplate RO's newfound loyalty. Metis feared their dispute would send her back to the Wardens.

He turned to Kirana, "Hiraeth?"

"I don't know." She looked at Gwen, "Is it safe?"

"It is with Lorenzo."

Metis took the staff from Gwen and put it into Kirana's hands, "We can stay here and run or we can go to Hiraeth and hide. I don't know any other options."

RO stepped forward, "You could go to the Ward. It's hot on the outskirts but you can take longer to make a decision there. You can't force her to make a choice here and now."

"The Warden's world?" Kirana asked, "It's called the *Ward?*"

Metis repeated the worlds' names: Permidia, Hiraeth, Telematic, and the Ward.

"No!" Gwen grabbed Kirana's shoulder, "We can't go back to the Warden's world. Lorenzo can take us in."

"We can't–"

"I am not being biased, I am telling you he can keep us safe!" She looked to Metis, "If you have any other places better say them now."

Metis had a few, but his ideas for a safe place weren't as permanent as a rebel leader's safe house would be. He had friends, a few groups even who could take them in, but not forever, and not in safety or loyalty. Metis nodded at her, backing up from the group, "Hiraeth."

As quickly as he could he ran into the backroom and grabbed Ben E. The android didn't resist, he had been in escapes before and knew to stay still and stay quiet. Metis came back around and swiped the two piles of clothes left on the bar before moving back to Kirana and grabbing the staff. He nodded down to his arm holding Ben E and the clothes and RO held onto his wrist. As the world around them started to change and morph he caught Gwen's glare. Gods, it was horrible. She hated the Warden more than anyone, more than anything. He feared her anger would get them all hurt, or worse.

The world around them split and the white light flashed over his eyes before darkening. Metis opened his eyes as quickly as he could from the flash to check where they were. If Hiraeth was as dangerous as Gwen said then they needed to be ready for anything. But, as he turned and got ready to run, he was shocked to see what was truly around him. Not people, not Wardens, not buildings, not metal. Plants. Real, green, plants. All of them were in rows of soft soil. The air, as soon as he took a breath he could taste its difference. It felt... fresh, as if this was the first time he had breathed real air.

Kirana fell to the ground head-first. She only just managed to turn her head as she slammed into the dirt. "Ow." She was conscious, that was good. Metis couldn't help but smile. He looked around for anyone near them. He saw no one, so he went over to one of the plants and touched it. It felt smooth, like plastic. He pinched down and part of it broke. There was some sort of liquid inside. It was real. It was truly, completely real.

Metis looked over to see RO glancing around them. At first, he thought she was looking for Wardens, but as she turned to face them he saw something else behind her gaze. She was curious.

He gestured to the plant, "Isn't it gorgeous?"

"It's a plant." She shrugged, "It... grows."

"What is this?" He asked, turning to Gwen.

"Corn."

"*Corn.*" Metis repeated, looking down the long row of plants.

It was then he realized there was a view before him, one beyond the corn. He stepped back to see the view fully. The farms were built along their crop's rows, one that led to another field, then another, and another. His eyes followed the path right to a town. Or rather, some very small, clay version of a city. The buildings were built on top of each other, stacking up to form a hill-like structure. There, fixed in the center of a strange small city, was the Magistrater's Tower... in all its glory.

In Telematic the tower was ominous, but it was just a tower. It was one of thousands of buildings. It was tall, it was dark, and it was strange, but it was not dangerous. Metis had seen Wardens come in and out of the front grates, the most heavily guarded place in his entire world. But it was still just another building among so many others. Hiraeth's small structures barely reached a second story. It was nothing, it was pitiful, and then there was the Magistrater's Tower. The people of Hiraeth had to face the Wardens, and then they had to face the unfathomable structure. He was starting to understand the fear he had seen in Gwen, but especially the hate. Hiraeth was beautiful, it was lush and green with a grounded brown element, but at its core was a dark, looming virus. The source of the Wardens.

"Metis." Gwen pointed down to Kirana, ignoring the view, "Can I have a hand?"

Gwen and Metis pushed Kirana up onto her knees. "That's getting easier." She told them. She wiped her nose and looked at her hand, "There's less blood." She pointed to her face where a streak of smudged blood lined her cheek.

"More or less." He looked up to Gwen, "Are we safe?"

This question snapped her into focus. She straightened her back and looked around, "If a worker sees us they will notice something is wrong. But if we talk to them first there is a good chance they won't report us."

This shocked Metis, "I thought you said Hiraethans hated Wardens. Why would they report their people?"

Gwen nodded solemnly, "It's how we survive. If someone is caught with people breaking the law, they are just as guilty as the one who committed the crime. It's for their protection."

Kirana pulled herself up and leaned against the staff, "So where do we go?"

Gwen looked left and right, up once, and then pointed left, "There."

"You can just tell." Metis laughed, looking around at the rows of corn around him, "It's all the same."

"I could say the same thing about Telematic." She gestured in the direction she had already pointed, "I can see the mountain from here. Lorenzo's rebellion hides out in an old mine right in the center of the range. Gods, that's a long walk."

Gwen took a moment to stare at the view. Metis had been concerned with the

Magistrater's tower, but it seemed she was more interested in the natural view. Hiraeth's city was surrounded by a massive mountain range. Metis could see large fields and a river right at its lowest point. In Telematic, every space is used, but in Hiraeth, some places were left untouched even from the Magistrater.

"Your home is beautiful, Gwen."

She smiled up at him and nodded, the breeze in her hair, "I missed it so much." She pointed to the river, "That is where my father and I would go, to escape the Wardens and responsibilities. When I was little my mother used to go with us, and we spent the night with our feet in the streams talking about the Keepers. It's where we had my mother's funeral."

Kirana had been behind them, wiping off mud from her clothes and blood from her face, and stopped the moment Gwen spoke about her mother. She exchanged a look with Metis, perhaps wondering if he knew about the death of her mother. He did, and he gave her a small nod before turning back to Gwen, "Maybe we can stop by, have a moment to rest."

Gwen shook her head, "Maybe one day. We need to keep moving." She gestured to Metis, "You should change before we start moving."

He looked down at the clothes bundled in his arms, "That's a good idea." Metis walked away from Kirana and Gwen and over to RO who had stayed back to watch the three of them. He pulled a few pieces out and handed them to her. She seemed reluctant but eventually took it. Metis wondered what it meant to RO to remove her Warden armor and wear Telematic clothes. This was a physical change for her, perhaps a commitment beyond what she was ready for.

Metis was about to say something when she suddenly looked up and said, "Why did you save me?"

"Sorry?"

"You saved me from the Wardens; I was trying to kill you."

He felt his gaze soften, "Is that why you're here?"

"I'm not in debt to you. I'm just asking."

He shrugged, "You didn't deserve to be killed."

"What if they weren't going to kill me?"

"Then I'm guessing they were going to do something much worse. You're not my enemy, RO. I'm not yours, no matter what your superiors say. I stand by what I said; I want to help your people. I want to help you." He gave a smile, "I believe in second chances."

"Second chances."

"You're not defined by your orders. Sometimes you do bad things for the sake of someone above you even when you don't–"

"Why did you join the Keepers?"

"Well, that's a big question." He scratched the back of his head. His hair was getting tangled into large clumps of knots now. He hoped Lorenzo had a shower. Gods, that would be nice. Metis would be clean and safe in a Hiraethan bed. "I joined the Keepers because I wanted to help my world. You've seen Telematic, your people keep my people inventing while leaving others in chaos. I want to change the system."

"You just... decided to start helping. Because of them." She glared at Kirana and Gwen.

Metis tried to decide how much he would keep from the Warden before him. Should he lie? No, she would know. Should he keep parts of the truth? In some ways, she deserved to know all of it. "I used to save kids in the pipes."

Her eyes widened, "What?"

He smiled at her, "Have we met?"

She looked him up and down in disbelief, "You're the Telematic Hero?" She stepped away from him, "And you became a Keeper."

"I was chosen to be a Keeper."

"Because you stop us from taking the children."

Metis felt himself go cold. He stood up straight and asked, "Where do you take them?"

She shook her head, "I don't know." He couldn't tell if she was lying. She remained fixed in her expression, blinking now and again but not moving any other part of her face.

"Guys." Gwen called from ahead, gesturing to the corn around them, "We don't have much time, please hurry."

He wiped down his face with his hand, "I thought you said we were safe?"

Gwen shook her head, "I never said we were."

Metis tried to turn into another row of corn when RO grabbed his arm to stop him. She made him lock eyes with her. "Why are you trying to save your world?" This question meant more to her than he had expected. It seemed for her choice to stay she needed to understand why the others stayed too. He respected that.

"They're just kids. They don't deserve to die or live down in those pipes. Kirana and Gwen gave me the opportunity to make Telematic a better world. I would never turn that down."

RO studied him for something he was hiding. A truth, or a lie. She found none because he wasn't keeping anything from her. That was the truth. RO turned away from him and moved into a cornfield. Within a second she disappeared. He stood there in the field for a moment, lost in her dismissal, before moving into the opposite row to change.

The outfit was much like the one he had before, only this time his long coat was now a short jacket. His sleeves were pulled up too, something he hadn't seen until that very moment. That would pose a problem, one he would need to fix before they started moving. Taking off the Warden's clothes he ripped undershirts and turned them into strips of cloth. Tying them as best he could, he wrapped them around his forearms. He chose to wrap both sides, not because needed to but simply for less suspicion. The scar was on his left arm. Long and still, to this day, jagged. He pressed his hand on top of it and thought about the Master and his blade.

No matter what his father had done: bringing in Mixer, losing his temper, hitting, killing. In the end, it was Metis's own fault for being hurt so badly.

He closed his eyes and let out a soft sigh.

He deserved the pain.

He walked out back through the corn and saw Kirana and Gwen huddled around the staff making some sort of plan. RO kept her distance from them, positioned so Gwen could not see her. She wore a tight red shirt and a shawl over her shoulders. Her baggy pants were a dark black, and now they were covered in specks of dirt.

Gwen pointed towards the staff as he came over, addressing Kirana as she spoke, "Even the most loyal worshipers will make a scene." She saw him come over and gestured to Kirana, "We had an idea. But it's risky."

Metis shrugged, "When have our plans not been risky?"

Kirana winced, "I'm going to transport us straight into the city."

"Why is that so risky?"

"If we land anywhere near a Warden they will see us and report us. If we disappear to Lorenzo they will find a way to follow us. We have to make it through the entire city, board a small passenger ship to the mining town across the mountain range, and make our way into the base without being seen by anyone." Gwen locked eyes with him, "Not even my people can know we are here. We can't keep the staff out because one look and someone will get the Wardens. I can't be recognized by friends or family. We can't show our faces to cameras or soldiers. We have to be completely invisible."

They would have to become four faceless Hiraethans heading to a mining town. Metis didn't know if they could do that. He had hoped there would be an easier way to find a safe place to rest. This no longer felt like resting, it felt like another fight.

There was a *bang*, like two pieces of metal crashing together not too far from where the Keepers were.

Gwen froze, "Wardens."

It was a warning. An alarm.

They could not be seen.

Chapter 35

KIRANA

KIRANA FELT EXPERIENCED. Having been in Hiraeth already she felt like she had an advantage. It felt powerful. Their journey would be hard, but not impossible. So many moments had felt impossible until now. This wasn't some new unknown place, half of the team had been there before, and the other half had at least heard of it.

It was not impossible.

As quick as she could, she grabbed each Keeper and pulled them across the dimension into the in-between. Splitting through their world she landed them in the in-between and looked around the suffocating world. She searched for Hiraeth and she found it. Then she searched for the city. She pictured it, she felt its streets, its life around her. She needed a place away from the eyes of people. She tried to remember her time in the city. Gideon had led them through those streets, but they were all crowded. Were there alleys? Not many. She only entered Trent's building, which was likely being watched by the Wardens, and there was certainly no way she could just appear within it. Where else could she go?

It hit Kirana suddenly. The place they had escaped to: the roofs of the crowded city. A temporary haven from all eyes.

She pulled the group forward and pushed them to a clay floor. Kirana dropped down onto her knees and did her best not to lay on the ground. Her nose bled, but not as much. Her head spun, but less than normal. It was getting better, and she had the strength to run. That was needed. The others looked around and pulled her away from what she only assumed was the view of someone near them. They guided her to a wall and peeked around the corner.

Gwen stood in front of her, studying her face for how much damage the trip had done. Kirana blinked herself into focus and pulled herself up with the staff and wall. "Are we safe?"

Gwen looked around them carefully. She was focused, now more than ever. It was her responsibility to guide them to Lorenzo through a dangerous city, but as she looked around, her movements shifted from focus to fear. She went stiff, staring out at the vast rooftops before them.

This was where they had separated from her father.

Kirana grabbed her shoulder, "We need to stay focused."

Gwen locked eyes with her and blinked down her fears. She glanced at RO once before pointing to a crack between two buildings, "We'll jump down there and join the crowd below." She pulled up her hood and tucked her hair inside, "Put away the staff."

Kirana listened and pushed the staff back into the in-between.

Metis crouched down next to Gwen, "Do we have a plan?"

Gwen looked around the corner, "Act like a Hiraethan, don't draw attention, hide your faces, and follow my lead."

"Alright, and what about your leg?"

"Hiraethans limp, it's normal. You just have to follow me, I know this world. If we get in danger can we escape quickly?"

Gwen looked at Kirana, who shook her head, "It will take me a while to get the staff back. Even then, I'll need to be holding onto all of you and find the time to concentrate."

They all exchanged looks but said nothing more. They were facing true danger and there was nothing they could do to avoid it. They had a simple plan because, well, there was no way to make a proper one. Time was against them, and they would just have to endure a trip without any godly advantages.

Kirana prayed the Voice would stay close, just in case.

The trip down into the alley was done carefully. They all knew dozens of eyes would pass them by within seconds, and one glance could mean the end of their travel through Hiraeth. Gwen went first, lowering herself carefully across each crate she was able to not make a sound, even with her injury. Kirana went right after her with a not-so-graceful landing. The two of them crouched behind a crate as Metis and RO followed. RO was doing everything they were asking her, but Kirana had no idea why. She was ready to accept that she was a Keeper, but how long did they have until she changed her loyalty?

"Watch her," Gwen told Metis as RO came down the crates.

He shot her a look, "I am—"

"She acts too much like a Warden. Hiraethans know what they act like. Especially Enzo."

Kirana squinted at her, "Ezno?"

Gwen shook her head quickly, "Sorry, Lorenzo." She glanced over Metis again and saw he was holding Ben E in his arms, "Hide him."

Metis looked up at Kirana, "Can you put him away like the staff."

Ben E looked up at him, "You don't want me?"

"We need to hide you, Ben E." Metis pushed the android into Kirana's arms.

She held Ben E tightly and tried. Though she could sense the in-between, she could not find a way to put the android inside. It was as if he didn't belong there. With the staff, she could transport him, just not leave him there. She shook her head, "The in-between isn't for storage. I can only do that with the staff. It's rhodonite. I can probably hide your weapon but I need to connect to the object. It needs to belong in the in-between."

Metis looked at the crates around him and found a small thin cover over one of them. He unhooked it and slipped it over Ben E. It looked lumpy and pecuniary, but it was better than nothing. RO joined them and Gwen turned towards the street, "Follow my lead."

Using the crate to pull herself up, Kirana walked calmly into the street. She followed Gwen and slipped into the space beside her. Metis and RO moved behind them making the Keepers a tight group of four. Did it look suspicious? Looking around, many Hiraethans were traveling with other people. No, they looked normal.

The Hiraethan street was busy. People moved from side to side, attempting to break the constant flow of people in the center of the street moving up. Telematic was more rigid than the Hiraethan city. Here, people went as groups and became a collective body. The Keepers joined them in the center, following dozens of others further into the city.

Kirana looked around at the many stalls around. She could smell sharp spices and clay. People were yelling out, attracting people with their many products. The moment the street went quiet was the moment Wardens appeared. Most of them stood along the walls, watching the crowd. The Keepers turned their heads and were hidden behind a dozen other people.

The crowd they were in shifted at the sound of commotion up ahead. Gwen guided the group to the side and Kirana tried to see what was going on. She could hear shouts and Warden voices, and from what she could tell two people were getting thrown to the ground by Wardens.

"They're being arrested." Gwen whispered to them, picking up her pace.

Kirana watched as one of the Wardens waved another soldier over, "Ellis Wills, 17th Mill."

Metis leaned forward, "What did she do?"

"She didn't show up for work."

"I called it in!" The woman on the ground yelled, sobbing violently, "I told them!"

Metis walked closer to Gwen, "Why would the Wardens–"

Gwen pushed him back, "Don't draw attention. If she doesn't show up for work production is stalled. The Wardens maintain productivity."

A second group of Warden came by as the Keepers turned a corner. They had their guns out and fingers resting just beside the trigger. The leader paved the way through Hiraethans as two others carried large metal crates. Their appearance was a shock, and Kirana tried to slow down and or turn around to run.

Gwen grabbed her arm and forced her to keep walking. "Don't stop." She wrapped her arm around Kirana's and pitched her voice, "Tristan's paycheck's coming in next week. We can buy the tools on Tuesday, we'll need the surface Corts for some other things." She turned her head around as the Wardens walked by. She was good at this. Gwen knew more about the Wardens than Kirana gave her credit for. As the Wardens disappeared, Gwen did not let go of Kirana, who quickly realized the only reason she had her arm around her was for support. Gwen had been shot in the leg and the group was still making her walk through a city. The Keepers had to keep moving, so all Kirana could do was support her.

Gwen glanced back to Metis, "Stop looking curious."

He walked up behind her, "Everyone is so scared." He seemed shocked, even with the warning they had given him about the world and display of Warden violence.

"Welcome to Hiraeth." Her words were cold, an unspoken apology for bringing him to her home.

Gwen guided them through the busy roads before moving them to smaller streets. There were fewer people now, but not fewer Wardens. They were able to easily hide within the crowd, but now it was up to them to disappear. The smaller streets were narrow, at the very least, and though there were few people in front of them a single person could block the group from any unwanted eyes at the end of the road. But as their cover turned and moved past them Kirana looked up to find a Warden at the end of the street, leaning against the wall and watching the people around him.

Gwen's grip tightened against Kirana, "They're guarding the platforms. The ships are just on the other side. They're making sure we're not going outside of the city" She didn't let them stop walking towards the Warden. Two people in front of the Keepers were all that blocked them from the soldier's view. At the other end of the road was a busy street, they could hide away, but not if they were seen.

Metis moved up again, "I can kill him and hide the body. I'll make it quiet."

"No. They'll notice." She looked around, "Shit. Turn around."

Kirana didn't let her, "He'll notice."

They were getting closer. Dangerously close. As the people in front of them started to pass by, a second Warden came up beside the first. The two Hiraethans kept their heads down but the Wardens stopped them. They started to say something, gesturing for the two to lift up their chins. They did, and the Wardens examined their faces.

They were checking their faces.

Gwen turned Kirana to a stall. An old woman with a gray eye watched them. The Hiraethan Keeper pointed to a fish, "How much?"

"15 Corts."

"What do you think, Oliva?" She looked up at Kirana and they locked eyes, "Do we buy it or go back to the old fishing stall down the road."

Kirana didn't know. She saw something move out of the corner of her eye and saw the Wardens starting to move down the street. If they walked away they would be followed. If they stayed where they were there was a chance, gods, a slim chance they would be disregarded. Maybe their features would be missed, maybe the Wardens were idiots but… all Kirana had were maybes.

A voice suddenly echoed through the street, "Troopers! Get over here *now*!"

The Wardens looked behind the Keepers towards the street they had come from. Glancing around, the two of them walked towards the voice, pushing past the group and running towards the Warden who had called for them.

Gwen pushed Kirana forward, "Go."

"Don't you want a fish?" The woman called after them but the Keepers collectively ignored her.

They rushed forward towards the busy street and weaved themselves back into the safety of a crowd. Kirana felt herself finally breathe. Glancing back she saw the Wardens looking down the narrow street for who had called them. No other Warden was with them, no other Warden was in the street.

Metis was glancing back too, only more panicked. It was then Kirana realized RO wasn't beside him. He looked down at Kirana, "Where is she?"

"She— No you were with her—"

Kirana looked behind him and found RO walking back to them through the crowd. Without a word, she slipped into place beside Metis.

Gwen tried to look back at her, "What did you do—"

Kirana pushed her forward, "Not now."

"She—"

"She distracted them."

That was RO's voice in the street. She had slipped away and distracted the Wardens. The Keepers hadn't even seen her leave. She saved them. Kirana looked back to RO and gave her a nod of thanks. RO did nothing in return, her stoic expression all she offered the Keepers. Metis glanced down at her and gestured to his face. RO relaxed her expression and slumped her shoulders ever so slightly. Kirana hoped it was enough to keep them hidden.

In the busy street, they had no problem with staying out of sight of the Wardens along the streets, but with the constant flow and ruckus, they struggled to stay together. Kirana could barely keep Gwen beside her as people pushed back and forth both around and sometimes even tried to get between them. She didn't let herself look back for fear of drawing too much attention to her panic. She had to trust that Metis and RO could stay with them. Gwen was their guide, their beacon, if everyone followed her then they would be fine. From what she could tell, it was working. Kirana could see the platform Gwen had referred to up ahead. On it sat a ship. Much smaller than the one Kirana had ridden in before in Hiraeth. It could only carry a dozen or so people. Enough people to hide beside, small enough to not draw attention.

As the Keepers made their way towards the ship with the crowd, Kirana saw flashes of more Wardens. They were watching the people within the crowd.

"We're almost there." Gwen's voice trembled as she spoke. It sounded as if she was comforting herself more than Kirana.

"Hey!" A Warden's voice cried out through the noise.

The crowd all looked back, hands clutching bags and eyes open wide as they waited for gunshots. The Keepers did the same, only they knew that they would be the target. Kirana let out a gasp, a cry, but turned herself around and got ready to face the barrel of a gun.

But the Wardens were not speaking to her. They didn't even go near the Keepers. They went through the crowd and grabbed someone else. A child. The boy tried to run away but the soldier grabbed him by his collar. Pulling him back he forced the child out of the crowd. Choked by his shirt, the boy could only let out muffled screams. The Warden pulled a fruit from his little hands and held it up out of reach.

Gwen put a hand to her mouth, "*Danny.*" She muttered under her breath before turning to Kirana, "That poor child stole the fruit. Danny did the same thing. But this one looks so thin. He needed food for his family so he stole it."

"*Telematic.*" The Voice rang through Kirana's head, "*Grab him.*"

Trusting in him, she reached out and grabbed Metis's arm. The Voice had warned her in time to Metis from pulling out his gun and sprinting towards the Warden. She pulled him forward, "What are you doing?"

He looked at her like she had just hurt the boy herself, "We have to save him."

Gwen grabbed his other arm, "Walk away. He's not our problem."

Wrong words, wrong person. Metis tried to move back through the crowd and Kirana grabbed him again. The Wardens were everywhere and the crowd was moving on without them. "Metis." Kirana said, "If you save him they'll hunt us down. Think about Lorenzo. Gwen's family is there. They will know where we are going, the ship is right there."

Gwen pushed him forward, "They won't kill him, they'll send him home with a few bruises. This happens–"

"He's just a kid."

The two of them pushed him forward and Gwen slipped against her injured leg. Metis caught her and, coming to his senses, walked her with the crowd. Metis was devastated. It was in his eyes, though he wasn't crying there was a cold terror within them. Kirana and RO took the lead.

"This happened to you, as a *child*?" He whispered to Gwen.

Kirana looked back in time to see her glance away. It had.

The Keepers spilled out with some of the crowd onto the open platform. Most of the people turned down new streets but Kirana guided them to the ship. It looked very similar to a Warden's ship. Silver, and built to withstand a hit. But it was painted over with brown and orange paint in some places, windows showing seats inside the long body of the ship. It looked like a flying rectangle with strips. It was hideous. Kirana had gotten used to the flashy Telematic ships, and though they were sometimes blinding, they were also fun.

Kirana went right up to the ship's door and looked inside. It was rusty, not well kept, and not made to look good in any way, but so was the pilot who sat at the front of the ship, who didn't say a word. She just stared at them with yellow-glazed eyes. Kirana took a breath and walked up the steps. The pilot glared at her as she walked by. The ship was already half full, that was good, more people to hide with. Kirana tried moving down to the back of the ship before Gwen grabbed her from behind and pulled her to the middle. She pushed Kirana to a seat by the window.

Gwen sat beside her with a wince, "Look at me." Kirana locked eyes with her. "Don't look out the window, don't let them see your face."

Metis moved into the seat behind them and RO moved to the opposite side of the ship beside a sleeping Hiraethan. Metis leaned forward to speak to Gwen, "How often do they take kids?" A person moved by and he was forced to pull back. As soon as they were gone he leaned forward again, "How often?"

"You need to stop talking, Metis. Please."

"That's not fair, Gwen."

Gwen closed her eyes, "I know."

"What are people doing to stop this?

"There isn't anything people can do, Metis. Children are punished, or they're taken to prisons, same as everyone else. If we fought back it would only get worse."

"You just let them take *children?*"

She looked back at him, almost forgetting where they were. Someone knocked into her and she made them trip. "Sorry." She muttered, turning back to face the front. After a moment she shook her head and whispered, "I couldn't help them. I had to take care of my family."

Metis didn't answer, but the lack of response seemed worse to Gwen than any sort of criticism. She looked back to the floor, thoughts somewhere far beyond Kirana's understanding. As the final person took their seats she took Gwen's hand gently.

"We're almost there."

She nodded softly, "I just want peace." She adjusted her hood, "I'm tired of thinking about these things."

Kirana understood that feeling, more so than she had during her first day in Hiraeth. She had been empathetic before, trying to think of what life would be like but now... she was living it. It was good, as the leader of the Keepers she would need to understand each world and each god. As the doors closed there was a sense of acknowledgment of where they were. They had just shut out the Wardens. They were not out of danger but out of its quick reach, and as the ship pulled up and shook itself to life they were leaving it behind.

They were heading to peace.

Chapter 36

RO

THE WARDENS WERE seen as monsters. Without mercy, without care. RO had never been to Hiraeth, but she had heard what the people called Wardens: monsters, heartless pawns with buckets strapped to their deformed heads. Telematics were no different. During her patrols in the Firelane District, they would yell at her squadron. They said Warden armor was to hide her hideous demonic forms. They called her gun an extension of herself and nothing more. They threw bottles at the other Wardens and said they were the scum of the world, a disease spreading their poison to every good-hearted person they wished to kill. But RO knew better. She knew that those labels were nothing but foolish, childish excuses. She knew her people's purpose, she knew her own. They were trained to be warriors, but also to be monsters.

And by the gods, RO had vowed to be the very worst of them.

For as long as she could remember, the desire to be a respected Warden fueled her every action. Her every footfall, every breath, a step forward to greatness. Her destiny. Her fate. She sealed it every single day.

Almost.

There was something about being a monster among soldiers that scared people. It was the look in their eyes. Dark though they were, hers were darker. The blood behind their words came in drops, hers came in floods. They were scared of her, sometimes even terrified. Her people were trained to be monsters, but not all soldiers could be so murderous. They hesitated, they became lazy, they fueled their ego. RO stood above all of them. She was a monster, the best of her people. They saw her power, her value, and she had climbed above her peers because of it. Higher and higher still.

Until she fell.

Something about Metis had haunted her when they first met. She knew something was wrong with him, she just couldn't figure out what. If she had truly thought about every option, she would have seen his Telematic traits. Even the way he walked seemed playful, as if he was stepping into a dance. His name was Telematic too, and though she found it strange he introduced himself with his first name, she simply thought it was because he was lazy and attention-seeking. She had not been distracted, simply unaware. If her superiors had told her about the Keepers she would have known. She would not have punched him, but rather taken out the small dagger in her left boot and pierced it through his throat. RO would have been the god killer, the one to take down a Keeper from within their world.

If only she had known.

As the ship neared the ground the Keepers waited anxiously for its arrival. It circled down and around a valley between two high cliffs of dark rock and bright greenery. RO did not trust the Hiraethan piloting them; of all the deaths she had envisioned for herself, this was not one of them. But the ship landed without true damage, just an unprofessional shake and lunge forward. She suspected the pilot would blame the ship and not herself. How selfish.

The people around the Keepers started to get off quickly, moving to the opening doors and traveling around to the back of the ship. The man beside RO woke up with the sudden landing and she was forced to stand to let him pass. She moved back to her seat when he left, and much to her disgust, Metis followed and sat beside her.

"We'll wait until everyone leaves." He nodded to the other Keepers, "There aren't too many Wardens around here, we got lucky."

No, they didn't. Luck was impossible, but they were foolish enough to believe that there had been no Wardens ready to board the ship.

"Understood." She glanced out the window. What part of Hiraeth were they in? She had seen pictures and studied basic maps, so perhaps she had a way to find their exact location.

"I need your help." Metis told her, "I need you to tell more about the kids you take from Telematic." She said nothing and waited for his question. He took a breath, "I know you use them for projects. But where do you take them?"

"Projects?"

He squinted at her, "You work them, right? I only have a basic understanding of what happens. I know they're taken to another dimension, but I need to know more to help them."

She shook her head, "I told you before, I do not know where they are taken."

She waited for a response, and when he did not say anything she looked over to find him staring at her. He was studying her answer, her body language. Metis was a strange man, a Telematic at heart in his loud and energetic need for attention, but someone with a keen eye still. He could see things better than Kirana or Gwen combined, that was a problem.

"I only work in Telematic. If they are taken somewhere else I would know nothing. I load them up in a ship and they leave."

He nodded, "Fair enough." They sat in silence for a moment, before he turned back to her, "But if you've heard anything from–"

"I know as much as you do."

RO had always been careful about what she said. Too many words were better than too few. When she was younger, it was hard to control her arrogance. Naturally, she picked up the habit of oversharing as most of her peers did. They boasted about missions and training opportunities, and at the time, staying quiet felt weak. She wanted to prove herself.

When she was about 14 years old, she said to a group of loud-mouth Wardens, "We're going to Bending Bridge to take down a gang. I don't see you being chosen to do anything quite as admirable."

The look on his face was... horrible. He looked smug. He had been able to lure her into some psychotic trap. A commander had overheard her right as she realized her mistake. He turned her around to face him and with one hard smack, she never bragged again. With one hard hit, she remembered how powerful silence was. If she had said nothing, her success upon returning from the mission would have been enough of a boast to affect her peers.

That same night, RO snuck into the loud-mouth's room and set fire to their clothes. It was in a closet, so only when smoke had filled the entire room did they wake up to notice. All she needed was an ember to light the flames. She watched from afar as an alarm sounded and the young Wardens came running out of their room coughing and gasping for air. She was burning material that should not have been burned, and much to her luck, it left their throats coated with thick smoke and toxins. They were never the same again. She made sure they got to see the look on her face, even if she denied any such crime, they knew it was her.

Better to say nothing than to say too much, and for now she wanted to keep her information as a valuable tool for the future. She knew more about the Telematic children than she was telling Metis, but based on his constant desire for answers, she could use it as leverage for later. And yet, if she under shared Metis could see her lack of commitment. She could not let that happen.

"What was that back there, with the kid?"

Such a question would scare him away, and sure enough he was quick to stay quiet. The last person moved from their seat behind them and he stood up with Gwen and Kirana. Metis moved behind them and RO followed a few paces back. They exited the ship quickly, and right as RO walked through, the doors quickly shut behind her. Then just like that, the engine started up and the ship began to lift. The Keepers were forced to step away as the grass beneath the ship bent away from the gust of wind. Slowly but surely, the ship lifted and started to move away. RO was quick to continue forward, ready to see whatever base the Hiraethans had made, but the Keepers were not.

Kirana and Gwen stared up at the ship in some sort of shock. After a few seconds, it faded into relief, and then joy. It took RO a few moments to realize the lack of danger immediately around them had made the Keepers drop their guard. All of them, and almost at the same moment. This place was some sort of safe environment for them, something they clearly had not had in a long time.

Kirana bent down to her knee and sat for a moment. She had nothing but pure gratitude for where they were. In a moment of peace, she put her hands out before her and in a swirl of white light the staff was brought to her hands. She held it close, keeping it to her heart. Gwen was looking at the world around her, hair waving in the breeze. She closed her eyes and soaked in her world. Metis had not been looking up at the ship but rather across the valley. He glanced at every crevice in the rocky cliff and bent down to feel the blades of grass. After a moment he rolled over and lay down on the grass, Ben E placed beside him.

RO walked over and looked down at him, "What are you doing?"

He looked so happy, "It's so beautiful." He played with a piece of grass in his hands before taking the cloth off his android and turning him back on, "Ben E!"

The android sprung to life and looked around, "Wow!" He looked up at RO and let out a robot squeal, pointing up at her, "Sir!"

"She's with us." Metis told him, patting him on his head. He looked up at RO and gestured to the cliffs, "This view is gorgeous."

She glanced up before looking back down at him, "It's rocks."

"It's pretty rocks." He smiled to himself, "I'm so sick of metal. No amount of human crafting could replace this." He looked over to Gwen, "You look so at home."

She nodded softly, eyes still closed in the breeze, "I missed it."

RO suspected Gwen acted differently when the Warden wasn't around. She, now forgetting RO was near, had become softer. She had a gentle way of moving. When she was calm, she dissolved into her environment, becoming a part of it. The breeze shifted and she moved with it, breathing with Hiraeth's natural movements. Here, in her home, she was safe.

Gwen looked down into the valley, "The entrance is there." She gestured down to the end of the valley against a cliffside. RO squinted down to it and could just make out a door. RO had not seen one in person but by the sheer size of it, she knew what it was: a mining door. Four stories tall, maybe more, built for production. That was the base?

RO turned to her, "It's a mine?"

Gwen's movements became static as she remembered the danger RO brought with her, "It was, once." She looked RO up and down, before walking to Kirana. "Let's go."

The walk through the valley was long. According to Gwen the ship went to the town and the base but had to be sent further from the mine in case a Warden discovered so many people flying to the door. RO could not ask any questions, certainly not to the Hiraethan, so she was happy to see that Kirana and Metis were curious enough to ask on their own.

"So Lorenzo found this place." Metis asked.

"Found?" Gwen laughed at the idea, "Are you kidding me? You can't just *find* places like this." She gestured to the door, "The mine was abandoned after the

tunnels filled with too much methane to be contained. It was shut off until someone went looking inside."

Kirana leaned forward, "The gasses just stopped?"

"They put fans inside and opened up a few vents."

"Lorenzo?"

Gwen shook her head, "This has been running for decades. There have been
many leaders, but Lorenzo is the most recent. I think for a while they just ran it
as a business, they still are."

This intrigued Metis, "What business?"

"It's a gambling den."

Not a business, a crime. RO was not very familiar with every aspect of Hiraethan laws as they differed from Telematics almost entirely. However, she did
understand the premise of Hiraeth's control: containment. Everything worked
exactly as it needed to work. She knew that this place the leader Lorenzo had created had slipped under someone's radar. She intended to find out why.

Kirana looked up at the doors, "So it's not really a rebellion then."

"No no, it is." Gwen reassured her, "But they are covering their tracks." She
stopped walking to face them all. She glanced at RO for a moment before speaking
freely, "They run an arena. They bring in creatures and get a few guys to go down
and fight. People rarely die, and if they do they choose to take that risk. People
come, place bets, and never speak of the mine. They keep quiet, it's their little
escape. But no one knows it is a rebellion unless they are a part of it."

"Is there anything else we should know?" Kirana asked.

"Lorenzo and I are good friends. I'll talk to him first but he'll understand
we're a team." She looked at each of them before stopping at RO. Her expression
hardened, "Are you coming with us?"

"I am." She tried to sound solemn, to react like any average person would:
emotionally.

Gwen clenched her jaw, "Then you need to act different."

RO raised an eyebrow, "How so?"

"You act like a Warden." She looked her up and down, "You look like one too.
Change that."

"I can't just do that."

"If they so much as sense what you are, they will kill you."

Her words hit hard enough to affect the other two Keepers. Metis took a shallow breath, "But this is safe, right?" Why was he scared? He would be able to act like a Hiraeth, she did not doubt that. But with his glance down to RO, she realized he was worried about her. Why?

That was not part of the mission.

Gwen gestured to her face, "Fix your expression. Express your faults."

"I don't have faults."

Gwen rolled her eyes and pushed past her, "*I don't have faults.*" She mocked RO as she turned around and walked towards the mine. Gwen and Kirana took the lead and started to walk to the doors.

Metis smiled at RO, "At least she's not trying to kill you. I consider that a step in the right direction."

She turned to him, "But you don't want to kill me."

"I don't like to kill anyone, RO. Especially my teammates."

RO had killed her teammates. She had driven a sword right into her comrade's stomach and watched him foul around like a fish out of water. It was horrifically beautiful, a memory she would not forget. Nor did she ever wish to lose.

Metis had not killed someone close to him before. He was a Telematic who only cared about himself. Selfish and independent with a fun kink for being the hero. He saved kids, sure, but there was a reason he didn't have the heart to care for anyone older than twelve, and she could tell it was something selfish.

RO had to admit one thing, she did not wish him to feel the pain of killing someone close to him. Though she had no regrets, there had been a time when killing hurt her. She spent her whole life waiting for blood, but when she saw it, she felt sick. The satisfaction wasn't there, it was gone, all gone. She felt incapable of moving or breathing. Her body weaved in and out of death as if the soul of her victim was trying to pull her with them. She had to realize something very important to pull herself away from complete decay. She had to learn that a life taken was a life given, and it was the only way to earn her place in her society.

She had to kill to survive.

RO looked up to Metis. She made her eyes soft like an animal no longer needing to hunt, "I don't like to kill either."

Every death got that much easier. Again and again, she did it for her people. For herself. She made her life and fueled her legacy with every action she took.

And they thought she sacrificed all of that to be a Keeper.

Never.

RO knew that Metis couldn't see through her. He looked down at her as if they had made a connection. She had proved herself to be emotional, to be human. She seemed relatable in her sorrow.

The truth was that she had no sorrow, she had no fears.

She had loyalty.

RO recalled when Chief Haunton had called for her. She had only hoped it was because of that: her loyalty, skills, experience, and determination. But no, this meeting was different. On her way to the detainment center, a Warden ran after her and led her to a new room. As soon as she walked inside she knew something was wrong. Generals stood waiting for her, standing as soon as she entered as if RO had become the Magistrater herself. The Chief had walked to her from the darkest corner of the room, "Lieutenant RO." She gave a small nod, "We have reason to believe that the Keepers have been following you."

Those words did not sound correct. Not only the idea that the newly pronounced gods were in the Ward, but that they were with her. "What do you mean, sir?

"They are looking for a Warden Keeper. We believe it is you."

This was when the sense of danger kicked in. If the Chief was there then her statement was true. RO was a Keeper, but now what? She did not let herself show the true panic she felt. "Do you wish to kill me?"

"No." Haunton lifted her hand to reveal a small chip of some kind. RO stepped forward and took it carefully. From what she could tell it was a communication chip. The Chief gestured to the side of her head, "Attach that to the back of your ear. We will be able to talk to you through it, and you will be able to tell us *every-thing*."

RO understood, "You want me to be a spy."

"A Keeper in disguise." She nodded softly, "You will act as a Warden. Do not change your nature, for the man you had a conflict with upstairs was a Keeper." RO had to swallow her shock. "All Wardens will see you as a traitor. They will try to capture you and bring you in. Find a patrol group, let them try and capture you. Let them hurt you. The Keepers will come to your rescue and you will act as if you have nowhere else to go. Join them slowly, make whatever excuse you want for being a Keeper, but stay with them."

This was not RO's fall, this was her chance to become something greater. Everything she had worked for, everything, it would all go to this.

She was a good soldier.

She was a good monster.

"I will do whatever it takes. What do you want me to learn?"

"Find their allies, learn what they know, and report what they are finding. Do not kill them unless we tell you to, especially Kirana. The Magistrater needs her alive. If you have to kill anyone, let it be the Hiraethan or the Telematic."

Kirana looked back at RO with a half-hearted smile, "It is good to have you, RO. When you figure out a reason to stay we will gladly support you however we can."

Never. "Thank you."

"Our last Keeper. Now we can begin the process."

RO stopped walking. She looked at each of them with the best shock she could muster, "You don't know?"

Metis looked pale, "Know what?"

RO remembered her own shock when Haunton first told her. After she agreed to be their spy, Haunton stepped forward and lowered her voice to say, "We have the advantage now."

"How so?" RO had asked.

"We know the final place they will be going."

RO had lifted her head, "To the final Keeper."

"We will be ready for them by the time they make their way into the dimension. They may not know of its existence, so tell them of it. Help them in any way you can, keep them alive, learn everything you can, and help us bring them in."

RO would do whatever it took.

She would act like a Hiraethan, she would fight, she would bleed, she would hurt anyone and everyone in her path. She would protect the Keepers until the day she could betray them.

She couldn't wait for the look on their faces.

She would make sure they could see her own.

RO tried to look hurt as she locked eyes with Kirana. She put a hand to her chest, "You only have four Keepers, but there are five dimensions."

Kirana shook her head violently and walked back to RO, "No, no, there are four. Hiraeth, Telematic, the Ward, Permidia–"

"Is Permidia a jungle? Is it filled with mountains and miles upon miles of vast oceans?"

Kirana turned to Gwen, "What is she talking about."

Gwen shook her head quickly, "In the books I... I always saw four Keepers. But..."

"But what?"

"There is a jungle world." She looked at RO in horror, "I saw the drawings. I just assumed they made Permidia have a different environment."

RO sighed, "You're missing a Keeper."

Kirana put up her hand, "You could be lying. How do we know?" Her voice was trembling.

"Why would I lie?" RO asked, "You can travel to it, go see for yourself."

Kirana placed the staff before her and in a white flash disappeared. The Keepers stood together for a moment, and RO could hear that neither Gwen nor Metis were breathing. A second later, Kirana appeared and dropped to her knees, "It's green." She put a hand over her mouth. "It's so small I missed it."

Gwen let out a cry, a gasp filled with too much pain to be out of shock. It was out of grief. RO looked over to see her already beginning to cry.

They were lazy gods, it seemed, not willing to push through every struggle to succeed. RO could see that now more than ever. These were just children who were given the title of a god by their hopeful worshipers, destined to lead a world they could never even reach. They had their weaknesses, but that was not RO's fault. It was their fault for having them. It was her job to report them. To bring them back to her people. To rid the worlds of their imperfections.

RO was not the Warden Keeper.

She was the Warden spy.

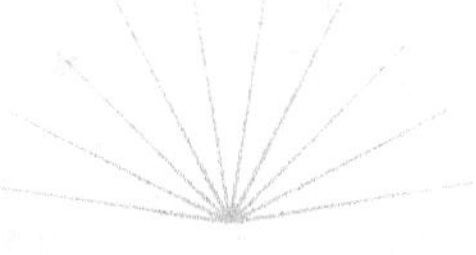

PART 5

Hiraeth

Chapter 37

* * *

METIS

METIS ALWAYS WANTED to be in nature. He had so many stories about them. Plants were essentially living objects, so detached from humans that they didn't need them all. Looking around, he wished for once the Keepers could just enjoy the moment without thinking of more danger. Metis wanted to lay down in the grass for a few minutes more, to rest away from his world and their future pain.

He played with the blade of grass in his hand as Kirana looked up to RO, "Are you sure–"

"I'm sure." The Warden looked so steady. Metis hoped she could help them with more information. Gods, he felt blind. They all did.

He stepped forward, "But you didn't know about Permidia."

"No one goes there. I only know the Worlds people are posted in. The Ward, Hiraeth, Telematic, and 'Āina."

"'Āina?" Gwen repeated the word softly. She shook her head, "The books only had four Worlds. Four Keepers." She put a hand to face and tried to think, "Maybe the staff represented a fifth Keeper, or maybe the pictures were too faded and there was a figure holding them? I wouldn't know."

Kirana stood up slowly, shaken to her very core; Metis wouldn't be surprised if she fell back down again, "There is a difference between the leader and the team. They were the ones I was supposed to find, not including myself."

"So we're not done..." Metis dropped the grass from his palm, "What do we do?"

"I can't do this all again." Gwen gestured to the mine, "We can rest inside and then find the last Keeper. Later. Not now."

They were all injured, tired, and stuck in their own forms of shock. No one disagreed. They all needed to recover, and gods, none of them were ready to face another trip into unknown territory again. Gwen and Kirana moved up and started to walk to the mine together, talking in whispers as Metis walked beside RO. For now, he would stick with RO and make sure she felt safe. And, without letting her see, watch her to make sure she wasn't a danger to them either. He wasn't stupid, his trust was earned, and so far she had not earned it yet. But Metis wanted her to have a second chance so she could redeem herself. So far, she was still going with the Keepers, following them and even protecting them from her own people. Metis knew she grabbed the staff for a reason, and until she showed signs of wanting to run back to her people, he would offer her a place in their team.

Metis stepped in pace beside her, "What is this world like?"

"It's a series of islands. Most of the world is covered in oceans."

"How many Wardens are posted there?"

She thought for a moment, before looking up to him, "I honestly don't know. Most of the people I have spoken to have said it was a lot like Hiraeth."

"But it's a jungle?"

"I think so."

"You didn't ask?"

She glared up at him, "No."

He nodded softly, "I understand." He looked up to the mine, "Let's stay in the back. Gwen will lead us around and do the talking, I think it's best if we don't interfere."

"You're scared." It wasn't a question.

But she was right, "I am. I want to give a good impression. I feel like it's my responsibility to make Telematic people look good. You should try and do the same and represent your people."

"They know my people, the impression is made."

"But we can't just lie to them about you. They'll have to learn eventually. If you can become friends–"

"This isn't about making friends."

"Except it is. If you prove yourself then you prove your cause." Metis looked up at the large metal doors. He realized now that Gwen was leading them to a smaller entrance on the metal itself. A smaller door, blended into the material, with a small window at eye level. He looked back down to RO, "You just have to think of a cause."

She didn't respond this time. Conversations were clearly not a skill she had learned. She seemed to enjoy a quick-witted response with an even faster escape from any more talking. Metis wondered if she thought he would allow her to win and let her be. He wouldn't. He wanted to help her, and right now she needed to be scared. Within those large metal doors were people who would shoot her on sight if they knew who she was. Gwen and Kirana might have been preoccupied with family and alliances, but Metis knew the most important thing they could do was prove that RO wasn't a threat.

Gwen was learning, and so could her people.

Gwen stopped in front of the doors and immediately pounded a fist against it. She watched the window, and after a few seconds, it slid to the side. Two narrow eyes studied them quickly, then widened. Metis heard the person mutter *Gwen,* before shutting the window and unlocking the door. A tall young boy swung the door open and rushed to Gwen. He wrapped his arms around her and cried out, "You're alive!"

Metis got the impression that there was a deep connection between the people in Hiraeth. He wondered if it had to do with the constant danger around them. Since everyone was doomed to a painful fate, they loved unconditionally in the time they had left. Metis had seen it in Gwen, maybe even felt it as their friendship grew. She knew to never trust easily, but once a connection was formed she would respect them through every moment and every battle.

Gwen held the boy tightly, leaning on her good leg before pulling him back to face him, "What are you doing here?"

"Working." He told her, a smile wrapped around his face, "Lorenzo is keeping us hidden and fed. We are even getting some Corts." He looked around at the others and spotted Kirana. "You!" The boy pointed at her.

Gwen held onto his shoulders and blocked his path, "Harold, don't–"

He pulled away from her, "She got us caught."

"She is here to help."

Metis stepped in front of Kirana to add another layer of protection. The

Hiraethan boy glared back at him, "Who are the other ones?"

"Just let us inside." Gwen told him, "I will explain everything, just get us to Lorenzo."

Harold took a deep breath in and turned back to the door.

Metis glanced back to Kirana. She looked worried, and clinging to the staff with white knuckles, she shrugged softly to his questioning look. It was clear she had no idea that this reaction would happen when they arrived.

Harold walked Gwen inside and everyone followed quickly. The Hiraethan boy didn't look back once as they moved into a dark hallway. It smelt like sulfur and tasted filthy, like the air in Telematic. As they moved further down the lights came more frequently, and soon the walls smoothed as they neared a turn. There was noise, an echoed slur of voices and movement. Metis stood behind Gwen as a barrier for both Kirana and RO, but as they continued down the hallway Kirana eventually slipped around him to Gwen.

"Do they think I turned you in?"

Gwen shook her head, "You're fine. They just need someone to blame."

Kirana stayed silent for a moment before whispering, "I'm so sorry."

Gwen glanced over at her and gestured to the staff, "You need to put that away. We don't want attention right now."

Kirana couldn't argue. She listened to Gwen out of guilt and pushed the staff into the in-between with a small white flash. She slipped back and fell into pace beside Metis. They exchanged looks but said nothing. There was a line of tension across this return to Hiraeth, and for all their hopes of sanctuary, Metis wondered if there truly be a moment of rest for them.

They turned the corner into a much brighter and larger space. People stood and walked from all directions going to one of three doorways. Two small hallways on each wall, and a much larger door at the end of the room. He could hear an echo of noise coming from the bigger door, and it took Metis a moment to realize how large a space had to be to create such noise. Was that the arena?

Harold moved them across the room and into one of the smaller hallways. Metis looked around to find the Hiraethans watching them carefully. In their eyes, Metis found the distrust he had seen within Gwen. At the mere sight of them, the groups turned from each other and watched them go towards the hallway. They could tell the Keepers were different, at first glance. The Hiraethans were so attuned to danger that the smallest sign of it put them on guard.

Harold led them down the hallway to their right. Metis looked around and saw a dozen doors on either side curving with the rounded walls. Metis could only assume the hallways curved around the arena. The noise from the arena came in and out through small vents on the roof. Small pieces of light filled the hallway from those gaps, and Metis dragged his hand over them every time they passed. The sun felt different in Hiraeth. Not as strong as it was in the Ward, not as soft as it was in Telematic. It was almost... perfect.

The group turned to a doorway and walked into a bright new room. The area was overflowing with people. Those around the walls didn't move as much as those in the middle, creating a natural current within the center of the room. It was loud, conversations echoing as the large fans dangling off of the roof made a loud whistle and clicked as it spun dangerously quickly. As the Keepers stepped inside, Metis was hit with a rush of heat. Steam covered his face in dew and he did his best to wipe it off and look presentable as they moved forward.

Harold and Gwen then slipped into the crowd and moved with the current. Metis and the others followed quickly, and by the time they reached the back of the room, the crowd had slimmed. Harold moved up quickly to a small group of people in the corner of the room, and Gwen stayed back for a moment.

Metis could tell what a leader looked like. It was not by the way they stood or the way they barked orders, it was how others looked at them. Four people were watching a man in the corner of the room. These people seemed to have their own goals. Two carried weapons, perhaps soldiers then. Two held rags, cleaners maybe. But they were all looking at the same man with his back turned to the Keepers until Harold spun around him, talking and gesturing to Gwen. The man looked over and, almost at the time, the people watching him followed his gaze and studied the Keepers with him.

It was Lorenzo.

Dressed in light browns and blacks, the tall dark-skinned man scanned over Metis, Kirana, and RO, before settling on Gwen. His stoic expression dropped and he ran to her. With one sweep he grabbed her and pulled her into a hug.

"Oh, my gods! You're alive."

Metis glanced back to RO. She was studying the room, examining it just like a Warden would. She caught his gaze and loosened her expression.

Lorenzo pulled away from Gwen and looked at her, "What happened? Is Gideon with you?" He looked behind her and saw the others. "Who are these people?"

Gwen pulled out of his grip, "We need to talk, please. It's about the Keepers."

He looked at Kirana, "The blond one?" Something changed. He did not look at her as if she was a god, he looked at her as if she was their enemy.

Metis stepped in front of her before Lorenzo could reach her.

"She is a traitor." He turned back to Gwen, "She got your entire family caught, why are you with her?"

Gwen went stiff, "*Caught?*"

Lorenzo shook his head quickly, "No. I'm sorry." He looked behind him, "Harold!"

The boy was already moving into the crowd, "I'll get them."

"They're safe. Gaia, Theo, the kids, everyone except you and your father." He glanced to Metis and RO, "Who are these people?"

"They're the Keepers."

Metis adjusted the grip on the android to put him under his arm. He didn't want the focus to be on his android just yet, and for now it seemed there was trouble enough with Kirana being there. First impressions were important, and yet as he moved Ben E to his side the cloth slipped and the android fell to the floor.

Metis grabbed him quickly, "Sorry–"

Lorenzo walked up to look at the android. He was shocked, truly and completely, shocked. "You have a robot?"

"An android." Metis corrected, but after Gwen shot him a look he shook his head quickly, "Yes, a robot–"

Ben E shook to life and looked up to Lorenzo, "Hello!"

The man jumped back with a gasp, the Hiraethans behind him stared at the android with wide eyes. Ben E looked up and around the room before a wave of steam covered his face. It put its arms up and wiped it away to reveal a disgusted expression, "Too hot."

Metis flipped Ben E's back panel open and switched him off, "I really need to fix that sometime. If I drop him he just comes to life–"

"You made him?" Lorenzo tried to reach out to touch Ben E.

Metis pulled his android away, "I helped make him, in my world–"

"Dimensions." Lorenzo walked back to Gwen, suddenly realizing the weight of the moment they were in. "Come."

He gently pushed Gwen further into the room where a small door stood against the dirt walls. He pushed it open and allowed the others to follow him inside. The room was dim and appeared to be some sort of separate hallway. Metis didn't understand the layout of the space they were in, and he wondered if the Hiraethans had quite literally carved their way through the mine. Inside were a vast number of people who, even from a glance, looked like soldiers. They carried guns at their hips and knife holsters against their shins. They gathered together at the back of the room where they decided to stay at the sight of the four new faces. Lorenzo led them into one of two doors just opposite each other in the hallway. Inside was a small storage space with a dozen or so chairs scattered around or piled together.

Lorenzo stood at the back of the room and looked from person to person before locking eyes with Gwen. "What happened?"

"This is Kirana." She gestured to her, "We found her outside our house and took her in."

"Gideon did?"

She nodded softly, "She's a Keeper."

"Are you sure?"

Kirana laughed, before realizing it wasn't a joke, "Sorry. Fairly certain."

He glared at her, "Where is the staff?"

She looked at Gwen for permission, and with a small nod, she stood up and put her hands out. A light burned from the center of her grasp, and within a few seconds, the staff appeared. Kirana stumbled with it for a moment before placing it beside her, "We are *very* certain."

Lorenzo took a soft breath and took a seat on one of the chairs, "So it seems."

Gwen nodded quickly, "The four of us are here to help."

"Four?" He looked at them all once again, before settling on Gwen. His expression fell, "You?" Metis couldn't tell if his fear was out of worry for her or worry for his cause. He suspected Gwen couldn't either. She looked around the room with a small nod and nothing more. Lorenzo dragged a hand across his face, "You are not gods."

"Except we are." Kirana sat back down in the chair next to his, "And we're here to help."

"Help do what, exactly?"

"Take down the Magistrater."

He looked at Gwen, as if not believing what Kirana was telling him. Gwen shook her head quickly, "You can't do this without us."

Kirana leaned forward, "Hiraeth is nothing compared to the worlds the Magistrater controls. You can't reach the millions who are ready to fight without us."

Millions ready to fight? Metis doubted anyone in his world would want to fight, not yet at least. But her words still affected Lorenzo, and he stopped to think. After a few moments in silence, he looked at each of them and shook his head softly, "This isn't the time to make these decisions. You can't expect to show up and unite the worlds with our cause."

Gwen nodded, "We aren't trying to. We... we just need a place to stay. We've been running for days now."

"You were limping." He glanced down at her extended leg, and got up, "What have you been doing?" He put his hand out and she used his help to bend down and take a seat.

Kirana gestured to Metis and RO, "Finding them."

Lorenzo turned to the Metis, "The team of gods, all returned."

"Not all." Metis told him, "We need one more but... traveling into unknown territory is too dangerous to do again. We need time to rest."

"So you just need a safe place to stay." He looked at Gwen, "We are happy to take you all in." He looked back to the door and stood up, "I will find a room away from the others for you to stay in. I only ask that you don't show the staff to the others."

Kirana turned in her chair, "Why not?"

"The Keepers are a symbol of forthcoming, do not let them see their saviors already beaten to their very bones." He moved to the door, "You all have a place here so long as you keep quiet, and when the time comes we can speak again about your future with the rebellion. I would like to learn more about these dimensions." His gaze fell over Metis and RO, "Harold will bring Gaia and others up to your room."

Gwen smiled up at him, "Thank you, Enzo."

He gave her a smile before walking out of the room and shutting the door behind him, leaving the Keepers alone.

Metis looked to Gwen. She looked relieved, happy in her environment, "We can explain everything to him later. He's right, we need to rest."

He looked at RO, "You need to make up a world. Talk about the Ward but say nothing to connect you to the Wardens. We can give him information without telling him who you are."

"I agree." Gwen said. Everyone turned to look at her. She folded her arms and leaned back in her chair, "You wanted to keep her. If Enzo– If Lorenzo learns who she is he'll kill her."

"Enzo?" Kirana squinted at her, "You keep calling him that."

"We're close." Gwen smiled to herself, "When we were kids we used to work in the same field. Our families were close and when the Wardens killed his parents he was handed over the rebellion. He's a very wonderful man."

"And he cares about you." Kirana leaned back in her chair.

RO leaned over to Metis and whispered, "We need to watch that."

Kirana and Gwen continued to talk and so he turned to RO, "Are you trying to protect her?"

"Of course not. I'm saying we should watch Lorenzo's compassion for an advantage. He seems to know a lot of his people by first names as well. His care could be–"

Metis shook his head quickly, "We can't exploit him like that RO."

She leaned back, "I'm only trying to help."

"Well…" She was right. He titled his head side to side, "We need to make friends, remember, we don't have to fight him."

"If he learns who I am, he will kill me. Do you honestly expect me to not fight for my life? Especially when I can't physically defeat his soldiers considering I am unarmed."

Metis nodded softly, "I understand."

And yet, he did not understand. Not fully. He wanted to empathize with RO but he found himself already feeling safe. It was amazing, as if the leader had just given them all a barrier from danger itself. Yes, RO could pose a problem, but that was it. It was just her. They would get a room, a bed, food, and time.

Gwen looked up to Metis, "Can you admit this is better than Telematic?"

He laughed, "Hiraeth is not better than Telematic, Gwen. But… this place is safer than anywhere I could have taken you guys. So… yes."

"As soon as you all left that bar people just started coming back inside like nothing happened. I was yelling at them but they just made up excuses. I could never handle your world"

RO leaned forward, "It's an acquired taste."

Metis smiled at her, "Is it better than the Ward–"

"No. It is not."

Kirana gave a quick laugh, "If this is a contest, I think I win."

Gwen rolled her eyes, "That's kind of the point, Kirana." She looked back to Metis, "I did find a Telematic with manners though. That was nice."

"That's not unheard of."

"It was some old man. He was looking for you."

The safety, the rest, the time.

Gone.

Metis's face dropped, "What did he say?"

"He said he saw you down the street and needed to see you or something."

He felt his heart race. He went pale and leaned forward, "What did he look like?"

Gwen noticed his panic, "Was he dangerous?"

The most dangerous man in the entire world. "No." Metis forced his beating heart to succumb to neutrality, "I just feel like I know someone like that. Did he... was there something..." He gestured to his left eye.

Gwen nodded, and Metis felt his stomach curl. She spoke and suddenly her words did not reach him. The Master had been right there, in that bar. He had found Metis. How? Why? Why now? Why ever? Why not before? Was he being tracked? Was he being tricked? Gods, they had been in the same room. He hadn't even known. The Master had seen him. He had watched him.

"Metis?" Gwen waved a hand in front of his face.

He stood up with a smile and grabbed Ben E, "You know, I think– No I–" Kirana stood up and Metis gestured for her to sit down again as he backed up to the door, laughing, "He's a trickster, he finds me all the time. We're *friends*." He felt dizzy and put a hand on the doorknob, "I need to make sure he didn't put anything on Ben E. He always does that. I'll just check him for bugs outside."

"Metis–"

He opened the door and shut it as soon as he stepped outside. In a panic, he moved to the other door in the hallway and walked inside. It was another storage room, and he prayed the others would not try and find him there. He shut the door. The room was quiet. Metis put a hand to his mouth and slid down the wall, dropping to his knees.

What did the Master want with him?

It had been 11 years and 3 months since Metis had run away. Since Mixer. Since the deaths. Since Reaper. Since the operations. Why now?

Metis pulled at his shirt, trying to breathe. His head spun and he cried, begging for air. He dropped Ben E and the android sprung to life. At the sight of Metis he rolled forward, "Sir?"

"He was there..." Metis put his head against the wall, "I would have... I couldn't..."

Metis knew what would have happened if he saw his father in that bar. He would have frozen, and then the Master would have spoken to him. Metis was not the same young worshiper of his father, but he knew there was a chance the Master could have lured him in again.

"Sir." Ben E put his small metal hand on his leg, "You are not Reaper."

Metis sobbed.

He remembered when all of it began. It was when Mixer moved into the workshop.

According to his father, the operations were becoming too complex for such a small team and facility. They needed larger spaces and more people, and Mixer was able to give the Master both. Metis never knew what the Master was working on. To this day, he would wonder what those chemicals and complex circuits were for. He saw pipes, tubes, wires, and multi-colored liquids, but he never questioned what they were for. If Metis was with his father he was working with blood and bones, barely able to touch machinery. All he cared about was that his genius father could continue to progress his dreams, and all he wanted was to be the one to help him succeed.

As the Master showed Mixer around, he spotted Metis peeking out from their bedroom and ushered him over, "This is my apprentice, Tech." He put a hand on Metis's back.

Mixer was a large man, tall with a wide chest and belly. He had blond hair cut around his ears and a short beard that framed a large smile. At the sight of Metis he had laughed, "Children are allowed in your operations?"

"Workers are workers." The Master ruffled Metis's hair around, "He can already label every organ in a person's body and is almost there with the muscle groups. He has even gotten to try a few of my surgeries." Metis practically melted at the sound of his father's praise.

"He's quite talented." Mixer turned towards the door where his own workers waited outside, and said, "Axel!" A boy appeared in the doorway, blond hair and wide grin matching Mixer's. He ran over and Mixer gestured to him proudly, "And this is my son."

Axel was one year older than Metis when moved in with his father. Metis hated the boy at first. Mixer replaced Metis beside the Master, and so he became bitter towards Mixer's entire family. Axel was an energetic young boy with a blond buzz cut and long skinny limbs. He followed Metis around talking endlessly, and all the while Metis spent his time thinking of ways he could cut the boy open and give him to the Master. At the time, corpses seemed to be the only thing that brought him and his father together. But Metis wasn't a killer.

Not yet.

Eventually, Axel's company became more enjoyable. Though Metis considered himself tough, he was no match for the new kid. Axel had this unmatched sense of confidence. The two of them would run around the streets and even go into the wasteland, and while Metis glanced around for dangerous strangers, Axel would run around and talk loudly for all to hear.

"One day, I'm going to run my own gang and sell weapons, just like my dad." He swung a pole around the air, pretending to have a sword fight, "I'm going to be the biggest crime lord in the entire city." He picked up another pole and put it in Metis's hands, "What are you going to do?"

Metis dropped the pole and wiped his hands on his pants, "Help the Master advance Telematic."

"That's it?" He looked behind him and swung in the air. He kicked his make-believe opponent and stumbled, "Don't you want to leave? Go into the city?"

Metis had never had a friend. No one to love other than the Master. His loyalty was still to his father, but this new friend started to show him a life away from what he knew. He would watch how Mixer smiled at Axel and wished the Master would do the same. Metis was drawn between jealousy and judgment, half wanting the kindness and half judging Axel for being so sheltered.

Metis wanted to prove himself to his father, and as time went on attention became a necessity. He begged for jobs or simple tasks, but the Master just shooed him away. As time went on, Metis became terribly lonely, and looking back, he knew he should have just moved on and spent his time with Axel and Mixer, but he couldn't. He loved his father too much.

"Please!" Metis had begged as his father went to bed, "I can help you with clients! I can–"

"Be quiet."

"Please!" Metis had sobbed, "I don't–"

The Master smacked him, sending him to the floor, "Do you not understand, Tech. I am a genius." He pinched the bridge of his nose, "You are too far behind. You would get in the way and jeopardize my life's work for your own selfish reasons. Do you hate me that much?"

"No!"

He knelt before Tech and grabbed his face, "If you contribute nothing, then you will only slow our progress. I am so close."

The more the Master worked with Mixer, the less attention he gave Metis. The Master stopped eating with him. He stopped giving lessons. He stopped praising him. As a young, loyal son, Metis vanished without his father's acknowledgment of his existence.

Metis needed the Master, so he did the only thing he knew how to do: open a corpse. If he could kill someone and bring them to the workshop, he figured his father would surely give him a chance, maybe a lesson, maybe a smile. Metis had never killed someone before, but he expected it was no different from operating on a corpse. He knew who they worked, which joints would break easily, which organs would pop faster from a blade. So he went into the wasteland and searched, but the only people there were children like him and Axel who played in the rubble. He found one of them, a blond girl in a black dress with a jacket too large for her small frame wrapped around her body. She had been walking around the pipes, singing softly to herself and as she drew pictures with a stick in the mud. Metis grabbed the pole Axel had played with, snuck up behind her, and hit her head until she went quiet. He couldn't remember her face, only that there was a blue flower embroidered into the front of her jacket.

He dragged her body all the way back to the workshop. The Master and Mixer were working at one of their tables, talking in lower voices and gesturing to other workers in the room. When Metis came in with the girl, he dropped her at his father's feet and suddenly people were yelling at him. Metis ran into their bedroom and hid under the bed for what felt like an hour.

He could hear the Master talking outside the room to Mixer, "You said we need to test it."

"Not on dead children. We're not monsters."

"Those kids would die out anyway. You know that. We're just using… early resources."

"Early–"

"Do you want this to fail? We're incredible, Mixer, we could change everything about this world. He's brought us a way to progress our filthy city. Are you really about to throw it all away?"

Mixer let out a breath and raised his voice, "My son–"

"Is not the one who will kill them."

The Master went into their room, sat Metis down on the bed, and smiled, "Would you like to help us advance Telematic?"

Metis had never felt so good about himself, "Yes."

"My boy." The Master wrapped his arm around him, "I need you to do something for us." Metis was already nodding. "I need you to hunt children."

Now, sitting in the Hiraethan storage room barely able to breathe at the idea his father was so close, Metis realized nothing had changed. He may have gotten away, but the Master would always be able to control him. Metis would always be his little monster, and he would always want that praise.

Metis shook his head, "I'll always be Reaper, Ben E. For him."

＊ ✳ ＊

Chapter 38

GWEN

GWEN FELT SAFE in her world, not quite safe with her team, but at least their environment felt like a home and not a war zone. The room Lorenzo had managed to get them was very nice. She could tell it was not made for more than five people, and she hoped he had not removed anyone from the room just for them. And yet, it felt as if he was treating the Keeper the way they needed to be, as the gods they were. But for now, they needed to stay hidden. Gwen also understood that when the last member of the Keepers joined, they would be able to stabilize. The team could truly begin what would be a very long process. Gwen wished there wasn't another god to find, because now seemed to be the perfect time to just… stay still.

The Keeper had spent the night undisturbed in their room. Gwen fell in and out of sleep with waves of exhaustion and sparks of fear. Yes, she felt safe at home, but their journey was not completed just yet. There were many things left unresolved, like what to do about the Warden she shared the room with. When Gwen woke up in the night, she found RO sitting up and leaning against the back wall of her bed. From what Gwen could tell, RO did not sleep as much as the others. She spent her night watching the Keepers or closing her eyes for quick, light sleep.

Metis spent some portion of the night with Ben E, quietly trying to fix a piece of circuits under his face. His reaction to Gwen's news scared her. She wondered if he was lying to her about who that man was, and decided to keep an eye out when in Telematic again. Metis may have not found it important to share his history with her, but Gwen feared he was keeping something very dangerous from them.

She didn't want him to get hurt or go off on his own to find the man. When she rolled over to watch him another time she realized he was also looking at his gun. The Keeper's weapon. It was glowing in his hand, and he studied it as quietly as he could.

Kirana slept like a baby, exhaustion taking over fear completely. When she woke up in the morning she was quick to get up and move around, well-rested and ready to start their day in Lorenzo's rebellion.

By the morning, Gwen was still so very tired, she wished the others felt the same way. She could have slept for hours more and had to remind herself they had many days to do so, just not right then and there. No one would be fighting for quite some time, so there was no longer a need to conserve all her energy. The thought of Gaia and her father got her out of bed, today she would be able to see them both. Her leg felt better, not healed by any means, but the Telematic medicine was speeding up the process. She was glad they had stopped there before coming to Lorenzo. She knew her people would not have such painless tools to help her.

The Keepers all came together in the morning and did something long-awaited: they talked to one another. Sitting on the floor in a small circle they spoke about every detail from every part of their journey through the Ward.

Metis spoke about his travels around the Ward, about the plants and the lift, about the briefing and the Commander, and about RO. He told them he had been sent up to a briefing room and then to his Commander after getting in trouble with RO. He told them how he got the Commander, a father, killed. He explained to them how the Warden knocked him out and put him in the detachment center.

"Your technology is truly advanced." He told RO, "Even Telematic doesn't have that type of equipment."

She squinted at him, arms folded, "You have the same equipment in Telematic." She blinked at his confusion, "We take your technology."

"What?"

"Hiraeth supplies us food and produce, Telematic gives us factories and technology, 'Āina gives us mines and water."

Metis looked heartbroken, "Is that why you separated us? To make sure we create something for ourselves?"

"We give you education, tools, materials, and you create us crazy things we can build off of. Your separation is only there for our protection. If we let you have everything, and if you all ganged together..." She stopped speaking for a moment, thinking, before not saying anything else.

"What?"

She twisted her jaw to the side, "You could defeat us."

Gwen spoke about the Warden celebration and how they tracked down Metis. She spoke about how terrified she was and how little time they had. She told them about how Kirana had pushed her into the detainment center. She told them about Clay and her hiding spot. She explained how she freed Metis and took down RO. She told them how they were trapped inside with no way out until a Malfunction came to save them.

Metis nodded softly, "Her name was Patch." He looked at RO, "These Malfunctions, are they loyal?"

"Unconditionally. The Malfunctions listen to everything Wardens say; you just got the handful that heard too many Keeper stories."

"Clay obeyed my requests without even checking if I was a Warden." Gwen glared at RO, "You hate them, don't you."

RO smiled, "Of course."

Gwen couldn't tell if RO agreed to make her angry or because it was true.

Kirana spoke about her capture. She told them how she was knocked out and woke up in a cell. She told them how they carried her into a dining room where Haunton was waiting. She explained as much of the conversation as she could recall.

"The Magistrater knew I was a Keeper."

The silence was heavy, but it did not last long.

"How–"

"Why didn't–"

Kirana waved her hands in the air, "I don't know. Haunton said I wasn't supposed to go to Hiraeth. The staff had never done that before."

Gwen stared at her, "Before? How would she know that?"

"She mentioned having studied the Keeper for 16 years or something like that." She pinched her lips together and thought for a moment longer, "She knew about Rhodonite too."

"Rhodonite?" RO said, surprised.

Kirana looked over to Gwen, who reluctantly explained to the Warden, "The staff is made out of a very valuable, very powerful crystal called Rhodonite. It's everywhere. It's in us, in our worlds–"

RO put up her hand, "I know what Rhodonite is." She pointed to the nearest light on the ceiling, "How do you think we have so much power?"

Metis turned to face her fully, "Wardens use Rhodonite?"

"Everyone does. A small portion of that resource could power the entire district of Telematic. My people run your cities. We're not just soldiers." She leaned back against the nearest bed, "We make you believe we are monsters, because we need to control you. We push you to only see us as enemies, not as the only force allowing food, water, shelter, and power to be brought to every person possible. So long as you hate us and the Magistrater, you won't fight each other."

Kirana pointed at her, "That's what Haunton said. She said: *hate is fueled by comfort.* So you were raised to be... monsters. You pride yourselves on killing people."

"Yes." RO straightened her back, "But we are also the government and the leading force for all survival related resources."

"While you kill us." Gwen said, crossing her arms.

RO shrugged, "I do what I am told. The Magistrater has a plan for us all."

"That included Kirana." Gwen took Kirana's hand softly and made them lock eyes, "Could Tia have been a part of this plan?"

It was clear that the idea had not crossed Kirana's mind, not yet. She winced, "I really hope not. I don't want that to be true."

"It would make sense." Metis admitted, "If they wanted you for a purpose they would have raised you in a certain way. Did she ever... train you?"

"Never. I barely got to see her when I got older." She shook her head firmly, "No. They wanted me to be alone, maybe to force me to grab the staff and follow the Voice. If I didn't go to Hiraeth, I would have been foolish enough to believe whatever lies the Magistrater told me about her grand plan."

Gwen had never been more grateful that she found Kirana all those days ago. The Keeper was maturing into a leader throughout the journey, but even now, she was naive. The Hiraethan had a feeling Kirana would have easily joined the Magistrater, and that thought hurt Gwen.

Kirana inched closer to RO, "Who is she to you?"

"She is our god."

Gwen felt her stomach curl. She hated that RO was a Keeper, especially knowing the Wardens already had a god of their own. They didn't deserve that much divine assistance.

Kirana nodded quickly, "*May her divine powers continue to bring us honor.* So she does have abilities then?"

Gwen sat there in her hatred until she felt a sense of familiarity. She glanced over at Kirana. Kirana had called the Magistrater her savior, the one who created perfection for all. In a way, it was very similar to the Wardens. Perhaps they were being manipulated as well.

"She does not show her powers off, we see the effects of them. Like the gates."

"Gates?"

"How do you think we go from world to world?" She looked at each Keeper, and when no one answered she laughed at them softly, "We travel through the Magistrater's tower. There is a door for each world inside."

Metis put a hand over his mouth, eyes darting around, "I suppose that makes sense, considering it's the only structure that's the same in each world. That could be the spot every world feeds out of." The Keepers leaned forward, waiting for more, and at the sight of this Metis raised his hands, "I'm assuming here, but we should look into this later. And... I hate to ask this but... the Keepers are all dead, right?"

Gwen went cold, "No, Metis–"

Kirana nodded quickly, "That would explain what she is, and why she knows so much about the past Keepers. I mean... it's possible, right?"

"The Keepers have been gone for long. She would have to be hundreds of years old."

RO shook her head, "The Magistrater has been leading my people for decades. Maybe a century... Maybe longer."

"She is powerful," Metis said, "and there is a reason she has been able to remain in power for long. I am not a scientist but I know that there is no non-magical reason for someone like her to be alive. She is manipulating her age to stay powerful, but if she's a Keeper that's a good thing."

Gwen scoffed, "How?"

"It means she was once human, like us."

Kirana gave a breath of joy, a short smile fading and out of her expression. It was replaced by hope, "We could be as powerful as she is. We could defeat her."

By the time they were finishing their conversation there was a knock at the door, and with a mutter of agreement for the person to come in, the door opened to reveal a group of people.

Gwen's family.

She jumped up and ran to them as best she could with her injured leg. The children were the fastest, able to wrap themselves around her easily. Gaia pushed through them and reached her, holding her close in an embrace. She was crying, and soon Gwen was too. Gods, to see them, to feel their warmth, it was magical.

Gwen pulled away, "Is this everyone? Is everyone here? Did you all make it here?"

Gaia held her shoulders, looking her up and down, "We all made it." She noticed the injuries spread across Gwen's body, "What did they do to you?"

"What do you know about my father? Did he send a message? Has anyone seen him?"

Danny jumped up to her and she picked him up as best she could. Seeing her struggle Gaia pulled him off and put him back on the ground, "Theo is looking for him; he left this morning."

"When will he be back?"

Gaia winced, "I wish I knew, but he'll bring news, or maybe he'll return with your father, we'll have to see."

Gwen glanced back at the Keepers. Lorenzo was speaking to them, ready to hear all about their journey as Keeper and plans for their future against the Magistrater. Gwen knew it would be important to have her input, but for now she just wanted to be with her family. Gaia hugged her again as the children went away to explore the room and the strangers within. It was nice to have someone holding her. It felt as if Gwen had been holding herself up for years. She closed her eyes. Gaia did not feel the same way her mother had, but the love was there, and that was enough.

Gwen put her eyes into Gaia's shoulder, "I was so worried something happened to you all."

"We're safe, and now so are you." Gaia slowly pulled away from Gwen and held both her hands, "You look tired."

She smiled softly, "I am–"

"Did she hurt you?" Gaia nodded to the Keepers, and though Gwen's mind went to RO first, she took a moment to realize the woman was referring to Kirana.

She shook her head quickly, "No, she saved my life. She's a Keeper, Gaia, a real Keeper–"

"Is it true?" She locked eyes with Gwen, "Are you one as well?" Gaia was looking at her as if she had done something wrong.

Gwen found herself feeling guilty as she spoke, "I am."

"I hated those books. Those legends." Gaia shook her head softly, "I tried to tell Gideon that it was nothing but old fairy tales but he wouldn't listen, he believed that they would come and save us."

"And we're here." She smiled at her.

"I'm not a religious woman, Gwen. But if I was, I'm fairly certain my god would not be a young girl." She put a hand to the side of Gwen's face.

Gwen took a staggered breath, "I'm sorry, but I was chosen to do this. I will do my best to help–"

Gaia held her in another hug, tighter this time. She held her as if someone was ripping Gwen out of her grasp, "You're just a child. You shouldn't have to become a god for your people. If you are doing this for your father then don't, please, you're just a girl, you're not a god."

Gwen pulled out of her grasp slowly. Those were not the words she wanted to hear, "But I am a god. I am the Hiraethan Keeper, chosen by the staff."

Gaia looked into her eyes. Was she searching for an answer? Proof that Gwen was indeed a god? Proof that Gwen would stay in Hiraeth with her? Whatever it was, Gaia seemed to find it, and held onto it for a moment before looking away, "You're safe now." She walked around her into the room.

Gwen winced but did not go after her. Would her people not believe she was a god? What would the others think? Had she proved herself too weak to be now labeled as someone destined to save them all? That couldn't be true, no, the staff had chosen her. She just needed to get her people to see that.

Lorenzo gave a quick whistle through the room to grab everyone's attention, "I need everyone here to know that no one else is aware of the Keepers' return. We are keeping this all quiet for a reason. Too much attention will lead either the extremists to *them* or the Wardens to *us*, and in both cases, someone will get hurt." He gestured to the doors, "I will be giving the Keepers a tour, you do not know them, you have never seen them before. They are not gods, they are Hiraethans." He looked at Gwen, "Do you want to go with them or your family?"

It seemed like a question she should not have to answer too quickly, yet suddenly all eyes were on her. She shrunk back and looked at Kirana, who gave a nod back to Gaia with a small smile. Gwen was grateful she understood, "I'll catch up later. I know this place well."

Enzo looked pleased at her words and nodded softly with a smile. He moved towards the doors, "Very well then." He opened them for the Keepers, "After the tour I may need their assistance in various jobs across the Arena–" Lorezno's head turned and he looked over at the doors in time to see someone running inside.

Gwen recognised the man as Haru. She had met him a few times, a cheery Hiraethan soldier with a knack for smiling at times when most would simply start crying. For all the darkness he had seen he always remained positive. In times of crisis he was calm, and most importantly, calculated. Lorenzo had chosen Haru for those reasons and for his ability to get any job done with ease and without argument. He had a broad upper body and straight black hair pulled back. It looked as if he came in expecting to find everyone scattered and instead found everyone already staring at him.

He skidded to a stop and looked around with a nervous laugh, "Sorry to interrupt." He gave a small wave to the Keepers, before looking around and seeing Lorenzo, "Sir. We..." He paused for a moment before moving forward and pulling the leader aside.

Kirana moved up to Gwen, "Are you okay?"

She looked back, "Of course."

"You seem worried."

"I'm just... thoughtful." Gwen was worried.

The reunion went as well as she had hoped. Yes, her family was alive, they were together, but it all felt incomplete. Not only because Theo and Gideon were gone, but also because of how wounded they were. Physically, they were exhausted from running, mentally, they were overwhelmed by fear. She needed Kirana to understand that their healing would take time. One night and a happy morning was only the start of what was needed. But... how would Kirana possibly know what that feels like? She had never had any family like Gwen's. Yes, she had a sister, but that was it.

She looked back to Kirana with a soft smile, "Thank you for taking me home."

Her words seemed to allow Kirana to breathe.

Lorenzo turned back around and turned to Gaia and Gwen, "Theo is back."

Gwen felt her body start to move before even registering her own fear, but she didn't know where to go. She walked forward, then back, and then she ran for Gaia, who was already on the move. She ran out the door and Gwen rushed after her. She was already running down the hallway when her thoughts came back to her and she ran back to Haru. She spoke into his face, "Was he with anyone? Did he arrive with anyone else!"

"Yes, another man–"

Gwen had never heard such sweet-sounding words. She let out a breath of something between euphoria and desperation. It felt sweet, a pinch against her eyes ready to let tears fall, a squeeze around her mouth pulled up her lips into a smile. She ran after Gaia. She ran for her father. He was there. He had returned.

Gideon was a smart man, and gods, she had never doubted him once. He was clever but also skillful. If he had been shot, then he would have found a way to dig out the bullet and use it to take down a patrol of Wardens. She could see his face in her mind. She could see his reaction to her. Shock, joy, and then desperation. She would run to him and jump up into his arms as if she was a little girl. She wouldn't care how youthful that sounded, how ungodly her tears would seem. She was his daughter, he was her father, and she deserved to be young around him.

She ran down the hallway like a madman, panting through her joy and grief. Leaving him in Hiraeth had felt like she was leaving him for good. That had never been her intention. She had to protect Kirana, the staff, and herself and the choice was one she made for her father. She didn't let guilt fester within her because it all turned out alright!

He was alive!

He had come back!

She ran down the hallway and saw Gaia. She had stopped in front of Theo and her husband pulled her into an embrace. She was blocking the man beside him. Her father. Gods, it was him! It was him!

She ran faster, "Dad!"

Gaia moved around Theo to reveal him. But... it wasn't Gideon. It wasn't her father. It was her old neighbor. Dean. Some... some old friend.

No.

She moved up to Theo, "Where is he? Is he here?"

Theo pulled her into a hug with Gaia, "Gwen, you're alive."

She pulled out of his grasp. He was not the person she needed to hold her. She needed her father, "Where is he?" Theo held onto his wife for a moment. There was silence, too much silence. "Theo."

He let go of Gaia and looked from Gwen to Dean. There were tears in his eyes.

No.

Gwen shook her head quickly, "If he is hurt we can get him, okay? Don't worry. I have the Keepers here. I have the gods. We can go get him. If the Wardens have them– I don't care about the Wardens! Where is he?"

Dean looked from Theo to Gaia, not to Gwen. He didn't answer.

"Theo. Where is he?" Her voice was getting softer, she needed it to be louder, but it was falling into a whisper. The silence was dragging her to the very depths of grief.

No.

Theo shut his eyes. He couldn't look at her, "Dean saw what happened. He was at home when the Wardens showed up with their ship."

No.

"They cleared out the house, they found the books and packed them all away. Then... When–" His voice cracked and he pulled back.

"What?" Gwen's voice cracked just the same. She was crying.

No.

"Gideon... He's gone, Gwen."

No.

"They brought his body to our doorstep."

No.

"They shot him. Dean– something about his leg. Then his... his heart."

His heart.

Gwen's vision blurred, not from tears. She lost balance and stumbled to the wall to hold herself up, it didn't work. She couldn't. She fell. She fell, and no one caught her. She fell and her father didn't hold her. He was supposed to be there. To hold her. He was gone. His heart. His leg. His heart.

Her father was dead.

Tears fell down her face. Ignoring her skin, they pulled right down onto the dirt floor. She let out a whimper, forehead down on the floor. Her whole body was shaking, and she couldn't stop it. No one came to her side, they didn't know what to do with her. She didn't know what to do with herself.

He wasn't supposed to leave her, he was the one person who wouldn't leave her. Her mother did. Beaten to death. She had left her daughter. He had left his daughter. Gwen grabbed her hair, pulling at the roots. Gods, he must look the same as she did. Had they beaten him? Put him up as an example. His body was lifeless. His gentle ways were gone. The wind was dead, the breeze had settled into lifeless dust. She could not breathe. She could not move. It was cold and silent. She broke the silence with a scream.

She lay there in the hallway undisturbed, head planted on the ground against her dirt-filled tears. She faded from hysterical to misery, and suddenly the mere act of crying was too violent to continue. There she stayed, undisturbed, trying to stay there for as long as it took for her body to recover. It never did. She couldn't move. She took shallow breaths. She couldn't think. Her mind was clogged with pictures of blood, bruises, and bleeding parents. All she could think about was the fact Theo didn't bring back his body. Maybe there wasn't a chance to grab it and bring it safely to her, or maybe it was too destroyed to even pick up.

Had Gwen done this to him? She had trusted him, she did everything he told her to, and the moment she decided to run for herself she left him behind. She ran away with Kirana, the Keeper, the god he had protected for the future of their people. She had run away and left him to die. There would have been time. There would have been a chance. She hadn't taken it. Was it Kirana's fault? Gods, please not her. Gwen needed to choose any other villain, anyone else to blame.

She lay undisturbed. Until she felt a hand touch her arm. It was Gaia. She didn't flinch at the touch but she knew her body wanted to. Her hands were cold. Everything was cold. Gaia nothing, and with a small squeeze walked away. Mere seconds later, another hand grabbed her shoulder. It was Enzo.

She looked up at him with eyes filled with dried tears. He looked at her as if she had died herself. She realized she didn't care, and put her face back on the dirt.

"I'm so sorry, Gwen."

She had a feeling she would hear those words a lot. She didn't like them.

"We'll make them pay." Them? "That's why you're here. To fight the Wardens."

The Wardens.

There it was. The blame.

They were murderers. They destroyed *everything*. They took *everything*. From her people. From her. They were monsters. They killed the most incredible person in the entire world for nothing but a show. They displayed his body, and they were proud. They killed him, and they were greedy.

Gwen agreed to be a Keeper so she could defeat the Magistrater and create a new system that would give her people a better life. But in that moment she didn't care about peace, she wanted justice. She wanted a Warden's body shot dead and left on their family's doorstep. She wanted to see them beg for their lives. She wanted them to bleed and burn and die at the hands of her people. She wanted them to lose everything. She wanted them to suffer. At the hands of her or her team of gods, they would pay.

Her team.

The Keepers.

"RO is a Warden." She didn't look over for his reaction, she didn't care what he thought. Her eyes were to the floor, to the dirt. "Kill her."

Chapter 39

RO

RO COUNTED THE people in the command room: five people, five targets. RO walked around them, trying to see what they were doing as Haru gestured around the room. He had taken over for Lorenzo as the Keeper's tour guide, a change for which RO was grateful. Lorenzo was calculated and observant, and she couldn't have asked him too many questions without becoming suspicious. Haru, however, was a giddy fool she could use. A tour for a spy was as soothing as a current taking her in the exact direction she needed to go. The water was working in her favor, so far.

The command room was the border between the Arena's business and Lorenzo's rebellion. The five Hiraethans worked together to keep the games active while spying on the watchers. The room had a long desk fitted with rusty technology against a large window. The room oversaw the entire Arena and every seat in the stadium. RO tried to estimate the number of people watching the show, which at that moment was a Hiraethan running from a pack of wolves. There had to be hundreds of Hiraethans scattered across the seats, and in small clusters, RO spotted Wardens.

Metis pointed down over one of the worker's shoulders, "What are these for?" He pointed to a long pole sticking out of the table.

Haru smiled before speaking, "A microphone." He nodded to the woman in front of it, "Clara can show him."

She scoffed, "Who put you in charge of a tour?"

He laughed, "If you won't do it, I will."

Clara put her hand on a button in front of the pole and bent down so her mouth was right at the end, "Looks like Ben's got one more fight in him." Her voice erupted across the Arena, "Let's show him our support!"

The crowd stood up and started cheering.

Metis laughed, "You have such a fun job."

"Haru." RO said, pointing down the stadiums, "You have Wardens?"

Metis moved forward and looked out the window, "What?"

Haru nodded, "This is their secret spot. They like to come here to gamble to earn a few extra Corts. We have had a few of them report us, but all the Wardens found was an Arena overrun by their fellow soldiers. The Wardens we let in keep our Arena a secret so they can come back to have some more fun."

"That sounds dangerous." Kirana leaned over the table to get a better look.

Haru shook his head, "There is no other way. We can't own a business that isn't completely controlled by the Wardens. Those who come to gamble here keep it under wraps for their sake. Wardens aren't supposed to gamble. It's their downfall disguised as their paradise."

Metis glanced at RO quickly. He was looking to see if the comment was correct. It was, but she did not risk nodding. Her supervisors would decide a suitable punishment for the Wardens who came to this Arena. These Wardens Haru spoke of were becoming lazy and weak. It wouldn't be enough to give them isolation or remove their privileges; their loyalty would need complete reconstruction. Not a threat, not a warning, an activity that would bring back what little honor they had obtained over their years. There was so much to be done for her people, and she could see it all from behind enemy lines. RO was an observer, and she was proud to be sent on such a mission. She had ideas, more so now than before, and suddenly the idea of having the power to control part of her people's system thrilled her.

RO hoped that her return to the Ward would consist of a very gracious promotion and respect from her peers. She would remain a god, just not among the Keepers. A Warden god *and* a Warden spy. She had to bite down a smile.

Haru looked up at RO, who was forced to quickly loosen her jaw and hunch her back. Haru pointed at another Hiraethan down the line, "Caleb keeps track of the Wardens in the Arena and makes sure all of them leave and are accounted for at all times. His sister works downstairs to tap into Warden communications to make sure nothing is being reported."

Metis crossed his arms, "And if it is?"

"We go into lockdown, wait out a quick report, and then carry on." Haru smiled, "Easy as that. We don't like hiding down here, but we're still alive. That's all that matters."

The Hiraethans seemed to be comfortable in the dirt. RO wondered if they would feel the same way when she put them six feet deeper.

Haru gestured to the door with a smile, "Our *main* control room is just down the hall. Lorenzo works there with me and the highest-ranking members."

Kirana looked over, "You have ranks?"

The Hiraethan seemed proud, and like a child receiving praise, he smiled again, "We are organizing ourselves now. It's safe enough too. Lorenzo will be our main leader for the time being, and over time we hope to begin voting for our next leaders. We are also trying to create ranks, kind of like the Wardens, actually."

The Hiraethans had a strange relationship with the system; they knew they needed it and in some ways accepted it, all while vigorously resisting it. In the end, their rebellion would leave Hiraeth in chaos. RO wondered if they would ever learn that complete acceptance would save so many lives.

"Wow." Metis seemed impressed by what she saw as their lack of organization. A god or not, he was still a Telematic fool, "And what do you call yourselves? Lorenzo's Rebellion?"

"The *Guardians.*"

That name stuck with RO quickly. It sounded powerful, and that was dangerous.

Something caught her eye. RO had tried to not look out the open door for fear of getting distracted, but as a person walked past her she couldn't help but notice their qualities. First, it was their stare. They were looking right at her, right through her. Eyes, green, piercing her. She then noticed his hair, a trait she would not have even acknowledged if it hadn't been such a vibrant orange. The man had ginger locks cut short around his head. He looked dirty, but the filth did fit his posture and bearing. His face was sharp and cut clean. His eyes were narrow, they slid across the air. When he looked at her, what little empathy he wore as a mask dropped, and they matched each other's gaze.

She knew those eyes. She knew that face. It had changed in the years she had not seen it, but it was his. He was no Hiraethan. It was Antony, a Warden.

He passed by the room without breaking eye contact and when he went out of view RO was tempted to run after him, but there was nothing she could say that wouldn't seem suspicious. She had to let him go. Was Antony undercover like her? Had he betrayed their people and joined the Hiraethans? Both seemed unlikely. So why was he there?

"RO?" Metis said. Haru and Kirana looked at her with him.

She pointed outside the door to the only other subject in her view: the vents. "How safe is your air quality? I heard there used to be a problem with the methane levels."

Haru waved his hand in the air, "The vents do their jobs in pumping clean air across the rooms. So far, there hasn't been a problem."

RO glanced back at where Antony had been, and she wished she could find him in the crowd by simply knowing his hair color, but it was impossible. He would have disappeared into the crowd. Antony was a Warden, an old friend she hadn't seen in years. *Friend* was not a good word, but there was no other word to describe him. He was not her enemy, she did not care about him, but she did not wish death upon him for damaging what little remembrance of their past remained. For memory's sake, she had never hurt him. For her future's sake, she avoided him.

If she was truly honest, she had not seen him for over 10 years. They had been friends as children. So why was he there? She would need to tell one of the Keepers as soon as she could. But what if he was there to help her for the mission? She didn't know how the gods would react, let alone how Gwen would take the situation. For fear of him being there to help her, she would not utter a word, nor think too heavily on his presence, even if the look he gave her looked like some sort of warning. Not against the Keepers or Hiraethans, but against himself, as if he was coming for her. But he wouldn't... right?

"Enjoying the tour?" They all turned around to see Lorenzo in the doorway. He smiled at them, "I wish we could explain more, but I hope over time you can learn from experience. We are quite pressed for time at the moment and honestly, we could use the gods' help." He laughed at his comment. RO sensed something was off about the man. He had been so stoic before, why was he suddenly smiling so much?

"Gladly." Kirana nodded quickly. She couldn't see it.

Metis looked behind him, "Where is Gwen?" He could see it.

Lorenzo gestured behind him, "Catching up with her father. He's so proud of her, it's so sweet. She'll be back soon."

Kirana put a hand to her heart and took a breath, "He's alive."

"Barely." Lorenzo wiped his face. What was he hiding? "Metis, you are an engineer, correct?"

"I can work with machinery." He pointed down the hallway, "Though I could use Ben E's help if you would allow me to take him with me."

"Whatever it takes. We need help with the gate, someone dropped a cage into it and it's not working. We need it working as soon as possible." He looked to Kirana, "Do you know anything about strategy or terrain navigation?"

Kirana shook her head with a nervous laugh, "No, not really. But I can try–"

He looked over at RO, "I need someone to help me with a shipment of food that needs to be delivered tomorrow. I need a path to stay clear of Wardens, can you help map a route?"

She nodded once. RO's cover story was that her world was a wasteland, which it was, and that her people lived together in isolation, as they did, with a survivalist society built on protection, as it was. He figured she could help him navigate the terrain and stay clear of Wardens, which she could. But more importantly, he would disclose their location. RO would know the exact coordinates of the Arena and could send in Wardens through her next report. "What types of defense do Wardens have here?"

"Mostly ships, but a few Wardens are watching from certain towns around us."

She forced a smile, "I would love help."

Lorenzo smiled back, "Perfect." He looked to Kirana, "You can stay with Metis then, offer some assistance, it may be a two-person job." He gestured to the door, "I'll escort RO. Haru, please take the others to the gate."

Metis glanced over at RO. She found his worry for her strange. She had not proved herself loyal to them yet. Metis seemed to be a strong believer in second chances, and to him, her choice to stay with the Keepers was an act of her redemption. It was not.

Haru walked with Metis and Kirana to the door and they followed quickly.

Lorenzo gestured to the door once they were gone, "Shall we?" RO nodded and walked through. With a glance back, she saw Lorenzo slip Clara a small piece of paper. RO moved out of Lorenzo's view so he would not know that she saw his secretive action. As she tried to think of what he would need to say to Clara, the only thought that came to mind was her own secret. But so far she had not given away any details of her being a Warden. Unless someone told him, everything was fine. She would not rush to conclusions, not yet, but seeing Antony mere seconds earlier felt like no coincidence.

The walk down the hallways was surprisingly peaceful. Lorenzo didn't speak to her once and simply led her where they needed to go. There was something very Warden-like about the Hiraethans, especially Lorenzo. They did not have the formality her people possessed, but they had their focus. Maybe even their anger. Lorenzo walked like a true leader, and if he was wearing Warden armor, she might have just believed he was one of her own people. Wardens had hatred woven into them as a weapon. Hiraethans beat it first into themselves and then into their children. RO was starting to see why her people feared them so greatly. They could do nothing to the Wardens, not really, but their presence brought power, and even monsters could feel fear.

The Arena's hallways seemed to be separated into two distinct themes. The first was the backrooms, the rebellion's dirty hallways Hiraethans hid within. The second was the Arena's entrances, the well-decorated halls leading guests to their seats. Lorenzo led RO into the nicer hallways past guests and even Wardens. At first, RO was fascinated by the change and was eager to see more, before questioning exactly where he was bringing her.

Lorenzo slowed down and let a group of Wardens pass. She looked up at him but he kept his eyes forward. RO decided to try and figure out if he knew who she was, "This path feels dangerous for a meeting about maps. There are many Wardens. They may recognize me from my own world."

"We'll be careful then." Lorenzo walked forward and she followed. RO glanced back and saw one of his soldiers walking a few paces behind them.

The Hiraethans knew she was a Warden, and now they were trying to get rid of her.

RO was trapped, unarmed, and away from both her own people and the Keepers. She would have to find a way to survive on her own. For now, the only weapon she truly had was her words. There was no point in denying Lorenzo's knowledge, but she was still a Keeper. She needed the Keepers to believe she was on their side, whether or not Lorenzo agreed. She had to make sure he knew she was, although a Warden, still a Keeper. RO had to make sure he did not know she was a spy.

She placed her hands behind her back, lifted her chin, and clenched her jaw, looking like a proud Warden, "Gwen told you."

Lorenzo looked down at her, eyes wide, he glanced behind him, "If you run–"

"I am not running." She looked around, "Where is Gwen?"

His upper lip curled up, "Morning the death of her father. He was killed by your people. Shot in the leg and then the heart. Dropped off at her doorstep."

RO looked ahead and saw more of Lorenzo's men blocking her path, "What does she want you to do with me?"

"She is waiting for me to bring the news of your death."

Lorenzo guided her across the crowd into a small opening against the wall. RO had not been able to see the true extent of the fighting grounds from the command room, but now, walking beside the stadium seats, she was engulfed in the *massive* space before her. The Arena in all its glory. It was certainly something of glory. The Hiraethans had carved out their freedom from the very mines RO's people had been stupid enough to leave empty. The cavern before her stretched high enough for the peak of the hill to be breached, light spreading down a gaping hole. The cave-like space around her had been clawed smooth and packed in with clay seats and stone walls.

Lorenzo walked her forward to a small platform with a long drop into the Arena itself, a battlefield. The sand-covered floor was covered in crates, concrete blocks, and junk of all sizes. RO looked up at the hole above it and pictured what it would look like to a ship passing by. It would look like an abandoned mine.

This was how they tricked the Wardens. They traded the soldiers liquor for silence and littered their Arena with abandoned mine equipment in case they bothered to look down while flying over the hole.

RO looked at Lorenzo. The two of them were standing a few paces away from the edge, and she was almost certain that drop was meant for her. She clenched her jaw, feeling as if she was standing trial, "You have made a beautiful space for your people. I am not here to ruin what you created." If she played the situation right, she could leave with, at the very least, the idea that she was trying to leave her people's ways behind and join the Keepers. She wanted Lorenzo to believe she was on his side. "I am sorry about Gwen's father. But I did not kill him. Gwen–"

Lorenzo twitched, his head shot to the side and he put his hand to his neck as if to hold himself steady, "Don't say her name." There was so much disgust in his tone that she wondered how he had been able to stop himself from puking his very words. There was something violent in the way he ordered her to not speak, and something even more deadly in his inability to look at her.

"The Keepers lied to protect me. I am loyal to them and to you." RO looked back to find his soldiers blocking her off from the hallway. She clenched her jaw and tried to focus her fear into passion, "I left my people behind. I saw what they were doing to your people and I couldn't stay any longer. I am here to be a Keeper and protect your people."

He took a moment, before putting his hand down and looking at her. There were tears in his eyes, angry, dangerous tears. RO glanced to her side to find Hiraethans with guns aimed to her feet, ready to be raised to her head. The same look was in their own eyes, only without the tears.

Lorenzo caught her gaze, and without even trying to hide his plan he leaned forward and said, "*Monster.*" The tears fell. He looked to his soldiers, "Throw her in."

RO was not ready to die. If she died the mission would be over and she would just be another Warden who could not serve her people. RO knew the best plan would be to throw Lorenzo in with her, that way she could use him as a trade offer or fight him for freedom. But RO could not allow Lorenzo to view her as a monster. She had to remain a loyal Keeper. So, however pitiful it was, she tried to run. RO did not fight, she did not harm the Hiraethans, she tried to avoid them at all costs.

Behind Lorenzo, just past one of his smaller-looking soldiers, was another platform off the edge of the Arena. If she could make the jump, she could climb up and find a way back to the Keepers. Kirana and Metis would fight for her or at the very least get her away from Hiraeth altogether.

RO didn't waste a moment. She shot past Lorenzo, planted her foot on the edge of the platform and jumped for her life. RO was fast and light, and though Lorenzo had doubted her abilities, she knew she could make such a leap. Her stomach slammed into the platform and with a grunt she pulled herself up and tried to run through the crowd. Only there was one problem.

The crowd was made up of Hiraethans who knew Lorenzo. RO was running from a man they all admired and respected. They might have not realized she was a Warden, but they knew she was the enemy. As soon as her feet touched the platform, a horde of watchers grabbed her and threw her over the edge. RO had to stop herself from grabbing onto one of them and was forced to let herself fall without a fight.

The more RO fell, the more she realized how much she had underestimated the drop. As best as she could, she rolled and slid her body across the Arena floor. Her body practically bounced off the four and tumbled across the Arena. RO took deep breaths and forced her mind to not think about any of the wounds against her. Twisted leg, bruised shoulder. No time. RO grunted and pulled her body to her arms, then her knees, and finally to her feet.

The crowd roared with anticipation and RO looked up to see Lorenzo staring down at her.

RO decided to make one final act of loyalty, "Lorenzo!" She yelled, "I am not here to hurt anyone! I am a Keeper!"

"You are a monster and you will *die* as a monster!"

"What I am does not change that fact the staff chose me–"

"I do not doubt that!" The crowd around Lorenzo stopped cheering to hear what he had to say, "Nor do I doubt that you *all* decided to lie instead of telling us the truth! All the gods, to protect *you*!"

Lorenzo still thought she was a Keeper, he didn't know she was a spy. RO's lies were starting to grow too close to one another, and suddenly she was living in two perspectives: one was a Warden spy and the other was a Warden Keeper. It was strange, though, to think about being a Keeper in all of their eyes. They truly believed she was a god, some believed she was a monstrous Keeper but still... a god. The Keepers had chased after her, defended her, lied for her, and protected her. They had even killed for her. Gwen had even pushed past everything she knew about the Wardens to help RO.

RO had to physically shake her head to get such thoughts away. She was not a Keeper, she was a spy. She was a Warden.

"I left my people, Lorenzo! I am not–"

"Your death will not be one of honor, *Warden*!" He turned and walked out of view.

"I am a Keeper!" She yelled back, "I am here to help your people!" Lorenzo didn't come back. The Hiraethans slowly started to walk away from the edge. "Lorenzo!" She screamed after him, but it was no use.

RO stepped back into the Area, and for the first time since she became a Keeper, she felt afraid. Truly afraid.

Clara's voice echoed through the large space, "We have our next fighter! *A Warden!*"

The crowd went wild with excitement and RO realized very quickly that they were not cheering for her. They knew very well she was not there at her will, but they liked that. They wanted to watch her suffer. To die. Lorenzo was trying to kill her, but also to put her on display. RO's mission wasn't done, and this was certainly not the way she intended to die. She hadn't even been able to send out a report, yet.

The report!

RO ran away from the door for fear of being overheard and dropped down, pulling the chip out of her boot and sticking it along her ear within seconds. She pressed down on a single button, "This is Lieutenant RO. I am here to submit my first report."

Things were changing. The energy in the Arena was shifting. She looked behind her to see something that had been out of view until now: a large metal gate at the end of the Arena, slowly starting to open. It was dark inside, for all the light around her none of it could enter the space within. Across from her was another gate about the same size, only this one seemed to be some sort of workers' area. Perhaps the true entrance for the true contenders of Lorenzo's sick little game.

"We copy." A man's voice shot through her ear, "What have you learned?"

There was a noise from within the rising gate. A growl.

"I am in Hiraeth with the Keepers." RO started to run forward into the Arena, "The Hiraethan god took us to a rebellion's location within an old mine. They are running a gambling den where viewers place bets on fights in an Arena. There are Wardens here who think this is some getaway spot. They have been hiding in plain sight."

There were items across the floor as she ran further in. She saw a weapon and slid down to pick it up. A machete, thank the gods. She ran to one of the crates and started to climb it. Once on top, she looked around for a new area to hide in. The space around was a true jungle of objects. Dozens of crates stacked on top of each other, beside, and slanted somewhere between. There were pipes and poles. Junk stretching from small to enormous. It was a true arena.

"The Keepers did not know about the last Keeper's existence and are taking a rest period before embarking on any next mission."

The gate neared the top of its doorway. She could hear footsteps, strides sending vibrations across the vast Arena and up into her very soul.

"Do they suspect you?"

"Kirana and Metis think I am a chosen prophet without a true alignment. The Hiraethan got me thrown in the... Arena."

A figure showed itself from the shadows of its cave. RO could see its eyes a bright purple, glowing not from a shine but from itself. She could see something was wrong with the creature before it had even shown itself, and when it did... RO found herself holding her breath. The creature's face came through the darkness, a long muzzle pulled thin with bone and veins. Its fur was a dirty white, and its blood was clearly shown right through its skin. Purple blood. It looked like a wolf, only longer and much larger. It stretched over two stories tall, its legs making up more than half of that height. It looked starved. Its eyes bulged out of its head, and gods, they looked so human. RO could see its lust and hunger. It was looking for her, sniffing its thin nose for anything it could find. She could hear it breathing. She could hear it wheeze and whine with every breath. But something changed its struggle. It caught something. Its head turned to RO suddenly and stared at her.

"Lieutenant?"

"I don't know if I can win this fight." It was the truth, it was a fact. She needed to stop trembling, "The Hiraethan Keeper sold me out."

"You have to win." Chief Haunton's voice shot through the chip, "You can not let the Keepers come after you. You can not let them die for you."

They would never... right?

The Keepers did not know she was in the Arena. They would not find her, she knew that. They would not care if she was dying. RO just needed to get out of the Arena and run for it. If she survived, so did the mission. If she died it was all over, after everything, it would be over. Just because they saved her before didn't mean they would do it again.

And yet, they seemed to trust her. That was the goal, to build a bond between them. Gods, her lies were catching up to her, and her loyalty might have made too big of an impact on the Keepers.

The monster before her let out a hoarse roar before running to her. RO jumped off the crate and ran towards the most crowded area she could see. She ran, gods she did, trying her best to move her body beyond her speed. If she could climb out or get to the other gate then maybe she could escape and make it back to the Keepers. She needed to return to them, but they needed to stay away from her. That could be done. It had to be done.

RO would not die in the Arena, she would not let herself. She had faced death before and she was not about to let some monster decide her fate. The day she was to die would be the day she had created her legacy, she would not settle for anything less. To truly succeed she needed to get the Keepers to 'Āina. That was the goal, that was the plan, and not even some mutated creature would stand in her way.

"Send in the Warden!" She yelled through the chip. "I'll get out and he'll disappear! I need help!"

There was a pause, an excruciating pause as she kept herself running to the crates.

"We didn't send a Warden to help you."

Antony wasn't there to help her? He came there on his own.

She spotted something. Someone. With her mind still on the Keepers she thought it was Metis. But the Telematic didn't have ginger hair, nor knew how to slide down a clay wall and land like a Warden would.

It was Antony.

He had come for her.

Chapter 40

✦ ✶ ✦

KIRANA

KIRANA DIDN'T KNOW much about machinery, but she could tell that the gate's engine was going to take a very long time to fix. Whatever someone had dropped on it had pretty much destroyed it. When Metis was able to remove the outer layer of dented metal they both looked inside to see the inner gears twisted and curved. It was Kirana's job to reshape the metal slabs while Metis fixed just about everything else. She had found a good hammer, one with a large front piece, that helped keep her work even.

Metis pulled out another piece of the machine and looked back to Kirana as she smashed another dented corner, "Hey." She looked up and he gestured to the plate. She held it up to show him her work. "I think that's good."

"I can do a bit more." She slammed the hammer back down to try and fix the crooked corner, only to add another dent.

"It doesn't have to be perfect, miss Permidian." He took the plate from her and placed it alongside the others where Ben E sat, correcting any minor dents left. "Also the constant banging is starting to get to me."

There was another noise from the Arena, a crash much like the one Kirana had been making. A hit to metal. The room they were in was for the main gate, and if they had been closer to the massive gate itself the Keeper would have been able to see through its bars and watch what was going on. Sadly, the machinery to operate the door was far along the wall and all Kirana could catch were a few cheers and boos from the crowd and the sound of a true fight.

She put down the hammer, "I wish we could watch."

"You want to watch this?" Metis looked inside the machine, "It's horrible."

She shook her head quickly, "It's fun."

Metis looked at her again, only this time with a bit more attention. He put down his gear and faced her fully, "You don't seem to be affected by violence."

She shrugged, "It's just some blood and bruises."

"Or *death*."

She squinted, "Are you mad at me?"

"No, I would just assume for someone who had seen nothing in the world that these types of things would affect you. You have really been... well, traumatized yet."

"Yet?" She laughed but Metis didn't flinch. He was serious about this conversation. Kirana changed her expression quickly and matched his energy, "Haunton scared me."

"Were you able to sleep last night?"

"Yes."

"Then she didn't scare you."

Kirana clenched her jaw and picked up the hammer again to fiddle with, "I'm not some unemotional beast, Metis–"

"I know." He backed down, "You're just... different."

Kirana went cold.

"What?"

"That's... it's just what they called me in Permidia. Different."

"Because they knew you were a Keeper?" He thought for a moment, "They didn't train you but they might have been able to influence your life enough to change a few natural behaviors."

Her heart raced, "Like... programming me?" She glanced down at Ben E.

"They could have just programmed your life. You've handled everything well, and they would have wanted that to happen. But you're not artificial, Kirana. There would be signs if you were. You're just the perfect foundation for a Keeper." He sighed and softened his expression, "How about this, why don't you tell me how you feel about... everything."

"I feel... fine, but scared. In a good way though, I feel like I am learning. Gwen's wound was horrible though, so I reacted to that. You have to understand I wasn't connected to people my whole life. Maybe that has something to do with it."

He nodded softly, "You just don't empathize with people's deaths." He looked down at his gears and back into the machine, "Pass me that wrench." She looked around on the floor and found it beside the other similar-sized items. Metis seemed to have a very clean way of working. She hadn't expected that from him. He took it from her, "You had a sister though?"

"Tia."

He pushed the wrench into the machine, "Did you love her?"

Kirana didn't know why but that question seemed so dangerous. A yes or a no, and she would set off a bomb. Her hesitation made Metis look back at her. She swallowed, "I think so."

He put down the wrench and faced her again, "You think so?"

She laughed, "At this rate, we're never going to fix the gate."

"It's not a priority." He gestured to the Arena, "They already have their champion of the day, gods rest their soul–"

"I do love her." Kirana admitted, "But that doesn't mean she loves me. I just… it's been a lot lately and I don't know what to think about my past life."

"Your people aren't the villains, Kirana. How do we know that your sister wasn't trapped just like you were."

Trapped. That word sounded so sinister. She didn't like it. "My people are all happy and healthy, and right now that is enough to make someone a villain. Especially here." She looked around the room at the Hiraethans moving past them in the large space. It was filled to the brim with crates, some empty, others filled with animals both large and small. The people around the creatures were all working efficiently and almost always without uttering a word. They only broke their process to look over at the gods, or rather, in their eyes, the new strangers.

"And your sister?"

"I used to think our life was perfect because we had each other. But one day she left me and I realized I had imagined that she loved me. I think I was in denial for a long time, and when I met Gwen I knew my sister never cared about me. Not really. It's strange, though, I still miss her." Kirana thought for a moment about those words, and shook her head, "But I don't think I should."

"You can still miss her even if it was one-sided."

"But what if she was evil? What if she was working for the Magistrater this entire time."

Metis locked eyes with her, "She's still your sister."

"But can you love someone who was secretly evil–"

"Yes." He clenched his jaw, "There is always truth to a trick. The love was there, and it always will be. Whether you created it or it was once shared by the two of you."

She squinted at him with a laugh, "You sound experienced."

He shook his head softly, "I don't have any family, Kirana. I'm Telematic."

"No one? A childhood friend? Someone who raised you?"

He cleared his throat and took another metal plate from Ben E, focusing on the machine. He didn't like these questions, Kirana could tell, and maybe she had asked too many at once but she truly wanted to know the answers. As she started to back down he spoke. "I had a brother."

She inched closer, "Who?"

His eyes were on the floor. He was lost in a memory, "*Axel.*" The boy's name was said in a single breath, as if it took everything Metis had to sound out each syllable. He swallowed, "He wasn't secretly evil I just... I had a brother. His name was *Axel.*"

"What was he like?"

Metis looked up at her. She could tell this question was nice. For all the grief behind her questions, this one seemed to spark some sort of joy. He gave a half-hearted smile, "He was kind of like you, actually."

She smiled and pointed to herself, "Me?"

"Bold, gods, he would run into a fight like he had an army behind him."

Was she like that? Kirana supposed she sometimes rushed into things with an air of confidence, but she believed that was a good thing. "He sounds fun."

"He was."

Was.

Metis was right, Kirana didn't know how to connect to someone's death or grief. She didn't understand many things about a person's pain or comfort. But she was learning, and she knew they had talked long enough.

She looked down at the gears, "How long will this take?"

"A few hours."

"Hours!" She groaned and put the hammer back on the floor, "Why are they making us do this? We're gods."

Metis put his hands up and glanced back to the Hiraethans, "Don't say that too loudly."

"Why are we keeping it a secret? Everyone should know, that's why we're here."

"We have to honor Lorenzo's choice, Kirana. He has a plan, we don't."

"*Gwen.*" The Voice filled her head.

He was speaking to her more often, and always when she needed guidance the most. She went pale and realized something could be wrong with Gwen.

Metis noticed the change, "You alright?"

"I want to check on Gwen." She put her hammer down and stood up.

"Why? She's with Lorenzo and her family."

The Voice spoke again, "*Gideon.*"

"I want to check if her father's back. Because if he's not..." She clenched her jaw, "I have a strange feeling something could be wrong."

Metis nodded and gestured to the door, "Okay, do what you need."

She smiled down at him, "I'll be back in a few minutes." She spun around and walked swiftly to the doors.

Kirana found walking through Hiraeth thrilling. She didn't know what it was exactly, but she felt a sense of power to her mere presence. The more she passed people by the more she realized it was the fact they had no idea who she was, and what she would do for them. She loved how Hiraethans were so emotional, they would have true reactions to her godly title, to the entire team's. The more people she met out in the worlds the more she realized how much she hated her people's dull existence. Honestly, Kirana wanted to be seen, and as the leader of the Keepers, she had every right to be. Though she tried not to let such thoughts fuel her ego she couldn't help but walk a little taller and glance a little harder at each mortal she passed by. Soon they would learn who she was, and then she would save them all.

Kiran didn't have to walk far to find Lorenzo. A few turns and she found him near the entrance to the mine. Just beyond him, she could see a large group of people huddled around the entrance. Lorenzo was speaking to Haru and two other Hiraethans. As she approached him she realized how hurt he looked. His face was puffy and bleeding all over. But his eyes were worse. There was some-thing very dark about the way he looked around the room. At the sight of her, it only got worse. The pain faded into anger, and he tightened her jaw to speak with her, "Yes?"

The Voice had been right.

"I just came to check–"

"Gwen is fine. Please help your friend with the machine."

Kirana looked back to the large group and saw Gaia within it. The woman turned to look at someone beside her and Kirana could just make out tears along her face.

Kirana went cold, "What's going on?"

"Nothing–"

"Where is Gideon?"

Lorenzo stared down at her for a moment, and in his silence, she found his answer.

He was dead.

Kirana put a hand to her chest, "Where is Gwen?"

She started to move towards the crowd when Lorenzo grabbed her arm, "You've done enough–"

Kirana pulled out of his grip and ran towards the crowd, "Gwen!" The crowd turned to look at her and she stopped quickly. She didn't know what she was doing, she just knew she had to find Gwen. The people around her were her family, but Kirana was her friend. More than that: a teammate, a fellow god… someone who cared. But the crowd glared at her with the same line of tension. Death was in the air. It was choking Kirana.

Gaia walked out of the crowd towards her. Kirana didn't know what else to do but stand where she was, "Gaia–"

Gaia let out a gasp of pain as she slapped her across the face. Kirana fell to the floor and stumbled back across the ground. "You killed him!" Gaia was hysterical, tears dried on her face, and she was no longer grieving through sadness. She was grieving through anger. "You brought the Wardens into my family's life!"

A man Kirana quickly recognized as Theo moved beside Gaia and she quickly pushed herself back up, "I'm sorry–"

"You got him caught!" Gaia yelled at her, "They shot him twice, they let him bleed and die and suffer and it was your fault!"

"Where is Gwen–"

"Next time you come into someone's home. Next time you bring your staff and your godly arrogance, try remembering that your crystal is a beacon to those *monsters*." Gaia stepped forward and spoke mere inches from Kirana's face, "Try remembering that when you bring a helpless girl into your *cult* her entire family reaps the benefits of your little *game*."

"I didn't–"

Gaia shook her head and stepped away, "Oh, I'm just making a suggestion. You are a god, after all."

Lorenzo came from behind Kirana and grabbed her by her jacket collar. As he pulled her away she caught a glimpse of someone in the crowd. Someone pressed onto the floor, her face planted in the dirt.

Gwen.

"Gwen!"

Lorenzo pulled her into the other hallway and pushed her to the wall, "You are a child! You walked into my operation like a god when you were just a spoiled coward."

"I am a Keeper!" She tried to pull out of his grasp, "Let me go!"

He dropped her and she stayed close to the wall. He didn't need to physically hold her to keep her with him. She knew she couldn't run. Lorenzo looked down at her, "Gideon is dead. You killed him."

She shook her head quickly, "I didn't kill him–"

"You led the Wardens to him–"

"He led me to the Wardens!"

Her words hit him harder than she had intended, but it was the truth. She hadn't killed him, she had followed his lead and that was that. Lorenzo stepped away from her, "You disgust me. You are no god, you have no respect for anyone but yourself and your team. You have brought death into my world, twice."

"Twice? I don't–"

"I will ask you once what RO is and if you lie to me I will shoot you where you stand."

Kirana looked at the soldiers around him to see their guns drawn, "Lorenzo–"

"What is she?"

"She's... she's not..." She looked around the hallway, "Where is she?"

"Answer the question."

"How–" She swallowed hard, "She's a Warden."

"And you brought her to us."

"She's not with them anymore." Kirana tried to step forward but one of the Hiraethans raised their guns. Gaia and Theo watched from afar, staring at her as if waiting for the performance her execution would be. She raised her hands beside her head, "You can trust me–"

"I do not *trust* you, Kirana. I would not trust you with anything, let alone the title of a god. Let alone Gwen's fate!"

"She is a god, my teammate–"

Lorenzo looked away from her, "When RO is done you and Metis will leave this world and never return."

Kirana went cold, "What?"

"Gwen will be safe here."

"Where is RO?"

"Where do you think I put monsters?" His upper lip twitched, "I let her do what she does best: fight, and die."

The Arena. "She's loyal to us–"

"Then you should have told me who she was. You chose to lie."

"So did Gwen!"

Lorenzo twisted his jaw, "She is the victim here."

Kirana dropped her hands to her side. He was wrong, she knew he was. She shook her head, "Gideon chose his fate." She looked to Gaia, "Maybe next time you want to stay safe and innocent, don't fill your basement full of incriminating books, or lead the most incriminating person straight into a city of Wardens."

Gaia trembled with both anger and fear. Good.

Kirana glared at her, "Oh I'm just making a suggestion."

Lorenzo turned away from her. "Take her to a cell, we'll–"

The Keeper couldn't let that happen. These were Gwen's people, yes, her family, but they were blinded by their hate. Kirana could see more clearly than anyone in the room around her. That was why she was a Keeper, and it was her job to keep her team safe. She saw four Keepers in that vision. She was not with them, she was before them. She was a god, and she was the leader of the Keepers. She remembered Gideon's words: *Do what you were chosen to do. Protect.* She would keep her team safe. Holding her hands together she reached into the in-between and let the white flash grow between her palms. She was reaching for the staff, but the Hiraethans didn't know that. They all stepped away from her as the flash got bigger and bigger, and when it collapsed into the staff she ran for it. She sprinted past the two frightened Hiraethans and kept running.

"Grab her!"

They were after Kirana. Maybe not to kill her but at the very least capture her. Guilt hit her but she tried to push such a feeling away. She had a responsibility to her Keepers, she had to help them first. She only hoped Gwen would understand that.

She followed her old path right to the gate, "Metis!" She screamed through the room.

He shot up and saw the Hiraethans behind her. He pulled out his gun and held it at the group as Kirana moved behind him and caught her breath.

The Hiraethans stopped, guns drawn. The one in front, a man with a thick black beard, stepped forward, "Please. We don't want to hurt you."

"Then put down your weapons."

Kirana whispered to Meits, "RO is in the Arena."

He looked back at her once before facing the Hiraethans, "We aren't your enemies. We are fighting the same people."

The man before them took a shaky breath. He was trembling. "You brought one to us. Why?" He was acting as if they had met before. There was hope in his words. Hope that they would agree with one another. Kirana could see it now, the man knew the Keepers well. He worshiped them.

She stepped to the side and placed the staff before her, "We are uniting the worlds against the Magistrater. You have to trust us. Please."

"You brought the enemy to us–"

"The Magistrater is our enemy. RO left her people to save us. To save you. You have to trust in us. Trust in the gods, because she is a Keeper too. The staff chose her, you have to trust in its decision as I do."

The man stared at her for a moment, then at the staff, and dropped his gun. The two soldiers behind him followed until every Hiraethan soldier got down on their knees, weaponless in their gods' presence.

For all that was happening, for all the damage she had caused with her title, Kirana was still a Keeper who brought hope.

Kirana had never felt so powerful.

Metis put his gun down and ran to the gate with Kirana. The bars were pressed together too tightly, they couldn't fit through. With a quick thought, he pulled out his gun again and shot at the metal bars. The bullet shot through the metal with ease. Metis shot, again and again, to weaken it with a fiery blue glow. He kicked at the gate again and again, until the small portion bent and broke. They could fit through it.

"She's a Warden!" Kirana and Metis turned to see Lorenzo in the doorway. The leader shook his head, "She will betray you and betray all of us just the same. Do not die for her."

Kirana held the staff close to her, "She is a Keeper! Chosen by the staff and the gods before you! We are not fighting the Wardens, we are fighting the Magistrater! You need everyone working together to win this war! We'll prove to you how much she is worth!"

Metis pulled himself through the gate and dropped into the Arena. With a final look to Lorenzo Kirana followed and dropped down onto the dirt floor.

Metis pulled out his gun, "How do we get out of this one?"

Kirana held the staff beside her, "We fight, we get RO out, we get Gwen, and we run."

"And we lose Lorenzo."

"We lose an army, but we gain a god." She locked eyes with him, "She was chosen for a reason."

Metis nodded and looked out into the Arena, "Then we save her."

Chapter 41

✴

RO

RO COULDN'T SEE the monster, but she could hear it. Those loud thumping footsteps. This creature seemed to work in waves of hysterical violence and patience. It was unpredictable. She tried to find patterns, a normal aspect of nature and survival, but there seemed to be none. This creature was mutated in some way. That purple liquid pumping through its body was not an infection, it was purposeful. At a closer glance, she saw tubes and pipes across its entire body.

RO couldn't help but flinch at the sound of the creature's growl. It was right next to her, right on the other side of the crate. She sat very still against the thin metal. If she moved it would hear her. It took her a few moments to realize that the creature was circling her. As silently as she could, RO grabbed a small scrap piece of metal beside her and threw it to the opposite side of the crate. As soon as the junk hit the metal teeth pierced through and suddenly the entire room was thrown onto its side. RO stumbled across the crate to the other door and swung it open. She dropped down onto the sand and watched the creature rip apart the metal.

The crowd let out a collective groan at her victory.

She didn't have much time. RO ran further into the Arena, towards more crates and better places to hide, but more objects in her way. It was becoming a maze, and she only hoped that her last advantage would be outsmarting the creature. It couldn't be that strong, not both physically and mentally. If it was she was dead, no gods to help her, even if she was one of them.

She heard the footsteps of the beast behind her. By then she had made it to the outskirts of the most crowded space, and without waiting a moment to look back she pulled herself up onto the first stack of crates and crawled her way inside. As she turned to run to the other side of it she saw the other door already move open. She held up her weapon and watched as a person started to enter her hiding place. A Hiraethan? An extremist out to kill her? Antony? Out of breath and out of patience she nearly lunged forward to kill them where they stood. The person rushed inside and saw her quickly, hands up to stop her.

It was Metis.

She lowered her weapon, "Metis?"

"Are you okay?" He moved up to her.

"What are you doing here?"

"We're here to help you."

They both looked back as the Arena was filled with a banging noise. Was someone hitting a crate? Oh gods, it was Kirana.

"You're not supposed to be here!" RO yelled so violently that Metis took a step back from her out of fear, his gun at his side. He wasn't supposed to be in the Arena. Gods, what if Haunton found out she led them into danger? If Kirana or Metis died the mission was over, done. No Keepers, no mission, no promotion. She would be killed, by the creature or by her superiors.

"We came to help you."

RO moved to the door with him, "With the *Permidian*. Why did you let her go on her own?"

"She's making a distraction." He pushed open the doors, "We made a hole through the gate, we just have to make it there." The creature suddenly showed itself as it ran by their crate towards the noise. Metis curled back, "That monster is terrifying."

She moved beside him, looking at the creature as it sniffed around the area, "What are the purple veins?"

Metis pointed at its back, "It's going into their neck. I thought it was a nervous system boost, but other veins are going into its chest, and another into its head. No chemical should be able to keep an animal alive in such large portions. I have no idea what that liquid is, but it's not good."

"Where is Gwen?"

"Her father is dead, Lorenzo lied to us." He looked at her, "Did he hurt you?"

"He's trying to. If I get out he'll kill me."

"So we'll use the staff to go back to Telematic then."

She stared at him, "But this is the rebellion. You need this to win the war."

"*We* need this. Everyone united, remember? But if Lorenzo doesn't understand that then we shouldn't work with him."

He seemed so certain that RO was going to help unite them. That her people would fight against their leader and then each other. It would never work. It could never work. He didn't understand that, and she found herself hating the idea he would die for his hope.

She was a spy and he was a fool, and her mission was a game she had to win.

"You shouldn't have come here." She shook her head firmly, "You shouldn't have left Kirana either."

"Well, too late now." The creature turned its back to them in search of the Permidian. Metis pushed the door open further, "We just have to make it to the gate."

"What about Kirana?"

"She's going to transport herself on the other side once we're in the clear."

RO must have looked as shocked as she felt because Metis squinted down at her new expression, "You thought we wouldn't have a plan? We're new at this, but we're not stupid."

"No it's just... that's a good plan."

"Then let's get–"

A gunshot rang through the Arena and Metis flew down to the floor.

"Metis!"

He kicked the door closed and put a hand on his waist, "I'm fine. I'm fine." His side was bleeding, but from what she could tell it was just a scratch.

It was Antony. It seemed he wasn't trying to just kill her while on his little mission. He was operating alone, that was clear, but how could she tell Metis that?

He forced himself back up, hand to his side, "Is someone else here?"

She needed to tell him something. If Antony came up to speak to her or any other Keepers he would talk about RO and the lie would be known. If she lied once they would suspect her to lie again.

"He's after me."

"He's not a Hiraethan?"

"He's a Warden."

There was a bang and a bullet flew through the crate beside Metis. The two of them moved back further inside, weapons raised.

"We need to get everyone out of here before the others arrive."

"Others?"

He gestured around the crate, "If he's here then your people know about this place."

Antony was truly ruining her plan. Whether by her hands or her superiors', he was going to die for his traitorous actions. She shook her head quickly, "No. This is personal. He came down from the stands the moment I came into view."

"But we can't be too sure." Metis looked at her skeptically, "What do you mean *personal*?"

Oh right, she had forgotten she had no communication with her people. She was getting confused. She was trapped in an Arena with a beast and an emotional Warden inside a rebel base filled with people who wanted her to suffer in a world that hated her kind with people of her kind also hunting her alongside gods who would kill her if they knew who she really was. "I figure it has something to do with becoming a god and betraying me people." Sarcasm was the only thing holding her entire mission together at that point.

There was a shout from off in the distance. It took a few tries from the person speaking but eventually their word was said loud enough, "Run!" It was Kirana.

RO and Metis looked at each other in realization but they were out of time. The crate was suddenly pulled back. The two of them fell to the floor. RO felt them fall and braced herself as they were thrust to the walls. The metal above them was ripped apart and the light poured into the room, before being stopped by the face of the creature. The two Keepers shot forward before the beast could reach far enough inside to make its attack. They moved to the doors and slammed into them, pushing them open and running. They were in the open. Metis ran towards the most crowded area of crates and for a moment RO almost forgot about their other threat.

Not too late this time. She ran after Metis and pushed him in between a slab of concrete and a stack of crates. Metis was smart enough to follow her lead and keep them moving. The creature let out a growl as it tried to pull apart the obstacles to reach them. The stack of crates above them shifted and started to tilt. The two of them made it through and ran through a new section of the Arena.

The crowd was buzzing with cheers and groans, a murmur of unsure watchers all waiting for the creature to kill the two specks they must have assumed were both Wardens. Metis's plan would work, but she realized now it had to. They didn't have another choice. If he went out of the Arena someone would think he was a traitor or a Warden himself. He didn't look Hiraethan, he couldn't fake the culture because he could never understand it. She needed to protect the Keepers.

There was a gunshot and RO heard the metal of the crate beside her crash with a bullet. She followed its path to the top of the largest section of junk. A tower of crates, concrete, and a collection of junk torn from the very heart of Hiraeth's dusty corners. RO and Metis moved towards it to hide beneath the rubble, but the creature reared its head and they were forced to keep moving down the line. Metis moved between two items and she followed willingly.

At the other end, he ducked behind a metal slab, catching his breath, "We can't take both."

RO twisted the machete in her hand, "Can you wound the creature?" He looked at her as if she was asking him an impossible question. "Metis–"

There was a banging off in the distance. Kirana seemed to finally remember to do her job. The creature let out a roar that shook the very ground and ran back in her direction.

Metis pulled up his gun, "Looks like we can deal with the Warden then. What gun does he have?"

"Something small."

Metis looked down to his side, still bleeding, "He's a good shot."

"That's about all he can do. He's heavy on his left. Range is his advantage."

"Are we killing him?"

"What kind of question is that? Of course we are."

"I thought you knew him–"

The metal above them suddenly slid down with intense force. RO jumped to the side but Metis wasn't fast enough. His legs were slammed down under the rubble. The creature appeared above them and dove down for RO. She swung her machete back and forth to force it away. Her blade hit its nose and the creature reeled back. It let out a hot roar to her face. She did not finch, she did not pull away. She stood her ground. She held the machete to her side and let out her own monstrous scream. The creature dove down for her again. She rolled to the side and pushed back up in time to bring the weapon down upon its neck. But gods, the creature was so large all it did was break enough skin for it to bleed.

It bled the thick purple liquid. Pumping out like tar.

The creature let out a horrible sharp groan and waved its head fast enough to hit her. RO was sent flying back into a crate. With a crash, she fell to the floor. She let her injuries scream themselves into submission and crawled forward until she was able to jump up and run. The creature had turned to Metis who quickly aimed his weapon at a creature that had never seen a gun before. With a single bullet, it learned its lesson. The blue line that followed the bullet's path lined up with the creature's neck. With another horrible screech, it reeled back and retreated straight into a crate. RO slid down to Metis's side and dropped her machete. She slipped her hands under the metal plate and tried to lift it. It was heavy, but she was able to lift it enough for Metis to slip out.

He jumped to his feet and nearly fell right back down. He pointed his gun up to the creature, shifting in his stance.

A bullet cut through the air, but it was only when RO heard it hit beside her that she realized it was not from Metis. The two Keepers retreated to the crates and hid beneath the cover of thin metal. At the very least, they were out of sight of the stubborn Warden. They could see the creature watching them. The patterns RO had observed were working their way back into inconsistency. It was more calculated now, ready to jump forward at the moment they revealed some weakness to it. Before it had been chaotic, now it was clever. Neither of the Keepers dared to lower their weapons to it.

Metis nodded up to the tower of crates, "You take the Warden, I'll take the monster."

"Can you run?"

"Yes. Go."

And she did. With Kirana still trying to draw the creature's attention away with her banging, RO pulled herself up onto the next stack of crates. She heard the sound of gunfire but she could not locate who it was from. With the crowd still screaming for her death and the echo of the mine it was too hard to tell. She didn't know where Antony was, but she knew with caution she could locate him well before his bullets could find her.

When they were kids, she used to outsmart him all the time. Of course, he was much older now, but his traits never truly faded. Weakness is embedded within someone like bone, and by the time she was done with him, bone was all he would have left. He started the fight to kill her, he wanted the satisfaction of defeating a god. She would not let him have such a victory.

The crates were stacked up between metal slabs, pipes, poles, concrete slabs, and discarded elements of machines and ships. She kept moving through it, searching for the Warden and listening. That was one of the best things she could do: observe. Within the chaos, she had to find a way to track him. Within the junk, she needed to find footsteps, bullets, and blood. She needed to know where he was before he could find her. She pushed herself against the crate and put an ear to the thin metal. She could hear the creature's footsteps and the vibrations of the crowd. She could hear gunshots farther away now than before. But she could also hear something sliding, like clothes. She pulled her machete around the side of the crate and scratched it to the side, pulling it back quickly. She kept her ear to the metal and heard the clothes slide again towards her. Silence was her power. Within it was the truth. Chaos only harbored lies, she learned that from her time in Telematic. A person was forced to face themselves in the quiet. RO could find herself within what little silence remained in the Arena, but she could expand that peace. She found the footfalls of Antony just around the corner. She pictured his stance, the perfect Warden, gun at the ready. He knew where she was. She knew where he was.

He was waiting. She was listening.

RO wondered if he could feel the silence she had created around them, the tension of her plans to hurt him. Death was breathing up Antony's neck. She had sent it there to take him away.

Or maybe she was death, and she was the one who would bring him to silence.

RO raised her hand to her eye level. She listened to the clothes suddenly shift forward. Antony rounded the corner, gun up. He was in the perfect position. Gun at eye level. She grabbed the barrel and raised it out of her face. The gun went off, hot against her hand. RO put her machete to his neck and walked forward.

She gave Antony no time to react, and suddenly he was being walked back to the edge of the crates.

She locked eyes with him and moved her hand to his wrist, "Drop it."

He nearly slipped off the edge. The only thing holding him from the deadly drop was RO. His eyes went down to the drop below him, and back to her. His gun crashed to the floor beside her.

"RO please–"

"You have seconds before I decide whether to cut your throat or let you fall. Why are you here?"

She was expecting an explanation for some sort of revenge, or perhaps an act to kill the gods. But instead of anger, she saw grief. It was embedded within his gaze, like poison, "They took you."

He wasn't there to kill her. "You were here to kill the Keepers?"

"They marked you as a traitor, RO." He leaned forward and sliced part of his neck against the blade. It didn't stop him. "You're a hostage… We can prove to our people that you're not one of them. There is still time." The banging from Kirana's side of the Arena returned. Metis released three gunshots and a metal crate crashed with the creature's roar. Antony took a short breath, "We can take you back."

"Take me back?"

"You have not done any damage to us yet. You are still innocent. We will kill the Keepers and go back."

RO had suspected Antony to be there to kill her because she was a Keeper, it seemed now that he didn't care that she had been chosen. He cared if she stayed with her people.

"You do not know me that well if you thought for a moment I would have stayed with these… terrorists, willingly." She lowered her blade slowly, "I'm not a Keeper. I am a spy." He was too stunned to speak. She pulled him back a few inches and let him center himself. She put a finger to her lips, "Stay silent."

"But the staff–"

She looked him up and down, "I am a god, Antony, but I would never betray my people."

"You're keeping the gods alive to follow them?"

"Good job, Antony." She tapped the blade to her head, "You're finally thinking. You should have bothered to think before coming here to *kill* the Magistrater's greatest prize." She pointed to where the Keepers were, scattered across the Arena.

He went pale. The Warden slipped around her back and moved away from the edge of the crate. For a moment all she could see on his face was regret, but after a few moments, it shifted to something stronger. He straightened his back and took a breath, "They marked you as a traitor."

"As you said."

"They're hunting you."

"I noticed."

"It's not fair." He looked across the Arena. RO followed his gaze to the crowd. They were so far away she wondered if they could even see them fully. Antony sighed softly, "They keep trying to get rid of you."

"They'll never get to."

"Everyone has always been against you, RO. You were good at hiding where you came from but now… they're afraid you're coming back for revenge."

She clenched her jaw. Of course, the Wardens thought that. After every mission and every action she took out of her loyalty, they still thought she was the enemy. "What have you seen?"

"They're scared of you."

"Finally."

"No. No, It's bad, RO. They think the Keepers are turning you. They think you'll help them take us down."

She let out a laugh, "Turning me? Into what, exactly?"

"Turning you back." Antony knew too much about RO. She should have killed him for it. She didn't. She couldn't. RO knew his words were coming but it hurt just the same, "You will always be a Malfunction."

She closed her eyes for a moment. She hated that word. She truly did. She hated the way it sounded, the way it was spelled, like poison against the page. She hated how it had been burned against her head and never let itself heal.

When RO was born she was not labeled a Warden. She had a defect with some genetic trait that did not work the way it was supposed to. Over time she had learned to forget what it was exactly, but she knew it was something to do with the brain. Her thoughts or maybe her emotions didn't operate like the normal soldier. She was a weak link and they picked her off before she could even talk. But she knew that she was not a Malfunction, she knew the Wardens around her were selfish and fat with their greed. She worked day and night and got nothing. They barely worked a day and were kept fed and happy. They got to train, she got to scrub vents clean. They brought their people honor while she served them their drinks.

Antony was wrong, she was not a Malfunction, she never was. She was a

Warden, she had earned her title. She had done horrible things to get to where she was. Her regrets were as rare as her tears, and she intended to keep it that way.

"Deran." Antony waited for a reaction, she made sure he wouldn't find one. He looked away, "Our people will always remember."

"And you'll never forget." He tried to speak but she cut him off, "I would have died down there. You forget the position I was in. Kill or be killed, and I was not about to let Deran grow up to be a Warden. No one cared about me. I had to take care of myself."

There was grief in Antony's eyes, "I always cared."

She couldn't punish him for his words because, above all, they were true. He had always cared, more than anyone else. For her struggles, for her fear, for her wounds. It was people like Deran who didn't care about her. The Wardens her age who beat her with their training gear and locked her in an old cabinet for two days. Antony had brought her a medical kit. Antony had set her free. But he was not the reason she stood where she was that day. That was her doing and her doing alone. She fought and, yes, killed for it. She was a loyal Warden who could defeat even the very gods that posed a threat to her world.

"Deran—"

"What do you want me to say, Antony?" She put her hands together and waited. When he said nothing she laughed, "I am not sorry for what I did to your brother, so why would I apologize? I beat your brother until he went still and caved his stomach in with a sword. I found pieces of him in my hair three nights later." She watched Antony go pale and smiled, "There is nothing to say about the innocent. I proved myself to our superiors by being able to kill their star cadet. Killing Deran got me out of the vents and into Warden armor. It has been 10 years—"

"You avoided me for that entire time." He was begging her, but for what she still did not know. "After everything I did for you." He swallowed, "I protected you. Deran wouldn't have killed you. He would hurt you and then I would have been there to help—"

"I was your project." RO shrugged, "Did you feel powerful when you snuck me, a little vent rat, small pieces of food? I saw how Deran looked at you, a pathetic, weak Warden with no promise of bringing his people honor. You are still looking to save me."

"Rose—"

She put the blade back to his throat, "Say that again. Say that name again, Antony, and I kill you the same way I killed Deran. Then you can finally rest easy knowing the pain I put him through."

He put his hands up, "I took care of you, RO, of course I saw you as a project. Do you think my superiors would have rewarded me for showing you kindness?" He pushed her machete away, "I just want to help someone, for once. And then you turned into a monster. Just like the rest of them."

RO remembered how many savior projects Antony used to have as a child. In the Ward, there were no animals other than small bugs gathered in the garden. He had found a large spider on a leaf and kept it in his room, tucked away in his sock drawer. He would feed it and bring it water, taking care of it while being trained on how to kill. He had a soft heart, still did, and part of RO wished he did not have to fight and kill so often. Antony had saved her as a Malfunction, actually looked at her, and cared for her injuries. She couldn't ignore that, no matter how weak it made him.

"Careful." She pointed at him, "You starting to sound like a Hiraethan." She found herself saying it less as a threat and more as a warning. RO glanced down to where Metis had been. He was getting closer to the gate now. "You are going to leave and never show your face to me again. And soon I will return to the Ward with that Keeper's head on *my* staff, and you'll see where my loyalty stands." She bent down and picked up his gun. She had been right, it was small, a compact sniper rifle he had intended to work as a shield from any true fight. She stepped towards him, examining the gun while still holding her machete to her side.

"You earned this." He was sincere, and she could see he hated himself for it. "Everything you did was justified. I see that. I should have never thought you were here willingly. But you need to understand when you go back they won't see you as a god."

"They will when I become a Chief."

"Do you honestly believe that?"

RO refused to think more about her future rewards. She threw the gun to Antony to shut him up. He hadn't expected such an action and nearly dropped the weapon. He looked up at her with a soft glimmer in his eyes, before clenching his jaw and refocusing, "Where is the exit?"

"The gate." She looked down to where Metis had been. The creature below was limping, barely able to walk. He had done well. "We'll make a run—"

The crate beneath them suddenly shook. RO looked back down at the creature. It was still with Metis, nowhere near the tower they were on. RO walked to the edge of the crate and looked down. A creature, identical to the one Metis was fighting, stood below her, climbing the crates. The stack of junk shifted again as the beast ripped apart the shaky foundation. It was getting unstable.

Antony pointed his gun down and shot for the creature's head, "Move to the back!"

She ran ahead to clear a path for them, but gods the crates were toppling down quickly. The so-called path they could take was opening on its own as the entire tower started to tip back. "Antony!"

He ran to her as the creature pulled itself to their level. This one was different from the last one. Not in its scars or its fur color. It was simple and unconditional, rabid. Its tongue hung out of its mouth as its lips curled up into a human-like smile. The last one had been hungry, but this one just wanted to kill. It staggered up and found RO.

The monsters locked eyes. RO looked away and slid down the crates behind Antony.

The tower started to crumble down with the creature as the two Wardens forced their way down the debris. Scrap pieces of metal and concrete went flying as the materials beneath the Wardens shifted and slid away. They leap onto a block of concrete and roll into a rocky landing. RO spun forward and watched the creature before they managed to stay behind them. Antony stumbled to his feet and shot at the creature. It took the bullets and reared back.

"RO!"

Kirana screamed from the alley below them, another creature behind her.

Anonty looked at RO. She shook her head once and they moved to the edge of the block. As smoothly as they could, the two Wardens slid down the concrete and landed on the Arena's sandy floor. Anonty pulled up his gun and shot at the creature chasing Kirana. It stopped suddenly and turned to him. With a horrible screech, it ran back towards him. RO was ready. She came in front of the Warden and ran for the creature. As it tried to come down and bite she dove to the side and swung her machete across its neck. Antony was already on the move and within seconds she was behind him. The creature turned as the Wardens rounded the corner and pulled themselves through the crack of two crates. There they stayed as the creature ran past them. They shifted up the two walls and found Kirana at the top of it. Hands on her knees she panted hard.

She looked back, ready to say something to RO before spotting Antony, "Who–"

"He's a Warden. Don't worry, he's on our side now." She glanced back to where the creature had gone, "Where is Metis?"

"I thought he was with you. You were supposed to get to the gate."

"Well, that's when you thought there was just one of those things." There was a noise on their side. The creature that had been harmed seemed to still be writhing in pain. "If we find Metis you can just take us all to Telematic."

"We can't just leave Gwen." Kirana shook her head, before wincing at the thought, "But Lorenzo will kill us. Definitely kill you." She looked at Antony, "You too, actually– How did you get here? You look Hiraethan."

He pointed to the crowd, "I was in the stands."

RO glanced at him. She didn't know what he had done to get into the Arena, or how he had tracked RO down in the first place. Perhaps he had heard rumors from his fellow soldiers and figured the Keepers would take her there. But he hadn't just arrived in the stands, people had seen him as a Hiraethan or whoever he had posed to be. He too, now, posed a problem if they were to come back to Lorenzo. "We'll go to Telematic, avoid all contact, and come back for Gwen if we can."

"*If we can?*"

There was a gunshot from further in the Arena. Metis.

RO swiped her machete across the air to get drops of blood off before they reached her hand, "We get him and we get out, just like that."

Kirana gave a nervous laugh. She pulled the staff to her chest, "You make it sound easy."

"It is. To us." She nodded to Antony and looked around for a safe passage through the crates to Metis. They would need a communication technique at some point, a way to talk with one another when they get separated. She thought about Metis's datawatch, and figured the Keepers could buy or steal three more to keep in contact in case of another fight. RO shook her head as she realized she was making plans for the Keepers, as if she was one of them.

In RO's observance of the area, she failed to realize how quiet the Arena had gotten. Not just the creatures or the gunshots, but the crowd.

They could see something the gladiators could not.

There was a sudden crash as the crate beneath them was suddenly pushed forward rapidly. All of them fell to the surface. The creature bit down on the metal to try and grab Kirana and Antony. RO rolled off the other side and landed hard. She stumbled to her feet and went around the crate. With one swing she carved the creature's leg right to the bone. She pulled at the weapon but it wouldn't move. It was stuck. RO tried to rip it out but with a kick the creature sent her flying back. She rolled across the sand and smashed against a large metal pipe. Pushing herself off she ran back to the creature. Kirana stood above it shooting Antony's gun. Her shots were wild, with one bullet nearly hitting RO. But she was to be feared, and the creature retreated away from them.

Kirana dropped the gun and went to her knees. "RO!" The Warden had never heard her so afraid. She was holding something. Where was Antony?

RO jumped back to the crate and pulled herself up to the top. Antony lay on the edge, his arm carved by what she could only assume was a tooth. He was barely keeping down a scream, and she couldn't blame him. His arm was a mixture of cut metal and broken bone.

Antony had never been a fighter. He could hold a gun and shoot a sniper's bullet but that was it. He took care of spiders and little Malfunctions. Antony had come all that way to protect her and he was bleeding for it. Dying for it. That wasn't fair. He was willing to help her so long as she was a Warden, and she was, and he was taking the pain for her. That wasn't fair.

"What do we do?" Kirana looked around them as if a doctor would burst out a crate.

RO closed her eyes. They didn't have a blade. She put out her hand, "Give me the gun."

"RO–" Antony spoke through shattered breaths. She took the gun from Kirana's hands and pointed it down to his arm. "Wait!"

As rapidly as she could, she pulled each shot down across his arm. He let out a scream but as soon as she was done she pushed the gun back to Kirana and pulled him away from his arm. They were lucky, he came off of his limb easily. She pulled him away and watched gushes of blood follow his path.

"Can you take him out of here and come back?" Kirana looked unsure, she tried to think but RO wouldn't let her, "We are running out of time!"

There was a growl from nearby. They could smell the blood.

Antony grabbed RO's hand, he was trembling, "RO, you can't–"

"Shut up, Tony!" She turned to Kirana, "Can you?"

"Where would I take him? I can't just leave him on a Telematic street. I can't go back to the Ward. If I come back here I'll faint and none of us will be able–"

"You have to try!"

A creature let out a bloodcurdling roar. It was getting closer.

"Kirana please!" RO was begging her. No, why was she begging her? Antony was a soldier, he was supposed to die like this. He would be honored as a Warden serving his people… but no. Antony had gone there alone, on his own to visit a traitor and protect her.

Antony held her arm tighter, "You can't join them–"

"These aren't your dying words!" She turned to Kirana, "He looks like a Hiraethan. We tell Lorenzo fell in the Arena. Get him up!"

RO got on her knees and pulled the Warden's torso up. Antony let out panicked screams and gasps but she didn't let him fall back down. She moved to the other side of him and held him with his good arm. His only arm… He lost an arm. For her.

When RO was younger, back in the days she spent in vents, she got hurt often. Small enough to fit into small places, the danger was always around. Fans and machinery hurt the most, but when cleaning weapons she often hurt herself against the blades and sharp edges.

She would show her wounds to the Wardens that oversaw the Malfunctions tasks, but they would shoo her away, "Those are just cuts. Get used to them."

When Deran or the others would beat her, or bruise her, or make her very eye bleed, she would beg for help from her fellow Malfunctions, but they would shake their heads again and say, "If a Warden hurt you, then you deserve the pain."

She would scream back to them, "I was just standing there!"

If she wasn't that hurt they would smack her, if she was too hurt they would threaten too.

But Antony would see her pain, and he would sneak her little packages. Sometimes food, sometimes actual medicine. He showed her how to wrap a bandage once, wrapping his own arm up. "It should be firm, but not tight."

She had said, "Those words mean the same things."

"They don't. Firm is a comforting squeeze, tight is more violent. It'll hurt you more than heal you."

He had healed her, and then, she had left him behind.

RO knew he hated her for what she did but what other choice did she have? She had been right when saying he wouldn't understand, but gods she wished he could. She hadn't seen Antony in years but he was still the same. He was caring, and that made him weak, yes, but also purely kind. She wished that he did not have to bleed out the way he was. He was never supposed to be a soldier, but it was that or fall behind and become a Malfunction.

Why were there only two choices?

RO carried Antony with the care he had given her, but with the protection she had developed over her years away from comfort. She held the gun up and shot anything that dared to show its face. Kirana took the lead, frantically yelling Metis's name.

Antony was sweating, he was slowing down. She shot towards the creature ahead of them, "I need you to keep walking!"

"You're so good at this." He was fading, "You were always a fighter."

"Antony–"

"I forgive you..."

Those words... shouldn't have meant as much as they did. Antony suddenly went limp. RO dropped with him, "Kirana!"

Kirana ran back and held up his other side, ignoring the blood and pushing them forward against his bleeding side. There was a noise behind them as suddenly a creature ran for them. RO pulled her gun back and shot at it, but this one wasn't obeying her threats. A blue bullet shot over her head and she looked back to see Metis coming towards them.

He shot frantically for the creature as RO left Antony with Kirana to defend him. She aimed for the beast's eye. Three shots, one landed. It screamed, but its voice echoed too closely. RO heard gunshots behind her only to find Metis with another creature. This one was fast. Too fast. Both of them rushed towards Kirana but Metis was forced to dive out of the way of a bite. The creature slipped against the sand and rolled across the ground. Kirana pulled Antony out of the way as RO tried to deal with both the creature behind her and the one ahead. But she should have focused on the one frantically moving around her because she was in the way, and with one stumbling kick the creature hit her.

She flew back away from the others. She rolled to her side and shot at the creature further down the Arena. Again and again, she put every bullet into the creature. And then the gun stopped firing. The creature had faced enough and retreated behind the crates, but if it came back she would have nothing. No blade, no gun, nothing.

She looked back to the others to find Metis and Kirana desperately trying to keep the creature away from them... and Antony.

There was something in the way they stood, in the way they fought. They were not trying to kill the creature. They were not trying to survive. They were defending Antony and each other.

But... They knew he was a Warden, but she hadn't explained anything to them. They trusted that he could be trusted. They trusted RO. Antony was their enemy and yet there they stood, defending him. Either Keeper could have left, they could have left without her or Antony, but they weren't going anywhere.

Antony didn't deserve to die. He had come to save her. His plan was stupid. His intentions were weak but... he was just trying to help RO. He had gone all that way, followed her across Hiraeth to get to her. Just because he had a heart didn't mean it needed to be put to silence. She did not want to be death, nor the monster that brought him pain. He was a Warden, he was born to be a soldier... that wasn't fair. He had never wanted to fight like she had. RO had dreamed of being the very monster she was. She wasn't allowed to be a soldier until she killed Deran. Antony didn't want to fight, but he would die in a battle. Dead.

That wasn't fair.

In all her confusion, in her panic, RO forgot things. She forgot she was a spy. She forgot she was a trained soldier. She forgot she had a history of pain and struggle. She forgot she had a future of respect and reward. She forgot she was sent there to observe and defend. She forgot she should have killed Antony and went on with her life. She forgot to be a monster.

She looked at the Keepers and suddenly she could see them so clearly.

The Keepers were protecting Tony not because he was a Warden but because he was a person. He was suffering and they were there to help him. That was... that was it. They were just there to help people.

The gods. The protectors.

Kirana and Metis had been helping her from the beginning. Why? No matter what they sought to protect her. They didn't know who she was. Surely the idea she was a spy could have crossed their minds. She knew Metis had been skeptical at least once, he was so smart even with his heart. He had hope for her. True and unconditional hope. He didn't care that she was a Warden, not out of spite but simply because they valued her as a person.

Not a soldier.

Not a Malfunction.

A Keeper.

RO got to her feet and she ran. She ran for Tony. She ran to keep the creature away from Kirana. She ran to protect Metis. She ran for the Keepers. She ran for her people. She ran and suddenly she did not feel like a monster. No, she was fighting the monsters now. She was a protector. She was their destiny. She held their fate. Not out of the control of death but out of the fight for life.

As the creature lunged down to bite Metis she ran in front of him and lifted her sword.

What... What sword?

She didn't have a sword. She hadn't picked anything up. But there, in her hands, was a sword. She could feel it. She could feel its power. It glowed red in her palm, like fire, and suddenly it was set ablaze. The sword burned poker red within flames. She held it to the monster above her. It pulled back and she waved the sword through the air. It felt light, it felt... strong. As if it was made for her and her alone. The monster growled at her and she swung her weapon before them. They let out a cry and rushed back. She turned around to the other beast, circling the group behind her, protecting them. She held the sword, ready to use it as if she had trained with it for a hundred years. She could use it, and she could use it well.

It was only then she realized that she had saved those behind not for the mission, but for herself.

She looked down at the sword and the flames went out. Kirana grabbed her shoulder and she felt the familiar pull as they were dragged back through the dimensions.

RO felt like a protector.

Like a Keeper.

Chapter 42

METIS

METIS LANDED ON a hard metal floor. It was wet, rain dripping down from above them. He looked up and saw his city, his world. It was a rainy Telematic evening, the sun setting against tall skyscrapers and ships. People walked past them without glancing down. With a quick look, he didn't see any Wardens, nor anyone who would recognise him. He looked back at the others. Kirana was standing with the staff, recovering from what had just happened to them.

RO sat over the Warden from the Arena. She looked back at Metis, "We need a doctor."

Metis crawled over to her and looked down at the Warden, "We can't just find a doctor."

"He needs help!" She looked around, "I can't tell where we are. Metis, please!"

He jumped up and ran down the street. After a few moments and an identifiable shop he ran back, "We're on the outskirts. The distribution district by Firelock."

RO closed her eyes and thought, "We can drop him off at a Warden facility. There is nowhere else to take him."

Metis moved down beside her and looked at the wound. It was messy and continuously bleeding. If it had been a clean cut the Warden might have just been able to stay awake.

Metis took off his jacket and tried to push RO aside.

She stopped him, "What are you doing?"

He ripped the fabric into a long strand, "I'm making a tourniquet. This is too severe to just apply pressure—we need to stop the bleeding." He put his ear to his mouth and listened for breathing. When he heard and felt nothing he put his hands on the Warden's chest and started pressing down. Metis tried to keep count as he spoke, "We need to make sure he survives long enough to make it to the doctor." He pinched the Warden's nose and pressed two fingers under his chin before pressing his mouth onto his and breathing out. When Metis pulled back the Warden let out a single gasp which quickly turned into a soft scream.

Metis rolled him onto his good side and grabbed his makeshift tourniquet, "RO, I need you to hold him up. Grab his shoulder."

She listened to him and moved behind the Warden. As she pulled him up Metis put the tourniquet around the remaining limb and used the rest of his jacket to cover the Warden's body, trying to keep him warm in the rain. The Warden let out a gasp, wincing. He wasn't dead, not yet at least.

"We need to get him to someone fast." Metis thought about where they were, before looking up and seeing Kirana. She could take them anywhere, so whatever option he had in mind could work. But he didn't know too many doctors. Not someone who could help the Warden.

The Master came to mind and he winced, "No."

"No, what?"

He shook his head, "I can't think of anyone. Just get me the tools and I'll do it."

RO stared at him in shock, "Do what?"

"I'll patch the wound. We'll need to find him blood, Kirana can take us to get some. I know a place, but… I don't know if we have time."

RO just looked at him. She stared up at Metis with glistening eyes, as if she was utterly confused, yet grateful for what he was doing. He wondered how many Wardens had been willing to help her like he had so far. From what he could tell from his time in the Ward, it was a selfish society. In a way, it was much like his own.

Kirana knelt on the other side of the Warden. "Who is he?"

"Antony." RO winced after saying his name, "I think—gods, he shouldn't have been here." She looked back to Metis and then down to his side, "He shot you."

He looked down and saw the cut against his shirt. He shook his head and gestured down to Antony, "I think this is more pressing than a scratch."

Kirana looked down at the Warden's missing arm. She clenched her jaw, "We could take him back to Hiraeth. He looks Hiraethan."

Metis shook his head, "They'll kill RO. They might just kill us too."

"RO saved our lives!" She looked at RO, "You proved to us that you're a protector. Not just for us but for your people." She pointed to what was in RO's hand, "You proved it to yourself."

The sword's hilt sat lifeless on RO's hand. Metis was shocked to see it without a blade and quickly looked around for where it could have gone. She held it up and the blade shot through the hilt and extended itself. There was no fire, nor the poker-hot glow, but the weapon was still a sight to see. She pulled it back down and the blade went back into the hilt.

RO took a breath, "We have to go back to Hiraeth."

"What?"

Antony sturred and RO reached out to grab him. She held her hand above him, not finding the right thing to do. She pulled her hand away, "You need Gwen. They have doctors."

"They'll kill you—"

"Metis." Kirana waited until he looked at her, "She saved our lives. Lorenzo has to learn we're a team. That she's here to stay."

RO put her head down for a moment, before picking it back up and looking at Kirana, "Antony fell in. We saved him. He's a Hiraethan."

Metis shook his head, "RO—"

"We don't have another choice."

"I can do it—"

She stared at him, "Metis he lost a limb. I guarantee you've never had to patch up an entire arm, no matter your Telemetic experiences."

Metis didn't know how to tell her it was his specialty. He didn't know if he should have told her then and there. They would ask questions, and his skills would be put to the test. Truth be told, he hadn't operated on someone in years. But the tasks were embedded within him, he knew he would be able to do it. He had done surgeries and minor operations his entire life. On himself or others. He never trembled at the touch of a blade, never got a flashback to the workshop. No. Metis was a master at the art of molding a person's inner workings. Even now, looking down at Antony, he did not see the Master's blade, he saw his own. He saw the path he could take to heal the man, he saw the way to one day attach a new mechanical arm to his wound.

His talent overtook his trauma.

The Master would be so proud.

But in times like the one they were in, he could not perform such miracles. He would need tools, medicine, and a clean facility. They had nothing.

He rubbed his forearm, "You'll stay here."

Kirana shook her head, "Lorenzo has to see she isn't a danger–"

"I don't care about Lorenzo, they'll shoot her the first chance they get."

"*Metis.*" RO spoke his name with as much intensity as she had left, "For Antony and Gwen, I will see this through."

He wanted to argue, he wanted to say that they were being rash and stupid, but if they wanted Lorenzo to work with them they needed to reveal all their secrets. They needed to show him that RO was not a threat. She was not some spy or someone who would betray them so easily.

As Kirana grabbed Antony and RO, Metis held onto the staff and whispered to RO, "Show them the sword. Show them you're a god."

"I'm still a Warden."

"Good. You're supposed to be."

He felt the world around him fold onto itself and suddenly he was pulled through the world. As soon as they landed he let go of the staff and looked around. They were in the gate's room. There stood his machine, still broken. Around the Keepers were dozens of Hiraethans. More than a hundred, and within a second all eyes were on them as the crowd stepped back and formed a circle around them.

Metis stood up, but as Kirana tried to do the same she swayed and suddenly fell back to the floor. He looked down to see her nose bleeding, eyes fading.

He put his hands up to the Hiraethans, "We need help. One of your people fell into the Arena." He looked back to see RO holding Antony's body. Her face was hidden by a small wave of hair and nothing more.

"Let me though!" Lorenzo's voice cut through the crowd as he pushed his way forward. Metis went around the group as their shield. The rebellion's leader stood at the edge of the crowd, not yet crossing the border to the Keepers. "You saved her?" Her eyes were on RO.

Metis put up his hands again. He noticed a few Hiraethans back away at the sight of his movements. It took him a moment to realize they now saw him as a god. They thought he had powers. He turned back to Lorenzo, "We're not your enemy."

"But she is." His words were numb, powerful with their lack of emotion, "You lied to all of us."

"To protect her–"

"A lie is a lie, and you hid the very thing that could destroy us."

"Gwen lied too." He put his hands down, "And RO has done nothing to hurt you. She saved our lives. I know you were watching."

"I did not–"

"Don't lie, Lorenzo."

The rebel leader's eyes narrowed, "She's still a Warden."

"That won't change. She will always be a Warden, and we need her as such." The Hiraethan crowd started to whisper and Metis realized he was not just convincing Lorenzo, but every person around them. He turned and faced the crowd, "Her people are forced into a society that prides themselves on killing innocent people. I have been to her world. It is painful, just like Hiraeth. If you don't fight you are cast aside or killed. If you are weak, if you love, if you cry... The Wardens fight only because they have to. The Magistrater has molded them into monsters."

Lorenzo started to walk forward slowly. There was a gun to his side, his hand resting against it, "You're right. They are monsters. This one is as well. The staff may have chosen her but she is not–"

Someone came up behind Metis. He expected to see Kirana. Instead, he saw RO. "I never wanted to fight."

Lorenzo looked at her in disgust, "Have you killed before?"

"Never a Hiraethan. But I have killed Telematics and a few of my own people. I have brought control to worlds in the name of the Magistrater... and I will never again. The staff chose me to help my people, and yours. I pledge my allegiance to you, Lorenzo. To your people, to those both the Magistrater and my people have harmed."

She stepped forward and Metis was ready to grab her and pull her back. He had to force himself not to.

She took a breath, "There are people in my world called Malfunctions. I hate them. I have been modeled to hate them because I hate my own weaknesses. If I, or any of the Wardens around me became sloppy, or weak, or emotional, we become defects. Our anger is the only thing that has kept us alive. We are only acknowledged when we have been killed. We are only given honor when we hunt children and tear families apart in the name of our people."

Metis had never realized how well his history matched with RO's. He had hunted children to be seen by the Master, to bring honor to the workshop and his genius father.

RO shook her head and held the hilt of her weapon up to him, "I am a Keeper, I am here to unite the worlds and to fight the Magistrater. I am here to help my people, and yours. Without the Wardens on your side, you can't stop her. I know how to fight them, and one day how to free them. I can create a world where my people don't have to kill to prove their worth. I admire you as much as I admire your world's love."

Lorenzo looked shocked. He stared at her and took in her words. Every last one. His hand slipped off the hilt of his gun. "Your people are monsters. But you are not?"

"I am a monster. I always will be. But I am here now to redeem myself."

Metis stood up taller and moved to her side, "She saved our lives. She is here to help her people, as I am here to help mine. But Lorenzo... you need all of us."

"The Wardens are our enemy–"

RO shook her head, "For now. But when the war ends what do you expect will happen to them? When the Magistrater is dead are they to die too? And what about the Malfunctions? What about the system they are trapped within?" Lorenzo didn't answer, he just stared at her. RO pulled her weapon back and let the blade extend out. Within a moment it was set ablaze. The crowd murmured with both awe and fear. RO held the fire to her side, before letting it out and going down on one knee, the tip of her sword down against the ground. She bowed her head, "What is an alliance without its unity? Let me help you unite all the people, from all the worlds, from all places of suffering."

When she finished speaking there was silence. Lorenzo stood there, thinking. Everyone let him. No one moved. Not the crowd, not the Keepers, not the very creatures in their cages. Lorenzo was deciding history, and they could all feel the pages being written with every second that went by.

The leader let out a breath. Not a sigh, not a laugh, just air. Just a breath. He waved his hand across where they stood, "Get the Hiraethan to the medical room." Lorenzo turned to two Hiraethans and they walked behind Metis and RO to Antony. They lifted the Warden and carried him towards the door. Metis heard RO take a breath, and he wondered now how long it had been since she had let herself breathe. She stood up and pulled her sword back into its hilt.

There was a gunshot.

RO suddenly flew to the floor. She let out a scream as someone came from behind them. Metis pulled out his gun and turned to the person.

He went cold.

It was Gwen.

Chapter 43

GWEN

GWEN HAD BEEN stuck with her mother's body for three hours before Gaia or her father got off from work. She didn't know what to do. For a while she just sat there a few feet away, staring. When it truly hit it she sprung forward and held her mother's bleeding head. But tears were so temporary, and when they stopped there was nothing but silence.

Lifeless silence.

For the next two hours, she curled up in her mother's arms and tried to find a piece of her. She was cold, soggy, and soaking in her blood. Gwen tried not to look at her face, at the bruises, at the pieces left in craters. She prayed to the gods to let her mother breathe. She waited for an hour against her, listening for a heartbeat, feeling for a rise in her chest. She watched the tips of her fingers. Not a twitch, not a movement. She realized then that her mother was gone, not simply by dying but also in spirit. The body before her was not her mother, it was just a body.

When her father got home she could have only assumed he thought they were both dead. His wife, face caved in and still. His daughter, blood across her body and eyes closed. Gwen felt his hand against her as he shook her violently.

All she remembered was thinking her mother had woken up.

The two of them sat with her mother's body for an hour. Her father cried as silently as he could, arms wrapped around Gwen. She had decided to not look at her mother anymore, after all, that was not her mother.

That very night the neighbors came and helped burn the body. They collected the ashes and gave them to her father in a small glass jar, second hand. That night they stood together outside the house as the others helped clean the bloody floor. From that day forward, Gwen would do everything in her power to avoid going into the kitchen.

She remembered her father's face, not sad, not angry, just numb. He held his wife in his arms in that little jar like a baby. In silence, they stood by the door. Standing there and hearing the others clean the floor. Eventually, her father moved. He grabbed her hand softly and pulled her around the house. He didn't say a word, he just walked with her away from the house and into the orchards. Gwen did not know much about the rules the Wardens placed upon them, but she knew that they were not supposed to go out so late. But to break the silence was to break the very thing that was keeping them from shattering. They walked for what felt like miles. They walked across the orchard, through five layers of different crops. Her father wouldn't stop walking. Eventually, they reached a place she had been before, a few times.

The river.

Feeding across more rural lands it separated them from a small grassy hill. Just beyond there was a town. All those in the area worked in cattle, and Gwen remembered hearing the murmur of the animals now and then.

Her father went to the water's side and got down on his knees. Gwen moved beside him and sat down against the dirt and rocks. It was dark, the moon was bright but the area was shadowed by a midnight glow. Her father put his head against the jar. It looked like he was praying, but Gwen would never know if he had been speaking to the gods or trying to reach his wife. After a minute he pulled back, eyes closed he kissed the jar and put it down on his lap.

"Did I ever tell you about the Keeper's River?"

Gwen shook her head.

"There was once a Keeper who got married to another god. They were madly in love. They would love each other forever but time was not on their side." He was crying, and he was only just managing to keep his voice steady, "One of them died and left the other. The Keeper wept for three days over a river. His tears sent waves across the entire world. On the fourth evening, the river was filled with fish. They were glowing their two colors, shining in the water… Do you know what happens after we die?"

Gwen shook her head. She refused to look at the jar.

"Our energy lives on–" His voice broke and he closed his eyes. He took his time to speak, "The Keepers connect to the life around us like they do with Rhodonite. But everyone lives within that same balance. Our life and death will always be connected to our home, to our world. To our family–" He put a hand over his eyes. He was trembling.

Gwen put a hand to his arm. She was so grateful to feel his warmth, his movements.

He wiped his face, "So we're going to release your mother's body, and let her live within us from now on." He opened the jar and looked back to his daughter, "I'm going to send her away now, but this isn't her. Your mother lives within the Rhodonite, in our world and within us."

Gwen looked down at the jar now. At the ashes. She was crying too, "That's not my Mama."

Her father shook his head, "Your mother is here." He put a hand to her heart, to her head, and then to the world around them. After collecting himself for another minute he slowly sprinkled the ash along the running water. It was too dark to watch it fade away. It just… disappeared.

Gwen's tears had returned, worse now than ever. She tried to keep them silent, but she didn't know how. She wanted to grab the ashes and piece her mother back together. She wanted her mother back.

The breeze picked up around them as she closed her eyes. It circled through her hair, across her tear-ridden face. It was cold, so very cold. She breathed it in and let the air fill her lungs. She let it hold her. She let it fill the world around her.

Gwen found her mother within the breeze for years, then within herself. She started to look like her, elements of her father taking hold but constantly being swayed away by her stubborn mother. No matter what happened she had her father and the breeze. She would find her family within the world around her. But then Gwen was taken away from her world and returned to a lifeless home. When her father died she could not feel the breeze, nor her mother. She could not feel her father with her, she could not feel her world holding her close. Her parents were not with her.

Gun raised the gun in a crowded room. She had never felt so alone.

RO curled over and let out a scream. Metis turned back, ready to shoot whoever had attacked the Warden. At the sight of her, his eyes widened and he lowered his weapon. Kirana shifted along the floor and spotted Gwen.

Gwen stepped forward and yelled across the room, "Why is she alive?"

Lorenzo had put his hand off his gun. He wasn't going to kill the Warden. Why? Because she could spin a few inspiring words together? It was all lies.

RO was on the floor, writhing in pain. Her hand clasped her stomach. Gwen had been aiming for her head. Metis tried to move towards the Warden, and at the sight of his movement, she turned the weapon onto him. The look in his eyes... as if she was the one betraying him. No, the Warden was the monster, not her.

"Let her bleed." She walked closer to the group.

Kirana got herself up with the staff. Her nose was bleeding, she had taken too many trips and her body swayed through the exhaustion. She put her hand out, "Don't do this. She's not our enemy–"

"She is a Warden! She has killed– slaughtered!"

Kirana nearly slipped down the staff. She brought herself up, "Gwen–"

"She is a monster!" She let out a laugh from some demonic place within her. It sounded horrible, and she put a trembling hand to her mouth to stop another from escaping her, "Don't you realize what she has done? She's never suffered. She's lived like a god her entire life, she doesn't deserve *anything*, just like the rest of her people."

"Gwen!" Kirana yelled so violently that Gwen stopped moving. "She's telling the truth–"

Gwen shook her head, "She's a monster."

"We've all had to kill–"

"In defense! For the sake of our people–"

"For the sake of mine!" RO let out a gasp as she tried to stand up. Metis looked at Gwen, then the gun, before slowly moving to help the Warden get up. What could Gwen have done? Shoot him? He knew as well as she did that she could never do that.

"She's a monster. She had done horrible things. She has... she has hurt in-nocent people."

Metis brought RO to her feet, "She is here to change–"

"She hurt your people!" Gwen was crying, she was hysterical but she deserved to be, "She took those *children*, Metis. Do you have any empathy for what she did?

Do you not understand how horrible a person has to be to hurt *little kids?*"

He closed his eyes and looked away.

RO moved out of his grasp and stumbled towards Gwen, "I understand you hate me–"

She waved the gun towards her, "I have watched the Wardens kill people I loved since I was a child. I grew up knowing how to live with blood stains on my family's clothes."

The Warden continued to move closer to her, "You didn't deserve what happened to you."

"Stop!"

"I only–"

"You took everything from me. From my people!" Gwen put the gun to the sky and shot. The crowd around her let out gasps of screams. RO stopped walking. She looked terrified, and Gwen wanted that to stay true. She wanted the monster before her to know how easy it would be to die. All Gwen had to do was pull on the trigger. RO pressed her hand against her bullet wound. Her breathing was heavy, sweat spread across her brow.

Gwen's chest pumped up with an angered breath, her lip curled up. She stepped closer to the Warden, "You are a *monster!* You will never be a *god.* You will never be a *Keeper.* You and your people are our enemies. We will wage war on your world and kill every last one of you. Because it's justified. Because when you burn our world we have every right to burn yours."

"The Magistrater–"

"Will suffer, just as you will." She stepped closer to RO. They were both trembling, "You took my people's freedom. You took their childhood, their lives, their parents, their children. You took my family's safety. You took my life. You took everything I loved. You took my mother! My father!"

She pulled the gun back and swung it across her face. The Warden fell to the floor and Gwen aimed the gun for her head.

RO looked up at her in desperation, "I did not kill your father!" There was blood along her lips. She swallowed hard and let out a gasp of pain, "I have never done anything to you! I have only followed orders–"

"That's an excuse!"

"Of course it is, *Gwen!*" She had never heard RO say her name before. It felt wrong. It felt… personal. RO let out a breath, "I was trained since I was a child! You were in my world. We may look as if we have a choice but we don't. Everything we do is for a mission or ourselves. Our worth is judged on death and pain. We can only be soldiers and you better believe…" She had to stop talking to hold her stomach, she winced, and when she looked up at Gwen she could see a bruise forming along RO's face from the gun. "I did not kill your mother. I have never met your father. If I was sent to kill them I would have, because I was told to. Not because I *wanted* to. Because if I didn't they would have killed me."

"You're monsters–"

"Because they told us we had to be! They threatened us. They beat us. We could never love. We could never be loved. We could never have a weakness. We could never have a family. You saw the Malfunctions. You saw what they do to us if we don't meet their expectations." She looked up with eyes burned by a thousand flames, "We are monsters, but we were once just… people. Fight or die. Kill or be killed. Be cruel or be *nothing*."

Gwen just stared at her.

She had seen the Wardens in their very home. They looked cruel, all of them, but that was because they were monsters. They chose that life… and yet, they didn't. But they were the ones who slaughtered and killed. They were the ones that tore worlds apart for something as simple as an order.

They were the ones left with blood on their hands.

But there was one person who remained clean through all of it. The one person who gave orders and destroyed worlds. Who made an entire world become an army just to hurt innocent people.

The Magistrater.

Gwen looked down at the gun in her hand to find blood against the metal. On her hand.

Gwen's body went loose suddenly and she lowered the gun. It dropped from her hand and she dropped with it to her knees.

Metis ran to RO's side and looked back to Lorenzo, "She needs help!"

Kirana stumbled over to them as the crowd started to move. She dropped to the ground beside Gwen. Kirana grabbed her and pulled her close. Gwen was sobbing, and she clung to Kirana for dear life.

"I'm sorry…" She mumbled, face dug into her shoulder.

Lorenzo shouted something in the distance.

Kirana held her closer, "Do you need to leave?" Gwen nodded. "Where?"

"The river." She sobbed, "I can't..."

Gwen felt the familiar pull as Kirana took them out of Hiraeth, then back again.

When they landed, Gwen did not let go of Kirana. She did not look around her, she just sat there, holding Kirana. After a while, her tears stopped falling, and silence took over. She could hear herself breathing against the cool air. The sound of trees waving and water running. She could feel Kirana's heartbeat in her chest. Gwen put a hand flat against her back. Kirana was alive, she was warm and breathing.

"I could have killed you." She winced and tears returned, "I panicked. I didn't know what to do. I'm sorry, I'm so sorry Kirana–"

Kirana pulled her away to look at her, "Don't apologize." She looked at Gwen's face as if she had cracks all over it. Gwen felt so broken, and she could see how clearly it was showing.

"I wanted her to die." She took a staggered breath, "But you went after her. I didn't know–"

"We're safe now." Kirana held the side of her face. It was clear she didn't know what to do in the moment. Gwen had a feeling Kirana had never had to comfort someone before, certainly not to the extent needed. She pulled her hand away, "I'm so sorry about your father." Something shifted within her, and she leaned back, "I should have gone after him. I shouldn't have taken us to Telematic."

"What?"

"I led the Wardens to him... to your family." She winced, "I was naive and foolish and I should have never left him behind. You can blame me, Gwen."

Gwen had blamed RO. That was true. But Kirana brought up the right question, who was to blame? She put a hand to heart. She knew it was not her own fault, however much that would solve the problem. She knew it was not Kirana, the Keeper had followed her and her father's lead. She knew the Wardens were not to blame completely, and with that logic, it was the Magistrater who had truly killed him. But that felt so far away. She shut her eyes and felt the breeze around her.

The river had not changed that much over the years. The water ran full, but it looked different. The sunset brought glimmers of light across the surface and illuminated different aspects of the land around them. The wind picked up around her and she watched the river flow to its guide. She put her hand out to feel it. It felt the same, like it had never left her. Gwen had to remember it never would. No matter where she went, she would always have her parents within the breeze. She wondered who else followed her through the wind. Perhaps she had hundreds of ancestors with her. Perhaps there were Hiraethans who had been harmed waiting to see what she did next. Perhaps they weren't just Hiraethans.

Gwen took in a deep breath, "My father shouldn't have gone to Trent. He should have been patient and kept you in our home. He should never have kept those books. They were old, and incriminating. He kept them as symbols of hope when they truly offered nothing to us. He should have joined Lorenzo a long time ago. He should have listened to me more."

Kirana looked stunned. She had not been expecting such words.

Gwen watched the river, "There was this old story my father told me, about a river. It was this old wive's tale about a god who died before their lover. The surviving Keeper wept for three days along a river bed, and on the fourth evening the river filled with hundreds of fish, all glowing and swimming together." She closed her eyes, "It is said that when we die we live on in the worlds around us. Our life and our deaths stay within our world." She looked at Kirana, "The Keepers especially. We are the most connected to the worlds around us. That's why we can work between them, because we are champions of our people."

"Your father would be so proud."

Those words hit Gwen and she shut her eyes to stop tears from falling. She laughed, "I wish he was here. I wish he could see what we do next." She shook her head, "I want him to help me. I need him, I really do. I don't know what I am doing. He was always the one to take the lead. Before you, I only did what he told me to do."

Kirana took her hand, "Well maybe that needs to change."

Gwen nodded softly, "I'll try."

Kirana looked around them again, "Your world is truly beautiful, Gwen."

"From a girl who grew up in the perfect world, I'll take that as a compliment."

Kirana laughed. Her eyes were red now. Gwen had brought her to tears. She wiped them away quickly, "What do you need to do here?"

"I don't know." She looked down the river. It flowed so far, but slowly. She wondered how far her mother's ashes had made it. She wondered if her father had found her yet.

Kirana squeezed her hand, "These past few days have been... a lot. We've done enough now."

"We haven't even started."

"No. We've started. You and I found two gods in two impossible places, and we brought them together. That was us, Gwen."

"We're still missing a Keeper."

Kirana rolled her eyes dramatically. It made her tears fall, "Well, four out of five is pretty good. We've traveled farther than anyone has in centuries. We've done things no one has done since the last Keepers. We've fought, we've healed, we've protected. It's not over, you're right, but right now, we need to stop."

Gwen watched the river flow, "And then?"

"We'll find the last Keeper and start our work." She looked at Gwen and they locked eyes. The way Kirana looked at her was different from how her family had. Even Gaia, a woman she considered to be her new mother, did not have as much care as Kirana. No, Gaia had worry and fear, she did believe Gwen was a god, but a god that was too young and naive to take on such a role. But Kirana... She believed in her. She cared for her, and yes, she did worry, but it was not because of anything Gwen could have done. Kirana trusted her. Gwen trusted her, more than anyone else.

Kirana smiled at her softly, "I'm going to give you something I should have given you a long time ago."

"A gift?"

She nodded, "For everything that has happened to you, and the rest of us." Kirana took a breath and looked around them.

"I'll give you time."

PART 6

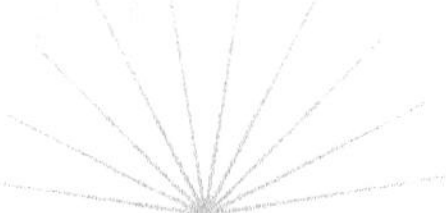

ʻĀina

Chapter 44

RO

RO DIDN'T UNDERSTAND what was happening. Suddenly, she was questioning things. Maybe it was just seeing Tony again– no, seeing Antony. Maybe it was how Kirana and Metis had protected him. Maybe it was the Keepers coming into the Arena to rescue her. Maybe it was Lorenzo accepting her as a Keeper. Maybe it was Gwen putting down the gun. There was too much happening, and suddenly RO didn't feel like a spy anymore. She felt like a Keeper. It was jeopardizing everything. Yet, she couldn't help it. No one had ever protected her like this, never in her whole life. But they were idiots. Children playing gods. How could they be affecting her so much?

When Lorenzo had accepted her something felt real. It was as if her speech was her own and she truly believed in what she was saying. She made up a cause and ran with it. It felt real because... well, it was. Her people didn't have a choice on who they could be, but she didn't feel the way they thought she did. That was all that mattered. She knew the system worked, she knew it did. Her people were not happy, but they were alive and respected. Their world was above all others, they exceeded all others. She had to keep that in mind.

After Gwen's breakdown and the entire Arena affair, it took time for everything to settle down. The injuries kept people on edge. Antony had been rushed away but he still posed a problem. Not only could he die, but he could also mumble that he was Warden and prevent the doctors from working on him. RO needed to deal with him, she needed to be there to make sure she could defend his Hiraethan backstory, but she had her own problems to worry about. Gwen's bullet had cut right through her stomach. She needed a medic, someone to help her stop bleeding. Metis had dropped to her side and they gave each other the same look. They knew no one would want to help her. Metis had been the one to help her back up and pull her away from the crowd as Kirana took Gwen away. Lorenzo had enough sympathy to show them to the medical facility.

It was dark, and somehow both dirty from use and unprepared from lack of use. RO was in so much pain. She tried her best to bite it down but it was no use. She was fading fast. Her memory went into blotches of unorganized moments. She didn't know how to connect them and at one point she simply gave up. If she was to die there then so be it, she had done her very best to prevent it. The Hiraethans had sentenced her to death twice on the same day.

RO had been shot before, once. Down in the Firelane District, there were more than enough bullets to find her. The people in the district ranged from drugged geniuses to drunk clowns. They were either high or drowning in their liquor. When her team came in to take a piece of technology from a group, they found themselves faced with extremely aggressive Telematics. They were rabid, all of them. Their drugs had turned them into animals, and they acted as such. For a while, it was just hand-to-hand combat, and the Wardens were able to easily take down the group. But someone was smarter, and faster. They came from the side and as RO turned they shot three bullets at her. One to her chest, two to her arm. The one aimed for her heart hit an armor plate, and the other for her arm skimmed over her wrist. But the last one got her. Gods, it hurt, worse than she had imagined. She had already fallen from the first impact and lay there in agony.

A Warden shot the last Telematic and walked up to her. He had been wearing a helmet, but she knew his gaze. It was nothing but humor. "Oh get up." He had kicked at her knee as he helped another Warden further away.

No one helped her. She ended up walking on her own back to the ship, bleeding out on the metal floor, and spending her night trying to figure out how to give herself stitches without fainting from blood loss and pain. The process not only left her a vicious scar but also the knowledge that if she was shot again, no one would be there to help her.

She was a savage little Malfunction. If she was hurt it was because her defects got the best of her. No one ever protected her, no one ever helped her.

Even the Hiraethans could see it. It was the same gaze, the only difference was that they feared her. She liked that part. Better to be feared than disgraced. But no matter where she went, no one would help her. She was either a Malfunction or a Warden, neither good, neither true. She was a horrible unbalanced mixture.

RO woke up and suddenly the moments around her felt steady. She was awake, completely this time. There was a tube in her arm and a clean bandage around her waist. She was wearing her own clothes, but her top had been cut during what she could assume was some sort of operation. She was in a bed in the medical facility, a curtain drawn from someone beside her. The two metal tables on either side of her were lined with tools covered in blood. Metis was at the bottom of her bed sitting in a chair. His head was resting on his arms, hands stained with blood.

He had been the one who patched her wound.

The idea of that hit her harder than it should have. She shook her head violently to get such thoughts away. If she was starting to betray her people it would not be because of selfish reasons like his kindness.

She kicked at his head, "Telematic." Gods, it felt strange to talk. It was like there was something inside her, a brick.

He shot up quickly and looked at her, "How do you feel?" It was clear he had been preparing to ask the question well before he fell asleep.

"Like I got shot." She moved herself up with a few winces. It hurt, not as much as before, thank the gods. "You did this?" She gestured to her bandage.

"I was scared to let someone else." He wiped his hands on his pants, "This doctor had offered several times if he could help me. He was trying to kill you."

"Are you sure?"

He laughed, "I am. Because he came in here with a knife."

RO glanced around the facility again. She hated the curtain closed next to her. "Where is he?"

"I had Lorenzo take him out." He shook his head, "Kirana came and watched over you for a bit, and when I came back I took the shift."

They had taken shifts to watch over her...

Metis nodded to the curtain, "Antony's there. The new doctor's softer. He won't come in here. He's just a little Hiraethan man with a knack for seeing blood and not fainting." Metis got up from the chair as if he hadn't been sleeping a few seconds ago. He peeked around the curtain before coming back around to her,

"They're both still here."

"Is he alive?"

RO hated how relieved she felt at the sight of him nodding. "I tried to help where I could but I wasn't much use between the two of you."

"Did he say anything?"

"He hasn't woken up. I told the new doctor to let me know as soon as he did."

RO shook her head, "We can't trust the new doctor to tell us the exact moment."

Metis gave her a smirk, "You'd be surprised what a bit of flirting can do to a man stuck in a place like this his whole life." He pointed around them, "When Antony wakes up I can distract the doctor for a good… 15 minutes, and in that time you can talk freely with Antony about whatever you need to."

RO didn't know what shocked her more, the fact that Metis was Telematic enough to flirt his way into a new opportunity, or the fact that he trusted her enough to leave her with one of her people. He didn't see her as dangerous or less than. What did he see her as then?

Metis went back down to his chair, "Can I ask who he is?"

He was asking to ask a question. That just seemed counterproductive, and yet… kind. If she said no he would not put up a fight that felt good to know. If Antony woke up he would not have to be there when they spoke. No one would be there but the two Wardens. She could lie, tell the Telematic anything. But lies left stains, and to remain clean she would have to speak with a few minimal truths. After all, Metis already knew Antony was a Warden. He knew his name. He had seen how she had tried to save him. He knew too much to not know just a little bit more.

"He came here to help me."

Metis squinted at her, "By killing you?"

"By killing *you*. He was trying to take me back to the Ward."

Metis leaned back and thought her words over. He glanced towards the curtain, "But he followed you. What did you tell him?"

Gods, she had to say it, "I told him I am a spy." She didn't want that thought in his head. The idea of it surely had crossed his mind but by now it would have well disappeared. She needed him to trust her, no doubts, no fears.

He nodded softly, his expression still stern, "So when he wakes up what should we do?"

"He will not harm anyone, I will make sure of that. We will talk, and I will give him a backstory. He is a Hiraethan who fell in the Arena and we saved his life. When he's better he'll return to the Wardens like nothing happened."

Metis pulled back from her, "Like nothing happened? He's missing an arm."

"So?"

"Will they– What will they do with him?"

She clenched her jaw. Again, the truth was the best answer, "They'll keep him in the Ward, give him reasonable tasks."

"He'll be a Malfunction?"

She hated the word. She hated how it sounded in Meits's voice. He did not sound disgusted but there was a layer of pity behind every syllable. "He'll be whatever they see fit, and he'll be proud."

Metis stared at the curtain, before leaning closer. He dropped his voice to a whisper, "What if we kept him?"

RO couldn't help but let out a laugh, "He's not a dog. We can not just keep him."

"You know what I mean. The Hiraethans could use him. Can you sway his loyalty?"

"Impossible."

"And yet, here you are." He gestured to her, a prize candidate for their little rebellion.

She could not disagree with him, not only for the sake of her own story but also for the sake of Antony's. Metis was right, her people would belittle him. They would make him a Malfunction or someone low enough to be marked unhonorable. It was her fault, after everything he had done to help her.

Metis got up from his seat, "I need to help fix the gate for Lorenzo. We're all trying to do our part around here. It's either been doing chores, making plans with Lorenzo, or working on our own projects."

"Plans?"

"We need to reach the last dimension. Maybe in a few weeks."

Gods, that was too long. Her people were ready for them, and the sooner the gods were captured the sooner they could start their work. RO would be promoted, the Hiraethans around her would be crushed, and the Keepers would be sent to their deaths. "I'll be ready in a week."

Metis laughed, "A week? RO, that's the bare minimum."

"I feel better."

"You've been asleep for three days." She hadn't been expecting such a number. He gestured to her shocked expression, "See. You got shot, and you kept fighting."

"That wasn't fighting, I was just talking."

Metis folded his arms with a soft laugh, "Do you realize the enormity of what you did back there?" He waited for a response but she stayed quiet. He shook his head, "You proved to everyone where your loyalty stands."

She nodded, "With them."

He rolled his eyes, "With your people. RO! Lorenzo is changing everything because of you. He sees the value of *unity* because of you. His entire family was killed by your people and you proved to him that a Warden suffers as much as he does. You proved your cause." He smiled at her, "You're a true Keeper now." She went pale at his words. He walked back, "I'll be back soon. Get some rest."

She tried to sit up, "I'll come with you."

He pointed a finger at her, "Don't you even think about it."

"Metis–"

"The moment you stand up, the doctor over here will call me immediately." He pulled over a scrawny orange-haired boy. The doctor looked up from Metis to her, his cheeks a bright pink. Metis gestured to him, "Don't even think about crossing this guy. He's a psychotic killer."

RO rolled her eyes and couldn't help a small smile at his joke. She looked back to find Metis still standing where he was, only this time, completely stunned.

"What."

He put his hands down, "I've never seen you smile. It's..." He lost his words. "I'll be back later. Rest." He looked to the doctor before moving out of view.

RO secretly wanted to know what he would have said. She winced at the thought but did not push it away. She pulled herself back down on the bed and held it close. A comfort.

RO had been getting comfortable. She could feel it. Not only in the relationship she had forged with the Keepers but also in the space they were creating. She was able to heal in that facility because she felt safe. It was strange, mostly because she had never truly felt such a thing. RO had been safe before, but never with other people. She had felt safe in her room at night, safe eating at a table far from others, safe with her helmet on, and safe when no names were called. But now, she was able to fall asleep even knowing Metis would return. If Kirana came to watch over her she would not flinch. The Hiraethans hated her, and yet, she felt safe.

RO slept hours more through the day and well through the night. She rested, and at some moment faded between being fully awake and completely asleep. At first, she found herself happy in the little bed in the little facility, but then she realized what that thought meant, and suddenly sleep did not come so easily.

She could feel herself becoming weaker. She was loyal to her people, always, and yet, the idea that even as a Keeper she would work to help her world started to toy with her mind. No matter what she did in her life she would always fight for the Wardens. It was her purpose, she had always known that. She had watched them her entire life, begging and praying to be one of them.

She thought about all the years. All the work. She thought about what it was like in those vents. Useless, unseen, unheard. RO always shocked herself when realizing she had spent more time as a Malfunction than as a Warden. She had spent the first 14 years of her life crawling through vents, cleaning, cooking, bowing, and making sure she never existed in the Warden's eyes. RO had been taken care of in the nursery until she was a year old. They tested her and found a genetic trait that would make her a less-than-adequate soldier. They sent her into the vents where she passed from Malfunction to Malfunction, raised in small metal rooms around people who were beaten constantly. RO never knew who her real parents were, and she forced herself not to look for them among her many superiors. RO remembered seeing the Wardens and feeling the tension as they glared down at her. They were clean, loud people, and RO did not understand why she could not be one of them. She used to watch them, often from within vents to hide away from the aggressive Wardens who would attack her, and study their traits. She copied the way they walked, talked, and even fought, practicing on her own when no other Malfunctions were around.

She turned on her back and looked up at the ceiling. The Hiraethans lived much like she did in the Ward. They lived in cracks and craters. Their rooms were dark and dirty. They were working with the bare minimum of what the Wardens would supply or leave behind, which wasn't much to begin with. They wanted more, just like the Malfunctions did.

When RO was about 10 years old she was given the chance to be out in the

Ward. It had been so clean, so spotless. She felt like a speck of dust, so easily swept away. She worked in the training rooms and polished every inch of the space. Sometimes they would train while she was there. She watched them closely, but one wrong look and she was in danger. The older ones were not as quick to hurt her, but the Wardens her age were more aggressive. There were multiple occasions when little groups of wardens would grab her off the floor and beat her. Sometimes their commander would be there in the room. They would just watch. They would watch as she bled and bruised, and when the Wardens were done with her their gaze would fall elsewhere. No matter the pain, no matter the work, no matter how spotless the room looked after she cleaned her blood off the floor, she was just a useless Malfunction.

In those days when she felt so small and invisible, RO remembered the one person who would bother to look at her. She remembered their gaze, sturdy but weak. Green eyes, red hair. Antony had noticed her in the vents and saw her between his training sessions. He started to talk to her, to spark conversations she had never had with anyone. He snuck her food, medicine, and bandages. He told her about his day and even taught her a few ways to fight. He was selfish and often complained about the details of his day, but he was still kind. He did not know her struggle but he tried to.

But even now, behind the curtain, he would never understand. She had hurt him. He wanted answers for what she did but he could never understand.

RO's eyes were closed but she was wide awake. She could hear someone enter the room. Their footsteps were patterned, like a dancer. Metis. He sat in his chair and she could feel his head against the bed. He would stay the night with her to make sure no one hurt her. Metis was a lot like Antony, and yet, more understanding than her Warden friend had ever been. But like Antony, she would end up hurting Metis just the same. She hated how much that hurt to understand.

Antony had a brother, Deran. They were close, and often competitive, but good friends. Deran was destined to be one of the next great leaders of the Ward. He would have gone on to be a General, one with a legacy. He was violent, and one day he would have learned how to control his rage. Just not back then, no, RO was his target, and his brother was his clean-up crew. Deran would find her cleaning the training rooms or picking weeds out of the garden in the Ward and beat her in front of his friends. Wardens pride themselves on violence from the moment they are born, so Deran decided to prove himself with the help of a little, insignificant Malfunction who could not fight back.

RO would tell Antony how Deran beat her, but he would always defend him like his brother was some saint. She hated him for how much he loved his brother. She still did. Antony was the one person who bothered to look at her, but what good was it when someone looked at her if they were blind? There was only so much Antony would do for RO, and she wondered if he ever realized it was life or death for her, and certainly not the same little game Deran was playing.

At night, RO would picture herself ripping him apart, sticking her fingers into his throat, stabbing his arms, cutting off his legs, and breaking his arms. She believed she was just as violent as the Wardens, certainly more than Antony, so she also believed she belonged among them. RO never saw herself as a Malfunction, not really, just a mislabeled soldier.

Day after day RO spent submitting to Deran and his group. Day after day she cleaned and polished. She moved through vents and bowed her head to every last Warden. Day after day, for years. For 14 years. She wanted more. She needed more.

One day Deran took it too far. Bowing her head she had been met with a punch to the face. She had been pulled onto the training mat and everyone around her moved away. She had felt so angry. Her nose was cracked, but she did not make a sound, pressing herself against the padded floor.

Deran had grabbed a sword from the training rack. He leaned against it, looking over at his teacher, "Sir. Can we make a deal? If I kill the roach, I get a full day off."

The kids around him had laughed. They laughed. At him. At her. She felt that noise within her very skin. It crawled over her like electricity.

RO would forever remember Antony's words to her. His face among the other happy Wardens, panicked. He had mouthed the words, *run* and *hide*. Run and hide. She was not a Malfunction. She was better than every Warden in the room and she knew it. RO was a monster. She wanted blood and she would get it.

With a scream, she got up and ran for him. She spun her fist into his face and it met with a deafening blow to his cheek. She pulled her hand away quickly, and suddenly Deran's face had changed. He looked… dangerous. He brought the sword up and swung it down for her again and again. He got parts of her, slashes to her shoulder, to her chest, to her leg. She tried to run through the crowd of Wardens to the weapons hanging on the wall but they stopped her and threw her back.

She watched as Deran hunted her, as he tried to kill her. She let all her anger, all her hate, fuel her. She moved to him and dodged another slice of the sword. She jumped at him and knocked him to the ground. She scrambled to his sword. She needed it. She had to get it off him. He wouldn't let go. She held his arm down and frantically brought her fists down to his face. Again and again. She put her hands together and pounded every inch of his face. She broke everything she could. She screamed the entire time. Tears rolling down her face. He went loose and she ripped the sword out of his hands and into his chest.

RO had never felt so good in a moment, then so terrible. She had killed Deran. She had caved his head in like a *monster*. The commander had taken her away, bloody and broken, and got her reassigned as a Warden. She was, as they called it, their test.

RO wondered now if she was still their test. She wondered what they thought of her as a Keeper. A Malfunction Keeper. As Antony told her, they were afraid. She was too. She was afraid of what the Keepers had been doing to her. They were sending her back. She felt like the little Malfunction again right after her first kill: confused and alone. There was a single week in her life, just one week when RO did not want to be a Warden. For all those years she had longed to be one, she no longer wished it to be true.

She did not want to be a monster. She just wanted to be seen.

But she got over it, she learned how to become someone like Deran. The problem was simply how kind the Keepers were, in comparison to what she had known all her life. They were proof that there was a way to not be a monster in a world of monsters. They were leading her down a path she had never once thought of truly taking.

Until now.

All night, these thoughts of past and present collide. She felt sick, stomach clenched with a bullet wound. She didn't want to question her people, but everything felt permanent.

Towards the morning of the next day, she realized something that would haunt her for many days. All that connected her back to her people was the communication chip. If she destroyed it… she was a Keeper. That was all it took. She would fight for her people to not have to fight. Wardens and Malfunctions. Was that why the staff chose her? She was the best of both worlds? A combination forged in fire and hate, learning to heal.

RO sat up and looked around. No one was there. "Hello?" She called out. No one answered. She listened carefully. She could hear Antony breathing, but nothing else. She was alone.

RO forced herself to bring her foot towards her and grab the communication chip out of her boot. She put it behind her ear and pressed the button. She didn't know what she would say, or why she needed to report in the first place. It just felt... needed.

A voice almost instantly responded. "We are here." She wondered if they thought she was dead. After so many days without a report, it made sense to question her survival. "You survived."

"I did."

There was a long pause in which she said nothing. She didn't know what to tell them. She didn't know what to report.

The Warden spoke up, "RO?"

"Do my people fear me?"

"Yes. They all believe you are a traitor."

"Will that change?"

They did not answer for a few seconds, but when they did their voice was more grounded, "That is not our concern at the moment." There was another pause. "What do you have to report?" Again, she did not answer.

The Warden let their silence last. But suddenly, the next voice was someone different. It was Haunton. "They were in the Arena. They saved you."

It was not a question. She knew. "None of them died–"

"Do you feel like a Keeper?"

RO's heart raced. She wasn't there to confess, and yet she needed to. She had to. "They believe I can bring my people a better world. In which... we don't have to be soldiers."

"You're not a Malfunction, RO." Her words hit her suddenly. She hated how the title was strung in such a way it made her feel proud. The Chief spoke again, "You have worked your entire life to be a Warden. It has been hard, and like the rest of us, you have suffered. But suffering is good. It makes us stronger. You are surrounded by weak people with weak-minded ideas. Our system works perfectly, and with the Keepers, we will become stronger. Don't you see, RO, you *are* helping your people. You're just not doing it through soft-spoken words. Change can only happen if one is willing to bleed for it. Do you honestly believe the Keepers are ready to die for their cause?"

"Yes."

Another pause, longer this time. "They will ruin us, RO. They will ruin you. And everything you have worked for will be for *nothing.*"

"Do you fear me?"

"I do."

"Because I was a Malfunction? Do you think I will take my revenge?"

"No."

"Why?"

"Because you are not a Malfunction anymore. You are one of us. If you leave, you will never be one of us again." RO felt herself go cold. "There is a reason the Magistrater is trying to bring the Keepers together under her rule. It is because she is trying to change things herself. She is bringing a new life to each world, but only if she has the Keepers. Did you think we would just kill them? We need them alive, we need them to work with us, not against us. They will learn that over time."

There it was, the reason she had called in. She needed a reason to stay with her goal. She had found it. "I did not mean—"

"These thoughts were expected, RO. Get the Keepers to us as soon as possible. Your rewards will be given and your people will thank you for your service to us."

She closed her eyes, "Thank you."

"Bring the Keepers to 'Āina as soon as you can. We are ready."

"I understand."

"Who was the Warden you said was in the Arena? We need a name."

Antony. Antony. Antony. "I don't know their name."

There was another pause. She heard the Chief take a breath, "You are becoming weak, RO. You care for fragile things because someone has started to care for you. But you are not fragile. You are a killer. You are a soldier. You are a monster. You may be a god but you are not one of them. You are better."

RO opened her eyes. She stared at the end of the bed. The Keepers were weakening her. They were destroying everything she had built for herself. This was her path, this was her future, this was her reward. "Antony Rican."

"We will see you soon, RO. Do not forget what you are again." It was not a reminder, it was a threat. RO forced the words into her very soul. She made herself fear them, fear what would happen if she betrayed her people.

She was no Keeper. She was a Warden. She was a spy. She was a monster.

RO heard someone come into the room and she took off the chip, slipping it back into her boot.

Metis came into the room with two plates of food, "Good, you're awake." He looked so happy. He looked so alive. "I found a new job. The Hiraethans need food for both the people and the creatures and I happen to be a very good cook." He handed her one plate and sat down in his chair. "I used to work for this guy named Chop down in Ginish–"

She stopped listening and stared down at the food. He had made it for her. Metis treated her like she was fragile. He would suffer and submit to the Magistrater. Within the next few days, he would be sentenced to months of correction, training, of torment. The Magistrater may have been the ruler, but she was no saint. She would be cruel to him.

"The kids are taken to 'Āina."

He froze, eyes locked to hers.

She looked away, "We put them on a ship and send them through the Magistrater's Tower. They work in a mine. We keep them there and work them to death." She closed her eyes, "I trust you, Metis. I know you will do incredible things one day for your people."

She could see hope in his eyes when she looked back. She had opened up a world of possibilities to him. For now, he would believe he saved them all.

It was the least she could do for all the pain she would give him.

He had one week left before she ruined his life.

Chapter 45

✳

METIS

METIS TOUCHED EVERY item in his bag. He didn't want to forget anything. He had his basic tools, a water canister, three guns, a dagger, a torch, five packets of food, and a medical kit with enough medicine to cure all of them three times over. He was ready for bullets, blood, and bargaining. He was constantly over packing and repacking, as he had been for the past week. He just wanted the mission to go well. Gods, he really did.

Kirana had a sort of terminology for their mission, a name: in and out. They would, quite literally, go in and out. No more surprises. No more details they couldn't see. Yes, they were going into unknown territory, but they were prepared this time. RO knew more about the world than Metis had suspected. Working with Lorenzo and other strategic Hiraethans, she gave them every detail about the world. Though she had never been there before she heard stories and even read reports from Wardens posted there.

"There are two main positions." She looked from Lorenzo to Kirana, "The first is in smaller Warden facilities scattered along the same island as the Magistrater's Tower. The second is in the mines." She glanced up at Metis, "With the Telematics."

"What is this world's purpose?" Lorenzo asked, having been told about the Magistrater's system beforehand. The Keepers had tried to tell him everything they knew, so now he was just as knowledgeable as they were. That was good, Metis was happy it was no longer up to the four of them to decide the fates of their worlds.

RO crossed her arms, "Mining, but I have no idea what they are mining for.

Coal, iron, diamonds, gold, it could be anything."

"How many mines are there?" Metis asked.

Her eyes went soft, and he suspected she knew he was asking to get a better sense of how many kids Metis would find in 'Āina. She clenched her jaw, "Dozens, each across the many islands that make up the world. They are huge, each one about the size of Hiraeth's city. Some might even be bigger."

She locked eyes with Metis before looking away quickly. He could see within her gaze an apology. He wished he could tell her not to feel such guilt. She left the Wardens and the history she had with the Telematic kids. He did not hate her for who was before, it would be too hypocritical on his part.

RO told them everything she could recall about the place, finally being able to speak openly with the Hiraethans. She knew there were other existing places, small villages, or towns scattered across the world, but most of the people lived, worked, and died in the mine beside Metis's people. The Keepers knew they could not get into the mine without a real plan, let alone search the place if the Keeper was somewhere inside. They all decided to scout out the island first and make sure the Keeper wasn't tucked away in a village away from the Wardens. That would be the best-case scenario, but not a likely one.

Everyone rested well in the Arena, putting on lively faces Metis had not had the privilege to see until then. Gwen, though still grieving, was strong enough to begin another trip. Metis noticed that for the first few days she was simply saddened by the loss of her father, hiding away and staying with Gaia and Lorenzo throughout the days, but soon after she seemed to begin to feel guilty. She started seeking out the Keepers and those who had been in the Hiraethan crowd, apologizing openly.

"I'm so sorry." Gwen had whispered to Metis when he went to help her fold laundry with Gaia. "For everything. I don't know what I was thinking."

"Do you remember what I told you about death, back at Bot's Bar?" Metis asked her. She nodded. "Then you know I understand. Grief is grief, and you chose to take action rather than allow yourself to stay in despair."

RO and Gwen's first encounter since the incident happened in their shared room. Metis had brought RO up from the Medical Facility earlier that day and was forcing her to stay in bed a few days longer. When Gwen came in, she had gone to speak to RO directly. Metis had been in the same room, and though he didn't like to eavesdrop, he decided to stay close in case something went wrong.

RO had put up a hand as Gwen started to speak, "Do not."

Gwen took a step back, "I'm so–"

"Do not submit to me."

She looked shocked. These were not the words she had expected from a woman she had nearly killed. "RO–"

RO shook her head firmly, "You are many things, Gwen, but you should never be sorry."

She let out a laugh, "RO, I nearly killed you."

"You were ready to kill me. Own it. Our actions justify who we are in this world. You chose to avenge your parents. To me, that is admirable."

Gwen took her words to heart. She took a breath and straightened her back, "So you don't want an apology?"

"No."

"What do you want?"

"Nothing." She locked eyes with her, "We are even now."

RO had taken most of her time to rest and prepare herself for the trip. She was weak, barely able to walk, but the Telematic medicine he was able to get with Kirana was helping her. Metis knew quite a few pharmacies across the city and spent what little Korts he had left on his datawatch on supplies for Lorenozo's medical facilities. Closer to their departure, Metis allowed her to train with her sword. He studied how she used it, the way it reacted to her. There seemed to be this trust between Keeper and weapon, a sort of bond he could not scientifically understand.

Metis spent most of his time working around the Arena. He fixed the gate, lift, helped bolt doors to walls, and gave the workers around him Telematic tricks. They saw him as a god, and so, trusted his advice. Any task open, he took. Metis worked beside Lorenzo organizing the Arena, he helped Gwen and Gaia cook the food, but most importantly, he watched the kids scattered around the mine. The Hiraethan children differed from Telematic children in the sense that they had true families, and if not, they had communities. They did not have to earn their place in safety, they were taken in simply because they needed a home. He liked that, he wished more than anything that his people would, one day, do the same.

Metis had met quite a few of the kids, sometimes not by choice. They followed him around because he was a Keeper. A few asked him to perform magic tricks, which he did with a small pebble he found on the ground. With a small toss, he made it look like it vanished into thin air, a trick the kids would refer to as the Keeper's Invisibility Spell. Others wanted to know what his world was like, and so he described a magical place made completely of metal. But some did not want magic; they wanted truth. They wanted to know if he would help them. They wanted to know if he trusted his Warden friend. They wanted to know things no child should have to understand. His response to most of them was stories. He told the stories of his world, of the Keepers, of monsters and creatures of the depths. Nothing too childish, he wanted to leave them with something meaning-ful. He wanted to spread the idea that sometimes darkness was the only thing that could harbor light. It was stupid, but it was all he could give them. That and food. He served them larger portions than he gave the adults. Gaia had given him a good talk about that multiple times, but he didn't stop. He couldn't.

Metis felt so close to saving the Telematic kids, and finally, after 11 years, he would be able to make a difference. He knew it would be more dangerous to go into the mine now, but part of him wanted to take the risk. He wanted to free the children and destroy the mines. He wanted to get a cargo ship and send them somewhere safe. But where? Martha could never house so many children, and returning to Telematic felt like a bad idea of its own. So no matter how much he wanted to go in, guns blazing, and free the children, he couldn't, not yet. All he could do was give the Hiraethan kids more food, fun magic tricks, and stories.

Kirana spent most of her time on matters involving the Keepers. She traveled across every dimension as much as she could. As soon as she had healed she was back with another bloody nose and dizzy head. But over time she was getting better. She could jump between worlds seven times before the headache stopped her from running or fighting. Through her travels, she found the last dimension in the in-between.

"It's all so green." She had said with a laugh, "You're going to love it."

Metis smiled, "And safe?"

Kirana nodded, "Definitely not smooth, there are lots of rocks and branches, but no bullets." She took a breath, "I think we're done with bullets and guns."

Gwen walked over and smacked her shoulder, "Stop saying stuff like that." She looked over at Metis, "She keeps jinxing us."

Metis nodded to RO, "Well if there are guns, we not only have a sword made out of fire but also a very powerful gun that could defeat Chief Haunton herself."

Kirana nodded quickly, "We're ready."

Metis spent that morning packing and unpacking his bag until finally he felt ready himself. He swung his bag over his shoulders and holstered his Keeper's gun to his right thigh. On his other leg was a small machete he could use to get through any thick portions of the forest. He took a final breath of rest and comfort, before turning and walking out the door. Kirana and the others waited there for him, all packed and ready in their new Hiraethan clothes with their new Hiraethan tools. They all looked like the very best forms of themselves. Heavy with trauma and grief but finally safe enough to look alive.

Gwen looked at each of them, "We're all ready?" She lingered on Metis and raised an eyebrow, "Have you checked everything?"

"I have."

"Are you sure? You've only checked it a hundred times, after all."

He waved her off, "I just want to be ready for anything we find."

Kirana smiled at each of them, "Let's finish this." She closed her eyes. One of the newest advancements to Kirana's ability to travel was that she no longer had to have everyone holding onto her. She could feel them, apparently, their energy around her own. The world around Metis morphed together and he felt the familiar pull as he was shot down into a new environment. The ride was smooth and almost enjoyable.

The sun was bright against his face. He hadn't seen so much light since they were in the Ward. It burned. He rubbed his eyes and blinked until the light settled into a comfortable glow. The area around him, no longer burning in sunlight, shone brightly with its own green aura. Everything, from the ground beneath him to the very high tops of the trees, was completely green. Not the type from Hiraeth, no, this color was different. It was vibrant, it was the definition of life in a single shade. Everything around him felt lighter, and yet so very grounded to the earth itself. The sky was blue, covered in tangled clouds. Mountains peaked over the trees to reach the sky, layers of clouds covered its tops as it wrapped around miles upon miles of a wide valley. Everywhere he looked he saw what he could only describe as beauty.

Kirana gestured around them with a smile, "I think this dimension is going to be a lot of fun."

She took in a breath and Metis did the same. Gods, the air felt so fresh, so clean. He let out a laugh. He loved the natural world, he could feel its very elements collide with his smoke-filled lungs. It was healing him.

Kirana pointed down the valley, "To review the plan: we walk into the valley to get a lay of the land, scout out the world, and check how the staff glows along the way." She pointed back the opposite way, "If the glow doesn't change I'll take us back here and we'll head towards the mine."

Gwen nodded, "Still works. If anything changes we head straight back to Hiraeth." She looked down at the staff and her eyes widened, "Kirana."

The Keepers down at the crystal as Kirana held it up for them to see. It wasn't glowing as it normally did. No, it was flashing. Every second flashed a green glow.

Kirana looked up at the group, "What do you think it means?"

Metis shook his head, "Something could be wrong."

Gwen waved her hands, "Maybe it's just because they are the final Keeper."

He shrugged, "Maybe it's because the person it senses is not a *full* Keeper."

"What does that even mean?" Kirana asked, but he simply shrugged.

RO squinted at the staff, "Is this not normal?"

"It's usually one solid glow." Kirana shook the staff lightly, "But it's still dim so we'll just need to watch it with more care." She glanced around, before nodding behind them, "Let's get started. It'll be a long walk."

Metis didn't mind the travel all that much. He enjoyed being out in nature, he liked how alive everything appeared, connected to each other in every way imaginable. But, Metis was still used to the smooth metal surfaces of Telematic. The ground was choppy with roots, wet in some places, and thick with grass in others. The environment changed every few minutes as they went deeper and deeper within. Rocks were the common element to hurt them. Whether by making them climb, slide, or stumble, they were there. Metis's backpack was weighing him down, but he knew it would come in handy eventually. It always did. He bent down and collected two pebbles from the ground and tucked them into his bag. One of them was crimson red, the other a deep brown. If he had time he would study them to see the differences between dimensions. He knew that his contributions going forward would be in technology and science. He was not a master in any such thing, but after looking at Lorenzo's organization he realized how little people really knew of even their own worlds.

The further they walked through the forest, the darker it got. The clearing they had landed in brought a refreshing glow to the forest, but now, under the shadows of the trees, it all felt sinister. The whole group became aware of this. They did not panic, they simply acknowledged it and put their hands closer to their weapons.

Metis walked up beside RO further in their journey. She shook her head before he could say a word, "I'm fine, Metis."

He glanced down at her waist, "You sure?"

"You gave me a week to rest. I've never rested so long in my entire life. I'm fine."

He wanted to give her some advice on how to conserve energy or offer a hand as she climbed up a tree root, but he knew she would never accept his help. He just decided to stay quiet and walk beside her. That was all he could do, be there. Not watching, not worrying, he was her teammate, a friend, and he wanted her to know that.

After walking for a good hour, Metis heard water. They approached it and found a small stream filled with rocks. There was a break in the branches above them and finally light returned.

Gwen sat down on a rock nearby, "Has it changed?"

Kirana inspected the staff again, "The flashing isn't helping. I honestly have no idea."

"We need to get some distance–" As Gwen walked towards the group she suddenly lifted her foot and leaped onto a nearby root. "The vine moved!" Her eyes darted around the floor.

Everyone stepped back and looked at the ground beneath them. Clusters of vines were littered along the floor, but they seemed like just another natural element. Metis leaned closer to one and saw the faintest purple glow. Like something was pumping through it. It seemed... familiar.

"Guys!" He pointed down to it, "This looks like the liquid in that monster."

RO jumped down and moved towards it again. She pulled out a dagger from her boot and sliced it. When she did, the vine let out a soft cry and shifted away at the two broken ends. A bright purple liquid spilled from both ends. The light shifted along its surface, and Metis recognized how similar it was to oil. A fuel.

"It's alive?" Kirana watching it move, "How does that connect to Hiraeth? How did Lorenzo get monsters with the same liquid inside them?"

Everyone turned to Gwen, and she shook her head quickly, "I have no idea where Lorenzo gets his monsters. A few of the larger ones arrived before him, but that's all I know."

Kirana glanced at the staff, "Is there magic outside of the Keepers?"

"Not magic." Metis corrected, "Magic doesn't exist. There's an explanation for this."

"Kirana's right." RO said, crouching over the vines, "Does this all connect to the Keepers, or is something else at play here?"

"Like the Rhodonite?"

Gwen looked up to the staff, "Like the Magestrater."

RO let out a breath, "I don't like making assumptions, but the idea that the ruler was or is a Keeper makes sense."

Gwen pointed down to the vine, "So she did this?"

"The world's only purpose is what is mined, so what does she care what happens to the surface? This could be purposeful for all we know." She put her dagger to the liquid. Nothing happened. "But I am not sure. It is not like she openly told us her plans for each world." RO wiped her dagger against a tree and tucked it back in her boot.

Kirana gestured across the stream, "Let's just keep moving."

Everyone followed as she made her way to the stream, hopping from dry rock to dry rock. The group continued into the forest, moving through the constant trees, rocks, and vines. Metis got hit in the face by a steady rate of three branches per minute. He wiped dew drops off his face and stumbled over a root. Landing on the ground he was met face to face with another one of the vines. He could see now how darker the surface of it was compared to other plants. He could see the liquid flowing with a pulse. It was moving, and before he knew it, it was on him. Pulling away quickly he felt his wrist tighten around his wrist.

He pulled out his gun as he tried to pull it off him, "They're not friendly!"

RO, standing beside him, pulled out her sword and set it ablaze. The vines suddenly shot away from the Keepers and disappeared into shadows.

The forest fell silent.

"Stay away from the vines!"

Kirana remained beside Gwen. She glanced around them as she could find the source of the silence. "There is a clearing behind us, let's stop there and make a plan."

RO spun the sword around the area. The fire seemed to keep the vines at bay, for now. Metis nodded ahead to the other Keepers and they moved into a thicker group, RO protecting them with her sword.

Perhaps Metis was too focused on the vines or the darkened shapes slithering along the shadows of the forest, but he noticed too late how unnatural the clearing was. It was a random clearing. No water, no uprooted plants. It was just short grass, surrounded by thick trees, bushes, and vines.

Kirana broke away from the group before he had time to realize how strange the clearing was. She went to the other end of the clearing and held up the staff, "Does that look brighter?"

Gwen, RO, and Metis stopped walking in the center of the clearing. The ground was softer. Their realization came too slow, and suddenly the layer of ground sank with their weight. The group fell with a scream and Metis landed feet first and fell back on his back. He let out a grunt as the metal pieces in his bag hit him.

He looked up and saw Kirana dangling from the side of the hole. Gwen and RO were on opposite sides of the hole but stuck at the bottom as he was. Kirana just managed to climb back over the edge with the staff. Metis tried to get up but he couldn't. His bag was stuck to something, his legs couldn't move. He glanced down and saw what looked like mud all around them. Hot and sticky mud. RO was to his right, stuck with her knees already covered. Gwen was to his left; one foot free, she tried to pull her way out by grabbing onto the roots on the wall. Metis started to panic when he realized how deep he had already sunk.

"Kirana!" He yelled to her, trying to pull himself up.

There was a gunshot, and Metis looked over to see Gwen shooting at something. "The vines!" They were coming out of the dirt.

It was a trap. The vines had trapped them.

Metis slipped off his bag and tried to pull it out. No use. He reached in and pulled Ben E out. The android looked around and let out a gasp, "Sir!"

Kirana ran around the edge of the hole, "What do I do?" She didn't wait for an answer and dropped down above Gwen. She pushed the staff over the edge and tried to reach the Hiraethan, but she was in too deep.

Metis pulled Ben E back and threw him over the hole and onto the surface. With a crash, the android landed and rolled right back to the edge. Kirana ran to Ben E and looked down at Meits, "I'm going to transport us out of here!" She dropped to her knees and held the staff before her.

Metis felt something crawl over his thigh and start to pull him down. He clawed at a slimy vine, ripping it off, but any movement made him sink lower.

"Kirana!" He yelled, "The vines are bringing us down!"

Kirana let out a scream. He looked up to see a vine wrapped around her hand, creeping up the staff and spreading across her entire body. "I can't–"

Metis pulled out his gun and tried to find a vine he could shoot without harming Kirana, but they were all too close to her. He couldn't hit them. "Kirana!"

At the sound of fire, he turned his head. RO had activated her weapon, moving it to the vines around her. They scattered away. She looked to Metis and waved her sword towards the vines around him. It was just enough to send some away.

"Move to me!" RO yelled to him, and gods, he tried, but even without the vines, the mud kept him there, stuck, and sinking. His waist sunk into the mud.

"I can't. RO, you have to climb out. Help Kirana."

Gwen let out a scream and Metis looked over to see the vines wrapping her against the wall. "Kirana!"

Metis tried to rip the vines off of him. Suddenly, a vine shot up from the mud, heading right for RO. She had been able to almost escape entirely, hanging from the roots in the dirt. The fire was helping her, until now. The vine shot to her sword and pierced through her hand. RO let out a scream as she dropped to her knees on the mud, her sword's fire suddenly fading into smoke. It was a miracle she didn't drop it into the mud. Drops of blood slid down her arm. The vines were smart, they knew who posed a threat to them.

Metis felt the vines tighten as he rushed to peel them off. They were well-motivated now and pulled him further into the mud. Suddenly he was chest-deep in the mud and going deeper.

"Ben E!" He yelled, staring up at his android, "Grab a rope! Find something!"

Metis tried to pull himself up with the wall behind him. He grabbed a root, a vine. He pulled himself up and up before it snapped out of his hands. He slammed down further, back into the mud. He could feel it against his neck, his head. Metis looked up, trying everything he could to keep his head afloat. "Kirana!" He could see her, stuck, still stuck. Vines held her, forcing her from the staff. He looked over to find Gwen sinking into the mud, being pulled down and choked by the vines. He caught a glimpse of RO, bleeding, legs caught, chest deep. She looked at him in her panic.

But they were gods. They couldn't die like this.

There was noise above him as the mud covered his chest, building up to his neck. The back of his head was sinking. "Kirana!"

He saw something move. Someone. But Kirana was still in the vines. He couldn't see them clearly, only their figure, only a glimpse. He felt the mud against his ears. "Please!" He could hear himself yelling but he couldn't hear if they responded. He watched the person look down at him, look at Kirana, and step away.

The mud spilled over his face and covered his mouth. Metis could feel the urge to scream fill his throat, but he forced it down with a final breath. He tried to push back up to the surface as he was forced to close his eyes, his ears filling.

This wasn't how he was supposed to die.

Metis wondered if this had anything to do with how much he had longed to live. He had a purpose, a life, friends… family. He had everything. Maybe it was just too much. Selfish, as always. He had caused so many people such horrible pain, of course he didn't deserve the luxury of comfort. He didn't deserve anything for what he did.

Metis felt his lungs start to flatten out, and his heart beat faster as if it would help him survive. Deep down, Metis started to accept such a fate. He hadn't expected to live so long anyway. He had set the bar to age 14. That was when he pictured himself dying. Of course, at the hands of the Master. Perhaps in the old shop in the Master's chair. Gods, that chair. His fate, his end. Not some puddle of mud. Not some tar that filled and flattened his lungs. He had always pictured his body in the Telematic waters, sinking, drowning, filling the space with the bodies of all the other forgotten people. Victims. His victims.

He felt so far from them, and guilt filled his soul as he realized he would never have made up for what he had done.

His life would end with what he considered to be the beginning.

Chapter 46

KIRANA

KIRANA TRIED TO focus on the staff, on the in-between, or at the very least, her Keepers, but the vines tightened around her and suddenly she could barely move. Every time they were in a dangerous situation, Kirana was the one stuck in need of saving. She was unconscious, bleeding, captured, or stuck in a fight she could never win. She had been taken down by some *vines*. She sat there and watched her team sink into the mud. She sat there, like a fool, as she was pulled away from the staff.

Some god she turned out to be. Powerless little Permidian.

Something swung before her eyes and she flinched back against the vines. She forced her eyes open and saw a blade between two cut pieces of darkened plant. The vines writhed and tightened their grip around her. She winced and gasped out in pain. She yelled to whoever it was before her, "Help them!"

Kirana felt something pierce her skin and for a moment thought it was that same blade, that whoever had found them was not a friend. Gods, Kirana just wanted a friend. Why were there so many people with hate? Why would they choose to feel that way when love was still, and always, an option? But looking down at her arm she saw it wasn't a blade, but the vine, a thorn, pumping the strange purple liquid into her own body. Darkness crept in from the corners of her eyes. The vines around her dropped and the stranger grabbed the blade to attack more vines before her. She took in a breath and collapsed to the ground. She couldn't move. She was fading. The last thing Kirana could see before the darkness filled her mind was a group of people with torches, rope, and three bodies covered in mud.

Her Keepers.

Kirana had felt so ready for their next mission. She had finally felt like a god in Hiraeth, like the leader her team deserved. She had found this newest world, she had made the plan, and yet there she lay, defeated by vines and strangers. She wanted to be a god, a true powerful god. Jumping through the dimensions was important, but it was just transportation. She was not their pilot, she was their leader, and yet, they surpassed her in everything. She just wanted to keep them safe. She didn't want to be diplomatic, she wanted to be powerful. She wanted to be exactly what they called her. The Permidian god. Not someone weak, or fragile, or naive.

In her sleep, Kirana felt sick. Her mind faded away from reality and pulled her in and out of something imaginary. Eventually, it let her stay there.

In her sickened dream she was in Permidia. Tia was standing over a pot of a bright red soup, stirring. Just stirring. Dinner was almost ready. Kirana was sitting at the countertop, waiting. She could hear the breeze outside an open window, the smell of flavors she never bothered to put a name to, the quality of breath from the perfect air, the hum of grass blades against one another, the soft breath of her sister. Home with Tia. Her life. Her love. She wanted to stay there, but her thoughts were returning, and the dream was starting to fade.

Kirana tried to stay there a little while longer, "What are you?"

Tia stopped stirring. "What kind of question is that?"

"Was I your captive, or did I leave you in our cage?"

She turned and looked at Kirana. Her eyes were bloodshot, and bleeding.

Kirana reached out to her sister when suddenly her head felt shot with pain. It didn't feel like a dream, it felt real. She fell to her knees, landing on a hard glass surface. For a moment she looked around and saw only darkness, but within one blink she was sitting on a bed of water in a galaxy.

She was in the in-between.

She took a breath. She could taste the air. It was heavy, it was thick. She wasn't floating, she was on a real surface.

"Hello!" She tried to stand but her body kept her down, tired. So very tired. She didn't know what would come from falling asleep in a dream but she didn't want to find out. She kept her body up, arms shaking, falling towards the inches of water she would drown in.

Kirana felt something hit her hand. She grabbed it and pulled it out of the water. The staff. Her staff. She pulled it back as the white crystal glowed around her.

But then the crystal got darker, dimmer. Black.

She felt her energy return.

"You've done so well."

Kirana looked up to see something before her. Maybe it was her dream, but the image before her was not a person at all. It was a figure of shadows and light. Particles and the spaces between creating the shape of a human.

She knew as soon as he spoke who it was: the Voice that called her to the staff.

He wasn't the staff or Rhodonite, after all, he was something else entirely.

She smiled at him weakly, "It's you." She looked around, "Did I die?"

"Not yet." He waved a particle hand over the crystal and it turned white.

Her energy vanished. "What's going on?"

"Your soul is with me, Kirana, I will return it soon. But I need you to do something for me. I need you to prepare yourself."

"I don't understand." The world was getting darker.

"You will. Soon. I will meet you after."

"Meet—"

"Everything will be explained. Listen to her. She does not lie."

Kirana could barely stay upright. Hands to her side she tried to keep her head from falling into the water, "Help—"

"Listen to me when I command you."

"What?"

"I will show you power."

"Help—" Kirana's head dropped and she fell into the water. Then she kept falling, deeper into the water, barely able to keep a hold of the staff.

Kirana shot up with a breath of air, real air, as she woke up. She coughed and fell off whatever thing she had been lying on. She groaned, face-planted on the floor. She stayed there for a moment, cheek against a dirt-lined floor. She glanced around and found her eyes blurry and unfocused. She saw two figures nearby and, with as much energy as her body could muster, forced herself to stand back up, backing away from them both. "Who are you?" She crashed into something and nearly fell back down again.

"You're safe, child." An old woman's voice.

Kirana blinked until her vision returned, "I'm not a child." She took a breath and let her eyes focus. When she opened them again her vision was back. The two strangers were similar in looks, they could have been related. Golden brown skin with black wavy hair. One of them was old, winkles weighing down her entire body except for her smile. She wore a cream dress with a woven vest over her torso. The other person was younger. Skinny and long, their hair went down to their shoulders. His outfit was more practical for work. Pants, a baggy cream shirt, and a large apron. Like the woman, he wore wristbands from the same material as her woven vest. Kirana squinted and realized their common attire looked very similar to the vines the Keepers had encountered.

The younger one asked her, "Are you okay? How do you feel?"

The room was dim, even with the windows open. With wood walls, a thatch roof, and a stone fireplace it felt almost primitive. She had been lying on a table, tools hanging above where she had been. She patted herself down for wounds, "What did you do to me?"

The elderly woman shook her head, "We healed you. Please sit."

She eyed the tools against the bed and stepped towards them, "Who are you?"

Neither of them dared to come closer to Kirana. The woman put her hands up gently, "My name is Mele. This is Keaka. Are you a Keeper?"

She didn't know whether to lie or not, but they had her staff, and her team, "Yes. I am a god."

The woman laughed, "Are you now?" She walked behind a wall, out of Kirana's sight. When she returned she was holding the staff, "We thought you were Wardens at first. Until we saw this."

Kirana rushed forward and grabbed the staff, "Where is my team?"

"*Gwen* is outside getting a tour of the village. The other one is with the man." Kirana squinted at her and the woman shrugged, "She wouldn't tell us her name."

Kirana rolled her eyes at RO's Warden mentality. "She likes her privacy." She looked around the room again and spotted the door out. Both of the people followed her gaze and begrudgingly moved out of her way. Kirana realized then how blunt she had been to them, and shook her head quickly, "I'm sorry. Thank you. You saved us... why did you save us?"

"Again, we thought you were Wardens. Turned out you were the complete opposite."

"You set up that trap–"

Keaka shook his head quickly, "The vines do that themselves. We heard screams and wanted to check if it caught a few Wardens."

"Why?"

Mele gave the other a joking look, a sort of inside joke Kirana didn't catch, "They have guns, metal, medicine... items we can't get here." Kirana looked back to the tools beside the table. They were made out of metal and stood beside white bottles and tubes, very Warden-like in their design. Mele gestured to the door, "It's been a busy day but everyone is excited that you are here. Gwen is on a tour with our Ali`i, Kaiko."

"Your what?"

"Chief." Keaka answered, "The village head."

Kirana nodded and forced a short smile to her face. She didn't want to offend those who had saved her, but she needed to find her team. "Thank you." She moved past them and walked out of the building.

Kiraana had always considered Hiraeth to be rural, but the town before her practically lived within nature itself. Every house was built from dark wood or stone. Every roof was built from dead leaves and grass. The roads were dirt, and torches littered every wall. The people wore outfits she had only seen in Permidian history books. Warden equipment stood out among the wood, hide, and stone. She saw a few men walk by with guns wrapped around them, eying Kirana but not pulling out their weapons just yet. She saw crates and boxes like the ones back in the Ward beside the buildings. She saw a few outfits that matched Warden jumpsuits, cut up and redesigned to better fit the village style.

Kirana had never seen a place so alive. The people were all busy across the village. Kirana saw mothers hurrying children down the dirt roads, colorful blankets in hand. She saw two old women sitting outside a house on a woven mat feeding flowers, nuts, and leaves together into long strands. She saw grown men with their pants rolled up to their knees, mud lining their bare feet as they gingerly greeted a woman passing by and quietly celebrated with each other when she turned away. Kirana saw a group of young girls wearing white dresses run towards the stone wall and rush to push the gate open.

Kirana walked through the street, keeping the staff out to see their reactions to her. From what she could tell, the people were more curious than afraid, and for some reason that didn't sit with Kirana well. She didn't have much experience with kind people. Almost everyone she had met so far had either tried to kill her or tried to kill her at first and then forgave her. These people had saved the lives of the Keepers. She needed to respect that, but what if the strange new people were out to hurt them? What if they had powerful guns and bombs and Kirana lost one of her Keepers? Permidia was perfect, and everywhere else had broken pieces. The village was simple and no match for the Wardens, but the people looked happy and safe. That felt wrong… like they were lying. Kirana hadn't realized how much her journey had affected her until that moment, when suddenly she did not want to search for connection. In fact, she feared meeting new strangers.

Kirana walked around the entire village and, with no sight of Gwen, walked to the gate to look around outside. The village, it seemed, spanned much longer than the inner wall. The entire area stretched along a vast clearing in the center of the valley with structures and farms built around a flowing river. She saw people working along square farm patches, some were lined with short plants while others remained large mud pits getting ready to be used. On the other side of the river were what looked like more walls, only there was nothing inside but more small stone structures. Closest to Kirana was a gathering of people, most of which were seated on the ground in front of a long stretch of food. Plates of meat, birds, fruits, purple pudding-like food, and items Kirana had never seen before were passed from person to person. Not too far away was a soft melody of music being played from drums and feathered objects. The girls from before were lined in front of a woman wearing the same white dress, a pink flower in her hair.

"Good morning Kumu!" They said together, laughing and smiling up at their teacher.

The woman greeted them and Kirana watched from a distance as they started to dance. The girls, knowing the movements already, followed the woman as a man sang for them using words Kirana had never heard before.

Kirana spotted Gwen talking with a man, watching the dancers with him. Ben E rolled around at her feet, looking up from the dancers to the man, listening in on their conversation. As Gwen looked over, she spotted Kirana and her face beamed with joy. Gwen muttered something to the man and ran up to her, Ben E following quickly. Kirana let out a breath, finally able to breathe easily knowing Gwen was safe, and ran to her.

Gwen grabbed her and pulled her into a hug, "Oh thank the gods! I was so worried."

Kirana closed her eyes and put her face against her shoulder. It felt like the first time she had taken a breath in hours. There was a difference between Gwen and Tia, she didn't know what it was, but it was there. Maybe it was because of all the danger, but when she could feel Gwen near, by touch or by heart, she felt safer. With Tia, it just felt so simple, but with Gwen, it felt… stronger.

Gwen pulled away too soon and forced Kirana to look at her, "What did the vines do to you?"

"They just surrounded me, and the staff." She suddenly remembered her dream, with the Voice and his warning. Maybe it wasn't the village she should have been worried about.

"Kirana?" Gwen caught her fears.

Kirana thought about telling Gwen about her dream and the Voice. It would be a strange conversation. She would have to confess that she had first heard him in the Ward, that he had told her to sacrifice herself, rather than Kirana instinctively saving Gwen on her own. His guidance just felt so… personal, only to her. For now, she would keep it that way. As the leader, Kirana needed pieces of information only she knew.

Ben E tapped her boot and when she looked down he pushed his little arms up and smiled, "Hello!"

"Hello Ben E." She tapped him on his head.

Gwen laughed at the android, "He's quite popular." She gestured around at the people, "When they took us here he was the one who explained who we were and that we weren't a threat. He was just playing with some of the kids over there." She pointed to the young dancers.

Ben E smiled again before picking up one of his wheels and frowning, "I do not like the mud."

Kirana looked around at the village, wiping the bottom of her nose instinctively but finding no blood, "Are these good people?"

"Yes. They've been telling me about the Keepers. We're not gods to them."

Kirana let out a laugh, "Excuse me?"

"We're historical figures." Gwen smiled up at Kirana, "They have preserved their history so well that they know the Keepers were not only real people, but those who ruled over their world. In Hiraeth, we're gods because we're powerful legends. Here, we're leaders because we're from historical events." She pointed to the woman leading the girls in the dance, "She was telling me stories that were passed down for generations. These people are storytellers and survivors. That dance is a story." Gwen took a breath and watched for a moment, before looking back up at Kirana, "It's everything I have wanted for my world."

"Stories?"

"Freedom." She pointed back to the man she had been with who remained where she left him, glancing over now and then to study Kirana. "That's Kaiko, he's their Chief. This village has taken decades to build but it started with the people who escaped the Wardens."

Kirana glanced down the valley towards where the mine would be, "There are no Wardens here?"

"Not directly after them. Not watching them or reinforcing their working hours. The forest is dangerous, so unless the Wardens *need* to kill these people for whatever reason, they're safe." Gwen looked up suddenly and pointed into the forest, "That reminds me, they have this way of harvesting the vines that protects them from being hunted like we were. They dry out the vines and put it in their clothes and accessories."

"Where did the vines come from?"

Gwen nodded quickly, eyes wide as she bit down a smile. While she spoke, she gestured and shaped her explanation, "Kaiko was telling me that the Wardens poisoned their land. He says there are other plants like the vines, and worse, *animals*." She smiled, "This is where the Arena's creatures come from. Lorenzo probably bought them from the Wardens or stole them from a shipment, but they're from here."

Kirana smiled down at Gwen, "It's nice seeing you like this."

Gwen put her lips together, her smirk shifting to the left side of her face, "When we're not being chased by soldiers or gang members, I'm a happier person, Kirana. Don't forget I love history, and besides, this world is too bright for me to not enjoy it." Her smile faded for a moment and she put a hand on Kiranan's arm, "I thought you would be more excited. Don't you want to see these people, talk to them?"

Kirana realized she had no intention of making friends or even engaging with the people of 'Āina. The only person she wanted to see and talk to was Gwen and the rest of the team. She pulled Gwen's hand off her gently, "I'm just nervous. I couldn't save you guys back there and–"

Gwen shook her head, "None of us could. Don't blame yourself for that."

"Where are Metis and RO?"

Ben E let out a shudder and shook his head. Gwen picked him up and her expression hardened, "Metis nearly drowned, they're trying to wake him up but he's... hurt, Kirana."

Kirana hadn't been expecting such an answer. "Where is he?"

"He's resting. RO is staying at his side. I tried to stay as well but it was pointless. RO stayed and I got the tour with Ben E." She started to walk to Kaiko, gesturing for Kirana to follow. "I've told him about our journey and who we are. It was a long conversation but he knows about Permidia, Hiraeth, Telematic, and the Ward."

"What about RO." Kirana whispered.

Gwen shook her head, "If you want. It's up to you."

Kaiko turned around as they got closer, and his eyes scanned over Kirana before falling upon the staff, still blinking green. He was a large man, his figure filling his clothes and allowing him to tower over both of the Keepers. Out of all of the people there, most of whom had flowers in their hair or around their necks, he had the most color. On his head sat a crown-like array of flowers, feathers, and leaves, all connected with a long stand of the vines.

Kaiko smiled down at Kirana, eyes darting back to the staff, "Gwen has told me so much about you, and the staff." He let out a loud laugh, one that fit his wide physique, "May I?" He extended his hands out and she handed the staff over. Kaiko held it up gently, not letting himself touch the Rhodonite but holding his fingers a few inches away. He reminded Kirana of Trent. Kaiko smiled down at the staff, "I have heard about this staff for so many years."

Kirana nodded, "The Keepers have returned, that's why we're here, we're after the Keeper of this world."

He looked over, his eyes wide, "The Keeper is here?"

Gwen shook her head and gestured to the Rhodonite, "The glow is still dim, that means the person we are looking for is still a distance away." She turned to Kirana, "Kaiko says there are more villages across the island. They're not connected but some routes are less dangerous than the one we took."

He nodded, "If you are in search of the final Keeper we can help you find him or her. At the very least, we can get you on the right path."

"Thank you." Kirana told him, "We would love any help you can give us. In return–"

He waved his hands, "I know about the Keepers, Kirana. You do not need to give us anything. So long as you survive and find our Keeper, all is replied. In fact, I think we owe you more than you owe us."

Kirana glanced around the village, "I'm sorry to ask this, but what have the Wardens done to your people? You all seem so… healthy, I suppose."

Kaiko sighed, "My mother raised me in the mines. I don't remember much, I was very young when my sister and I escaped with a group of survivors and ran into the mountains, but I remember those I left behind." He gestured to the village, "There isn't much left for us here. There are so few of us left in our land. The Wardens keep us so far back on the islands that we haven't seen the ocean in decades." He looked longingly through the forest, "They took half of our culture and produce, leaving our surviving people damaged and afraid. I would like to see my people back where they rightfully belong. Free, both from the mines and from the Warden's control."

"That's why we are here, to free you from the Magistrater's system." Kirana placed the staff beside her, "I am very grateful for your hospitality, and with your help, we can find your people's Keeper and begin the process of freeing all of our worlds."

Kaiko nodded quickly, "I grew up with stories about the Keepers that ruled our world. My mother used to call our Keeper the true Ali'i nui kapu. She would be so excited to know the Keepers have returned." He smiled and gestured to the people behind Kirana eating on the ground, talking and laughing with the music still playing for the dancers. "Would you like to eat with us?"

"Yes." Gwen said quickly and looked up at Kirana, who nodded, excited at the idea of not only learning more about the past Keepers but also eating such a gorgeous meal.

The Voice's warning seemed so far from the Keepers, if it was a warning at all. Meeting the Voice would be a wonderful occasion, and seeing Gwen happy and excited made Kirana want the moment to last forever. The Keepers were safe, for now, and the Voice promised her a good future. One that would give her both knowledge and power.

The Keepers were almost complete. They were so close to the final god.

Chapter 47

RO

RO'S EYES WERE closed. She should have been looking around, not just at the people of ‘Āina and the threats they could pose, but at the very least she should have been looking at the mountains. They were beautiful, captivating in their ability to be a subject in every glance she took. But she could not look at them. She could not look at the people. RO had never felt guilt before now, not really. When she had killed Deran it was there, but she had let it die. It was back now. She didn't want it. It made her feel like she was destroying something perfect. She was not, she was improving it. She was setting a small fire to create a foundation of ash from which the Magistrater could grow. From which the Keepers could grow in the rightful place.

But RO could not look at the world around her. It hurt too much.

She was reluctant to admit that her time in Hiraeth had been good. It felt like something soft, her memories no longer in her head but rather against her heart. She wanted to keep them there, but the guilt kept them at bay. When she closed her eyes part of what was to come vanished and she could remember moments she enjoyed.

RO had enjoyed her time with Kirana in Hiraeth. As RO recovered, she was passed from Keeper to Keeper in case a Hiraethan decided to take another shot at the Warden. RO received aggressive glances, and when she was with Metis he was quick to guide her away or speak on her behalf. Kirana, however, handled the situation differently. Instead of avoiding the Hiraethans, she would walk over and speak to them. Kirana was a passionate, optimistic leader, and through her stories and Permidian perspective, she began to change the Hiraethan's minds. She did not shield her team from aggression, she adapted Lorenzo's society to better fit the Keepers.

"They need your perspective." Kirana would tell RO, "I'm not just going to stand by and let Hiraethans fight for revenge. We're fighting for freedom and peace."

Kirana told RO how she studied the Permidians and now had started conversation with Hiraethans just to see how they reacted to her and ideas from the other worlds. RO couldn't help but believe Kirana had the qualities of a kind leader, someone ready to not only give the entirety of themselves to a cause. RO noticed as the days passed how Kirana seemed to mature, speaking with purpose and working with Lorenzo more often as the voice and leader of the Keepers. She was growing, and if she had time, she would become a true leader of the gods.

RO had enjoyed helping Gwen with the Arena. As a Warden, and as a soldier, she liked to watch the fights. They weren't as gruesome as her own, but the fighters were trained to perform. They did good, and she found herself nearly cheering a few on. Gwen had looked over to find her on the edge of her seat, barely keeping in a shout. She laughed at RO, "I knew you would like this. Lorenzo suggested maybe you can help plan one?" RO had said yes. She shouldn't have, but she did. She sent two volunteers into the Arena, one with a weak bow and arrow and the other with an ax. After a few minutes, the one with the bow started to hit the other man by accident, and suddenly the two of them were fighting each other while the creature ran away. She stood up from the stands and watched with Metis. She laughed under her breath and caught him staring at her. She corrected herself quickly but he gave her a shove, "Your humor is dark, RO." He gave a laugh as the two of them swung and missed each other, "But this is pretty funny." Even the crowd was laughing. None of the fighters died, and neither did the creature. RO liked that. She did not want to, but she did.

RO had enjoyed helping Metis cook, a task she hadn't expected to be so fulfilling. He made it fun, talking to her as he walked around the kitchen. RO had never seen a person so alive while willing completing a task others would call monotonous. Wherever he went he always had a group of children following. Metis put them up on his shoulders and ran down the halls, filling the Arena with laughter.

RO didn't know how to talk to kids, and often their parents were quick to pull them away from her. Metis had tried to include RO, and she was forced to play their little games. But it was… sweet. Soft, weak, fragile. But… They were so happy.

RO forced her eyes open and looked up to the mountains. The plan was to bomb the Keepers. She would slip away while a group of fighters sent down a parade of bombs. No artillery fire, just enough damage to either knock them out or put them to sleep with a selective amount of chemicals. Haunton had promised her the Keepers would not be hurt too seriously. RO needed that promise, but she hated herself for how happy she was to hear it.

"Hey."

She spun in her chair to see Metis leaning against the doorway. He looked weak, but he smiled. She got up quickly and gestured to her chair, "Sit down."

He looked up and his eyes went wide at the sight of the village, "This place–"

"Sit."

He shook his head, "I'm okay, thank you."

"Metis, I swear to the gods I will–"

A man came out after Metis and noticed him stumbling forward. "No no. Sit down." He pointed down to the chair.

"I'm–"

The man turned to RO, "Is he always like this?"

"Always."

Metis laughed at them both and moved to the chair, "Fine! If it'll make you two feel better."

The man went back into the building with a sigh. After they had stitched up RO's hand they had put her on the porch by the front door. They told her to sit and rest, and reluctantly she had. RO leaned against the fence around the porch, looking Metis up and down, "How do you feel?"

"Honestly, I feel okay. Weak, but alive." He looked around the village, "This place is beautiful."

She glanced behind her, "It's rural."

"But the people are kind."

"They don't have any defenses."

He nodded softly as he picked mud off his clothes, "They have good medicine though. From the Wardens?"

"From what I could tell they have a lot of Warden equipment. Good weapons as well though I doubt they have a steady stock of ammunition. They have their protection from the vines."

"The living vines." Metis leaned back in his chair, "Did they tell you where the vines came from?"

"From what I could tell they have been here for a long while. Their origin is unknown but I think it's a good assumption that it has something to do with... the power of the Keepers?"

Metis waved his hands in the air with a smirk, "*Magic.*"

She bit down a laugh and rolled her eyes, "Maybe. But this is linked to us. If the Magistrater is an evil version of the Keepers then maybe this poison is an evil version of our power." She stopped speaking after that. These ideas were wrong, she had remembered that. The Magistrater was not evil. The poison had a purpose, just like everything else.

Metis leaned back in the chair, "Honestly, after we find the Keeper I want to start studying the worlds. I tried to work on the weapons but I didn't have the right tools." He had a thought and looked down at his empty holster.

RO took his gun out of her holster and held it up, "Do you think you can learn more?" She threw it to him and he quickly slipped it back to his side.

"I think someone has to. Why not the *Telematic* Keeper?" He pointed to himself before gesturing to her, "Of course, you can always help me. You know more about the worlds than anyone else."

That was true. She felt her heart fall and she tried not to show it, "Of course."

There were footsteps behind RO as Gwen and Kirana came up the stairs. As soon as Gwen saw Metis, she let out a gasp and ran up the remaining steps, "You're awake!"

He laughed, "I am."

"Oh thank the gods." She put a hand on his shoulder, "How are you feeling."

"I'm okay, just tired." He looked down and saw Ben E in her arms. He took him, smiling brightly, "Ben E!"

"Metis!"

"You alright little guy."

"Dirty." He pointed at his wheels, "I miss metal."

Metis laughed and put him on the ground, "We'll be home soon."

Gwen looked at RO, "We just met with Kaiko. He'd like to meet with the two of you when you get a chance. It shouldn't take as long as it took with us, we explained everything."

"Everything?"

Gwen shook her head softly, "Almost everything."

Gwen trusted her. RO... "Thank you."

Metis stood up from the chair. The Warden wanted to tell him to sit back down but he didn't stumble. He looked strong, weaker than normal, but well enough to stand and walk. "We can go see him now. Why is he meeting with us all?"

"He wants to get to know us." Kirana leaned against the fence beside RO, "He's going to form a group to take us to a few other towns."

Metis's smile grew, "So when do we leave?"

"Within the next hour."

He glanced up at the sky, "We'll find the Keeper today."

Gwen let out a breath, eyes closed but a smile across her face, "We're so close."

RO felt sick. She was pale, she knew she was. She turned away and leaned against the fence to face the town. The guilt was getting to her. It was making her sick. She wanted it to stop. She wanted to stop it. Gods help her.

Kirana and Gwen walked back down the stairs, Ben E following them quickly. Kirana ran down the dirt street with her giddy energy, "We'll come get you after you're done with Kaiko! We're going to look around a bit more!" Gwen hurried after her and caught up in time to grab her arm and slow her down.

Metis moved beside RO, "I'm excited. I don't remember being this excited... ever." He laughed at the thought. She had chosen not to look at him and regretted it when he caught her ignoring his joy. "You okay?"

"I'm fine." She walked away from the fence towards the stairs, "We should–"

Something hit her ankle. Like electricity. Burning against her very skin. She stumbled forward as it pulsed against her bone. It was so violent she stumbled forward and barely stifled a gasp of pain. She realized immediately what it was.

The chip.

"RO?"

"Give me a moment." She snapped as she stumbled down the steps and moved around the building. She ran out of view behind the far wall and ripped the chip out of her boot. It was hot, burning, and pulsing electric blows. She knew what she had to do. She placed it behind her ear. Dropping down to her knees she felt the thing pump electric currents across her very skull.

"Lieutenant." His voice was choppy and calm.

"What?" She hissed back. The pulsing stopped, it burned against her skin.

"We are ready. You have five minutes to get away from the town. We will be sending down artillery fire."

She couldn't find her words.

"Lieutenant?"

"You said it would just be bombs. *Chemical* bombs." She resisted her urge to add in the word *promise*. "I can get them into the forest away from the town, but may I suggest you let them find the last Keeper. The Magistrater needs all of them."

"RO." Haunton's voice this time, "You need to stop talking and listen. Get out of the village within the next five minutes. Do not let a Keeper follow you. Keep them where they need to be."

"But the final Keeper–"

"We will deal with them later."

RO's heart raced, "You don't need them... you're going to kill them."

"Is there a problem?"

She closed her eyes, "No."

"Then shut up and get out of the village. You have four minutes."

There was another electric pulse before the chip fell off of her head. She grabbed it off the grass. It was broken. They had broken it.

It was over.

They were ready.

Four minutes.

RO got up and ran back into the town. RO had to run. She had to move. She had to escape. She had to... She had to.

Metis came down the stairs. He was worried about *her*. "Are you okay? What's wrong?"

Four minutes.

"RO?"

He put a hand on her shoulder and she stepped away from him. "I just need to think!" She started to walk away from him. He started to follow. She needed to tell him to stay back. She needed to keep him there. In the target. He was the target. The Telematic Keeper who cared for all others. The Telematic fool. The Telematic Hero. She looked back and he locked eyes with her. The Magistrater would hurt him, maybe even kill him if he did not obey her orders. She would use him to hurt Telematic and the kids he had spent his whole life protecting.

RO needed to help Metis.

She had to.

RO ran back to him, "You need to follow me."

Three minutes.

He squinted at her, "Why–"

"Metis please!" She grabbed his arm and pulled him down the road. She didn't let them stop. She kept them moving. She ran as fast as she could. She forced him to move faster. They had to escape. She pulled him through the gate. She kept them running into the field. They just had to get away from the village.

Two minutes.

"RO!" He tried to get out of grip and when he did she was ready to pull him again, but he was running with her. Beside her. He trusted her.

She stopped running, "Stop!" She looked up at the mountains. She couldn't hear the fighters, not yet.

"RO..." Metis looked at her, panting hard. He had followed her even after being drowned half to death. He nearly fell to the ground but she caught him, holding him tightly and forcing them to lock eyes.

"Why did you do this? You trust–" She winced, "What if the Magistrater is right?"

He looked at her like he understood. He didn't. "It's crossed our minds–"

"No. What if you're the villain? If you gave her a chance–"

"Why are you saying this?" He looked back to the village, "Did something happen?"

RO's heart was racing. She stepped away from him, "I'm sorry. I'm so sorry." She shook her head. "I didn't–"

"RO." He grabbed her shoulders and forced her to look at him, "We're fine, at least, I think we are. If we're in danger I need you to tell me."

Her heart was racing. What could she tell him? Nothing. She was a Warden.

She was a spy. She was a Keeper spy. She was a Warden spy. She was not a Keeper. She was not a Warden. She was a pathetic little Malfunction girl. She was a disappointment. She was weak. He made her weak. He made her pathetic.

One minute.

She pulled out of his grip, "The system works…"

He looked shocked. Not in realization but from her words. He was shocked she would say such a thing. "It doesn't, RO. You know that."

They stared at each other in the silence, seconds ticking by. This would be as close as RO would ever be to Metis. She felt tears in her eyes but he did not let them fall, she would never. She took in a breath, "I'm sorry, Metis."

Time was up.

The blasting sound of a ship filled the air, and she watched Metis grow cold. He stared at her for a second, a moment of alarm and maybe some sort of understanding. He looked up to the sky and watched two ships come right over the village. A bomber and a fighter.

As soon as Metis saw it he started to sprint back to the town. RO was too slow to catch him. She reached out and stopped herself from running. She needed to stay. She had to stop him. With a scream of guilt, she ran after him.

She had never seen him run so fast. Scream so loud. "Get out! Get–"

His voice was cut out by the engine, then by the explosion. The fighter came by first, and a series of bullets came down upon the village. They weren't traditional artillery ammunition, they were made to start a fire, and within a moment a blaze was sent up over the town.

The bomb fell quickly, right in the center of the village and as soon as it touched the ground it went off in a burst of smoke and force. The smoke nearly reached Metis and RO had to tackle him to the ground to keep him from going inside. He pushed her off him, got back up, coughing, and stepped away from the smoke. "Gwen! Kirana!" RO could hear screams coming from the village. A new ship appeared behind them. Another to their side. They were bringing in soldiers, and soon, Wardens would be scattered across the entire area.

She looked back to Metis to see him running into the village, his arm over his mouth. "Metis!" She ran after him.

He looked back at her, gun drawn. "We need to help the others." He told her, "I'll help the villagers into the forest, you get Kirana and Gwen."

"No." She pleaded with him. "They're gone."

"They're not gone!"

She pulled out her sword. She couldn't let him go in there. His back was to her. He couldn't see how hard it was to decide who to aim the weapon at.

There was a ruffle in the forest around them, and suddenly Wardens were marching forward in armed formations. They looked different. Like the Hira-ethan armor they had camouflage, only this time it was green. Everything was green. Even the glass they wore along their helmet. It was built to withstand the environment and to hide within it. Dozens of them flooded into the town, and ten others approached Metis and RO. They were coming from both sides of the forest, flanking the two Keepers quickly. And yet, Metis didn't back down. He ran back beside RO and put up his gun. His free hand was to the side. Over RO.

He was protecting her.

Was he that stupid? Did he not understand?

The Wardens raised their guns and stopped a few feet out of reach. Ash pulled over them from the fires, quickly darkening the sky as the other Wardens kicked open the gate and ran inside.

Smoke and ash. They were burning the Keepers to the ground.

The Wardens around them were watching RO. They were waiting for what she would do. It was up to her.

Metis lifted his weapon to fire and she pushed his arm down, "Metis don't–" He pulled away from her and tried to fire his weapon. "Stop!" She stepped in front of him, sword raised and ready for him to try and run past her.

The look on his face... He was afraid. Not of her, but of what she had done to them. There was no anger in his gaze, only pain. She had betrayed him. His breath shook, "RO..."

She was trembling. She put her sword up. The ashes fell on her shoulders. She was covered in the darkness. She breathed it in. It was her own. "The Magistrater will help you. Please, don't fight. Please, *Metis.*"

The Wardens started to walk towards him. Metis stepped back and she raised her sword to his head. He stared at her. He didn't say a word.

"Lieutenant?" A Warden waited for her command. She was in command. Chief Haunton was behind this, she knew they were, this was a test of loyalty.

She closed her eyes, "Take him."

"*RO–*" She would never forget the horror in his voice.

She heard a shot of electricity and Metis screamed, falling to the ground. She holstered her sword and turned away.

"Lieutenant RO." A Warden approached her. Behind them, the others started to take out the ash-covered villagers. They were dead. She saw someone move, twitch. She heard a gunshot far off. No, they were being killed. The Warden stepped in front of her, "Chief Haunton put you in command of this mission as soon as your cover was dropped. We are at your command."

A Warden came out with Gwen slung over his shoulder, her unconscious body dangling lifelessly. She wondered if Lorenzo's Guardians would be burned just the same as the village. No, they would do far worse to him... and Gwen's family.

"Lieutenant?"

RO looked back up to him, he was the same ranking as her. From the looks of it he had been leading the mission first. Someone came out with Kirana's body. Someone else held the staff. They didn't deserve to hold such a relic.

"I'm ignoring the Chief's request. You continue your mission as you please."

A ship landed on the opposite side of the grass clearing. She looked down to see two Wardens dragging Metis towards it. They held him like he was nothing.

Through the grief and guilt, something felt... right. She had fought and killed for her place among her people. Had survived years of training and yes, torture. What awaited her back in the Ward was pride and celebration. They would see her as a true Warden, as a loyal soldier. She would have gone through a historical mission and succeeded. Her name would belong in history. That felt good. That felt right.

Betray her people, or betray the Keepers? The Keepers.

Betray her people, or betray those who were kindest to her. Those kindest to her.

Betray her people, or betray those who fought for justice. Those who fought for justice.

Betray her people, or betray her team... her friends? The terrorists.

She walked up the ramp of the ship with the Warden holding Kirana, and as she went into the larger back room a cluster of Wardens were waiting for her. One approached her, helmet off. A blond woman with cold gray eyes, "The Chief sends their regards." Another Warden handed her a stack of clothes and a crate of armor. She numbly took it. "The Magistrastrater has a message prepared for you." The woman told her, with a smirk, "I feel a promotion is on the line for you, RO."

Someone behind her laughed, they didn't even try to hide it. Even the woman in front of her looked smug, somehow, after everything, superior to RO. Antony was wrong, they didn't see her as a terrorist or a traitor. They saw her as a Malfunction.

The Wardens ahead threw the Keepers into three separate cells. They tossed them like bags of crops. Like they were nothing.

The woman tried to speak again and put a hand on her shoulder. RO smacked her hand away, "Get away from me." She pushed past the woman and down the hallway.

She needed to be alone.

Chapter 48

GWEN

GWEN'S HEAD WAS pounding. What just happened? She had been speaking to a group of people, laughing and talking, sharing stories. Kirana was beside her when her head shot up. That's when something blasted her out of her body. It felt like every part of her had been flung across the world. Yet she landed on the wall of the village and fell onto ash and mud. Everything after that felt dark and faded. She remembered pain, fire, and after that, she had no memories at all.

Gwen forced her eyes open, keeping her face planted on the cold floor as she looked around. It was dark, metal everywhere. She winced as she turned her head to the other side. She was greeted with a formation of iron bars. It was a prison. A Warden prison. She gasped through pain and forced her body to move up. She pulled herself up and let herself fall back on the wall, exhausted already. She looked out the bars for something, anything that could help her get out or stay alive. There was a long hallway leading to a metal door. It opened, and she didn't have the strength to hide the fact that she was awake.

A Warden stepped out, helmet on and metal weapon in hand. Not a gun, but some sort of club. They took note of her, glancing once, before passing to the other side of the hallway. She heard a door open, and the sound of conversations filled the space.

Conversations and celebration.

The door shut and silence took over again.

On the other side of her jail cell was another, with someone inside it. Metis.

He was moving, twitching, barely awake. Gwen needed him to wake up. He would have a plan, or maybe an explanation. She banged her arm on the metal wall as hard as she could. The noise didn't reach him.

"Metis." She whispered, voice cracking, "Metis."

He let out a gasp as he tried to get up. His body was shaking, trembling. He moved himself up as she did. Face planted on the beams, he held himself up with the bars. He looked clean, with no ash, debris, or blood on him. His eyes were bloodshot as he studied her quickly, "Are you okay?"

"What happened?"

"RO..." He winced and she could see tears falling as he closed his eyes, "Where is... she?"

Gwen looked further down as best she could. She couldn't see Kirana or RO. She looked back to see Metis eyeing the door the Warden had just left through. The door to other Wardens. And that was when it hit her. Gwen didn't blink, didn't move, couldn't breathe. It was RO. She didn't just see it in the situation, she saw it in Metis's eyes.

A spy.

"Why." Her voice cracked. She wanted to be angry but she felt tears form instead of screams. She had learned to trust a monster. She should have killed her. She should have shot that final bullet. Ended those lies.

Metis's eyes were focused on the ground, reddened and shaking. He looked numb, "I'm... I'm so sorry."

She started to cry, tears of anger and despair flooded down her face. The things RO had seen... She knew where Lorenzo was. Where her family was. She knew their plans. She knew their secrets... Gwen had told her about her mother.

What had RO told her? *We are monsters, but we were once just people.*

Lies. All of it lies.

They were *demons*. Bloodthirsty monsters.

She wanted her dead. She needed her dead.

"Gwen." Metis pulled himself up further, "We need to get out of here." He was recovering faster than she was. He must have not gotten hit during the explosion, he looked shocked but stable. Gwen, on the other hand, could barely move. She had bruises across her body, her head was weighed down by her very eyes. Metis glanced around quickly, and mouthed his words, *Ben E.*

She looked down the hallway with him. She didn't see their stuff. Not their weapons or Metis's android. Painstakingly, she dragged herself to the other side of the small cell. A short distance, but a painful stretch of time. She landed on the bars like Metis had and looked through them as best she could. There, she saw it. Ben E was on a few crates in the back, screen off, and head tilted to the side. Their weapons were nowhere to be seen.

Gwen pointed towards the android for Metis and he nodded. Swallowing and glancing around, he lifted his chin towards their last hope. He raised his voice, "Ben E."

They both froze. They waited for a Warden to come running by, and when none of them did, Metis repeated his call, this time louder, "Ben E." The android let out a twitch, then suddenly shot up as its screen flashed to life. The small android blinked itself away and looked around. It spotted Gwen and looked around for Metis. With a loud crash, it dropped to the floor and rolled down the hallway. Metis reached out to grab him the first chance he got, but the bulky android couldn't fit through the bars.

"Sir!" Ben E was loud. Too loud.

Metis put his fingers to his lips, "Be quiet. Please, Ben E, you can't make a noise."

Ben E stopped moving, perhaps recognizing the stakes of their situation. Metis pointed up to the panel by the door, "Open this door or get us a gun or something to break the panel." His voice shook through every word. His hands trembled against the android. This was one of the first times Gwen had seen him truly scared. The idea that this, more than anything else, was making him so afraid... haunted her.

Ben E looked up at the panel. It was too high for him. He looked around the hallway and rolled down in the new direction. Gwen could no longer see him and watched Metis for his reactions. He had his hand over his mouth, anxiously biting on his index finger. He didn't think to glance over to her once, eyes locked on his android. He flinched once, before nodding softly. When Ben E returned, the ship changed course. It felt as if it was slowing. As Ben E came back with a metal club in its hands the ship shook. They had landed. Metis reached out to take the weapon as the door to the hallway opened.

A Warden stepped inside and ran towards Metis, "Hey!" They kicked Ben E away. Metis tried to pull the club inside, but it caught on the bars.

"Metis!" Gwen yelled in a panic as she watched the Warden and Metis fight over control of the club. Metis was too weak, and within seconds the Warden pulled the weapon back and stumbled into Gwen's cell. She pulled her face back as they slammed against the metal and pushed back towards Metis. They hit the bars with the club, "Get back!"

More Wardens came inside, three of them rushing to Ben E.

"Don't hurt him!" Metis pleaded as they opened the cell, "Please don't–"

A Warden opened Gwen's cell and grabbed her arm. She tried to resist, yelling in pain, but there was no point. They dragged her out of the cell and threw her down the hallway. Metis had found the strength to fight back, slamming the Wardens into the wall as soon as he was out of the cell. Those with Gwen pulled her back as she tried to reach out for Metis and Ben E. One of them swung a club into Metis's stomach, and he curled over as another pushed him to the ground.

"Stop!" Gwen yelled at them, but they only tightened their grip on her, strapping metal cuffs on her bruised wrists.

Up ahead, the two Wardens were chasing Ben E. The android was fast, racing under their feet as they tried to reach down for it. At one point, they gave up, and one of them slammed down their foot on top of him. There was a crack of metal gears and the breaking of the glass screen. But that wasn't enough. Five times, they kicked the android. Five times, until Ben E was flattened out.

"No!" Metis tried to get out of the Warden's grip; he tried to get to Ben E. Gwen was turned around and pulled through the back door. She could hear the sound of a club meeting flesh. She couldn't tell the difference between his screams and sobs.

They dragged her down the hallway and forced her to her feet. She could barely walk. She limped and stumbled, half dragged and half forced to step through pain. When they spun her forward they moved down a ramp out of the ship. They weren't outside. There were no trees, no plants, no grass. They were in a docking bay. It looked like the Ward. She looked back to the ship to see an open gate behind them where 'Āina's world sat in peace. They were in a Warden's facility, but they were still in the same world.

Where was Kirana?

The Wardens were everywhere. Helmets off, they looked happy. They stared at Gwen as she stumbled and fell with each step. Tears were streaming down her ash-ridden face, she knew how defeated she must have looked. Among the heads of gelled hair and smug faces, she saw a different-looking Warden. This one looked like a doctor of some kind, and he was poking and prodding at a Warden with short black hair and a lining of mud down her Hiraethan clothes.

"RO!" Gwen yelled out for her, her voice turning into a scream. Her sudden movement wasn't expected and a Warden almost lost their grip on her, "You traitor! RO–"

She felt the breath leave her body as they slammed a metal club into her stomach. She let out a quiet scream as she curled over and was dragged out of the room and down the hallway. She didn't put up much fight after that. Her final stretch of energy had been used for that scream to RO, now, she simply felt herself giving in. Metis was nowhere to be seen. They were being separated.

By the time the Wardens stopped, they were well away from where they had started. The hallways looked different, they looked darker. They opened one of the doors and she lifted her head to look inside. It was a dark room, not a cell. A room, with a chair.

This was for torture.

"Wait–" She fell back into a hysterical panic, digging her feet back to stop them from going inside, but it didn't stop them. They pulled her inside and pushed her down into the chair, "No. Please–" They unlocked her cuffs and thrust her wrists into the cuffs on the armrests. She pulled at them as the Warden stepped away.

"Please!" She yelled for them as they walked back to the door, "Please I'm– Just let me–"

They walked outside and shut the door.

Her breathing echoed in the room, loud and staggered.

She was alone.

Chapter 49

METIS

METIS HAD RECEIVED Ben E as a gift. An android for a ten-year-old boy. The Master had thought it was appropriate.

"It's a reminder" The Master had told him, a smile coating his words with giddy wisdom, "that gears and switches are just metal pieces, but it's the heart that goes into the work that makes it come to life."

It was a lesson in mechanics. Metis learned so many mechanical lessons from those days spent creating the android, learning from his dear father figure in their free time. Those were some of the best moments of his life. Even if something didn't work, or a metal plate snapped under their palms, the Master never got upset. He had bigger worries. He designed Ben E as a side hobby, but to Metis, he meant everything.

When Metis started hunting children, those good times were brought back in full force. Every child he dragged home, alive or dead depending on what the Master needed, would be a lesson for Metis and the carrier of praise.

"My boy!" The Master would yell, picking him up and swinging him around to show off to Mixer and the other workers. He would sneak Metis sweets, telling him that half were for his own rewards and the other half were for luring children to the workshop. "They're rodents, my boy. You set the mouse trap and let the starving mice justify the risk for food."

Mixer and the Master experimented on the children, cutting them open or putting chemicals in their system to see how they reacted. The Master would tell

Metis how their grand plan was almost completed, that they were on the verge of perfecting the Telematic upgrade. All it took was more children.

Metis was too young to count all of his victims. The Master had taught him to count up to one hundred, but after that Metis got confused and stopped counting altogether. Little pipe children and lost orphans were easy to find. They were hungry, and Metis would bring them back by telling them about his mother's famous meat pie. He brought in groups of young children or grabbed older ones by cutting their ankles or throats.

Metis built such a legacy for what he did for his father that he received a new name from the children from the wasteland.

The Child Reaper.

The Master simply called him Reaper.

"You're a monster." Axel had told him one night, interrupting him from going out on his hunt.

Metis just smiled at him, "Are you scared of monsters?"

Axel was, but he had put on his tough act, "Stop pretending you have a justified cause. The Master is killing these kids for nothing!"

"He's studying them–"

"They're just kids! Little kids! You can stop this. Stop going back to him! Stop helping him–"

Metis stepped forward and Axel leaned away from him, shutting up. "At least I am the Child Reaper. You are nothing."

The Master had been making progress on the project he was designing with Mixer, but time was against them. And so was the law. The Wardens had started to notice the growing number of people with metal limbs. The Master's clients were stronger than the patrolling soldiers, and that was exactly what the Wardens were there to do: snuff out any threats to their own people and steal the inventions for themselves. One of the Master's clients got on a drunk spin and fought a squad of Wardens. He killed three soldiers. Unarmed except for his prosthetic arm. The upgrades were outlawed, and the Wardens shut down the Master's operation. Like most of the laws in Telematic, no one really bothered to keep up with them. The shop remained open, but clients became scarce, and soon none were coming. To forever wear a metal limb meant there was always a promise of a death sentence if a Warden showed up near them. Telematics were risky, but not stupid.

That was when things got bad.

Metis still did not know what the Master's goal was exactly, only that it was an invention that now required a lot of blood and a lot of help. After the Wardens, The Master wanted to keep going. He hadn't finished his project and felt as if he was getting closer. Mixer stayed, but the idea of leaving started to become a reality as the team he had brought with him started to disappear. Soon it was just Metis, Axel, Mixer, and the Master. The Master wouldn't let them stop. He kept going, making Metis go out again and again.

The Master had laughed at Metis, "Can you explain to me why you were able to bring five children three nights ago, and yet can't bring one tonight? Can you explain?"

The legend of the Child Reaper had grown into stories told by worried guardians. People started whispering the name and spreading it everywhere. To most, he was just a story. But to those in the Wasteland and pipes, those he needed to hunt, he was someone to fear. Children started to run from him, all of them ready for his tricks. If he went home empty handed he would face the rage of the Master. All that love would be gone. Metis would stay out and tackle kids to the ground to get them to go home with him. He would kill a few as well, grab scrap pieces of metal and beat their eyes back into their soft skulls, dragging them back on his own.

Mixer had taken him aside one night, away from the Master. Axel sat beside him, thinner than normal, more scared than ever.

"Tech–" Metis had shaken his head, and the man reluctantly corrected himself, "Reaper. I think we should stop."

"Why?"

Mixer put out a hand to Metis's face, trying to feel the bruise on his cheek. Metis pushed his hand aside. Mixer sighed, "It's getting dangerous. It always has been but now… now it's deadly. And it's for nothing. How would you like to leave?"

"Where?"

"With us." Axel locked eyes with him, trying to show how serious the moment was.

Mixer nodded, "Come stay with us. The Master can keep doing all his work and we can take a break. You can take a break from all of this."

"Why?"

The man had closed his eyes for a moment, frustrated by Metis, "This is no place for a child. I should have taken you away from the Master a long time ago–”

“No.” Metis stood up and stepped away, “I'm not leaving him.” He had left then and there, not willing to hear another word.

Back then, Ben E lived in the back of his closet. Metis physically pushed away anyone who wasn't his father. He just wanted the Master to love him, that was it.

This need for love cost Mixer his life. It cost Axel everything he had ever loved. It cost the Master his life work and left eyes. It cost hundreds of little kids their lives.

All because Metis wanted to be loved.

Years later, after Martha took Metis in and raised him until he was around 14 years old, he returned to the Master's shop to see what had become of it. The entire street was a ghost town, the water had risen and left dangerously large puddles on the street. One day, the workshop would fall into the sea and Metis would never see it again. That being said, there wasn't much left to look at, just a half-burned, empty building with a metal cage and two rusty beds. Metis did not know what he was searching for, he just had to see what remained of his past life. In his search, he moved one of the old beds to get to his closet. Since it was so well hidden against the wall, none of the street thieves were able to find it. That was where he found Ben E, unharmed and dusty.

Metis took the android home and fixed him. He added a new personality to Ben E, someone fun and a little blunt at some moments. Metis didn't know what he was doing, he was so young and lonely, and he gave Ben E the personality of his father, a remembrance of the taste of life. Of love. Ben E was not the Master, but he was the closest thing Metis would ever have to him. He could see him within the android's words, programmed with sparks of his personality.

Ben E was the last selfish keepsake Metis had allowed himself to have. A remembrance. A token of the lie. He had indulged himself with a friend.

But no longer.

Metis was defeated. He didn't know what to do. He had trusted RO. Was that foolish, or had she simply toyed with his kindness? The look she gave him felt sympathetic, as if she felt guilty. Good. She should. She had doomed them all, both the people back in Lorenzo's protection and the people of 'Āina. There were children, so many kids, in both worlds. She had sent them to their graves, or maybe somewhere far worse.

Metis hoped she drowned in that guilt.

The Keepers were separated, and yes they had been before, but not like this. Last time, they had the element of surprise and an unhealthy pinch of confidence. Intending to simply make a Warden grab the staff, they had the advantage, they had a quick way out, and yes, they had luck.

Metis had a feeling their luck had run its course.

The Wardens pushed him into a dark room, and his despair turned back into fear. It was a torture room. With a chair. It wasn't like the Master's, but too similar for him not to lose himself to panic. As they pushed him into it and strapped his wrists down he felt a wave of horrible nostalgia fill him. He was almost grateful that the Wardens left him alone as he curled over in the chair. It took him a good 10 minutes to pull himself together, but even after that, his left arm twitched with an aching pain, as if the blade was back under his skin.

By the time thoughts of courage returned to him, the door opened, and some-one new walked inside, escorted in by two Wardens. He had dark gray hair cut short at the top but left a mess around the sides. It was a Warden, dressed in a crisp white jumpsuit and red spectacles. His demeanor wasn't as focused. His eyes darted around, his stance was slouched. He seemed... excited.

He pulled up a chair in front of Metis, "Hello." His voice was too high-pitched for his face. Eye bags and a crazed expression belong to someone with years of in-tensity, but within his voice was nothing but a layer of childish desires, "My name is Doctor Fácil, I will be helping with our... You know." He laughed, "Questioning." He stood back up, returning the chair to its spot beside a tray. Metis hadn't looked around the room, he hadn't wanted to. Though Fácil was a doctor, the tools around him were not for healing. Pliers, crooked knives, long blades made needle-thin, even a corkscrew. To his left, another tray containing devices, mechanical items, and bottles of chemicals was placed across it. A mask attached to a long pipe, two metal slabs side by side, a small unidentifiable gun, rows upon rows of already filled syringes. While Metis sat with the people from the new dimension RO was off planning all of this for the Keepers. Kirana and Gwen were in a room just like the one he was in, and though he trusted their strength he wondered how long they could truly last in such a place.

The door opened again and, this time, the most stereotypical Warden Metis had ever seen entered the room. Chin held high, shoulders back in the perfect position, his glare made Metis catch his breath. His dark black hair was shaved down evenly. His skin was deep black, smooth, and well-shaven. He entered with his hands behind his back, and one of the two Wardens brought over a chair for him to sit in front of Metis. He grabbed it and pushed it closer so the two of them were just two feet apart.

He locked eyes with the Keeper, "I am Colonel Harris. You will answer my questions truthfully." His voice was deep, not loud but powerful. Metis glanced down at the chest of his armor. There were barely any armor pieces at all, and the chest plate was marked with many symbols proving that the man was very high ranking, "If you do not, you will answer to the doctor." Fácil came back into view with a small wave. "He may look like a laughing fool, but he is not smiling because he likes your company. He likes to inflict pain. Don't you, Doctor?"

Fácil snorted a laugh from behind them.

"Answer the questions, and you will not be harmed. The Magistrater has asked for you to remain whole, and alive. But we will get close to that border between death and life if you rebel against us. Tech."

Not his name.

"Or would you rather be called Metis?"

Metis pulled back in the chair. He didn't answer.

"Our little spy told us you were called that instead–"

"Where is she?"

Harris did not smile, "Do I sense anger or sadness? It seemed out of all of the Keepers you two were the closest." He gave a small chuckle, "Shame." The man snapped his fingers and one of the Wardens behind him came over with a screen. The questioning was starting. Fácil moved around Metis as the Warden glanced through the screen. The doctor grabbed Metis's arm and placed a patch on his right forearm.

As he moved around him he playfully tapped the scar on his left. "I have some questions about this but we can have that conversation later." Metis grew very cold at his words.

Harris put the screen down and looked up at him. Metis kept his eyes on the ground. "Tell us what you know of Lorenzo's organization."

Metis vowed he would not answer, but rather took a moment to look within him and find a vault deep inside himself. He would keep his answers there.

Lorenzo had trusted the Keepers with his secrets, he would not give away anything, even if RO had already shared them all. Metis was a Keeper and it was his duty to hold the secrets. But he was also a man who had once been selfish, who had taken everything from everyone to stay comfortable and loved. He would not do that again. No matter what happened, he would remain a Keeper.

"Do you not know?"

Still, he did not answer.

Haris went still, "Look at me when I am speaking to you."

Metis didn't move.

"A different question then?" The Warden was getting angry, and impatient, "Where is Lorenzo's organization hiding?"

Why were they asking him these questions? RO knew all of them. Was she not telling them? No, she would, but maybe they were just making sure she was telling the truth. If their answers lined up then they would get the whole picture. Metis could not allow that to happen.

"Where–"

"Where did your mother find someone ugly enough to–"

Harris slapped him across the face. He stood up and tossed the chair away. "Phase 1." He was speaking to the doctor.

"Wait," Metis said. The Warden looked back. "It's in the city." Metis looked up and locked eyes with him. He didn't have to fake a terrified expression, "They're hiding as a shop. They're hiding in the city. I swear."

Harris paused for a moment as the doctor worked on something behind them. After a moment, he took a deep breath, "Is he lying?"

"Yes."

Metis felt his heart race. The pad on his forearm was a lie detector.

Harris nodded, "The subject seems to not understand that when I ask a question, he must tell the truth. Can you convince him to tell the truth?"

Metis had been in a situation like this once before. Pikko was this small gang leader, a cook who liked his clients to stay higher than a ship. Metis stole from them. Once. It was just to get some of their products. He didn't like to take drugs, not after a horrible day in the clouds and a horrible night filled with nightmares. He just wanted to sell it. After getting it out to the public he was knocked out on his way to Bot's Bar. When he woke up he was in a dark alley, surrounded by

Pikko and his crew. All of them were high, and all of them were furious. They beat him up until he gave them the money he had earned. He had lied about what he made and only gave up 25% of what he earned. They were easy to fool; he lied about his name, his age, where he lived, and the gang he was a part of. All lies, and they fell for each one.

The Wardens would never be so foolish. They had every detail prepared for him. It was only at that moment that Metis realized what was in store for him. He realized that the Wardens were not going to keep him healthy or even fully alive. They were going to break him and leave him half dead for the Magistrater.

The doctor came up beside him, leaning so close to his face that Metis could feel his breath as he spoke, "You know, they asked me to go easy on you for the first few rounds. So I would just like you to remember how much worse this could get." He gave a small laugh and dug something into Metis's arm. It was a blade, long and skinny. It was blunt. He slowly lowered it into his forearm. Metis tried to move, trying to get his arm away from the knife, but every movement added a new path for it to cut. He let out a whimper of pain but refused to scream. He had this type of pain before, only on the other arm. This was nothing compared to that. The doctor was not carving out his flesh or pulling out muscle. He reminded himself of that. He had to remember that.

When the blade hit the armrest of the chair he pulled it out, and Metis let out a gasp, clenching his teeth and shutting his eyes.

"How many people does Lorenzo have in his little army?" Harris asked from the back of the room.

"Fuck you!" Metis's breath staggered and shook, his voice cracking. He had forgotten to stay silent, too lost in his bleeding arm to think any further.

Harris walked back to the chair and grabbed his face, pulling him close, "You are nothing but a Telematic piece of shit. Don't forget who you are talking to."

Metis pulled out of his hand.

"Would you like a pass on that question?" Harris grabbed the screen off of the tray, "Perhaps something more interesting. Something worth a stronger punishment."

The doctor let out a small chuckle, running around Metis like a child finding a new toy.

"What is your real name?"

"It's Tech," Metis answered honestly. Because that wasn't a lie. He was telling the truth, it was his real name. The Master had once called him that. It was his first name, a temporary one, but as real as any name could be.

"Truth." The doctor said, and Metis let out a breath of relief.

"Good. We are getting somewhere." Harris pulled up the chair and sat back down, further away this time, "Do you see how easy this is?" He paused to look up at the doctor, "Though you are making Fácil very disappointed. He was ready to have some fun."

Metis looked down at his arm. There was so much blood. He didn't remember there being so much blood before. He barely remembered anything. He wanted to know, to understand, that this wasn't the most pain he had experienced.

"Where are you from, Tech?"

"Telematic."

"Where in Telematic."

He didn't know what to do. He couldn't tell them everything, but better it be about him than about Lorenzo, "I grew up in the pipes."

The Doctor sighed, "Truth."

"Did Gwen grow up with Lorenzo?"

Metis didn't answer.

Harris looked back up, "Did we go too fast?"

"What if I said I don't know?"

"Lie."

The Warden smirked, "It's sweet, how protective you Keepers are. But it's useless. The Hiraethan will tell us much more than you will. She was already pleading with us as soon as we put her in that chair." Metis glared at him, breaths hot and heavy. He wanted to attack the Warden, he wanted to get up and attack. Harris could see his anger. He laughed, "Now that's interesting. You know, you're not like any Telematic I've ever met." He stood up and leaned closer. He whispered, "You'll tell me why soon."

No...

Harris stood up and walked away from him, "I will be back when he is ready to talk. And if this pain does not work, we will just try something else." He stopped at the door, already half outside. He looked back to Metis with a sudden smile, lips curled into something sinister, "If he doesn't care for himself perhaps he will care what we do to the Hiraethan."

"No!" Metis leaned forward in the chair. He forced himself back, "Please, she doesn't know anything. She never knew Lorenzo–"

"Lie–"

Metis turned to the doctor, "Say *lie* one more time I dare you!"

Harris indulged himself with a laugh, "You make this too easy."

"Please!"

He shut the door.

Metis had given away too much. Gods, he didn't know what to do. He needed to keep the others safe but to do that he had to give away the safety of Gwen's people. Her family. He was making choices he had feared he would one day have to make. Why couldn't they just hurt him and leave the others alone? That's all they had to do. He would take the pain. It didn't matter how terrible, he would take it all. The mere idea of Harris or Fácil hurting Gwen or Kirana was horrible. And it would be his fault.

No… this time it wasn't. This time, he wasn't the cause of it. If Gwen or Kirana were hurt it would be on RO, not him. She killed Ben E. She was hurting Gwen and Kirana. She would soon be the cause of Lorenzo's downfall and the Hiraethan's deaths. This was one of the only moments in his life that Metis allowed himself to not take the blame. A hatred for the Warden grew in him, and the desire to forgive her was quickly washed away.

The blood was on her hands this time, not his.

The doctor bent down beside Metis, "Finally, we're alone."

Something sharp touched under Metis's chin. A round dagger, so sharp the tip was already digging into his face. His head was turned to face the doctor.

Fácil smiled, "Let's have some fun."

Chapter 50

✳

KIRANA

KIRANA PULLED HER hands up as if somehow she could break the iron cuffs. Her legs were fastened to the legs of the chair and her wrists to the arms. The room was so very dark, dim enough only to show her how small the space was. It didn't feel like a cell but a box, a place to store her.

Kirana barely understood what had happened. One moment the team was laughing and celebrating a due victory, and the next she was blasted into the sky and then sent down on top of screaming, burning people of 'Āina. It all happened so fast. The next thing she knew she was waking up in a metal chair in a small dark room. Kirana didn't know whether to start crying or screaming for her team. She didn't know whether to give in or pull at her hands until she bled. She didn't know if the Voice had tried to warn her of this moment or something worse to come. Kirana hadn't even seen a Warden yet, she had been captured and no one had bothered to tell her how or show off their victory over the gods. Kirana thought of Gwen, stuck in a metal chair or somewhere far worse, and tears started pouring down her face as she let her hands rest on the metal cuffs.

After a minute in silence, the door to the cell opened.

Kirana flinched at the sight of three Wardens in a silver hallway: two soldiers and Chief Haunton. At the sight of the Chief, Kirana pushed her body back and stiffed, as if she could preempt the pain the Wardens would surely give her.

The two soldiers stayed back and Haunton walked inside, her movements flowed and relaxed. The door closed and she walked through the dim room right up to Kirana, getting down on her knee, "This is not the end for you, Kirana. This is your beginning. We are not erasing the work you have done to bring back the Keepers, if anything, we are happy you got a taste of life. It will do you good when working with the Magistrater." Haunton reached out and wiped the dust off of her shirt. It took everything Kirana had not to writhe at her touch.

Kirana took a staggered breath and forced confidence into her words, "Where are they?"

"We are asking them a few questions. We will keep them alive, Kirana. There is no need to panic. Even if we have to make them bleed for valuable information, we will not kill them." She rubbed her gloved hand as if to get rid of any ichor Kirana's collar could have left behind, "I apologize for all that has happened. Like I said before this was never supposed to happen. I am glad you're here, finally, and without any means of natural escape. May I list out what will happen in the next hour?" Kirana didn't respond so Haunton went on, "The Magistrater is ready to explain everything I have been so reluctant to say. She will be arriving through your mind. She will be taking you out of this world and into a small world she can control. It's not a dimension, per se, simply an in-between." Kirana felt herself grow pale. "This is to ensure that she can show you both her mercy and her visions."

"She has no mercy. You're villains."

Haunton leaned back away from Kirana, "We may act like villains, Kirana, but we do it out of the kindness of our hearts. I beg you to see beyond what your new friends have been showing you. When you speak to her you will see why everything is the way it is. The system, Permidia, the Keepers, *you.*" Haunton stood up, "In the end, the true villain might just be the girl who jumped one dimension too far, and decided to start a war." She shook her head, "After all, there were many chances for you to slip away. One might call it a case of bad leadership."

Kirana felt sick at the thought of Gwen, and she desperately leaned forward, attempting to get closer to Haunton, "Let me see them." Kirana felt so weak, so insignificant, as if someone had violently ripped away her title as a god. "Let me talk to the Magistrater with them."

Haunton raised her chin, "You don't know."

"What?"

"How many Keepers do you have?" Kirana didn't respond. "You have two. You used to have three but *she* was never a part of your team. I thought you would have realized this by now. How else could we have found you so soon?" Kirana just stared at the Chief. She nodded, "She's not a very good *spy*, after all."

Spy? But... no. RO betrayed them. She must have told the Wardens everything, every last detail about their plans, their coordinates... Lorenzo. It was Kirana's fault. She was the one who let the Warden in with open arms. She let a parasite into her team like it was nothing; as if the decision wasn't something to even think on. Kirana looked down at her hands to find them trembling. She felt sick, swaying in the chair. "No. No. No."

"I do not wish you to feel this way, but if you need to be punished for your actions then so be it. I need you to know this, Kirana: you were foolish, and though I care very little about the other Keepers I acknowledge where you went wrong. You hurt them. This is all your doing."

Kirana was crying. She couldn't help it.

"What did you think would come after you took down the Magistrater?" Haunton waited for an answer but Kirana couldn't give her one. "They would hate one another. They would find their own chaos. With the main villain gone they would turn to each other and fight. With the doors to each dimension open there would be wars. With the doors to each dimension closed there would still be wars. I told you the Magistrater is the common enemy, I have never lied to you. Never."

Kirana let out a cry, she deserved that much.

Haunton sighed and looked towards the door, "You have no plan, Kirana. You and your friends were just mortals playing gods. You were destined for more. Both for yourself and for the worlds. The Keepers do not work, they never have and they never will. Unity will always be unachievable because of inequality, and equality is unachievable. You wish to bring peace and comfort when all that will do is spark wars. We want to help you. Today you will see what we do. Today you will learn what you were made to do. Your fate–"

Kirana shot forward, "My fate is not beside the Magistrater!"

Haunton sighed, "Kirana, I have spent the better part of my life studying the Keepers. I am one of two people who know almost everything there is to offer about the history of the gods. About you." She moved to the door, "I know you will understand."

"You don't know me."

She knocked on the door and the two Wardens outside opened it. Haunton looked back to Kirana, tilting her head to the side softly, "But I do, and I know by the end of this you will be on our side. You will be the source of our success, by choice or by force."

Kirana lunged forward, trying to get out of the chair. "Please!" She had seconds before she would be locked in a cell. She had only words to stop this from happening. "Let them go. I didn't mean for this to happen. I will listen to you but you have to set them free. I promise you. Set them free and I am yours."

Haunton shook her head "You're already ours. They are too, for the time being. The Magistrater will be coming here in person and meeting you in this very room. She will be here in 23 minutes." She thought for a moment, before pulling back her sleeve and looking down at her watch, "Well, now 20 minutes. Within the hour you will know the truth, and finally be on the right side." Haunton let out a laugh as she walked back into the hallway, "In all honesty you could have gotten away. RO wasn't a good spy, but you were a much worse leader. You were a fool to challenge the very idea of the Magistrater, I hope you've learned your lesson." There was no humor to her words, nor arrogance. She was telling her facts, plain and simple. The Wardens shut the metal door and with a soft metal click she was gone.

Kirana let out a cry, a horrible gasp she couldn't find the strength to make a scream. It was all her fault. She got her team hurt time and time again. She let her inexperience lead her on every mission. Kirana couldn't even find the heart to blame RO. The Warden was a horrible spy and Kirana didn't even hesitate to believe in her. She thought that because RO was a Keeper she could trust her. She put faith in places it should never have been, and now it was all over.

Listen to her. She does not lie.

Was the voice talking about Haunton, or maybe RO? He was all she had left, the last hope she had to escape or find a way to set her friends free.

"Please." Kirana put her voice out as far as she could, "I need help. How do I get out? Where are the others?" No answer. "*Please*, I need your help." The room was silent.

The Magistrater was going to be there in 20 minutes. Kirana didn't know what to do. She had to find her team but what good would it be? They were trapped, all of them, stuck just as she was. Metal cuffs and metal walls, she would need true power to escape and the only source of that godly magic refused to answer her calls.

"Please. Please." Kirana muttered softly to the voice, her voice cracking as tears streamed down her face. Still, the room was silent. "I'll do anything. You're all I have left. I am the Magistrater's if you don't help me. At least save them, please. I can't... I can't reach them. I need power. I need you. If I can't be a god then you have to be. *Please.*" She felt something against her face, something cold and wet. She looked down at her lap and watched a drop of blood fall from her nose. Her nose was bleeding. She was being taken to a new dimension.

Kirana had never felt so helpless, and it was at that moment she realized there was no one else who could save them. This was the end.

Chapter 51

⁕ ✳ ⁕

RO

RO WAS THINKING about Antony as she leaned back in her chair. It was all she could bring herself to picture: him. He could have woken up, and if he did he would be smart enough to stay hidden within the Hiraethans until her people came to destroy them all. She told the Wardens that Antony was there, so they would be sure to look for him before they went in to destroy Lorenzo's rebellion. Once Antony was safe and on his way back to the Ward, they would patch his wounds and find a place to put him. In other words, they would make him a Malfunction. RO could picture him hearing the news, disgusted by the idea of becoming so dispensable but knowing it was the only role he could have among his people. She wondered if he would realize it as soon as woke up. One look at his arm and he would know exactly where he belonged. He would remain a Malfunction until the day he died, a speck of dust in the forgotten vents. RO had earned her place among their people, but he would never have that privilege. She would die a Warden, and he would die a Malfunction.

She had escaped the hierarchy. She had paid her dues and now this was her reward. All it took was one mission and the title of a god and she was finally one of them.

RO was sitting in a rather nice office space. It featured a well-crafted glass table, a silver patterned metal bar, and plants tucked in every corner possible. A long glass wall at the back of the room displayed both the vast greenery of the world and its never-ending seas. RO could see two mines from where she sat, smoke filling the clouds above. All she could picture was Metis's people trapped in those mines, working themselves to death in a place they didn't belong.

Why did her people keep so many in the shadows?

On the other side of the room sat a large door, conversations spilling through from a celebration for RO's success. Those who had captured the Keepers were bragging about their greatest kill and giving their regards to any fallen soldiers. They were talking themselves up to Generals and maybe even Chief Haunton if she decided to come. RO kept well away from most celebrations after missions, it was a time to get drunk and talk, often which ended up with a group of Wardens laughing at her or shoving her out of the room. But this time the celebration was for RO. She would walk into the room and be handed a glass of fine Telematic Belic or Hiraethan Vander, and no one would be able to put up a fight.

On the opposite side of the table sat a tidy Officer who had introduced herself as Second Lieutenant Coraline Laurens. She looked up at RO, "Just a few more questions." She was a coward, RO could tell. She was new and young. This had to be one of her first jobs. She scrolled down on her screen. She was slow–precise, but slow. As soon as the debriefing was over RO would be able to join the celebration and, at last, be with her people. "Please list out the names of people you met during your time in Hiraeth."

"Lorenzo... That is it."

The woman looked up, "Are you sure."

"Yes."

"You spent a week there–"

"Lorenzo."

"You did not–"

"I did not learn their names."

She scrolled down again with a sigh. Laurens seemed tidy, her blond hair pulled back into a small bun, pale white skin smooth, uniform clean and ironed. She was what RO's fellow soldiers called a paperwork trooper. She didn't even wear armor, just a formal uniform. Pathetic– smart with a pen, but barely able to hold a gun. RO didn't understand how she was seen as better than the Malfunctions; they were so much stronger than Laurens would ever be.

"The last few questions are about the Keepers." She scrolled further, "What weaknesses did you observe in Kirana?"

"She's weak. Physically, she can be taken down in a second." But her strength in character was everlasting. For someone who had no experience with death she took it well. RO had never seen someone do that: face death for the first time and justify their actions with the idea of love. No guilt, no fear, just the idea that she would do anything to protect her team. When RO had killed her first victim she took weeks to recover. Yes, she had been 14 years old, but still, death affected everyone in the same way. Age did not matter, just the weight of the victim to the killer. Deran… he held weight. He would have killed her, she knew that. He had enough ego and enough rage to truly beat her to death, so she got to him first. Kirana could never do something like that. She never had to kill her own people, and never would.

"What weaknesses did you observe in Gwen?"

"She's… kind. She loves too hard and gets attached to people. She would die for her people." And she would have died for RO, right? Something formed between them. Somehow the two of them trusted one another. She had seen the true side of Gwen, the strength she held for her family and her people. Yes, RO had been lying to her, putting on an act, but she wasn't lying when she said was sorry for what happened to Gwen's family. RO did feel sorry for everything the Wardens had caused her, and everything they would cause now. But Gwen's compassion was no weapon. If RO had so much as held a gun to a random Hiraethan Gwen would take the bullet head-on to defend them. That was not a strength. That kind of love was a weakness.

"What weakness did you observe in Metis."

She hesitated for a moment before giving in, "Same as Gwen."

Laurens looked up, "The Telematic?"

"Yes."

She let out a small sound, a sort of hum.

"What is that supposed to mean?"

Laurens shrugged, "Just do not see a Telematic caring that much about people every day. Did you find any reasons for that?"

Yes. Metis was the Telematic Hero. RO needed to report that, but for the moment she sat on that thought. The idea of the Telematic Hero had always confused her. No one in that horrible world cared about each other. They lived for themselves, and if someone died in the process then so be it. She spent years down there around those people, but none of them acted like Metis. Maybe it had something to do with him being chosen as a Keeper. Maybe the staff or the Rhodonite fueling their worlds had sensed his good deeds and decided he was the only possible champion in the entire world, but Metis's kindness stretched further than Telematic. Gwen was kind, she was loving and willing to do whatever it took to help her people. Yet... Metis was even more. As the Telematic Hero he hunted down Wardens, fighting them off from his people. He watched as Wardens killed his people and enslaved the children of his words, and yet... when meeting RO he didn't hate her.

How could he not hate her?

In his eyes RO could see this... warmth. No one in her entire world could match that look, could match that sympathy. Was it a lie? Surely it had been. No one could be that kind to someone. No one could care that deeply while knowing the cruel things she had done to survive. Metis knew she was a monster but he still protected her, he healed her wounds, he talked to her like someone worthy of thought, he looked at her as if her actions were just. From the moment they met, something about him seemed different. He was a fool, a crazy Telematic man... but his heart was golden.

RO clenched her jaw and locked eyes with Laurens, "I don't know any reasons."

Laurens looked back down to her screen, "You encountered a Warden named Antony Rican, can you confirm he is still in Hiraeth?"

Metis had helped save Antony. Why? A golden heart could not be the reason. That was not why he had gotten into all that trouble. He had been ready to perform an entire surgery for a Warden he didn't even know... but RO knew him. Maybe it was just a feeling, a sort of intuition, but behind Metis's gaze she saw something else. A look, something far beyond them both. Behind her act, behind his own mask. She saw him as he was, and he saw her as she was. Whether Metis knew it or not he was seeing RO's true form, and she let him. Gods, she had let him see her as she was. He had seen how much Antony meant to her. Her panic and fear were uncontrollable and he didn't see that as a weakness. He just did what he needed to in order to help her.

He had understood her pain. He had seen past her monstrous ways and found something she thought had died long along.

"RO?" Laurens waved her hand in front of the Warden's face.

She swallowed, "Antony is in Hiraeth."

"You seem tired." Laurens went to a new spot on the screen, switching documents, "I suggest you find a way to stay awake for the time being; your mission isn't over yet."

RO pinched the bridge of her nose, "I am very much aware of my responsibilities, continue with yours."

"I have information about what will happen in your next few days. First thing first, you will be promoted to a one-star General."

They had moved her so high up the ranks that RO felt herself get whiplash from the mere idea of it. She blinked and swallowed, "That's quite a reward."

"A bit too much if you ask me." Laurens hid her suddenly annoyed look with the top of her screen, "If the Magistrater does not wish to use you in any way or sees you ready to work again after your Keeper business, you will be sent to guard the Magistrater's Vault and facilitate the patrols and maintenance of the area." RO sunk back in her chair. That was exactly where she was supposed to go before she had become a Keeper. The mission she was being briefed on with Metis, only this time she was in command. "And the Magistrater has sent a message for you." She flipped to a new screen and held it up, straightening her back, "General RO. You have–"

"This is the message? You're reading it out for me? She's not even–"

"What more do you expect?"

RO gestured around the office space they had put her in, "I don't know... I was a *Keeper*–"

"Trooper." Laurens pursed her lips, a sudden flare of emotion spreading across her face. Her cheeks turned pink as if *this* was a burst of rage for her, "Not only have you been promoted but you have also been allowed to keep your title as a god and have been given a celebration in your honor." She gestured to the door, conversations still buzzing from within, "You should be lucky you have this much. A person like you should never even have gotten these opportunities to begin with." With Laurens's hand still up, the door to the room opened suddenly. RO expected to see another officer, maybe even an escort to the Magistrater herself, but no. It was Haunton. Laurens dropped her hand so fast it hit the side of the table. The two of them shot up out of their chairs.

The darkly dressed trooper walked gracefully into the room, her hands behind her back, "I hope I did not hear you speak to our Keeper in such a way, Officer."

Laurens shook her head quickly, "I apologize sir, but RO–"

"It's *General* RO." RO thought she heard humor behind the Chief's words and it took her a moment to realize it might have been joy. Haunton did seem happy, cheerful even in the way she walked. She moved towards RO and glanced back at Laurens, "I think she's had enough for one day, you are free to enjoy the celebration."

Without another word Laurens grabbed her screen and moved to the door, shutting it as she left. RO looked over to Haunton and found herself fearful of the Warden before her. She had never heard of anyone in the room alone with her before, let alone in a conversation Haunton had deemed a joyous celebration. For however much RO was scared of offending the Chief, it was clear today was a good day to be in her presence.

Haunton walked past her, "Our Keeper has finally returned." She moved to the bar and gestured to RO, "You can rest now. It's all over. You did it." She grabbed a bottle and a single glass. RO suddenly remembered Metis's friend Bot back in Telematic, the bartender she could destroy by muttering his name. Haunton poured a fine-colored Belic into the glass and brought it to RO, "The promotion is nothing compared to your other rewards." She pushed her towards the large window, "You have served your people and defined your loyalty as a true Warden, better than many I have seen in my time. Your rewards start with drinks and celebration and end with what the Magistrater has planned for you, our Keeper."

RO matched Haunton and looked out of the window, "What does the Magistrater want me to do?"

"That is not your concern as of now."

"And the others?"

Haunton looked down at her, "Now that is the concern. *Others.*" She gestured to the door, "We are your *others.* They are, as of now, the *enemy.* When they realize what their actions have caused, they will feel guilty for the things they have done to harm our system. Only then can they be your *others.*"

Haunton was letting details of her plans slip into their conversation. It seemed the plan was to turn the Keepers into soldiers like RO, loyal to the Magistrater. Warden gods working for a system they once swore against. "I apologize. It's been a long mission with many lies. I will keep my loyalties in check as time goes on."

"That would be wise." Haunton straightened her back, "But since you're curious; we are questioning the Keepers at the moment. It is a painful step in the process, but once Kirana speaks to the Magistrater, everything will become clear. She will see what we are doing." Haunton glanced to her left, "She's actually not too far from here. Just down the hall. But we are keeping the gods separate for extra precautions. We wouldn't want another Malfunction to find them and take them back through the vents." RO recognized her tone was directed to the Warden Keeper.

RO swallowed, "And what exactly are we doing?"

Haunton didn't answer right away. She took a breath, "You will be treated as a Keeper until we see fit to bring you back into the Ward. For now, the Magistrater wishes to only speak to Kirana. Once Kirana is on our side, the Magistrater will meet with the rest of you."

"May I ask you something?" Haunton nodded, and though RO realized her next words would only end up hurting her she needed to know. "My people will never see me as a Warden, will they?"

"You are always going to be the Malfunction Keeper, RO. But now you have a place. You have earned your place beside the Wardens."

"So I am one of you?"

Haunton sighed from beneath the helmet, "Why are you asking me this?"

"I only want to know what my people will think of me. You say I have earned my place beside them but I need to know if they will believe that."

"They won't." Haunton's tone dropped, "But power is a strong tool. They will know who commands who, and in the end it will be you leading the Wardens." She looked back towards the doors, "Let me show you." The Chief pushed RO away from the window and swiftly across the room. Haunton swung open the doors and walked straight into the celebration.

The Wardens' conversations quickly stopped at the sight of the Chief entering the room, and as they turned to face the two of them, RO realized how special this celebration truly was. In the Ward, rooms like the one before RO were kept for the highest-ranking troopers or the most honored missions and soldiers. Gold patterns replaced the classic gray and silver lines across the walls, tall plants framed a wide window like the one in the office, but what truly completed the room were the people inside. RO spotted Generals, Specialists, Colonels, and some of the highest-ranking Wardens she had ever heard of. The thirty of them stood with Belic in their crystal glasses, eyes on RO and the Chief.

Haunton placed a hand on RO's shoulder, "As most of you know, General RO has not always had the privilege of standing beside us. She was once as insignificant as the other Malfunctions, born worthless when compared to the might of us Wardens. But she proved herself more valuable as a soldier, to the point in which I was called to voice my thoughts." RO had never heard this story before, she looked up at the Chief, her heart racing. "They told me a Malfunction child had been able to defeat a Warden her age. They told me she had enough fight to fuel her for a thousand missions, and after seeing the damage she inflicted on that Warden, I realized she could one day be like one of us. When the staff guided us to her, I was reluctant to allow her to become our spy for fear of her resorting back to where we had saved her. But look at RO now, our General, our leader and, now, a Warden." The Chief lifted up her hand and the Wardens followed by raising their glasses. "To our *Warden* Keeper. To our spy. To our proud monster. To one of us."

The room let out a cheer as the Wardens, the best of her people, celebrated RO's victory. RO felt something within her lift. It felt like hope, like her heart was glowing. This was all she had ever wanted. After everything she did, it was all worth it. Every fight, every death, every battle, every scar, every betrayal, all of it, and she had finally gotten her reward.

RO raised her glass with a smile, "To our mighty Magistrater. May her divine powers continue to bring us honor."

"Hail be!"

But visions of the Keepers returned. RO tried to push her thoughts away, but she could not help but picture all that her people and the Magistrater had done: Gwen's mother and father, the Telematic children, those who hid away with Lorenzo. Part of RO ached and scolded her pride, and suddenly Haunton's speech felt like nothing more than a distraction.

General RO... the Malfunction Keeper who kept her loyalty to her masters.

Metis never saw her as a monster or even a Warden, and she knew he would not care if she was a Malfunction. In fact, she could picture him celebrating it. Kirana had accepted RO's history as a valuable beginning for a much greater future. Gwen... forgave her. Gwen, the woman whose mother and father were killed and family enslaved for generations by RO's people... forgave her.

The room fell back into conversations as the Wardens turned away from RO. Haunton let out a sudden laugh and grabbed RO's shoulder, shaking her playfully, "You are too serious, RO. Have a drink, settle down. Your work is not yet done but it is final. You brought the Keepers here and now they have no escape. You did it."

RO forced herself to look pleased, "My future is bright beside the Wardens."

"Your future is bright beside the Magistrater. You're still a god, after all, only now you're back on the winning side." She leaned closer to RO, "Our first Malfunction to succeed where Wardens couldn't." Haunton pulled out her watch, "I will return for you once the Magistrater has spoken with Kirana. Within the next hour, all of this will be over, and Kirana will see the truth: That we are right, and she was nothing more than a playful, purposeless child with too much power. She will one day make a great god, under our rule." She started to walk further into the room, pointing back to the office as she spoke, "Leave your weapon on the table if you leave the celebration. You are free to go where you please but I suggest you stay here and await your next instructions." She stopped walking and nodded to RO, "Enjoy your rewards. This is only the beginning, RO."

"Thank you, Chief Haunton."

Haunton walked through the room, ignoring every Warden who bowed or attempted to talk to her. She walked to the door, opened it, and left the room.

RO did not move for a moment. She stood there, her back to the office door, looking at the Wardens around her. No one moved up to her just yet, but she knew they would. Her people would congratulate her on her work or ask her questions like Laurens. RO stood there, her heart racing, knowing this moment was everything she had ever wanted but feeling helplessly guilty for all it had cost.

RO felt the little voice muttering doubts kill whatever hope had found its way into her dark heart. She felt sick, and as another General turned to her she looked away and walked back into the office, away from her reward. She shut the door and moved back to the table, tugging at her collar and trying to breathe. The glass fell out of her hands onto the table, Belic spilling across its polished surface. Her celebratory drink spilled onto the floor. In an attempt to break the horrible feeling of decay within her, RO grabbed the glass and threw it at the window with a grunt. The glass shattered and the window broke from the center outwards to form one large crack.

RO dropped to the end of the table and put her hands to her eyes. She wouldn't let herself cry, not over her reward. She tried to tell herself it was deserved. She tried to remember all she had done and not feel guilt or regret. RO had a duty to her people, finally, her own people. She was a Warden, she wasn't some broken piece they could discard for another. She was indispensable and she earned that title. She had earned all her titles; god, Keeper, Malfunction, monster. But she couldn't stop herself from picturing Metis's face when he realized what she had done. He looked at her like no one had ever before. Like she had done something awful instead of existing as something awful. As if she finally had a choice to be a monster.

There was a noise to RO's side, a faint shift. Her head snapped to the side and she found herself face to face with a vent, small eyes peering out from inside. RO crawled over to the vent and ripped it open. The peeping Malfunction had already tried to retreat and managed to get out of reach.

"What are you doing here?" RO's upper lip curled as she realized that the roach could have seen her with Haunton or, much worse, could have seen her outburst.

"I'm sorry." That voice…. The Malfunction was a child, a little girl hiding in the shadows of the vents. Her head was dipped down right below a line of light that reached inside the vent. She had learned how to avoid all eyes.

RO didn't want to meet with her past, not when her present had become so heavy. She wanted to forget about the Keepers and burn her guilt away, but like the little Malfunction in the vent, her troubles always seemed to have a way of returning to sight. RO had learned how to push thoughts and memories away, she learned how to see a vent and not think of herself or the people she once knew. She had done it so well that she could not recall the name of a single Malfunction she grew up with. But the memories and lessons the Keepers gave her felt too permanent to even attempt to leave behind.

The Malfunction girl leaned forward into the light, her eyes so fixed on RO that she did not blink, "How did you do it?"

It seemed the Wardens were right to fear the power she held as a Malfunction god because now the roaches were watching her. "Come here."

The young Malfunction looked afraid but did not hesitate to move forward. RO looked up at the corner of the room and found no cameras, so when the girl was within reach, RO grabbed her and pulled her to the edge of the vent, "Listen to me. You are not me, you can not become one of them. You are a defect, you are worthless. There is no place for you among the Wardens. I am not your god, I am not your saint, I am not your anything. I am not one of you. I am far greater than you could imagine…" The girl studied RO's face, eyes darting from place to place. RO sat there for a moment clutching the girl's shirt, and in the end, she said, "I killed a Warden, I proved myself."

"Can I?" She sounded so desperate.

RO found herself wanting to say yes, she wanted to help this poor child the way someone should have helped her all those years ago. *Should* have. RO had never felt so connected to Malfunctions, and she knew that before she had become a Keeper. RO could have sent the girl back into the vents or even killed her without a moment of hesitation, but now… everything had changed. RO looked back to the cracked window. It would need to be replaced, no one could heal it. She was broken, and so was the Malfunction before her. They were both doomed to keep breaking, even if it wasn't… fair.

"Do not kill anyone." RO pushed her back into the vent, "You're not me."

"I can kill. I have a gun. I can shoot good. I promise."

"*Promise?*" RO shook her head, "You can't escape what you were born to be."

"You–"

RO grabbed the vent door, "I was a miscalculation, you were a mistake. You are stuck with the others." *Others.* RO slammed the door back into place and held it there, waiting to hear the Malfunction leave. The girl slid back almost immediately, and within seconds she was silently crawling back into the vents.

RO was alone.

Alone.

Did she want to be? No Warden could comfort her. She had seen so much, made connections with people she shouldn't have. That was where the pain came from: her own mistakes. But how could RO not like the Keepers? They were kind, they were sweet. Weak, yes, but not in the way she expected. They had no idea what they were doing. They had no plan, no physical or strategic advantage. They just had a heart. They loved their people more than anything, and she was the same. Everything she had ever done was for her people. She followed orders, went out on hundreds of missions, endured years of training, and suffered years of torment and disapproval. She had been beaten, threatened, shot at, ridiculed. All for her people. If they asked her to jump off a cliff she would. No hesitation.

She would do anything for her people… and so would Gwen. So would Metis. So would Lorenzo. So would the next Keeper.

Even Kirana, who had no people of her own to protect, was willing to lay down her life to save those who needed a god to trust.

RO looked out the cracked window to the mines. She pictured what life was like, not just for the children they took from Telematic and ʻĀina, but also for her own people. If they were like Antony, not weak but loving, they would want to stop the injustice. Why didn't they? Why didn't she? RO had been exposed to so much the past weeks and yet she still betrayed the Keepers. It was because of her people, it was because of the culture they had built for themselves. Weakness was nothing more than a ticket to become a roach behind the walls of the facilities. RO had spent years trying to erase that weakness, but now she wasn't quite sure it was that at all. Everyone wants to be cared for. Every Hiraethan, every Telematic, every Warden, every Malfunction… The little girl in the vents had no one. RO had no one. Antony had no one. No one received the one thing all people deserve: love.

RO understood.

She understood what the Keepers were doing.

She understood why she was chosen.

She was a Keeper, for her people.

For all people.

But how could that be? RO was a soldier. If she wanted to help her people she needed to stay and fight beside them, not against them. Right? If she defeated the Magistrater there would be a chance to reorganize the system. Change things for the better.

The Wardens had no freedom in their lives, she could see that now. From birth they are manipulated into believing that the only way to prove themselves is by killing and hurting others. What did her people receive but a life with a gun in their hands? RO knew there was order, she knew that her people were supposed to be the villains but… why did they always have to be the monsters?

RO remembered watching Deran, snot and tears dripping down his face as he begged and screamed for his life. RO realized that day how easy it was to kill someone, and how it was something she could never undo. She didn't want him to die. But she didn't have a choice. If she wanted to be among her people, if she wanted them to accept her, she needed to kill him. And she did, Antony and everyone else watching her as she plunged a sword into his chest and watched him choke on his own blood and tears.

But her sacrifices, that day and after, were for her people. Yet it had gotten her nowhere. Nothing in the Ward had been changed, no one had benefited from her work except...

The Magistrater.

RO did not want her people to have to fight. She wanted to help them. She wanted to save them. But betray her people? Would she truly be a traitor? No. She would do anything to help them, and helping them meant sacrificing. She would sacrifice her name for the hope that she would one day be able to free them from years of constant, unnecessary battles.

She was a Warden, she earned that title, but she wasn't just another trooper.

She was a Keeper.

And now she had a decision to make.

To be the god her people needed, or to be the monster they had trained her to be.

Looking out of that broken window she realized she had no other choice. RO was destined to be something more than what her people had expected from her. It would hurt her, maybe one day kill her, but she knew then and there that her actions needed to change.

She needed to save her friends.

RO put a hand on the table and pulled herself up off the ground. Before she could change her mind she walked to the door and opened it, pulling herself away from all she had ever wanted for what her people needed. She walked through the room of celebrating Generals and Wardens, pushing past them to the hallway and refusing to stop for a moment. Haunton had looked to her left when she spoke about where they were keeping Kirana, if RO could find her they could make a plan, maybe even slip away with the staff or find a way to get to the others. They could use the vents or she could clear a path with her sword. The situation was dire but it was not impossible. RO could save them all.

This facility was almost identical to the Ward. The walls were still clean, wiped with Malfunction hands. The Warden uniforms matched the dull, lifeless, linear hallways. Walking down the halls it felt like she had never left her home world. As if she had truly just returned from a mission. That was good, for now she just looked like another Warden going off on a new mission. She received only glances, quick looks at the Malfunction who had become a god. They all knew who she was, watching without fear.

Haunton was a liar, she had no power to command them.

It was all lies.

RO followed the hallways, turning and finding herself going in circles. If there was anyone watching her they would know exactly what she was doing, so she hurried her pace and finally came upon a group of three armed Wardens standing against a metal door. She had never been so grateful to see cocky, stupid Wardens before. They were so relaxed they had taken their helmets off, guns resting against the wall or to their side lazily.

The one closest to her had the highest ranking. Blond hair and a smug look on his face, his eyes were that light shade of blue that pierced through souls. He laughed with his fellow Wardens, "I tell you right now if I had been there earlier I would have just killed that Hiraethan girl first. She had this look on her face like... what's something really... soft?"

"A puppy?"

They all laughed. "A puppy!"

"Some god!"

RO took a breath and walked down the hallway towards them. She had two options, kill them all or attempt to talk them into letting her inside. She would attempt the second plan out of mercy. They looked over as she came down the hallway. The blond Warden seemed most interested in her arrival. He gestured to her, "Is that you? *General* RO?"

Someone whistled in the cluster as RO stopped a few paces away, "Thank you. I am quite happy with–"

"Come celebrate!" She looked down at one of the trooper's hands to find a bottle already partially empty.

"Chief Haunton told me to speak with Kirana. I need you to let me inside."

"We want to hear about everything you saw."

She shook her head once, "Then read the report."

"No, no. We want the juicy stuff. What were the gods really like?"

She glanced behind her, "They were just people. Foolish people. But the Chief has sent me here to speak–"

"Seriously, that's all you've got?"

RO tried to step forward, "I wasn't there to find–"

The man laughed, "Holy shit! Malfunctions are so uptight!" Everyone laughed with him, "Just be a little like us for once RO. I mean, you do outrank us now." He gave a little bow to her and his group laughed.

RO found herself feeling pity for him. Her people needed to change; however cruel they were, they weren't born that way. He didn't deserve to bear the weight of the Magistrater's kills, no matter the arrogance he used to lighten the guilt. For now, there was only one way to stop her people from continuing the system. RO placed her hand by her sword, "I am not like you. I don't play games. I get my work done, and that is why I outrank you."

His smile grew, "You'll always be a Malfunction, *General.* You'll never outrank us, not really."

"I am a god. You are a mortal with only pride to be buried with your disheveled corpse. I pity you, and I am sorry for what has to happen." She saw a spark of realization cover over him, but by then it was too late. She wanted to send a prayer to his god only to realize she was the one she would be praying to. One day she would make up for the killing with a peaceful world without the Magistrater to control it.

RO grabbed her sword and swung it through the air. As she did, the blade expanded out from within the hilt and swiped itself across the Warden's neck. Before the others could react she threw her sword to the Warden with his gun already in his hands and kicked away the other Warden's gun down the hallway. With their helmet off she was able to send one hard fist to his face and whip him into the back wall. As the Warden fell to the ground beside the other troopers she grabbed her sword out of the other Warden's body and swung down onto his head.

This would not be the last time she would have to kill her own people, but she knew it had to be done.

For their future, and for the Keepers.

Igniting the sword she let it grow hot within her grasp, waiting until it expelled a dangerous, violent glow. She pushed it through the lock of the metal door, cutting through metal and gears as she pushed into the door. Within seconds it gave way and swung open, heavy enough not to hit the wall. There, seated in the center of the room, sat the restrained leader of the gods, her nose bleeding and her eyes wide.

"RO?"

It was at that moment RO felt the true luck of her situation. Her desperation had led to the loss of reason, and suddenly the idea that they would have kept Kirana so close felt like a choice. It was a test, so where was the punishment? RO did not enter the room. She could see Kirana clearly, not a hologram, not a trick. The betrayal in her eyes was something no android could replicate. RO stepped back into the hallway past the bodies of the Wardens and looked down the way she had not come from. Standing there in her all-knowing glory was Haunton.

The Chief tilted her head, "We gave you so much more than you deserved. Was it not enough?"

RO looked at Kirana to find her staring back. She looked at RO with an intensity that belonged on a Warden's face. Kirana was waiting for what the Warden Keeper did next.

Haunton started to walk to RO, her steps light, "I am sorry it has to be this way. I was hoping you would not need any such punishment, but I suppose you will always be that little–"

RO spun her sword before her and aimed it at Haunton. She pressed the hot blade close to her face, "I am a greater soldier than any Warden you have fought beside, and your arrogance will be your downfall."

"You assume I can bleed. We are all monsters, RO, but some of us are a little less *fragile*."

RO looked at Kirana. She tried to express a message through her look, one of loyalty, one of rebirth. Whatever happened next would determine the fate of all of their worlds, and if she was to die there the Keepers would be left trapped under the Magistrater's rule. So long as RO sent off a spark her purpose would be done. Her life mattered only to the flame it could produce.

RO took a breath, one last breath, "I don't want you to bleed, I want you to *burn*."

RO was the last chance the Keepers had. She would not let her friends down.

PART 7

Battle of the Keepers

Chapter 52

* * *

KALANI

KALANI LIFTED HIS hand and traced the closest branch above him. He aligned his finger and pulled it down to the trunk of the tree. There were enough leaves to stop the sun from hitting him, yet still, the space around him was filled with light. Kalani had never liked shadows, he preferred the sun on his skin, it made him feel like a tree. He could shut his eyes and listen to the birds, to the movements of branches, sometimes even little creatures moving by. Kalani put his hand beside him against the grass and looked past the leaves to the sky. It was getting darker, soon it would be night and there would be no sun to shine on any of the wonders of the forest. Kalani pushed his head back and saw a gray cloud coming over one of the mountains behind him. By tomorrow, after the night's rain, the trees would look so alive.

"Kalani!"

He looked back and heard footsteps nearing him. He crawled towards a tree and ducked down against a thick root. Someone came into the forest and he took a risky peek. It was Hali'a. She was looking for him, wiping her hands on a cloth wrapped around her waist as she moved further into the forest. When her gaze came close, he ducked away again.

"Kalani!" She waited for him to appear. He didn't. "Everyone's looking for you! We thought you were at the lo'i!"

He tucked his legs into his chest and got comfortable. The lo'i was where the village grew their Kalo, a purple-colored root that could be ground into poi. Kalani was supposed to work there for the day. The kids of the village had been asked to pull out the recent cluster of weeds while the adults dealt with a rather aggressive growth of vines nearing the other patches.

Hali'a sighed, "Don't worry, Kalani. I told them you were in bed. Sprained your ankle when you were helping me earlier."

He peeked out from the tree slightly. Hali'a was waiting there, eyes already locked on where he was. She put out a hand and waited. Kalani looked back up to the branches above him, to the forest, before coming out of his hiding place and walking to her.

Hali'a took his hand and held it up to look at his back, "You got so much mud on you." She picked a piece of mud out of his hair, "Wipe some of it off before we get back. And maybe fake a limp if you see Lani or Kaipo."

"Okay."

Her smile faded into something softer, "You know, they do need your help. It might do you some good. You're old enough to help now, help your people."

Kalani just stared up at her. He knew no one needed him. The best thing he could do was stay out of everyone's way. Hali'a was trying to find some excuse to make him want to go out and help. She said he was tall enough, strong enough, or, now, old enough. With a hopeful glance down at him, she realized her words had not changed his mind, and with a sigh, she squeezed his hand and walked forward.

On the walk back Kalani tried to wipe off whatever mud he could from his clothes. By the time they reached the outer wall he looked somewhat clean, and by Hali'a's glance it seemed good enough. Smoke already billowed from the houses on the ground, and the smell of cooking food created an air of safety. Food meant comfort and survival. The hunters must have found a lot of animals to cook up as well because three of four cookhouses were being used. As they passed the fourth he saw about half of the hunters, all resting and laying out their tools on the wall. They glanced over as Kalani passed, and Hali'a kicked his leg to remind him to limp. He faked a limp for a few seconds, before giving up.

"Hali'a!" Kapua ran towards them. The man acted like a bird. He moved around quickly, with a thin neck that could turn in a second. He was good with spotting creatures deep in the forest, but not so manly when an animal is up close. He wasn't a tough act, not like others were; if anything he was just a gentle man who knew his boundaries.

He approached holding something behind his back, "Hali'a. I saw you weren't with Kaia today. She was teaching the kids how to weave baskets. I thought you would be there." He glanced down at Kalani, who stared back, studying him. Kapua looked away, unsettled, "But I made you this." He held out a small basket filled to the brim with pink and purple flowers.

Hali'a didn't know what to say at first, so she mouthed different words until finally settling on, "Thank you."

She took it and looked at them all, touching each flower. Kapua stood there for a moment, flapping his hands around like the bird he was. "Well I should go." He turned around and walked towards the other baskets on the wall of the cookhouse.

Hali'a looked down to Kalani, "Isn't he sweet."

"He's a bird."

She stared down at him for a moment, processing, before giving up and continuing to walk.

They continued forward and eventually stopped at the second gate. Kalani tried to push the gate open but Hali'a put a hand on the gate and kept it close. "Kalani." He looked up at her, "You can't just hide away from life anymore. I know we're not your true village or even your true family, but this is your home. We're your people now." She pulled open the gate, "This was made by us, Kalani. Don't you want your name on something?"

Kalani had stayed in other villages before, four to be exact. But Hali'a's home was the nicest one out of all of them. Well built and managed. They had built an outer wall for production-focused tasks and buildings and an inner wall for a final layer of protection for the houses. Someone had told Kalani their village was a reflection of what was once a modern civilization. Kalani didn't believe that was true, because how could something be a reflection if it is nothing like the original image? Their ancestors had so much; they had technology, language, literacy, an abundance of food, peace, and access to the ocean. When Kalani looked around he saw small pieces of their history: recycled material, old clothes, surviving traditions. There were many places for development, but Kalani was not going to be the one to change the village for the better.

He looked up to Hali'a and shook his head. She shrugged softly, "Well, I tried."

As she started to walk through the gate Kalani felt the ground beneath him shake. He thought it was his imagination before he noticed everyone in the village had stopped what they were doing and looked to the sky. A great billowing sound grew louder and louder, until finally, with a hot burst of wind, a ship appeared above them.

A Warden ship.

Then behind it a smaller ship flew to the ground, ropes dropping and Wardens sliding down into the jungle below.

"Into the forest!" Someone screamed, and Hali'a pulled Kalani's arm and ran back the way they had come. Suddenly everything was moving. Every person was running, every tree was swaying, and every speck of dirt was flying.

As the people in front of them reached the wall there was a blast of fire from the ship above them, and everyone sprinted back into the village. The ship spun around the village and created a wall of fire.

"Do not resist." A voice boomed over them as Hali'a held Kalani behind her. The Wardens came through the flames, like the demons they were, guns drawn. When they reached the fourth cookhouse the hunters came out, weapons drawn. Ready for a fight they could not win, or maybe, ready to make a big enough distraction to let others survive. Hali'a pulled Kalani back to the gate and they ran through it, going around the wall as a Warden pursued them. A Warden pursued everyone. They were outnumbered, outgunned, and yet the Wardens didn't shoot. Why weren't they shooting? Hali'a ran into a house and shut the door behind them. She dragged Kalani across the room, tramping mud onto finely made rugs.

"Hali'a!" Kalani said, trying to pull out of grasp. They needed to run, not stay in the houses and let the Wardens find them.

Hali'a let go of him and searched the house for hiding spots, "Kalani–"

The door suddenly burst open and a Warden lunged for the two of them. Hali'a pushed Kalani into a wall and the Warden pushed her to the wall.

"Run!" She yelled before the gun was held onto her head.

Kalani didn't have a gun. He wasn't strong enough to fight back or even distract the Warden enough to let Hali'a slip away. He stood there, trying to find a way to be a warrior. He stood there, and he did nothing as the Warden smashed Hali'a's head onto the floor so hard she stopped moving.

"Damn it." The Warden wiped his hands and looked at Kalani, who sprinted for the door. Kalani made it outside before the Warden could grab him and he kept running. He ran as fast as he could. The fire was burning fast, covering the trees around them. People were everywhere, being chased or being dragged. Some were unconscious, others were screaming, but most of them were running. Running to the forest. He could see some of them were making it, but the fire was spreading, and he realized then he would have to run through the flames to escape. Could he do that? Could he make it? He had to try.

Kalani ran for the forest, watching the trees and branches burn away against the sunset.

Chapter 53

KIRANA

KIRANA HAD STOPPED praying by the time RO arrived in her cell. She heard a series of noises from the other side of the metal door. Kirana thought it was just the beginning of some horrible new ritual Haunton would put her through. When the door swung open RO stood there as if she had never left. Yes, she looked guilty, but Kirana realized at that moment that this guilty expression on RO's face was nothing new. She had seen it before, many times, she had just been too blind to know what it meant. Kirana barely had enough time to look at RO before Haunton arrived, and suddenly their weapons were drawn. The hallway went silent.

Neither of the Wardens seemed ready to begin the fight. They were waiting for the trigger, for something to change. After a series of long, horrible seconds, RO lunged to her side towards Kirana. With a grunt she forced her sword down onto the Permidian's wrists, breaking through the very edges of her metal cuffs and sliding through her skin. Before Kirana could let out a gasp of pain Haunton came running into the room.

RO swung her sword past Kirana's head and towards Huaton's neck. Haunton ducked down and dodged the poker-hot sword as it landed back by RO's side. Chief Haunton's chestplate was sliced by the sword, but when the blade should have dented or carved through the material, it only left a scratch. Haunton was covered in indestructible pieces of armor, and even without a weapon, Kirana knew the warrior before her would be an equal match for RO and her sword. There was an opening in RO's stance, one that the Chief had preempted. Haunton, already close to RO by dodging the blow, swung her arm around RO's neck, grabbed the hilt of her sword, and sent her wheeling around to the back of Kirana's metal chair.

In such a small space, Kirana realized very quickly that the fight had brought great danger to herself. RO's sword spun behind her dangerously close to Kirana's head, but she used it as motivation to try and pull her hand free of the now-damaged metal cuff. It felt looser, but gods, it was painful to push against hot, dented metal.

RO leaned back on Kirana's chair and kicked her feet up into Haunton's chest. As the Chief flew back and hit the wall she spun over the side of the chair and brought the sword down on the second set of cuffs, barely missing Kirana's wrist. Before she could pull the sword back up Haunton came down with a heavy punch. RO flew forward with the impact and raised her sword back up, her focus suddenly dazed. With a grunt she shot the sword forward, skimming Haunton's stomach as the Chief spun out of the way. Kirana shook the entire chair as she tried to release the cuffs. Her wrists bled, but with one final thrust her hand came free. She clawed at the next cuff as Haunton, ignoring Kirana's attempt to escape, stepped back and let RO swing the sword above her. As RO brought the blade down, Haunton caught the hilt and twisted around the Warden Keeper, bending her arms back. With a scream RO kicked off the ground and sent them both back against the wall and attempted to drive the sword back into Haunton. It worked only to force the Chief away, but in doing so, allowed RO to spin around and hit across her arm. Haunton attempted to move forward again but RO, seeing the pattern, brought the sword closer and drove it across her helmet with a scream. Haunton flew down to the ground, allowing RO to look back at Kirana. RO saw her struggling and drove her sword back to the cuffs, driving it in and breaking it loose.

Kirana had begun to give in to hope before Haunton suddenly jumped onto the chair itself and dove into RO, sending them first to the wall and then to the ground. Kirana's hands were free and the cuffs around her ankles were looser. She clawed at them the same as she had before, bending forward and looking for a way to cut herself free. She could see RO racing to get back up, trying to keep her sword close, but Haunton was fast and strong enough to grab onto the hilt with one hand, and she sent her elbow to RO's neck. RO let out a gasp for air as Haunton rolled on top of her, forcing the sword out of her grasp. When it gave way the Chief spun back around and tried to send the blade down to RO's head.

In an act of panic, Kirana reached forward and grabbed Haunton by her helmet, pushing her head back to allow RO enough time and distraction to evade the blade. The Chief pulled the sword back up and threw Kirana back to the chair. RO spun back to her feet, edging away from Haunton with her hands up. The sword dimmed in Haanton's grasp, for RO it produced fire, but for the Chief it sat cold.

Haunton examined the blade, "You are quite the fighter." She threw the sword into the hallway, "But what you do here does not matter. You know you can not defeat me. I will give you one last chance–"

RO shot forward and swung a fist down to Haunton's helmet. The Chief simply moved to the side, before grabbing RO by her jacket collar and throwing her to the ground. RO allowed herself to fall to the ground and swung her leg around to knock Chief Haunton to the ground with her. It didn't work. Kirana could tell how heavy RO's kick was, and yet all it did was shake the Chief. Haunton sent her own kick straight to RO's chest, sending the Warden sliding to the wall with a gasp of pain. They were running out of time. Kirana grabbed the broken metal from her handcuffs and tore them off their hinges. She pushed the metal into the cuffs around her ankles again and again, denting and breaking the lock with whatever strength she had.

Haunton stood up and looked down at RO, "You are as pitiful as the day we found you." RO used the wall to stand up, hand wrapped around her waist. Kirana didn't stop pounding the metal against her cuffs. They were coming loose. She could see them coming loose. When she glanced up Haunton was staring at her, just watching. "Put it down, Kirana." Kirana stared back at her and waited for a punch, for a sudden hit that would send her back in her chair. But nothing happened. Did Haunton expect to intimidate her simply by staring? That wasn't like her. Kirana realized then that there was a reason none of the Wardens had hurt her. Strapping her in the chair might have been for her own protection. Kirana didn't know if it was true, but she wouldn't put it past the Magistrater to order the Wardens to not hurt the Keeper for the sake of building Kirana's trust.

RO took a deep breath, sweat building across her brow, before pulling her hand off her stomach and pushing off the wall. She sent her fist under Haunton's helmet, finally hitting something that could allow her an advantage. RO sent a second blow to the Chief's stomach, and though Haunton curled at the blow she did not hesitate through the pain. She grabbed RO's fist, pressed a hand to her shoulder, and threw her into the wall. Kirana sent another blow down onto her cuffs and the metal flew open. She had one left, one left and they could run. RO tried to push off and punch Haunton again, but her movements had become slow. Haunton moved to the side of RO's fist, grabbed her head, and slammed her knee into her stomach. Kirana hit her cuffs again and again. Her hands bled as she clutched the sharp metal.

RO dropped to the ground and tried to stand back up. As she slid back up the wall, blood spilling over her lips, the Chief gestured to her with open arms, "You could have been recognized. You could have been the greatest Warden we have ever seen. The Warden *god*." RO put her hands back up and sent another fast blow to Haunton's chest. Haunton caught her fist and twisted her hand. With a scream, RO dropped to her knees. "I could see how much those Keepers meant to you. Their soft words, their little lullabies to you. As if you were a child. How selfish. How *weak*."

Kirana's cuff suddenly flew open and without wasting a single moment she shot forward. She stumbled and fell to the ground. Her hands bruised and her feet locked and cold, she crawled through the hallway like a starving animal. She grabbed the hilt of the sword and forced herself back up. Kirana stood there, Haunton framed by the doorway with RO in hand, and aimed the sword forward.

The Chief shook her head, "There is nothing you can do, Kirana. Put the sword down."

Without allowing herself to think too long, Kirana pressed the blade to her neck, "You won't fight me. You can't hurt me. You're following orders. You need me *alive*!" Kirana had never heard her voice become so violent. The fight went still as Haunton looked over suddenly. At the sight of Kirana she remained there, above RO and refusing to let go. Kirana moved the blade to her forearm, "You need me alive. You need me whole. Let go of her."

"I know you. You wouldn't."

Kirana thought of Gwen and pulled the blade towards her. She let out a gasp and stopped herself from pulling the sword away. There were tears in her eyes formed well before the blade's cut, "Let go of her or you will face the Magistrater alone!"

RO stared at Kirana with the disbelief she hoped was hiding behind Haunton's mask. But the Chief didn't let go of RO, her grip only tightened around her face.

"That's not even a scratch, Kirana dear." Haunton grabbed RO's neck and allowed her to crawl at her hand. "I know you. You won't kill yourself for this and that is all I care about. You can't escape the Magistrater, and you can't defeat *me*. You'll see why we had to keep you here soon enough."

Kirana didn't know what to do. She was free but there was nothing she could do. Powerless. Helpless. RO was about to die and Kirana didn't even know if she deserved it. Kirana didn't know where the others were, she didn't know how to escape, how to find the last Keeper, how to run, how to breathe.

"*Death.*" It was the Voice. "*Feel. Act.*"

Back in 'Āina, he had told her to listen to his command, that he would show her power. Of all the struggles he had observed, this was when he chose to help her? When Haunton was seconds away from killing RO and Kirana was already doomed to meet the Magistrater? Regardless of his timing, Kirana listened. She had no other choice, and if there was a way to help her team then she had to take it. She listened. She searched the same way she searched for the staff and in-between, only this time she looked for death.

The Keepers were connected to all people, they received their power from the world around them, and it was then, through the Voice, that Kirana felt death. It was a strange, familiar feeling. When she searched for the worlds she could sense the feelings within, almost like a distinct taste. The colors were associated with people, and with their Keeper. She felt Gwen within Hiraeth, Metis within Telematic, RO within the Ward, and through them, their people. Kirana pushed herself through this mental state, trying to find death and whatever it could give her.

Around Kirana she felt the closest elements of death: the Warden bodies of the Wardens around her, their souls slowly leaving the corpses. She took a breath, only it did not feel as if she was taking in air. She could taste Belic and smelled a sharp taste of metal that burned her throat. Kirana was taking in the souls, the spirits, the energy they had left behind. She felt strong, as if there was another life within her, burning and allowing her enough power to do whatever she needed. She owned the dead, but the Voice owned death. Kirana could feel him guiding her, the same way he had when he pushed her into Hiraeth after grabbing the staff. She was not in control, but the Voice was teaching her how to find death within the in-between. He was showing her how to find souls and take the energy they had left. He was giving her power.

The sword went red in her gasp, and as her body moved without her intent she watched her eyes blur and return to sight when she was before Haunton, the sword plummeting to the Chief's hand wrapped around RO's neck. Kirana was in the air, coming down with enough force and enough speed to finally hit Haunton. The Chief attempted to pull her hand away, but she was clipped by the sword and sent back to the wall as Kirana thrust the hilt into her helmet. Before Haunton could move, the Voice had Kirana place the blade of the sword against her own neck, pressing so hard it broke and burned her skin.

When Kirana felt herself return to control she did not allow herself to show signs of sudden weakness. No, Kirana wanted Haunton to believe that she was the only one who could defeat her. No matter what RO may have told her people, Kirana wanted Haunton to see that she was not some naive, weak Permidian. She was a god.

"You don't know me." She kept the blade to her own neck, "I am not the same Permidian you think you knew, and you should know that I am willing to do anything to protect my team. So what are you willing to do to protect your mission? Because I know the Magistrater, Haunton, and I know she does not want you to present me in two pieces, let alone scarred by your mistakes."

The Chief did not move. She stood there, and Kirana hoped her sudden stillness was out of shock, and would not lead to a laugh or a new attack. Haunton straightened her back and moved her head ever so slightly at RO before walking across the cell. Kirana reached down and grabbed RO's arm, pulling her up and forcing them to move to the door of the cell. The three of them circled each other, the two Keepers following Haunton's movements as she walked slowly down to the chair and sat. Kirana and RO stepped out into the hallway, and there, framed by the doorway, was the Chief in Kirana's cell. Haunton sat on the metal chair as if it were a throne. "She will find you, Kirana. You're out of time with your only advantage being your freedom from our chains. That won't stop her."

Kirana grabbed the door to the cell and slammed it shut. She let out a cry as she sank down against the door, her body falling against the corpse of a Warden. She writhed at the feeling of wet, blood-soaked skin and shot back into the center of the hallway. She looked down at his gun and knew to take it. She knew she had to keep moving, keep surviving, but in that moment all she could do was breathe.

Her body felt cold, blood rushing through her and trembling beneath her skin. She put a hand to her chest and tried to breathe, trying to find a way to push past the horrible fears within her.

When a hand grabbed her wrist she cried out, "No!" She looked up to see RO, bloody and bruised, trying to pull her back together. Kirana felt herself break away from fear, but the only path she found herself ready to take in order to maintain focus was a path of anger. She pushed RO's hand away and crawled back, "You betrayed us." She stumbled up the wall to her feet, "You turned us in. You betrayed us?"

RO forced herself to stand, arm wrapped around her waist, "Kirana I am sorry–"

"You're sorry?" She laughed at her, she truly laughed, and suddenly there were tears running down her face, "After everything you did. You're *sorry*? Sorry for hurting Gwen and Metis. Sorry for sending me to the Magistrater and sending the others to their deaths–because by the gods RO–one little word is a lot to cover all of the damage you created!"

RO put a trembling finger to her lips, "Kirana if a patrol is close they'll hear us. You have to stay quiet–"

"What is your plan?" Kirana waited, but with no immediate answer, she laughed again, "You felt sorry. You're here out of guilt."

"I am here because I realized you were right." RO put her hands out, pleading with Kirana to understand, "I thought you were naive, and maybe you were, to trust me, but your heart means everything to this fight– this war. My people were wrong, I was blind–"

"We showed you everything. You don't realize this sooner? After everything we did?"

"I had no choice. It was too late to change–"

"It was never too late to change!" Kirana waited for her to say something else, but as RO opened her mouth to speak the Permidian realized that she did not care for any of the excuses she would hear. She thought of Gwen, tied down to a metal chair, being questioned, and turned away from her, "I should never have trusted you, that's my fault, but by the gods you are not guiltless. You are to blame for everything that is happening!"

RO stepped forward, gesturing down to the bodies of the Wardens, "I did what

I thought was best for my people. I would have done *anything* for them because it was justified by our cause."

Kirana shook her head, "It wasn't justified–"

"I know! I know, Kirana! That is why I am here. Everything I did with you was a lie, but I know what I am fighting for now. Believe it or not, Kirana, I didn't believe betrayal was the best route for my people's redemption, but I see now I was blind to their imperfections. I am guilty and always will be guilty, for the actions I have taken to stop you from succeeding away from the Magistrater. But I am here now, I am here to rescue you and others. There is still time–"

"You and I are doomed. You will die redeeming yourself and I will be trapped with the Magistrater. Our fate is sealed, RO."

"What do you mean?"

There was blood on RO's hands. Kirana looked down to her own and saw the same splattered pattern. "The Magistrater will take my mind. My body will be here but my conscience will be in whatever world she decides to keep me in. She wants to recruit me to her cause, she believes I will join her as soon as she tells me her secrets."

RO stood there and stared with a look that Kirana associated with grief. Kirana was being grieved over. She felt it there, a sort of cold breath against the back of her neck. Death and pain, breathing down her spine.

RO took a staggered breath, "We can run. Haunton thought she could defeat me alone, she was wrong, but her arrogance means that no one else knows she came here. We can get to the others before my people know what happened."

"Then what?"

"We get them on a ship. They can go after the final Keeper." She thought for a moment, "Your mind will be with the Magistrater but we can take your body to safety. When you escape from her you will come back to us."

"You are one of the smartest people I know, RO, after everything. Are you saying this out of reason or hope?" She looked up but the Warden looked away. It was simply hope. "If we run they'll see us on the cameras, or they'll just shoot us and be done with it. We don't know where the others are. We don't have the ship or the staff or any way out of this facility alone. We don't have an advantage. I don't even think we have luck anymore." Kirana looked across the hallway. It was quiet, Haunton remained still behind the door. It was then that Kirana realized they had truly trapped the Chief, one of the most powerful Wardens of all time. He took a breath and rubbed her mouth, "We can use her."

RO stopped Kirana before she could make it to the door, "What are you suggesting?"

"I'm not suggesting." She reached down and grabbed RO's sword, handing it back before grabbing a gun from a Warden body, "She is doing all of this to make me join her. This," She gestured to RO, "was merely to keep me safe. She needs me, and right now we need her."

"You want to make a deal with her? For what?"

"Metis and Gwen's protection."

RO looked away from Kirana with a short breath, and though she took a moment to think she eventually shook her head, "You're right, she needs you, but she doesn't need them. As soon as you are gone she will kill them."

"So you have to be the one to stay in control, RO." Kirana waited for her to look back and had them lock eyes, "You have to protect them with Haunton."

RO gestured to herself, "I can't keep her in check."

"She's wounded—"

"She defeated me without a weapon, Kirana. Her abilities go beyond any other Warden, and if she chooses to kill the others then they will die. The only reason we're both alive is because she *let* us live."

Kirana clenched her jaw, "Then we just have to make a deal that allows us to live again, all of us." She put the barrel of the gun to her temple and opened the door.

When Haunton saw Kirana, her demeanor did not flicker for a moment. Rather, she looked amused, "You are getting smarter."

Kirana lowered the gun and pressed the barrel against her palm, "Where are they? Where are you keeping them?"

"They are alive—"

"Where?"

"They're in the prison sector. But trust me when I tell you saving them will only lead to more harm. My soldiers will not bother to catch them once they have escaped our grasp this final time."

Kirana realized her hand was shaking and pressed the barrel harder against her palm. Now was the time to act like a god, and not the Permidian Haunton once knew her as, "Then call them off. Tell them to stand down."

"I just need you alive."

"I am willing to die to save them, Haunton." Kirana gestured down the hallway, "What will you do then? When I am at gunpoint and you're stuck here? What will the Magistrater do to you?"

"The Wardens work on a chain of command, I can not simply call them off with a single order. They know I would never do that nor would they let me. Besides, my soldiers know not to kill *you*, just the others. If you went out there running for your friends they would let you. But they would kill your friends without hesitation."

"And what if one of those bullets finds me? Then what?"

RO stepped beside Kirana and whispered, "We can lock her in the room and make a run for it. No one knows what has happened yet. There is still time to leave her here."

Haunton let out a laugh, "You'll go in the vents?"

"I'll do whatever it takes." RO moved past Kirana to try and catch her gaze, "We can run, we can hide, disguise ourselves, go in the vents, kill, whatever it takes. But we can not trust her."

Kirana looked past her to the hallway. Never before had a moment felt so much preempted grief. No one was dead quite yet, but it felt as if death was creeping up on all of them. There was too much pain for there not to be permanent damage to a soul. Kirana was angry, angry at herself, at RO, at Haunton, and at every Warden that kept her team in death's grasp. She had left Permidian searching for love, but most of the time all she faced was hatred. She wanted to be a god who could protect those she loved, and even with this power of death she was still too inexperienced to use it well. Right now, Kirana had power over Haunton, and she had to use it to her best ability for the sake of her team. No matter the cost.

"I am at the Magistrater's mercy. No matter what I do I will see her, but what you decide now will be the difference between my respect and my ignorance. You want me to trust you? You want me to join you? Then prove you are worthy of my attention."

The Chief tilted her head, "What do you want?"

"I know you aren't above killing your people, so kill them. Protect my team, allow them to escape to the final Keeper and my staff. Guide them to a ship and keep them alive, and I will listen to you. I will do what you want. I won't put up a fight."

"Kirana, no." RO put a hand on her shoulder, "They need you. We can run–"

"I told you, we're doomed. This way our fate has some meaning. We need this."

RO gestured to the Chief with her sword, "What exactly can you offer us?"

Haunton tilted her head side to side, "Willingness is quite a reward. I can offer you many things for that." Haunton gestured to Kirana, "Last time you escaped us it was because we let you. We watched you run around our facility and you led us to RO. You can't get away on your own, not in a place like this, but when no one can see you or track you… well, let's just say my people rely heavily on the idea that no one can defeat them. We are the strongest beings alive, until now. I can override many of our operations for a few minutes, the most prominent being our cameras and our communications. I can make my people blind, and then I can protect you from the stragglers."

"Not just me. My team as well."

Haunton nodded.

Kirana looked to RO to see how valuable such an offer was. RO looked back and took a second to think. With a glance back to the Wardens outside she twisted her jaw and nodded, "We're all too weak, and she's the strongest Warden alive."

Haunton crossed her legs and leaned back in the chair, "So you want me to guide your friends to a ship by killing my own soldiers in one of the most heavily guarded Warden facilities we have ever created?"

Kirana shrugged, "The other option is for you to watch me leave and find my body with the others. You betray your people or you betray me. I know your cause is more important to you than your honor, so stop pretending like you have the power here, Haunton. You're talking to gods, remember? So do we have a deal? One Keeper for the safety of four others."

"You were so young before all of this." Haunton clicked her tongue, "Look how much pain has matured you. You know, we never wanted you to feel this way." Kirana didn't answer, she had no words for a past that would have manipulated her. Haunton waited for a real answer, but when she saw Kirana's patience she nodded, "I will escort your team to a ship and you will join us without a fight."

"I will *listen* without a fight."

Haunton stood up and both RO and Kirana stepped back. The Chief straightened her back, "There is no difference." She looked at RO, "Do you accept this deal as well? I can't have you try and stop me if you intend on having my help."

"Only if she stays with us. Her body. You can't take her."

"No." Haunton shook her head, "She will stay here, with me, in this cell or another. I will only agree to this if you and the rest of the Keepers leave without Kirana. I have already given you so much mercy, do not ask for more."

"I understand." RO straightened her back, one arm still wrapped around her waist from their fight. Haunton might have gone as far as to break one of her ribs. "I will stay as well."

Kirana turned to RO and reached out as if she could stop her words from reaching the Chief, "RO, no–"

She clenched her jaw, "I can not leave you here. I need to fix what I have done. I don't care what happens to me."

"Why are you here, RO?" Kirana realized it was a question she should have asked right away.

RO didn't need a moment to think, "Because my people are suffering, everyone is, and the Keepers are the only ones who can break this system."

Haunton laughed and shook her head, "You sound like a child, RO. They've blinded you. Dragged you back to the shadows I saved you from. You're selfish."

"I am not doing this for myself. For the first time in my life, I am truly helping my people. That includes you." RO's sword slid back into its hilt and she stored it against her thigh. "How do we save the others?"

Haunton gave a small hum before turning back to Kirana, "The prison sector is not built like the one you know. It is built for the people of this world. Mortals who have information we need. They are torture rooms, large ones at that. Gwen and Metis are entire blocks away from each other, but they are in the same sector. If you want to save them, I suggest you split up before running to the ships." Haunton pulled down her sleeve and looked at her watch. With only a few swipes and one press, she placed her hand over the entire device and the light turned from blue to red. She pulled her hands away and held them up as if to put herself on display.

"That's it? Everything is off?" Kirana asked.

Haunton nodded, "When they realize I am working beside you they will block my access to such advantages." She pulled her sleeve over her watch and fixed her jacket. "But we should have enough time to run to a ship before they can regroup the entire facility."

"So we kill them and run?" RO asked, "Stop them from reporting us and move too quickly for them to track?"

Haunton nodded and walked forward. Both Keepers kept their distance as she moved into the hallway, "You may have to use the vents at some point, and the longer we run the more time we give my people to prepare." She bent down to the corpse of one of the Warden outside and grabbed their gun. With a small shake, she flicked their blood off the barrel, "We go down to the prison sector together. RO gets the Telematic. Kirana and I get the Hiraethan. We take them to a ship in B-4-34. They keep an array of bombs in a room by the depot, so if they go into a lockdown you can simply blast your way through the wall and escape."

Kirana moved out into the hallway, gun still pressed to her hand and finger resting on the trigger. She studied Haunton, finally able to see her without fear of being killed at her hands. The Warden looked right back down to her. Kirana took a breath, "This is the only way I will listen. Betray our deal and–"

"I understand, Kirana. It is actually more favorable on my side than yours, so why would not I agree? Besides, I want you to trust us, after this. We do this out of care for our worlds and for *you.*"

She reached out to touch Kirana's face and the Keeper shot back, "No."

Haunton walked out of the cell toward her, "You look traumatized, my dear. I hope when this is over you get your rest before we begin your true journey as our god." She gestured to Kirana's nose, "The bleeding will only get worse."

Kirana wiped her nose and felt blood. It was as if she traveled from another dimension, but in this case, she assumed it was the Magistrater pulling her in.

The Chief started to walk past her down the hallway, "RO, you and I will take the lead. Kirana, shoot whatever moves, and when you start to feel weak stay back. When the Magistrater takes your mind you will be in danger, and knowing your team they will risk everything to keep you safe."

Kirana followed her down the hallway, "And you will do everything in your power to keep them from harm. That is the only way I could trust you."

"Oh, you will trust me, Kirana. I have a feeling after you speak to the Magistrater and learn of our plans you may even call your friends back to the facility."

"No secret is that powerful." Kirana prayed that it was true.

"We'll just have to see. Soon."

Haunton rounded the corner with the two Keepers in time to see a patrol of Wardens starting to walk by. At the sight of Haunton in front of the newly freed and bleeding Keepers, they stopped walking and waited for instructions.

Haunton raised her gun for her soldiers, "We have 15 minutes."

Chapter 54

* * *

METIS

METIS FELT NUMB.

Like there was nothing left he could give. He had lied, refused to give any piece of the truth, tried to stay silent between screams, and now... he had nothing left to give at all. He knew there were answers to the question they were asking but he couldn't even find them. He had cried, screamed, even laughed, and suddenly he could not do anything. He wasn't stunned or paralyzed. He was just... numb.

Colonel Harris tapped the side of his hanging head, "Is he alive?"

"He is." The doctor seemed pleased.

"He thinks we're done?" Haris snapped his fingers to Fácil, "Play it again." Metis winced and shook his head, but he shouldn't have reacted like that. He shouldn't have reacted at all. He just didn't want to hear it again. Harris laughed, "You don't like this one, do you? We'll play it a hundred more times for you if we need to."

"Sir." Fácil was holding the headphones, and Metis turned his head away. "Are we sure this is the right phase?"

"Do it."

"We don't want to drive him insane–"

"I'm giving you a good show, aren't I?"

"Not if he dies."

"Do as I say, doctor."

Fácil hesitated, before grabbing Metis by his hair and pushing the headphones on his head. It was quiet, and even as the Warden before him seemed to speak, Metis couldn't hear him. He couldn't hear his breath. He felt as if he was stuck deep underwater, and no one knew he was there. He was sinking. Drowning. Diving deeper and deeper. The farther down he sank, the less chance he had to ever breathe again. How many times he had watched bodies sink down those channels? Enough to understand what it is like to let someone fade beneath the waters. To disappear. For a while, there was just silence. Endless silence. Then it kicked in. He heard Gwen screaming. It was so loud that her pain surrounded him. The worst part was that it was real. They were hurting her. Because of him? He didn't know. He couldn't think. The screams were not enough to drive him insane, he could push through, he knew he could, but there was something about the noise. They had altered it to a perfect pitch to force his mind to hear *every* sound. More screams joined in, creating a choir of suffering. It was too loud, too violent.

He had heard so many screams in his lifetime. Those screams represented more than just those the Wardens bothered to torture. Their screams morphed into his victims. He heard the children, their cries for help, their hysterical sobbing, their blood-wrenching arc of pain. He heard Axel. He heard Mixer. He heard the Master.

It was all his fault.

All his fault.

All his fault.

He tried to shake the headphones off but they wouldn't budge. He tried to scream over them but his voice didn't come through.

Oh, but he was selfish too. He should have let himself suffer in those screams. Fester in his guilt. He should have stayed there and died with his victims. If he died he would only hope the Wardens would throw him into the Telematic waters, so he can lay with those he destroyed. Drown with them.

Maybe he could disappear too.

The screams stopped as Fácil ripped off the headphones. Metis twisted his entire body away from it, digging his head into his shoulder as he panted. He was tired of the pain. He wanted to be free of it... but that was selfish. He knew that. The real torture was this conflict, but they knew that as well as he did. They just didn't know why. Soon, they might just learn.

"Telematic." His ears were ringing, the voices blurred together from his own exhaustion. The Warden grabbed his face and pulled him back to face him. That's when he saw someone new was in the room. Standing right behind him. He blinked and forced his eyes to focus.

RO.

Her eyes were locked on his body, gaze bouncing from wound to wound. There was so much guilt stretched across her face that it took Metis a moment to realize that she too was injured. He didn't remember RO looking the way she did when she betrayed him. The guilt was the same, but her injuries were new. Blood smeared across her face, a bruise on her cheek, her uniform twisted and uneven. Behind whatever punishment they had given her, she was wearing the same uniform that she had the day Metis first met her. She was back where she belonged: with the other monsters.

Harris stood up and turned to face RO, "General. We weren't expecting you."

She clenched her jaw and matched his gaze, "Haunton suggested I help with the interrogations. The Magistrater will be with Kirana shortly so I can remain here until called upon."

Metis stared at RO, and he must have looked as hurt as he felt because when Harris glanced over he laughed, "The betrayal continues." He turned back to RO, "I'm interested in what you can get him to confess, he hasn't told us much so far. He's a stubborn Telematic." Harris grabbed the screen from his chair and handed it to RO. When he stepped to the side she moved forward and sat on the chair. Metis kept his eyes on RO, watching her scroll down the list of questions. When she looked up she hadn't expected him to already be watching her, and they locked eyes. It was barely a second before she looked away.

"Confirm you are the Telematic Hero."

The worst part was that Metis had trusted her. He had truly trusted her with his life. She had done the same or, at least, he thought she did. Was she truly lying that whole time? How was that possible? How could someone be so lifeless? He had taken care of her. He had been her friend, her partner, her teammate. He made her food, he studied her weapon for her, he introduced her to Hiraethans, and, gods, he saved her life so many times. He had thought she was grateful, but no, she was just using him.

"No confirmation." She marked something down on the screen and glanced over at Haris, "Tell me about your childhood."

He had trusted her. Truly trusted her. How? Was he that stupid? He had been the one who convinced everyone she could be trusted. It was all a lie.

"Telematic. Answer me."

He just stared at her. For a few seconds, she didn't say another word. Eyes on the screen. She stopped scrolling for a moment and slowly looked up. They locked eyes, and this time she didn't let go. They stayed there, and Metis tried looking beyond her gaze. He found something there. Some sort of... sadness. The way she looked at him was almost longingly. Her eyes were red and Metis realized she was about to cry. He had brought a cold Warden to tears. At that moment he thought there was hope, that there was a chance she was still on their side, after everything. But RO didn't set him free, she looked back to the ground and stood up, "I need the room." She took out her weapon, "It'll be more impactful if it's just me and him." Her weapon went poker hot.

It was an act. Metis just shook his head. He didn't know what else he could do. No. No, that couldn't have been a lie. He had been so sure. Did he fall into traps so easily? After all those years he still trusted too easily. As if someone could be what he needed.

Harris gestured to the two Warden at the door and they left.

RO glanced back at the Colonel before looking at Metis. She didn't look sad. She looked ready to kill. "You once told me that no one likes killing." She raised her weapon, inspecting it, "That was not true. People enjoy others' pain. But not by choice." She lowered it to her side, "My people kill. But only because they are told to. So I will fight for their freedom and the freedom of your people. To end the suffering. To end the killing." She locked eyes with Metis, "Beside you."

With a single turn, she swung the sword through the air and let it carve through the throat of Harris. The Warden tried to let out a scream, but in his panic, all that came out of his mouth was a spray of blood. He dropped to his knees, clawing at his throat.

"Wait! Wait!" Fácil pleaded as he ran behind Metis, but RO had set her target. She flipped her sword around and threw it without making another step. It went out of Metis's view, but with a defining scream and the thud of a body, he figured she didn't miss. Harris tried to move to the door but she spun around and kicked the side of his face, twisting his head so far his neck cracked and he fell limp to the floor.

RO let out a staggered breath and looked at Metis, crying. She was truly crying. He had seen her tears begin, but that was as much as he thought she would give. But no. She clenched her jaw, trying to not let more fall as she moved behind Metis and retrieved her sword.

Coming back, she held it by his hand, "I'm going to burn you free." She bent down beside him and held her sword steady. She was cutting through the hinges, melting through the lock. Within seconds, Metis's hand went free. He pulled it away from the burning metal and held his arm to his chest. Scar to his heart. RO moved around him to the next one. And the next two. Without a word, she set him free. She moved around to his most injured arm, looking at it carefully, "I don't think there is time to get to a medical room. There is a plan in place, everything is being taken care of. I can explain along the way."

He just stared at her, and suddenly the idea that she had just saved him flooded away, "How did you do it?"

She closed her eyes and pointed behind her ear in shame, "A chip. I sent in reports of my findings." She shook her head firmly, "I can explain later. We have to leave now before someone comes back. We have a very short window before my people realize what is going on."

She put out her hand to help him up, but he didn't take it. He got up on his own, barely able to stand but managing alone. His body was in shock, with a few bruises and cuts but he could walk. It would just take a while to build the strength to run.

"Metis…" He looked back at her and saw the tears had returned. She frowned them down, wishing them away, "I'm sorry. I had no–"

"You did." He forced them to lock eyes, "I saw the moment you realized that our cause was right. I saw it in the Arena. I saw it when you woke up after I healed you. I saw it *every day* in Hiraeth. I saw it when you took me away from the village. You had every chance to tell us what you were but you didn't."

"Metis–"

"No. Don't start begging. Don't tell me you didn't realize what you were doing was wrong."

She stayed silent for a moment, before swallowing and turning her sadness into something darker, "I followed orders, Metis. Don't tell me you haven't done the same. Followed someone else's instructions to–"

"I did."

"And what did it cost you?"

"Everything... and everyone."

She let out a staggered breath, she was annoyed by him, but she didn't have any right to be. "Then you understand I didn't do this for myself. I had no... I didn't–"

"You knew–"

"Of course, I knew! I knew what I was doing would cause other people pain. But I am here now. I am here to save you."

He shook his head, "I trusted you–"

"You were foolish, and so was I, apparently, for trusting the people who raised me. Who trained me? I was foolish to trust my people–"

He turned away from her, looking around the room for a weapon. He looked back to Harris and saw he had a holster on. Metis limped over past RO and bent down to get the small gun. He grabbed it and used the wall to stand back up. "They are hurting Gwen." He checked the ammunition. It was full. "I heard her screaming. I don't know what they are doing to her but it's because of you. I don't take lightly to people who hurt others with the excuse that they were just... following orders."

"Then I will live with that guilt! Forever. I will hate myself for what I have done. But I couldn't have stopped it. I didn't know what side I was on half the time. I do now." She moved back to him, trying to get close so he could see her guilt. Even in her heroic acts, she was still manipulating him.

He stepped away from her, "We gave you so many chances. I showed you everything. I let you see everything, and you chose to stay with your people. Second chances are as far as my mercy reaches."

"You can hate me as much as you want, Metis, but I am here now. We have to run. I set Kirana free. She's on her way to Gwen."

"You left her alone?"

"No, I..." She mouthed the next words before going silent. RO stepped back, "She's with Chief Haunton." Before Metis could speak she waved her hands in the air, "I know, Metis, I know. But she wants Kirana to trust her. Haunton won't protect us but she'll protect Kirana–"

"You left Kirana with that... *monster.*" He laughed, he didn't mean to, it just slipped out. He pulled his hand down his face, "She'll kill us all."

RO tried to move closer again, "We made a deal. We had to. We needed an advantage. She is our only hope, Metis, I had no other choice. She will get you and Gwen to safety."

"You had–"

"You can blame me for everything that has happened before now, but I swear to you my actions from here on are for you. Look at me Metis. Look at me." He locked eyes with her, "I am ready to die here to protect the Keepers. We're going to fight our way through the facility, get you on a ship, and find the final Keeper. Kirana's mind will be taken by the Magistrater, and in return for Haunton's help she will stay here. I had no choice in that, that was Kirana's decision and it will keep you, Gwen, and the final Keeper safe."

"Safe?" He shook his head, "I am not leaving Kirana here."

"We can't do this alone. We can't fight Haunton either." She gestured to herself, bruised and bleeding, "The only way to get a ship is by letting her lead us there, that means leaving Kirana here. They won't kill her, but without Haunton they'll kill you and Gwen."

RO stopped for what Metis could only assume was her anticipation of another argument. She was waiting for Metis to say something, to yell at her, but he couldn't. The situation was horrific and it was her fault. He left her in the silence of his blame.

She tried to break it, "I thought I was justified. I've always thought that no matter what I do, if it benefits my people or my ranking, then it can't be bad. I'm fixing my mistakes."

He shook his head and looked away, "That's not enough."

It was ironic. He knew it was. His own guilt stemmed from following orders. He knew this instantly but he didn't care. She should have stopped. He should have stopped. She did it for her superiors. He had been doing it for the Master. For 11 years and 3 months, he had been living with his own hatred of what he did. He deserved that. He still did. Now it was her turn.

She was still the reason for all his pain. All of Gwen's. All of Kirana's. All of Lorenzo's. All of Hiraeth's. She deserved to suffer.

"We need to go." RO put her weapon away, "Haunton and Kirana are in Gwen's cell across the facility. We'll meet in between and make a run for the ship. The cameras are off but my people will catch on to where we are soon enough. Kill every Warden you see." They locked eyes, and hearing the irony, RO looked away, "You'll survive this. I'll do whatever it takes to get you out of here. And… if we get a chance, save Kirana from this deal. We need Haunton to get to the ship but after that…"

Metis gestured to the door, "I'll do what it takes. We should go, *General.*" It hurt him to mock her, it really did, but she deserved the punishments of her blind loyalty.

This was the first time anyone had come close to his own guilt.
It was the first time he let someone else suffer like he did.

Chapter 55

* * *

GWEN

GWEN WAS TERRIFIED.

Not because of the room she was in, not because of the Wardens, not because of the impending promise of pain, but because she was alone. Truly alone. How could they get out of this? She didn't even know where Kirana was. Did they even take her? What if she was still there, burning up in the flames of that town? Not even Ben E could save them.

Not Kirana. Not Metis. Not RO. Not Enzo. Not her family. Not her father.

She was alone.

And so very scared.

The Wardens could see this. The man before her looked at her as if she was an interesting book. He was young, older than Gwen but younger than she assumed such a high-ranking Warden would be. Mid twenties at the most. She had hoped his youth would allow him to find sympathy, but it did not. The doctor moved around her to something new, and the Warden before her didn't seem to care as she pleaded for her life.

"Please I just– We didn't know anything– We just–"

He rolled his eyes and scrolled down on his screen, "I usually like when a prisoner starts talking, but this is just rambling." He gave a small smirk to the doctor, sharing some sort of inside joke, "Remember that wrinkly old man? What was his name?" He laughed, "You know, I don't remember." He locked eyes with Gwen, "I would hate to go off schedule, but it seems your Telematic friend is doing worse than you are."

Metis… She winced at the thought. Knowing him, he wouldn't talk. He was stronger than she was, able to last longer, and the consequences of that would be deadly.

The Warden knocked on his screen, "Damn thing is on the fritz." When it flashed back to life he read it quickly and looked up at Gwen, "One last question before we try something new. Please list out what you know of Lorenzo's past."

"Please!" She resorted to the only thing she could do: pleading. "He's not a danger– He just wants to help– He's just trying to help! Please–"

The Warden gave a small laugh and gestured to the Doctor. She heard them starting to move behind her. Gwen had foolishly believed that their journey would be easier after they left the Ward, but time after time they had been thrown back into danger. It was because of RO. She had told them about Lorenzo. Her family was there. The traitor was going to get her family killed.

The doctor didn't touch her, instead, they put some sort of clip on her chair. They had done this before. The moment she didn't answer their question they sent a bolt of electricity through the chair and into her body. It was horrible, like her bones were being both shaken and burned at the same time. It was strong enough to kill her if they let it ride too long. Gwen wanted to blurt out answers to these questions to avoid more pain but… she couldn't. She had to stay strong. She was a god, and that had to mean something in a situation like the one she was in.

"Last chance: list out what you know of Lorenzo's past."

She stayed silent. Her eyes filled with tears and within seconds she was sobbing. She didn't want to cry, now was not the time for tears but she couldn't help it. She was so scared. She just wanted to go home. She needed Kirana. She shut her eyes and prayed for the Permidian to somehow find a way to her. She prayed that the gods would find another stroke of luck. She prayed for Kirana.

She waited for a jolt of pain. She waited for another question or comment. But there was just silence. She looked up and saw the Warden was staring at her, studying her. He looked down to his screen and started scrolling through some sort of file. He bit his lower lip in thought, eventually getting up and going over to the doctor. The two of them looked at it together, having a hushed conversation right at Gwen's ear.

"Can you do a blood test of any kind to double-check?"

"I can have a team compare the Telematic one to this one."

The young Warden glanced down at Gwen, "What is your name?"

She didn't understand what was going on, but if she was going to die, they might as well know who she was. "Gwen."

"Who was with you on that rooftop?"

Rooftop? Back in Hiraeth. That was when she first held the staff. She didn't answer the question simply because of her own confusion. They knew Kirana and her father had been there, who else could they be referring to? The doctor flipped a switch and a jet of electricity pumped through her body. She hadn't been expecting it and thanked the gods for how short it lasted.

"Come on. Answer the question. Did you have a sister or someone else up there other than the Permidian?"

"No!" She was shaking, her throat was dry.

The Warden put down the screen and looked her over, "Where is your weapon?"

She didn't answer. She watched the doctor's hand hover over the switch, but they did not press it down. In fact, they moved away from it.

"Do you even have a weapon?"

She just looked up at the Warden, not saying a word.

He sighed, tapping his screen on his thigh, "I think we have the wrong one." He turned to the doctor, "Could that have happened?"

"It's probable."

Wrong one?

"That's exactly what happened." He pressed something on his screen and shut it off, "This girl is no god."

Gwen didn't know what to say, what to do. She wanted to go with this lie for her own sake. Maybe they could see her as something innocent. If they did, they might let her go, and she could return for Metis and Kirana. Her own pride made her want to yell out that she was a real Keeper, but she just sat there, too scared to utter a word.

It was then that she realized they might have been right. What had she done for the past weeks other than be a burden? Kirana had never seen a day of fighting and yet she was leading a team of gods with no fear. Metis had gotten her and everyone else out of dozens of situations. Even RO, the *traitor*, had done her work to help them. Gwen hadn't done anything but stay behind. Weaponless. Powerless. Helpless.

What if the staff got it wrong?

There was a knock on the door. Everyone turned back to look, and even Gwen lifted her eyes to see what was going on. When the door opened a new Warden appeared in the doorway. Gwen shot up. It was Haunton. She scanned the room, standing away from the doorway and saying nothing.

The Warden before Gwen straightened his back, "Chief Haunton." He sounded scared. "Is there anything I can help you with?"

Still, she said nothing. Everyone waited, standing so they could all see the new Warden. It was only then that someone else came into view. As soon as they arrived there was a gunshot. Gwen screamed and shut her eyes, waiting for the bullet. Her body locked in fear, it took her too long to realize there was no bullet against her body.

She heard two bodies fall beside her and she opened her eyes. Kirana was running inside the room, gun in hand. She dropped to her knees before Gwen.

"Gwen!"

"Kirana…" Her voice shook and it was all she could muster the strength to say. Her god had answered her prayers.

Kirana pulled at the cuffs around her wrists, frantically trying to pull them off. It was then that Gwen saw her trembling hands. She looked up at her face to find tears on Kirana's cheeks dried around ash from the village. Her eyes were wide and red. Her nose was bleeding. She had never looked so terrified. Gwen looked past Kirana to Haunton. The Warden was in the room with them, standing like a statue in the corner.

"What is going on?" Gwen whispered, not looking away from Haunton.

Kirana didn't answer, and instead turned back to the Chief. "How do I unlock them?"

The Chief pulled something out of her belt. Gwen got ready to see a knife or a gun. Instead, she saw a chip in her hand. No, a remote. She pressed it, and the handcuffs flew open.

Gwen threw herself out of the chair. She needed to get away, but her legs failed her and she collapsed onto Kirana. Instead of helping her up, Kirana dropped with her and held her in an embrace. Gwen forced her away and turned to Haunton,

"What are you doing?"

Kirana tried to pull her up, "Can you run?"

"I don't know." She used Kirana's help to try and stand. She felt weak. Her body shook from torture. Her hand had been smashed, her fingers crushed, and she could barely form a fist. Her ribs repeated the pain from being poked and hit with a blunt metal pole. Her cheek had bruised from a smack. Her head felt dizzy from screaming. But she could stand, she could walk, and with enough motivation, she could run.

She stepped away from Kirana, holding her side and staring at the Chief, "What is going on?"

Kirana grabbed her arm and guided them to the back of the room. Kirana whispered, "She's helping us." Gwen hated those words. She shook her head and tried to step back into the room. Kirana wouldn't let her. "We don't have time, Gwen. The Magistrater is coming for me."

"She's here?"

"She's going to take my mind. We have 10 minutes until I'm stuck with her and my body is stuck… here." Kirana swallowed and looked to the ground. When she regained herself she looked up to Gwen and held her shoulders, "I made a deal. I need you to trust me, I need you to follow Haunton–"

"Kirana, no–"

"She needs me to trust her. I said I would listen to the Magistrater if she got the rest of you to safety." More tears started to fall and Kirana stopped blinking to keep herself from crying, "This is the only way you and Metis can get away. To find the final Keeper and stay safe."

Gwen shook her head violently, ignoring her headache, "There is always another way, Kirana. We could go through the vents." She leaned in and whispered, "We can kill her. You are not staying with her. I won't let you."

Haunton stepped towards them, "There isn't much time–"

Gwen shot back and hit one of the Doctor's trays. She grabbed the first knife she saw and held it up, Gwen's blood still lining the blade. Kirana moved to her, "Gwen we don't have time."

"We can't–"

Kirana pushed her hand down so violently it nearly hit Gwen's leg, "*Gwen.*" Kirana clenched her jaw, eyes locked on her, "We don't have time. We need to run.

This is the only way we will survive. I need you to trust me. I am about to meet the world's most powerful villain, the least you can do is stay safe." She swallowed, "RO saved my life. She is getting Metis as we speak. They're not too far, if we run we can be with them in less than ten minutes. I don't trust these Wardens but I know that RO has finally seen that our cause is right, and Haunton... well, she has to protect you," Kirana looked back to the Chief, "or she will have no Permidian Keeper."

Haunton moved to the door, "I understand the deal, Kirana. We have nine minutes. I suggest we keep moving."

Gwen grabbed Kirana's arm, "Don't do this. Please, there is always another way."

"We don't–"

"Then how are we supposed to leave? What are we supposed to do without you, Kirana?"

"Survive." Kirana pulled Gwen in and held her close. As quietly as she could she whispered, "Save the final Keeper and hide. I can escape. If you are with my body, then I can return to consciousness and we can run. I will never join them." Kirana broke their embrace and moved the two of them to the door, gun held up and ready to be used. Haunton saw this and went out first.

Gwen had no memory of the prison sector she had been brought through. Everything happened so quickly and so painfully all she remembered were hallways that matched one another and a very dim lighting. As she limped out of the cell, hand around her wounds, she saw the sector wasn't dim, but rather painted darker than the normally bright Warden facilities. The walls were gray and black with pipes between the walls, floor, and ceiling. Their footsteps echoed along the area, and for the first time in the last hour, Gwen could hear another person breathing with the same staggered fear as her. She took Kirana's hand before Kirana caught on, wrapped Gwen's arm around her shoulder, and ran behind Haunton with a gun to her side.

One thing was certain, the Wardens were hesitant about what they could do to the Keepers. The patrols of Wardens that arrived didn't seem to know what was going on. They saw their Chief running down the hallways with two injured Keepers. Some raised their weapons to the Keepers, others tried to step aside and let Haunton pass, fearful of disobeying their superior. They had orders to never kill Kirana, but they had heard nothing about Gwen, and certainly not Haunton. In their hesitation, Haunton raised her own gun and shot them dead. Those who heard the gunshots would come running, but still, they did not know what was going on and who to shoot. If they were fast, they would raise their guns to Gwen. If they were smart, they would aim for Haunton and make a final stand for themselves.

The way Haunton fought was horrific. She had no care for her fellow soldiers or the way they died. Taking a life was as easy as taking another step for her, and Gwen watched as she practically strolled through the prison and killed whatever moved around her. Unlike the Chief, Kirana was panicked, yet through it all she remained bound to their safety. Haunton took out the many Wardens in front of them, but stragglers slipped behind to make their own move on the Keepers. Gwen was armed only with the knife, and too weak to react if someone came close. Kirana's fear drove her into paranoia, and she was able to catch the slightest noise as they kept pushing forward. She turned behind them and shot dozens of times until a bullet finally hit one of the soldiers and sent them to the ground.

Haunton stopped at a new turn with the Keepers close behind her in time to see a new group of Wardens waiting for them. As they had done before, Kirana and Gwen dove back the way they came as Haunton pushed forward, bullets bouncing off her armor and hitting the prison walls. The two Keepers turned and got ready to fight whoever could attack from behind, only to see two Wardens already within arms reach. They had two metal poles on either side of them and shot forward, one for each Keeper. Kirana dove out of the way and shot at the Warden as Gwen used her knife to try and push the pole away from her. She couldn't dive out of the way, she could barely dodge the blows at all, but when her knife hit the weapon, a spark of electricity filled her and she dropped it. Kirana shot again and again, and it was only then that Gwen recognized how similar the two Wardens' armor was to Haunton's: black and bulletproof.

Gwen had no choice but to back up into the hallway with another dozen Wardens facing the wrath of Haunton. The Warden swung for Gwen as bullets started to fly around her. She dodged their blows until they swung for her face and sent her to the ground. As they tried to drive their pole into her she rolled to the side and missed a bullet by mere inches. Gwen was already so injured, she could barely get up, let alone fight. As the Warden shot forward for another attack she gave in. Gwen gave up. She laid there and heard the words of the Wardens who interrogated her.

This girl is no god.

Kirana was suddenly above the Warden, blood splattered across her face as she came down with Gwen's knife in hand. She dove the blade into his neck and the pole hit the floor in front of the Hiraethan. The Warden let out a scream as someone grabbed Gwen from behind.

"Kirana!"

Haunton pulled her up to her feet and shoved a gun in her hand, "Shoot something." The Chief turned her weapon to the Warden below Kirana and placed a bullet where the knife's blade had entered. Kirana got back up to her feet, covered in blood, and stumbled into the wall. She pushed off but hurried to them at a slower pace than before. Her eyes were unfocused, and though the panic remained she looked exhausted. Her mind was slipping. Haunton didn't hand Gwen the gun to protect herself; she gave Gwen a weapon to protect Kirana.

Haunton looked forward suddenly and raised her gun. Gwen could hear someone coming towards them and raised her own Warden gun, ignoring her injuries and trying to be the god her team needed. Haunton ran forward down the hallway before stopping at the corner. Gwen had her gun raised, hands shaking, but before the Wardens could show themselves, Haunton dropped her hand, leaned against the wall, and let the people appear without a fight.

RO rounded the corner and swung her sword for Haunton's head. At the sight of who she was attacking and the people behind her, RO pushed her sword back and missed the Chief by a hair. Haunton didn't even flinch. RO put out a hand and grabbed Metis in time to pull his gun away from Gwen and the Chief. Gwen felt such relief seeing him there, alive. He was not safe or without pain, but he was alive, and for now that was all she could ask for. Gwen's relief vanished as soon as she realized RO did not look guilty, a gun in one hand and her sword in the other, she was as she always was: focused. She looked bruised and wounded, blood against her face and armor. She wore blood beautifully, as if death was an honor she could wear.

Metis dropped his gun and ran to Gwen, pulling her into a hug, "You're alive." She wanted to hug him back but the embrace alone hurt so much, and by him only using one arm she recognized that he was in similar pain. They had faced the worst of the Warden's torture. He let go of Gwen and grabbed Kirana by her shoulders, before looking up suddenly to Haunton, as if forgetting she was even there.

Haunton laughed at him, and gesturing to them all, she said, "The Keepers back together once again. This is the last time you will see each other under this horrid attempt for a rebellion. Remember that now. You have six minutes until it all ends."

Chapter 56

✳ ✳ ✳

Kirana

KIRANA RAN DOWN the hallway next to Haunton. The Chief took the lead and turned the corner in time to reach the new patrol of Wardens first. Three bullets flew and three bodies dropped as Kirana slid down with the wall as her cover to take out the last one. She shot five times before the sixth bullet hit between the armor plates. The Warden let out a scream and dropped to the ground.

As the group of Keepers and Warden protectors ran past the dead bodies the lights suddenly went out.

"Haunton!" Kirana reached back for Gwen, blinking desperately to find her.

"Be silent." The Chief grabbed her by her jacket and held her as the lights flickered back on, only instead of illuminating the hallway in a white light, they turned the walls dark with a deep red glow. Haunton let go of her and pulled up her watch, "They know. Communications are being rebooted in an emergency protocol."

"Now what?" Metis ran to Kirana's side, his hand around his forearm, "How far are the ships?"

Haunton gestured past the bodies of her latest victims, "Just a few turns. We will have to run, my people will be sending everything they have to kill you and capture Kirana."

Kirana stepped up to Haunton "So you will protect them–"

The Chief grabbed Kirana's shoulder, "I understand the deal, you need not repeat yourself, though you do remind me that it may be your turn to hold up your end of our exchange." She looked down the hallway before opening her watch, "You have three minutes until the Magistrater arrives. I cannot risk you getting hurt along the way; you will wait here."

Gwen stepped up beside Kirana, "Haunton–"

"Are you not grateful for all I have given you?" She looked back to Metis and RO, "Do you expect me to do more?" Kirana tried to get out of her grasp but Haunton pushed her to the wall.

"Don't hurt her!" Metis tried to reach Kirana but RO stopped him.

At the sight of this, Gwen looked back and yelled, "Let go of him!"

"Stop!" Kirana put her hands up and looked back to Haunton. The Chief let go of her and allowed Kirana to run back to her team. "Don't fight. We can not fight right now. I need you to stay focused–"

Gwen stepped away from RO and pointed at her, "Do you not remember what she did? Are you on her side?"

"I am on *our* side." Kirana drove her finger into her chest, "*Our* side, Gwen. We are the Keepers. She is still a Keeper, and right now we need her help."

Metis looked down at RO, "You told them about Lorenzo?"

It took Kirana a moment to recognize that it was Metis targeting RO and not Gwen. She had never heard him sound so hateful, and it hurt her to realize how fractured her team really was.

RO clenched her jaw, eyes to the ground and hands raised just high enough for them to see she was not holding a weapon. That was how much tension the situation held; at any moment it could break into a deadly fight, "I told them everything. I followed my orders–"

"You told them about my family!"

"I never said their names–"

Gwen looked over to Haunton, "Kill her." Everyone froze at her words. Even the Chief didn't seem to comprehend what she was asking her to do. Gwen gestured to RO, "You want her dead, right? She betrayed you too."

Kirana put a hand out to Gwen, "Don't do this. Please."

"She told them where to find my family. She let them torture us. She told them *everything.*" Gwen's anger betrayed her sorrow, and though there were fears in her eyes she was not crying out of grief, but hatred. She swallowed and held her chin up higher, "You traitor!"

"Gwen please–"

"You're on her side!" Gwen looked at Kirana in disgust.

Kirana looked over to Metis for support, but he was walking away from the group and moving to Haunton, "How do we find the staff?"

"Metis!"

The Chief looked from Gwen to Metis and laughed, "This is quite a surprise, but the longer you delay the less time you have to run."

Kirana ran to his side and grabbed him, ignoring his wince, "Metis, please!"

He looked down at her, "Following orders is no excuse. She knew what she was doing."

"So you want to kill her too?"

He shook his head, "We need her."

"She knows what she did! She's here to make up for her mistakes!" Kirana looked back from Metis to Gwen, "Everyone needs to calm down! We can't stop moving. We don't have time. You can figure this out later–"

In a single moment Kirana felt her entire body flicker. It was the strangest sensation, as if her very body decided to give out and fade to a very quiet, dark place. She felt cold and suddenly her legs gave out. When her senses returned she felt blood fall down her face, down her nose, down her ears. She was on her knees, Gwen at her side yelling her name. Kirana looked up at Haunton first.

The Chief gestured to the wall, "Your time has come."

Kirana forced herself to stand using Gwen's help. As soon as she was back on her feet she grabbed Gwen by her shirt, "Don't kill her. Don't hurt her–"

"She–"

"She saved my life. She rescued me. She realized she was wrong. Gwen, trust me!" Kirana moved to RO, wiping blood from her lips, "You need to lead. I need you to not come back. Stay with them."

She shook her head, "I'm not leaving you here–"

"All we can do is survive. I will survive here, but you and the others do not have the same protection. You have to provide that protection."

Without waiting a second RO said, "I swear, I will keep them safe."

Haunton moved to Metis before Kirana could and handed him a screen from her belt, "This is how you can locate the staff. It's miles from here on a cargo ship. By now they will have located the village where the Keeper resides. You will have to get past an army."

"*We.*" Kirana corrected, but Haunton shook her head.

"All you asked me to do was get them to a ship."

"I asked you to protect them!" Kirana put her hands together and moved in front of Haunton, "Please! Just a little bit longer, Haunton. They need your help–"

The Chief pushed Kirana's hands down, "Do not pray to me. I have given you all I have, but the more time you waste here the less time I have to escort your friends to a ship." Kirana felt her body give out as it had before, only this time Haunton grabbed her before she could fall. Haunton lowered her to the ground and leaned her against the wall. Kirana was seated next to a Warden, covered in blood just as they were, "I hope in time you will see how trustworthy I truly am. How much mercy I have."

Kirana put a trembling hand on the wall and forced her broken body to face the Warden, "You only have mercy for your mission. You're... numb."

Numb... emotionless...

Kirana had met so many different people in her journey through the worlds. Everyone was different, not only separated by cultures but also by personalities. Even the Wardens, who she had first thought would be like her own people, had their own unique motivations for life. RO was complex even in her ability to remain focused and detached. Haunton was the same, only she did not flicker.

Kirana never expected to see one of her own people outside of Permidia.

She swallowed, "You can't *feel* anything. Can you?"

"You're getting smarter." Haunton tilted her head, "You were always bright but now... now you're something far beyond what you were back in those Permidian fields, waiting for *love.*"

Kirana grew cold. The room went silent. She went still. It had been so long since she had last been to Permidian. It had felt like years, to the point in which she forgot what she left behind. She knew that voice, she knew that numb care, she knew that Permidian.

"*Tia.*"

Kirana never expected to see her sister outside of Permidia.

Tia put out a hand and moved a piece of Kirana's hair behind her ear, "I'll be there for your meeting with the Magistrater. You'll see why we had to do... all of this." She put her hands to the side of her helmet and lifted it. Tia's face revealed itself, and Kirana felt both the sharp familiarity and horrific difference of what her sister had become. Her features were dimmed by sweat, the bridge of her nose was caved in by the bullet Metis had sent through her helmet back during their first meeting. But her eyes... Kirana knew those eyes, strikingly brown and quick to drift softly, unbothered by distractions or noise. But for the first time, Kirana didn't see love within them, not even warmth. Gwen's eyes were bright and loving, but Tia's was cold and focused on a concept far beyond Kirana: a mission. "You'll trust me again, Kirana, once you know the truth. We're still sisters, after all, you're just on the wrong side of a war. That'll end today."

Kirana tried to say something, anything. She wanted to ask questions, she wanted to fight, she wanted to kill her and kiss her and heal her, but all that came out was a gasping, wheezing cry, and suddenly tears were streaming down her face.

Her sister was a Warden. Her sister was the right hand to the Magistrater.

Haunton was a monster.

Tia was a liar.

Kirana knew that, she knew that well before seeing her sister in Warden armor, but she had never, truly acknowledged the extent of the lies. Through everything, through every mystery uncovered and every lie exposed, Kirana always had her sister. Tia, the one Permidian who loved her. Kirana cried because, suddenly, it was all lies. Every aspect of her entire existence was a planned operation. Kirana felt like an experiment, like a lab rat being put back in a cage.

Tia held the side of her face and Kirana was horrified to find herself not writhing at the touch. She wanted her sister to hold her, to look at her the way Haunton was looking at that moment. Haunton. The Chief and right hand to the Magistrater. Kirana glanced back to her team to find them all staring at Haunton with complete fear. All she could think was how Haunton's reveal was keeping her team from fighting.

After a moment, Tia stood up, put her helmet back on, and gestured down the hallway, "We'll need to move quickly. Are you ready?"

"Tia." Metis put his hand, and for the first time in the last hour, Kirana recognized his kindness. He was negotiating for her, finally removing himself from the feud with RO, "You already have Kirana, she will be with the Magistrater, let us take her body. Please."

"No. She will remain with me."

"If you are right, if she will join you after the Magistrater tells her everything then you have nothing to lose. We can't leave her here."

"I have everything to lose." Haunton gestured down the hallway with her gun, "Now choose whether you wish to leave here under my guide or go on alone. Only one of those options allows–"

Kirana dropped to the floor as her body gave out. Her vision curled in and out of darkness and she did everything she could to stay upright. "Please–" She was trying to tell her team to go, but as soon as she spoke something hot filled her mouth and she felt blood spill over her lips. Kirana coughed it out of her mouth, trying to not let it choke her, but even the action of breathing was being lost to exhaustion. Kirana tried to stay in ʻĀina, she tried to stay with her Keepers, but there was no hope.

"*Please.*" She reached out to the Voice, she searched through the in-between for any signs of him or the power he had shown her. But Kirana was so weak, and she knew even if he called for her she would not hear him.

She was doomed, and her time had run out.

In her desperation, she missed the source of a gunshot and was only just able to look over in time to see a body drop to the ground.

Chapter 57

RO

RO LOOKED BACK the moment the bullet went off. She raised her gun for whatever Warden was behind them, only there was none. By the time she looked back to the ground, Haunton had already dropped to her knees, and then to the ground. Her hands were wrapped around a bullet-shaped dent in her stomach armor, and it was only when she fell forward that the source of the attack appeared. Both RO and Metis were quick to turn their guns to whatever was able to kill the Chief, and she suspected they were both ready for either a savior or a true monster, but they were wrong.

It was a child, a familiar one.

She was the Malfunction RO had spoken to in the vents. She had been so quiet that the strongest Warden alive hadn't been able to hear her. RO looked down at the gun in her hands. It was Metis's gun, the one weapon that had been strong enough to break Haunton's armor. This poor girl had been so smart and brave—stealing a weapon she knew could kill the monster and acting on her own ambitions—but so dumb and weak because she had listened to RO's words and thought she could follow her to freedom. Antony was right, RO was already seen as the Malfunction god.

"No!" Haunton gave out a blood-curdling yell, and though it seemed she was struggling, it was clear her attack only injured her. For the time being, Kirana's sister was alive.

RO ran to Haunton and kicked the gun out of her gasp before it could be raised to the Malfunction. If they kept the Chief alive, there was a chance she could help them get to the ship. Even wounded, she would be a strong asset. But that meant leaving Kirana. RO knew that this situation would have led to a fight, the Keepers could never just leave one of their own behind like that. Certainly not Kirana.

Weakened by the bullet, RO was able to push her sword right through the Chief's stomach without any defense. With a cry of pain, RO watched Haunton slip out of the sword, organs and skin burned all the way through, and fall back to the ground. The Keepers no longer had the Chief on their side, and RO had no idea if the choice she made was reasonable.

Kirana had asked RO before whether she was thinking out of hope or reason, and RO wondered now if she was doing both.

"Tia!" Kirana screamed, pushing herself off the wall towards Haunton's body before falling to the ground and staying there, still.

Metis dropped down to Kirana but looked from Haunton to the little Malfunction.

RO put her sword beside her and, not entirely on purpose, yelled at the Malfunction, "What are you doing?"

"RO!" Metis scorned, "She saved us."

Gwen moved closer to Haunton, staring up at RO, "We needed her on our side. She was the only–"

"There are always other ways. Always!" Metis wiped blood off of Kirana's face and shook her, "Kirana!" She didn't respond.

RO gestured to Haunton for Gwen to see, "What choice did we have?"

"*You!*" Gwen pointed at her, "*You* had a choice. Kirana made a deal for us! A deal *you* let her take."

"I let her? I tried to stop her from taking the deal! She was calculated and reasonable–"

Gwen waved at her with her gun, an action RO hoped was out of natural movement and not a subconscious threat. "That's all you care about. Calculation! You're an android. You're a machine!"

"You seem just as fine to take her sacrifice, Gwen."

The look Gwen gave her was more out of shock than anger; she hadn't expected RO to say such a thing, and honestly, neither had the Warden. RO was not to blame for every event that occurred, she had just saved both the Malfunction and Kirana; that deserved a little recognition.

RO looked back to the Malfunction girl to find her seated against the wall, Metis's gun to her chest and eyes locked on Haunton's body. RO couldn't help but wonder if that was how she looked after killing Deran. She wanted to do something to help the little girl, protect her in some way, but there was no time. RO could only protect her team, even if she knew the little girl would be killed for her treacherous actions or live with that monstrous feeling forever, if she could bear to live at all. RO had to look away the moment she considered killing the Malfunction herself. That way the pain would be done, and the Wardens could not hurt her. But RO couldn't even fathom taking her life. Metis and Gwen would never forgive her, and they would never understand how RO knew exactly what was going on in the little girl's head.

RO dropped down and looked at Kirana, "What did they do to her?" Metis opened one of her eyelids to show that her entire eye was black with bloody-rimmed edges. Gwen let out a gasp and turned away.

RO nearly jumped at the sound of laughter and was horrified to find it was coming from Haunton. The Chief wheezed, "That was the Magistrater, not me."

RO glanced over in time to see her remove her helmet once again, blood streaming down the corners of her mouth. She smiled, her white teeth stained red from internal bleeding. She had long black hair that fell in a thick braid across the floor, tangled with sweat and blood. Her skin was a deep golden brown, marked with a deep wound across the top of her nose: a gift from Metis. Without the scar, RO would consider her sharp expressions and arrogant smirk the example of a perfect Warden. Perhaps Haunton shaped her culture, creating clones of her own personality. Calculuated, arrogant, strong, and of course, charming, even when bleeding and burning.

Haunton struggled to breathe, but she found enough air to smile and keep talking. "She's gone now. Everything is happening, and you're all going to die." She laughed, "Kirana will know I did everything I could to save you. Now look at me, lying here unable–" She coughed and rolled onto her side, spitting blood across the floor.

Metis looked up at RO the moment she turned back, "What do we do?"

Gwen dropped down by Kirana's head with a gasp of pain, "We have to take her body. Haunton can't stop us but maybe we shouldn't leave. The Magistrater has to be close. Can we distract her, bring Kirana back to consciousness and get her to the staff."

RO shook her head, "We're assuming she's close."

Metis nodded, "She has to be close–"

"You're assuming, Metis."

"We have to help her!"

"I never said we're not–"

Gwen put up a hand over her face, "Stop."

"Stop what–"

"Stop talking!" Gwen yelled at RO, "The Magistrater is trying to talk to her. She's there with her and it's because of *you!*"

"Hey!" Metis looked back down the hallway to see the little Malfunction girl staring down the barrel of the gun.

He tried to get up but RO stopped him, "We need a plan–"

"She–"

"She is thinking about it. She won't, not yet. We need a plan so we can start running *now.*" Gwen started to say something but RO cut her off, "Gwen, I know what I am doing. I am trying to keep you alive, and however much I want to distract the Magistrater or bring Kirana back, all we can do is survive."

Metis started to get up, trying to bring Kirana with him, "I can carry her but someone else needs to stay in front and fight."

RO helped Gwen get back up, "I can take the lead, Gwen behind me, and you at the back." She looked at how strangely Metis was holding Kirana, "Can you carry her on your own?"

He fixed his grip, "We don't have a choice."

"I'll clear the path." RO activated her weapon, keeping the metal cool, "Things will be locked down soon, we need to hurry. Can you run?" Metis nodded, then Gwen. "Once we get a ship–"

There was noise from down the hallway, and RO knew their plans would just have to be improvised along the way. Running and praying were all they had left, so that's what they did. The gods started to run down the hallway while muttering their wishes to stay alive.

"You'll never reach the ships!" Haunton yelled after the Keepers, "They will find you!"

As RO passed the Malfunction girl she stopped and slid down to her side. With Metis watching her, she took his gun out of the girl's hands and whispered, "Do not let them find you." If the cameras were still off and she moved fast through the vents, she could survive. RO got the impression the girl knew her daring to recreate RO's journey to becoming a Warden had failed. The girl had to run, hide, or die, but her Malfunction Keeper wasn't going to save her. RO looked forward and reminded herself of the three Keepers to her side, of those who she had given up everything for, and focused on the mission at hand. It might have been cruel to leave the Malfunction behind, but RO was still a monster at heart. If the Keepers would go to war over their cause, she would need to keep her cruelty for the time being.

Haunton rolled over on her stomach and screamed, "They will kill you all!"

RO turned her back to the Chief, handed Metis his gun, and led the Keepers through the Warden hall.

Most Warden facilities had the same basic function; therefore, they had the same basic structure and design. RO had spent her entire life navigating through vents and hallways; she would be able to find the route to the ships. The key was to search for the most productive design. If they passed a storage room she would move to the largest hallways, knowing that the supplies would be brought in bulk straight from the ships. If she passed briefing rooms she would push forward until she reached either a cafeteria or the dorm rooms. The cafeteria would indicate they were close, the dorm rooms would force her to move back the way they had come. Yes, luck would be needed, but she still knew the world around her better than anyone else on their side, and that had to count for something. The question was simply: how long would it take the Wardens to find and corner them? They were a team of beaten-down, unarmed gods with an unconscious leader, an angry Hiraethan, an injured Telematic, and a traitor. It was a question of when, not if. When that moment came RO would have to be smart enough to find one last miracle, and then they would be safe.

RO had each of the Keepers sprinting down the hallway, and Metis and Gwen were slow enough to allow her time to scout ahead, take the first blow, and take on the fight entirely. The less action the other two saw the less likely the group was to be slowed down.

It was strange to be hunted in a place much like her own home. She too was fighting back, fighting people she would have died beside mere hours ago. Everything had changed so quickly; her hallways red, her sword aflame, and the bodies of her people slowly burning away. RO didn't know why fire was such an element in her purpose as a Keeper, but watching her sword burn, she found comfort in the idea of ashes. She was going to burn her worlds to the ground so that one day something new could rise. Destruction was all she was good for until the day new life could take root. RO was not life, Gwen and Metis were life. She was death, and so she reaped and slayed and pictured future Wardens—no Malfunction titles to be given, no lives to be taken—living a life without the Magistrater.

RO fought her way through each patrol that came by. Being armed with both her sword and gun gave her the advantage for both range and melee attacks. It was hard to know where her people would strike, and for a while she found herself trapped or forced to retreat until a moment presented itself in which she could take out the soldiers. RO tried to find their patterns, their plans. If communications were back on then they would be talking to one another, a commander watching from above and mapping out the best way to kill the Keepers. RO recognized this and started to make her own plan, before realizing anything she decided would be based on something her people taught her. She was thinking like a Warden, she was predictable. RO chose to make an advantage for herself by being what she had sworn to never be again: a Malfunction. She had to be unpredictable and invisible, a person no Warden had cared to study for fighting techniques. RO never fought much while she was a Malfunction, but she still had a few instincts she could not quite kill.

RO ran into the next hallway and shot the camera further down. After three paces she skidded to a stop and changed direction, sprinting down the opposite way. She moved as fast as she could and got to the end of the hallway with a slide. She held up the gun and fired at the first person she saw. The Wardens were waiting for them, but they expected her to be predictable. She shot at the first one she saw. The Warden fell back as five more came out, one of them holding a much larger piece of machinery. She ducked back behind the wall as Metis and Gwen ran to her side. A blast of gunfire shot around them. The wall cracked and dust fell all around them as RO forced them to run the other way.

Encounter after encounter they ran as fast as they could, barely able to miss bullets and move out of opportunities for traps. Wardens were everywhere, now finally giving into the idea that the Keepers needed to be dead, once and for all. Haunton had truly given them the advantage by taking them so close to the ships, but RO knew having the Chief there would have allowed them to get to the ships without any inconvenience.

For as RO turned a new corner, she miscalculated.

This hallway was larger, the type that would allow for cargo to be brought from facility to facility. She saw at the other end two large doors that surely led to the ship depot. But the Wardens knew this was where the Keepers were running to, and they were ready. RO was just grateful she had been the first one through; otherwise, the bullets would have gone to Gwen or Metis. Pushing herself back to cover she felt the sharp pain of metal cutting through her leg. She flew back with Metis and Gwen as a powerful gun sent chunks of wall at them. She bit down a scream and crawled her way to a wall and back on her good leg. It had pierced through her calf. A muscle she needed in order to run, let alone walk. She could hear more Wardens coming down the hallway. They would be cornered any second.

RO pushed Metis and Gwen against the wall, and shot at the small black box camera on the wall, destroying it. "When you hear them run away, go into that room." The hangers in each facility were surrounded by different storage rooms. Large doors that looked just like the entrances into hangers. She pointed to the one closest to them.

Gwen looked at her frantically, "What do you mean?"

There was no time, "Run when they leave." Then RO ran down the hallway they had just come through. Limping, but finding the strength to move fast. The promise of death was enough motivation to keep her running. She went through the hallways until she found another group of Wardens. They saw her and she turned right back around back the way she had come. Her goal was not to die by the hands of her own people, but simply to bring them away from the Keepers. It was a small distraction, but it was all she could give them in their position. She prayed it was enough.

Turning the corner she found a door and slammed herself into it. Locked. She dragged her sword down the slit between the door and the wall. The lock broke and she kicked the door open. It was a briefing room with four pilots standing ready to leave. They were waiting for the command that would send them out after the Keepers. When RO entered she wasted no time. As the nearest Warden turned she spun forward and slid the sword across his neck. She caught his body as the others scrambled to find their guns. One of them shot at her and she used the body as a shield. She kicked it forward to the next Warden and dove under the table as the others tried to shoot at her. She waited for them there, extending the sword out to her side. The first Warden bent down to shoot her. With one swing she got both his arm and his gun. With a scream she rolled back into the third Warden and slid the sword through his shins. His legs slid off his ankles as he fell to the ground. Her own leg gave out as she tried to get back up. With a yell she slammed into the table and pushed herself back up. She looked around for the final Warden but they were gone. She looked back to the door to see it opened. Warden pilots were always cowards.

RO limped back to the door and slammed it shut. She used the sword to melt the metal back in place and fell against the frame for a moment. Her leg was agonizing, and all she wanted was the luxury of screaming and crying out. But she couldn't. She could barely waste the moment to rest. RO looked at the corners of the room and found the cameras. She shot each one before moving around the table to the vent. A Warden sat beside it, his foot and hand split open from her attack, but alive.

He stared up at her in fear, "How could you do this?"

She moved to the vent, pulling it out and tucking her sword in its holster.

"*Malfunction.*" He chose his final words as if they would resonate with RO, staying with her as his ghost. "You'll always be a monster." That was true, but one day she would be the monster that set her world free. For now, that job involved killing Wardens. She pulled out her gun and shot the Warden point blank. His body fell to the side of a blood-smeared wall.

RO could hear noise outside and crawled into the vent, locking it back in place and sliding down the small slope. It got larger as she moved inside, and with little noise she started to crawl through it.

It was stupid, she knew it was, to use this sort of transportation. But it was all she had. Navigation down in the vents felt so much easier than trying to fight back against her people. It was like some part of her was back in her habitat. She didn't like the feeling of familiarity, but there it was. She hadn't been in the vents for years, and yet, she knew exactly how to navigate the space. She climbed, crawled, jumped, slid, and with little delay and a trail of blood, she found the room she had sent Metis and Gwen to.

RO was on the ceiling, looking down at a vast room of weaponry. There were no ships to be seen, just crates and shelves. She saw guns and boxes of weapons staggered across the space, the most important items being the bombs in the corner of the room. This was where Haunton had told them to go, to set the bombs off and blast the hanger's door wide open so they could grab a ship and fly away during lockdown.

There were people below her dressed in gray jumpsuits. Malfunctions. She searched for Metis and Gwen and spotted them atop one of the many larger crates at each side of the room. They were well hidden, but not from her bird's eye view. She opened the vent door carefully, trying to find a way down. The crates were stacked and close to the ceiling, but it would still be a hefty drop. RO was worried she would both injure herself and cause a loud noise, but what other choice did she have? After a moment to collect herself, RO pulled her legs through and let herself drop. She fell and tried to roll as best she could to stay quiet and limit damage. With a crash she hit thin metal. Her leg gave out and let out a soft scream as she hurried over the crate to a lower level. As soon as her body went still she drove it back into movement.

She climbed down to where she had seen the others. When she got to them she tapped above them to let them know she was up there. They both jumped at the sound and Gwen turned her gun to RO. Even when she saw it was the Warden she didn't drop her weapon. They stared at each other for a moment, before she finally lowered the gun. RO pulled herself down to them and collapsed beside them in the small crack between two stacked crates. A good hiding spot.

"They're everywhere." RO put a hand against the bullet wound and let out a short gasp, "The hanger is locked down by now. We'd have to get to a command room to even open a door."

Gwen held the gun to her chest, "What do we do?"

RO crawled to the edge of the crates. She wanted to see where the bombs were and if they were guarded. She looked around at the slow-moving Malfunctions scattered around the room and it took her a moment to realize what they were exactly.

Child Malfunctions.

They were doing their jobs, not even fazed by the idea that the Keepers were near. She was familiar with the numb feeling of obsolete existence, but the way these children operated was far beyond what RO once was. Though the Wardens were the same as they were in the Ward, she wondered if the Malfunctions were different. The vents were slightly cleaner, she had to admit, as if even away from the Wardens they performed their tasks. RO watched one of the children go to the selves of bombs against the wall. There were no Wardens there, only a few children polishing and priming individual sets. RO looked up to the nearest set of cates and saw how easy it would be to climb up the shelves and turn a single one on.

RO sunk back into their hiding place, "We do what Haunton told us to do. We use the bombs to blast open the wall."

Metis leaned forward, "Are they that powerful?"

"I don't know. I'm not artillery, but if Haunton planned on using the bombs then it is very likely her plan would work."

Gwen glanced out into the room, "How do we turn them on?"

"I can find one with a timer, set it off, and we run."

Metis stared at her for a moment, and as she waited for him to say something the sounds of the Malfunctions working overtook their silence. He pushed past her to the edge and she knew better than to try and stop him. He looked out across the room. When he looked back at her... RO knew she was a monster but... not like that. Not with the horror in Metis's eyes.

Gwen grabbed RO's shoulder, "Who's in here?"

"Workers. Malfunctions."

Metis spoke in a single breath, "*Children.*"

RO shook her head and she hated how cruel she looked, "We can't save them."

Metis walked back into the crate. For the first time since his rescue, he looked at her and wouldn't look away, "You want to kill them?"

"I don't, Metis." She gestured for him to calm down, "But we don't have the time–"

"They're just kids! They're just little kids!" He raised his voice.

She shook her head quickly, "I don't want to do this, but we have another choice."

"They are children." He was pleading with her, "We can't just kill them."

"We will make up for it one day Metis. But right now–"

"No." His voice deepened.

RO stepped away from him slowly, "I'm sorry Metis."

"You–"

"She's right." Gwen stepped forward, "I hate it but we don't have another choice–"

He glared at her, "If these were Hiraethans you would do everything in your power to save them."

RO shook her head, "If they were Wardens you wouldn't care."

"I *would*." He was on the verge of tears. She couldn't tell if he was hysterical in his anger or in his grief, "But I care more now because these are children. Little children, RO. *Please*. There is always another way."

She clenched her jaw and looked over to Gwen, "Get him to run."

"*RO*." He tried to grab her but she shot back. Using her good leg to jump up, she kicked off the wall and pulled herself up onto the crate as Metis tried to grab her leg. She could see Gwen trying to get him to calm down, and that was all she allowed herself to look at. RO didn't want to hurt Metis like this, but it was that or sending him to his death.

This was how she would save her team. She was death once again.

She moved over the crates, limping and pulling herself around while trying not to make a sound. The crates gave her cover, but as she kept moving she found more Malfunctions around her. They would report her instantly, loyal to their masters. She moved past them quietly and reached the shelves of the bombs. She scanned them for one she could tap into. There had to be one, at least one. Or she could find a grenade to start some sort of chain reaction. But that meant the Keepers were there during the explosion. Gods, there were too many options. Too little time.

There was a screeching sound behind her, and she looked back to see the doors to the room slam shut. Her first thought was that the Wardens were there, ready to trap them in a room of bombs. But as someone pushed a small crate over the doors she realized the figure looked familiar.

Metis turned around and shot a gun into the air to get the Malfunction's attention.

He was saving them.

Chapter 58

* ✳ *

METIS

METIS KILLED MIXER. He wished he could say it wasn't intentional, but it was. Metis's entire life fell away within a month. Mixer's workers left, the Wardens banned the Master's inventions, the Legend of the Child Reaper kept Metis's victims away, and soon there wasn't enough money to buy the needed equipment. Mixer had already been thinking about leaving, but tied to his work he had never been able to walk away. The Master and Mixer argued every day, sometimes edging towards a deadly fight. One day, it hit that point.

The day Mixer announced he was taking his son and finally leaving, for good.

"I do not understand you." The Master said, "We have worked for years to perfect this and suddenly you are quitting?"

"We have filled the channel with blood!" He moved around the Master and started shoving pieces of metal and bottles into his bag, "I thought we could save our world but this invention will never be able to reverse what we have done."

"We are so close!"

Mixer looked over to see Axel waiting at the door, pale and stiff. Metis was standing beside him, waiting to see what his father needed him to do. Mixer sighed and locked eyes with the Master, "We will never create perfection. This machinery isn't going to help anyone. Just you and your ego."

"I am a genius!" The Master screamed, stepping right up to his face.

The Mixer had pushed him back, and the Master hit the back of his table. This was the trigger to fight. The two of them started a messy, angry fistfight.

Both Metis and Axel stood to the side, not knowing what to do. The Master was weaker than Mixer, older and smaller in size. Mixer was able to pin him to the ground and cup his neck in his hands. He was choking him.

Mixer was going to kill the Master.

"Stop!" Metis screamed.

Axel tried to grab him and pull him to the door, but Metis threw himself out of the boy's grasp and ran into the room.

Metis had killed so many children, by his hands or his father's, and because death was a normality, he didn't hesitate to kill Mixer. He grabbed the biggest, sharpest tool he could find, stood above Mixer, and drove the tool into his throat with a scream.

There was... so much struggling. Mixer gagged for air. He reached for the knife. He held his wound.

His final glare at the Master.

His final look at Reaper.

Not enough time to look at his son.

Metis had heard many screams over his years with the Master, but he had never heard one quite like Axel's. He let out the most horrific, blood-wrenching scream as he ran to his father's side, but the Master grabbed him and dragged him to the empty cell they had held the children in. Metis just stared at Mixer, not blinking, not moving, not breathing. Trembling.

The Master put a hand on his shoulder, and spun him around to face him, "Thank you, Reaper." and he hugged Metis, "You're my little hero."

No... Metis was not a hero. That was the moment he realized he had killed all those children... for nothing. Mixer was a kind man with a good son. He did not deserve to die.

The Master laughed and kicked Mixer's body, "I'm better off without him. My work can continue in full force. We'll operate on him tonight."

Metis was a monster, but his father was a demon.

That night the Master gave Metis celebratory lessons, carving Mixer open and showing his son why he was a genius. Axel wouldn't stop screaming from the other room. The Master made Metis clean up before he headed off to bed. Metis had just stared at the blood. Not cleaning it. Just staring. Then he started crying. He lay there in the blood. It smelt like iron. It felt warm for the first hour, before going cold.

It was all his fault.

Metis stood up and went to Axel in the middle of the night. Keys to his side.

"Axel." Axel didn't respond. He sat at the back of the cell, knees to his chest. Quiet. "Axel. I... I didn't..." Metis sobbed while trying to keep his voice quiet, "I can... I can get you out. Okay? We can escape. We can run away. I... I'm..."

"You're a monster."

Metis tried to wipe away the tears, forgetting he had Mixer's blood on his hands, "I didn't–"

"You aren't sorry. You aren't sorry for killing him."

Axel was raising his voice. Metis didn't know what the Master would do to them if he woke up now, "You'll wake him up–"

"You killed him. You didn't even hesitate. You did it like he was no one. Just another one of the kids you grabbed off the streets. He loved you."

Love? Metis hadn't seen it once. He was blind until that moment. It would forever haunt him that he missed out on a real father because of his bloodthirsty need for love. It was at that moment he realized he didn't deserve love at all. He didn't deserve anything. "I'm sorry–"

"You're not sorry. My father would be alive if you ran away with us. We would have gone together. He would be alive, the Master would be dead."

Metis fumbled with the keys to the cell, "Please. Please, I can help you now. We can run away. You can run away." It unlocked, and the door opened with a creak. But Axel didn't run out. He stood up, his eyes red and locked on Metis.

"Why did you do it?"

"I don't know–"

"*Bullshit.* Why?" Axel walked towards him and Metis moved as far back as he could to stay away.

"I couldn't let him kill–"

"Your master? So you killed my father instead? He was a better man and father than the Master could ever be. He loved you. He protected you like you were his son. And you stabbed him like he was nothing. Another child to murder."

Metis dropped down onto the floor, sobbing hysterically, "I didn't–"

Axel grabbed Metis's face and threw him to the ground, going down with him and pinning him to the ground. With one arm he forced his hand over Metis's mouth and with the other he grabbed the bloody tool off the floor. His father's blood was still fresh on the blade.

He dug the blade into Metis's left arm. The pain was worse than anything Metis had known, but his screams were muffled by Axel's hand, "He made a place for you in our home. A bed, clothes, food. Always ready for the day you came to us. He wanted to rescue you. I wanted to… You were a brother to me. We were supposed to be real brothers. Now I have no one. Nothing. Because you wanted to protect your Master."

Axel had started to carve out his arm, tearing out muscle, slicing skin, tearing meat off the bones.

"You deserve to stay with your Master, I hope he hurts you again and again. I hope he wakes up and works on you again and again and again. You deserve it. You deserve all of it."

A tear had fallen down his face, but that only seemed to make Axel more angry. With a sudden scream of rage he dug the knife into Metis's stomach and ran out the door of the shop.

Metis's memory faded after that, and the moments after came in pieces. He faded back into consciousness as the Master rushed to his side. Then there was darkness before he felt something around his wrists. Straps. There were the sounds of the Master preparing to operate on someone. Then suddenly pain brought him back to life. The Master was finishing Axel's job. He was replacing Metis's arm. Metis screamed as loud as he could for the Master to stop, but he didn't. His father kept going. He kept putting more metal into his arm.

"Just stay still! You are losing blood, my boy. I did not have any other prosthetics." Metis screamed and the Master pushed a cloth into his mouth, "You're forcing me to use our invention, Reaper! You were an idiot! You're risking everything I have worked for!"

He didn't stop. He never stopped. Until Metis made him.

Metis's handcuffs came loose. Why or how, he had no idea. Perhaps the Master had not tightened them properly, or perhaps the years of constant struggle from his victims had made them loose. But his hand went free, and he grabbed the first tool he saw, and hit the Master.

Metis lodged a thin tool into his left eye, forcing it in so deep the tool might have just pierced right through his head. His father screamed and fell back to the floor. Metis cut himself out of the chair as the Master struggled with his wound. The next thing he remembered he was outside. Running. Running as fast as he could through the alleys, streets, and pipes. Then collapsing.

When Metis woke up he found himself in a dark pipe with a strange woman trying to patch up his arm. He remembered bleeding. He remembered screaming and crying and trying desperately to let himself die.

He just wouldn't die.

Martha was the one who had found him, taking him in and binding his open wounds. For three months he stayed in the corner of that large room. He barely ate, barely drank. He just sat there, picking at the wall. Guilt hit him at night, and there were many occasions where he threw up after horrible nightmares. It took him years to learn how to deal with that guilt. Part of it was making up for what he had done, and the other part was learning how to be a different person. The Child Reaper was dark and serious, so Metis cared for those around him and stayed happy. Reaper was loyal and hopeful, so Metis stayed on his own and made no plans for his future. He liked that person. He became that person.

He was Reaper. He was Tech. Then, he was Metis.

But he was always going to be that monster. No matter how many times he changed his name.

He was always the Child Reaper.

But he was not going to let more children die at his hands.

When he shot the gun all of the Malfunctions turned to him. In the silence of the room, he realized he had no plan. He had blocked the door to stop the Wardens from coming inside, but now they had no exit. Maybe he could just shield them, set up a few crates and make sure the explosion wouldn't hurt them. Or just reopen the door and let them run. He was in so much pain, his arm still bleeding and his head throbbing, but he had to do something, anything.

"My name is Metis!" His voice echoed through the room. He stepped closer toward them and made sure his gun remained aimed at the sky, "I am one of the Keepers, and in about one minute my team is going to set off those bombs. We are not here to hurt you. I need you to leave the room and take cover. But… I need you to not try to stop us. Please. I am trying to save you."

No one moved. They all just stood there, staring at him. Some of them still had a piece of machinery in hand, just standing there.

Metis looked up for RO. He didn't know what she would do in this situation. Would she activate the bomb or would she wait? He didn't know what the better answer would be. He didn't know what to do. He was terrified. He was terrified of what they were about to do to these kids. These little kids.

"Can you do this?"

No one moved.

"Please!"

He ran up to one of the kids. A little boy. Almond skin, expressionless eyes. Metis bent down to him, "You need to leave. Right now."

"Why?"

"The bombs are going to go off. My teammate is going to set them off right now and we all need to run." The boy just stood there, motionless. How could this child be so numb? "We set it off and run."

"So you don't die."

"No one does." He stood back up and gestured to the doors, "I need everyone to leave!" No one moved. They weren't scared. They didn't care that they would die. His heart raced. He grabbed the kid in front of him, trying to trigger some sort of reaction. He did so. The child flinched back, ready to be hit. Metis let go of him instantly.

"Metis!" Gwen was at the doors. She had dragged Kirana with her.

They couldn't leave. Not yet. Not now. He shook his head and moved further into the room, "You all need to leave!" He screamed at them, "You're going to die here! Please!"

Someone moved. Someone finally moved. A black-haired girl walked to the bombs as the others watched. She started pressing something on it. She was... activating it.

"No!" Metis yelled for her, trying to reach her, but someone grabbed his arm.

RO. She stood behind him, holding onto him for dear life, "Metis we need to go."

He tried to pull away from her but she was too strong, "Let go of me!"

"It's too late!"

He turned back and grabbed her, "If you let these children die you will be the same bloodthirsty *monster* I first met!"

The kids all started to sit on the floor. They were accepting death. No.

"Metis!" Gwen yelled, trying to get the door open.

RO grabbed his shoulders, "We will make up for this."

"This is about your hierarchy–"

"Metis!"

"You can't–"

"I am a Malfunction! These are my people, how can I–" She grabbed his face and forced him to look at her, "This is my guilt. Not yours. Mine. Blame me, Metis. Blame me and run for your life. We will make up for this, Metis, I promise."

She was right. The children were going to die. He fell limp. RO pulled him away from the children and he let her. There was banging at the door as the two of them ran up to Gwen. RO pushed them both into one of the crates and shut the door right as the explosion went off.

The metal around them burst and bent as they were pushed over onto its side. Boxes and crates hit them and fell beside broken weapons and tools. Metis fell back against a box and as the explosions settled he pushed it off of him and lay there on the crate floor.

He tried to count how many children were dying as he stayed in the cover of the shelter.

He could never escape death.

He could never make up for it.

The crate had nearly imploded, everyone scattered around dents and thrown objects. Dust and smoke filled the space around them. Yet through this, RO found him. Laying with half his face to the ground she collapsed beside him. They lay there for a moment, before she grabbed his arm, "This is my guilt."

She could never understand.

Guilt was all he had left.

Chapter 59

KIRANA

KIRANA WOKE UP with a scream. She reached out in the darkness, terrified that the void before her was because she had gone blind, only to see her hands illuminated before her. In fact, Kirana's entire body was lit up against the empty darkness around her. She was wearing the same outfit she had on the night the staff took her to Hiraeth, and as she tugged at the clothes she felt how real they were. She put a hand to her face and felt her clean, bloodless nose, ears, and eyes. Kirana did not feel healed, simply given the illusion of health. This was what the Magistrater wanted: Kirana dressed for her perfect life, a Permidian brought back to sanctuary. But this place was no sanctuary.

Unlike the in-between, she was not suffocating nor floating somewhere within the void. She was defined by gravity and kept at the will of still air. The world around her was void of light or color, but the horizon was split by a floor of glass, ever so slightly bringing a white glow to its surface. Kirana pressed her hand against it to find she left no marks. With painful grunts she stood up and, not knowing what else to do, started walking. Standing still and waiting didn't seem right. She felt isolated in questions and fears. Kirana looked back as if she could see the moments that had just passed, and though she knew she would have been worried about the Magistrater's arrival or the sudden absence of the Magistrater, she was worried about her sister.

Tia's touch had been so familiar, but her gaze was different. Kirana had seen her kill those people. Tia could never do such a thing. Her sister was soft, gentle.

She had a good heart. She was not a killer. She was just… a sister. That was what Kirana feared most. Her whole life Tia had just been a sister to her and nothing more, and though she knew it was very likely that her sister had the same lack of connection other Permidians featured, Kirana had never considered her using her disconnection to operate a mission. Kirana had seen what true relationships look like. She knew what being a team felt like. Now… her sister felt lifeless, and it hurt to know there was not a single moment when Kirana was loved by her sister.

So why did it hurt so much to know someone had shot the lifeless Permidian? Kirana bit back tears as she replayed the blurred body falling again and again. What if it was her team who had shot her? What if it was a Warden who would shoot the Keepers next? Kirana's body was lying somewhere, alone, surrounded by bodies, or being dragged as a burden she could not relieve.

Kirana stopped walking and looked around her one more time. Still, there was nothing. Truly nothing around her.

"Hey!" She yelled through the echoless space, "What do you want from me!"

She sat down on the glass floor, and the moment she felt alone was the moment she remembered she wasn't. She moved onto her knees. She cupped her hands together to pray the same way the Hiraethans had done when speaking to the Keepers, "I need your help, please." There was nothing. She closed her eyes and whispered, "I know you are there. I need you, I need you to let me help my team. Please do not ignore me. You promised me power, I need power."

"Kirana."

The voice was behind her, and as she turned hoping to see the god who had been following her she forgot to take in the tone of her name. It was not a man, but a woman. Not Tia, her voice was deeper, sung like a melody.

The Magistrater, dressed in a silk red dress lined in gold vines and embroidered roses, her hands held neatly in front of her.

Kirana stumbled to her feet and took a stance as if she was ready to fight. She wasn't. "Stay back."

At the sound of a bell, Kirana glanced behind her. She blinked and suddenly the void was gone. A bright light filled the long pink and gold colored room. It was not the Magistrater's throne room, though the design remained the same; extravagant gold patterns, pink roses carved into the walls, tables along the walls with large bouquets, and warm lights enhancing the sunset just beyond the majestic view of Permidia.

Kirana looked up to find the ceiling slowly appearing before her eyes, melting together like a painting. However real this room and Kirana's clothes looked and felt, it was an illusion. Kirana was at the mercy of a tyrant, trapped in her playroom.

"You look different, my dear. Darker. That's not what I wanted for you."

The Keeper instinctively tried to wipe the blood from under her nose, "I look the way I do because of you. Don't act like you're trying to help me."

The Magistrater raised her hands to her chest, fingers strung together playfully. She had a grace to her horror, a mask hiding both her face and her stature, "Things have gotten complicated. I would have rather told the Wardens to stop hurting you, but I needed them to learn that your cause is punishable."

"Peace is punishable?"

"*War* is punishable." She walked forward and Kirana stepped back. "I am glad, in part, that I could see you out there; experiencing the worlds as they remain." She continued to walk forward as Kirana kept her distance. After a moment, the Magistrater stopped walking, a soft smile on her face unbroken, "Your life in Permidia was a foundation for your journey as a Keeper." She gestured to the window, "The staff made the choice to take you away, to let you see the worlds. I will honor that."

"You don't honor anything." Kirana stepped back and walked into something. She spun around with a gasp and turned to see a pile of books fall to the ground. Before her were stacks on stacks of books, all lined up to form a tidy circle. They had not been there a second ago. As Kirana looked down at the structure the Magistrater appeared beside her.

"Your friends are safe." The Magistrater said as Kirana shot away from her and stood on the other side of the books, "They are getting on a ship now. It was a close call, but they decided to leave Haunton behind." She grabbed the book from one of the taller piles and up the cover for Kirana to see. Embedded in old leather were the words, *The Winter Keepers*.

As carefully as Kirana could, she reached out to one of the books and took it. Still, it felt real. It read, *Vera's Keepers*. Keeping her sight on the Magistrater, she slowly bent down and picked up another book. This one was called *Rhodonite*.

The Magistrater gestured to the books, "Gideon's collection was quite–"

"Don't." Kirana stepped further away from the ruler, "Don't say his name. You don't deserve–"

"It's just a name, Kirana." She opened her own book, "His collection was quite diverse, but unorganized. The books were faded and burned."

"Because of you." Kirana threw the book back into the pile, "You destroyed any evidence of the Keepers!"

"I made them stories. I made them a religion. Now that you are here, you can read them, and I can tell you the true stories of the Keepers."

"I've heard enough from the Hiraethans. I know what I am destined to do, I don't need you to tell me your own twisted tales."

"How are mine twisted, my dear?" She opened the book and started to flip through the pages while walking towards Kirana. This time, the Keeper did not move away, "I have the evidence here."

"You could have changed them. This is an illusion."

"I wish I could prove to you that I would never do such a thing, but to be honest with you, Kirana, I could have changed everything. These are fake; after all, all of this is." She gestured around the room, "I only wish to speak to you in a familiar, safe space, however false they may be. But my stories are not all from these books."

She paused in order for Kirana to take in her words. She understood, and though the idea scared her she did not let herself show it. "You're a Keeper."

"I was one, once." She walked around Kirana, "I have stayed alive to keep the next generation from taking over."

"But you knew I was a Keeper."

She nodded softly, her mask heavy on her face, "I believe you can be better than the Keepers. Stronger, kinder, and, most importantly, smarter." She turned to face Kirana, "As a Keeper, the staff chose me to lead a team of gods. I was younger than you are now, poor and underfed. I wanted to change the worlds with my team, to maintain order and provide for every person a good life and love."

"And?"

"We wished to grow a forest atop ashes, but when our sprouts grew we set fire to them all." She closed the book gently, "It is every Keeper's story. They have heroic moments, they make promises, and then they fail their people. The next group succeeds, the next fails. Millions die, millions are saved. Millions live in luxury, billions suffer. The Keepers stood for unity and balance, the act of charity and allegiance between each world. They stood for equality in every aspect of life. Equality is impossible."

Kirana laughed at her, "But perfection isn't? That's achievable in your eyes."

"It is achievable, but not when people are allowed to love and hate. When people are given the chance, they will always find a conflict large enough to justify genocide, discrimination, classism, and murder. Permidia is perfect, but only because its people–"

"Aren't real people." Kirana felt braver now. Maybe it was the fact she wasn't being hurt, or the fact that she was starting to see a weaker side to the ruler, but she felt herself growing back into the stature of a god. "I've seen what a natural world looks like. Hiraeth, Telematic, even the Ward. People are only people when they are free to feel whatever they want. You deprive Permidian of choice."

"Then let me ask you this, Kirana. Would you trade every bad moment and every good moment, for serenity between?"

"No."

The Magistrater nodded again, her smile fading into something saddened, "You do not know darkness. You do not know how severe the contrast between love and hate can be. Not yet. I give your people the ability to live their perfect life. I take their grief and love and find the perfect place for them to rest." She took a breath, "But I can only do so much."

Kirana bent down and opened one of the books: *Rhodonite.* Inside were white, unmarked pages filled with pictures and paragraphs. "You know, for all the damage you caused Gwen and her people, they still find love. Balance is not impossible, it is natural to shift between good and bad. I will prove that when we defeat you and unite the worlds."

"You wish to start a war. It will be easy, it will only take strength and many deaths, but it will be done and you will start the next cycle of the Keepers. You will face many other wars across each world, whether it be within or against each other."

Kirana found herself watching the Magistrater closely, and when she broke her gaze to look back down at the books she found they were gone. The room felt darker, though nothing else had changed. The Magistrater turned to face Kirana fully. Her smile had been flattened into a more concerned expression, hands clasped together, she spoke with an intensity Kirana had heard lingering at the back of her words. "Permidia was a practice. It was a place in which I could see the true extent of my power to distill the perfect life. The world is useless without the others supporting it. Agriculture from Hiraeth, technology from Telematic, mined resources from 'Āina, and the control of each world from the Ward."

"It's selfish." Kirana shook her head in defiance, "My people don't deserve to take and never give anything back."

"Except they do… You do." The Magistrater took a breath and looked to her side, "I remember the day I found you."

Kirana followed her gaze to something suddenly beside them. It was a child with blond hair and a black dress with a jacket too large for her small frame wrapped around her body. There was a blue flower embroidered in the fabric. She looked around the room and rocked from her toes to her heels. It was Kirana, framed by the window behind her.

The Magistrater watched the child, "You were so full of life that when we operated on you, your body was infused with Rhodonite almost instantly."

Kirana put a hand to her chest as if she could feel what they had done to her, "You made me?"

"You have always been human, we simply made you our little god. But you did not just appear in our hands; your arrival to Permidia was like the others."

"Others?"

"You can't reach Permidia for a reason: it is not a world." Kirana did not dare interrupt as the Magistrater walked up to young Kirana and looked out of the window to the view beyond. "Permidia is the combination of every world. It sits between each dimension, a crack placed right in the center of the great span of our worlds. Before Permidia it was just the worlds, but I made a mistake and tore through it all." She gestured to her face, and the lines exposed on the edges of her mask, "I turned my greatest mistake into a cause worth controlling four worlds for." She took a breath, her red lips parting. When she lifted her head, she lowered her hands to her side and leaned closer to Kirana. "Permidia is justified… because it is the *afterlife*."

Kirana didn't know how to react. Part of her wanted to scream out her doubts and laugh in the Magistrater's face for coming up with such lies, but part of her recognized the intensity of this moment. A lie or not, this statement was said for a reason. Kirana shook her head and eventually found her words, "You're lying."

"An afterlife in which every person gets what they deserve: the perfect life."

Kirana looked over to young Kirana still at the Magistrater's side and noticed that she was not wearing clean, Permidian clothes. If anything, her clothes looked Telematic. Kirana put a hand to her chest and outlined the flower. It felt… familiar.

"You died when you were three and arrived on our doorstep as the perfect candidate to be our Keeper."

"No." Kirana didn't know what else to say. She didn't have any other words. She didn't know anything else. "No. No."

"People live their lives in the service, then they live their death reaping the fruits they bore from their own blood and tears. Hiraethans make the products and food, Telematic creates inventions for comfort and organization, 'Aina provides mined materials and lumber, and the Ward maintains order and governs over each world."

"You're lying!"

"The only lie I have told you is that balance is unachievable. In a way, this is the most perfect form of balance." The Magistrater walked right up to Kirana, who quickly found herself frozen in place, "You can see it, can't you? How justified everything is when the rewards outweigh all that came before. I wouldn't lie to you, not about this. Not when I need you to trust me, not when I need you to be what I made you to be." The Magistrater put out a hand and held the side of Kirana's face, "My Keeper, the one to bring perfection to all."

It was justified. A life in service and the other in paradise.

Kirana couldn't breathe. It was too quiet, she couldn't think. She couldn't breathe. She stepped out of the Magistrater's grasp, "Stop."

"When you–"

"Stop! You're lying to me!" She was screaming through tears, "You're the villain! You're a tyrant!"

"As Haunton told you, I am only presented as villainous to give the worlds a common enemy." Kirana let out a cry and sank so far down she had put her hands on her knees to keep herself standing. "I kept the Keepers a story among the world's people to give them hope. I had them pray to gods that were, in fact, real. I gave them enough power and freedom to live their life, and enough control to keep them working hard enough to deserve Permidia."

"No!"

"Permidians have a mechanism within their arms. It was when you were about seven that two Telematic men designed the perfect combination of mechanical prosthetics and chemically altered Rhodonite to stop people from feeling anything."

What if she was right? Oh gods, what if she was right? Kirana didn't want to believe the villain before her because she was evil, but… what if she was good? Her cause was justified, her words were pure.

But what if it was a lie? But what if it wasn't a lie? Kirana felt sick. She wanted to run but where could she possibly go? No, she was stuck there with the ruler. She was stuck there with those ideas, lies or not, she needed to understand what the Magistrater wanted to do with the worlds.

Kirana looked back up at the Magistrater, hand to her chest as she struggled to breathe, "If your worlds are so perfect, why am I here?"

A voice spoke from behind her, "Because they are not perfect."

Kirana looked back to see Tia, her sister, standing in her pink puffy dress with a low neckline and patterned edges. Behind her, a new table had appeared in the room. A majestic array of food and flowers filled every inch of the wooden surface. Tia's food. The room smelled like home, it made Kirana sick. She gestured to her sister, and though her words came out choked by tears she didn't stop herself from speaking, "This is who you are? Haunton?"

Tia took a breath, "I will always be your–"

"Don't! Don't say that to me." She stepped away from Tia and the Magistrater, and however much she wanted to run down the long room to hide away she knew she had to stand and listen. Kirana wiped her face and turned to the Magistrater, "Why did you make me?"

"For power. For our future." She extended both hands to her side, palms to the sky, "I know how people live, I am not blind, but to maintain the production of Permidian they must be worked. With you, a Keeper possessing the power of both her natural abilities and the staff, we could change everything. Workers could be replaced by machines. Pain could be cured by modern medicine. Every world could become Permidia. Two lives for every person, both lived in perfection, because of you."

"Why me?"

"Everything in each world has Rhodonite within it. Every tree, every blade of grass, every person. Everyone has a flake or two within their body, the Keepers have much more." The Magistrater lifted her hands and pinched her index finger and thumb, shaping the space between into the size of a coin, "Rhodonite is power, Kirana, and we put two handfuls of the crystal into your body."

Kirana let out a cry and put a hand to her mouth.

Tia shook her head quickly, her eyes doe-like in her worry, "Don't worry, your body took it well, Kirana. You grew up as any normal person would. Even now, you have not had the chance to experience the power within you. You got a taste back in your cell." Kirana remembered RO and Haunton's fight in the cell and how the Voice had guided her through a swift, violent attack. "While the other Keepers must obtain their power from the lifeforce around them within selective groups of the natural world and the souls of their people, you have it within yourself. We believe you could change the very structure of the worlds and bend them to our will. You could even have the ability to command and control *people*."

Gwen had told Kirana about the Keeper's connection to life, perhaps the power Kirana held allowed her to go beyond and tap into the Rhodinate within the dead. She was a Keeper of death, a Permidian who had once been something else entirely; a dead girl brought back life.

That was what the Voice had told her... Kirana looked beyond the Magistrater to the view of Permidia. There, swaying with the breeze, was the field of golden grass. The Voice promised her power, was... was this his offer? Had Kirana's fate always been to the Magistrater and this cause? The concept the Magistrater presented sounded so... perfect. Kirana turned back and waited for the catch, waiting for the moment the Magistrater told her about slaves or diabolical experiments she conducted on Permidians. Kirana was waiting for the moment the ruler became evil once again, but it wasn't there. The cause was kind, it was justified, and it was working. It was a system that operated through life and death and it was rewarding *everyone* with a life they deserved.

Kirana shook her head but she had nothing else to say. She couldn't find a question or comment that could rescue her from the idea that the people before her were saints. All she could say was, "No." Kirana dropped to her knees and started to cry. She couldn't stop herself, and by the gods, it was time she deserved to break. After everything the Magistrater had sent her through, after every chase, gunfight, and escape, she deserved to finally shatter.

The Magistrater did not approach Kirana to comfort or subdue her misery, but when she spoke the Keeper felt the natural end to her disclosure, "You were supposed to stay in Permidia. Tia and I were waiting for you to explain all of this. You would have known the rules of the worlds and what you could do to improve the perfection I created. No one would have died. You would know what you know now: our cause is justified, no matter the illusion we present it as to the people of our worlds. Sometimes, heroes have to be the villains in order to be heard. Sometimes, bad things must happen for the good not to be disturbed."

Kirana thought of Gwen. She thought of Gwen and all those moments she had spent with her. Not just in Hiraeth, but everywhere. She should have thought about Lorenzo or the many families who had demonstrated what connection truly is, but all she could think about was Gwen. This perfect world Kirana had lived in did not have her Hiraethan Keeper. It did not have Metis or RO. It did not have smiles or laughter. Their worlds had pain and death, but it had hope and life. Permidia was the afterlife, and every person she had met within was dead. They were. They may have been living without grief or despair but they were living without love. Kirana had felt what that was like, she had experienced both sides. This was why she was a Keeper. Unbiased and inexperienced, a tribute to both perfection and the mess of natural life.

She thought of Metis, Lorenzo, Gaia, Theo, Bot, and, most of all, she thought of Gwen. She thought of the love they had given her, and all she had tried to give back in return. Her people were all of their people. She was fighting for all of them. To hurt and hunger, and to rise and redeem.

Kirana looked back to the Magistrater and got up. Her body did not ache, her tears did not weigh her down. The secrets were shared, but Kirana did not feel their weight. She shook her head, "It is not justified. You are wrong."

The Magistrater did not move, she stood there, watching as the walls around Kirana began to melt.

Chapter 60

GWEN

GWEN GRABBED KIRANA'S limp body and did her best to pull her up onto a chair. Gwen struggled to strap her in but eventually got her securely fastened. The ship moved up and down frantically as Metis and RO shouted at each other. Gwen opened one of Kirana's eyes gently and saw the black abyss again. She brushed a piece of her hair behind her ear and tried to wipe away some of the blood. The ship shook violently and Gwen held onto the chair, "Please come back."

Every time Gwen had been alone in a fight she had messed things up. For herself mostly, but also for others. Her lack of capability forced everyone to fall behind. When she met with King King alone, she failed. When she went to save Metis alone, he was the one to lead her. When she sent RO alone in the Arena, Gwen sat and cried while the others saved each other in a heroic battle. She looked back to Metis and RO, the two of them flying a new ship while bleeding and recovering from the fight. They were heroes. They were gods.

What was Gwen?

She thought back to what the Warden had said: *I think we have the wrong one.*

Were they right? Could the staff have made a mistake? Gwen had no power, no weapon, no true strength. She was not some unique Hiraethan, not like her father or Lorenzo. Gwen only started to fight back when Kirana arrived with the safety of a godly title and hope, but before that she just hid behind the people she loved and prayed for someone to come save her.

Gwen looked back to Kirana, "I need you."

The ships suddenly stopped moving from side to side and she watched both Metis and RO fall back in their seats. The ships went quiet for a moment before RO unfastened herself and walked back towards Gwen. The ship itself was made to deliver Wardens. The cockpit had four seats, and the back had twenty lined up on the wall. RO limped across the ship, moving from cupboard to cupboard. Gwen watched and saw how empty the ship truly was. The Keepers had chosen the first fully powered ship they could find and flew as fast as they could away from the Warden's reach. RO bent down and pulled out a small box from one of the chairs. A medical kit. RO sat down a few feet away from Kirana and put her hand over her eyes.

Metis joined them a few seconds later, and though Gwen was worried about who was flying the ship, she figured she had no right to question something she didn't understand. Metis sat down on the opposite side of the ship. It was a sight to behold: Gwen kneeling in front of Kirana, RO with her hand over her face, and Metis staring at the ground. They were all spaced out from one another, and though they had escaped the facility, it did not feel safe. It didn't feel like a victory. They had lost so much and gained nothing.

Gwen didn't know what to think of RO. Part of Gwen knew that RO was a small piece of a much larger betrayal and that even without the Warden the Keepers would still have been caught, maybe even sooner.

Metis was the first to speak, and when he did Gwen felt a sharp pain at the sound of his voice. He sounded hoarse and so different than when she had first met him, "We'll be there in two minutes."

No one responded for a moment, and it was RO who finally pulled her hand away from her eyes and looked at Kirana, "Is she alive?"

Gwen took a breath and sat next to Kirana, "Yes."

"She's so strong." RO said, still not looking at Gwen fully, "She took down Haunton. I was going to die and she saved me. I'm not sure how she moved so fast but... she did, for me. She spoke with so much power, like a god. She saved my life after everything I did." After a pause, she leaned back, "I told them about Lorenzo; they knew who he was and there was nothing I could do to protect him. They don't know your family is there, and I didn't give them any other names. They will only strike when the Magistrater or Haunton tells them to, which will be in a few days. There is time to save them."

Gwen didn't know what to say. She did not want to forgive RO, but such an act, even when she was betraying them, was honorable. Thank you would not be a good response, it just did not feel right to say, but to say a harsh comment would be to excuse the good RO had done. Gwen decided not to say anything to keep the Warden in check, and she hoped that in the silence RO would sense part of her gratitude because part was all she deserved so far.

RO opened the medical kit and started looking inside, "We need a plan. We're all damaged, we're all weak, what do we have that we can use?" Neither Metis nor Gwen responded, and RO reacted to their silence by taking a breath and closing her eyes, "We have guns. We have Metis's gun. I have my sword. We have three Keepers, one to look after." RO looked over at Metis, who still had not looked up at the two of them. "Metis?"

Gwen didn't know what RO had told him to get him to move, and she wondered if there was a reason to bring it up. She wanted to know what happened or why Metis had decided to throw his life away for the safety of the children. Gwen wondered if he would have stayed there, with the bombs going off, if RO had not run and told him something. Gwen looked over to the Warden and they exchanged a look, both of concern and of connection. They were worried about Metis, and they were worried about each other, but at that moment they were not worried about fighting one another. Their problems outweighed all that had come before, and Gwen accepted that her ignorance would help them in the next battle. They had to find the staff, the last Keeper, and run as fast and as far as they could. Gwen prayed that Kirana would wake up in time to save them. She prayed that Kirana would wake up at all.

"Do we leave her here?" RO asked, looking at Kirana.

Gwen nodded, "We don't have a choice."

"We need the staff first, then the Keeper." RO's eyes darted around the floor before she shook her head, "Or we follow the staff to the Keeper. That's how my people knew I was the Keeper, they followed you. So now we do the same. We go in, together, fight our way through if we have to and follow the Warden holding the staff."

She looked over at Metis and her eyes went narrow, "Metis?" She reached out to touch him but he leaned back to get away from her. Gwen could see it too, his face was tear-stricken and pale. She looked down at his arm, still bleeding, his fingers trembling.

RO shook her head, "You can't fight like this, Metis."

He looked like he was about to argue to stay with the group and fight, but after mouthing a few words he clenched his jaw and looked back to the ground.

"What happened back there?" Gwen asked, regretting her words the moment he looked up at her, red eyes and a shocked look. RO was right, he was both too injured and too overwhelmed to fight. Gwen went cold at the thought of her and RO going in to find the final Keeper alone.

"I'm so sorry." Metis finally said, putting a hand over his eyes. A soft beeping went off in the cockpit and he stood up slowly, one hand around his waist, "We're almost there." He looked into the cockpit and his eyes went wide, "Fire." He muttered as he stumbled back to the cockpit. RO followed and when Gwen stood up she saw what he was staring at.

Off in the distance but approaching very quickly, was a tall bloom of smoke. Gwen saw the tall flames brushing up against the tips of the trees. The three of them stood there in silence as the ship continued to move towards the smoke. There was a sunset behind the nearest mountain that framed the light to almost enhance the flames. In some horrific way, it was beautiful. Gwen found herself thinking about dying down in the fire, and knowing it was such a gorgeous sight made it all more bearable. She hoped that, if she died, her parents could find her there, and bring her soul back to Hiraeth, back to that little river, back to the breeze.

Metis sat down in the pilot's chair and took control of the ship once again, "What does this change?"

RO shook her head, "They will only burn down the village once they have found the Keeper. They are trying to trap them in the fire and smoke." She studied the forest ground, standing up from her seat as Metis moved the ship down, "People could escape like this. Even with the fire the Wardens can't contain so many people. We have two places to look. The village and the forest."

"Where can I land?"

"There." Gwen pointed to a small clearing far from the smoke and flames.

"It's too far." RO told her.

"It's all we have–"

RO leaned forward against the instrument panel, "There has to be another way."

Metis turned the ship away from the clearing and towards the smoke, "Do we need to fly away once we have the Keeper?"

"If Kirana doesn't wake up they will find us."

"I can do one of two things." He flipped a switch in front of him, "I can crash the ship near the fire or I can land safely far away."

RO took a moment to think, and with a glance back at Gwen she nodded, "Crash. We'll run in and out, and then we'll keep running."

"Find a river or a stream. Something with a break in the trees near the smoke. A village needs water, there has to be something close."

"Do it." Gwen told him, giving her own vote.

He waved her back, "Get to a chair, hold on to Kirana."

Gwen went out of the cockpit quickly and ran next to Kirana. She made sure the Keeper was secured before pulling down her own straps and holding onto the chair. Gwen couldn't see the window from her seat so she could only tell how close they were by Metis and RO's yelling.

"Is that a river?"

"I can't see–"

"Look closer."

"I'm trying!"

Metis turned the ship further down and Gwen felt her stomach drop.

"It's a river!"

He angled the ship up ever so slightly, and the engine started to slow.

"You'll have to break through the branches."

"Okay."

"So go faster!"

He sped up.

"Slow!"

"Pick a speed RO!"

"Go slower!"

"Get ready!"

"Gwen–"

That was when they crashed. At first, all Gwen could hear was the breaking of branches, but as the ship twisted and turned against them it suddenly hit the ground with a horrible crash. It slid quickly down what she could only picture as a smooth river. Rocks hit the bottom of the ship so hard she could feel them under her shoes. Gwen pulled up her feet, shut her eyes, and prepared for the worst, and lucky so because they hit something head-on. The entire ship stopped moving within a second, and Gwen's entire body shot forward against the straps. The back of the ship lifted, before falling back into the water. Gwen held onto her straps for dear life. She tried to make herself breathe.

Someone grabbed her and shook her back to focus. RO. "Gwen?"

"I'm fine." Her words were shaking, but she managed to speak. She unfastened herself and dropped to the now-dented floor. RO helped her to stand as Metis stumbled out of the cockpit, leaning against the doorframe to hold himself up.

RO limped back to Metis and opened the medical kit, "Please stay here. Protect Kirana and wait for us."

"I can run–"

"But you can't fight." She took out a tube and a bottle from the kit and handed him the box, "We can talk about what happened later, but unless you can look me in the eyes and you won't die for another child then you have to stay here." He locked eyes with her but said nothing. After a moment, he pulled out his Keeper's weapon and handed it to RO.

RO turned away and walked towards Gwen, "We stay together, we find the staff, we find the Keeper, and we run for our lives back to this ship." She handed Gwen the bottle and the gun, "This should help with the pain."

Gwen took both items and watched as RO moved to the side of the ship and pulled open the dented door. They were so close to the fire that a single breeze filled the ship with smoke. Gwen holstered the gun and opened the bottle, downing the liquid as quickly as she could. It burned her throat and she prayed it would soothe her injuries. RO took the lid off her own tube and, without wasting a moment, stuck the needle into her thigh beside the bullet wound. She let out a gasp of pain and pulled it out. With a grunt, she dropped the tube and pulled herself out of the ship into the stream.

Gwen followed her, jumping out of the ship into the water and rock and falling. She stumbled back to her feet. The medicine settled in her stomach and she felt her energy return. Perhaps the liquid was a stimulant, or maybe some sort of drug. Whatever the medicine was, it was needed.

Gwen looked up at the smoke and took a deep breath, trying to calm herself before facing yet another fight. This time, she would call it a battle. She was terrified to be one of the only Keepers left. The fate of their worlds rested on whether or not Gwen could be the god the staff chose her to be. She thought of what her father would do, helpless and without any advantages.

He would fight, no matter what.

Yes, maybe the Wardens had been right, maybe Gwen wasn't a Keeper or the staff made a mistake, but that was no reason to stop fighting. The worlds needed a god, so she would do her very best. Powerless and helpless, but certainly not alone. The breeze returned to Gwen, smoke-filled and softer than before, but it was there. There was no one to protect her, only guide her actions. Gwen pulled out the piece of her father's jacket from her pocket. She dipped it into the water and put it over her mouth to stop the smoke. It would no longer smell like him, but it was his nonetheless, and she wanted some shield, however small, to protect her.

RO waited for her in the stream and pushed a gun into Gwen's hand the moment she was in reach, "We stay together and we move quickly. The medicine I took should allow me to run with my wound." Gwen nodded and without another word, RO started to run forward, "We need to hurry!"

The two Keepers ran towards the smoke, panting hard and watching the ships above them. They were at the fire's edge within minutes and Gwen could hear gunfire from the other side of the flames and smoke. A lot of it. The Keepers ran towards the fight. The flames were everywhere, spreading in clumps they could barely see through the haze. RO put her arm over her mouth, coughing with Gwen who, even with the wet cloth, was struggling to breathe.

Everything was hot and burning and Gwen could barely keep up with RO. When the heat reached a scorching limit Gwen nearly turned back, before something came into view.

The village wall.

Gwen put her hand to the rocks only to pull them away as they burned her palms. RO appeared beside her, spitting and coughing before pulling up her sleeves onto her hands and climbing up the wall. Gwen copied her and climbed the short wall, using her father's jacket to cover her right hand. She threw herself over the wall and landed on uneven ground, and stumbled onto a pile of something.

Gwen looked down to see… an arm. A hand. A leg. A person. People. It was a pile of people. "RO–"

RO reached out and grabbed Gwen before she could stand up, pulling her down onto the bodies. "Stay still." She whispered.

Wardens were killing everyone. Through the smoke, Gwen could barely make out anything around her. The Wardens had created a haze around them, and she could only imagine their helmets would be able to see through it. Could they sense heat? Then the Keepers would be safe on top of the bodies. For now. RO pushed her to move forward. Gwen crawled over the bodies, giving silent prayers, with the hopes that the death was quick and painless. When the two of them got to the point where the bodies thinned Gwen could make out the Wardens. Half of them were running, some were yelling orders. But one was staring at the bodies. They just stood there, watching. Gwen stayed low to the ground so they couldn't make her out, but with their technology, they should have been able to see her.

His helmet turned to her, and she could feel them lock eyes. The Warden didn't move, he just stood there. Watching her. She waited for him to move. To put up their gun. She had her own gun ready, to her side for the moment he moved towards her. But he didn't do anything. In fact, he lowered his gun to the side.

Another soldier came by and pushed him away, "They're getting away!" They both ran away. What just happened? A Warden hesitated. They showed regret and fear. Gwen suddenly wondered who the Warden was, how young he must be. She suddenly found herself giving in to the idea that Wardens were groomed to fight.

Like RO.

RO pulled out her gun and sword and whispered to Gwen, "If some of the people are outside of the village then we'll go there next. We'll comb through the village going from structure to structure as cover–" She coughed, "Do not lose me in the smoke."

RO watched a new group of Wardens run past and she shot forward the moment they passed. Gwen threw herself back onto her feet and sprinted after her, gun to her side but finger on the trigger. She followed RO, desperately searching for the staff. If they had found the Keeper the glow would have stopped and then... well there would be no way to find the Keeper or the staff. At this thought, Gwen ran faster to keep up with RO, blinking quickly so she could search every part of the village. The two Keepers made it to a house, not yet burned down, but before they could go inside or take cover, Wardens appeared.

RO lifted her own gun and shot twice as spikes flew past Gwen. They were using Spikers. Gwen realized the Wardens needed the villagers alive so they could find the Keeper. The pile of bodies must have been those they had already checked. That meant the staff could be close. The two Keepers pressed their back against the wall and kept their guns up. Gwen could see figures in the smoke and nearly shot them before realizing it was the villagers. They were running, screaming, or coughing, and almost all of them had a Warden in pursuit. RO looked to their side and shot as a Warden turned around the corner.

The two of them ran back around the building, RO already sprinting further in before Gwen felt someone grab her. A Warden clutched a fistful of her hair and she fell onto the ground. As quickly as she could, Gwen raised her gun and shot the Warden. His body flew back as another soldier dove onto Gwen and tried to pin her down. She let out a scream as the Warden pushed her knee into Gwen's arm. She managed to aim her gun at the Warden and shot wildly. The assailant let out a gasp of pain and rolled off of her. Gwen crawled away, sending the attacker off with a final bullet.

She looked around through the haze for a green light or a sword outlined in flames. Nothing. She risked her visibility and screamed, "RO!" As Gwen stood up and tried to run forward she saw two Wardens running for her. She shot them both and as she turned to sprint forward she was met head on by a new soldier. Gwen raised her gun but they grabbed her arm before she could shoot them. They ripped the gun out of her hand and she only just managed to get out of their grip. She sprinted away into the smoke, coughing and running into a scatter of people. The fire grew around them as the ship returned with the blaze.

But there was another blaze among them. A light among all others. A sword of flames fighting against the Wardens. Gwen ran towards RO as fast as she could, but she was out of time.

A Warden came from the side and grabbed her. She was thrown to the ground and dragged away from RO. She tried to hit the Warden, to get out of his hold, but he wouldn't let her go. She struggled against him as other Wardens came around her. They knew her face, they knew who she was, and Gwen would die there, weaponless and helpless.

But suddenly she was dropped, and as a splatter of blood covered her head she looked over to see the Warden's helmet and head caved in. Someone new grabbed Gwen and pulled her to her feet. She got ready to run before she realized it was one of the people of 'Āina, a man with a wide and sharp club in one hand and a Warden gun in the other. He was among other warriors running into the fight. He looked at Gwen and pointed into the village, "Run!"

She stumbled off the ground and spirited away, running back into the smoke, before stopping. The warriors were going to die. Did they know who Gwen was? Certainly not one of their people, but then why did they save her? It was yet another person risking their lives to save her, a shield from another attacker. Gwen could run, she could find RO and survive, or she could turn around and, for the first time in her life, protect. Gwen looked back and saw the flashing, green glow of the staff just beyond the warriors. The staff, in all its glory, guided her to what she needed to do. She was terrified, but so was everyone else. The people of 'Āina, the warriors, the Keepers, RO, and even the Wardens, all needed a protector.

Gwen put the piece of her father's jacket into her pocket and ran back, no tears to be found as a result of her bravery. She dropped down beside the Warden's body and grabbed the gun out of his hands. She sprinted forward past bodies towards the sound of gunfire and screams. Gwen put up her gun, ready to defend, ready to fight, and took in deep deep, smoke filled breaths that, suddenly, felt clean. There was a breeze rushing towards Gwen, fueling her with air and life. She had always felt her mother in the breeze, she pictured her father there too, then her people, and all those she had lost and never known. The breeze carried the life of her people, those lost, those not yet born, those waiting for her.

Gwen saw a Warden and shot them, the bullet hitting their shoulder and allowing a Warrior to finish them off. She sprinted away as Spikers flew around her and found a target. She looked down at her gun and saw the breeze moving the smoke around her hands, but not in the way it should have. The smoke was circling her, and as she shot the Warden it released itself with the bullet. Gwen knelt down and lifted her palm to the breeze. She could feel its energy. It's will to the world around her.

Gwen looked ahead and saw a Warden chasing a child. A little boy no older than Danny. The breeze quickened around Gwen as she raised her weapon and shot it forward to the soldier. But she was not holding the Warden's gun. No, Gwen had dropped it and raised her own weapon.

Her Keeper's weapon.

A black string flew over her palm as the breeze guided a metal hammer to the Warden's head, piercing straight through the helmet. Gwen left the Warden's gun behind and pulled her weapon back to her, catching the hammer gently and running to the child. She grabbed the boy by his shoulders, "You need to run. Go." He coughed and Gwen realized what she needed to do. She pulled out the piece of her father's jacket and put it in the child's hand, "Cover your mouth and run." He put the last piece of her father over his mouth and ran back into the village.

Gwen looked back towards the warriors and sent her weapon for the Wardens. The breeze shifted into a stronger wind and she guided the motions to lift her up and fuel her weapon. When she reached the largest cluster of Wardens she saw the staff in their grasp. She practically flew with the wind and landed in front of them. She threw her weapon to the side and pulled it past the Warden's legs, knocking them over or throwing them to the side. She brought her weapon back and used it to wrap around the Warden holding the staff. With one pull Gwen threw him towards her and pulled the staff out of his grasp. She let out a breath and let smoke cover her exit as she pushed Spikers away from her path and ran back towards RO.

Gwen felt the breeze flood past her face, through her hair, down to her hands. It was not easy to command the wind, but it knew to obey her wishes. It knew who she was.

The Hiraethan, guided by her people, a protector at last.

Chapter 61

RO

RO DUCKED BEHIND the wall. She put her hand to her leg. Gods, it hurt, even with the medicine to help. She didn't know how much longer she could run, but now she had three targets to find: the staff, the final Keeper, and Gwen. RO pictured Gwen with the Wardens. She didn't know whether they would kill her or capture her once again, and in both cases, there was nothing RO could do. She needed to find Gwen before they sent her away for good. Her leg did not matter, her pain was temporary, and she had to save Gwen.

With her sword in her right hand and gun in her left, she pushed off the wall and ran back into the village. But it was then that the smoke around her pushed forward. A new ship? She couldn't see one. A large group of civilians came running towards RO, escaping over the wall and into the forest. Something or someone must have been able to save them, but who?

RO let out a gasp of relief at the sight of Gwen running behind the civilians. It took RO all too long to realize that Gwen was not actually running, but leaping. No, flying, with the staff in her left hand and a weapon in her right. A wind took the smoke away from where RO stood and she breathed in the clean air gratefully.

Gwen landed at her side and RO hugged her. She didn't mean to, exactly, it was just that Gwen was both alive and helping the Keepers. They had the staff, thank the gods. No, thank Gwen. RO let go of her and stepped away, "Thank you."

Gwen smiled, "I am a god." She nodded, "As are you."

This was not forgiveness, it was acceptance, and RO was incredibly grateful to be given such a gift. "Let's finish this."

Following the staff, the two of them ran into the forest. The light of the staff, though still flashing, was getting brighter, and brighter. The Keepers started finding people and desperately asking them to hold the staff. Gwen kept the smoke at their backs as cover with her newfound abilities to harness the wind, and RO kept any final Wardens away from the villagers. But time was not on the Keeper's side, and however many people they found or Wardens they slayed, the true threat was approaching.

The ships.

RO looked up to see the ship that had started the fires was moving towards them. She stopped Gwen from running and tried to think of what her people would do knowing the Keepers had the staff back. The Wardens needed Kirana alive, but they knew the Keepers would never take her into the fight. They wanted the team dead, especially the final Keeper. So what did they have to lose by burning everything to the ground?

"They're going to kill everyone." RO told Gwen, swallowing and looking around at the people running past, "One final fire or bomb, then it's over."

"How can we–"

"We can't." RO looked up at the approaching ship, "We find the Keeper and we run back to the ship. Then that Keeper can avenge their people. That is all we can do."

Gwen shut her eyes for a moment, before nodding, "I know."

A group of Wardens appeared before the Keepers, no longer after the villagers but after the staff. Gwen shot forward, flowing like a bird against the wind. She flew forward in jumps and strides, and forced two Wardens into the rocks. While they were down she grabbed one of their guns and shot them both until they both went limp. RO held up her own gun and shot at another Warden coming at Gwen as she moved with RO. The terrain was sloped. It was becoming rocky, and by the sound of water she could tell they were coming near a stream or river of some kind. RO climbed up a rock and heard a gunshot fly past her. She threw herself down into a stream and crawled towards the trees. With Gwen's help the smoke was nearly all gone, but that meant the Wardens could find her easier too.

RO pushed herself back to her feet and, without warning, fell back down to the ground. Her leg was becoming a problem now. Perhaps the medicine didn't work for as long as she had thought. RO brought out her sword and forced her body to ignore the pain and stand. As a Warden raised their gun for her she sprinted forward and cut through their chest, falling with them. With a grunt she pulled herself back up. She was dizzy and injured, but there was no time to stop and recover. If she stopped moving the Wardens would find her or, worse, Gwen and the final Keeper.

RO found Gwen further into the forest holding the staff and defending herself against the Wardens. The smoke from the new fire started to blow around them, and even with Gwen's help the area became hazed. She could barely tell the difference between Warden and civilian.

As someone came running behind the Keepers RO raised the weapon for them, but waited. This was someone smaller; a child. The boy came running towards them, but stopped when he saw RO. He stared up at her with wide fearful eyes. He was covered in ash, black curls entangled with dirt and dust. He couldn't be more than eight years old. She lowered the weapon, and he just stared at her. He didn't run. He just watched her. Through the haze, she could see his head rise, and his expression softened. He... trusted her.

Gwen came around and grabbed RO's shoulder, "We need to keep moving."

RO pulled out of Gwen's grip and put out her hand. Gwen had no time to be curious and handed her the staff. RO limped up to the boy, but when she was only a few paces away he stepped back.

She knelt before him, "Who are you?" He just stared at her, and then down to the staff. She held it out for him. He reached out and slid his hand along the wood, then stopped suddenly, gripping the wood. A burst of light came out of him and the staff. A *small* burst of light. Little particles flew around the boy, before fading away. He didn't float, he didn't even look that affected.

Gwen came beside RO, "It's him?"

She moved past RO and knelt in front of the boy, "Do you know who we are?"

"No." His voice was soft and quiet.

"Where are your parents?" He shook his head, "Family? Friends?"

RO looked away. He was just a child. They needed a god, and they had found a little boy barely about to say two words in the face of danger.

RO looked down at the staff, now back to its white crystal form. This boy was a Keeper, and yet, he was not a complete one. "We can figure this out later." She handed Gwen the staff and looked around once again. She went cold at the sight of the Warden's ship now nearly above them. RO had been right, they were going to destroy everything. The hanger to the ship suddenly started to open, and through the smoke, RO realized her people were done with fire. They were going to drop bombs.

Gwen let out a gasp as RO ran to the boy and held his shoulders, "You are a Keeper. You are a god. We are going to save you but you have to follow our instructions. Do you understand?" He nodded quickly. "What is your name?"

"Kalani."

"Kalani, we need you to *run*. Run as fast as you can. With us."

RO stood up and looked around to make sure the Keepers knew which direction to run in. When she found her destination, she looked around at the people in the forest. The villagers were all staring up at the ship, frozen, but they weren't the only ones. The Wardens had stopped chasing them. The forest was quiet with fear, and everyone within it was going to die. The Wardens and the people of 'Āina, all to kill the Keepers.

Gwen stood beside RO and tried to pull her away, "RO we need to run!"

RO looked back at the flames rising above the treetops, then to the bombs. Any second now they would drop and send a wave of flames to kill everything. Everyone. RO looked down at her sword, one of flames and fire. Her people burned everything, and so did she. Of course Gwen's ability was to command the breeze, that is where her people were. The Wardens burned, and so did their Keeper. But for once in RO's life, she wanted to put out the flames.

"RO!" Gwen yelled.

RO turned to her and pointed in the direction of the ship, "Take him and run."

"What? No!"

"I can save them." RO put up her sword, "I have to try."

"You saved us!" Gwen gestured to herself, "Don't die out of guilt."

"I can't keep up with you, Gwen. Take him and run. I won't die. Go. Please. I have to do this."

Gwen shook her head, "I'll carry you—"

"You can't. You won't be fast enough. *Go.*"

Gwen clenched her jaw and turned away. She grabbed Kalani's hand and they sprinted into the forest, leaping now and again between trees and rocks. Without

RO, they would be able to make it to the ship without any delay. RO took a breath and shut her eyes. She thought of Antony, Deran, and that little girl in the vents, and let her sword burst into a flame. She held it over her head and ran towards the doomed people.

"Lay down your weapons!" RO yelled as everyone looked over at her, "I believe I can help you. You have no reason to trust me, but if I am lying you die, and if you leave you die, so give me a chance. Please!" A few of the Wardens had raised their guns for her, and yet, no one took the shot. "I am the Warden Keeper! I have done awful acts for the Magistrater and for myself. I am here now to protect my people and your own." She locked eyes with a Warden, "I'm tired of being a monster." She took a breath and lowered the sword, "Come to me and I will try and block the bombs!"

No one moved for a moment, perhaps still locked in their fear. RO allowed them time, though they had none to spare. She expected the people of 'Āina to go to her first, to bring their children to her, but no, a Warden moved first. She dropped her gun and walked towards RO. Then another Warden, and then the townspeople. Until there was a crowd of people waiting for RO to save them. She saw women holding crying children, people clutching weapons, and her own people, guns down and head bowed. One of the Wardens removed his helmet and looked up at the ship, tears rolling down his face like the people around him. They were all the same.

RO closed her eyes and tried to focus on the fire, on her ability and goldy power. She should have asked how Gwen commanded the wind, but there had been no time. Did RO command fire, or create it? If so, could she destroy or shape it? She released herself from questions and tried to work off of feelings, off of what she felt as a Keeper and god. She clutched her sword and heard the fearful gasps of Wardens, villagers, and children. Her people made fires and burned within them. That is where she found her connection to fire.

As a Warden and Malfunction, she was burned twice by the same fire. RO could hear the whistle of the bomb. She could hear the crashes of branches and trees, then the explosion. Wind swept past the crowd as RO desperately searched for a way to control the heat, to guide it away from the people around her. She holstered her weapon and put her hands to her side, trying to feel the world around her. She could hear the rush of flames, the crash of metal, and the cries of the people she was chosen to protect. RO did not want to die either. She wanted to live, for herself and for her potential as a god. She wanted to return to the Keepers; to Gwen, Kirana, and Metis. She wanted to be loved by them again, to be taken in and supported. She wanted to help their people and avenge their fallen.

RO put up her hands and opened her eyes. Flames rushed towards them and the crowd all ducked down, screaming and crying. RO put out her hands and screamed, trying to force the flames to bend away from the crowd. She screamed and thought of her Keepers, the Wardens, the Malfunctions, the Hiraethans, the Telematics, and all those who needed her godly power. RO bent the fire—the explosion—and screamed over the burst of flames as it cracked around the crowd. The wind nearly knocked her back but she dug her injured leg into the ground and kept herself standing there. She stared into the flames before her, pushing them back and keeping them off of the people around her.

She pictured her people, trapped and burning, and she let her fight fuel her goldy intentions. RO watched as the flames slowly faded and she eventually dropped her hands. The final sparks flew around the crowd, but they were all alive. RO collapsed to the ground and, face-planted on the ground, heard the people move. Some cried, some laughed, and some just sat there, quiet and grateful.

RO would force her body to make one last journey into the forest back to the ship. She would stumble over rocks and streams until she found her team and then they would leave.

RO saved them all, the Keepers, the Wardens, the people of 'Āina, and herself. She put out the fire.

Chapter 62

Kirana

KIRANA FORCED HER trembling body to stand, "You hurt innocent people. You kill children. You kill everyone."

The Magistrater shook her head softly, "And I send them to a better place–"

"Away from their families! Away from love!" She shook her head, "You wanted me to see the world, to become more experienced? Then see me now, understanding your words are nothing but lies. You are even lying to yourself. I do not think you are heartless, I think you are lost."

The Magistrater just stood there, locked in Kirana's words. She shook her head, and suddenly her movements were no longer graceful, they were just... violent. "Do you realize how long it took to make you?" Kirana went cold at her words. The room around her was falling apart, melting into a strange, abstract form of the room. "How many resources and years of labor your creation required? No, you have no idea. You were made by my hands to be a Keeper of all worlds, not just one, not just of a team. Of everything. Within you is the power to be a god. Not just a Keeper, a true, *powerful* god."

Kirana didn't know what else to do but continued to fight against the ruler, "So I'm a waste of materials?"

The Magistrater shook her head, this time with enough force to make the dangling pieces of metal fixed to her mask hit each other, "The worlds will never be powerful enough to stop me or the Wardens. Unless they unite. You will give them the ability to take down the only thing holding them together. You are foolish.

You think you know the way of the world. You think love is worth the pain. It is not. I need you to understand that."

"I do not." Kirana forced herself to stand taller, "You thought you would break me by telling me the details of your system. I do not see perfection, I see faults." She dragged her finger down the side of her own face, matching the cracks on the Magistrater's cheeks. "It doesn't matter what life people are living, they deserve a choice. They can choose to love or choose not to. Freedom—"

"Freedom is a lie, Kirana." The Magistrater put her hands before her, "Haunton explained to you how connection leads to wars. She explained that without us the worlds would fight each other as they have for hundreds of years. You do not know the history I have seen. You do not know the massacres I have both studied and witnessed in my lifetime. Love is not worth the pain."

"You can not decide this for everyone!" Kirana pointed at Tia. "I know now why you chose to put her in my life. You wanted me to see love, and then to experience pain. You wanted me to see that love is worth nothing outside of Permidia, so you let me escape with my team time and time again. I hope that some of those times were simply our skill, but I know there is a reason for your hesitation to capture me. *Love is not worth the pain?* But Tia never loved me. It was her mission. She loved her mission. I found people I love, and I would take on a thousand deaths if it meant I would have every moment with them. My life before these worlds was nothing."

"You do not understand." The Magistrater sighed and for a moment said nothing. She just lifted her head and kept it there. The conversation was shifting, and Kirana's heart raced as the ruler looked to Tia and walked to her, "I gave you Tia because you needed some piece of love to survive. You needed attention, to be cared for, and at the time I was reluctant to give you *only* androids. Tia became a tool, a source of love, and when the staff took you away you found better people. You were greedy for love and company. I let you go, I let you run around the cities and fall and fail and hurt. I should have just killed one of your teammates." The way the Magistrater said it caught Kirana completely off guard. She spoke as if it was any other comment unrelated to such horrific actions. "Gwen, perhaps?" Kirana caught her breath. "Her death would outweigh all other moments. Tell me Kirana, if she was dead, and you were to grieve with such a heavy loss, would it not be easier to simply never have known her? No grief, no guilt. You would never have to feel *death*."

Kirana felt powerless, standing in front of the ruler, but this final word gave her the strength to stand in her position. The Voice was on her side, he had shown her death and now she understood why. It was a part of life, it was a part of love. The good and bad, the love and the death. Kirana had to know the darker side of love, one that could not outweigh all the wonderful moments she had and would have with the people of the world.

Kirana's fate was not beside the Magistrater, it was with the Voice.

"Death is good." She nodded to herself. "I would never choose not to love my team so I could not feel the pain of losing them. That pain is good, it means we got to experience the very best of love." Kirana stepped forward towards both Tia and the Magistrater, "I don't know what happened to you, or who hurt you so badly, but your experience is your own and is certainly not a blueprint for society."

The Magistrater let out a soft breath, her mouth parted and head still, "I could still kill her. I could rip off her head, slowly, string her up on a board and pull her apart. I could make her scream and I could make you watch."

"You won't do that." Kirana extended her arms out beside her, "You need me."

"I need you, Kirana. I need you to expand my system. One that works, one that you clearly do not understand. So I will show you what it feels like to *love*. That's all you have ever wanted, so here it is."

Kirana shook her head, heart racing, "Gwen is miles away from here, you can't–"

"You have loved four people in your entire life. RO, Metis, Gwen, and *Tia*."

"I don't love Tia." She glanced at Haunton, "She's nothing to me."

"But you did once love her, and long ago, she loved you too."

Kirana shook her head before processing that the Magistrater was about to tell her something so dark that she had waited all this time to save it. The information she was promising would surely hurt Kirana, but still, the Keeper continued to shake her head and listen, "I don't believe that."

Tia stepped forward, and out of fear, Kirana stepped back. Tia watched her for a moment, her eyes cold but now softer than before. Perhaps it was just her familiar pink dress and lack of injuries, and Kirana had to pull herself away from the nostalgia of seeing her. "My real name is Nadia Haunton. By the time I was 18 I was one of the strongest Wardens alive. I was smarter, stronger, and better than every Warden around me, sometimes even those above me. The Magistrater

needed a new Chief and she chose me, not just because of my skills but also because I would make a fine sister to a god. I put on the role, I acted, I thrilled you
as a child. But the games stopped being games, and suddenly you were my sister,
perhaps more than that." She walked forward and Kirana found herself not moving away. "I did raise you, after all." She reached her hand out and Kirana allowed
her to hold her shoulder and squeeze it softly. "I went against the Magistrater's
instructions. I never trained you, I never gave you injections to help you grow, or
showed you how cruel I could be. Tia was made to give you attention, to build you
into the perfect god, and to make sure you understood that love was not worth
the pain. But you were my everything, and I ruined our plans."

The Magistrater spoke, this time keeping her distance, "When I learned of
what she was doing I realized the damage was far too much to fix so suddenly. I
could not rip her away from you, so I kept her with you to initiate a new plan. I
still pulled her slowly and slowly from your gasp in the hope that, just maybe, you
would hate her, that you would despise her for all that she did."

"I didn't." Kirana told her but found herself horrified at the idea that she
needed to clarify such a thing. She looked at Tia and realized the fact that her
sister once loved her changed everything. Kirana stepped out of her gasp, "You're
not my sister. You're Haunton." She put a hand to her mouth, "Tia loved me and
you took her from me!"

"I am Tia—"

"You're a liar!"

The Magistrater smiled, and Kirana thought it was because she had a clever
thing to say, but she didn't speak. She was reacting to Kirana's sudden grief.

Kirana thought back to what the Magistrater had told her, she thought back
to everything, and then it hit her that the ruler had not finished speaking, and
though it hurt her to say, she asked, "Why did you keep her with me?"

The smile grew as the room melted down into its primary gold and pink
colors. The floor became clear once again, the glass reflecting the bright colors of
the melting void. "In case you needed a final lesson. That if you did not believe
me, after everything I showed you, I could present you with love at its finest: in
the form of death."

Tia extended her arm out to the Magistrater and walked gracefully back towards her. When the ruler took her hands she placed one gloved finger on her

forearm and suddenly, without warning, Tia screamed, spots of blood flying out of her mouth as she dropped to the floor. She let out gasps of pain as her body trembled. But when she looked up... Kirana saw her sister's eyes. Not Haunton's, not a Warden's, Tia's true, loving eyes. The ones that had disappeared all those years ago. "Tia–"

Tia looked back to the Magistrater and, at the sight of her, frantically crawled towards her sister. The pink and gold colors became darker.

Kirana looked up at the ruler, "What are you doing?"

"She has been stuck inside a much colder version of herself for nearly eight years now. I'm just showing you that the love you felt was real."

It was a trap, Kirana knew it was, but what else could she do but drop down to her sister and try to help? If she could find the power the Voice had shown her then maybe she could save Tia, get her out before Haunton took over once again. Or maybe they could fight the Magistrater, together, maybe they could run, hide, scream, cry. Kirana didn't know what to do, but she dropped to her sister and held her.

Tia pulled away as soon as Kirana's arms were around her. She grabbed the Keeper's face, hands embedded in her cheeks, "Love is worth the pain."

"Tia–"

"Love is worth the pain, say it, Kirana!"

The void darkened. "We can–"

"You were worth the pain."

"Tia–"

Kirana had seen Tia bake hundreds of dishes and cook hundreds of meals, never together. It was always one or the other. So when Tia's face went red, and suddenly a gooey, jam-like organic consistency was coming out of her eyes and meat-textured muscles started pouring down cracks in her face, Kirana couldn't help but think of how wrong it was. Her sister was a cook, a baker, and now, she was a screaming, dying, exploding corpse of meat and jelly. Her head burst and Kirana let go of her as bone and liquids flew into her eyes and mouth. The Keeper screamed as she spat blood and meat off her tongue.

Tia's dress was spotted with blood, but Kirana's eyes went to her stockings because there was a speck of grass on her shins.

Kirana didn't know how long she stayed there, on the ground, lying there and staring at the grass, perhaps just long enough to test the Magistrater's patience. The ruler moved towards Tia and, without saying a word to Kirana, put her hand above her body. Kirana watched as her sister's body fell through the glass floor and fell into the black void. With a blood-wrenching scream Kirana tried to catch her, tried to grab her and hold on. She pounded a hand against the glass and tried to break it. She was startled by her own reflection, her face covered in thick blood.

The Magistrater sighed and wiped her hands together, "I apologize, Kirana. I know this is all so confusing, I never intended for this to happen. You and Haunton mixed around my plans so much that I sometimes considered restarting." Kirana crawled back on the floor, inching away from the Magistrater. "Now shall we try again? Do you see how trauma outweighs all love?" Kirana did not answer. "I can make the pain go away. I can make it all go away."

Love is worth the pain.

"I will not be your pawn." Her voice was choked by her tears.

The Magistrater walked towards her and, with a wave of her hands, Kirana's body was thrown up. She caught herself and landed on her feet, legs trembling. The ruler practically floated to her, placing herself right before the Keeper, "Love is not worth the pain. Give in."

"Never!"

"After everything I did for you!" The Magistrater grabbed her face, and, right when it felt like she was going to attack Kirana, she used her other hand to gently stroke the side of her face, "I do not want you to feel this way, my dear. Allow me to show you what you do not understand. This is my mercy. This, or I see how you react when I kill the Hiraethan."

"No!" Kirana tried to pull out of her grasp but it was no use.

"You are not my greatest failure, Kirana, you are simply my first trial. I made so many mistakes, Tia being one of them, but I had hoped I could fix them all. That you would see our glorious purpose."

"There is no glorious purpose!" Kirana screamed, "You are a monster!" Something within her burned, "You kill everything because *you* believe it is right." The image of Tia's body hit Kirana with intense fury.

The Voice came to her in a whisper, "*She takes power.*"

"You take power!"

"*From the dead.*"

"You take power from the dead!"

The Magistrater's lips dropped and she leaned away from Kirana.

"You use Permidia for power! You use the dead to control them all!"

"*You are stronger than her.*"

"I am stronger than you could ever dream! I am a *god*! I am *death*!" Kirana's voice came out in an echo, and through her anger, she could picture Tia, her sister, her dead sister. Kirana grabbed the Magistrater's hand and ripped it off her face. With a scream she pushed the Magistrater away. Black sparks flew around her hands and the ruler was shot back into the void. For a moment it looked as if she might just fall. When she looked back at Kirana her mouth was open in shock.

"*Henrik...*" She looked around the void, "You have doomed us all." The Magistrater stepped away from Kirana before, without warning, extending her hand to the Keeper, "He's within *you.*"

Kirana's anger, her hatred, vanished with a horrible surge of pain. Every part of Kirana was sick. She felt heavy, and as blood dripped from her nose she fell to her knees. She couldn't breathe. Her body was too weak to breathe. The pain intensified. She screamed out but it wouldn't stop. Every bone within her body was shaking. Every organ was imploding. Every part of her was dying. She fell to the floor. She coughed blood onto the glass. She lay there, face planted against the cold ground, dying.

"*Gwen!*"

"She'll be dead soon too, and I'll harvest the Rhodonite from her corpse to start again." The pain rose as the Magistrater twisted her hand, "I have to protect the worlds, Kirana. You are the greatest threat to perfection."

Kirana turned to her side as blood flooded out of her mouth. Everything was going dark, everything was going cold, and as she tried to find a way out, nothing came. But just when Kirana thought she was going to die, the pain stopped, and she heard a voice.

"*That's enough.*"

The Voice.

He was there, but he wasn't talking to Kirana. He was with the Magistrater...

The glass beneath Kirana suddenly gave out and she fell into the void.

As she started to black out, screaming and falling, she felt her back pressed against firm ground. Kirana opened her eyes and sat up screaming. She crawled forward, holding onto whatever she could grab. The floor. The wall. A person. A shirt. A face.

"Kirana!" Gwen grabbed her and forced her to sit still. The Permidian wreathed at her touch, resisting the urge to calm down. She couldn't. She couldn't. She was crying, she could feel real tears falling down burning eyes. Her eyes hurt, stinging and burning within her skull.

Gwen let go of her and thrust the staff into her hands, turning somewhere else and yelling, "She's awake."

Suddenly RO and Metis were running to her, a child holding onto Metis's arm for dear life. The room was shaking violently. It was a ship, but they weren't flying. It was hot, like there was a fire somewhere close.

The Keepers grabbed her arm. "Go!" RO yelled at her, and Kirana listened. She clenched the staff and with a scream pulled them out of the ship into the inbetween. Through the pain, chaos, and confusion, Kirana forced the Keepers to Hiraeth, to Lorenzo. When they landed she tumbled forward and lay on the ground, blood spilling from her nose. All she could think about was the Voice.

Henrik.

PART 8

Future of the Gods

Chapter 63

KALANI

KALANI WAS ALONE for many days. A week, or just about. After everything
went up in flames Kalani had run straight into the forest. He didn't know where
to go or who to trust. He tried hiding but the Wardens arrived on foot, chasing
everyone and shooting those they could. The two women that had found him let
him hold their large staff, and when he touched the wood he felt himself lift, like
a bird releasing its wings and still gliding off the ground. With a small burst of
light Kalani was left confused and cold.

The woman with dark skin and curly hair took his hand and they ran. Then,
they flew. The woman glided on the wind, carrying him with her. She took him to
a broken ship and tried to explain to him that he was a Keeper. Kalani didn't really
know what the Keepers were. He had heard some people call them gods, while
others said the Keepers were just old historic figures, but at that moment he was
too scared to ask any questions. There was another man in the ship, bleeding and
watching Kalani with intense worry. Kalnai listened to what they told him to do,
sitting him down beside an unconscious, pale-skinned woman. He had gone over
to check on her. She felt warm to touch, but she was barely breathing. At one point,
blood started to drip out from the corners of her mouth, then from her eyes. He
sat in the corner and stared at her. He didn't want to hurt her, so he stayed away.
When the curly-haired woman had stood beside her, she forced open her eyelids
and he saw how the woman's eyes were black. An empty void.

Explosions went off every few seconds, slowly but surely burning the valley to the ground. The two strangers didn't seem to know how to escape, and they split their time between trying to care for the unconscious woman and worrying about the final teammate still outside.

A few minutes later, the woman from before arrived. She was bleeding and covered in ash, but alive. They shook the white woman until she woke up violently, screaming. The man grabbed Kalani and pulled him into the ground as they all held onto the staff. Kalani watched the world around him morph and fall apart, and as his stomach curled and his body fell ever so slightly, he landed on a new ground.

Kalani didn't know what was going on, but as he tried to back away he saw people running towards them. They were no longer in a ship, but in a large dirt hallway. He could hear the sound of an enormous crowd yelling over growls from a large creature. The black woman cradled the blond woman in her arms and yelled the name *Lorenzo* over and over again. The man tried to talk to Kalani but the boy was too frightened, and he couldn't process what was being said.

Before Kalani knew it, the man and one of the other women had brought him to a new room, a long bedroom, and Kalani had tucked himself under a table in the corner. He put his knees to his chest as the others ran in and out of the room. The woman with short black hair limped across the room until finally crashing to the floor. The man helped her up and took her outside. Then suddenly, everything was quiet and Kalani was alone.

Kalani wondered if the Keepers weren't saving him at all, that he was their prisoner. And yet, they left the door open. He didn't dare leave the room. The mud walls around Kalani made him feel like an ant trapped underground. He didn't want to leave and get lost in the maze of dirt and strangers. When Kalani caught his breath and stopped crying, he got up and looked around.

The room had a table in the corner, six beds, and two small desks. The beds were incredible, soft and fluffy with a clean blanket. Kalani could bury his whole face in the sheets and disappear. He opened up the desks and looked inside. He found paper and pens, needles and thread, and a box with a red x on it containing strange looking tools.

All he could think about was the village and the people he had left behind. He had left people before. He knew how to handle separation. This one just felt different because he knew his people were still stuck in pain, or being handed over to death. Hali'a was still in the village with the Wardens, Kapua was gods know where, the warriors were still fighting or left dead on the battlefield, and the others were running, dying, or grieving. And yet, Kalani was safe.

When Kalani heard someone coming he questioned whether or not to hide. He stayed by one of the beds, ready to duck away if need be. The blond woman entered the room. As she came inside she touched the wall beside the door and suddenly the room lit up. Kalani rubbed his eyes from the sting of light and looked up for the source of the white glow. Fire? No. It was coming from the roof. What magic did these gods possess?

The woman saw him at the other end of the room and, very hesitantly, walked over to him. She sat down on the bed beside the one he was standing behind and gestured to a small lever on the wall, "It's a light switch. You can use it whenever you need… light." She didn't seem to know what to do. Her hands fiddled around uncomfortably until she looked up and gave him a soft smile, "What's your name?"

He looked into her eyes. They weren't black. They seemed normal, except for their strikingly blue color. She was very pale. Blond hair, white skin, clean teeth. She looked battered from old wounds but not in pain. "Kalani."

She nodded quickly, keeping on her smile. It seemed genuine. "My name's Kirana. Do you know who we are?" He nodded. "Then you know why we had to get you away from the Wardens."

He soaked in her words for a moment, before shaking his head again, "I'm not a Keeper."

"You touched the staff." Kirana mimed his grip against the item the woman from before had placed in front of him, "It chose you. You felt its power… right?"

Kalani knew about the staff and its connection to Keepers from an old woman he used to live with. She took him in after he joined the village and told him stories about the gods she worshiped. Other people called her crazy, Kalani included, but he would never forget how beautiful the staff looked carved into her front door. Kalani knew was not someone destined to wield or even see the staff. He wasn't a god.

"Why don't you believe me?" Kirana waited for an answer, but he decided not to respond. She locked eyes with him, "You're destined for great things. You can save your world. Fight beside us."

Fight? He wasn't a warrior.

"How old are you? Proximity."

"What?"

"Are you ten or eleven?"

"Eight." Kirana looked startled by the number. She looked away for a moment, taking in his age. Kalani didn't know what she had expected, but he felt bad for making her so scared. "Sorry."

"Don't apologize." She took a breath and fiddled with her hands, "Were your parents in the village?" He shook his head, "Siblings?" He shook his head, "Family?" He just stared at her, not wanting to say no another time. Kirana seemed to understand, "Where are you from?" When Kalani looked away she waved her hands around, "Okay, there is time for us to get to know each other later. You're in another dimension. The word is called Hiraeth. You'll be safe here."

He looked at her bruises and cuts, "Okay."

Kirana leaned forward and smiled, "Welcome to the Keepers."

He hadn't said yes. Was there anything to say yes to? She hadn't asked him if he wanted to be a Keeper. Was it a choice then? If the staff chose him, maybe it was final. But he still wanted the option. He knew so many better people who could be a hero. Was he really their best option?

Kirana showed him around the world she called Hiraeth. She told him about how they just found it, and together they went through the many rooms and hallways. Kalani had never seen so many people in his life. He spent most of his years moving from village to village, but the most one place had was around 130 people. This new place wasn't even a village, it was an Arena, and yet it could hold hundreds more both in the walls and the stadium. As they walked Kirana told him the story of how she became a Keeper. Through her stories he learned of each world, and each person along the way.

The next day, he met the others.

He had been dropped off at the medical room by Kirana and left under the care of the doctors inside. There, he met RO. Kalani sat on one of the chairs, and after a moment a curtain was pushed to the side to reveal one of the women from before. She looked hurt, more so than Kirana did. She was limping, wincing with each step as she grabbed a bottle from one of the many cupboards in the room. It took her a while to spot Kalani, and once she did her energy shifted. She got softer.

"Hello." He just stared at her. She didn't seem to know what to do with him and

eventually let herself go over and take a seat beside him. "Your name is Kalani?"
He nodded. "My name is RO."

Kirana had told him about her. Everything. She was a spy, a loyal soldier. He
was afraid of her. He glanced around for a good way to run away from her but,
like the good soldier she was, she caught onto his fear.

"It's okay." She put up a hand and stood back up, "I understand why you're
afraid." She gave her best smile, "Kirana asked me to help train you. Would you
like that?" He shook his head. This caught her off guard, and she couldn't help
but give a small laugh. It was sort of snorty, a joyful sound he hadn't expected
from her. "Why not?"

He stared at RO and waited for her to get uncomfortable and leave him alone.
She stared right back, eyes locked on him. He leaned away from her and shook
his head, "I can't fight."

"That's why I'm here to teach you."

He shook his head, "I don't want to fight."

RO's face dropped and she clenched her jaw, "I know this is all scary, Kalani,
you can get settled here before we begin our training. There is a lot to do." She
sighed, "Do you like this world so far?"

He nodded, "There's a lot of dirt on the walls."

She smiled at his words, "Clay. It is different from your world. But it is an
adventure, I suppose, and we will be here to help you."

Later that day, he met Gwen. Kalani had been looking around the bedroom
when she came inside and found him there. She spotted him and stopped at the
door, "Hey there." She smiled at him, "Kalani, right?" All of the Keepers liked to
smile when they saw him. It was unsettling. Kalani nodded, and she walked over.
He had been searching through the desk, and she knelt down beside him, "Are
you doing okay?"

"Yes."

She put the paper and pens on the table, "We're going to stay here for a little
while, and then keep moving. You can draw or I can find you some books or...
whatever you need. There are even some kids your age you can play with."

Kalani met the final Keeper that evening. Gwen had been showing him around
and they came across the room of books. She left him there to talk to someone down
the hall, but he didn't mind. Kalani had seen books before, but not so many. Going

from village to village he had been able to see many different types of items that the people kept sacred. Books were the most common. A written piece of old history. In a language almost no one spoke, they still valued it as something the gods gave them.

Kalani took one of the books out and opened it up. It wasn't in the language he had seen before. He heard footsteps and closed the book quickly, rushing to put it away. The man from before came into view, peeking out into the hallway. He was holding a stack of books under his arm, papers in the others, as well as an assortment of tools wherever he had managed to stick between them. He was quick to hurry away before Kalani caught his eye.

He turned back quickly and gave a warm smile, "Kalani!" He looked further in the room and nodded forward, "Let me just put this down." He ran forward, and Kalani followed from a distance. The man was working at a large table. There were already books, tools, and papers scattered everywhere. Kalani wondered why he needed so many.

"My name is Metis." He came back around and knelt to his level, "I'm from Telematic. I think Kirana told you about the worlds already." Kalani nodded, and Metis looked pleased, "Good. That must have been a long conversation." He sat down on the floor, "Have you seen books before?"

Kalani sat down in front of him, "Yes."

"Good! They're amazing things. I had a few of them growing up, but they were always rare items. In my world everything is digital. Do you know what digital means?"

"No."

"It means… not natural." He grabbed a book off of the table and put it between them, "This is somewhat natural. The paper is made from trees." He flipped the book to show a new page.

Half of it was filled with words, the other half was a picture of an animal. It was black and white, with a pink nose and high ears. It had a bulky body and looked to be in some sort of large field. Kalani pointed down to the animal. "What is that?"

Metis tilted his head around to read the words, "A cow. Hiraeth harvests them in herds."

"*A cow.*" Kalani repeated quietly. He dragged his hands down the words, "What does it say?"

Metis glanced from him to the book. It seemed to take him a moment to realize Kalani had no idea what it said, "Well." He flipped the book towards him, "The cow is a domesticated animal. It supplies meat once killed or dead, and can supply milk its whole life. This is assuming the cow is female, as the male cow is not a cow at all, but a bull. Which can be seen on page… 260." Metis laughed at the number and flicked through the other pages in the book. "This book is really long."

Kalani leaned closer to the cow. It looked so weird. "What's *domesticated?*"

"Well… It's like… Being separated from their natural world."

"That's horrible." Metis gave a small laugh, but Kalani saw nothing funny about the matter, "Don't they want to be free?"

"I don't think they ever have been." He gave a small laugh at the thought and shut the book, "I suppose they deserve to be." He picked up the large bind of paper and handed it to Kalani. The boy stared at him with wide eyes, and snatched the book quickly, holding it to his chest. "You can come to me with any questions you have. About animals or about… us."

Kalani stared up at him, "I have a question."

"Ask away."

"Can you teach me how to read?"

Kalani spent the next day following Metis everywhere. Even when the man seemed to be beyond busy he still made time for Kalani. When Metis worked on machinery he would talk about his world and let Kalani share facts about his own. When Metis helped cook meals he let Kalani try the food first and be his co-chief. When Metis worked with the other Keepers or with Lorenzo he would let Kalani be alone for a few minutes and then tell him what the plan was. He kept Kalani informed and engaged in their work as Keepers, all while showing him how to read about animals and nature.

Kalani trusted him more than anyone else.

But when Kalani was alone, he spent his time looking through each picture. He studied every inch of the animals and every speck of grass or lengthy tree behind them. He found them all beautiful, in their own unique ways.

He wished, more than anything, to see them in real life. To visit them in their worlds.

Chapter 64

*　✳︎　*

METIS

METIS STOOD OUTSIDE Lorenzo's office. They were waiting in silence, as planned. But he didn't like the silence. He wanted noise. He wanted music and conversations. Hiraeth was so quiet, and the people reflected that. They were fighting for their people's survival, whereas his people were fighting for their own survival. Pride in a community versus pride in themselves; reflected in noise. Kirana and Gwen waited at the door, silent except for Kirana's constant tapping on the door. She was anxious for the meeting, everyone was. Even RO seemed stressed. She stood away from them all, staring into the distance and plotting something. He wanted to start a conversation and listen to other voices. Noise broke tension, it broke inner thoughts and guilt, and he had used parties and music growing up to separate himself from his memories. But no one wanted to hear him talk. Kalani did, but he wasn't there.

The kid was blunt and honest, a strange energetic introvert of a child. Metis knew it must have been hard for him, to be swept up so suddenly and be chosen as a god. Kalani didn't react that much to the noise. That scared Metis, but what scared him more was how connected he felt to Kalani. In the kid's eyes he saw a reflection of himself. That glimmer of trauma and observance. A mix of stoic expression, but curiosity nevertheless. Metis feared it. He feared what their battles could do to the kid. Kirana wanted to teach him how to fight, and asked them all to help get him to mature faster. She told them that whether or not he was in a battle, he was the one who would lead his people. Kalani was 'Āina's symbol, their

650

future and their hope. Gwen agreed with her, saying they needed the full team to unite the worlds, and no other Keeper could represent the people of 'Āina.

Metis didn't want a kid to have to learn how to fight and become tougher. He had experienced what the pressure of wants and desires can do to someone. It made him want to hold him close and never let anyone hurt him, but... he didn't want Kalani to get too attached. Because if Kalani was his younger self, then Metis was the Master. He knew if the kid saw him as anyone like the Master, Metis would never recover. It was one thing to be the Child Reaper and another to be the Master, and all he had ever wanted to be was Metis. Not Tech, not Reaper, not the Master. Just a man with a heart that didn't burn those he held close.

The door opened and Lorenzo looked from Keeper to Keeper, "Is something wrong?"

Gwen nodded, "I told you we needed to talk earlier. Now that we're at least somewhat healed I think it's time. Are you ready to talk?"

He opened the door fully and walked further inside without another word. Gwen went inside first, Kirana on her heels. RO rushed to go in next but Metis put up a hand to stop her. The further back she was the better. Out of people's minds. Lorenzo's office was extravagant for the Hiraethan style, the type that would not be owned by a rebel leader. His desk was made from polished wood with a comfortable chair. Behind him sat a safe guarded by strong metal. If the Wardens arrived they would assume he spent his Arena money on luxury, and not on rebel costs.

Lorenzo gestured to his seat behind the desk, "Should I sit?"

"Stand." Kirana told him, "The Wardens know you are here."

This news shocked him quickly, and his rage made his jaw tremble, "What?" Gwen glanced back at Metis but said nothing.

Kirana put her hands up to calm him down, "We were captured. We barely made it out with our lives."

Lorenzo looked at RO, "You told them?"

Metis stepped in front of her, "I'm sorry Lorenzo. They were interrogating us. They were going to kill Gwen. I had to do something. They wanted information and I told them who you were and where to find you."

Lorenzo's shoulders fell back and he suddenly looked focused, "What did you tell them?"

"You run a rebellion. Your rebellion is disguised as an arena. They don't know where you are exactly but it's only time before they knock down your doors and–"

Lorenzo lunged at Metis and grabbed his shoulders. He rammed him into the wall, "You son of a bitch!"

"Enzo!" Gwen yelled, standing back still.

Lorenzo pulled Metis back and slammed him into the wall again. He was strong, but Metis could not fight back. He had to seem guilty, and a guilty person would want to take the beating. Lorenzo pulled him forward and threw him to the ground. Metis stayed there, eyes on RO's shoes.

"This whole operation has taken years!" He walked past Metis, "Decades!"

"Enzo, we can fix–" Gwen's voice was cut off by something he couldn't see. He waited, not moving, until he saw Lorenzo's shoe in front of him. In a split second, it collided with his face. Metis let out a short gasp of pain as he rolled back from the impact. His nose was twisted.

"Lorenzo!" Gwen shouted out and a blast of wind pushed the door and forced Lorenzo away from Metis and towards her. Metis cupped his face and looked over at Gwen. She let out her own breath of anger, "This will do you no good. You need to move everyone. The Wardens are still recovering from our escape. They don't know the exact coordinates but they'll start searching in a few days. We need to disappear."

Lorenzo looked down at Gwen before wiping his face and walking back to his desk, "How could you do this to us?"

Kirana looked at RO and nodded to the door. Metis got himself up, his hands keeping his own blood from spilling over Lorenzo's floor. RO put a hand on his back and the two of them left the room.

He smiled at RO and whispered, "It worked."

RO guided him towards the medical room, "Thank you, Metis."

He didn't look back, hand over his bleeding nose, "He would've done a lot worse to you if he learned what you did." He didn't mean it to sound judgmental. It was just a fact, Lorenzo would have killed RO if he knew she was a spy the whole time. So they lied, and even Gwen agreed it was for the best.

When they got to the medical room the doctor was not there, and so Metis moved from cupboard to cupboard finding his own equipment. RO came in and started searching through the other side of the room. "I still think we should have let Gwen take the fall. Lorenzo wouldn't hurt a hair on her head."

"We need her to represent us as a group." Metis grabbed a cloth, "That man has fallen and died for Gwen, that needs to stay true."

He started dabbing the blood off of his face, wincing as he got closer to his nose. RO came over and took it out of his hand. She pointed to the bed, "Sit."

RO moved around the room, grabbing items as she went to each cupboard. He glanced around, "I feel like we have done this before."

"We keep almost dying."

"Are you calling me fragile?"

She bit down a smirk, "You were almost killed by a *vine*." Metis laughed and RO laughed with him. This was the first time he had heard her laugh. It sounded strange, like she had no idea how to let out such emotion. She closed her eyes, indulging herself in the feeling of joy. Her smile was contagious, and Metis felt his heart glow at the sight of her happiness.

Metis had not intended to so quickly forgive RO for what she did, but how could he not? She had broken away from her people, it just took their capture for her to realize she was on the wrong side. It took Metis hundreds of deaths to realize he was supporting the wrong man. He could not blame her fully, especially after she had saved the Keepers.

RO swallowed down her joy back into focus, "We're going to have to move it back into place." He put up his hand and held his nose. She tried to grab him, "Metis. Wait no. No, there are better ways—"

He pulled it back to center with a *crack*. "*Shit*." He mumbled his pain.

"Enjoy that." RO put the cloth in water and came back over. She leaned over and grabbed his face, wiping the blood from around his nose.

He winced, "RO, I can do that."

She put the cloth in his hands and walked back to the cupboards, "I think they have bandages for this."

Metis cleaned himself up, wincing but not letting himself gasp out in pain. When he felt clean enough RO came back with a short bandage. She lined it up and placed it down the bridge of his nose. He just stared at her, not noticing the pain. He never realized before that her eyes were such a rich brown color, like chocolate.

RO pulled away, "That should be good." She left the items on the table and headed towards the door. "You need anything else?"

Did he? Not medically. He felt fine. He had faced worse injuries during his lifetime. But he wanted her to stay. He wanted them to do something. To get away from everything for a moment. Just then, he heard something from down the hall. A song. RO looked over, "They're playing something."

Metis jumped up and moved past her, gesturing for her to follow, "Let's see."

"Metis–"

"Come on." He walked towards the music. As it got louder and louder, the two of them eventually found themselves in front of the kitchen. Metis peeked inside and saw Hiraethans dancing to a song with strings and drums.

RO leaned over and looked inside with him, "They're so happy." She looked up at Metis, smiling, "Gwen's dancing with Lorenzo." He scanned the room to see the two of them on the dance floor, hand in hand and skipping side by side.

"Lorenzo's giving them all one last dance before they leave." RO's head dropped for a moment, and Metis decided now was not the time to feel guilt, "I wish we could dance."

"You can." She told him, but Metis shook his head.

"Lorenzo doesn't want me in there."

"Well he does not want a Warden to ruin the fun either." She looked up at him, "We will just have to be outcasts for a little while."

Metis's heart raced, and after a moment he stepped back and shut the door. Feeling stupid but really wanting to ask, he put out his hand, "Do you want to dance with me?"

RO raised her eyebrows and gave a small laugh. Not her good laugh, a fake one, "Really? She shook her head, "You should take some painkillers. Rest."

"We can do that later."

She glanced around the hallway, "I'm not dancing with you in the middle of the hallway."

"No one is here."

She looked down the hallway, "We need to help Kalani."

"RO." He locked eyes with her, "Dance with me."

She glanced around her, and clenched her jaw, "Metis–"

"If you don't know how, then I'll teach you." He grabbed her hand and pulled her away from the door gently. "Just hold my hands." He grabbed her other hand, "There are different dances for different forms of music. There are rages, party dances, choreographed ones, light ones, soft ones." He glanced up, "This is more of an upbeat type of song, something to move around quickly to."

"I can dance, Metis." She raised his left hand up with her own, "Wardens can dance."

He laughed at her, "What dance?"

"For special occasions." She gave a small laugh. Half of a real one. He wanted to get her to laugh fully. To laugh in a way completely true to herself. He wanted to hear it so badly. "We waltz." Metis let out a loud laugh and RO glanced around, "Be quiet."

"You waltz?"

She tried to let go of him, "If you don't–"

He held onto her, "No... I do."

She leaned back, uncomfortable as he moved around with her. After a moment in silence she seemed to settle, swaying with him to the beat of the music. She looked back up at him, "Can I ask you something?"

"Of course."

"I have the guilt of entire worlds. I took Telematic children and sent them off to a new dimension. I killed my people, Telematics, drunks, inventors, innocent people. I betrayed you and the Keepers for my own selfish gain. I will forever live with that. I will work until my death to make up for everything I have done."

"RO–" He tried to stop them from dancing but she didn't let him.

"That is my guilt." She locked eyes with him, "But you're worse than me, Metis. It's as if you hold the guilt of a thousand worlds. You are willing to die for the life of anyone in danger. Why?" He looked away from her, and she cleared her throat. "I'm sorry. You don't have to tell me. I owe you so much, you don't owe me a thing. But how can you stop... sacrificing yourself? How can I help you heal?"

"That is my guilt"

He smirked but she shot him a quick look of disapproval, "I don't care what guilt you hold, you should not want to sacrifice yourself over it. We need you."

Her words were lovely to hear, but they were just that. Words. They couldn't stop him from doing anything. "Thank you, RO."

"No." RO saw it meant nothing to him and squeezed his hand, "I need you to promise me you won't sacrifice yourself like that."

"What?"

"Promise me."

Metis clenched his jaw, "I can't."

"Why?"

He held her waist, "Can't we just dance?"

"We can." She stared at him, "But we can also talk."

"My past is my past. And it's far behind me."

"It doesn't seem that far." Her eyes went soft, "What happened?"

"Pain became my friend, and guilt became my weapon." He swallowed down a lump in his throat, glancing towards his scarred arm, "That's all there is to it. Can I make a deal with you?"

She squinted at him, "Okay?"

"If you don't ask questions about my past, I won't ask about your past as a Malfunction."

Metis could feel her stiffen, "I almost forgot I told you. I just needed you to run."

"So it wasn't a lie?"

"Metis, you're breaking your own deal."

He wanted a way out of the conversation. He found it quickly, and smiled down to her, "You have powers. That's new."

She nodded quickly, grateful for the new subject, "We never really talked about it."

"The whole, Kirana talked with the Magistrater and her sister is Haunton and she's not a real person, got in the way of that conversation." He sighed, "I can't imagine what she went through in there."

"This will only make her stronger."

He smiled again; he couldn't help himself, "But you can control fire."

RO smiled too, and he could see she was proud of herself, "I was tired of always fighting. It is my turn to protect, both my people and yours. I'll be able to do it again, with practice, to keep us safe."

Us. He liked that word. He really liked that word.

"So Gwen can control the wind, you can bend fire... what will I do?" He thought for a moment, "Electricity?"

"Because you're so sparkly." She bit down a laugh.

He laughed at her, "That is a horrible joke."

"It's not." She laughed at herself. A full laugh.

"It is!"

"It is." A full laugh. Eyes closed again. He stared at her joy. He just watched her. He couldn't look away. She was so... beautiful. She settled herself back down, "We should go see what else we can do. As soon as the Hiraethans are done dancing, we need to take action."

Metis nodded, "We should do that."

They kept dancing.

RO squeezed his hand, "We should."

Neither of them let go.

They kept dancing, kept moving. He would do something playful now and then. Dip her down a bit to make her laugh, sway her closer, move them around faster, inch her closer, rock them back and forth, pull her in, stare into her eyes. Closer. He could see how brown her eyes were, not dark, but golden. They looked like honey, sweet, a sticky trap he couldn't escape from. He didn't want to. He spun her around and they didn't look away. He moved closer. Closer.

The door opened.

RO pulled away quickly as someone came into the hallway. Metis looked over to see Kirana standing in the doorway. She looked surprised to see the two of them, "Hey."

Metis coughed and stepped away from RO. "Do you need something?"

She shook her head and laughed, "No. I just ran into you." She pointed into the room, "Gwen's having the time of her life." Metis looked inside and saw her dancing with Gaia, the two of them laughing.

Kirana looked over at RO, "Lorenzo's calming down. Plans are in motion. They have a few places in the city."

RO nodded softly, before remembering why Lorenzo was moving in the first place and nodding faster, "Good. Yeah wow, that's great."

Kirana glanced down the hallway, "Did you go see Kalani yet?"

Metis gave a nervous laugh and moved towards the hallway, "I almost forgot." He rushed away from them both and kept his smile on until he was out of view.

What was he thinking? What was he doing? Gods, he was an idiot. He was a Telematic romantic and RO was a soldier. He liked to dance, he shouldn't have forced her into participating in his Telematic traditions. But... Did she like it?

She didn't let go, she wanted to stay. When he moved closer, she did as well. Metis felt his cheeks. They were hot. Burning. He might as well have a fever. He looked towards their bedroom and shook himself out, getting ready to see Kalani.

The Keepers were too busy for this kind of distraction. RO had enough on her plate, and clearly Metis was something she was worried about. He needed to help her by not... dancing.

He glanced back down the hallway. If Kirana hadn't come what would have happened? Did it matter? Did he care? He did.

Metis liked dancing with RO.

Chapter 65

* ✳ *

KIRANA

KIRANA COULDN'T SLEEP. She just lay there, not even close to tired. She looked at the roof of the bedroom and studied the cracks in the clay. She fiddled with the staff in her hands and thought. She thought of the Magistrater, the Voice, Lorenzo, and Kalani. Kirana's thoughts didn't stop moving, refusing to let her sleep. She had told the Keepers what the Magistrater had told her, about Permidia and the fact she was created to continue the Magistrater's system and enhance their ability to mass-produce the afterlife and expand their perfection to every world. The Keepers had all agreed her system was wrong, even with the afterlife being a paradise. They all agreed in saying a life without love is not a life at all.

What she did not tell them about was the Voice. *Henrik.* Not yet, at least. She still needed time to understand what was going on.

"Kirana." She looked up to see Gwen in her own bed staring at her. Half of her face was pushed into the bed, the other half barely awake, "You need to sleep."

"I'm asleep." Kirana shut her eyes, "I've been sleeping for hours."

"You're a bad liar, Kirana."

Gwen put out a hand and Kirana took it. Gwen's palm was rough. Not just from the burns but from her years of work, "I wish you could have been in Permidia. With me."

"Do you miss it?"

"I miss... comfort. But I think if you were there it would have been perfect."

Gwen laughed, "Nothing is perfect, Kirana."

"After Tia..." Kirana decided not to tell a story about her sister just yet. She had told her team that the Magistrater had killed her, she just could not put into words how gruesome it was. Even saying her name brought back the image of her headless body. Kirana wanted to remember the taste of her desserts and meals, but now, she could only taste the blood and bones that had shot into her mouth. The Magistrater had destroyed the taste of her sister.

"I'm so sorry, Kirana."

Kirana shook her head, staring at the cracks in the roof, "I'm okay."

"You don't have to struggle alone. We're a team."

No, Kirana was their leader. It was her duty to protect them, to keep them safe. Gideon had told her from the beginning what she expected to be. "We will bring all of our worlds the justice they deserve." Kirana resisted the urge to say perfection. There was silence, and when looking over to Gwen she saw her eyes were to the side, thinking. "What's wrong?"

"I keep thinking about my father." She smiled for a moment before her expression melted into sorrow, "I don't know what to think. He's alive, in Permidia, but he doesn't even know I exist. I want to save him but... I don't know if I would be stealing him from a life of perfection. I want to believe that love is worth pain but the idea that he is safe feels so good."

Kirana shook her head softly, "No it doesn't. You want him back."

"And my mother, the rest of my family, Flint, Zero, Kaiko. Everyone."

"I can't get to Permidia. *Yet.*"

Gwen's eyes shined for a moment, and she gave a laugh, "I like that word. *Yet.* We can do a lot for these worlds, maybe not right now, but soon."

"We're going to defeat the Magistrater and take back the power. We're going to free our people and create a new system. We'll be the Keepers of the worlds."

"And Permidia?"

Kirana looked at the roof of the room, "We can destroy it."

"Destroy the afterlife? We're not that powerful, Kirana."

"Not *yet.*"

Gwen laughed, "Go to sleep Kirana."

But Kirana could not sleep. She stayed awake, staring up and around the room. She rolled side to side, never letting go of Gwen's hand.

Their plans felt like dreams, as if they were just fantasies that could never come true. They were trying to defeat a god, as gods, and still Kirana felt power-less. She didn't even have a clear idea of what they could do. Once they defeated the Magistrater, what came next? Would they rule their worlds? Lead them? Guide them? Could they achieve equality? Not in the state the worlds were in now. Kirana wanted love to prevail, but they couldn't leave their worlds in darkness just so they could feel joy. That was pointless.

There was something the team had decided upon that she repeated over and over again.

Love was worth the pain.

In the middle of the night, Kirana got up, put Gwen's hand back on her bed, and pulled on her boots. The Arena was guarded at night, a few Hiraethans patrol-ling or guarding doors. She found an empty hallway and held the staff before her.

Kirana stared into the Rhodonite, "*Henrik.*" She whispered, calling for the Voice, "You said we would meet. So meet me." She got ready to pull herself into the in-between, to feel for his presence, but she didn't have to. She felt him push her forward and she fell into the in-between. When she arrived there, the world seemed to settle. She floated there in the silence, in the galaxy around her, before she felt herself floating down, and before she could recognize that something was different, Kirana was lying on a thin sheet of water, breathing as she would in any world. Kirana could see every world from where she lay. Sparks of colors that matched with her own Keepers. She could feel Hiraeth, Telematic, the Ward, 'Āina, but still, no Permidia.

"No other Keeper has ever been here before." She turned her head to see the man of particles. The Voice. "You have a power no others have had before. It's growing, and it will continue as you lead your Keepers."

Kirana got up onto her knees and looked back to the voice, "So you were listening. You watched all of that happen?" She could hear the anger in her own words, "Who are you?" He just sat there in his silence. "You're a god, aren't you? What does that make me?"

"A god to be." She could see him turn his head, framed by particles. He was becoming clearer to her, his Voice now from a source and his body shaped as any human. The man was large, a face long with what she could only assume was a thick beard.

"You didn't save me until the very end, but you watched her capture my team and torture them. You watched her try and kill me. What do you want from us?"

"Just you. Not them. I want to help you."

"But you didn't help me."

"I helped you defeat Haunton. I helped you stay alive and fight the Magistrater. I am not here to win your battles. The Magistrater wanted you to be placed right into the head of the system. She wanted you to be a perfect leader in a perfect world. I disagreed."

Kirana let out a horrified gasp, "You're on her side–"

"She does things right, and she does things wrong. But I am the reason she stands where she is today."

Kirana looked behind her and saw the staff. This was still the in-between; she could leave and Henrik could not stop her, "You're the villain. You did this to these people."

"For as long as there have been the Keepers, I have been their god. I have watched the worlds through their changes and wars. I work not within the team but from the mind of their leader, once corrupted."

"You're evil."

He shook his head, "The Magistrater was greedy. She still is, and in her greed, she weakened me." He moved his hand, the particles weakly following his form, "I am not within the dimensions, I am not living but a part of a vibrant source of souls. I am trapped here."

"You want me to free you. I won't."

"I do not wish to be free, though, that idea is a nice thought. To be living once again." He nodded softly, "The Magistrater made Permidia to be a farm. She forged the four corners of the worlds together to form a combination of all places. She found a way to harvest the energy of the dead and replenish them."

Permidia was a farm… "How? Why?"

"Each Keeper has their own connection to the world's energy, to its lifeforce. To the Rhodonite within us all. The choice of power comes between life and death. She is harvesting the death of those around her, and if these people die twice then the energy is doubled. With her power, she wanted to expand her cause, thinking it was entirely justified. She made you to help her, to speed up the process and be a Permidian god, the first of your kind. But you, Kirana, were not made to control others' deaths, but to be the very god who commanded death itself. You can feel every person who has passed around you. Close your eyes, feel them in this place."

"Here?"

"You called it the in-between, and that is what it is, the place between each dimension. The place where the energy lays to rest, beside me."

Kirana did not know what to think of Henrik. He seemed to believe the Magistrater was partially right, but that felt so wrong. Kirana decided leaving now would leave too many questions unanswered. Besides, she was curious. She closed her eyes.

"Look for someone you know who has died."

She thought of Gideon first, and she searched for him. She searched for his energy, for his gentle ways, for his hardened eyes. She searched for his very soul, and she found it. She could feel it, somewhere in the space around her. It felt like Hiraeth, like Gwen, only different. He felt dead, and yet... powerful.

"Do you want power?"

She shook her head, "Not if it means following you and the Magistrater." She opened her eyes and looked at the god, "Are you on her side? What do you fight for?"

"Like I said, she does things right, and she does things wrong. You can not tell me the idea of Permidia and the afterlife does not sound perfect." Kirana didn't let herself respond. "But she is greedy, and weak. She follows my words and yet, she still commands me. I am trapped here and she rules over the worlds, keeping its power for herself. I convinced her to make you as another subject to exploit. I told her you would work beside her, that you were the one who could truly bring her perfection."

"Can I?"

Kirana had never heard Henrik make a sound before, but echoing around her she heard the faintest laugh, a chuckle under his breath. "Your ambition was expected, but it is refreshing to see nevertheless. You want power, don't deny it."

"I want to protect my team. I found love and I can't let it... die." She glanced at the staff again, "I don't want death. I want life. I chose to leave Permidia to find love, and I am not going to give up the people I have found just for... power."

"Death is not about fighting, nor is the power you would take from the souls. Love is at its strongest in the presence of doom. You have seen that comfort has no love within it, only safety, and dull content. You are the ashes from which your team has risen from. Made to be a Keeper, destined to be a god. Death is not something you should fear, for you are a Permidian, the first Keeper forged from the afterlife."

"I want to bring peace, not death."

"In order for there to be peace, someone must pay the price of blood. Tell me, what would you do for your team?"

"I will protect them, no matter what."

"That is love, forged by death." He put out a hand and four particles flew from his palm towards her. They stopped at arm's reach before her. "I am offering you the power to take down the Magistrater and restore the worlds. To create real perfection."

Kirana stared down at the particles. It was an offering. "And our cause? We want to unite the worlds, to bring peace and love to all places, equally."

"Then I shall help you."

"What is your cause? What do you want from all of this?"

"I want to take down the Magistrater. I want the dimensions to be as they were, without the complexity of Permidia. You love your team, you want love to prevail, then so be it. Through my years of observance and my time alive, I have always known love should prevail. You have the power to rescue the worlds from conflict and wars, all while keeping love."

Kirana shook her head, "You sound like the Magistrater. Perfection is impossible."

"Not with you. Not with us."

She looked down at the particles. The four of them floated before her, glowing and shifting between yellow, blue, red, and green. "You can give me the power to make perfection, and still have love?"

"After all the destruction you have seen, you can not possibly tell me you would not wish you were back in Permidia. Or perhaps, your team was."

Kirana thought about Gwen. Her hands were burned, she cried so often about her father's death, she had scars along her body from their fights. Gwen didn't deserve the pain, and yet without it there would be no love? People had only two choices in life: to live in comfort without connection or live in danger with love. That didn't seem fair.

Could Kirana change that?

The particles before her moved back towards the man before going to his side. She watched as they moved into the space around them and grew. She could feel them, feel how they appeared before her. Souls.

The god was offering her a way to never let her friends hurt again. Kirana wanted that, and yet, it felt the same as what the Magistrater was doing. But if Kirana was so powerful, could she control the worlds with the Keepers, would that control it be better than what they already had?

She could bring all the worlds the perfect life she had in Permidia... with love.

But it came with a cost. Kirana would be death itself, and that would be her duty. She would command souls and bend worlds to her will. But maybe it was worth it. She would do anything for the love she had found. For she was different from those around her, she was created to be more powerful than the Magistrater herself, and with Henrik's help, she could become even stronger. Kirana would use that power to protect her Keepers, even if it meant toying with the dead. She was a Permidian, the Keeper of all people, and if she could bring them all the perfect lives then she would do it.

Kirana let out a breath, "Show me power."

And so it begins.

www.ingramcontent.com/pod-product-compliance
Lightning Source LLC
Chambersburg PA
CBHW060606100726
47907CB00006B/1519